POLITICS UK

POLITICS UK

Bill Jones (Editor)
Andrew Gray
Dennis Kavanagh
Michael Moran
Philip Norton
Anthony Seldon

With additional material by Peter Hennessy and Bill Jenkins

HARVESTER WHEATSHEAF
PHILIP ALLAN

New York   London   Toronto   Sydney   Tokyo   Singapore

First published 1991 by
Philip Allan
66 Wood Lane End, Hemel Hempstead,
Hertfordshire, HP2 4RG
A division of
Simon & Schuster International Group

Typeset in 10/11$\frac{1}{2}$ pt Times by MHL Typesetting, Coventry

Printed and bound in Great Britain at
the University Press, Cambridge

British Library Cataloguing in Publication Data

Politics UK
  1. Great Britain. Politics
  I. Jones, Bill *1946–*
  320.941

   ISBN 0-86003-826-2
   ISBN 0-86003-827-0 pbk

5 95 94 93

Contents

Authors

Bill Jones studied International Politics at the University College of Wales, Aberystwyth, before working for two years as an Assistant Principal in the Home Civil Service. In 1973 he joined the Extra-Mural Department at Manchester University as Staff Tutor in Politics and has been Director of the department since 1987. His books on politics include *The Russia Complex* (Manchester University Press, 1978), *British Politics Today* (with Dennis Kavanagh, Manchester University Press, 4th edn 1991) and *Political Issues in Britain Today* (Manchester University Press, 3rd edn 1989). He also undertakes regular consultancy work for radio and television and writes books and articles on political education and continuing education. He was chairman of the Politics Association 1983–5.

Andrew Gray is Senior Lecturer in Administrative Studies, Board of Studies in Accounting, and Director of the Public Sector Management Unit, Canterbury Business School, at the University of Kent at Canterbury. He was previously at the University of Exeter and Manchester Polytechnic and, latterly, a visiting professor at the University of Southern California and California State University, Los Angeles. His interests in accounting and public administration have taken him to China, South East Asia, the USA and Europe. His chapters are written with Bill Jenkins, with whom he has carried out extensive research into public sector management, including the book *Administrative Politics in British Government* (Harvester Wheatsheaf, 1985).

Dennis Kavanagh studied government at Manchester University and returned to lecture at that university for a number of years before becoming Professor of Politics and Head of Department at Nottingham University. He is author or co-author of fifteen books, including (with David Butler) the series of Nuffield studies of British General Elections. Among his better-known books are *British Politics: Continuities and Change* (Oxford University Press, 2nd edn 1990), *Thatcherism and British Politics: the End of Consensus* (2nd edn, Oxford University Press, 1990). He is also a regular contributor on British politics to *The Times* and other newspapers.

Michael Moran began his academic career at Manchester Polytechnic before joining the Department of Government at Manchester University, where he is now Professor of Government and Director of the European Policy Research Unit. He has written widely on British politics and comparative public policy. His current interests lie in welfare systems of the European Community. He lectures on the main introductory undergraduate course at Manchester and is a frequent lecturer to Sixth Form Conferences. His publications include *The Politics of Banking* (Macmillan, 1986), *Politics and Society in Britain* (Macmillan, 1989) and *The Politics of the Financial Services Revolution* (Macmillan, 1990).

Philip Norton is Professor of Government at the University of Hull. Among the many books he has authored or edited are *The Constitution in Flux* (Martin Robertson,

1982), *The British Polity* (Longman, 2nd edn 1990), *Conservatives and Conservatism* (Temple Smith, 1981), *The Commons in Perspective* (Martin Robertson, 1981), *Parliament in the 1980s* (Blackwell, 1985), *Conservative Dissidents* (Temple Smith, 1978), *Dissension in the House of Commons 1945—74* (Macmillan 1975); *Dissension in the House of Commons 1975—79* (Oxford University Press, 1980), *Legislatures* (Oxford University Press, 1990), *Parliaments in Western Europe* (Frank Cass, 1990). He has served as President of the British Politics Group in the USA and has given evidence to parliamentary committees in the UK and Canada and to a New Zealand Royal Commission. He has been described by the *Sunday Times* as 'Britain's foremost parliamentary academic'.

Anthony Seldon was educated at Oxford and the London School of Economics and Political Science. After writing his first book, *Churchill's Indian Summer* (Hodder, 1981), he established the British Oral Archive of Political and Administrative History at the LSE. His interest in interviewing bore fruit in *By Word of Mouth — Interviewing Elites* (Methuen, 1983). In 1986, with Peter Hennessy, he established the Institute of Contemporary British History and became a co-director. He has helped to establish three journals: *Contemporary Record*, *Modern History Review* and *Twentieth Century British History*, all of which he edits or co-edits. His edited publications include (with Peter Hennessy) *Ruling Performance* (Blackwell, 1987); (with Dennis Kavanagh) *The Thatcher Effect* (Oxford University Press, 1989) and (with Andrew Graham) *Governments and Economics Since 1945* (Routledge, 1990).

Preface

Politics is an exciting subject. We, the authors, are naturally biased in thinking it offers its students very special attractions. It is a subject you digest with your breakfast. Each morning its complex canvas unfolds with the daily papers and broadcast news; by evening new details have been painted in and the scene subtly, sometimes dramatically changed. Politics is unpredictable, dynamic, it affects us, it is about us. In one sense the canvas *is* us; a projection of ourselves and our aspirations, a measure of our ability to live together. Politics is arguably the most important focus of study on the human condition. We hope that this volume on the politics of the United Kingdom does the subject justice.

This book is designed to provide a comprehensive introduction to British politics both for the general reader and for the examination candidate. With the latter group in mind, we have fashioned a text which is a little unusual by British standards. When we were studying 'A' levels twenty years or more ago (forgive us for not being more specific about our ages) the transition from 'O' level to the new textbooks was quite difficult. This was hardly surprising, because many of our 'A' level texts were the same as those we went on to study at University, partly because of the shortage of good books and partly because of shared assumptions about 'A' level and University students. It was believed that they should be treated as mature intellects (good), but also that it was up to them to extract meaning from texts which — in the name of standards — made no concession to their possible unfamiliarity with the subject (not so good). In the circumstances it is not surprising that so many aspirant university students gave up before the intrinsic interest of their subjects could capture them.

Things have improved since then — in the field of politics textbooks remarkably so. Syllabuses have become much wider, of course, and now embrace stimulating new areas like political sociology and current political issues. This has helped authors produce more interesting work, but a revolution has also taken place in the production of other kinds of teaching materials. Variety, clarity and visual appeal have become important aims, using devices like audio and video resources, theme packs and educational journals. *The Social Studies Review* appeared in 1985 and quickly established itself as a superb vehicle for the teaching of politics and sociology. Articles are concise and usually written in fresh, readable prose; layout owes much to the daily and weekly press, with extensive use of diagrams, tables and photographs. Three years later the Politics Association brought out its revamped *Talking Politics* with a similar style.

It will be immediately obvious to the reader that this book has been written and produced within this new tradition. To this extent, it is a new kind of textbook — though in America the approach has been around for some time. Rather like American texts, *Politics UK* aims to be comprehensive, addressing the core elements of all the 'A' level and university syllabuses on British government. Inevitably, it cannot be all-encompassing — it excludes some topics which arguably should have been included — and its content also reflects two particular biases. Together with the Institute for Contemporary British History (its director is one of our authors) the authors of this book believe political science has moved quite properly into the mainstream of social sciences since the 1950s, but to some extent at the expense of its historical base. We do not believe it is possible to understand British politics without a thorough grounding in British history, particularly since 1945. We therefore devote a section to history and each author, to a greater or lesser extent, has included a historical dimension in his contribution. The second bias favours the study of political ideas — a neglected subject on most introductory politics courses. Consequently, a section of the book concentrates on political ideologies.

Otherwise, the structure of the book focuses initially upon **context** — historical, social and ideological — before moving on to **process** — representative, legislative, judicial and executive. The final section concentrates upon the **policy process** and addresses five major policy areas. A feature of the book is that each major section is concluded by a comment (editorial) upon some relevant, sometimes topical subject. Throughout extensive use has been made of diagrams and illustrations from *Social Studies Review, Contemporary Record, The Economist* and other publications as well as illustrative material in the form of 'boxes'.

Special thanks are owed to Philip Cross at Philip Allan for helping the project along so tirelessly in its early stages; latterly to Clare Grist, who equally tirelessly saw the book through its final months of gestation; to Peter Hennessy, for his cheerful encouragement and assistance; to Andrew Bennett MP, Keith Bradley MP and John McHugh; and finally to Judith Martin for undertaking a disproportionate amount of the typing, usually at short notice and under pressure.

Bill Jones (Editor)
Andrew Gray
Dennis Kavanagh
Michael Moran
Philip Norton
Anthony Seldon

Manchester, 1991

Acknowledgements

The authors and publisher wish to thank the following who have kindly given permission for the use of copyright material:

A. Bilton *et al.* for information from *Introductory Sociology*, 2nd edition, Macmillan, 1987.

Butterworth Heinemann for figure from Colin Padfield, *British Constitution Made Simple*, 1972.

W & R Chambers Ltd for three diagrams from *The Business of Government* by J. Dennis Derbyshire, 1987.

The Controller of Her Majesty's Stationery Office for Crown copyright material from *Social Trends* and *Regional Trends*.

Ivor Crewe for table from his article, 'How the Working Class Voted', *The Guardian*, 15 June 1987.

Susan Crosland for an extract from her article in *The Sunday Times*, 28 January 1989.

David Denver for table from *Elections and Voting Behaviour in Britain*, Philip Allan, 1989.

The Economist for extracts from various issues of *The Economist*.

Grafton Books for figure from R. Tressell, *The Ragged Trousered Philanthropist*, 1965.

The Green Party for information on the history, ideology and structure of the Party.

The Guardian for extracts from various issues of *The Guardian*.

The Rt Hon. Roy Hattersley for an extract from his article in *The Guardian*, 30 September 1989.

Peter Kellner for an extract from his article, 'The War that Started a Revolution', *The Independent*, 28 August 1989.

J. Lundskaer-Nielsen *et al.* for material from *Contemporary British Society*, Akademisk Forlag, 1989.

Manchester University Press for material from B. Jones, *Political Issues in Britain Today*, 1989; J. McIlroy, *Trade Unions in Britain Today*, 1988; A. Adonis, *Parliament Today*, 1990; and B. Jones and D. Kavanagh, *British Politics Today*, 1978.

John McHugh for his chronology of key events in Northern Ireland.

Howard Newby for an extract from his article in *The Guardian*, 6 September 1989.

Oxford University Press for the table from M. Burch and M. Moran, 'The Changing Face of the British Parliamentary Elite 1945–1983', *Parliamentary Affairs*, **138**,

Winter 1985, p. 15, and two maps from Redcliffe Maud, Lord & Wood, *English Local Government Reformed*, 1974.

Philip Allan Publishers for various material from *Social Studies Review* and *Contemporary Record*.

Clive Ponting for extracts from his book, *Whitehall: Tragedy and Farce*, Hamish Hamilton, 1985.

Donald Shell for table from *The House of Lords*, Philip Allan, 1988.

The Study of Parliament Group for table from M. Rush, 'The Members of Parliament' in M. Ryle and P.G. Richards, *The Commons Under Scrutiny*, Routledge, 1988.

Talking Politics for various extracts.

Tyne Tees Television Ltd for material from *Is Democracy Working?*, 1986.

Unwin Hyman Ltd for table from B. Headey, *British Cabinet Ministers*, 1974.

Every effort has been made to trace all copyright holders, but if any have been inadvertently overlooked, the publishers will be pleased to make the necessary arrangements at the earliest opportunity.

1 Introduction: Explaining Politics

Bill Jones and Michael Moran

This opening chapter is devoted to a definition of 'politics' and the way in which its study can be approached. We discuss decision making and identify what exactly is involved in the phrase 'political activity'. We then go on to describe how the more general activity called 'politics' can be distinguished from the workings of 'the state'. In the second section, we describe some of the most important approaches used in the study of politics and examine the chief reasons for its study in schools and colleges. The third section explains the purpose of studying politics. Looking forward to later chapters, the fourth section sketches some of the themes raised in the study of British politics.

Definitions and Decision Making

Is politics necessary?

'A good politician' wrote the American writer H.L. Mencken, 'is quite as unthinkable as an honest burglar.' Cynical views of politics and politicians are legion. Any statement or action by a politician is seldom taken at face value but is scrutinized for ulterior personal motives. Thus, when Bob Hawke, the Australian Prime Minister, broke down in tears on television in March 1989, many journalists dismissed the possibility that he was genuinely moved by the topic under discussion. Instead they concluded that he was currying favour with the electorate — who allegedly warm to such manly shows of emotion — with a possible general election in mind.

Given such attitudes it seems reasonable to ask why people go into politics in the first place. The job is insecure: in Britain elections may be called at any time, and scores of MPs in marginal seats can lose their parliamentary salaries. The apprenticeship for ministerial office can be long, hard, arguably demeaning and, for many, ultimately unsuccessful. Even if successful, a minister has to work cripplingly long days, survive constant criticism — both well- and ill-informed — and know that a poor debating performance, a chance word or phrase out of place can earn a one-way ticket to the backbenches. To gamble your whole life on the chance that the roulette wheel of politics will stop on your number seems to be less than wholly rational behaviour. Why, then, do politicians fight for such dubious preferment?

Cynical views on politics and politicians

Politics: 'A strife of interests masquerading as principles.'
Ambrose Bierce

'Politics . . . has always been the systematic organisation of hatreds.'
Henry Adams

'Politics are . . . nothing more than a means of rising in the world.'
Samuel Johnson

'Politics ruin the character.' **Otto von Bismarck**

'Men who have greatness within them don't go in for politics.'
Albert Camus

'Politicians are the semi-failures in business and the professions, men of mediocre mentality.' **W.P. Pitkin**, US writer

'Politics is the diversion of trivial men who, when they succeed at it, become important in the eyes of more trivial men.'
George Jean Nathan, US editor and critic

'All politics are based on the indifference of the majority.'
James Reston, US political commentator

'Politicians are the same all over. They promise to build a bridge even when there is no river.' **Nikita Khrushchev**

'In argument truth always prevails finally; in politics falsehood always.' **Walter Savage Landor**

Not all judgements on politicians are cynical however . . .

'I reject the cynical view that politics is inevitably or even usually dirty business.' **Richard Nixon**, US President, nicknamed 'Tricky Dicky', who resigned following the Watergate Scandal in 1974

Biographies and interviews reveal an admixture of reasons: genuine commitment to a set of beliefs, the urge to acquire power and exercise it, the desire to be seen and heard a great deal, the trappings of office such as the official cars and solicitous armies of civil servants. Senator Eugene McCarthy suggested politicians were like football coaches: 'You have to be smart enough to understand the game and dumb enough to think it's important.' A witty remark, but true in the sense that politics is an activity which closely resembles a game and which similarly exercises an addictive or obsessive hold upon those who play it. But is the game worth playing? Words like 'betrayal', 'opportunism', 'exploitation', 'distortion' and 'fudge' are just some of the pejorative terms frequently used in describing the process. Would we not be better off without politics at all?

In his classic study *In Defence of Politics*, Bernard Crick disagrees strongly. For him politics is 'essential to genuine freedom . . . something to be valued as a pearl beyond price in the history of the human condition'. He reminds us of Aristotle's view that politics is 'only one possible solution to the problem of order. It is by no means the most usual. Tyranny is the most obvious alternative . . . oligarchy the next'. Crick understands 'politics' as the means whereby differing groups of people with different, often conflicting interests are enabled to live together in relative harmony. For him 'politics' describes the working of a *pluralist* political system

Bernard Crick, author of *In Defence of Politics* and champion of the cause of political education.

'in advanced and complex societies' which seeks to maximize the freedom and the power of all social groups. The system may be imperfect but it is less so than the various authoritarian alternatives.

This line of thinking provides an antidote to overly cynical analyses of politics. The compromises inherent in the process tend to discredit it: few will ever be wholly satisfied and many will feel hard done by. Similarly politicians as the imperfect practitioners of an imperfect system receive much of the blame. But without politicians to represent and articulate demands and to pursue them within an agreed framework we would be much the poorer. Whether Crick is right in reminding us to count our democratic blessings is a question which the reader must decide and we hope that this book will provide some of the material necessary for the making of such a judgement.

Defining politics

Politics is difficult to define yet easy to recognize. To some extent with the word 'politics' we can consider current usage and decide our own meaning, making our own definition wide or narrow according to our taste or purposes. From the discussion so far politics is obviously a universal activity; it is concerned with the governance of states, and (Crick's special concern) involves a conciliation or harmonization process. Yet we talk of politics on a *micro* as well as a *macro* scale: small groups like families or parent/teacher associations also have a political dimension. What

How much do people know about politics?

The answer would appear to be 'surprisingly little'.

The Observer (17 September 1989) commissioned a polling organization to ask a sample of 2,275 adults fifteen (relatively easy) general knowledge questions. Average scores according to party affiliation were as follows:

Green voters	9.26
SLD/SDP	9.12
Conservative	8.78
Labour	7.66

Answers to the political and historical questions were as follows:

'Who was Prime Minister before Margaret Thatcher?'
38 per cent answered correctly: James Callaghan (47 per cent of men but only 30 per cent of women)

'What are the dates of World War Two?'
71 per cent knew the answer: 1939–45

'Which of the following countries are not in the EC: Spain, France, Switzerland, Greece, Sweden?'
Only 31 per cent knew the answer: Switzerland and Sweden

'Who is the President of the USA?'
86 per cent answered correctly: George Bush

Source: taken from an *Observer* poll, 17 September 1989

is it that unites these two levels? The answer is: the conflict of different interests. People or groups of people who want different things — be it power, money, liberty, etc. — face the potential or reality of conflict when such things are in short supply. Politics begins when their interests clash. At the micro level we use a variety of techniques to get our own way: persuasion, rational argument, irrational strategies, threats, entreaties, bribes, manipulation — anything we think will work. At the macro level democratic states establish complex procedures for the management of such conflicts, often — though famously not in Britain's case — codified in the form of written constitutions. Representatives of the adult population are elected to a *legislature* or parliament tasked with the job of discussing and agreeing changes in the law as well as exercising control over the *executive*: those given responsibility for day-to-day decisions in the running of the country.

Is the political process essentially peaceful? Usually, but not exclusively. If violence is involved on a widespread scale, e.g. war between states, it would be fair to say that politics has been abandoned for other means. But it must be recognized that:

1. Political order *within* a state is ensured through the implicit threat of force which a state's control of the police and army provides. As John Adams (nineteenth-century US President) pointed out, 'Fear is the foundation of most governments.' Occasionally passions run high and the state's power is explicitly exercised — as in the 1984–5 miners' strike.
2. There are many situations in the world, for example in Northern Ireland or the

Lebanon, where violence is regularly used to provide both a context for and an alternative to peaceful political processes.

So, while political activity is peaceful for most of the time in most countries, the threat of violence or its reality are both integral parts of the political process. We should now be able to move towards a definition:

> *Politics is essentially a process which seeks to manage or resolve conflicts of interest between people, usually in a peaceful fashion. In its general sense it can describe the interactions of any group of individuals but in its specific sense it refers to the many and complex relationships which exist between state institutions and the rest of society.*

Peaceful political processes, then, are the alternative, the antidote to brute force. As the practitioners of this invaluable art politicians deserve our gratitude. It was interesting to note that in July 1989 when Mr Rafsanjani emerged as the successor to the Iranian extremist religious leader, Ayatollah Khomeini, several Iranians were quoted in the press approving him as 'a political man': someone who would be likely to steer the country away from the internal violence which religious conflicts threatened at the time.

Does this mean that cynical attitudes towards politicians should be discouraged? Not exactly, in our view. It is wrong that they should be widely undervalued and often unfairly blamed, but experience suggests that it is better to doubt politicians rather than trust them unquestioningly. After all, politicians are like salesmen and in their enthusiasm to sell their messages they often exaggerate or otherwise distort the truth. They also seek power and authority over us and this is not a privilege we should relinquish lightly. Lord Acton noted that 'all power tends to corrupt' and history can summon any number of tyrants in support of this proposition. We are right to doubt politicians but as John Donne advised, we should 'doubt wisely'.

Decision making

Much political activity culminates in the taking of decisions and all decisions involve choice. Politicians are presented with alternative courses of action — or inaction — and once a choice has been made they have to try to make sure their decisions are accepted. Two examples follow which illustrate the micro and macro senses of politics and which also introduce some important related terminology.

Decision making I: micropolitics

A 17-year-old girl wishes to go on holiday to Greece with three other girls — replicating a similar holiday taken by her brother two years earlier. Her father is strongly opposed to the proposal on the grounds that she is too young and vulnerable for such a risky undertaking.

On the face of it, this familiar argument has little to do with politics — yet it is an example of politics with a small 'p' or 'micro-politics' and political science terms can be fruitfully used to analyse the situation.

Interests in politics are defined as those things which people want or care about: usually financial resources but other things too like status, power, justice, liberty or the avoidance of unwanted outcomes. In this example the girl's interest lies principally in gaining permission to enjoy her first holiday abroad without her parents. Her father's interests clearly lie in sustaining paternal protection and avoiding personal worry.

Political actors in this instance include the two principals plus mother, brother and other friends, relations and neighbours who may be drawn into the debate.

Power in politics is the ability to get others to act in a particular way. Typically this is achieved through the exercise of threats and rewards but also through the exercise of *authority*: the acceptance of someone's *right* to be obeyed.

The power relationship in this case might be seen in the following terms. The daughter could offer 'rewards' to her father in terms of a promise of mature and responsible behaviour both on holiday and thereafter, substantial self-funding of her holiday and a firm resolve to work hard for next year's examinations. Her 'threats' could include a unilateral decision to defy her father and go on holiday; a prolonged period of misery which could disturb the harmony of the family; or difficult, rebellious, retaliatory behaviour.

Father could offer to pay the full cost of a 'safe' holiday or other financial inducements, but his hand is perhaps better stacked with threats, such as a refusal to fund the trip at all, extended cuts in pocket money or 'curfew' regulations on regular evening activities. He is obviously in the stronger position: he has both financial power and 'authority': the acceptance by his daughter of his right to respect based upon his years of caring for her from birth. The outcome of the conflict will depend upon a number of factors.

1. *Political will:* how prepared are father and daughter to offer rewards, or more importantly here, implement their threats?
2. *Influence:* how open are either actors to rational argument, appeals to loyalty and so forth? The daughter can obviously argue that it is unfair and inconsistent of her father to deny his daughter a privilege freely extended to his son. But will her father be receptive to this argument? For his part he can cite examples of young girls being attacked while on holiday abroad.
3. *Manipulation:* how effectively can daughter or father involve the other actors? The girl might persuade her brother to support her case, cite the permission given by the parents of other girls or indeed enlist their support. Her father would also, no doubt, seek support from other fathers or like-minded neighbours. Perhaps the decisive role would be played by the girl's mother; in this situation she might well determine the balance of power.

The political process would take place largely through face to face contact. Extended negotiations might feature attempts at rational persuasion, stormy displays of emotion and attempts at compromise solutions, for instance: Father: 'I'll pay for you to go next year but not this'; Daughter: 'I'll agree to ring home once or twice a day while I'm there'. Both major actors might damage their cases by overstatement, alienating potential allies or failing to press home their argument at crucial times. Experience of family life suggests that eventually a compromise would be achieved.

Decision making II: macro politics

One of the civil service unions seeks a pay increase three times the rate of inflation in order to, as it claims, 'catch up' with pay settlements in the private sector. The government offers only a rate of inflation increase, but offers to discuss further pay increases along with proposals to increase productivity and weaken terms of employment.

This familiar situation is quintessentially political.

Interests. The government's interests are clearly financial: it wishes to restrict public expenditure or at minimum 'sell' a pay increase in return for measures which would increase efficiency and save money in the future.

The union's interests are primarily financial but it will also wish to resist any erosion of its members' job security or status.

Actors in this particular drama are potentially numerous: other government departments, especially the Treasury; other civil service unions; other public and private sector unions; the Trades Union Congress (TUC); the Confederation of British Industry (CBI); political parties; both Houses of Parliament; the Cabinet; the media; local government pressure groups. The degree of involvement will depend upon how protracted and intense the process becomes.

Power. The power relationship in these circumstances would naturally be influenced by the ability of each side to deliver rewards or enforce threats. The government can 'reward' the union by giving way on the pay demand in exchange for union flexibility on the other issues. As paymaster, however, it can threaten to withhold any reward, sit out strike action and impose its proposals notwithstanding.

The union can reward the government by giving way on the award-related proposals. Its principal threat lies in its ability to disrupt government activity and possibly national life, through industrial action.

Authority. Two kinds of authority are in conflict here. The government can claim that its victory in the general election gives it a 'mandate' to rule and the right to be obeyed. Union leaders, however, assert their right to disagree with the government on this particular issue and also claim the right to obedience from their own members.

Which side is the stronger? On the face of it *the government* holds the key cards, especially in the context of weakened trade union power since Mrs Thatcher came to office. Ultimately the government controls the resources which the union wishes to release. However, like any employer it retains a key interest in maintaining good relations with its own work-force. *The union's strength* will depend upon a number of factors, principally the degree of rank and file support for the leadership; the density of union membership within the civil service; the perceived strength of the union's claim and the degree of public support for it; the willingness of other trade unions to render support; the union's financial resources; and the negotiating skills of its leaders. The outcome of this conflict will also depend upon the following:

1. *Political will.* How prepared are both sides to implement their threats; in the union's case indefinite strike action and in the government's case indifference to such action?
2. *Influence.* How open is either side to influence by third parties? Will they accept arbitration from some disinterested agency like the Advisory, Conciliation and Arbitration Service (ACAS)?

3. *Manipulation.* How effectively can the government undermine the union's membership through the media, private persuasion of civil service chiefs and so forth? Can the union win wider support via the media from the public, the unions, the TUC, MPs and others?

The political process in this case will be much more formalized and will take the form of long, tough negotiations between official delegations. Discussions will be secret but both sides will 'leak' to the press. If industrial action is involved the number of actors will multiply and the process will become more public and visible featuring public meetings, picket lines, banners, chants, leaflets, lines of marchers no doubt singing 'Here we go, here we go, here we go', and so on. Both sides throughout are seeking to communicate to each other the message that they are determined, united and powerful. Much of politics involves the pursuit of objectives through displaying strength rather than exercising it. These situations resemble games of poker in which the style and demeanour of the players is almost as important as the cards they play. There was much in ex-Prime Minister Harold Wilson's tongue-in-cheek comment that 'much of politics is presentation, and what isn't is timing'.

The Critical Political Questions

Because politics studies the making and carrying out of decisions, the student of politics learns to ask a number of important immediate questions about the political life of any institution.

1. Who is included and *who is excluded* from the process of decision making? It is rare indeed for all the members of a community or organization to be allowed a part in the decision making process. Mapping the divide between those taking part and those not taking part is the most important initial task of political enquiry.
2. What matters are actually dealt with by the political process? This is sometimes called 'identifying the political agenda'. Every community or body has such an agenda — a list of issues which are accepted as matters over which choices can be made. In a school the agenda may include the budget and the curriculum; in a church, the religious doctrine of the institution; within the government of a country such as Britain the balance of spending between defence and education. But the range of subjects 'on the political agenda' will vary greatly at different times and in different places. In modern Britain, for instance, the terms on which education is provided by the state is a major item of political argument. But before 1870, when compulsory education was first introduced, this was a matter which did not concern decision makers.
3. What do the various individuals or groups involved in the political process achieve? What are their interests and how clearly can they be identified?
4. What means and resources do decision makers have at their disposal to assist them in getting their way? When a decision is made, one set of preferences is chosen over another. In practice this means that one person or group compels or persuades others to give way. Compulsion or persuasion is only possible through the use of some resources. These are highly varied. We may get our way in a decision through the use of force, or money, or charm, or the intellectual

weight of our argument. Studying politics involves examining the range of political resources and how they are employed.

Politics, Government and The State

Every human being has some experience of politics, either as the maker of decisions or as the subject of decisions, because politics is part and parcel of social organization. An institution which did not have some means of making decisions would simply cease to be an institution. But this book is not long enough to deal with the totality of political life in Britain; it concentrates upon politics inside government and the organizations which are close to government.

The best way of understanding the special nature of politics with a capital 'P' is to begin by appreciating the difference between *the state* and other institutions in society. In a community like Britain there are thousands of organizations in which political activity takes place. By far the most significant of these is that body called 'the state', which can be defined as follows.

> *That institution in a society which exercises supreme power over a defined territory.*

Three features of the state should be noticed.

1. *The 'state' is more than the 'government'.* The state should not be equated with 'government', let alone with a particular government. When we speak of 'a Conservative Government' we are referring to the occupancy of the leading positions in government — such as the office of Prime Minister — by elected politicians drawn from a particular party. This in turn should be distinguished from 'government' in a more general sense, by which is meant a set of institutions, notably departments of state such as the Treasury and the Home Office, concerned with the conduct of policies and everyday administration. The state certainly encompasses these departments of state, but it also embraces a wider range of institutions. Most important, it includes the agencies whose role it is to ensure that in the last instance, the will of the state is actually enforced: these include the police, the courts and the armed forces.

2. *Territory is a key feature of the state.* What distinguishes the state from other kinds of institutions in which politics takes place is that it is the supreme decision maker in a defined territory. Other institutions in Britain take decisions which their members obey; but power in a family, a school or a firm is ultimately regulated by the will of the state. In Britain, this idea is expressed in the notion of *sovereignty*. The sovereign power of the state consists in the ability to prescribe the extent and limits of the powers which can be exercised by any other organization in British society.

   It follows that this sovereignty is limited territorially. The British state lives in a world of other states, and the extent of its rule is defined by its physical boundaries — which inevitably abut onto the boundaries of other states.

   Disputes about the physical boundaries of state sovereignty are among the most serious in political life. It might be thought that an 'island state', which is how

Britain is conventionally pictured, would have no difficulty in establishing its boundaries. In practice, identification is complicated and often leads to fierce disputes with other states over claims to territory. In 1982 a rival sovereign state, Argentina, had to be expelled by force when it occupied territory (which Britain claims for its own) in the Falkland Islands of the South Atlantic. Another source of dispute arises from the fact that the boundaries of a state are not identical with its land mass: states like Britain also claim jurisdiction over the air space above that land mass and over territorial waters surrounding the land. In recent decades, for instance, Britain has extended its 'territorial limits' — the area of sea over which it claims sovereignty — from three miles to two hundred miles beyond the shoreline, in order to possess the fishing and mineral exploration rights of those waters. This extension has often caused disputes between rival claimants.

The fact that there exists on earth only a finite amount of land, sea and air space means that the sovereignty of a particular state over territory is always subject to potential challenge from outside. Occasionally the ferocity of this challenge may actually lead to the destruction of a state: in 1945, for instance, the defeat of Germany at the end of the Second World War led to the destruction of the German state and the occupation of all German territory by its victorious opponents.

A state's sovereignty is, however, not only subject to external challenge; it can also be disputed internally. In 1916, for instance, the boundaries of the British state encompassed the whole island of Ireland. Between 1916 and 1921 there occurred a military uprising against British rule which ended in agreement to redraw territorial boundaries, creating an independent Irish state covering most of what had hitherto been British sovereign territory.

3. *State power depends on legitimacy.* As the example of the Falklands, the destruction of the German state after 1945 and the creation of an independent state in Ireland all show, control of the means of coercion is an important guarantor of sovereignty. But the sovereign power of a state depends not only on its capacity to coerce; it also rests on the recognition by citizens that the state has the *authority* or *right* to exercise power over those who live in its territory. This is commonly called *legitimacy*. It would be extremely difficult for a state to survive if it did not command this legitimacy. Britain, like most other large communities with sophisticated and advanced economies, is far too complex a society to be governed chiefly by force. This is why the state in Britain, as in other advanced industrial nations, claims not only to be the supreme power in a territory, but claims to be the supreme *legitimate* power.

This right to obedience is asserted on different grounds by different states at different times. The German social theorist Max Weber offered a famous distinction between three types of legitimacy: traditional, charismatic and rational—legal. The first of these rests on custom and appeals to continuity with the past. It is the principal ground, for instance, by which rule through a hereditary monarchy is justified. The second appeals to the divine-like, 'anointed' quality of leadership: in our century many of the greatest dictators, like Adolf Hitler, have commanded obedience through their charismatic qualities. Rational—legal legitimacy rests on the ground that in making decisions agreed rules and agreed purposes are observed.

Weber's three
kinds of
legitimacy

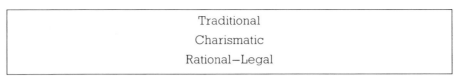

Traditional

Charismatic

Rational—Legal

Although in any state elements of all three sorts of legitimacy can be identified, they will be emphasized in different ways. In Britain, *charisma* is relatively unimportant. Although some politicians are occasionally described as 'charismatic' personalities, this is no more than a journalistic way of saying 'exciting' or 'appealing'. Political leadership in Britain does not rest on a claim that governors are 'anointed' with divine-like qualities. *Tradition* in Britain, by contrast, does have some importance. The crown is the symbol of political authority and the Queen's right to that crown of course rests on inheritance — she was born to the succession, like the monarch who preceded her and the one who will follow her. However, the legitimacy of the state in Britain rests only in part on tradition; for the main part it is *rational—legal* in character: its actions are taken in accordance with agreed procedures, in particular, laws passed by Parliament. It is an absolute principle of the exercise of state authority that the state cannot legitimately command the obedience of citizens if its demands do not carry the backing of legislation, or the *force of law*.

Approaching the Study of Politics

We now have some idea of the nature of politics as an activity. It is the process by which conflicting interests are managed and authoritative choices made in social institutions as different as the family and the firm. The most important set of political institutions are conventionally called 'the state', and it is the state which is the focus of the discipline called 'political science'.

Political science is now a large and well established academic discipline in both Europe and North America. For instance, the American Political Science Association has 12,000 members and in Britain the Political Studies Association and the Politics Association have over 1000. However, this is a relatively recent development. The emergence of political science as a separate discipline organized on a large scale in universities and colleges first developed in the United States in the early decades of this century. Even now, the overwhelming majority of people called 'political scientists' are American. Before the emergence of political science the subject was divided between specialists in different disciplines (see Figure 1.1). Constitutional lawyers studied the legal forms taken by states. Historians studied the relations between, and the organization of, states in the past. Philosophers discussed the moral foundations, if any, of state authority. In large part the modern discipline is the heir to these earlier approaches. It is important to be aware of the main approaches, because the approach employed in any particular study influences the kind of questions it asks, the evidence it considers relevant and the conclusions it draws.

Three important approaches are sketched here: the institutional, the policy cycle and the socio-political. These, it should be emphasized, are not mutually exclusive. They are indeed approaches; and just as we usually gain an appreciation of a physical

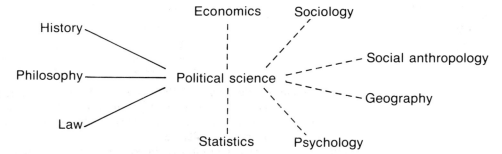

Figure 1.1 *Some of the disciplines contributing to political science*

object like a work of art if we look at it from a variety of angles, so we understand a system of government better if we examine it in a similarly varied way.

The ***institutional or constitutional approach*** to the study of politics was until recently dominant in the study of government in Britain. It has three distinctive features: its focus, its assumptions and its choice of evidence. The ***focus*** of the institutional approach is upon the formal institutions of government. In Britain this means a concentration on the bodies at the heart of what is sometimes called 'central government' in London: the two Houses of Parliament, the Cabinet, the individual Ministries and Ministers and the permanent civil servants in those ministries. The working assumption of this approach is that the legal structure of government and the formal organizations in which government activities happen have an importance in their own right. In other words, they are not just the reflections of other social influences; on the contrary, they are assumed to exercise an independent influence over the life of the community. In practical terms this means that the approach is dominated by an examination of the legal rules and the working conventions which govern the operation of these formal institutions.

It is sometimes objected that this approach is static, that it has a tendency to stress the character of government at one fixed moment, and to neglect the fact that political life is characterized by constant cycles of activity.

The ***policy cycle approach*** tries to capture this cyclical quality. Government is examined as a series of 'policy cycles'. It is pictured as a system of ***inputs*** and ***outputs***, as shown in Figure 1.2.

Political activity is pictured as a series of stages in the making and execution of decisions about policy. At the stage of ***policy initiation*** there exist both demands and resources. At any one moment in a community there will be a wide range of views about what government should do, which will manifest themselves as demands of various kinds: that, for instance, government should provide particular services, such as free education for all under a certain age; that it should decide the appropriate balance of resources allocated to different services; or that it should decide the exact range of social activity which is appropriate for government, rather than for other social institutions, to regulate. Making and implementing policy choices in response to these demands requires resources. These are the second major input into government and include: people, like the administrators and experts necessary to make policy choices and to implement them; and money, which is needed to pay

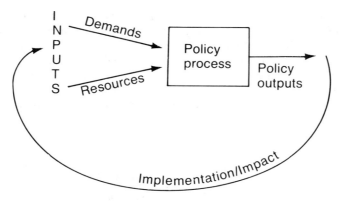

Figure 1.2 *The policy cycle*

government personnel. These resources can be raised in a wide variety of ways; for example, revenue can be raised by taxation, by borrowing or by charging for the services that governments provide.

After examining the initial stages of resource raising and allocation, the policy cycle approach describes the processing of inputs; in other words, how the balance of different demands and the balance between demands and resources is allocated to produce policy choices. Finally, the process of what is sometimes called policy implementation and policy impact (see Figure 1.2) studies how government policies are put into effect and what consequences they may have for the subsequent balance of demands and resources. It is this emphasis on the linked nature of all stages in the policy process which leads us to speak of the *policy cycle* approach (see also Chapter 23). This approach is also distinguished by its particular focus, assumptions and choice of evidence. Although it resembles the institutional approach in concentrating attention on the institutions of government its focus is primarily on what these institutions do, rather than on how they are organized, because the most important assumption here is that what is interesting about government is that it makes choices — in response to demands and in the light of the scarce resources at its command. In turn this affects the sort of evidence on which the 'policy cycle' approach concentrates. Although much of this evidence concerns practical functioning and organization of government, it also involves the wider environment of government institutions. This is necessarily so because the demands made on government and the resources which it can raise all come from that wider society. In this concern with the wider social context of government institutions the policy approach shares some of the concerns of the socio-political approach.

The socio-political approach has two particularly important concerns: the social foundations of the government order; and the links connecting government to the wider organization of society. Close attention is paid to the wider social structure and to the kinds of political behaviour which spring from it. It is a working assumption of this approach that government is indeed part of a wider social fabric, and that its workings can only be understood through an appreciation of the texture of that wider fabric. Some versions make even stronger assumptions. For instance, most Marxist scholars believe that the workings of government in a community are at the most fundamental level determined by the kind of economic organization prevailing in that community. The focus and assumptions of the socio-political approach in turn shape the kind of evidence on which it focuses. This includes not only information about the social structure, but also about the social influences which shape important political acts, such as voting and the kinds of economic and social interests (like business and workers) who influence the decisions taken in government. Table 1.1 summarizes the differences between these approaches.

Table 1.1   *Summary of important approaches to the study of politics*

Approaches	Focus	Main assumptions	Examples of characteristic evidence examined
Institutional	Formal machinery of government	Formal structures and legal rules are supreme	Structure of Parliaments, Cabinets, Civil Services
Public cycle	Choices made by government	Government action shaped by mix of demands and resources; policy affects wider society	Kinds of resources (money, etc.). Patterns of policy making and implementation
Socio-political	Social context, links between government and society	Structure and production of government shaped by wider society	Economy and class structure; organization of interest groups

Why We Study Politics

It is not difficult to understand why many individuals wish to take part in political activity. Some people have a desire to control the lives of their fellow human beings; most people wish to control their own lives. Political activity offers the chance to exercise such control. But the study of politics is an altogether different matter. It offers the chance of gaining understanding rather than power. What is the purpose of attempting to acquire this understanding? In a country like Britain, the reasons are threefold.

1. *Training in citizenship.* Even when not studied as part of an examinable course, knowledge of how the system of politics works is an important part of training in citizenship. Citizenship conveys the right to make choices: between different parties at elections; between different forms of political activity, or no activity at all; between opposition to, or support for, the policies designed to meet the pressing problems of the day. Making these choices sensibly and intelligently obviously demands some thought about, and knowledge of, the substance of the issues involved. It is not sensible, for instance, to form definite views about how the National Health Service should be organized without knowing at least a little about the problem of providing health care for the community.

   But another kind of knowledge is necessary to make a sensible choice as a citizen: knowledge not just about the substance of the issue in question, but the means by which decisions can be made and the processes by which they can be put into effect. This latter sort of knowledge comes from an examination of the political process in a community like Britain. Wishing a particular result is, in politics, a very long way from achieving it. The effective citizen who wishes to have some say over how the community is governed needs to be in a position to make some appreciation of political and administrative possibilities. This is particularly important in Britain because, as we will discover, one of the characteristic features of the British political system is that citizens are offered choices by fiercely competitive teams (political parties) who wish to be selected as governors of the country. Assessing the realism of the competing promises made by these teams demands a knowledgeable and educated citizenry — educated not only in the substantive nature of particular policies, but also in the realities of political power and in the administrative capacities of the state. The study of politics is, then, about the way a person can become educated so as more effectively to play the part of a democratic citizen. But there is also a second use to which political knowledge can be put.

2. *Improving the effectiveness of government.* Political institutions are in part the product of conscious human design. They are created by people in particular circumstances to achieve certain purposes. The civil service in Britain, for instance, was reformed in the later decades of the nineteenth century in an attempt to produce an efficient and corruption-free administrative machine capable of putting into effect the laws passed by Parliament. Because political and administrative institutions can be designed, they can also be changed and reformed in order to ensure that they achieve their goals more effectively. One purpose of the study of politics is to examine institutions with a view to assessing that effectiveness and discovering how it can be increased. Judgements of this order are far from simple. Different institutions have different objects, so the assessment of effectiveness will vary greatly: what constitutes effectiveness in a political party will be very different from what constitutes effectiveness in a civil service department. Nor is producing increased effectiveness a straightforward matter. The kind of knowledge we acquire from the study of politics does not allow us to engage in social engineering. A malfunctioning engine or a defective bridge can be dismantled and rebuilt to cure defects; the problems of an institution such as the House of Commons cannot be solved by simply abolishing that body and starting again.

Nevertheless, the study of politics can make a practical contribution to the workings of institutions. It encourages discussion about the goals to which they should aim; it examines cases of successful achievement and of failure and offers the possibility of making recommendations for reforms and improvements.

Part of the purpose of the study and teaching of politics is, then, to encourage citizens to become more knowledgeable and sophisticated and to produce a better appreciation of the purposes and functioning of institutions in order to improve their working effectiveness. But the study of politics is not simply an activity whose existence has immediate practical justifications. Understanding political life also illuminates the wider nature of a society.

3. *Understanding British society.* The political life of a community is part and parcel of its total social life. Nobody could claim to understand Britain who knew nothing of its history or its literature. In other words, political life is an integral part of the culture of a community, and understanding the culture of Britain demands

a knowledge of British political institutions. Therefore, we study British politics in part for exactly the same reasons that we study English literature or the history of the country: it is quite simply a necessary part of any person's knowledge of the experience of being British.

Themes and Issues in British Politics

Britain's system of government is one of the most intensively examined in the world; not surprisingly, therefore, there is no shortage of issues and themes. We conclude this introductory chapter by selecting four which are of special importance and which recur in different ways in the chapters following. These themes are: democracy and responsibility; efficiency and effectiveness; the size and scope of government; and the impact of government on the wider society.

Democracy and responsibility

British government is intended to be democratic and responsible: it is meant to be guided by the choices of citizens, to act within the law and to give an account of its actions to society's elected representatives. The issue of how far democracy and responsibility do indeed characterize the political system is central to the debates about the nature of British government. Defenders of the system point to a variety of features. Democratic practices include the provision for election — at least once every five years — of the membership of the House of Commons by an electorate comprising 43 million from Britain's 57 million inhabitants. The membership of the Commons in turn effectively decides which party will control government during the duration of a Parliament's life, while all legislation requires a majority vote in the Commons. In addition to these formal practices, a number of other provisions support democratic political life. Freedom of speech, assembly and publication allow the presentation of a wide variety of opinions, thus offering the electorate a choice when they express a democratic preference. The existence of competing political parties similarly means that there are clear and realistic choices facing voters when they go to the polls in elections.

Democracy means that the people can decide the government and exercise influence over the decisions governments take. *Responsibility* means that government is subject to the rule of law and can be held to account for its actions. Those who think British government is 'responsible' in this way point to a variety of institutions and practices, some of which are formal in nature. They include the right to challenge the activities of government in the courts and to have the actions of ministers and civil servants overturned if it transpires that they are done without lawful sanction. They also include the possibility of questioning and scrutinizing — for instance in the House of Commons — government ministers over their actions and omissions. In addition to these formal provisions responsibility rests on wider social restraints which are intended to hold government in check. The mass media report on and scrutinize the activities of politicians and civil servants while a wide range of associations and institutions, such as trade unions and professional bodies, act as counterweights in cases where government threatens to act in an unrestrained way.

Against these views a variety of grounds have been produced for scepticism about the reality of responsible democratic government in Britain. Some observers are sceptical of the adequacy of democratic institutions and practices. Is it possible, for instance, to practise democracy when the main opportunity offered to the population to make a choice only occurs in a general election held once every four or five years? It is also commonly observed that the links between the choices made in General Elections and the selection of a government are far from identical. The workings of the British electoral system (see Chapter 11) mean that it is almost unheard-of for the 'winning' party in a general election to attract the support of a majority of those voting.

Even greater scepticism has been expressed about the notion that government in Britain is 'responsible'. Many observers argue that the formal mechanisms for restraining Ministers and civil servants are weak. Widespread doubt, for instance, has been expressed of the notion that the House of Commons can effectively call ministers and civil servants to account. Indeed, some experienced observers and participants have spoken of the existence of an 'elective dictatorship' in Britain: in other words, of a system where government, though it requires the support of voters every four or five years, is able in the intervening period to act in an unrestrained way. There have also been sceptical examinations of the wider mechanisms intended to ensure restraint and accountability. Some insist that the mass media, for instance, are far from being independent observers of the doings of government; that, on the contrary, they are systematically biased in favour of the powerful and against the weak in Britain. Similar claims have been made by observers of the judiciary — a key group since, according to the theory of responsible government, judges are vital in deciding when government has acted in a way which is not sanctioned by law. Finally, some radical observers go further and argue not merely that 'democratic responsibility' is defective, but that there is a 'secret state' in Britain; in other words, a system of unchecked power which operates outside the scrutiny of public institutions and which is able to act systematically outside the law.

Efficiency and effectiveness

Arguments about democracy and responsibility touch on the moral worth of the system of government in Britain, but government is not only to be evaluated by its moral credentials. It also is commonly judged by its working effectiveness — and justifiably so, for the worth of a system of government is obviously in part a function of its capacity to carry out in an effective way the tasks which the community decides are its responsibility.

Until comparatively recently it was widely believed that British government was indeed efficient and effective in this sense. Britain was one of the first countries in the world, for instance, to develop a civil service selected and promoted according to ability rather than to political and social connections. In the last quarter century, however, the efficiency and effectiveness of British government have been widely questioned. Critics focus on three issues: the skills of public servants, the evidence of the general capabilities of successive British governments and the evidence of particular policy failures.

The most important and powerful public servants in Britain are acknowledged to be 'senior civil servants' — a small group of senior administrators, mostly based in London, who give advice about policy options to Ministers. This senior civil service is largely staffed by what are usually called 'generalists' — individuals chosen and promoted for their general intelligence and capabilities rather than because they possess a particular managerial or technical skill. However, critics of the efficiency of British government have argued that the nature of large-scale modern government demands administrators who are more than generally intellectually capable; it demands individuals trained in a wide range of specialized skills.

The absence of such a group, drawn from disciplines like engineering and accountancy, at the top of British government is often held to explain the second facet of poor effectiveness — the general inability of British government to manage its most important tasks effectively. In recent decades the chief task of government in Britain has been to manage the economy. That task has, measured by the standards of Britain's major competitors, been done with conspicuous lack of success. In the 1950s Britain was one of the richest nations in Western Europe; by the 1980s she was one of the poorest.

The debate about the general competence of British government has been heightened by a series of more particular instances of policy failure in recent decades. One observer, surveying the history of British policy initiatives, concluded that there existed only one instance of a major policy success (the introduction of 'clean air' legislation in the 1950s). On the other hand, every observer can produce numerous instances of policy disasters: the Concorde aeroplane, which should have assured the country a first place in modern aircraft manufacture, and which turned out to be an expensive commercial failure; a series of financial and technical disasters in the field of weapons development; and a comprehensive disaster in the building, during the 1950s and 1960s, of uninhabitable high-rise tower blocks in the effort to solve the country's housing problems.

The belief that the efficiency and effectiveness of British government have been defective has dominated debates about the organization of the system in the last thirty years and has produced numerous proposals for reform in the machinery. A few of these have even been implemented. Local government, for instance, was reorganized in the early 1970s into larger units which, it was believed, would deliver services more efficiently. Within the last decade, however, a new argument has entered the debate. The belief that the problems of efficiency and effectiveness were due to a lack of particular skills, or lack of an appropriate organizational structure, has been increasingly displaced by a more radical notion: that the failings of the system were intrinsic to government, and that more efficient and effective institutions could only come when government itself was reduced to a more manageable size and scope. In other words, there is a link between the debates about efficiency and effectiveness and our third theme — the size and scope of government.

Size and scope of government

British government is big government. Major public services — the provision of transport, health care, education — are performed wholly or largely by public institutions. Many of the institutions are, by any standards, very large indeed, for example the National Health Service. As we will see in Chapter 4, Britain has a 'mixed' economy. In other words, goods and services are produced by a combination of private enterprise and public institutions. Nevertheless, an astonishing variety of goods and services are provided by what is commonly called 'the public sector'. What is more, until very recently this sector was steadily growing at the expense of the private sector.

The growth of government to gigantic proportions has prompted two main debates, about its efficiency as a deliverer of goods and services; and about the impact of a growing public sector on the wider economy. The 'efficiency' debate we have already in part encountered. In the last decade, however, many free market economists have argued that government failures are due to more than the failings of particular people and structures. They are, it is argued, built into the very nature of government. According to this view the public sector lacks many of the most important disciplines and spurs to effectiveness under which private firms have to work. In particular, say its critics, the public sector rarely has to provide services in competition with others. Because the taxpayer always stands behind a public enterprise the discipline exercised by the possibility of losses and bankruptcy, which guides private firms, is absent in the case of government. Thus government has an inherent tendency towards wastefulness and inefficiency. Defenders of the public sector, on the other hand, while not denying the possibility of waste and inefficiency, argue that failures also happen in the private sector; and that, indeed, one of the most important reasons for the growth of government is the failure of private enterprise to provide vital goods and services on terms acceptable to consumers.

A more general argument about the problems of having a large scale public sector concerns the resources which are needed to maintain this sector. In the 1970s perhaps the most influential explanation of the failings of the British economy rested on the claim that Britain had 'too few producers'. It was argued that non-productive services had grown excessively at the expense of the sector of the economy producing manufactured goods for the home market and for export. A large proportion of the excessive expansion of the 'service' sector consisted in the growth of public services such as welfare, health and education. These were in effect 'crowding out' more productive activities. Against this view, it has been argued that the growth of 'services' is more a consequence than a cause of the contraction of manufacturing in Britain, and that in any case 'non-productive' services, such as education, are actually vital to sustaining a productive manufacturing sector.

Whatever the rights and wrongs of these arguments we will see in succeeding chapters that critics of 'big government' have, in the 1980s, enjoyed much influence over policy. Many activities once thought 'natural' to the public sector — such as the provision of services like a clean water supply and energy for the home — have been, or are being, transferred to private ownership. Arguments about 'privatization', as these transfers are usually called, have also cropped up in the final major theme we sketch here — the impact of government.

The impact of government

We already know from our description of the 'policy cycle' approach that government has powerful effects on the wider society. Modern government takes in society's resources — money, people, raw materials — and 'converts' them into policies. In turn, these policies plainly have a great effect on the lives of us all. On this there is general agreement, but there is great disagreement about the precise impact of government. This disagreement has crystallized into a long-standing argument about the extent to which the effects of government activity are socially progressive or regressive — in simpler terms, whether the rich or poor get most out of the policy process.

The most important way government raises resources in a country like Britain is through taxation. The taxation system in Britain is guided by the principle of 'progression': in other words, the wealthier the individual or institution, the greater the liability to pay tax. On the other hand, the services provided by government are either consumed collectively (for instance, national defence), are consumed individually but are freely available to all (such as free art galleries) or are designed for the poor (such as supplementary welfare payments). By contrast, it is difficult to think of a public service which is designed to be consumed only by the rich. These considerations should ensure that the impact of government is redistributive between rich and poor. At the extremes of poverty, for instance, the poor should contribute nothing to taxation but nevertheless be eligible for a wide range of benefits paid for from the general taxes paid by everyone else in the community.

Critics of the view that the impact of government is redistributive in this way rest their case on several arguments. Firstly, some services of government, while not designed for the benefit of the better-off, may nevertheless be worth more to the rich than to the poor. An efficient police service, for instance, which deters theft, is correspondingly desirable according to the amount of property one stands to lose to thieves. Secondly some services, while again designed to be universally enjoyed, may in practice be almost totally consumed by the better-off. In the arts, for example, opera attracts large public subsidies but is rarely patronized by the poor and is highly fashionable among the rich. Thirdly, some services, while designed to actually ensure equality of treatment for all, or even preferential treatment for the deprived, may nevertheless in practice be more widely used by the better-off than by the poor. It is widely alleged, for instance, that the National Health Service in Britain actually disproportionately devotes its resources to caring for the better-off. This is partly because the poorest in the community are least knowledgeable about the services available and least willing to make demands for these services; and partly because the actual distribution of resources inside the Health Service is alleged to be biased towards the more vocal and better-off groups in society.

Most of the argument about the redistributive effects of government focus on where the services provided by the public sector actually end up, but some observers also question how far the formally 'progressive' character of the taxation system is realized in practice. It is commonly argued that the very richest are also the most sophisticated at minimizing their taxation obligations by the use of skilled advisers like accountants and tax lawyers, whose speciality is to arrange the financial affairs of a company or an individual so as to minimize the amount of tax which must legally be paid.

This opening chapter has discussed the meaning of politics, the characteristics of the state, approaches to the study of politics, reasons for studying the subject and some important themes and issues in British politics. The rest of the book, organized in eight parts, follows directly from the definition we adopted on page 5.

Politics is about conflicting interests: Parts I and II provide the historical, social and economic contexts from which such conflicts emerge in Britain. Part III, on ideology, examines the intellectual basis of such conflicts.

Politics is also centrally concerned with how state institutions manage or resolve conflicts within society. Parts IV, V, VI and VII deal respectively with the representative, legislative, executive and judicial processes whereby such management takes place or is attempted. Finally, Part VIII examines how these institutions handle the major policy areas.

References and Further Reading

Crick, B., *In Defence of Politics*, 2nd edn (Penguin, 1982).

Duverger, M., *The Idea of Politics* (Methuen, 1966).

Jones, B. and Kavanagh, D., *British Politics Today*, 4th edn (Mancheser University Press, 1991).

Laver, M., *Invitation to Politics* (Martin Robertson, 1983).

Leftwich, A., *What is Politics? The Activity and its Study* (Blackwell, 1984).

Renwick, A. and Swinburn, I., *Basic Political Concepts*, 2nd edn (Hutchinson, 1987).

PART
1

The Historical Context

The authors of this book heartily agree with G.K. Chesterton's observation that 'the disadvantage of men not knowing the past is that they do not know the present. History is a hill or high point advantage from which alone men see the town in which they live or the age in which they are living.' Historical understanding is a neglected but vitally necessary skill needed by political scientists. Without it they skate on the surface, their facts have no purchase and their ideas are two-dimensional. The following two chapters on the historical context of British politics are, therefore, necessary underpinnings for subsequent sections of the book.

2 Britain and the World since 1945

Anthony Seldon

This chapter deals with the dramatic economic and political decline in Britain's world role during the two decades after the Second World War, which subsequently did much to determine the nature of domestic political events. It pursues three analytical themes up to 1979: defence policy, decolonization and entry into Europe. The record of the Thatcher governments in defence and foreign policy is dealt with in Chapter 28.

The World in 1945

In 1945 the biggest war in the history of mankind ended. Unlike the First World War of 1914–18, which was largely a European affair, the Second World War was truly international, spreading from the Far East through the Indian subcontinent, the Middle East and North Africa down to the South Atlantic. By 1945 the world was exhausted.

Germany was decisively beaten, and the Third Reich, which Hitler had said would endure for a thousand years, lasted just twelve. The combination of countries fighting against her proved too much for Germany. The British contribution to the war effort was eclipsed by the USSR and USA, but up to their entry into the war (in 1940 and 1941 respectively) she had fought almost alone against the menacing wills of the German and Italian dictators.

Long before the surrender of Germany in May and of Japan in August 1945, it became clear that Britain would not be able to compete on equal terms after the war with the Soviet and American superpowers, in either military or political terms. Both these countries had vastly greater military might than Britain, the former by virtue of its concentration of economic resources on defence, the latter backed up by its almost limitless economic wealth. The war had shown how dependent on other countries for economic resources, and for physical protection, Britain had become. As with the First World War, the war would not have been won without the intervention of the USA. Great power status had moved away decisively from Europe.

Whereas the former European great powers had constantly jockeyed for power, no major doctrinal difference had separated them. Yet the USA and USSR were indomitably opposed, each championing respectively the opposed ideologies of capitalism and communism. Within months of the ending of war in 1945 it became clear that these two nations, allies during the war from 1941—5, would now become implacable enemies. The world was quickly dividing itself into two hostile camps, with a numerically large but politically weak 'non-aligned' group of nations in the middle. The high ideals which launched the United Nations (UN), the international body which superseded the ill-fated League of Nations of the inter-war years, quickly foundered on the rocks of the 'Cold War' — the war of words and propaganda fought between the East and West.

Where stood Britain in the face of this rearrangement of the balance of power in the world? It is necessary to appreciate how devastating a blow the war was to Britain. A quarter of a million dead, with many more wounded, often for life, provides a clue to the extent of the trauma. Britain's homes and factories were severely damaged, especially in London, south eastern towns and in towns with ports. The whole economy was severely dislocated, with debts and loans much increased and exports devastated, never fully to recover. The USA also suffered with a similar number of dead, but the ability of the US economy to recover from the expense and shock of the war drain was far greater. Britain, in truth, was already in relative decline by 1939: the war merely provided another decisive downward push.

Yet we should not write off Britain in 1945 as already a second-rank power; to do so would be quite wrong. Although weak economically, she still had great power expectations. She was one of only five nations (alongside the USA, USSR, China and France) to have a permanent seat on the UN Security Council, she presided over a vast empire and she was shortly to become (in 1952) the world's third nation (after the USA and USSR) to possess nuclear weapons.

By 1979, however, Britain had become almost the sick man of Europe, economically declining, her former status as a leading nation submerged in the European Economic Community, very much the junior partner in a fairly cool 'special relationship' with the USA and in possession of a mere handful of scattered overseas colonies of no great economic or military significance.

How did this *volte face* occur? The story breaks down into three main parts: defence policy, decolonization and entry into Europe. They will be discussed separately although in reality all three are inextricably interconnected.

Defence Policy 1945—79

The strain of maintaining Britain's vast overseas empire made itself felt long before 1945. During the late nineteenth and early twentieth centuries, Chancellors of the Exchequer frequently had cause to complain about the excessive drain on the economy caused by the cost of Britain's overseas empire. The First World War (1914—18) strained the nation to breaking point and left the empire vulnerable in many areas. The inter-war years continued to be a period when need outstripped capability to the extent that, in 1937, the British government decided that no army could be sent to France in the event of war with Germany due to shortcomings in men and military equipment.

These earlier stresses pale into insignificance when contrasted with the burden posed by the Second World War. Britain found herself in 1945 not just with a massive accumulated debt but also in possession of ever more overseas territory. Some responsibilities were only temporary, including Indo-China and Indonesia, which were soon returned to their former colonial rulers, respectively France and Holland. But other fresh commitments were to be of longer duration, and included Britain's occupation of former enemy territories — most conspicuously the British zone in Germany, Trieste and Libya.

NATO

The primary objectives of defence policy, once the war was over, returned to the staple tasks of defending the mainland and British territories overseas with maximum efficiency and minimum cost. From the late 1940s, Britain was able to run down its military presence. A number of factors was responsible, principally the stabilizing (if not defrosting) of cold war relations with the Soviet Union. The granting of independence to India in 1947 and the ending of the Palestine mandate the following year both freed large numbers of troops. Withdrawal from India heightened the importance of the Suez Canal Base, from which some 200,000 British troops were supplied or stationed. The Middle East, with the Canal Base as the hub, became the focus of Britain's overseas attention in the late 1940s. Europe was almost of secondary importance in Britain's defence plans: had Stalin decided to invade Western Europe, his troops would have encountered very little resistance, bar the threat of nuclear retaliation from the USA. It was against this background that the Brussels Pact and the North Atlantic Treaty which became NATO were signed in 1949, mainly at the instigation of the British Foreign Secretary, Ernest Bevin. NATO, however, did not lead to any immediate reinforcement of British troops in Europe: this only came later. At the time, European security did not seem to be a pressing issue.

This complacent picture was overturned rudely by a series of events from the late 1940s. The successful testing by the USSR of an atomic bomb in 1949 ended the Western monopoly of nuclear weapons much earlier than had been anticipated and opened up the prospect of Soviet atomic bombs landing on Paris, London and New York. The communist takeover of China also came in 1949 and at a stroke altered the balance of power in the Far East, putting under threat a whole range of territories allied to or possessed by the West.

Korea

Worse was to follow with the outbreak of the Korean War in June 1950, which further alarmed an already anxious West. The invasion by North Korea of the South was interpreted in both London and Washington as a Soviet-inspired move to divert Western resources to the Far East, leaving the front door open in Europe to further Soviet advance. At the time, many thought that a Third World War was imminent: with hindsight, the fears appear exaggerated if not unfounded.

The Attlee Government responded to the Korean War with a massive rearmament campaign in 1950 and 1951 and a shift in focus of British defence policy from the Middle East to Europe, where it has remained ever since. The British Army of the Rhine (BAOR) was increased from two to four divisions, and at the same time deployment of NATO forces was moved forward from the Rhine to a new line near the East German border, thus protecting German industry and further deterring the Red Army.

The crisis passed. A truce came in Korea, with the communist North Koreans pushed back out of the south. Further stiffening of US nerve came with their successful testing of the altogether more deadly thermonuclear ('hydrogen') bomb in 1952. It was left to a Conservative government under Winston Churchill to cut back on the defence build-up, which had damaged the British economy and, ironically, played its part in the defeat of Labour in October 1951.

With Europe now indisputably the focus for defence planning, the question of the organization and structure of the West's defence effort became paramount. Heated discussions took place in the early 1950s which were eventually resolved by the proposal of Foreign Secretary Anthony Eden in 1954 to include West Germany in NATO and a revived Brussels Treaty Organization, to be renamed Western European Union. Eden pledged the indefinite maintenance in Western Europe of Britain's armed forces, namely four divisions and a tactical air force, where they remain to this day.

Britain a nuclear power

Other profound changes were meanwhile occurring in Britain's defence thinking. Britain exploded its own atomic bomb at the Monte Bello islands off Western Australia in October 1952. The explosion came as the culmination of a six-year operation initiated by a secret decision of the Attlee Government in 1946 that Britain should not be left out of the race and should become a nuclear power. Possessing nuclear capability enabled defence planners to realize that reliance on the deterrent effect of these horrific weapons could greatly reduce dependence on conventional forces and hence save money. Britain accelerated the production of the long-range 'V-bombers' to deliver the weapons, and the first Vulcan bomber squadron became operational in 1955. By this time, too, preparations were well advanced on Britain's own hydrogen bomb, initiated in 1952 and tested in May 1957. The Victor bombers came into service at the same time, capable, unlike the Vulcans, of reaching Moscow.

The full flowering of this new thinking came in the Defence White Paper of 1957, long associated with the name of the then Minister of Defence, Duncan Sandys. This paper spoke explicitly of the need to consider defence spending in the light of Britain's economic and financial capacity to pay. Nuclear weapons, it said, were a cheaper and better way of providing defence for the future, and hence would become the cornerstone of Britain's defence policy. What role then would be left for conventional (i.e. non nuclear) weapons? Essentially it was to be one of defending colonies and undertaking limited operations in overseas emergencies. Further, their role was to deter attack from enemy conventional forces. The document thus reflected foresight, because such has indeed been the role of Britain's conventional forces ever since.

Conventional forces were much reduced. Total armed services manpower fell from 690,000 in 1957 to 375,000 by 1962, and national service, the system whereby every adult male had to spend two years in one of the three armed services, was phased out by 1960. The Suez Canal Base had already been abandoned in 1956, in line with the down-playing in importance of the Middle East, and Cyprus became the principal base in the Mediterranean region, which it remains today.

Consistent with the new policy, Britain also came to rely more on arrangements for collective security and multilateral treaties. With NATO and WEU in place in Western Europe, Britain built up the Central Treaty Organization (CENTO), or Baghdad Pact, to defend the Middle East against a possible Soviet invasion from the North. This pact consisted of Turkey, Iran, Iraq and Pakistan, but in reality it never had much substance and shortly fell apart: as the Chiefs of Staff admitted in 1955, 'we have neither the men nor the money to make the Baghdad Pact effective militarily'. In September 1954 Britain acceded to another loose mutual defence arrangement, the South East Asia Treaty Organization (SEATO), which consisted of the UK, the USA, France, Australia, New Zealand, Thailand, the Philippines and Pakistan. With NATO, CENTO and SEATO, the Soviet Union and China were effectively encircled by anti-communist alliances.

Suez

The year before the Sandys White Paper Britain had witnessed the single most traumatic episode in its post-war history, the Suez crisis. When President Nasser of Egypt unilaterally nationalized the Suez Canal, which was jointly owned by Britain and France, in July 1956, he placed both nations in a dilemma. How should they respond? To do nothing might be seen as a sign of weakness by their colonial empires, and as an indication that they could strike out with impunity and gain their independence. But to respond with force might invite international condemnation.

For several agonizing weeks the French and British Governments debated the options and with an acceptable compromise position (as they saw it) being unforthcoming, they decided on the latter course, i.e. force, in association with Israel after top secret discussions at Sèvres in Paris. The military operation in November 1956 backfired badly, and Britain and France found themselves isolated on the world stage. Most painful for Britain, her old ally the USA was one of the strongest opponents of military action. After a few days of fighting to regain the canal the Anglo−French operation was forced by international pressure to stop. It proved to be one of Britain's last major overseas operations, until the Falklands War in 1982.

Technological dependence on USA

Britain was deeply humiliated by Suez and from January 1957 the new Prime Minister, Harold Macmillan, worked hard to restore Britain's international standing. But the myth — for such it was — that Britain was still a great world power underpinned by its own independent nuclear weapons system began to break down for a number of reasons in the later 1950s. Nuclear deterrence as a policy became progressively more expensive and far beyond Britain's capability to maintain and modernize herself. Britain was thus forced to abandon her own home-built delivery systems and buy US missiles — which succeeded bombs carried by planes as the most effective vehicle for delivering warheads. Thus, British nuclear defence since the early 1960s has been based on the US-built Polaris missiles, negotiated at the Nassau meeting with President Kennedy in 1962.

Pressure on financial resources also lay behind Britain's efforts to reduce the size of BAOR. In 1957 Britain announced it was cutting the size of BAOR from 77,000

Harold
Macmillan —
Britain's post-
Suez crisis
Prime Minister

to 64,000, and in 1959 to 55,000 men. Her European partners protested that this was going against Eden's 1954 pledge, but Britain defended these cuts by arguing that although numbers were being reduced, the effectiveness of the force was not. This was because British troops were being supplied with tactical (i.e. 'theatre' or limited) nuclear weapons designed to compensate for any fall in numbers. This argument failed to impress her partners and Britain was prevailed upon not to go ahead with a further reduction to 49,000 troops, announced in 1960. Financial pressures also played their part, as we shall see in the next section, in accelerating Britain's move towards granting independence to her colonial possessions.

Withdrawal East of Suez

The growing realization that Britain could no longer afford to be a great power, coupled with an awareness that the much-vaunted special relationship with the USA, like the Commonwealth, carried little international weight, produced a major rethink in Whitehall. It was decided that Britain's future lay with Europe rather than as an independent world power. A reaction had also set in against the human (and financial) cost of a number of limited-scale overseas operations in which British troops had become engaged to protect her colonial interests — Malaya and Kenya in the early 1950s and Malaysia again in 1963–5.

The gradual acceptance that Britain's economic future lay in Europe had a dramatic effect on defence planning. Prime Minister Harold Wilson, who told Parliament in

1964 that Britain had no intention of relinquishing her world role, had by 1967 changed his view, and the following year announced the ending of Britain's East of Suez interests. So Britain, free at last of her main overseas commitments, redoubled her commitment to European defence and NATO. Yet Labour, which had initiated Britain into nuclear weapons in 1946, did not seek to eliminate them between 1964 and 1970, although that was precisely what those on the left of the Party wanted.

The Conservatives, always more attached to notions of 'strong defence' and higher defence spending than Labour, promised while in Opposition (1964–70) to revive some of the defence commitments abandoned by Labour. But back in office (1970–4) they found themselves subject to the same financial pressures and were forced to leave pledges unfulfilled. In addition, commitment of troops to Northern Ireland from 1968/9 placed new and increasing demands on defence spending. When Labour was returned to power in 1974, with unemployment rising and the economy refusing to come right, there was neither the will nor the means to extend the defence effort beyond Europe.

Defence policy after 1979

So what was the thrust of British defence policy in 1979? The vast bulk of the effort was focused on the BAOR in West Germany, with Northern Ireland remaining a major commitment. Small garrisons were retained elsewhere overseas, notably in Cyprus, Gibraltar, the Falklands, Hong Kong and Belize, but only the first base was of any size. The nuclear deterrent was still based on the Polaris missiles housed in four nuclear submarines and operating from their base at Holy Loch in Southern Scotland. The navy's surface (i.e. non-submarine) role was minimal, to protect convoys in the event of war, to defend the fishing fleet, most particularly in the 'Cod War' with Iceland, and to offer protection in the unlikely event of Britain's overseas territories being threatened. The 'unlikely event' occurred in 1982 when Argentina invaded the Falkland Islands: the action provided a reprieve for the navy, which at the time was faced by the prospect of some savage cuts. The Falklands War in any case was an aberration: for many years before Britain's defence effort had been focused on Western Europe. The fact that Britain's two most spectacular overseas post-war military operations — the Suez and the Falklands — occurred outside Europe should not distort the general picture of British defence after the mid-1960s as very limited in range and scale compared with the vast international defence role it had fulfilled in 1945. (See also Chapter 28.)

Empire into Commonwealth, 1945–79

The story of Britain's empire and the gaining of independence by former colonial territories is of central importance to an understanding of post-war British history and politics. Colonial policy was an area in which bipartisan consensus existed. Labour liked to see itself as the party with the more modern, progressive outlook, keener on granting independence to the colonies, and it liked to paint the Conservatives as the more reactionary party, committed to out-dated notions of empire

Imperialism

> In imperialism, nothing fails like success. If the conqueror oppresses his subjects, they will become fanatical patriots and sooner or later have their revenge; if he treats them well and 'governs them for their good', they will multiply faster than their rulers, till they claim their independence.
>
> Source: **William Ralph Inge**, *Patriotism, Outspoken Essays,*
> First Series, 1919.

and wanting to keep the colonies subjugated and economically dependent upon Britain. The truth was rather different, with both Labour and Conservative forcing the pace of decolonization when in government.

But before considering the causes of decolonization, some history and terminology needs to be clarified. It is necessary to distinguish two separate entities within the British empire, which together constituted the areas coloured red on old maps and which were made up of eleven-and-a-half million square miles and over 400 million inhabitants. Commonwealth countries, formerly Dominions, were totally self-governing and recognized as such since the Statute of Westminster in 1931, but they accepted Britain's monarch as their head of state and followed Britain's lead in defence and foreign affairs: these were, in 1945, Canada, Australia, New Zealand, Eire and South Africa. The second 'part' of the empire was the colonies. These were not self-governing, but were under direct rule from Whitehall in London via a British-run administration in each territory supervising road-building, providing schools and medical services and other benefits. The colonies were principally in Africa, for example Kenya and Nigeria, but were also to be found in the Far East (Singapore, Hong Kong), the Mediterranean (Malta, Cyprus), the Caribbean (Jamaica) and elsewhere. These territories had in the main been acquired in the nineteenth century and were a source of raw materials, e.g. palm oil from Nigeria and tin and rubber from Malaya, and were at the same time an important market for British goods. In the post-war period, as colonies gained their independence, almost all chose voluntarily to join the Commonwealth.

The empire as a whole was based on four main elements.

1. *Partnership with the Commonwealth*, of importance for both economic (as a market for British products) and strategic (contributing vital manpower and supplies in both World Wars) reasons.
2. *Dependence on India*, which since the early nineteenth century had underpinned Britain's influence in Asia, and which continued to be of utmost military and economic significance to the mother country.
3. *Dominance in the Middle East*, of central importance because it made possible naval dominance in the Indian Ocean and Eastern Mediterranean; guaranteed access through the Suez Canal; provided air bases which could strike directly at the USSR; and protected the principal source of that vital raw material, oil.
4. *The key importance of Britain itself*, as a market for raw materials and food and a source of investment, trade and manpower.

All four were under strain by 1945. The former cosy notion of the old Commonwealth countries looking to the mother country for their lead was the first to go. In 1948,

Eire, which had been neutral during the Second World War, left the Commonwealth. In the same year in South Africa a Boer-dominated Nationalist government came to power whose hard-line policies on the majority black African population placed it at loggerheads with successive British governments. South Africa eventually left the Commonwealth in 1961. In the early 1950s Australia and New Zealand joined in the so-called ANZUS pact with the USA, from which Britain was excluded, and in general both countries, as well as Canada, began to look more to the USA for protection than to Britain.

India

Of greater importance in the winding down of empire were events in the Indian sub-continent in the early post-war years. Before the outbreak of war, Britain's long-term plan for India was for it to become an independent pro-British Commonwealth country which would preserve the benefits to Britain of the former relationship. British demands on India during the war, exacted without consultation, tipped the balance of opinion in the ruling Congress Party against cooperation with Britain. Gandhi launched the 'Quit India' movement, which found an enormous popular appeal. The Attlee government, which came to power in 1945, saw it was useless to delay independence; Lord Mountbatten was sent out to bring it about quickly and with a minimum of bloodshed. Independence came in 1947 but it was at the price of partition, with a Muslim Pakistan (in an East and West) being separated from the predominantly Hindu India. The haste of departure and the anti-British feeling within the new Government led by Pandit Nehru meant that Britain's hopes of a close relationship with India were dashed. Britain would no longer be able to depend upon the mighty Indian Army to bolster her position in the Far East, and the whole of Britain's East of Suez policy was called into question. India and Pakistan did at least choose to remain in the Commonwealth (although the former did not recognize the British monarch and became, therefore, a republic). In 1948 Burma and Ceylon became independent, the former choosing to leave the Commonwealth altogether.

The Middle East

A further blow to Britain's influence in the Indian sub-continent came with the undermining of her position in the Middle East. In 1945 her influence was impressive. She had close relationships with many territories, including Jordan, Iraq and Libya. Following the collapse of the Turkish empire, Britain had exercised a mandate (i.e. ruled) over Palestine. Sudan was, in effect, an Anglo–French colony and Egypt, although never formally part of the British Empire and technically independent after 1922, was subject to British military occupation. This influence rapidly washed away after 1945. Britain surrendered her control of Palestine in 1948 in the face of violent Jewish unrest and a Jewish state of Israel was established, to Arab protest. In 1951, Britain was openly humiliated when Mossadeq, the Iranian leader, unilaterally nationalized the Anglo–Iranian Oil Company's oil refineries. Although a CIA-inspired coup in Iran in 1953 led to the return to power of the pro-West Shah, notice was nevertheless given that the British could be pushed out with impunity.

That message was certainly received by Nasser of Egypt, whose nationalization of the Anglo-French Suez canal in 1956 has already been described, and which had a massive impact on Britain's position in the Middle East.

Post-Suez

Whether or not Suez hastened the end of empire is a subject on which scholars differ, but what can be asserted without fear of error is that the pace of decolonization quickened substantially from 1957. That year saw the first grants of independence since 1948, to Malaya and Ghana. Both territories were, not coincidentally, the first colonies to pose major problems for Britain after 1945. In Malaya a communist-inspired guerilla war broke out in 1948: unlike the French and later the Americans in Vietnam, the British were successful in defeating the communists. At the same time, Britain realized she could not hold on to Malaya indefinitely, and confident that a friendly government would take over after they left, granted independence. Riots, albeit on a smaller scale and not communist-inspired, also occurred in 1948 in the Gold Coast (as Ghana was known pre-independence). Again, the will and the ability to preserve Ghana as a colony in the face of agitation for self-government and a strong nationalist political movement, headed by Nkrumah, was called into question. The granting of independence to Ghana in 1957 was not, however, intended to unleash a torrent of further moves to independence; yet it happened.

In the mid-1950s independence for the bulk of the colonies was still perceived as many years away. This was especially so for colonies such as Kenya where a large (but minority) white settler population feared its privileged position would be eroded should a black government come to power. The British government tried various expedients, including that of trying to link several colonies together in a series of 'federations', but such devices broke down in the face of internal pressure for independence.

By the time Labour was returned to office in 1964, self-government had been granted to several former colonies, including Nigeria, Cyprus, Tanzania, Sierra Leone, Jamaica and Uganda. Labour continued the deolonization policy largely unaltered, especially after 1968, and by 1979 only isolated colonies like Gibraltar, the Falklands and Hong Kong remained dependent. The one major problem was Southern Rhodesia. Here the white settlers in 1965 led by Ian Smith, alarmed by the prospect of the British government forcing independence, free elections and a black government on them, declared unilateral independence. The new Smith government, like its neighbouring government in South Africa, had no intention of allowing blacks to vote. Years of pressure from London yielded no fruit until 1980 (see Chapter 28).

End of empire

What reasons can be found for the rapid demise of the British empire? There are three main explanations.

1. *The British economy*. This had underpinned the empire in the years before 1939 and was becoming too weak in the 1950s to maintain its key economic and financial relationship with the colonies. The government had imagined in the late 1940s

Ian Smith, Prime Minister of Southern Rhodesia, who led the 1965 move towards unilateral independence for the white settlers. The situation was to remain unresolved until 1980.

that the economy would again revive and would become the largest and most dynamic in the West outside the USA. But such notions were pipe dreams: huge war debts, loss of exports, the running-down of Britain's staple industries and low productivity saw to that. Other economies in Europe and Japan rivalled and then overtook Britain; her economy could no longer provide the colonies with the economic resources, especially loans, at pre-1939 levels (see Table 2.1). The 1960s were an even more painful decade for Britain economically, culminating in the devaluation of sterling in 1967 and the announcement of the withdrawal of Britain's role East of Suez. Economic performance and overseas influence are critically interdependent.

2. *Britain's eclipse as a super-power* relative to the USA and USSR. The crunch came in the Middle East. Before 1939, Britain had been able to exclude other powers from influence in the area. Not so after 1945. The Arab—Israeli conflict brought in both the USSR and the USA, each competing with the other to offer arms and economic aid to states they wished to cultivate and offering resources

Table 2.1   *The relative decline of the British economy*

Growth in gross domestic product (percentages)							Shares of world exports of manufactures (percentages)					
	UK	USA	W. Germany	France	Italy	Japan		UK	USA	W. Germany	France	Italy	Japan
1950–60	2.6	3.2	7.6	4.4	5.9	8.1	1960	12.7	17.9	14.8	7.4	3.9	5.3
1960–70	2.5	3.8	4.1	5.6	5.5	11.1	1970	8.6	15.3	15.8	6.9	5.7	9.3
1970–80	1.8	2.8	2.8	3.7	4.0	5.3	1980	6.8	11.5	13.9	6.9	5.5	10.4

Source: New Society, 24 May 1984

The end of empire: a chronology

1919	Government of India Act (Montagu–Chelmsford reforms)
1922	'Independence' of Egypt
1931	Statute of Westminster: constitutional equality of the dominions
1935	Government of India Act proposing eventual federation
1939	Palestine White Paper proposing close limit on Jewish immigration
1942	Fall of Singapore, loss of Malaya and Burma; Cripps Mission to India; 'Quit India' movement
1945	Recovery of Burma, Malaya, Singapore and Hong Kong; preparations for constituent assembly in India
1946	Abortive Cabinet Mission to India to prevent partition; US loan to Britain
1947	Breakdown of Anglo-Egyptian negotiations over British withdrawal; sterling crisis; independence and partition of India
1948	Independence of Burma and Ceylon: Burma and Eire leave the Commonwealth; British withdrawal from Palestine; riots in Ghana (Gold Coast); outbreak of Malayan Emergency; election victory of National Party in South Africa
1949	Sterling devaluation; London Conference approves India's membership of the Commonwealth as a republic
1950–51	Korean War and crisis over rearmament in Britain
1951	Anzus Pact
1952	Mau-Mau emergency begins
1953	Creation of Rhodesian Federation
1954	Anglo–Egyptian agreement; onset of crisis in Cyprus
1956	Independence of the Sudan; Suez crisis
1957	Independence of Malaya and Ghana; end of conscription proposed in Britain
1959	Emergency in Central Africa; Devlin Report
1960	Lancaster House conference recommends majority rule for Kenya; Harold Macmillan's 'wind of change' speech; onset of Congo crisis; independence of Nigeria and Cyprus
1961	Independence of Sierra Leone and Tanganyika (Tanzania)
1962	Independence of Jamaica, Trinidad and Uganda
1963	Dissolution of Rhodesian Federation; independence of Kenya
1964	Independence of Malawi and Zambia
1965	Rhodesian independence unilaterally proclaimed
1967	Devaluation crisis in Britain; withdrawal from East of Suez announced
1973	Britain enters the European Community
1980	Independence of Zimbabwe following supervised elections
1982	Falklands war
1984	Anglo–Chinese Hong Kong agreement

on a scale Britain could not match. Oil only heightened the two superpowers' interest in the area, to the exclusion of Britain. The Suez crisis of 1956 showed forcefully how impotent British influence had become in the area. Worse still the USA, notionally Britain's closest ally, was deeply suspicious of British colonialism, and tried wherever possible to quicken the pace of decolonization.

3. *Nationalist movements*. Before 1939 inhabitants of colonies were, by and large, content to accept the British presence: some factions may not have liked it but there were no mass movements backed up by military action to persuade the British to leave. After 1945, there was a swift and rapid rise of nationalist (i.e. pro-independence) movements, which fired the imaginations of the colonial masses. The British responded by trying to encourage moderate black Africans who would be content to accept the need for moving slowly on the political front — much as the white government has attempted to do in recent years in South Africa. But nationalist leaders — Kenyatta in Kenya, Nkrumah in Ghana, Nyerere in Tanzania — were not prepared to accept British insistence on slow political progress: they wanted total African control, and they wanted it not later but immediately. They also looked to other governments, and often to Moscow, for support — to London's horror. Hopes that friendly governments could be left behind after the British flag was lowered for the last time appeared to be in jeopardy. As decolonization was bound to come, British governments reasoned, it was better to leave sooner in the hope that some goodwill from the new independent governments could be salvaged.

The European Community

The third and final piece of the jigsaw which completes the picture of Britain's post-war external position is her attitude to Europe. The origin of the movement for greater cooperation between European nations was the Second World War itself. For the second time within the space of thirty years Europe had plunged itself into a long and violent war. Politicians across Europe realized that the way to prevent a recurrence of such a tragedy was some form of post-war integration. War damage in mainland Europe, especially in Germany, was widespread and most national economies lay in ruins. The imposition of Soviet influence over Poland, East Germany, Czechoslovakia, Hungary, Bulgaria, Yugoslavia and Romania forced the USA to act. Its European Recovery Plan, or Marshall Aid, served to unite Western Europe behind the USA in that it provided their main, perhaps only, hope for survival and recovery. Economic aid therefore preceded the joint action on defence which followed with the Brussels Treaty in 1948 and NATO in 1949.

Factors other than the idealistic hopes of avoiding further war and the need to work closely in defence to deter possible Soviet advance were also propelling Europe towards closer union. To prevent West Germany reuniting with Soviet-controlled East Germany, it seemed sensible to bind it in closely with other West European countries. The rise of the USA and USSR as the two super-powers of the post-war world also played its part in promoting European unity: if Western European nations were to retain any political influence on the world stage, they should speak with a common voice. A further impulse towards closer cooperation was provided by the USA itself, which from 1945 onwards promoted closer integration to strengthen resistance against possible Soviet aggression. Indeed, the USA saw Western Europe as its first line of defence against the USSR, helping to found NATO in 1949, and remaining its most powerful single backer since. The USA especially urged Britain into closer ties with its Western European partners — but with scant success throughout the 1950s.

Britain cool on Europe

Initially Britain stood aloof. Content to station part of its army in Europe and, indeed, from 1956 to make Western Europe the focus of its defence effort, it nevertheless shied away from economic union. The government argued that Britain stood at the centre of three overlapping circles — the empire, the special relationship with the USA and Europe (see Figure 2.1) — and it could not throw in its lot too single-mindedly into Europe for fear of damaging its relationship with the other two. Further, Britain still saw herself, in the late 1940s and early 1950s at least, as a great power, with an independent nuclear deterrent and world-wide interests. Nor had she been invaded in the Second World War, and hence the appeal of a multi-national body to reduce the risk of war did not carry the same emotional force as on the continent of Europe.

Therefore, during the first fifteen years after the war, Britain remained detached from proposals to effect a closer union. She was unwilling to join the Coal and Steel Community in 1952, the brainchild of the French Foreign Minister, Robert Schumann. Nor did Britain take part in the talks in Messina in Sicily in 1950 which led to the 1957 Treaty of Rome and the creation of the Common Market (as the European Economic Community (EEC) was initially known), comprising France, West Germany, Italy, Luxembourg, Holland and Belgium. Neither the Labour nor Conservative party was keen on economic integration, nor were the two men who dominated British foreign policy after the war, Ernest Bevin (1945—51) and Anthony Eden (1951—7, as foreign secretary until 1955, then as Prime Minister). Foreign Office civil servants were also in the main against closer economic cooperation.

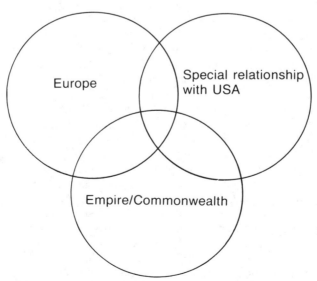

Figure 2.1   *The three interlocking spheres of post-war British foreign policy*

Britain applies in 1961

Britain had expected the six founder members to make a mess of the EEC and fondly imagined they would then look to Britain to help them get out of it. They did not do so, and far from coming unstuck, the EEC flourished. Britain was forced to retaliate and in 1959 organized a competing bloc of trading nations, the European Free Trade Association (EFTA). But this proved less successful and in 1961 Britain applied for membership of the EEC, while acknowledging that she would have to honour, if admitted, her existing trading obligations to the Commonwealth and to EFTA.

To Britain's anger de Gaulle, the French President, vetoed Britain's application in January 1963, arguing that Britain was insufficiently free of overseas ties, especially to the USA, to join in an economic community with other European nations. A second attempt was made by the Labour government of Harold Wilson in 1967, which was subjected to a second French veto in 1969. In 1970 the Conservatives were returned to power and Edward Heath, who had led the discussions in the first bid for entry in the early 1960s, was now Prime Minister. As important, de Gaulle was no longer President in France, having been succeeded by a man more sympathetic to Britain's new-found European enthusiasm — Georges Pompidou.

This third attempt proved successful and in January 1972 a treaty admitting Britain into the EEC was signed; in January 1973 she joined along with Ireland and Denmark. Britain's future in the community was called into question, however, shortly after. Labour returned to power in February 1974, and was deeply divided over Europe. As a device for holding his party together Prime Minister Harold Wilson called a national referendum — the only one to have been held — in June 1975. The result, in the event, recorded a 2:1 majority in favour of remaining in the EEC. Wilson had, meanwhile, obtained some minor financial concessions in Brussels but the debate about the pros and cons of entry continued to divide the Labour party and indeed the nation.

In 1979 the three interlocking circles of British dealings with the outside world were still relevant but all of them had shrunk in absolute terms, in accordance with Britain's modified power position, and the US and Commonwealth spheres in relative terms to the European one. Britain's victories in the two twentieth-century world wars had proved pyrrhic: triumphant but exhausted in 1945 she had no option but to observe how the logic of geography and economics turned her into a middle-ranking rather than a major world power. British defence and foreign policy since 1979 are dealt with in Chapter 28.

References and Further Reading

Bartlett, C.J. *A History of Post-war Britain* (Longman, 1977).
Carlton, D., *Britain and the Suez Crisis* (Basil Blackwell, 1990).
Childs, D., *Britain since 1945: a Political History* (Ernest Benn, 1979).
Darwin, J., *Britain and Decolonisation* (Macmillan, 1988).
Dockrill, M., *British Defence since 1945* (Basil Blackwell, 1988).
Freedman, L., *Britain and the Falklands War* (Basil Blackwell, 1988).

George, S., *An Awkward Partner: Britain in the European Community* (Oxford University Press, 1990).

MacDonald, C., *Britain and the Korean War* (Basil Blackwell, 1990).

Madgwick, P.J., Steed, D. and Williams, L., *Britain since 1945* (Hutchinson, 1982).

Morgan, K.O., *Labour in Power, 1945−51* (Oxford University Press, 1985).

3 The Rise and Fall of the Post-war Consensus

Anthony Seldon

In the aftermath of the war, Britain was relatively united in its approach to peace. A reforming Labour government introduced economic, social and foreign policies which commanded bipartisan support for the next three decades. By the late 1970s, however, consensus was wearing thin and could not survive for long the onset of Thatcherism. This chapter analyses the rise and fall of the post-war consensus and ends by speculating on whether a new consensus has been created.

Origins of the Consensus

The 'post-war consensus' is a key concept in understanding the recent past. It describes the overlap between the economic, social and foreign policies of both Labour and Conservative governments throughout the post-war period until its breakdown in the 1970s. The word 'consensus' is Latin for agreement, and its use implies a set of common assumptions and a continuity between the policies pursued by both the main parties when they were in power. It does not mean that there were not disagreements: there were many. But it does suggest that the differences in the policies practised when the parties were in office were relatively small rather than fundamental.

The term permits the existence of major differences between the radical elements within each of the main parties, but it recognizes that when the parties were in power they were dominated by moderates for whom continuity and slow change were more important than major policy departures. Most writers now accept that the term 'consensus' is a useful or adequate description of British politics from 1945 until the late 1970s, when it began to be replaced by a new, Thatcherite, consensus.

The post-war consensus was largely consolidated by the post-war Labour Government (1945–51), presided over by Clement Attlee, but its genesis is found in the war years, 1939–45.

1. *Six years of war united the country* against a common enemy while the privations of war instilled a widespread desire for a new and better beginning. The comradeship of war had also helped blunt some of the sharper edges of British class differences.

Clement Attlee,
leader of the
post-war Labour
Government
(1945−51) and
architect of the
post-war political
consensus.

2. *Coalition government 1940−5* had fostered social and intellectual links between socialists and conservatives. The common everyday effort to defeat Hitler had taken much of the bite out of ideological differences between the two parties.
3. *Acceptance of Keynesianism* had been evident both in Chancellor Kingsley Wood's 1941 Budget and in the 1944 White Paper which commanded full support from all three main political parties for its aim of 'full employment'.
4. *Planned economy*. Conservatives had always maintained that central planning of the economy would not work, but the spectacular success of the government's tightly controlled war economy supported the case for planning.
5. *Trade unions*. In 1940 Ernest Bevin, General Secretary of the Transport and General Workers' Union (TGWU), was appointed Minister of Labour in recognition of the unions' importance to the war effort. Their enthusiastic cooperation was vital to success and established a strong claim for regular post-war consultation.
6. *Welfare*. The famous *Report on Social Insurance and Allied Services* in 1942 associated with the name of its principal architect, William Beveridge, commanded widespread support for the post-war welfare state.

By 1945 all the ingredients for a new widely supported consensus were present in the political culture. All three parties went to the polls in 1945 committed to a broad range of economic and social policies of a qualitatively different kind to anything envisaged in the inter-war years. The stage had been set.

The Attlee government, 1945−51

A major problem with history is that one can never know with any certainty what might have happened had circumstances been different. It is possible that, had the Conservatives won the General Election of 1945, they would have implemented as radical a set of policies as those enacted by Labour. But it seems most unlikely that the Conservatives would have gone as far as Labour did, or executed policies in quite the same way. The Attlee government has been chiefly credited with creating the post-war consensus. As the historical examination above has made clear, it did not create the consensus, but it did consolidate it and gave it its particular form. The post-war consensus can be said to have six main aspects or 'planks':

1. *Full employment.* The Attlee government pledged itself to abide by the 1944 White Paper on Employment to achieve full employment. This meant in practice a mix of interventionist economic and fiscal policies to ensure that unemployment never rose above a minimum level of 2−3 per cent. This contrasted markedly with the high levels of the inter-war period.
2. *Mixed economy and Keynesian policies.* This entailed a mixture of private and state ('public') ownership of industry and services. The 1945 Labour manifesto advocated nationalization of public utilities and an extension of state ownership over other aspects of the private sector. Once in office, it proceeded to nationalize hitherto private companies, for example coal (1946), electricity (1947), railways (1947) and gas (1948). Major manufacturing industries, however, remained in the private sector. Keynesian principles of economic management were now accepted as orthodoxies.
3. *Welfare state.* The government's social policies from 1945 to 1951, which included setting up the National Health Service (NHS) in July 1948, an expansion of free education, public housing, sickness benefit and family allowances, far exceeded the tentative groping towards a welfarism before 1939. The core principles of this aspect of the consensus included universal and free welfare benefits for all in need.
4. *Trade unions.* The Attlee government, for the first time in peacetime, brought unions into both formal and informal contact with government in a continuing relationship. They gave the unions the feeling that they had a virtual 'right' to be consulted.
5. *Equality.* The Attlee government pursued active economic and social policies to try to *reduce* (if not eliminate) inequalities of income, wealth and region. Heavily progressive taxes were thus pursued to flatten out inequalities in salaries and wages and an active regional policy was followed to bolster employment and income in areas of higher than average unemployment, such as the north east of England.
6. *Foreign policy.* It is tempting, but wrong, to see the consensus wholly in terms of the continuity in economic and social policies pursued by Labour and Conservative governments. There also existed a marked overlap in the foreign

and defence spheres. Thus it was Labour which decided in 1946 that Britain must be a nuclear nation, which forged NATO in 1949 with full Conservative support, and again it was Labour which decided in 1950 that it could not submerge Britain in the European Coal and Steel Community.

The elements of consensus

1. Full employment
2. Mixed economy and Keynesianism
3. Welfare State universal services
4. Trade unions as partners in government
5. Equality as objective of social policy
6. Pro-US foreign policy

Selected social security legislation

Family Allowances Act 1946. This granted a non-contributory allowance, to be paid to the mother, for each child other than the first. 1945–52 5s (25p) per week; 1952–68 8s (40p) per week; 1956–68 10s (50p) per week for third and subsequent children; 1968 15s (75p) per week for second, £1 per week for third and subsequent children.

National Insurance Act 1946. This Act provided a new scheme of insurance replacing the national insurance and contributory pensions schemes with effect from 5 July 1948. All persons over school-leaving age, except certain married women, became compulsorily insurable. In addition to provisions for unemployment benefits payable were retirement pension, widow's benefit and death grant.

National Insurance Act 1966. This extended the period of widow's allowance, introduced a scheme of earnings-related supplements to unemployment and sickness benefits and included a widow's supplementary allowance.

Ministry of Social Security Act 1966 repealed and amended much previous legislation. It provided for the abolition of the Ministry of Pensions and National Insurance and the National Assistance Board and the establishment of the Ministry of Social Security. The Act also provided for a scheme of supplementary benefits to replace the system of allowances which had previously been administered by the National Assistance Board. The benefits were paid as of right to those people whose incomes were below the levels set in the Act and not according to national insurance contribution records.

Family Income Supplements Act 1970. Created new benefit for families with small incomes.

Social Security Pensions Act 1975. This provided for social security pensions and other related benefits to consist of a basic element and an additional component related to higher earnings and made various other provisions in relation to pensions. Made full National Insurance contributions obligatory for women except widows and women already on reduced rates.

Child Benefits Act 1975. Replaced family allowances with child benefit and provided for an interim benefit for unmarried or separated parents with children.

Selected
health
legislation

> **National Health Service Act 1946**. By this Act, hospitals were transferred from local authorities and voluntary bodies and were to be administered by the Minister through regional hospital boards, general medical and dental services through executive councils, and other health services by county and county borough councils. Health centres were to be provided by local authorities for general, mental, dental and pharmaceutical services, but few were built. Almost all services under the Act were to be free.
>
> **National Health Service (Amendment) Act 1949; National Health Service Acts 1951 and 1952** and **National Health Service Contributions Act 1957—8**. These made modifications in the original scheme by imposing charges for certain parts of the scheme (prescriptions, dental treatment, etc.).
>
> **Mental Health Act 1959**. The Board of Control was abolished and its functions passed to the new Mental Health Review Tribunals, local authorities, and the Minister of Health. The Act redefined the classifications of mental disorders, provided for further safeguards against improper detention, and extended the provisions for voluntary and informal treatment of patients.
>
> **Prescription Charges** were ended in 1965. They were reimposed in 1968 with exemptions for some categories.
>
> **Chronically Sick and Disabled Persons Act 1970**. This placed more stringent obligations on local authorities to seek out and provide for the chronically sick and disabled.
>
> **Health Services Act 1980**. Made provision for increased access to Health Service facilities by private patients and made other alterations to the law regarding private health care.

The Consensus Endures 1951—5

In October 1951, the Conservatives won the General Election. It was a narrow victory of just seventeen seats, and in fact they won 200,000 fewer votes overall than Labour. But for the vagaries of the British electoral system, therefore, the Conservatives would have lost the election. What type of Conservative government would there now be? Labour had warned during the election campaign, as it had done during the earlier campaigns of 1945 and February 1950, that if elected the Conservatives would return to their inter-war policies.

They did not do so, although there were some minor modifications to the consensus. A variety of factors explains why they chose to accept rather than reject so much of the Attlee settlement. The narrowness of the majority had much to do with it. For 1952 and much of 1953, the Conservatives were not performing strongly in either the opinion polls or by-elections: unpopular moves were ruled out and to have cut back on, for example, the welfare state or to have been confrontational towards the trade unions were deemed likely to lose support. (The popularity of privatization was only discovered after 1979, when the climate of opinion had changed considerably.)

Major education reforms

Education Act 1944. This Act changed the title of the President of the Board of Education to the Minister of Education. Primary and secondary eduction was divided at '11-plus', and secondary education was generally provided under this Act in three types of schools, grammar, technical and modern. Some local authorities preferred to use their powers to amalgamate these into comprehensive schools. Provision was made for compulsory part-time education between the school-leaving age and eighteen in country colleges, but this has not been implemented. The minimum school-leaving age was raised to fifteen (in 1947) and provision was made for raising it to sixteen. Powers were granted under this Act, which led to a great expansion of technical colleges. No fees were to be charged in schools which were publicly provided or aided by grants from the local authority.

Comprehensive Schools. In 1965 the Department of Education asked all local authorities to submit plans for reorganizing secondary education on comprehensive lines, with a view to ending selection at 11-plus and the tripartite system. The policy of universal comprehensivization was suspended in 1970 but revived in 1974 by Government Circular 4/74. In 1976 the Direct Grant system was phased out (119 of the 170 Direct Grant schools decided to become independent) and the **Education Act 1976** required Local Education Authorities to submit comprehensivization proposals (seven had earlier refused).

Nursery Schools. In 1972 the Department of Education (Cmnd 5174) accepted that within ten years it should provide nursery education for 90 per cent of four-year-olds and 50 per cent of three-year-olds.

Education Act 1980. The Assisted Places Scheme was established to provide financial support for some students in independent education, and various other changes were made to increase parental choice and participation in the schooling of their children.

As important was the fact that the Conservative right wing lacked cohesion, leaders and even supporters. Potential leaders of a right wing reaction were either not given jobs by Churchill (PM 1951–5), for example Waterhouse, or were to an extent marginalized as in the case of Lord Salisbury.

Churchill's own continued presence was of considerable importance in explaining the continuation of moderate policies after 1951. Churchill, who as a younger man had often been identified with radical policies, now saw himself as a conciliator. His policy preferences, his appointments and his very presence were central to the consolidation of the consensus.

The Conservative party too had changed its spots since 1945. Reforms to parliamentary candidate requirements meant that it was no longer necessary to have private capital to stand as a Conservative. In consequence the 1950 election saw a vast influx of a new type of middle-class Conservative MP, typified by the grammar school-educated Ted Heath. On policy, R.A. Butler, the wartime Education Minister, had been reforming and modernizing party policy at the Conservative Research Department. Aided by some bright young assistants who went on to play major parts in the subsequent history of the party (Reginald Maudling, Iain Macleod and Enoch

Powell) Butler was responsible for a stream of policy documents and statements, notably the *Industrial Charter* (1947) and *The Right Road for Britain* (1949). These documents played a part, albeit a small one, in assisting the transfer of the Conservatives from an arguably *laissez-faire* party before the war to an interventionist one after it.

A final factor that accounted for the Conservative acceptance of the consensus after 1951 was the collapse of the centre vote. 1951 was the worst result ever for the Liberal party: 2.5 per cent of the votes cast, and six MPs. Many middle-class voters abandoned not just the Liberals but also the Conservatives, either not voting at all or voting Labour. The Conservatives knew they had to woo back these left-inclined voters if they were to consolidate their hold on power.

In consequence, all areas of the consensus were held up largely intact. *At the Treasury* the moderate Butler was appointed Chancellor rather than the right wing Oliver Lyttelton who had been tipped for the job. Butler's economic policies, aimed at full employment, were so similar to those of the Labour Chancellor Hugh Gaitskell that *The Economist* coined a new term 'Butskellism' to honour the continuity.

The mixed economy was retained virtually intact. Only two industries were privatized (or 'denationalized' as it was then called), both in 1953. But one of these, iron and steel, had barely had time to be nationalized and even after 1953 retained a large measure of state supervision; the other, road haulage, was scarcely of first rate significance.

The welfare state was accepted, and in some areas was extended. Initial plans for instituting cuts and other economies were dropped. There was no doctrinal attack on welfare, nor was there any social policy offered by the Conservatives that could be said to have been distinctly Conservative.

At the Ministry of Labour (currently called the Department of Employment) Walter Monckton was preferred to David Maxwell Fyfe, a more hard-line politician who had shadowed the Ministry in opposition. Monckton was given precise instructions from Churchill to avoid industrial confrontation. Trade union leaders quickly realized that Monckton was a soft touch: no wonder he was regarded as their favourite post-war Minister of Labour — of any party. As employers were encouraged not to resist wage demands, Monckton earned himself the title of 'the oil can'. Union leaders meanwhile were frequent visitors at 10 Downing Street and in the corridors of Whitehall. There was to be no return to their second rank stature of the interwar years and before.

The concept of equality, albeit of opportunity, was also subscribed to by the Conservatives. An Excess Profit Tax was introduced to howls of protest from businessmen. Progressive income taxes were retained, as were regional policies.

On the foreign and defence fronts, there were no right-wing hawkish policies. Defence spending, following the close of the Korean War, was cut back. Following the death of Stalin in March 1953, a policy of trying to bring about closer relations with the Soviet Union was actively pursued by Churchill, to the intense annoyance of the USA. Progress towards decolonization was continued, especially in West Africa. True, the government did decide to build the hydrogen bomb in 1953, but this decision was a logical follow-on from Attlee's decision to build the atomic bomb (tested in 1952).

High Noon of the Consensus, 1955–70

The Churchill government of 1951–5 set the tone for the entire period of Conservative rule to the Labour victory in the General Election of October 1964. The policies that Labour inherited were strikingly similar to those it had bequeathed the Conservatives in 1951. No further denationalizations occurred after 1953; the welfare state was little changed; trade unions became an even more permanent fixture, with the formation of the National Economic Development Council in 1962, of which they were partners; full employment policies were still being pursued; and Britain's defence and foreign policy stances were maintained. Indeed, the period after 1955 witnessed a great acceleration in the granting of independence to Britain's former colonies. The Conservative party, once the party of empire, was now the party of decolonization and self-government.

Labour won a narrow victory in 1964 but consolidated it with a ninety-six majority in the general election of March 1966. The party held office until June 1970. In opposition before 1964, Labour had made radical policy proclamations, as parties tend to do when relieved of the shackles of office, and when the (usually) moderate leadership is less able to marginalize the fervour of its back-bench followers. In 1960, for example, the Labour Party Conference voted against nuclear weapons, which would have meant sweeping changes to Britain's defence and foreign policy commitments. The party leadership managed to persuade Conference to reject the proposal the following year. But radical zeal was not quenched, and when the apparently left-wing Harold Wilson beat the right-wing candidate, George Brown, for the party leadership in 1963, the stage looked set for a future Labour government which would advance radical socialism, thereby breaking the consensus. But Labour in power from 1964 was not a radical force: moderation, continuity and pragmatism continued to be the order of the day.

Britain's poor economic health was the reason given for the conspicuous lack of radicalism. 'Socialism costs money' was the answer given to an increasingly restless left wing, 'But when the economy recovers . . . '. The economy, however, never did recover. True, there were some left-wing policies — comprehensive schooling (in place of grammar and secondary moderns) was given a decisive push and the steel industry was renationalized in 1967. The government also presided over a wide range of permissive reforms in divorce, race relations and abortion.

None of these policies, however, could be regarded as a serious challenge to the consensus. The Conservatives from 1951 to 1964 had themselves done little to discourage the drift towards comprehensivization. The renationalization of steel was denounced, but no serious plans were made to re-privatize it. And the reforms in the personal sphere owed more to the traditions, and occasionally even the instigation, of the Liberal party.

Hence, there are two related problems in understanding why the consensus continued until 1970: why the Conservatives adhered to it after Churchill's departure in 1955; and why Labour did not abandon it after 1964. The first is probably the easier to explain. Churchill was succeeded as PM by the moderate Anthony Eden and when he resigned prematurely, in January 1957, the even more middle-of-the-road Harold Macmillan took over. With a leadership determined to stick by consensual policies and their proven popularity at the polls (the election victory in May 1955 was followed by an even bigger one in October 1959) there was neither will nor incentive to introduce new-style policies. Why bother when the present mix appeared to be working? Alternative policies, moreover, were not on offer: no one in the parliamentary party was seriously suggesting abandoning the principles of the welfare state, pursuing wholesale privatization, suppressing trade union power or arresting the pace of decolonization. Those voices raised on the far right of the party were few and far away from the mainstream.

Radicial anti-consensus policies were, in contrast, being widely advocated by Labour. Why then did the consensus hold after 1964? In practical terms, a left wing Labour programme would have entailed a massive nationalization programme, which would have tipped the scales away from a mixed economy; abolition of private education and health care; and unilateral nuclear disarmament and a withdrawal from NATO. Economic difficulties provide part but by no means all of the explanation why such policies were not pursued. The small size of the majority (five) after the October 1964 election, and the desire not to repel potential voters, helps explain why radical policies were not followed before the March 1966 election, but not after it. One could make a case for saying that Labour lacked the time, in the four years between 1966 and 1970, to introduce anti-consensus policies. But the evidence does not suggest that Labour would have produced more radical policies if it had remained in office after 1970. The overwhelming reason why Labour did not abandon consensual policies wholesale between 1964 and 1970 was the lack of desire by senior figures in the party to implement left wing socialism. Had they really wanted to introduce radical anti-consensual policies, they could have done and would have done.

The moderating influence of the Civil Service also played a part, if an unquantifiable one, in explaining why the consensus continued throughout the period. Civil servants tend to like continuity and moderation and to resist sudden change. The general unpopularity of, even unfamiliarity with, non-consensual economic and social philosophies, is also important. Both Labour and Conservative parties until the 1970s broadly accepted the ideas of Keynes and Beveridge. Those who seriously challenged their prevailing orthodoxy were regarded as mavericks and outsiders.

Consensus Under Stress, 1970—9

The election of the Conservative government under Mrs Thatcher in May 1979 can correctly be identified as the principal catalyst in the breaking of the consensus. It had, however, come under severe stress between 1970 and 1979, first from Conservatives, then from Labour. Not all commentators, however, would agree that the period saw the consensus under stress: in particular, Martin Holmes (1988) argues that the post-war consensus reached its high point only in the years 1972—6. This period, he argues, saw trade union involvement in government, welfare spending, state control in industry and Keynesian economic policies all reaching new heights.

There is much in what Holmes says. But one should not overlook that the pre-1972 Conservative government under Edward Heath offered the most serious challenge the post-war consensus had faced up to that point. It also provided the first taste of the right wing economic and anti-union policies which after 1979 became known as 'Thatcherism'. Heath's government was elected in June 1970 determined to free

A challenge to the post-war consensus, or its highpoint? Conflicting opinions on the Conservative government 1970–4, led by Edward Heath. Heath lost the election of February 1974 after failure to bring the miners' strike of that year to a satisfactory conclusion.

industry from wide measures of state control, to legislate on trade union power and to promote the free market and self reliance in place of welfarism. In the event, as unemployment rose above half a million, Heath lost his nerve when the unpopularity of his policies was felt, and in consequence he brought about the so-called 'U-turn' in 1972. From that point until the election, as Holmes describes, the government embraced consensual policies. Nationalization was even extended, unique for a Conservative post-war government, and the 1972 Industry Act greatly increased state controls, in direct contrast to the direction of policy between 1970 and 1972. Trade union leaders were consulted as never before and it was ironical, and personally very painful for Heath, that it was the failure to bring to a conclusion the strike with the miners that precipitated his decision to call an election for February 1974. He lost.

Labour returned to power with a minority government led by Harold Wilson. A second election followed in October when he was able to achieve an outright, though wafer-thin majority of three. Several senior Labour figures, notably Tony Benn and Michael Foot, whose views were well supported on both front and back benches, now pressed hard for the introduction of radical policies, in particular: withdrawal from the European Community, which Britain had joined in 1973; unilateral nuclear disarmament; and an extension of state ownership and control.

Not one of these policies was adopted. Wilson, and then Callaghan, who succeeded him as PM in 1976, were both able to outflank the left, to its growing dismay and anger. Labour's small majority, which disappeared altogether following by-election defeats in 1977, was offered as one reason. The 'Lib—Lab pact' of 1977—8, when the tiny Liberal party maintained Labour in power, provided another reason for the government to reject doctrinaire policies. Recurrent economic difficulties, which resulted in the International Monetary Fund (IMF) being called in to help out the government in 1976, also help explain Labour's moderation in office, especially as the IMF made the setting of monetary targets and cuts in spending a condition of the provision of stand-by facilities.

Other policies, normally associated with right of centre governments, followed the IMF loan, including the imposition of cash limits on many departmental programmes and the sale of some government shares in British Petroleum to the private sector. At the same time Labour was gradually abandoning its commitment to Keynesian beliefs in spending one's way out of recession, and hence to full employment. Without the twin constraints of no parliamentary majority and a weak economy, Labour might conceivably have adopted more genuinely socialist policies after 1974. As it was, the consensus was still virtually intact when Mrs Thatcher entered Downing Street in May 1979. It had largely survived the twin attacks on it in the 1970s, from the right in 1970—2 and (ironically) from Labour, 1976—9.

Why the Consensus Broke Down

Why was there a fundamental change in the policies pursued by British governments after 1979? Kavanagh (1989) lists three main reasons, which together explain the breakdown.

1. *Ideas*. No challenge to the prevailing Keynesian—Beveridge orthodoxy had captured the imagination of a critical mass of policy makers from the war until the 1970s. The challenge came from the right (what has become known as the 'radical right') which exalted free enterprise in place of state control and provisions. The new ideology rested heavily on the work of two men: F.A. Hayek, in his influential book *The Road to Serfdom* (1944) who subsequently argued that state power was a potential menace to individual liberty and should be everywhere curtailed if individuals were to enjoy maximum benefit. Milton Friedman spearheaded an economist's challenge to the principles of Keynesianism, and in attempting to overturn his teaching substituted a new theory, popularly known as monetarism, which laid great stress on the control of the money supply and the reduction of inflation, even at the expense of maintaining full employment (see also Chapter 8).

   The ideas of Hayek, Friedman and others were initially articulated in a little known international annual Conference, the Mont Pelerin Society, formed soon after the war. Like-minded academics, mainly economists, met at this forum and advocated many of the ideas which were later adopted by Mrs Thatcher. The Mont Pelerin Society provided the spur for the establishment in London in 1957 of the Institute of Economic Affairs which, together with the later Centre for

Was there a post-war consensus?

The 'post-war consensus', little heard before the 1980s, became in that decade a buzz-word among political scientists and contemporary historians. Controversy surrounding it focused on three areas. Did it, in fact, ever exist? If so, when did it reach its high point? Was it a net benefit, or a cause of the nation's decline?

Prime among the sceptics of consensus is Ben Pimlott (1989), who argues that 'the consensus is a mirage, an illusion that rapidly fades the closer one gets to it'. He argues that it is only from the perspective of the 1980s that there appears to have been harmony before; during the period from 1945–79 the divisions were bitter and almost continuous, and politicians from both main parties never regarded themselves as belonging to a 'consensus'. Keynes and Beveridge, the intellectual fathers of the alleged consensus, Pimlott argues, were by no means accepted uncritically by the Labour and Conservative parties, particularly by their radical wings. The notion of a consensus, he argues, has a rose-tinted view of what the electorate felt. Ordinary voters were, he says, more divided during the period of the so-called consensus than since its conclusion after 1979. Pimlott sums up his views in a memorable expression: 'Sandbagged in their electoral trenches, the early post-war voters can be seen as the anonymous infantry of two implacably opposed armies in an era of adversarial politics, with the middle-way Liberals floundering in no-man's land'.

Lowe (1990) produced an altogether subtler distinction. He argues that there is a need to define more closely exactly what is meant by consensus, and whether it is a consensus about interpretations of the past or about what should be done in the future.

Lowe's qualifications are salutary. It does indeed depend on what is being claimed for the consensus. If we take it to mean what parties did when in office, as opposed to what they said or did when in opposition, there is no doubt that the consensus is a notion that implants meaning and coherence to the history of post-war politics in Britain.

Policy Studies (1974) gradually persuaded academics and politicians of the benefits of 'free enterprise' policies over Keynesian state involvement.

2. **People**. Ideas need people with political weight to articulate them and give them force if they are to have any significance. The earliest influential convert in the Conservative party to the radical right was Enoch Powell, and after his dismissal from the Shadow Cabinet in 1968 the banner was kept flying by John Biffen and most importantly Keith Joseph. Joseph in turn had been influenced principally by Peter Bauer, a London School of Economics (LSE) economist, and by Alfred Sherman, a journalist and propagandist; he did more than anyone to persuade Mrs Thatcher of the virtues of free enterprise policies. And it was Mrs Thatcher who possessed the single-mindedness and personal conviction to see that the policies were carried through without deflection after 1979.

3. **Circumstance**. Ideas and people alone would not have been sufficient to bring about the major policy shift; circumstance provided the opportunity. Without the collapse and discrediting of Keynesian social democrat policies in the 1960s and especially the 1970s, as described by Marquand (1987) and Skidelsky (1988),

'Thatcherism' would never have had its chance. The policies with which Keynesianism was associated — demand management and income policies — were shown to have failed as unemployment and inflation both rose and governments seemed incapable of running the government effectively, or indeed of containing the trade unions. Mrs Thatcher seized her opportunity with both hands.

The Consensus After 1979

Although John Vincent (1987) has argued that what was remarkable about Mrs Thatcher was how little, not how much, she changed, such a stance distorts her historical importance. Most of the six planks of the consensus were overturned, or at least seriously modified, by Mrs Thatcher after 1979. Four aspects of the consensus listed below went through absolute transformation.

1. *Full employment* policies were never pursued by her. Heath had panicked when unemployment threatened to reach one million in 1972. Mrs Thatcher kept her nerve and watched unemployment rise to more than two and then three million, levels that had existed in the dreaded inter-war years. No one had believed before 1979 that unemployment would ever be allowed to rise that high, nor that a government would survive if it were allowed to happen. They were wrong on both counts. The reduction of inflation, in line with the teachings of Friedman rather than Keynes, were placed above the lessening of unemployment.

2. *Trade union industrial and political power* diminished greatly in the 1980s. Consultations, almost a veto, over government policies had risen to an all-time high in the 1970s. Mrs Thatcher decided that she was not going to continue the cosy relationship and in consequence formal and informal contacts between union leaders and government ministers and officials all but ceased. Trade unions were effectively pushed to one side in policy formulation.

3. *The mixed economy* was also changed beyond recognition. The steady programme of privatizations — gas, steel (again!), electricity: the list is long and well known — decisively pushed the balance in the economy in the direction of private rather than public ownership. The rise in private share ownership was mirrored by the increase in home ownership through the government's policy of encouraging tenant purchase of council properties.

4. *Mrs Thatcher also denied that governments have a duty to further equality.* In place of equality she appeared to prefer a 'stimulating inequality', believing that differential pay acts as an incentive to effort and enterprise, and that intervention by the state distorts the operation of the free market. Regional aid to reduce inequalities between different parts of Britain was consistently cut back after 1979, with the result that differentials between north and south have increased markedly. The steady reduction in income tax rates have benefited the better-off, and helped increase inequalities in income. Although many sections of the working class saw their prosperity rise after 1979, the numbers in the 'underclass', comprising the long-term unemployed, single-parent families and those dependent on state benefits, grew considerably in size. Britain became a more polarized country as a direct consequence of Thatcherite policies.

The remaining planks were not removed. ***The welfare state*** remained largely intact during Mrs Thatcher's first two terms of office (1979−87). Its survival was in some ways paradoxical. Bodies such as the Institute of Economic Affairs had for many years been campaigning for a move away from the universal to selective provision of welfare benefits and at the same time advocated the extension of market forces throughout the various parts of the vast welfare empire. But partly for fear of risking unpopularity, partly because the government's hands were full with other matters, the welfare state was left intact. In Mrs Thatcher's third term (1987−90) the NHS in particular was subjected to new market pressures but it would be wrong to exaggerate the extent to which Mrs Thatcher disturbed the welfare state. Its key principles, which include universal and free provision, and flat rate benefits, remained. Private provision increased but the welfare state continued to provide support for those who either could or would not pay. Mrs Thatcher realized it would be electoral suicide for her to do anything else. (See also Chapter 25.)

The foreign and defence consensus has also continued very much intact. Policy since 1979 has been based upon Britain's continued maintenance and upgrading of her nuclear deterrent (Polaris to Chevaline); grants of independence to some remaining colonies (notably Zimbabwe in 1980); close cooperation with NATO and the USA; and qualified support for the European Community. If one includes a determination to contain terrorism in Northern Ireland and to remain there providing military and economic support then the continuity of consensus policy is complete.

A New Consensus?

Did Mrs Thatcher manage, in largely breaking the old, to forge a new consensus? The immediate response must of course be that we do not yet know. Returning to the definition of consensus given at the opening of this chapter, it matters not what parties say in opposition (when they tend to make pronouncements more extreme than they carry out in office): it is their policies in power that matter. We do not yet know what a future Labour government may do if and when it regains office. Only when their policies are manifest can a definitive answer be given to this question.

And yet it is already possible to see Labour becoming more moderate. Its high point of non-moderation came in the period 1980−3 after Michael Foot succeeded James Callaghan as party leader. Its 1983 manifesto was as socialist as any since 1945, promising the unilateral abandonment of Britain's nuclear weapons, extensions of nationalization, as well as opposition to the (capitalist) EEC.

After 1983, however, with Neil Kinnock replacing Michael Foot as party leader, the party progressively moved away from left-wing policies. Labour's 1987 election programme was moderate. The defeat further stiffened Kinnock's resolve to fight off his left wing and remove from the party doctrinaire policies which no longer commanded the support of the electorate. Old-style left-wing figures such as Tony Benn and Eric Heffer were gradually marginalized, a task made easier by their defeat in their challenge for the party leadership in October 1988. Kinnock was assisted in his task by his deputy Roy Hattersley and by the promotion into senior front-bench positions of able pragmatic figures like John Smith, Bryan Gould and Gordon Brown.

One view of consensus politics

The mood of the times was captured by Ernest Bevin, Churchill's minister of labour in the wartime coalition. In a speech to the Commons in June 1944, Bevin recalled visiting troops in Portsmouth as they prepared for the Normandy landings: 'They were going off to face this terrific battle with great hearts and courage. The question they put to me when I went through their ranks was: "Ernie, when we have done this job for you, are we going back on the dole?" Both the Prime Minister and I answered: "No, you are not." '

After the war, the Conservative Party opposed Attlee's reforms at first, but soon embraced them; thus the post-war consensus, lasting more than 30 years, was born. It has become fashionable during the 1980s to deride this consensus as a drag on Britain's modernisation. In *The Audit of War*, published in 1986, Correlli Barnett argued that the welfare state diverted resources from the more vital task of industrial reconstruction. More generally, Mrs Thatcher blames the post-war consensus for undermining Britain's economy, for example by protecting sloppy state industries and bloated trade unions.

An alternative analysis is available. It is that Britain emerged from the war virtually bankrupt, but still managed to create a civilized post-war society, with full employment and faster economic growth than during any other 30-year period of British history.

Those observations do not obliterate the weaknesses: inadequate investment, a diminishing share of world trade, regular sterling crises. Whether these were exacerbated by the post-war social reforms is, however, highly debatable. A strong case can be mounted for arguing that their roots lay elsewhere: in lingering illusions about Britain's — and sterling's — world role, in diverting too much of our research and development into military projects and in allowing finance to retain a higher status than manufacturing in our economic culture.

In other words, the British economy has suffered not because the post-war reforms went too far but because they did not go far enough. 3 September 1939 unleashed the nearest thing since Cromwell to a British revolution. Sadly it remains incomplete.

Source: From **Peter Kellner**, 'The War That Started a Revolution', *The Independent*, 28 August 1989

The endorsement given by the party conference in October 1989 to the party's pragmatic policy review was a major endorsement of Kinnock's policy of 'modernizing' Labour's policies. In practice this meant that the party had come to realize that if it clung to its traditional socialist politics, it would never again be elected. The class composition of the electorate has been changing throughout the post-war period in favour of the Conservative party. With the exception of its strong showing in the March 1966 election, Labour had undergone a steady loss of support at every election between 1951 (48.6 per cent) and 1983 (27.6 per cent). The 1987 result was a slight improvement at 30.8 per cent of the popular vote, which could have been interpreted as an endorsement for Labour's more popular policies, but the party was still 10 percentage points behind the Conservatives.

The period since 1979 has seen the pace of social change increase. From 1979 to 1987, according to the opinion-polling organization MORI, union membership

Prime Ministers and leaders of the opposition since 1945

Government	Prime Minister	Leader of the Opposition	
1945–50 Lab.	Clement Attlee	Winston Churchill	Con.
1950–1 Lab.	Clement Attlee	Winston Churchill	Con.
1951–5 Con.	Winston Churchill Anth. Eden (Apr.–May 1955)	Clement Attlee	Lab.
1955–9 Con.	Anthony Eden (1955–7) H. Macmillan (1957–9)	Hugh Gaitskell	Lab.
1959–64 Con.	H. Macmillan (1959–63) A. Douglas-Home (1963–4)	H. Gaitskell (1959–63) Harold Wilson (1963–4)	Lab.
1964–6 Lab.	Harold Wilson	A. Douglas-Home (1963–5) Edward Heath (1965–6)	Con.
1966–70 Lab.	Harold Wilson	Edward Heath	Con.
1970–4 Con.	Edward Heath	Harold Wilson	Lab.
1974 Lab.	Harold Wilson	Edward Heath	Con.
1974–9 Lab.	Harold Wilson (1974–6) J. Callaghan (1976–9)	Edward Heath (1974–5) M. Thatcher (1975–9)	Con. Con.
1979–83 Con.	Margaret Thatcher	J. Callaghan (1979–80) Michael Foot (1980–3)	Lab.
1983–7 Con.	Margaret Thatcher	Neil Kinnock	Lab.
1987– Con.	Margaret Thatcher (1987–90) John Major (1990–)	Neil Kinnock	Lab.

fell from 30 to 23 per cent, home owner-occupation rose from 52 to 62 per cent, share ownership increased from 7 to 19 per cent and households defined as 'middle-class' rose from 35 to 42 per cent. Much of the increase in Conservative support in the 1983 and 1987 elections came from those affected by these changes. They gained 36 per cent of the working-class vote in 1987, the highest percentage in any post-war election, and did especially well among those living in the south who worked in the private sector (see Chapter 11).

Two responses are possible from Labour. Either they could adapt their policies to appeal to the new electorate or they could argue, as the left does, that the reason for the defeats was because the party was insufficiently socialist. From the perspective of the early 1990s it seems that the moderates have won the argument and the battle for power.

So what policies might a future Labour government adopt? The likelihood is that they would have to accept most of what Mrs Thatcher did in the same way that the Conservatives after 1951 accepted much of the Attleean consensus. In doing so a new consensus could be forged comprising: higher acceptable levels of unemployment than Labour has envisaged hitherto; an arm's-length relationship with the trade unions involving the retention of some Thatcherite legislation; and acceptance with only minor amendments of the major privatizations. Labour would, however, revive equality policies like increasing the higher rate of taxation (though not as high as in the 1970s); increase spending on the welfare state; and pursue a less idiosyncratic and isolationist foreign policy. A partial consensus perhaps but a Thatcherite legacy which will long survive her departure from power in November 1990.

References and Further Reading

Hayek, F., *The Road to Serfdom* (Routledge, 1946). First published 1944.

Holmes, M. and Horsewood, N., 'The Consensus Debate', *Contemporary Record* (Summer 1988).

Kavanagh, D. and Morris, P., *Consensus Politics* (Basil Blackwell, 1989).

Kavanagh, D. and Pimlott, B., 'Is the postwar consensus a myth?', *Contemporary Record* (Summer 1989).

Kellner, P., *Independent*, 28 August 1989.

Lowe, R., 'The Second World War and origins of the consensus', *Contemporary Record* (Summer 1990).

Marquand, D., 'Postwar consensus and its decline', *Contemporary Record* (Autumn 1988).

Skidelsky, R. S. (ed), *Thatcherism* (Chatto and Windus, 1988).

Vincent, J., 'Mrs Thatcher's place in history', *Contempory Record* (Autumn 1987).

The Reversal of National Decline

It is likely that the great majority of British school-children in the mid-1950s felt a frisson of excitement when contemplating a map of the world. They made no distinction between Commonwealth and colonies and were thrilled to see, coloured in red, an empire on which the sun never set. No doubt their parents experienced a more mature but substantially similar version of this youthful pride. In 1939, after the USA, Britain was the richest country in the world. Following her heroic struggle against Hitler Britain had emerged victorious from the war, her empire intact and in some places even augmented. It is easy to understand (if impossible to justify) why British people felt that indefinable sense of superiority to foreigners.

Ten years later, however, it was as if all that red had been suddenly washed away. The 'wind of change' which Harold MacMillan had spoken of in 1960 had raged throughout Africa and elsewhere, scattering in its wake new independent countries with indigenous leaders and transplanted 'Westminster Model' constitutions. To lose an empire so quickly and in some cases so ungraciously was a shock to the national psyche. Dean Acheson, the US Secretary of State, struck a raw nerve in 1962 when he observed with undiplomatic accuracy that 'Britain has lost an empire and not yet found a role'. The USA wanted Britain to help lead Europe but British prime ministers — and sections of public opinion — still hankered after the world role which Britain's ailing economy neither merited nor could support.

This sense of lost greatness was reinforced by a growing awareness that many countries — including the defeated Germany and Japan — were flourishing economically while Britain languished, e.g. British motorcycles which had dominated the world in the late 1950s had succumbed both internationally and domestically to Yamahas and Suzukis by the mid-1960s. Britain may have won the World Cup in 1966 but in the international prosperity league she had slipped to around twelfth and was still falling. A sense of national decline set in which weakened morale, helped erode the consensus supporting Attlee's post-war settlement and contributed towards the rancour of political strife in the 1970s. The British public felt bitter at being denied the improved standard of living they had expected and perhaps even felt they deserved.

Morbid introspection followed. Analyses of 'the British Disease' abounded and even Britain's political system — previously venerated as a model for all to follow — was found wanting by a series of critiques, reports and Royal Commissions. National economic and political revival became the Holy Grail which all politicians claimed they could find — if only they were voted into office and given time.

Mrs Thatcher received both privileges. After ten years she felt able to claim that her medicine had revived Britain both economically and internationally and created a new national consensus based around her own ideas. While there is some evidence for these claims, they are challenged by both her opponents and academic experts. Less at issue is the claim that Mrs Thatcher's conduct of the Falklands War made the mass of British people feel good about themselves for the first time in many years. This extraordinary adventure appeared simultaneously to fulfill a moral mission and satisfy a gut desire of the British to take on a foreign country and win by force of arms. Rightly or wrongly the majority of Britons revelled in the action; perhaps it was the imperial resonance of this far-away war which further helped to make it wildly popular. For others, however, it merely highlighted the irrelevance of our few remaining stale crumbs of empire and exposed the true scale of Britain's decline since 1945.

PART II The Contemporary Context

Thirty to forty years ago the structure of this book might have surprised political scientists. Their discipline had emerged basically from history and law and in those days the emphasis was upon the Constitution and the institutions of government. This approach was too narrow; scholars began to realize the impossibility of understanding the politics of a country without detailed knowledge of its economy and social structure. Moreover, other social sciences like sociology and economics were beginning to use their perspectives to produce profound insights into political activity.

A new approach to the subject, therefore, began to evolve which drew upon the major social sciences. Arguably, this approach has not gone far enough and the boundaries between disciplines concerned with the study of society should be broken down still further. This section of the book reflects these developments by addressing, in turn, economic structure, social structure and political culture and participation.

4 The Economic Structure

Michael Moran

Every society has an economic structure because every society has an economy — a set of social arrangements for producing at the very least the means of material life. In some societies, especially poor ones, the structure is simple. Britain's, by contrast, is exceedingly complex, shaped by a long history of economic development and technical change. When we look at the economic structure we will examine a wide range of features: the balance between different kinds of economic activity in the community; the evidence about who owns and controls the means of activity; and the patterns of work and of employment in our country.

The economic structure is vital to the political system in Britain for many reasons, of which three are especially important. Firstly, the way property is distributed and work allocated in the labour force is a major influence over political organizations in the community. As we examine elections, political parties and pressure groups later in this book we will see that the voting behaviour of citizens, the divisions between parties and the structure of pressure groups are all closely tied to the wider economic context. Secondly, in the economy lies, obviously, the wealth of the country — and, therefore, the resources on which government can draw to support its operations. Finally, in Britain today the management of the economic structure and the cure of economic problems is the most visible task of government: as the US President Woodrow Wilson commented 'Prosperity is necessarily the first theme of a political campaign'. The relevance of the economic structure influences political organization, provides the resources of government and involves major responsibilities of government.

Economic Organization: Public and Private

Britain has a market — or as is sometimes said a *capitalist* — economy. This means that economic resources are predominantly in private hands. However, in no capitalist economy is activity completely controlled by the private sector; and in all modern capitalist economies the state is a major participant in economic life (Lindblom, 1977).

Although most debate about the role of the state in the economy concerns what is usually called 'public ownership', this is only one way among many by which state influence is felt. Public intervention in the market economy actually takes six main forms: ownership, partnership, regulation, licensing, purchase, supply.

The government as owner

Public ownership is the most visible form of state participation in the economic structure. Government has long been a major owner of productive property: for instance, the Crown was already a great property holder when land was the main source of wealth in the community. In the nineteenth century government established a public monopoly in a major new industry of the time, posts and telecommunications. In modern Britain government is still a major owner of society's natural resources, like coal, oil and gas. (The right to exploit these is only given by licence to private firms.) However, the best known instances of public ownership are the result of what is usually called *nationalization*. The nationalized industries are the product of conscious political choices. For most of the century until the start of the 1980s the nationalized sector grew, with successive governments of different political outlooks adding to the range (Pollard, 1983). In the years between the two world wars, for instance, industries as different as broadcasting and electricity supply were nationalized (by the creation of, respectively, the British Broadcasting Corporation and the Central Electricity Generating Board). The years immediately after the Second World War saw a substantial increase in public ownership: coal, steel and railways were all taken into the state sector. The main reason for the post-war growth of public ownership was the belief that the enterprises, if left in private hands, would be run inefficiently or would even fail. This motivation also explains many of the important pieces of nationalization accomplished in the 1960s and 1970s. These included shipbuilding and important sections of the aircraft and motor vehicle production industries.

Until the mid-1970s it seemed that the continued expansion of public ownership was an irreversible trend in Britain. However, Mrs Thatcher's Conservative administrations of the 1980s destroyed this assumption. Through a programme of 'privatization' they sold into private hands about 40 per cent of what was in public ownership at the start of the decade. The 'privatized' concerns include many once thought 'natural' to the public sector, such as the gas supply and telecommunications industries. Privatization marks a radical shift in the balance between the state and the market in Britain (Grant and Nath, 1984). For more on privatization see Chapter 20. However, the retreat of state ownership does not necessarily mean that total public participation in the economy is in decline. On the contrary, in most of the other five cases which we will consider the importance of government is apparently growing.

The government as partner

The state can act as a partner of private enterprise in numerous ways. Publicly controlled institutions in the financial sector commonly provide investment capital to allow private enterprises to set up or to expand. The major area of growth in partnership in recent years, however, has been at the local level. Faced with the need to redevelop declining and derelict areas of the cities, local authorities and local development corporations have embarked on numerous joint developments with private firms. Some of the best known examples of policy initiatives at the local level — such as the redevelopment of London's docklands — are the result of precisely such partnerships.

The government as regulator

Most debate about public intervention in the economy is focused on questions of ownership. Yet it is arguably the case that the structure of the market economy in Britain is less influenced by ownership than by public regulation — in other words by sets of rules either contained in law or otherwise prescribed by government.

Public regulation is of three kinds. First, the state sets a general framework for the conduct of life, including economic life, in the community. Criminal and civil law defines and enforces commercial contracts, identifies what constitutes honesty and dishonesty and provides a means for detecting and preventing fraud. Without this general framework of enforced rules the market economy could not operate.

A second category of regulation is directed more precisely at particular industries or sectors of the economy, governing the conduct of affairs inside individual enterprises. For instance, there now exists a large body of law governing relations in the work-place. Industrial relations law places obligations on both employers and trade unions in industrial bargaining. Health and safety legislation prescribes rules governing the detail of work processes, in the interests of safeguarding the life and health of employees.

Finally, there is a growing volume of regulation governing the relations between firms in the private sector and the rest of society. The importance of this kind of regulation has grown greatly in recent years. Two of the most important instances concern pollution control and consumer protection. Pollution regulations govern the nature of industrial processes and restrict the emissions which firms can allow into the atmosphere. Consumer protection regulates the content of many products (in the interests of safety), how they can be advertised (in the interests of honesty and accuracy) and the terms of competition between firms (in the interests of ensuring fair prices) (Cranston, 1979).

One important form of regulation is sometimes called 'self-regulation'. Under this system an industry or occupation determines its own regulations and establishes its own institutions for policing and enforcement. Some important professions (like the law) and major industries (like financial services and advertising) are organized in this way. But most self-regulation should more accurately be called regulation under public licence, because what happens is that the state licenses a group to regulate itself — thereby saving the difficulty and expense of doing the job directly. This links to our next instance of public participation in the market economy.

The government as licencee

When government does not wish to engage directly in a particular economic activity, but nevertheless wants to retain close control over that activity, it has the option of licensing a private firm to provide goods and services under prescribed conditions. This method is historically ancient: in the seventeenth and eighteenth centuries, for instance, government often granted monopolies to private corporations to trade in particular products or in particular areas. In the modern economy licensing is used extensively. The exploitation of oil reserves in the North Sea has largely been accomplished by selling licences to explore for oil to privately owned companies. The service of providing commercial radio and commercial television is handled in a similar way, though licences are at the moment given rather than sold: thus, the licence or 'franchise' to provide a commercial television service for the north west of England has been held by a private firm, Granada TV, since the foundation of commercial television. (These arrangements may change as a result of recent legislation.)

One of the most common ways of allocating licences is through a system of competitive bidding; the government, of course, can also use the competitive system by going to the private sector as a customer for goods and services.

The government as a customer

We saw in the opening chapter that government can use a variety of means, including coercion, to raise goods and services. But government in Britain in fact normally uses the market. In other words, it employs the state's revenues (from such sources as taxation) to buy the goods and services it needs. A glance around any classroom or lecture theatre will show the importance of the public sector as a customer. The room itself will almost certainly have been built as the result of a contract with private firms of builders and architects. The teacher at the front of the room is a private citizen hired on the labour market. Virtually every piece of equipment in the room will also have been bought from private firms. This simple example is illustrated on a wider scale throughout government. Take the example of national defence. Although we usually think of government as providing the defence of the country, it actually buys most of the means of defence in the market-place: soldiers, sailors and airmen have to be recruited from the labour market in competition with other recruiters of labour, like private firms; most defence equipment is bought under contract from the private sector; and the everyday necessities of the forces — from the food eaten in the regimental Mess to the fuel used by a regimental staff car — is bought in the market-place.

The government is a customer in the market economy, but it is a very special kind of customer. Because government is the biggest institution in British society it is also the biggest customer. In some important areas it is to all intents and purposes the only customer. To take the example given above, in the supply of most important defence equipment — rockets, military aircraft, warships — the public sector is the sole purchaser. In these circumstances the 'producer—customer' relationship is obviously a very special one. Firms producing defence equipment, while nominally in private ownership, operate in such close contact with government agencies that they are in practical terms often indistinguishable from public bodies.

That the state is a customer of the private sector is well recognized; but in understanding the country's economic structure it is as important to emphasize the role of the public sector as a supplier of goods and services.

The government as supplier

Picture the following example of a politics student on a course at a Polytechnic. She lives in a flat rented from the local council and travels to the Polytechnic by a local train service. She is learning Spanish in her spare time at a class in the nearby adult education centre. In her last vacation she walked the Pennine Way, using a guide book bought from the local branch of Her Majesty's Stationery Office. At the end of the walk she was soaked in a downpour, caught pneumonia and had to be treated in hospital.

What unites these activities and experiences is that they all involve goods and services supplied by public institutions: education, housing, books, health care. The example shows the great variety of conditions under which government acts as a supplier. Some goods and services are free at the point of consumption: this is true of most health care and, at the moment, of a Polytechnic education; but whereas health care is available to everybody in the community, higher education is restricted to a qualified group. Some goods and services are available to everybody at a price which is nominal (there is usually a small fee for adult evening classes). Some are available to all at a substantial price, but are nevertheless subsidized to keep that price below the full commercial rate (rail transport). Some are available on similarly subsidized price terms but only to a qualified group (council housing). Finally, some are available to all on payment of a commercially established price (the guide books published by Her Majesty's Stationery Office).

The various ways in which the state is a pervasive presence in the economic structure are illustrated in Table 4.1.

Table 4.1 *Varying roles of government in the economic structure*

Forms	Examples
Ownership	Minerals, land
Partnership	Development schemes in inner cities
Licensing	Oil exploration, commercial radio and television
Regulation	Health and safety at work
Purchase	Defence contracting
Supply	Health care, education

The list is significant both because it shows how important the state is in the economic structure and because it shows how far the issues that are argued about in British politics concern the balance between the various kinds of role. Take the single example of ownership. In the 1980s government 'privatized' many enterprises like gas supply and the telephone service. At the same time it set up public bodies to regulate the newly privatized concerns: to fix prices and other conditions under which services are supplied to customers. Arguments between supporters and opponents of privatization are not, therefore, arguments about whether or not government should be present in the economic structure; they turn on differences about whether, in particular cases, it is better for the state to be an owner or a regulator.

(Note the sectoral shift from manufacturing to service industries reflected in Figure 4.1. Figure 4.2 shows the breakdown of developments within the service sector.)

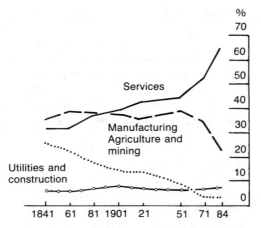

Figure 4.1 *Employment patterns (Source:* The Economist, *30 November 1985)*

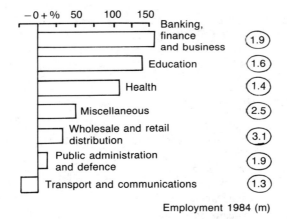

Employment 1984 (m)

Figure 4.2 *Services: per cent change 1954–84 (Source:* The Economist, *30 November 1985)*

Economic structure: the balance of sectors

The role of public institutions is obviously a key aspect of a country's economic structure, but just as important is the balance between what are sometimes called 'sectors'. We often speak of Britain as an 'industrial' economy, but the kinds of industries dominant in the economy have changed greatly in the recent past and continue to change. These alterations have momentous wider consequences: they affect the social structure, noticeably the class structure, and thus feed through to politics. For instance, the declining proportion of manual workers in the economy has been a cause of declining votes for the Labour party, once the party of most manual workers.

Table 4.2 *Gross Domestic Product by industry*

Gross Domestic Product by Industry	1977		1987	
	£ million	per cent	£ million	per cent
Agriculture, forestry and fishing	3,307	2.6	5,901	1.7
Energy and water supply	8,625	6.7	24,184	6.8
Manufacturing	37,972	29.5	85,552	24.1
Construction	7,840	6.1	21,524	6.1
Distribution, hotels and catering: repairs	17,057	13.2	48,963	13.8
Transport	6,955	5.4	16,227	4.6
Communications	3,259	2.5	9,688	2.7
Banking, finance, insurance, business services and leasing	15,034	11.7	63,903	18.0
Ownership of dwellings	7,516	5.8	20,180	5.7
Public administration, defence and social security	8,964	7.0	24,895	7.0
Education and health services	11,198	8.7	31,681	8.9
Other services	6,867	5.3	22,366	6.3
Total	134,594	104.5	375,064	105.7
Adjustment for financial services	− 5,844	− 4.5	− 20,545	− 5.8
Gross domestic product at factor cost (income-based)	128,750	100.0	354,519	100.0

Note: Differences between totals and the sums of their component parts are due to rounding
Source: Britain 1989: An Official Handbook

It is conventional to make a distinction between 'primary', 'secondary' and 'tertiary' (or 'service') sectors. The 'primary' sector covers those activities, mining and quarrying, concerned with the fundamental activity of extracting wealth from the natural world. The 'secondary' sector is most closely involved with manufacturing — in other words, with turning raw materials into finished goods, be they cars, refrigerators or aeroplanes. The 'tertiary' (or 'service') sector refers to activities designed neither to extract and process materials, nor to manufacture goods, but to deliver services; hence the alternative, commonly used name. We saw in the last section that many important services — like health and education — are provided by public institutions; but others, ranging from catering and tourism to financial services, are provided by privately owned firms operating in the market.

The three categories of sector are extremely broad, but their changing importance illuminates aspects of the developing economic structure. The decisive historical event in the evolution of the British economy was the Industrial Revolution. It began in the latter half of the eighteenth century and within a hundred years transformed the country. This revolution involved a shift in the balance between sectors. The key change was the decline in significance of agriculture as a source of wealth and as a source of jobs. At the same time the economy began to depend increasingly on the production and sale of finished goods — at first cotton, then a wide range of manufactures based on the iron and steel industries. Thus the Industrial Revolution coincided with the rise of the 'secondary' or manufacturing industries. But in recent decades there has occurred a second stage in structural change: the decline of

**Manual/
non-manual
workforce**

> Before the 'industrial revolution' most economic activity involved agriculture
>
> After the industrial revolution manufacturing was supreme
>
> In recent decades service industries have become increasingly important
>
> This is changing the class structure from one dominated by manual to one dominated by non-manual workers

manufacturing and the rise of service industries in the 'tertiary' sector. In part this change is not specific to Britain. It reflects the characteristic development of most industrial economies. The reasons for the expansion of service industries are various. Technical advance has made the activities of extraction and manufacture much more efficient than in the past: in agriculture, for instance, a work-force which is the tiniest in Britain's history produces more food than ever before because of the use of advanced technology on the farm. At the same time, growing prosperity has created an increased demand for services of all kinds, ranging from education to catering and tourism. Britain, because it is a classic example of an advanced industrial economy, has shared in this common experience of economic change.

But in Britain the widespread pattern of 'sectoral' change has been especially marked — so marked, indeed, that some have argued that we are experiencing the 'deindustrialization' of the economy (Bacon and Eltis, 1976). The great industries on which Britain's nineteenth century industrial might were built have almost universally declined — both in world markets and as components of the British economy. Coal, shipbuilding, steel and iron — all once major centres of economic power and employment — have become much less significant. This decline can be traced back over a century in the case of many industries, but in recent decades it has accelerated: since the beginning of the 1970s the number of jobs in manufacturing has fallen by over 2.4 million, while the number in service industries has risen by over 2.1 million (Central Statistical Office, 1987, p. 74).

The important changes in the balance between the sectors are also reflected in another important feature of the economy — the structure of ownership.

The structure of ownership

We have already examined one aspect of ownership in Britain's economy — the balance between enterprises owned and controlled in the public and private sectors. But the simple phrase 'private ownership' is complex, and deserves close scrutiny. The legal vesting of the ownership of productive property — factories, equipment and so on — in private hands is an outstandingly important feature of the British economy. The changing structure of that ownership has implications for the functioning of the whole social system and for the kinds of policies which governments can pursue.

In the early stages of the industrial revolution Britain, like many other capitalist economies, was marked by what is sometimes called ***the unity of ownership and control:*** firms were for the most part small by modern standards; they were controlled by families or by partnerships; and the legal owners were also usually those who

The 'ownership and control debate'

Has 'the separation of ownership from control' changed the market economy in Britain?

The arguments for: owners no longer control firms; managers, who make decisions, are socially responsible and are paid salaries not profits

The arguments against: many managers are also part-owners; many firms are still effectively controlled by a small number of shareholders; even salaried managers have to make profits in order to survive

took the main part in daily management. Like much else in Britain, this pattern has changed in modern times. Three developments are important: the separation of the managerial function from the role of ownership; the changing structure of legal ownership in the most important enterprises; and the changing size and scope of firms' activities.

The development of *a division of functions between those responsible for the daily control of firms and those vested with legal ownership* actually began in the nineteenth century; it is now predominant among larger firms in the economy. It has been prompted by the growing complexity of the task of running a large business enterprise which has resulted in the emergence of a wide range of specialized managerial jobs covering finance, production, personnel, sales and so on. No one seriously disputes that there now exists in most large corporations a separation between, on one hand, individuals responsible for the daily running of the enterprise and, on the other, groups vested with legal ownership. There is, however, a serious argument about the implications — including the political implications — of this shift. Some commentators argue that Britain is only one of a range of advanced capitalist nations where there has occurred a 'separation of ownership from control'. In other words real power in firms is no longer exercised by owners, but by salaried managers. The consequence is that one of the traditional characteristics of the capitalist system — the concentration of economic resources in the hands of private individuals motivated largely by the desire for profit — has been modified. Salaried managers, it is argued, have a wider set of motivations than pure profit and are responsive to the needs and wishes of the community. Other commentators argue that, by contrast, the rise of the manager has only allocated traditional tasks in a new way. Managers, it is claimed, run firms in the traditional interests of owners — with profits in mind above all. They do this because many managers are also in part owners; because owners who are not managers still retain the power to dismiss managers who ignore the pursuit of profits; and because in any case most managers accept the philosophy that the point of a firm is to make profit.

The original notion that owners were no longer powerful in big firms arose because of changes in the legal nature of firms. Most big enterprises in Britain are no longer family owned firms or partnerships. They are 'joint stock' companies — which means that ownership is vested jointly in a multiplicity of individuals who own the stock, or shares, in the firm. Where the owners are many and scattered, and managers are few and concentrated, it is natural that the latter should more effectively control decisions inside the company.

This connects to our second main development identified at the beginning of this section — *the changing form of legal ownership*. The largest and most important firms in the economy are typically owned jointly by many people scattered around the country — and in some cases around the world. The recently privatized British Telecom, for instance, has about two million shareholders, most of them owning no more than a few hundred shares. Since important decisions — like contests for membership of the board of directors — are decided by majority votes, with shareholders allotted votes in proportion to the number of shares owned, it is virtually impossible for numerous small shareholders to combine together in sufficient number to control decisions.

In recent years, however, changes in the nature of share ownership have altered this state of affairs. Although the number of individuals owning shares in Britain grew in the 1980s — principally because of widespread buying of the stock of newly privatized concerns like British Telecom and British Gas — the proportion of total shares owned by private individuals has shown a long-term fall over recent decades. In place of the private shareholder, ownership is increasingly in the hands of what are conventionally called 'institutions', notably insurance companies and pension funds. This change has an important implication for the debate about the separation of ownership from control. The institutions' shareholdings are concentrated in the biggest and most important firms. Hence, the argument that managers have the power to wield influence over a dispersed mass of owners no longer holds. Indeed, there have been striking cases in recent years where the institutions have wielded their numerical resources to control and discipline managements of individual firms.

The rise of the giant firm is the third important feature of the structure of ownership in the private sector which should be noticed. Most firms in Britain are tiny, but a small number of giant enterprises nevertheless dominate the economy (Utton, 1982). This is the result of a long-term trend: the domination of big firms has grown greatly in the twentieth century, a change mirrored in other advanced industrial economies. The giant firms dominant in the economy are also usually *multi-national* in character. A multi-national firm is a concern which produces its goods in different nations, and sells them in many different national markets. The most sophisticated firms operate an international 'division of labour': it is common, for instance, for different components of a motor car to be produced in a variety of factories in different countries, and then to be assembled in yet another country. In the years since the Second World War the significance of multi-national companies in Britain has grown greatly. Many of the biggest British concerns have taken on a multi-national character: though conventionally thought of as British, they actually only locate a minority of

The structure of private enterprise

The structure of private enterprise in recent decades has been marked by three great changes:

1. The rise of a specialized group of salaried managers responsible for the main functions inside firms
2. The concentration of share ownership in the hands of 'institutional' investors like insurance companies
3. The domination of many sectors by giant firms — multi-nationals — organizing their markets on a world scale

their workers in this country and only a minority of their revenue comes from British activities. British markets have also themselves been deeply penetrated by foreign multi-nationals. Britain is one of the most popular locations for American firms expanding abroad, and even when firms are not located in Britain there are whole markets — for instance in motor cycles, electrical goods and automobiles — where the products of foreign multi-nationals either dominate or are a substantial part of the supply.

Work and unemployment

Work is a central part of each individual's life — whether the worker is the unrewarded housewife or the trader in the City of London earning £250,000 yearly. But the nature of the work is also important for wider social reasons. ***Occupation*** is the single most important influence on the social structure. The kind of work done is a key determinant of the material rewards and the status an individual enjoys. Indeed the class structure in Britain closely corresponds to the occupational structure. Definitions of class commonly mean ***occupational class:*** 'working class', for instance, usually refers to those people -- and their families — who earn a living from 'manual' jobs. The central place of occupation in the political life of the country is well illustrated by the case of voting and elections, where ***occupational class*** has been, and remains, a key influence on the way people vote. Work is central to the life of the individual: but it is also central to the economic structure. Five aspects of this centrality are notable.

Most people in Britain live by selling their labour

Britain is a market economy in which the only significant tradeable resource controlled by the majority of the population is their labour. There are indeed exceptions: a small minority of the wealthy control sufficient productive property to be able to live on the returns of that property; a larger minority — like pensioners, the unemployed, some students — live off state-provided benefits. But most individuals either live off the returns of their own work or — as in the case of children — are dependent on 'breadwinners'. These are obvious points, but they merit emphasis because they explain the central place of work in the social structure. The proportions are illustrated in Table 4.3.

Table 4.3 *Employed and self-employed, 1987 (millions)*

	Men	Women	All
Full-time employees	10.9	5.1	16.0
Part-time employees	0.5	4.2	4.7
Self-employed	2.2	0.8	3.0
Government schemes	0.3	0.2	0.5
Total in work	13.9	10.3	24.2

Source: Jackson, 1988, p. 84

Most people sell their labour to private firms

We saw earlier in this chapter that the state is a major presence in the economy. Nevertheless, only a minority of the work-force is employed in the public sector. Until the beginning of the 1980s there had occurred a long-term increase in the size of this minority — so marked that some observers argued that excessive growth of public sector employment was a main cause of Britain's economic difficulties. As Table 4.4 shows, however, this trend has been reversed. A combination of cuts in numbers employed in public services and the privatization of many important industries means that the dominance of private firms as employers has been reinforced in recent years.

Table 4.4 *Public and private sector employment, 1961—85 (millions)*

	Public sector	Private sector
1961	5.9	18.6
1971	6.6	17.8
1981	7.2	17.2
1985	6.6	17.8

Source: CSO, 1987, p. 73

Changes in the balance between private and public sector employment are connected to a third notable feature of the work-force — the changing balance between sectors.

Service employment is displacing manufacturing employment

Great economic changes always produce changes in the kind of work done in an economy. The industrial revolution meant, in the long run, that agriculture ceased to be the main source of jobs in Britain. For several decades, as discussed above, an additional stage in the industrial revolution has shifted jobs into the 'service' or 'tertiary' sector. There are both proportionately and absolutely fewer workers in industries like steel and coal and more in banking, insurance and health care.

These changes are sometimes described as involving a shift away from manual, working-class occupations to non-manual, middle-class ones. It is certainly true that there has been a long-term increase in the number of 'professional', highly qualified workers in Britain. It is also true that most of the new 'service' jobs involve little of the strenuous physical effort or extreme working conditions associated with a job such as mining. But it is not the case that the service sector necessarily demands skilled work. On the contrary: in recent years some of the fastest growth has been in areas like cleaning and catering, which provide unskilled and usually casual or part-time jobs.

The expansion of the service sector as an employer is also sometimes equated with the growth of public sector employment. This is an exaggeration. It is indeed the case that some services — like education and health care — which have seen large increases in numbers employed in recent decades are 'delivered' by the public sector. But some of the industries where numbers have declined most rapidly —

like coal and steel — are also publicly owned. By contrast one of the fastest growing industries in the last decade, financial services, is largely privately owned.

Women are becoming important in the work-force

Women have always worked but they have not always been paid for working. For example, until the beginning of this century 'domestic service' was a major source of paid employment for women. Social change has since almost eliminated domestic servants and their jobs are now done for nothing by mothers, wives and daughters. In recent decades women — especially married women — have taken paid employment in large numbers: in 1931, for instance, only 10 per cent of married women were in paid jobs; now the figure is over 50 per cent (Halsey, 1987, p. 13).

Three features of women's work should be noticed. Firstly, it is disproportionately concentrated in the 'service' sector and in what is sometimes called 'light manufacturing' — work involving, for instance, assembling and packing components. Secondly, while just over half the population are women, far more than half of working women are in jobs with low pay and status and far less than half are in high status jobs: a disproportionately high proportion of women clean in universities, and a disproportionately low number of women teach in them. (Table 4.5 shows the proportions of women in the professions.) Thirdly, women occupy a disproportionate number of casual and part-time jobs in the work-force. This observation links to the final feature of work and employment on which we focus.

Table 4.5 *Percentage of women members in leading professional associations*

	Total members	Women (per cent)
British Medical Association	17,692	29
Chartered Institute of Bankers (UK members)	18,912	20
Law Society	13,261	20
Institute of Chartered Accountants	8,768	9
Institute of Mechanical Engineers	771	1

Source: Jackson, 1988, p. 84

Unemployment and part-time work have become more common

There has always been unemployment in Britain (see Figure 4.3). For over three decades after 1940, however, it was conventional to speak of the existence of 'full employment'. Only a small proportion of the work-force was out of a job: as recently as 1975, for instance, there were only 838,000 registered unemployed. Unemployment, moreover, was largely accounted for by individuals who were unemployable (for instance through ill health); by those who were temporarily between jobs (usually called frictional unemployment); and by relatively high levels of joblessness in a

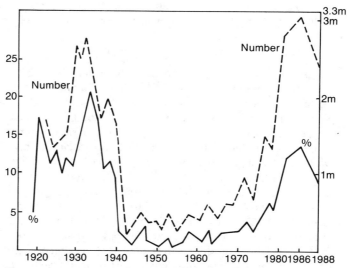

Figure 4.3   *Unemployment in Britain, 1920–88 (Source: McIlroy, 1989)*

few depressed parts of the country (for example, in communities over-reliant on a single declining industry).

This era of full employment has gone. For over a decade now, large-scale unemployment has been the norm: the figure for registered unemployed topped one million by 1976, two million by 1981 and three million by 1984. Even more significantly, unemployment has ceased to be a transient experience because the numbers of long-term unemployed have grown greatly: for instance, 30 per cent of unemployed men in 1986 had been out of a job for over two years (Central Statistical Office, 1987, p. 81). The unemployed are disproportionately concentrated among predictable groups: those with few or no formal educational qualifications; those who live in areas where the local economy is depressed; and those who come from some ethnic minorities.

It is often pointed out that even in an era of mass unemployment the overwhelming majority of adults are nevertheless in work and that while jobs are lost in some industries they are being created in others. This is correct, but simple measures of job numbers fail to reveal important changes which are occurring in the structure of the work-force. Full-time jobs in manufacturing have been lost and have been disproportionately replaced by temporary or part-time jobs in the service sector. This hints at a division in the population which may in time become as significant as the divide between the employed and the unemployed. To an increasing degree large employers are dividing their work-force into a 'core' and a 'periphery'. The 'core' consists of workers in secure, long-term employment. There is also a tendency for these to be the better qualified and to enjoy the best pay and fringe benefits. The 'periphery' consists of a shifting group of temporary employees who can be taken on, and laid off, according to demand. There is a corresponding tendency for these workers to be disproportionately women, to be doing less-skilled jobs and to be comparatively poorly rewarded. The 'dual' labour market, as it is sometimes

Labour power as an economic resource

> The vast majority of employees in Britain are united by one single important feature: their labour power is their only significant economic resource.
>
> But otherwise employees are fragmented into numerous groups:
>
> public sector and private sector workers
>
> manual and non-manual workers
>
> workers in service and manufacturing sectors
>
> part-timers and full-timers

called, offers considerable advantages to employers. Temporary and casual labour is comparatively cheap, most workers are poorly organized in unions and legal protection against such eventualities as dismissal is more limited than in the case of the permanent work-force. Thus employers can use their 'peripheral' work-force in a highly flexible way to respond to changing market conditions.

In this chapter we have examined three key aspects of the economic structure: the balance between public and private sectors in the economy; the structure of the private sector; and the outline of the most important market in the British economy, the labour market. Each of these, we will see in succeeding chapters, deeply influences both the structure of government, the content of political debate and the way political activity is organized in the wider community. The different roles of the state in the economic structure — whether owner, regulator and so on — are the central themes of political debate. The changing organization of ownership and of labour markets feeds through to the kinds of parties that are found, to the sorts of electoral support those parties can generate and to the kinds of interests that are organized as groups to exercise pressure on government.

The economic structure also has an additional importance: it is intimately connected to the wider social structure, the concern of our next chapter.

References and Further Reading

Bacon, R. and Eltis, W., *Britain's Economic Problem: Too Few Producers* (Macmillan, 1976).

Cranston, R., *Regulating Business* (Macmillan, 1979).

Central Statistical Office, *Social Trends* (1987).

Grant, W. and Nath, S., *The Politics of Economic Policymaking* (Blackwell, 1984).

Halsey, A.H., 'Social trends since World War II', in *Social Trends* (1987) 11—28.

Jackson, P., 'Women and the economy', *Social Studies Review* (November 1988) 84.

Lindblom, C., *Politics and Markets* (Basic Books, 1977).

McIlroy, J., 'Unemployment and the economy', in B. Jones, *Political Issues in Britain Today*, 3rd edn (Manchester University Press, 1989).

Pollard, S., *The Development of the British Economy 1914—80* (Edward Arnold, 1983).

Utton, M.A., *The Political Economy of Big Business* (Martin Robertson, 1982).

5 The Social Structure

Michael Moran

Every community has a social structure — indeed, were it otherwise it would not be a community. The social structure refers to the institutions into which life is organized. This covers social institutions which we would immediately recognize as such because they are part of our daily experience: the family in which we are reared, the school or college in which we are educated, the church we may attend. But it also refers to social groupings which have a less immediately recognizable form. For instance, every society has social groupings which arrange members into hierarchies, whether the hierarchies are those of wealth, esteem or power. These hierarchies are also an aspect of the social structure.

The social structure is therefore an all-encompassing term covering a wide range of groups and institutions. Our purpose here is obviously not to provide a complete description of these complicated features; it is to select the aspects of the social structure that, as subsequent chapters will illustrate, have impinged most directly on UK politics. Not surprisingly, these aspects arise from the most elemental features of social life: birth, death and how people live in between. In this chapter we will be looking at how valued social resources are distributed in society. These resources are not distributed evenly: people enjoy unequal prosperity and unequal health. It is the examination of these resources that forms the shape of the chapter: health, housing, wealth, self-betterment and education are examined in turn, and the way some of these are *geographically* distributed is then described.

Birth, Death and Health

There are near 57 million people in the United Kingdom, and one of the shaping forces on British society is the balance of birth, death and health which maintains and changes this number. The size and structure of the population has evolved through a number of important stages. The growth of an industrial society saw a rapid increase in numbers: a figure of just 22 million people in 1851 had grown to over 50 million a century later. In recent decades this increase has slowed down to a point where population growth has virtually ceased. The impression of stagnation conveyed by total figures is nevertheless misleading. Important changes continue to take place in internal composition. The most important reason for the changing curve of population growth is well known: there has occurred in recent decades in Britain, as in most other industrial societies, a sharp fall in the birth-rate. Indeed, the

Table 5.1 *Population in the United Kingdom*

	England	Wales	Scotland	Northern Ireland	United Kingdom
Population ('000, mid-1987 estimate)	47,407	2,836	5,112	1,575	56,930
Area (sq km)	130,439	20,768	78,772	14,121	244,100
Population density (persons per sq km)	363	137	65	112	233

Source: Britain 1989: An Official Handbook

population total would have shrunk were it not for another development at the opposite end of the life span. Growing prosperity and improvements in the quality of medical care have raised average life expectancy: for instance, in 1951 there were just over 1.5 million people aged 75 years or more; by 1981, the date of the last census, there were over 3 million. At the same time the number of children aged under five years fell by over 800,000. In short, Britain has an ageing population.

The changing balance between the young and old has momentous implications both for social organization and government policy. It is altering the balance of economic demands in the community, especially because the real income of old people

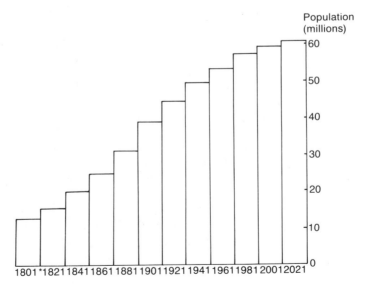

Notes: Census figures are mid-year figures except those for 1941 and 1981
* Includes estimate for N. Ireland

Figure 5.1 *Growth of UK population (Source:* Social Studies Review, *November 1985)*

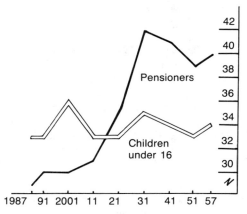

Figure 5.2 *Dependants per 100 people of working age (Source:* The Economist, *13 October 1989)*

has been rising in recent years: the food, clothing and holidays bought by the over-50s are obviously very different from those purchased for young children. In addition to changing the demands in the market-place it is also altering demands for public services: for instance, there has been a sharp decline in the demand for school places, but a sharply increased demand for places in institutions catering for the very old and infirm.

Even the distinction between the balance of the old and the young only begins to hint at the changing structure of the population. Birth-rates vary greatly between different social categories: births to single women, for example, now account for nearly a fifth of all those born; at the beginning of the century the figure was less than one-twentieth (Central Statistical Office, 1987c, pp. 11, 29).

More striking even than the variations in the rate of birth of children in different social categories is the fate of those babies so born. 'Infant mortality rates' — the proportion of newborn children who die at or near birth — have fallen dramatically in Britain in the twentieth century, because of factors like better feeding for mothers and offspring and higher standards of medical care. There nevertheless remain striking variations in the chances of survival among the children of different social groups. The crucial influence is usually summed up as 'class'. There is a wide gap between the death rates experienced among the majority of babies and those born to the mothers from the very poorest classes: the differences are illustrated in Table 5.2. These

Table 5.2 *Infant mortality rate for children born into selected classes by social class of father (deaths per thousand live births)*

Professional	Skilled manual	Unskilled manual	All legitimate births	All illegitimate births
6.4	8.8	12.8	8.7	12.4

Source: CSO, 1987a, p. 116

figures are illuminating because they illustrate the distribution of the most important of all values, life itself, and because the fate of babies is revealing about the health of parents, the distribution of health care services and the wider material conditions in which babies of different classes live (Black, 1980).

The 'class' influence also operates at the other end of the life spectrum. Life expectancy generally has increased in modern times, but for the families of the unemployed and the unskilled it remains shortest. There are three reasons for this. Firstly, many of the jobs done by the very poor are particularly dangerous and injurious to health. Secondly, the diet and life-style of the poor are not well attuned to the requirements of health and long life. Finally, when the lives of poor people are actually endangered by disease they use medical services less readily than do the better-off; and when they turn to these services the quality of the care given is lowest for the poorest in the community. Within the population, therefore, there exist great variations in the chances of people from different classes surviving the early weeks of life and, once having survived, of living to a robust old age.

The opportunity to live, and to live in good health, is obviously critical to everybody. But the dwellings where life is spent are also important. Housing is our next concern.

Housing and the Social Structure

The way a community organizes the task of housing its people is highly revealing about the social order, because housing is one of the most important services enjoyed by individuals and their families. The quality of this service varies greatly in different geographical areas and between different social groups in the community. Thus variations in the quality of housing, and the different types of tenure enjoyed, tell us a great deal about the way the resources of a community are allocated (Dunleavy, 1980). In addition, in a community like Britain housing is a considerable source of wealth — indeed, since most Britons live by selling their labour in the market-place house ownership is just about the only alternative means available to most as a way of acquiring substantial capital.

Understanding the significance of housing to the social structure involves an examination of what is usually called forms of 'housing tenure' — in other words, the legal arrangements under which groups occupy dwellings. In essence there are three major types of housing tenure in Britain: owner-occupation, renting from public authorities (mostly local councils) and renting from private landlords (Saunders, 1980). The changing balance between the three is illustrated in Table 5.3.

The most common form of housing tenure in Britain is owner-occupation — which in practice means that most houses are being bought by their occupiers on mortgages supplied by banks and building societies. The single most distinctive feature of the housing market in Britain is indeed the dominance of owner-occupation — and the apparently unstoppable increase in this form of tenure. The extent of domination is shown in Table 5.3. The reasons for this growth are various, but they are all traceable to the effects of public policy. Owner-occupiers have for decades been able to exercise tax privileges, notably because the interest on a mortgage is subject to tax relief. This considerably reduces the real cost of house buying, thus making

Table 5.3   *Housing tenure in Britain (percentage in different groups)*

Form of Tenure	1914	1945	1951	1961	1971	1981	1987
Owner–occupation	10	26	29	43	53	54	64
Local authority rental	0	12	18	27	31	34	26
Private rental	90	62	53	31	16	12	10

Source: Jewson, 1989, p. 132

the investment additionally attractive. In some parts of the country, notably the south east of England, a combination of planning restrictions on new house building, high population density and a high level of real incomes has made demand even more intense.

The second major form of housing tenure, that created by the supply of publicly owned housing to rent, has been in decline in the 1980s (McMahon, 1987). Most public housing is owned and administered by local authorities. The development of local authority housing as a significant sector dates back to the period immediately after the First World War, but expansion was sharply accelerated by post-Second World War housing 'drives' to replace slum dwellings with a better quality of public housing. These rapid spurts of redevelopment, especially the drive associated with the creation of housing estates dominated by multi-storey blocks of flats in the late 1950s and 1960s, produced huge numbers of dwellings which were soon revealed to have construction flaws and housing estates which rapidly developed serious social difficulties. Only some of these difficulties were due to the construction and planning of estates. The most serious social problem on public housing estates in the 1980s, for instance, was mass unemployment — a consequence not of planning, but of the concentration on the estates of the kind of people who suffered most from the rise in general levels of unemployment in Britain in the late 1970s and 1980s. Nevertheless, by the 1980s publicly rented housing had become widely perceived as synonomous with social failure and there developed a widespread belief that the stock of dwellings would be better managed if most or even all were owned by their occupiers. This led to widespread public support for a policy of 'privatizing' public housing. Demand was intensified by the realization of many tenants that the purchase of a council dwelling was often a considerable bargain. There thus developed during the 1970s pressure from tenants in the better quality public dwellings for a right to buy. Although public housing had been sold for many years before the 1980s, legislation passed by Mrs Thatcher's administration considerably speeded up the process: from 1980 to 1985 over 750,000 local authority dwellings were transferred to private hands; the present figure exceeds one million (Lee, 1989, p. 210).

The fact that sales have undoubtedly been disproportionately of the most desirable council dwellings has had considerable consequences for the management of the remainder. Public housing construction has in recent years dwindled to insignficance. Thus, local authorities have been left with the management of a declining housing stock composed of the poorest dwellings often occupied by the poorest of tenants. The economic and social problems created by this state of affairs have led to further demands for change. Some local authorities have disposed of their very poorest dwellings, either by physical demolition or by selling them at low prices to private

The political significance of housing tenure

> Housing markets are vital influences in government and in the wider political system because:
>
> 1. Governments help regulate the cost of housing, through tax policies, subsidies and interest rates that affect the cost of housing mortgages
> 2. Owner-occupiers and those in rented dwellings have different interests and compete with each other politically
> 3. In the 1980s the Conservatives made the sale of council houses to sitting tenants a major part of their electoral strategy

developers. But this has not stilled the demands for change. There now exist proposals for radical alterations in the form of tenure: these include the transfer of ownership to housing associations, to cooperatives of tenants and to private landlords.

The council sector, although in decline, has as yet experienced nothing like the catastrophic fall seen during recent decades in the number of privately rented dwellings. Before the First World War renting from a private landlord was the most common form of tenure; now only just over a tenth of all dwellings are in this category. The reasons are again traceable to public policy. There exists a long history of public intervention to protect tenants, notably by restricting the level of rents and restricting the powers of landlords to displace tenants from occupancy. This limit on the powers of landlords has in turn deterred investment in dwellings for rent. The result is that not only has the privately rented sector declined in numerical importance; it has also declined in quality. At its fringes it shades into what is in effect a fourth condition in the housing market, loosely called 'homelessness'. Few people in Britain are literally homeless for long, if only because few can survive the British climate without some sort of shelter. But there is a growing minority, whose exact size is unknown, which is forced to live in various kinds of temporary accommodation: for instance, in hostels and in cheap private hotels paid for by public authorities.

One of the major reasons why housing is important to the social structure is that it is an important economic resource. For the owner-occupier it is, in particular, a substantial form of wealth. But obviously wealth comes in many other forms — and it is these forms which we now examine. (For more on housing see Chapter 25.)

Wealth, Property and the Social Structure

Only one thing can be said with certainty about the distribution of wealth in Britain: it has long been, in statistical terms, highly unequal (Atkinson, 1974). But the meaning and even the accuracy of the bald statistics are perhaps more uncertain here than in any other area of British society. Beyond the general proposition that a statistically small group owns an arithmetically large amount of the nation's wealth, there exists little agreement.

Debate starts with the very significance of inequality. For some, the existence of a minority of very wealthy people in Britain is a good thing and any diminution of the wealth of the few a bad thing. According to this argument, great wealth is desirable because it shows the ability of the market system to reward the enterprising with great incentives, thus encouraging innovation and risk-taking in the economy. In addition, the wealthy are a socially important group, because although a minority they are still, in absolute terms, large in number. This means that they support social diversity by, for example, sponsoring a variety of political causes, charities and artistic activities. Without the wealthy, according to this view, society would be dull, uniform and dominated by the state. On the other hand, critics of the social order in Britain maintain that control of great wealth by a minority is illegitimate. It appropriates what is properly the wealth of the community for a few and contradicts the aim of democracy by lodging wealth — and thus power — in the hands of a minority.

These arguments are, in the long run, inconclusive because they involve competing notions of what is a just and morally desirable social order. But they have also proved inconclusive for a more mundane reason: nobody can agree on how definitively to measure wealth and its distribution. Most of us think we could recognize the existence of great wealth — but we would soon disagree about what exactly to include as a measure of wealth and how to value what is actually included. We could probably agree, for instance, that the great landed estates still owned by some aristocrats are a form of wealth and should be counted as such. But should this also be said of even the most humble property, such as the family semi-detached house? In an age where domestic houses often fetch high prices, and where over 60 per cent of dwellings are owner-occupied, this decision can make a big difference to estimates of the distribution of wealth. Similarly, there would probably be general agreement that ownership of a body of shares in a large business corporation is a form of wealth. But should this also be said of more indirect stakes in ownership? We saw in the previous chapter that in many of the largest corporations in Britain a substantial proportion of shares are owned by 'institutions' — organizations like insurance companies and pension funds, which invest the proceeds of the contributions of individual policy-holders or those paying into pension schemes. Since an individual making such contributions is entitled to a return on the investments, just as certainly as the direct shareholder is entitled to a dividend, it may be thought that participants in insurance schemes and pension funds should be counted as owning some of the wealth of the economy. If this is indeed so, it suggests that not only is wealth quite widely distributed but that it has become more equally distributed in recent decades, because the beneficiaries of life insurance and pension schemes have grown greatly in number. (For instance, in 1953 only 28 per cent of workers were in a pension scheme; thirty years later the figure was 52 per cent.)

These technical arguments affect the kind of judgements we can make about the extent of inequality in Britain. For example, Table 5.4 suggests very striking inequality. This table, however, refers to marketable wealth — property that could be disposed of by sale in the market. If we included pension rights — which cannot be traded, but are undoubtedly an entitlement to income — the share of wealth in 1984 claimed by the richest 1 per cent in the community sinks from 21 per cent to 12 per cent.

On the other hand, the sort of property rights conferred by ownership of a house for purposes of occupation, or membership of a pension fund for the purpose of providing income in old age, are very different from those conferred by ownership of a landed estate or of a block of shares in ICI. The rights to a pension, for instance, can be cashed, but they cannot be traded in the manner of shares and they rarely

Table 5.4 *Distribution of marketable wealth in Britain, Inland Revenue estimates*

Marketable wealth Percentage of wealth owned by:	1971	1984
Most wealthy 1%	31	21
Most wealthy 5%	52	39
Most wealthy 10%	65	52
Most wealthy 25%	86	75
Most wealthy 50%	97	93

Source: Halsey, 1987, p. 17

confer, as do shares, the entitlement to a direct say in the important decisions taken by the board of directors of a company.

An additional complication is introduced by the difficulty of actually valuing wealth, even when we agree on what is to be included in a definition. The values of shares in companies, for instance, are decided on the open market. Falls in share prices can thus drastically reduce estimates of the riches of the (mostly wealthy) groups of large shareholders.

It is important to bear these cautionary remarks in mind when discussing arguments about wealth distribution and in interpreting the figures presented in Table 5.4. Nevertheless, three observations seem beyond reasonable doubt. Firstly, there is indeed a minority which owns a statistically disporportionate amount of the community's total wealth. Secondly, there is a very large group at the other end

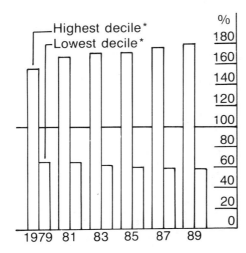

*Earnings exceeded/not reached by top/bottom 10 per cent of population

Figure 5.3 *Gross weekly earnings as percentage of each year's median, men only (Source: The Economist, 13 October 1989)*

of the social scale which is virtually propertyless. Thirdly, there is occurring over time some redistribution of wealth away from the very richest, but the trickle of resources down the social scale is slow and uneven.

Arguments about wealth redistribution touch on an even wider matter: the extent to which social hierarchies in Britain are fixed or changing. Figure 5.3 deals with gross weekly earnings and shows how much better the top 10 per cent of earners fare than the bottom 10 per cent. It also shows that between 1979 and 1989 the gap widened noticeably. The issue of 'social mobility' is our next concern.

Mobility and Social Structure

In the most general sense the British are probably more mobile now than at any time in their history. As recently as a generation ago it was the usual pattern for people to live their whole lives in the neighbourhood where they were born, and even to restrict their leisure travel to a few popular seaside resorts in Britain. In the last three decades this pattern has been revolutionized: the changing structure of the economy has emptied large numbers out of some regions into others; while the changing character of transport — especially the spread of the motor car — has drawn large populations from the cities into suburbs and small towns (see Figure 5.4).

Changing forms of leisure have also broken traditional patterns of mobility: in the years immediately after the Second World War hardly anybody took a holiday abroad; now nearly a fifth of all holidays are to a foreign destination. All these results

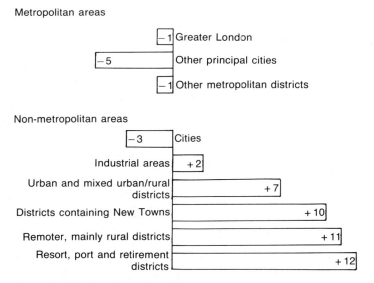

Figure 5.4 *Average annual population growth rate by district (Source: The Economist, 23 September 1989)*

have made British society more cosmopolitan — prompting changes ranging from fundamental alterations in the structure of the family to comparatively trivial changes in eating habits.

Britain is, therefore, a highly mobile society and is becoming increasingly so. But most discussion of 'social mobility' in Britain has focused on something other than the geographical mobility of the population: to wit, the extent of mobility up and down the social hierarchy.

It is usual to distinguish between two different kinds of social mobility, normally called *intragenerational* and *intergenerational* mobility. The first of these is typified by the archetypal 'self-made man': in other words by an individual who rises in the social scale during adult life, typically by individual economic success. The second usually refers to a successful rise in the social scale achieved over two generations. The common form of intergenerational mobility in Britain has involved success in the education system, allowing individuals to acquire qualifications which launch them on a career superior in prestige and pay to that enjoyed by their parents.

Three features of social mobility in Britain should be noticed. Firstly, because we are talking about mobility on a kind of ladder — the social hierarchy — it is perfectly possible for change to take place either way, up or down. Indeed, everyone can think of cases from their own acquaintance of individuals who have 'sunk in the world'. In recent decades, however, the most common form of mobility in Britain has been upward mobility and, significantly, almost all discussions on the subject are couched in terms of the extent and causes of movement up the social hierarchy. Secondly, while there exist numerous people in the community who have achieved intragenerational mobility, its significance is often greatly exaggerated by journalistic concentration on a few spectacular examples, commonly involving individuals who began their working lives in humble circumstances and achieved great success by building up large businesses. This progress from 'the shop floor to the boardroom' was historically held out as one of the great achievements of the free market system. The most widely publicized cases of 'self-made millionaires' are indeed of political and social importance. They contribute to the stability of the social order by spotlighting the possibility of success for the restlessly ambitious among the poor; and, where they manage to establish enduring businesses, they renew the vitality of the economic elite. The numerically most important kind of social mobility is, however, less spectacular. It consists of acquiring qualifications through education and then converting those qualifications into a career. Organizations in both the private and public sectors draw their pool of future top managers mostly from the educationally successful. The result is that access to the top positions is, in the biggest organizations, increasingly blocked off to those who do not acquire appropriate initial educational qualifications. The progress from the shop floor to the board room is becoming less common than the progress from the examination hall to the boardroom.

The third notable feature of social mobility in Britain can be simply stated: it is very common. This is a comparatively recent finding. It was widely assumed in the past that comparatively few people moved up the social scale and that movements which did occur involved modest changes in people's place in the social hierarchy. But the most comprehensive study of the nature of social mobility in the years since the Second World War — the 'Oxford mobility study' — has found British society to be much more open than was commonly supposed. The reason can be inferred from our discussion earlier of the changing structure of the work-force. There has been a long-term expansion in the number of 'non-manual' jobs — and thus a long-term demand for recruits to those occupations from the ranks of the families of manual workers (Heath, 1981). In this process of social change our next subject, education, has been immensely important.

Education and the Social Structure

Education is one of the most valuable services provided in society. Access to education in a country like Britain enhances both the quality of an individual's life and the likelihood of that individual enjoying economic success. It opens up the store of the community's cultural wealth and is increasingly also the key to a share in the community's material wealth. The better one's education the better the general quality of life, job satisfaction and material affluence. Education is thus a highly valuable service — and like most valued things in Britain access to the best education and the capacity to benefit from the educational experience are distributed unequally.

This inequality begins at the earliest stages of life. Although all children in Britain are legally entitled to free schooling, the experience of education is very different for different classes. No more than 7 per cent of the age group are educated in fee-paying schools — conventionally called 'public schools'. The products of these institutions, especially of a small number of expensive boarding schools drawing their pupils overwhelmingly from the families of the well-to-do, are disproportionately important in the education system and in the wider society. The occupants of positions of power and wealth in the community come disproportionately from the best public schools, which also provide a disproportionate number of those enjoying the most desirable forms of post compulsory education — in the universities, especially in the most prestigious universities of Oxford and Cambridge. The predominance and the staying power of the public schools as producers of elites is well illustrated by Table 5.5.

The special position of the public schools and of their products at the very top of the education system is, however, only a reflection of a wider pattern of inequality in the educational system. From the very beginning of education there are marked differences in attainment between children from different social groups — stretching

Table 5.5   *Percentage of selected administrative elites educated at fee-paying schools, 1939–83*

	(1) 1939 (%)	(2) 1950 (%)	(3) 1960 (%)	(4) 1970 (%)	(5) 1983 (%)
Ambassadors	73.5	72.6	82.6	82.5	76.3
High Court judges	80.0	84.9	82.5	80.2	79.0
Major Generals and above	63.6	71.3	83.2	86.1	78.9
RAF Vice-Marshals and above	66.7	59.1	58.4	62.5	41.1
Civil servants, under-secretary and above	84.5	58.7	65.0	61.7	58.8

Source: Moran, 1989, p. 166

in a ladder of achievement from the children of the very poorest at the bottom to the offspring of the professional and business families at the top. These differences have shown a remarkable persistence over time, despite the great changes in British economy and society in recent years, and despite the great changes in the nature of educational provision in the last generation.

It is worth examining higher education in some detail. Britain's colleges, polytechnics and universities provide education for just over one-eighth of those aged 18 or 19. These students are a privileged minority who, if successful on their courses, are virtually guaranteed a professional job, or at least one removed from the stress of manual work. The elite of this privileged group, chiefly from the most prestigious universities, will eventually rise to positions of great power and wealth. This privileged minority in higher education is much larger than in the past: in the mid-1960s it was just over 300,000 annually ; twenty years later it was nearly 550,000. This reflects some of the economic changes which we earlier sketched, notably the economy's demand for better educated workers in the expanding 'service' sectors. Among the chief beneficiaries of this expansion have been women (whose participation in higher education has, in recent years, risen greatly) and children from the homes of manual workers, far more of whom now enter higher education than was the case in the past. Nevertheless, the most striking feature of the social structure of the student body in higher education is the statistically low representation of those of working-class origin and the corresponding over-representation of those from what are conventionally called middle-class homes (Table 5.6). Success in education in Britain is tied to class origins. Entry to higher education in Britain now depends almost totally on achievement in examination results; social connections only matter in a tiny minority of cases and even those are declining. Yet middle-class students do as well — perhaps even better — in the competition for entry as in the years when selection procedures and funding arrangements discriminated in their favour. The example of the highest level of the education system illustrates a general point about the educational experience in Britain: it is closely tied to the wider structures and hierarchies of British society.

Social organization affects the distribution of many different valued social goods. The most obvious are economic in form, wealth and income. But of equal, or even greater importance, are health, quality of housing, educational opportunity and the chance to rise in the social scale. The distribution of all these is unequal, and the nature of the inequalities reflects deeply rooted features of the social order.

Table 5.6 *Class origin of entrants to university 1984, based on occupational class of parent, per cent in classes*

	Social class					
	I	II	III (Non-manual)	(Manual)	IV	V
University entrants (%)	22	48	10	12	6	1
All 18-year olds (%)	5	20	10	40	18	7

Source: Ball, 1988, p. 60

Thus far we have largely considered the United Kingdom as a single unit. But in fact a variety of regions and nations is 'united' under the British Crown. It is the significance of territorial differences which is our next concern.

The Parts of Britain

National and regional differences

Britain is a 'multi-national state': that is, it is a political unit ruled by a single sovereign authority but composed of territories which historically were different nations, and whose populations still retain strong senses of distinct national identity (Rose, 1971). This multi-national character has in the past been central to political history. In particular, the relationship between the Irish parts of Britain and the sovereign government in London has been, and continues to be, a source of immense political difficulty.

There are at least five different national groupings in the United Kingdom: the English, Welsh, Scottish, Irish and those (mostly Protestants in Northern Ireland) who are attached to an 'Ulster' identity (Rose, 1982). The matter of identity has been complicated still further by the phenomenon of immigration. The United Kingdom has periodically received waves of immigrants from abroad and in the 1950s and 1960s received particularly large numbers from what is conventionally called the 'new Commonwealth' — notably from our former colonial possessions in the West Indies and the Indian sub-continent. These immigrants and their children are for the most part permanently settled in Britain and are citizens of the community. They are conventionally called 'black Britons' but this oversimplifies the question of identity. Groups from the Indian sub-continent, in particular, often retain close connections with their place of origin and in Britain retain their own distinctive cultures, language and religious practices.

The question of national identity in Britain is therefore more complicated than the simple existence of a political unity called the United Kingdom would suggest. But there is a further aspect to territorial differences. Even the most casual traveller in Britain soon realizes that within national areas there exist striking variations — differences ranging from the most profound cultural and economic matters to the most mundane aspects of everyday life. Even inside the biggest nation in the United Kingdom, England, there also exist striking regional differences.

Although the actual figures change with time, for several decades real income in the south east of England, and accompanying measures of well being like employment, have been more favourable than in any other part of the United Kingdom. Conversely, areas like Northern Ireland and the north west of England have for decades been among the poorest. The scale of this is illustrated in Table 5.7.

The regional differences noted here have been widely noticed in recent years and have given rise to the argument that in Britain there exists a 'north–south' divide between the prosperous and the poor parts of the United Kingdom. But despite the undoubted gaps in the wealth of different regions, such characterizations are, at best, only a part of the truth. There exist numerous prosperous communities in the north of Britain; and in the heart of the prosperous south, in parts of London and Bristol

Table 5.7 *Regional inequality in Britain, 1987*

	South east	West Midlands	East Anglia	South west	East Midlands	Wales	North west	Yorks and Humberside	North	Scotland	Northern Ireland
Persons aged 16 and over in managerial/ professional occupations, 1986 (%)	17.1	13.2	13.7	13.2	12.6	11.1	11.8	11.5	10.8	12.3	10.5
Average weekly income per head (£), 1985−6	106.3	77.4	87.5	90.1	82.1	77.7	80.0	76.3	74.9	81.7	66.4
UK total Gross Domestic Product (%)	35.7	8.3	3.5	7.7	6.6	4.3	10.5	8.0	5.0	8.4	1.9
Households with deep freezer (%)	70.0	58.0	71.0	70.0	65.0	63.0	60.0	56.0	57.0	51.0	43.0
Unemployment rate, (%) 1987	7.7	12.1	7.6	9.3	9.9	14.3	14.0	12.7	15.3	14.5	20.3
Perinatal mortality rate, 1984−6	9.1	11.6	8.8	9.3	9.5	10.4	9.9	10.8	10.3	10.3	10.5
Cars per 1000 population, 1986	356.0	323.0	359.0	366.0	303.0	298.0	282.0	272.0	249.0	243.0	267.0

Source: Moran, 1989, p. 9

for instance, there are communities so impoverished that they have in recent years been the source of serious social unrest. Part of the reason for this is that overlaying any divisions between regions are important differences between various parts of urban areas in Britain.

Urban problems and the city

It is common to speak of the 'urban problem' in Britain or, in the same breath, of 'the problems of the inner city'. But there is actually a wide array of social features summed up in a single phrase like the 'urban problem'. Similarly, although in the 1980s the 'inner city' became a byword for poverty and misery, many areas of inner cities (witness parts of London) are the homes of the rich and fashionable, while in outer suburbs and even in rural areas there are, especially on public housing estates, areas of deep poverty. Nevertheless, a number of long-term social changes have combined to change the character of the giant cities which were the characteristic creation of Britain's industrial revolution. Two should be noted.

Firstly, long-term shifts in population have changed both the numbers living in many inner city areas and the social balance of the population. The figures of movement tell the story. Between 1980−5, for instance, the population of Cheshire rose by 1.2 per cent; the population of the adjacent city of Manchester fell by 3.0 per cent. In the 'booming' south east the population of the borough of Newham fell by 3.6 per cent, while the population of Buckinghamshire rose by 8.1 per cent.

This shift of population out of established areas of cities to suburbs and small towns reflects a second change: population decline is commonly a reflection of economic decline and social crisis. The cities of the industrial revolution have seen their economic foundations decay as the traditional industries have decayed, with important consequences for prosperity and financial stability. The example of the Borough of Newham in Greater London, cited above, illustrates the point. Despite loss of population it has the highest proportion of under-15-year-olds in the Greater London area (33.5 per cent); has also the highest population of school leavers finishing education with no qualifications; and in 1987 had over 17,000 unemployed, more than 40 per cent of whom had been out of work for more than a year (Central Statistical Office, 1987b, p. 47).

The social structure of a community provides the framework within which that community's politics takes place. In Britain the key aspects of the structure concern the allocation, across different geographical areas and different social categories, of social goods — whether wealth, health or educational opportunity. But the variety of political forms that can take place within the social structure is highly varied. One key set of influences on the kind of politics practised is summed up in the phrase 'political culture' — the subject of the next chapter.

References and Further Reading

Atkinson, A.B., *Unequal Shares* (Penguin, 1974).
Ball, S., 'Education: The search for inequality', *Social Studies Review* (November 1988).
Black, Sir D., *Inequalities in Health* (DHSS, 1980).
Central Statistical Office, *Social Trends* (1987a).
Central Statistical Office, *Regional Trends* (1987b).
Central Statistical Office, *Annual Abstract of Statistics* (1987c).
Dunleavy, P., *Urban Political Analysis* (Macmillan, 1980).
Halsey, A.H., *Change in British Society* (Oxford University Press, 1981).
Halsey, A.H., 'Social trends since World War II', in *Social Trends* (1987).
Heath, A., *Social Mobility* (Fontana, 1981).
Jewson, N., 'No place like home: Sociological perspectives on housing', *Social Studies Review* (March 1989).
Lee, G., 'The politics of housing policy', in B. Jones (ed.), *Political Issues in Britain Today*, 3rd edn (Manchester University Press, 1989).
McMahon, P., 'The sale of local authority houses in Britain', *Geography* (1987), 169−71.
Moran, M., *Politics and Society in Britain* (Macmillan, 1989).
Rose, R., *Governing Without Consensus: An Irish Perspective* (Faber, 1971).
Rose, R., *Understanding the United Kingdom* (Longman, 1982).
Saunders, P., *Urban Politics* (Penguin, 1980).

6 Political Culture and Participation

Michael Moran

We used the terms *social structure* and *economic structure* in the preceding chapters to show that there exist certain patterns of organization which can affect government. But the politics of a community is also affected by something less tangible, which we usually try to sum up under the term 'culture'. This word, though not easy to define, is inescapable for anyone wanting to grasp the influences shaping British politics. 'Culture' as employed by social scientists means something much wider than its everyday usage. This chapter explores and explains the concept and also addressess briefly the subject of political participation.

Political culture refers to the patterns of beliefs and practices which govern social life in a community. It thus covers an immense range: the character of religion and morality, the conventions and customs governing everyday social life — and the beliefs and practices concerning the conduct of politics. It is usual to refer to the last of these as the ***political culture*** of a community. The political culture governs the 'rules of the political game' in a society. It encompasses beliefs about the nature of political leadership and authority, about the proper and improper way to settle political differences and about the proper and improper functions of government. Thus, when we try to decide whether the British have a special respect for the monarchy, we are examining an aspect of the political culture. Similarly, when we examine the attitudes of the people of Britain to the role of violence in settling political differences we are also looking at a part of the British culture. And when we try to decide how far there exists in Britain general agreement about how much the state should control our lives we are looking yet again at the political culture.

Two things should be noticed about this notion of political culture. Firstly, it is obviously both part of a wider communal culture and is affected by that wider culture. In a society where violence is a generally accepted way of settling social differences, for instance, it will also be a generally accepted way of settling political differences. Secondly, although we speak in a shorthand way about the patterns of beliefs and practices in a community, this does not mean that there always exists an agreed set of cultural values held by everyone. On the contrary, in all communities there are some disagreements on the fundamental rules of the political game. In most communities there is a 'dominant' political culture adhered to by those who exercise most power, and a set of 'sub-cultures' which mark off various minorities. In some important communities — for instance, Northern Ireland — there actually exists a deeply divided political culture in which there are fundamental disagreements between groups about the rules of the political game.

The political culture concerns the rules by which politics is conducted in a community; and in analysing those rules we should begin with a distinction between those relating to how decisions are taken, and those relating to the substance of the policies which government can pursue. In other words, we should separate ***procedural*** and ***substantive*** aspects of the political culture.

Procedure covers much more than formal rules in a body like Parliament. It also encompasses more general views about how decisions should be taken and how those decisions should be put into effect. How far, for instance, is government a matter for the public at large to decide, and how far is it an activity left to a specially qualified minority? Under what circumstances, if any, is force used in political conflict? When, if ever, do citizens resist the decisions of a government to the point of breaking the law? These are all questions about the political culture of a community. They illuminate a particularly important point: political culture consists not just of what people believe, and say they believe, about the rules of politics; it also consists in what they actually do. If citizens say — for instance in opinion polls — that the law should always be obeyed, however bad it may be, this tells us something important about an aspect of the political culture. But to get a full picture we are also obliged to look at whether in reality laws are indeed obeyed. It is perfectly common in politics, as in most other areas of life, for us to say and believe one thing and to act in a quite different way.

A moment's thought will now show that the political culture involves something much wider than attitudes to the formal machinery of government. As the example of opinions about law-breaking suggests, it spills over into social life generally. We can infer important evidence about attitudes to authority from such apparently 'non-political' matters as the extent to which people obey regulations like those governing traffic speeds or the declaration of income to the tax authorities.

The procedural element is certainly the most important part of a political culture, because it goes to the very heart of politics — how decisions are to be taken and how they are to be put into effect. But this should not lead us to neglect the importance of the ***substantive*** part of the political culture. What people think government should do is no less important than their views about how politics should be conducted. How far, for instance, is there agreement about the substance of what government should do, and to what extent is political debate dominated by fierce divisions between conflicting political philosophies? Of course, there always exist in any group some differences between members about the content of the decisions which the group should make — whether the group is a family, a school, a firm or a government. But in a nation as large and diverse as Britain these differences will inevitably be more numerous, and more clearly organized.

Any examination of a political culture therefore involves (see Table 6.1) four different aspects of the 'rules of the political game' in a community:

(a) what people say about the procedures by which government should be conducted;
(b) what we can infer from behaviour about how those procedures actually work;

Table 6.1   *Examining the political culture*

	Procedure	**Substance**
Action	*Example*: how far laws are actually obeyed	*Example*: how far political parties actually implement radically different policies in government
Opinion	*Example*: popular views about when laws should be disobeyed	*Example*: how far political parties express radically different political philosophies

(c) what is said about the fundamental purpose of governments;

(d) what we can infer about this from practice.

It can hardly be stressed too strongly that it is important to look at both what is said and what is done. If a nation has a large political party whose programme demands the fundamental overthrow of existing social institutions, this constitutes an important piece of evidence about the nature of the political culture. But we should also look at how far that programme is reflected in the actual behaviour of the party. For instance, many West European countries have in the years since the Second World War had Communist parties with a large following, formally committed to the overthrow of capitalist society. Britain has no such well-supported Communist movement. This is often taken as a sign that left-wing radicalism is weaker in Britain than in Europe. Yet the actions — as distinct from the slogans — of Communist parties in France and Italy often suggest movements which are more cautious and conservative than many parts of the labour movement in Britain.

It should by now be obvious that identifying the nature of the British political culture demands a wide range of evidence. There is one other subtlety which should also be borne in mind. We find it a useful form of shorthand to speak of 'a' British political culture, because it is indeed the case that it is possible to identify a pattern of beliefs and practices which is dominant in the country. But we should always bear in mind that we are indeed talking about precisely that — the **dominant** political culture. Britain, like any large and sophisticated society, is highly diverse. There are many significant groups whose way of life — including political way of life — does not conform to, and in some cases seriously challenges, that dominant culture. In conducting our examination, therefore, we begin with the dominant pattern and then describe the most important patterns of minority dissent.

The Dominant Political Culture

Four features of the dominant political culture in Britain are noteworthy: deference, secrecy, civility and consensus. We will explain the meaning of each in turn and sketch its significance.

Deference

The first great essay on the nature of English attitudes to politics was Walter Bagehot's *The English Constitution*, which appeared in 1867 (Bagehot, 1867, 1964). Bagehot's work also popularized the single most influential idea in the study of the country's political culture: that we are a particularly *deferential* people. When we speak of the 'deferential' part of the culture, we are usually referring to a number of different things. Perhaps the most common modern meaning refers to a tendency to defer to the commands or wishes of public authority. Until recently in Britain this sort of deference was widespread. Law-breaking on any large scale was uncommon. This meant not only the comparative absence of any riotous behaviour but, perhaps even more significantly, the readiness to obey the law and the officers of the law in everyday matters. This readiness was reflected in numerous ways: for instance, in the willingness of the population to obey without close supervision regulations like those governing traffic; and in the fact that for the most part the police could enforce the law without being armed and with only occasional use of significant force.

This kind of deference is probably in decline. A second kind, of great importance in the past, is also certainly less common nowadays. When Bagehot spoke of deference he was thinking not of the tendency to defer to authority in general, but of preference for government by rulers born into a separate governing class. In other words deference was not to *any* authority, but to the well-born as the natural wielders of authority.

The respect and affection in which the monarchy has long been held in Britain is a shorthand expression of this sort of deference. A sizeable group in the population believed that government should be the prerogative of those born to rule. Although sections of the working class received the vote as long ago as 1867, and the whole adult population has had the vote for over sixty years, those selected by the population to govern were disproportionately drawn from groups connected to the traditional aristocracy. A significant proportion of manual workers habitually supported a party, the Conservatives, precisely because the Conservatives were associated with, and were often led by, people with aristocratic connections.

Deference is an attribute of the population at large, but it has had an important effect on the culture of the governing groups in Britain. In particular it helps explain a second key feature of the political culture: a strong attachment to secrecy in the theory and practice of British government.

The Ponting affair

> The Ponting affair tested the limits of Official Secrets law in Britain. After the Falklands War in 1982 there were allegations that an Argentinian ship, the *General Belgrano*, had been sunk with loss of many lives for unnecessary political reasons, not on military grounds. Clive Ponting, a senior official in the Ministry of Defence, anonymously leaked Ministry papers to a critical Labour MP. When Ponting's identity was discovered he was prosecuted under Official Secrets law. Ponting argued that he owed a duty above the letter of the law to inform an MP about a major constitutional impropriety. The jury, despite strong guidance by the judge to bring in a guilty verdict, acquitted Ponting.
>
> Source: Peele, 1988

Secrecy

The secretive character of the British political culture is built into the very structure of the law. Most countries have legislation prohibiting the publication of 'official secrets' — on grounds, for instance, of national security. But Britain's Official Secrets Act is recognized to be especially comprehensive. In recent years, for instance, prosecutions have included those of Clive Ponting, a civil servant who leaked documents to a Member of Parliament. But the significance of the Official Secrets Act lies in more than its substance. It is a reflection of a widespread predisposition favouring the conduct of government out of the public gaze. British government was historically ruled by the monarch and a small number of aristocratic advisors. The democratic politics which we now associate with Britain was accompanied by the survival of a traditional assumption that government was the proper business of a specialized class. This is reflected in a variety of characteristic British institutions. The 'Lobby' system, for instance, is an arrangement under which an accredited group of journalists is given confidential, anonymous briefings about government on condition that they observe prescribed limits on what they report. The doctrine (as it is usually called) of **collective Cabinet responsibility** similarly tries to ensure that Cabinet discussions and arguments remain secret, by binding each member of Cabinet not to dissent in public from decisions collectively arrived at. The doctrine of **individual ministerial responsibility** also serves the function of preserving secrecy in important parts of government. The formal meaning of the doctrine is that Ministers are answerable for actions taken by their department. This shields from public scrutiny the many civil servants who in reality take numerous decisions in the Minister's name.

These practices and constitutional doctrines are themselves a product of an important foundation of the traditionally secretive aspect of British government. Until comparatively recently there existed in Britain an identifiable governing class — an 'Establishment', as it was sometimes called. This group was quite small in number and tended not only to work together but to share a common social round in London and in upper-class society. A great deal of the business of government was therefore carried out in a private and informal way. The 'secrecy' of British government was therefore not a conspiratorial secrecy; it was the reflection of the sort of closed social world inhabited by the rulers of the country. As we will see shortly, the decline of this socially united governing group has placed the institutions of secrecy under great strain.

Civility

The term 'civic culture' was coined over twenty-five years ago by two American scholars to describe a kind of political culture of which Britain was held to be a prime example (Almond and Verba, 1963). 'Civility' in this connection means not the everyday usage which suggests politeness, but a certain attitude to authority and to the settling of political disputes. It signifies a willingness to respect the views of lawful authority, and is therefore related to the phenomenon of deference. But it also conveys something wider: a tolerance of opposing political views and a readiness to settle political differences by peaceful means rather than by resort either to violence or to aggressive public demonstrations. Political civility is also part of a wider social civility — in other words, part of a readiness in everyday life to tolerate others of different views and to respect the differing sensibilities of others in social life.

The judgement that Britain's was a 'civic' political culture was heavily influenced by foreign comparisons. By the standards of most countries Britain's modern political history has been remarkably peaceful. The last great armed struggle over the nature of political authority on the mainland of Britain was in the seventeenth century. Violent street clashes between political rivals or between political factions and the authorities were largely unknown in modern times. Trade unions have only once (in 1926) used a General Strike of all members to try to impose their views on an elected government, and then in only a half-hearted way. Popular support for those using or advocating violence, or some more limited means of direct action designed to secure concessions from government, has been low: such groups have in modern times never gained the support of more than a tiny minority of the population in, for instance, election contests.

This political civility seems to be part of a more general social civility. Though comparisons between countries in this respect have to be treated with caution, it really does seem to be the case that social relations generally are in Britain less abrasive and more peaceable than is common elsewhere. Support for this view comes in part from the admittedly unsystematic reflections of foreign observers but also from more systematically gathered material. Violent crime is, for instance, low by international standards, while the most violent of all crimes — murder — is at a miniscule level compared with the USA.

Thus far we have identified aspects of the political culture which bear most closely on the procedural rules of the political game. The final element which now commands our attention — consensus — links more closely the theory and practice of the substance of politics.

Consensus

The everyday meaning of consensus is agreement in opinion, but when we speak of consensus as an aspect of the British political culture we mean something more limited. The consensual character of British politics refers to an extraordinarily high level of agreement, both among the population at large and among the politically active, about the economic and social system which should prevail in Britain and about the proper function of government in that system. Of course, in a society such as Britain, with a diverse and sophisticated culture and a complex economy, there exist many disagreements about the particular policies which governments should pursue. Underneath these important differences, however, there also exists almost universal support for two sets of institutions: for constitutional democracy under a constitutional monarchy; and for a market economy supported by a substantial state sector. This consensus can be summed up as support for *liberal democracy* and the *mixed economy*.

All the major political parties in Britain in this century — Conservative, Labour and Liberal — have overwhelmingly supported the political principles on which the country is governed. 'Liberal democracy' indicates the joining together of two sets of principles: the practice of 'liberal' freedoms (like freedom of speech, worship and association) with a democratic method for changing or confirming the party which controls government. This democratic method involves periodic competitive elections in which almost all adults are entitled to vote. These two principles also have important consequences for the daily practice of politics. For instance, freedom of association and freedom to voice opinion mean that in British politics there are numerous groups (conventionally called pressure groups) who demand, and receive, the right to be heard in the process of policy making.

The consensus about the liberal democratic nature of the British political system remains relatively unshaken. As we shall see, this is not so true of the consensus about the mixed economy. Nevertheless, for over half a century disagreements in this area concerned only the exact 'mix' of the mixed economy, not the principle of its existence. The Labour party, the most important radical force in the country, never challenged the continuation of the market order. In the party there exists a group of socialists who would like to replace capitalism, but they have always been a minority in a varied alliance of reformers and radicals, who wish only to regulate capitalist institutions more closely. Similarly, there were until recently few in the Conservative party who wished to develop an economy in which the state did nothing more than cater for a few traditional functions like public order and external defence. In both parties leaders sometimes found it expedient to use language suggesting that they did not support the mixed economy. It was common for Conservative leaders to make strongly 'free market' speeches and for Labour leaders to attack capitalism, when addressing audiences made up of party activists. But the gap between what was said on these occasions and what was actually privately believed, and actually done, in government was very wide. This illustrates to perfection the point made earlier: in assessing the nature of a political culture we must attend to what is done as well as to what is said. This is especially true in a country like Britain, where the demands of democratic politics force politicians who wish to win elections to adjust their speeches to the particular audience they are addressing.

This sketch of a 'dominant' political culture has in parts deliberately been phrased in the past tense, because in recent years the extent to which it is open to challenge have become clearly marked. We now examine these challenges.

Challenges to the Dominant Political Culture

The account of the British political culture which we have just outlined undoubtedly describes a historically important aspect of British life — and an aspect which still powerfully endures. But it would be wrong to imply that this is the whole picture. There exist powerful challenges to the prevailing orthodoxy. Two sources of minority dissent are particularly important. The first is **nationalism**. Britain is, in Rose's phrase, a 'multi-national state' and its constitution and boundaries have been the subject of controversy and even of armed conflict (Rose, 1971). In recent years substantial minorities in Wales and Scotland have supported parties advocating separation from the United Kingdom — and have also supported the demands for independence of those parties. But the most important source of nationalist dissent has come from the Irish. Until 1921 the 'United Kingdom' encompassed the whole island of Ireland, and Irish constituencies sent Members to Parliament in Westminster. In that year, after five years of a war of secession, the Irish Free State gained independence. The episode displays many of the features — fundamental disagreement about the nature of the state, the use of violence to challenge authority — conspicuously absent from the dominant political culture. This source of challenge has been renewed in the last twenty years. Since 1969 British troops have been required in Northern Ireland to combat a violent campaign for secession organized from within a part of the Catholic community which believes in Irish nationalism as an alternative to British rule.

A second source of challenge can be found in *class organization*. Although the British labour movement has undoubtedly been marked by a special respect for the authority of elected governments, this respect is far from universal. At periodic moments in the country's history — in the years immediately before and after the First World War, in the so-called 'General Strike' of 1926 and in a wide range of individual strikes in the 1970s and 1980s — trade union militancy mounted a significant challenge to existing political and economic hierarchies. In many individual working-class communities — especially those formed around heavy manual occupations like coal mining — there have long existed powerful and deep-rooted radical traditions which reject many aspects of the dominant culture, especially the consensus favouring a market economy. To some degree this dissenting culture based on class coincides with the dissenting culture based on national differences, because many of the most important centres of class dissent have been in such places as the South Wales coalfields. This observation alerts us to an important point. The features usually described as characteristic of the ***British*** political culture are not so much British as English and, at that, are particularly characteristic of the southern half of England.

The dissenting challenges of nationality and class are not new in British politics, but cultural change in recent years has made us more sensitive to their challenge. The political culture of a country is neither fixed in content nor independent of the wider society. On the contrary, it is intimately affected by the wider pattern of social institutions and it will be subjected to change and stress as the wider social surroundings change. British society has, in recent decades, changed greatly. The structure of the economy has altered, with important traditional sectors in decline. The ethnic composition of the population in selected areas has changed as a result of large-scale immigration in the 1950s and 1960s. The traditional organization of family life has altered greatly, notably in the expanded numbers of people living either alone or in single-parent families.

Partly as a result of social changes a number of important challenges to the dominant political culture can be observed. They can be summarized under two headings: the challenge to deference and the challenge to consensus.

Although considerable argument exists about how widespread 'deference' ever was in Britain (Kavanagh, 1972) there is no doubt that, however defined, its level has fallen in recent years. The evidence for this comes from systematic surveys, from observation of political practice and from more general changes in forms of social behaviour (Kavanagh, 1980). We saw earlier that one important form of deference consisted in a preference for rule by individuals with aristocratic connections. These preferences are disproportionately held by older people and are thus literally dying out. The everyday conduct of political life also indicates a growing unwillingness simply to take authority on trust. For instance, the reporting of politics by journalists has displayed a growing readiness to question politicians sceptically. The signs of this include the rise of more investigative styles of journalism and the challenges now being mounted to the 'lobby' system of political reporting. Indeed, the decline of 'deference' has had important general effects on the 'secrecy' with which British government is conducted. Secrecy became a major issue in the 1980s. The traditionally secretive character of the system was sustained by a deference among political journalists and political activists towards the governing class. The strenuous attempts made by governments in recent years to preserve the secret nature of the government system reflect the declining hold of these traditional attitudes. It is much more common than was formerly the case for official documents to be 'leaked' to newspapers, increasingly common for civil servants to be discussed by name in debates about government decisions, and perfectly common for divisions expressed in the supposedly 'confidential' Cabinet room to be widely reported in the newspapers. The problem of leaks and of the inadequacy of their present means of control was dramatized by the Ponting case.

The declining hold of deference is also plain at the level of popular participation. There has been a growing willingness, especially on the part of the young, to participate in politics outside the conventional channels represented by elections and by membership of old established political parties. Membership of the dominant parties, Labour and Conservative, shows a long-term decline (Moran, 1989). On the other hand, participation in a wide range of loosely organized movements has grown. The 1980s were a booming decade for the Campaign for Nuclear Disarmament (CND) and a wider 'Peace Movement' in Britain. At one time, CND claimed over 100,000 members. It is possible that Peace Movements are now in decline, but they are only part of a wider shift to new kinds of political activity — in the Women's Movement, in groups formed to protect the environment and in numerous particular groups formed to campaign on local issues (Byrne and Lovenduski, 1983).

The scale of this shift into participation in new sorts of social organization is very well illustrated by the recent rise in membership of organizations concerned with the protection and care of the physical environment, as Table 6.2 shows. Not all members of these organizations are 'political' by any means — but the organizations themselves are often significant pressure groups. If we set alongside this growth the declining membership of more conventional groups, like trade unions and political

Table 6.2 *The rise of the 'Environmental Movement' (group membership 000s)*

	1971	1985	1988
Friends of the Earth	1	29	65
National Trust	278	1,200	1,634
Ramblers Association	22	50	65
Royal Society for the Protection of Birds	98	509	540
Worldwide Fund for Nature	12	90	147

Source: Social Trends, various years

**Political
activists**

Political activists are often represented as rather unusual, perhaps even a little odd. The reality is often reassuringly mundane. In August 1986, Tyne Tees television screened a series, *Is Democracy Working?* One of the programmes featured three party workers in the north east of England.

Mrs Karen Johnson, Chairman of her Constituency Conservative Women's Committee, helped her husband run his business: they were comfortably well off and sent their children to private school. She subscribed to the Conservative values of 'freedom, good housekeeping and the individual . . . Capitalism is a better way than the state being in charge of everything in that under Capitalism individuals have a chance to prove themselves.'

Mr Wal Hobson was born into a working-class family but became a Careers Officer. He was an active ward member of the Labour Party and believed 'Socialism is the only political theory that is really concerned about the ordinary people . . . social justice is the key word for me — and equality.'

Mrs Jane Young was Chairman of the Liberal Party in Newcastle North and a schoolteacher. She saw Liberals as standing for 'tolerance, rights of the individual — as long as those rights don't infringe on anyone else's liberty . . . consensus and cooperation.'

While these values obviously differ and clash all three saw politics as a practical and effective way of realizing them. As Mr Hobson put it: 'I think politics does determine how your life runs . . . If you do work at grassroots politics you can improve things for ordinary people . . . It's everything I've ever believed turned into something real, instead of just abstract ideas inside my head.'

All three were united in their concern for the democratic process. 'I am defending democracy by being active in a political party', said Karen Johnson. 'I do think it's important that some people are prepared to do it. I only wish that more people would be prepared to give a little of their time.'

The Liberal's view was similar. 'I bother because I think it is important to be a participating member of a democracy. If you are not willing to participate then I feel you have no ground for complaining about anything that is done. If you want things changed and you want to improve conditions for yourself and for the country as a whole then to be involved in very important.'

These activists did not come over in any way as power-hungry ideologues. Rather, they seemed hardworking, intelligent, sincere and public spirited. But are they typical? Of political activists, probably, yes — but not of society as a whole. Of the 4 per cent of the population who are party members, less than 1 per cent can be described as genuinely active. It would seem that the democratic links between government and society are becoming increasingly tenuous. And this is worrying if, as the American economist Henry George once said, 'We cannot safely leave politics to politicians. The people themselves must think.'

parties, we get a striking sense of a changing culture and a changing balance of group participation.

Research by MORI pollsters Jacobs and Worcester (1990), moreover, detects a slight decline in formal political participation since 1979. While over two-thirds of the population vote in general elections and one-third help in fund-raising drives of one kind or another, the 32 per cent who urged someone outside his/her family to vote in 1979 had fallen to 10 per cent in 1989; the 18 per cent who had urged someone to get in touch with a local MP or councillor had fallen to 15 per cent; and the 17 per cent who lobbied their councillor had fallen to 13 per cent. Other indices of participation included 13 per cent who had made a speech before an organized group, 13 per cent who had been elected an officer of an organization or club, 5 per cent who had written a letter to an editor, 3 per cent who had taken an active part in a political campaign and 1 per cent who had stood for public office. 17 per cent of respondents had done none of these things, an increase of 3 per cent on the 1979 figure. Of this apathetic group one in four were from social groups C2, D and E while only one in ten were from social groups A and B, confirming the rule that middle-class people tend to be more politically active than the working class.

Why should apathy have increased during the Thatcher years? Jacobs and Worcester (p. 172) speculate:

> It may be that one side effect of the Thatcher decade has been to reduce people's belief in the value of political activity of any kind. Perhaps just by being there for so long she has mesmerized the nation into believing that she is as unmoveable a part of the political landscape as Big Ben . . . and that there is nothing worth doing that will make any difference to that overwhelming fact.

Whether Mrs Thatcher's departure in November 1990 will make any difference to this situation remains to be seen.

If the 'procedural' part of the political culture is changing, the same is true of the consensus over the substance. The consensual nature of British politics was until recently one of its characteristic features. For most of the period since the end of the Second World War there was agreement across the political spectrum about the broad content of public policy: in particular, on the desirability of full employment, state provision of extensive welfare and the existence of a large number of publicly owned industries providing goods and services. In the 1970s and 1980s this agreement came under great pressure. The most important reason was the increasingly severe crisis of the British economy.

In the 1950s — the period when consensus was especially strong — the nation's prosperity grew rapidly. While Britain was not as successful as many of its international competitors, there nevertheless existed full employment and sustained economic growth. From the early 1960s increasingly severe problems appeared and by the middle of the 1970s a full-blown crisis was apparent: inflation was at a historically high level, unemployment was rising and international confidence in the economy was declining. Governments began to abandon key parts of the post-war consensus, beginning with the commitment to full employment (Plant, 1988). But the most radical departures came in 1979 with the election of Mrs Thatcher's first government. Since 1979 the country has been governed by administrations consciously intent on rejecting the post-war consensus. In the view of Mrs Thatcher's erstwhile supporters the state sector of the economy is inefficient, public spending is a burden destroying the ability of the people to create wealth, and many welfare services sap the capacity of the people to act in an enterprising and independent way. Since 1979 therefore the government has offered increasingly radical alternatives to the post-war consensus. These have included the large-scale disposal of public industries to private shareholders; the sale of council houses to their tenants; the closure of industries held to be too inefficient to compete in world markets; and the subjection of welfare, health and education provision to increasingly strong market forces (Gamble, 1988).

It is possible that the Conservative party's competitors, witnessing the electoral success of these radical policies, will adopt many of them and thus create a new consensus in British politics. But at the moment the story since the close of the 1970s has been the destruction by a radical Thatcherite Conservative party of many of the old understandings which formed a central part of the political culture.

We have seen in this chapter that the cultural context of British politics is a mixture of stability and change. In some ways it is astonishing how little Britain has altered in this century. The British have experienced two World Wars, decades of economic decline, the loss of an Empire, a revolution in welfare provision and forms of housing tenure, astonishing changes in technology and a transformation of material standards of life. Yet the country remains recognizably what it was in 1900: a rich capitalist society formally governed by parliamentary institutions. Politics and government are closely connected to the social structure, but plainly they are not just moulded by that structure. The relationship between the political system and its social, economic and cultural surroundings consists of a subtle and varied interaction. Precisely what kind of political practices and institutions have resulted from that interaction we will discover in the following chapters.

References and Further Reading

Almond, G. and Verba, S. *The Civic Culture* (Princeton University Press, 1963).
Almond, G. and Verba. S. (eds), *The Civic Culture Revisited* (Little Brown, 1981).
Bagehot, W., *The English Constitution* (Watt, 1964; original publication 1867).
Byrne, P. and Lovenduski, J., 'Two new protest groups: The peace and women's movements', in H. Drucker *et al.*, *Developments in British Politics* (Macmillan, 1983).
Gamble, A., *The Free Economy And The Strong State* (Macmillan, 1988).
Jacobs, E. and Worcester, R., *We British* (Weidenfeld & Nicholson, 1990).
Kavanagh, D., *Political Culture* (Macmillan, 1972).
Kavanagh, D., 'Political Culture in Great Britain: The decline of the civic culture', in Almond, G. and Verba, S. (eds), *The Civic Culture Revisited* (Little Brown, 1981).
Moran, M. *Politics and Society in Britain* (Macmillan, 1989).
Peele, G. 'The state and civil liberties' in H. Drucker *et al.*, *Development in British Politics* (Macmillan, 1988), 144–75.
Plant, R., 'Ideology', in H. Drucker *et al.*, *Developments in British Politics* (Macmillan, 1988).
Rose, R., *Governing Without Consensus* (Faber, 1971).

Dominant Values or Hegemony?

'Nothing appears more surprising', wrote David Hume, 'than the easiness with which the many are governed by the few.' This question is implicitly posed by the foregoing description of a society which, like other developed western countries, exhibits great inequalities of income, wealth and power between different groups in society. Why do the less well-off majority accept such blatant inequalities? Clearly the answer is connected with the dominant ideology discussed in the last chapter but why don't the masses rise up and cast off their chains as Marx exhorted them to do?

Marx himself (with Engels) offered an explanation relevant to all societies:

> In every epoch the ideas of the ruling class are the ruling ideas, that is the class that is the ruling material power of society is at the same time its ruling intellectual power.

In other words, those who own the wealth are able to control the machinery of government and impose their ideas upon society. Just as slaves are led to accept the rectitude of their slavery, so the proletariat in capitalist societies is persuaded to accept their inferior status and position as legitimate. A 'false consciousness' is created whereby the working classes come genuinely to believe, for example, that theirs is properly a subordinate role, the ruling class is more competent than they to rule, the private enterprise system is both fair and efficient and great inequalities of wealth are acceptable.

Antonio Gramsci, the influential Italian Communist thinker, developed this idea. He argued that while the machinery of the state enabled the ruling group to dominate society through coercion, its much more important 'intellectual and moral leadership' gave it success 'through consent'. This was achieved through the subtle manipulation of 'civil society': the major interlocking institutions in the country, e.g. the Church, schools and especially the media. The result of this process was a dominant, all-embracing 'hegemony' of society by the ruling class.

> The proletariat wear their chains willingly. Condemned to perceive reality through the conceptual spectacles of the ruling class, they are unable to recognise the nature or extent of their own servitude.
>
> Femia, p.31.

During the 1960s the sociologist David Lockwood tried to explain the same phenomenon. He distinguished three types of 'conceptual spectacles' closely related to occupation and local community (Bilton *et al.*, pp. 228–39).

1. Workers in traditional industries living in closely knit communities (e.g. mining and shipbuilding workers) are likely to subscribe to **proletarian traditionalism**,

**A metaphor
for capitalist
society**

American novelist and reformer Edward Bellamy, in his novel *Looking Backward: 2000–1887* (published 1888), dramatically visualizes nineteenth-century capitalism by comparing it to a carriage being driven along a road:

By way of attempting to give the reader some general impression of the way people lived together in those days (latter half of the nineteenth century), and especially of the relations of the rich and poor to one another, perhaps I cannot do better than to compare society as it then was to a prodigious coach which the masses of humanity were harnessed to and dragged toilsomely along a very hilly and sandy road. The driver was hunger, and permitted no lagging though the pace was necessarily very slow. Despite the difficulty of drawing the coach at all along so hard a road, the top was covered with passengers who never got down, even at the steepest ascents. These seats on top were very breezy and comfortable. Well up out of the dust, their occupants could enjoy the scenery at their leisure, or critically discuss the merits of the straining team. Naturally such places were in great demand and the competition for them was keen, every one seeking as the first end in life to secure a seat on the coach for himself and to leave it to his child after him. By the rule of the coach a man could leave his seat to whom he wished, but on the other hand there were many accidents by which it might at any time be wholly lost. For all that they were so easy, the seats were very insecure, and at every sudden jolt of the coach persons were slipping out of them and falling to the ground, where they were instantly compelled to take hold of the rope and help to drag the coach on which they had before ridden so pleasantly. It was naturally regarded as a terrible misfortune to lose one's seat and the apprehension that this might happen to them or their friends was a constant cloud upon the happiness of those who rode.

It must in truth be admitted that the main effect of the spectacle of misery of the toilers at the rope was to enhance the passengers' sense of the value of their seats upon the coach, and to cause them to hold on to them more desperately than before. If the passengers could only have felt assured that neither they nor their friends would ever fall from the top, it is probable that, beyond contributing to the funds for liniments and bandages, they would have troubled themselves extremely little about those who dragged the coach.

I am well aware that this will appear to the men and women of the twentieth century an incredible inhumanity, but there are two facts, both very curious, which partly explain it. In the first place, it was firmly and sincerely believed that there was no other way in which society could get along, except the many pulled at the rope and the few rode, and not only this, but that no very radical improvement even was possible, either in the harness, the coach, the roadway, or the distribution of the toil. It had always been as it was, and it always would be so. It was a pity but it could not be helped, and philosophy forbade wasting compassion on what was beyond remedy . . .

(Source: Edward Bellamy, *Looking Backward: 2000–1887*, 1888)

a perception of a world in which workers needed to defend themselves against the dominant class. Unsurprisingly, many solid trade union and Labour party supporters would be found among such people.

2. Workers in agriculture and small family businesses, on the other hand, were more isolated and hence more likely to accept values of the dominant class. These *deferential traditionalists* were unlikely to support left-wing alternatives.

3. Workers in new industries, however, earning relatively high wages and living on new housing estates, tend to replace traditional perspectives with a new one based upon money and the cultivation of home and family. Theirs is a pecuniary image of society, ideologically less likely to support Labour unless clear financial advantage is involved.

Overall Lockwood's analysis suggested that challenges to the dominant philosophy were likely to decline along with traditional industries and their bedrock Labour supporters.

Another sociologist, Frank Parkin (1971), believed views on inequality were formed more by exposure to influences at the societal rather than the local level. He identified three *meaning systems* to which working class people were exposed.

1. Like Gramsci, he perceived a *dominant value* system permeating society via its main institutions. This led workers to accept inferior status as both natural (*deferential consciousness*) and fair in that it provided opportunities for advancement (*aspirational consciousness*).
2. *Radical value systems* in the form of revolutionary or socialist party analyses could inculcate an *oppositional consciousness* but in many societies such organizations did not exist and where they did a shift had invariably taken place from radical alternatives towards reform of capitalism through parliamentary means.
3. This helped to explain the *subordinate value system* associated with working-class communities attempting to come to terms with inequality through concentrating upon achieving the best possible deal via piecemeal trade union action.

Mann's explanation of working-class quiescence reflected Parkin's third category. He saw a *pragmatic acceptance* by workers of the status quo: they were not fooled by apologies for capitalism but in the absence of anything better they simply adapted to its requirements. Dominant values are so powerfully ubiquitous workers cannot avoid absorbing them, but their social and work subcultures foster 'deviant' values in an unsystematic non-ideological way. The resultant admixture of values reflects the confusion that working people, perhaps understandably, feel.

Mann's explanation seems to make sense. Working people may not swallow dominant values uncritically but it is unlikely that their circumstances would allow them to formulate or adopt any consistent radical critique of capitalist society. Working people *have* to be pragmatic and realistic. While their wages may be a fraction of their bosses', they do earn enough for themselves and their families to survive and, in relative terms perhaps, even prosper. Radical strategies, on the other hand, carry the risk of economic hardship, widespread social dislocation or violence, with no proven alternative economic model to guarantee a superior way of life. In other words, the poor cannot afford a revolution; the rich-who-can do not need one.

References and Further Reading

Bilton, A., *et al.*, *Introductory Sociology* (Macmillan, 1987).
Femia, J.V., *Gramsci's Political Thought* (Oxford University Press, 1987).

Hall, S., *The Road to Renewal* (Verso, 1989).
Mann, M., *Consciousness and Action Among the Western Working Class* (Macmillan, 1973).
Parkin, F., *Class, Inequality and Political Order* (McGibbon & Kee, 1971).
Simon, R., *Gramsci's Political Thought* (Lawrence & Wishart, 1982).

PART III Political Ideologies

If actions are the direct products of thoughts then what people think politically is clearly of key importance. So far we have examined general questions regarding the nature of politics together with the historical, social and economic underpinnings of British politics. Ideology provides the final contextual element before the book moves on to consider political processes. Modern British ideologies occur within the intellectual and institutional framework of liberal democracy, which originated in the thinking of British liberal (note the small 'l') philosophers in the eighteenth century. Chapter 7 briefly discusses the nature of ideology before investigating these founding ideas and tracing their incorporation into party political progammes — beginning with the Liberal Party.

In Chapter 8 traditional Conservatism is analysed and the impact of Thatcherism — arguably closer to nineteenth century classical liberal thought — assessed. Chapter 9 makes a historical analysis of the various stages through which British Socialism has passed — both the left-wing and revisionist varieties. Chapter 10 addresses the centre ground of British politics in the form of modern Liberalism (latterly the Liberal Democrats) and the (now extinct) Social Democratic Party. The ideas of the Green Party are also covered in this part though it is appreciated that while it gains support right across the political spectrum Green Party thinking on social and economic issues is by far the most radical of any of the major political parties. Part III concludes with a brief examination of the ideas expressed by David Marquand in *The Unprincipled Society*.

7 The Liberal Tradition

Bill Jones

This chapter begins by discussing what we mean by the term 'ideology'. It goes on to explain how liberal ideas entered the political culture as heresies in the seventeenth and eighteenth centuries but went on to become the orthodoxies of the present age. Classical Liberalism in the mid-nineteenth century is examined together with the birth of modern Liberalism in the early twentieth century.

What is Ideology?

For up to two decades after 1945 it seemed as if 'ideology' as a factor in British politics was on the wane. The coalition comradeship of the war had drawn some of the sting from the doctrinal conflicts between the two major political parties and in its wake the Conservatives had conceded — without too much ill grace — that Labour would expand welfare services and nationalize a significant sector of the economy. Once in power after 1951 the Conservatives presided over their socialist inheritance of a mixed economy and a welfare state. Both parties seemed to have converged towards a general consensus on political values and institutions: there was more to unite than to divide them (see Chapter 3). By the end of the 1950s some commentators — notably the American political scientist, Daniel Bell — were pronouncing 'The End of Ideology' (the title of Bell's book published in 1960) in western societies.

The faltering of the British economy in the 1960s, however, exacerbated in the early 1970s by the rise in oil prices, industrial unrest and raging inflation, reopened the ideological debate with a vengeance. A revived Labour left hurled contumely at their right-wing Cabinet colleagues for allegedly betraying socialist principles. Margaret Thatcher, meanwhile, Leader of the Opposition after 1975, began to elaborate a position far to the right of her predecessor Edward Heath (PM 1970–4). The industrial paralysis of the 1978–9 'winter of discontent' provided a shabby end for Jim Callaghan's Labour government and a perfect backcloth against which Mrs Thatcher's confident assertions could be projected. Since 1979 'ideology' in the form of 'Thatcherism' or the New Right has triumphed over what has subsequently been labelled the 'post-war consensus'.

Ideology as a concept is not easy to define. It is to some extent analogous to *philosophy* but is not as open-ended or as disinterested. It shares some of the moral commitment of *religion* but is essentially secular and rooted in this world rather than the next. On the other hand, it is more fundamental and less specific than mere *policy*. Perhaps it is helpful to regard ideology as *applied philosophy*. It links philosophical ideas to the contemporary world; it provides a comprehensive and systematic perspective whereby human society can be understood; and it provides a framework of principles from which policies can be developed.

Individuals support ideologies for a variety of reasons: moral commitment — often genuine whatever cynics might say — as well as self-interest. Clearly ideology will mean more to political theorists active within political parties, elected representatives or the relative minority who are seriously interested in political ideas. It has to be recognized that most people are ill informed on political matters and not especially interested in them. It is quite possible for large numbers of people to subscribe to contradictory propositions — for example, that welfare services should be improved while taxes should be cut — or to vote for a party while disagreeing with its major policies. But the broad mass of the population is not completely inert. During election campaigns they receive a crash course in political education and leaving aside the more crass appeals to emotion and unreason most voters are influenced to some extent by the ideological debate. The party with the clearest message which seems most relevant to the times can win elections, as Labour discovered in 1945 and the Conservatives in 1979, 1983 and 1987.

Classifying ideologies

This is a difficult and imperfect science but the two approaches below should help clarify.

The horizontal left—right continuum

Left   Centre   Right
|——|

This is the most familiar classification used and abused in the press and in everyday conversations. It arose from the seating arrangements adopted in the French Estates General in 1789 where the aristocracy sat to the right of the king and the popular movements to his left. Subsequently the terms have come to represent adherence to particular groups of principles. Right-wingers stress *freedom* or the right of individuals to do as they please and develop their own personality without interference, especially from governments, which history teaches are potentially tyrannical. Left-wingers believe this kind of freedom is only won by the strong at the expense of the weak. They see *equality* as the more important value and stress the collective interest of the community above that of the individual. Those occupying the centre ground usually represent various kinds of compromise between these two positions.

The implications of these principles for economic policy are obviously of key importance. Right-wingers champion *free enterprise*, or *capitalism*; the rights of individuals to set up their own businesses, to provide goods and services and reap what reward they can. Left-wingers disagree. Capitalism, they argue, creates poverty amidst plenty — much better to move towards *collective ownership* so that workers can receive full benefit of their labour. Politicians in the centre dismiss both these positions as extreme and damaging to the harmony of national life. They tend to argue for various combinations of left and right principles or compromises between them: in practice a ***mixed economy*** plus ***efficient welfare services***. The left—right continuum therefore relates in practice principally to economic and social policy.

Left	Centre	Right
Equality	Less inequality	Freedom
Collectivism	Some collectivism	Individualism
Collective ownership	Mixed economy	Free enterprise

The vertical axis or continuum

The inadequacies of the left—right continuum are obvious. It is both crude and inaccurate in that many people can subscribe to ideas drawn from its whole width and consequently defy classification. H.J. Eysenck suggested in the early 1950s that if a 'tough' and 'tender' axis could bisect the left—right continuum, ideas could be more accurately plotted on two dimensions. In this way ideological objectives could be separated from political methodology — so 'tough' left-wingers, e.g. communists, would occupy the top left-hand quarter, tough right-wingers, e.g. fascists, the top right-hand quarter and so on. The diagram below illustrates the point.

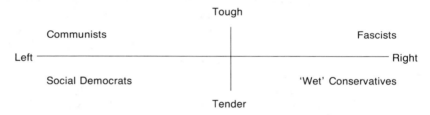

The vertical axis can also be used to plot other features.

1. An ***authoritarian—democratic axis*** is perhaps a more precise variation on the 'tough' and 'tender' theme.
2. A ***status quo—revolutionary*** axis is also useful. The Conservative party has traditionally been characterized as defending the established order. Mrs Thatcher, however, was a committed radical who wanted to engineer major and irreversible changes. It was Labour and the Conservative 'wets' who defended the status quo in the 1980s. This approach produces some interesting placements on our two-dimensional diagram.

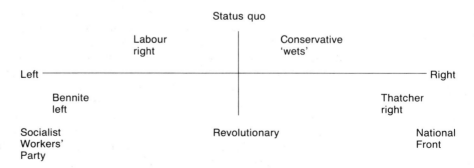

Ideas and values in politics

> In politics, ideas and values cannot exist in isolation. They need a vehicle by which they can be transformed from abstract ideology into practical legislative effect. The vehicle is the political party . . .
>
> The party politician is constrained by the beliefs of that party and the convictions of its members. In any economic crisis you can expect the Tories to bend in the direction of lower public expenditure and higher personal incentives. Labour will incline in the direction of welfare and protection . . .
>
> It is more than nostalgia that justifies the party system. It is essentially the belief that some of the 'ideas and values' of politicians have a permanent importance. The policies by which those ideas and values are implemented may change with time and circumstance but the ideology abides.
>
> *Source*: Roy Hattersley, *The Guardian*, 30 September 1989

Political parties and the left–right continuum

Despite its inadequacies the left–right continuum is useful because it is commonly understood: it will be used as a guide to the following sections, but first a word on the way in which political parties relate to the political spectrum.

For most of the post-war period the major ideological divisions have not occurred between the two big parties, but within them. The Labour party has covered a very wide spectrum from the revolutionary left to cautious Social Democrat right. Similarly, two major Conservative schools of thought developed in the late 1970s: traditional ('wet') Conservatism and the New Right or Thatcherite Conservatism. The centre ground for many years was dominated by the Liberal party but during the 1980s it was first augmented by the Social Democratic Party (which split off from the Labour Party in 1981) and then was fragmented when the merger initiative following the 1987 election resulted in the awkward progeny of the Social and Liberal Democrats plus the rump Social Democratic party led defiantly by David Owen until May 1990 when the party formally folded. 1989 also saw the arrival of a new player in national politics: the Greens.

The Liberal Tradition

The word 'liberalism' was originally a pejorative term used to describe radical or progressive ideas. Since then, like so many other political labels coined as forms of abuse ('tory' was once a name given to Irish outlaws) the word has lost its derogatory connotations and fully traversed the ground between vice and virtue. Now liberalism denotes opinions and qualities which are generally applauded. Most people would like to think they are liberal in the sense of being open-minded, tolerant, generous or rational. This is partly because the ideas of the English liberal philosophers from the mid-seventeenth to mid-nineteenth centuries became accepted as the dominant elements in our political culture. These were the ideas which helped create our liberal democratic political system in the late nineteenth century and since then have provided its philosophical underpinning.

An important distinction clearly has to be made between liberal with a small 'l' and the 'Liberalism' associated with the party of the same name until the 1987 merger. The Liberal party always claimed a particular continuity with liberal philosophical ideas but so deeply ingrained have these views become that most political parties also owe them substantial unacknowledged philosophical debts. For their own part Liberals made contributions to political, social and economic thinking which have been hugely influential and were plundered shamelessly by other parties. It makes sense, therefore, to open up with some consideration of the liberal tradition of both the 'l' and 'L' variety.

Philosophical liberalism

Bertrand Russell attributes the birth of English liberal thought in part to the French philosopher, René Descartes (1596–1650). His famous proposition 'I think, therefore I am' made 'the basis of knowledge different for each person since for each the starting point was his own existence not that of other individuals or the community' (Russell, p. 579). To us such propositions seem unexceptional but in the mid-seventeenth century they were potentially revolutionary because they questioned the very basis of feudal society. This relied upon unquestioning acceptance of the monarch's divine right to rule, the aristocracy's hereditary privileges and the church's explanation of the world together with its moral leadership. Feudal society was in any case reeling from the impact of the Civil War (1642–9), the repercussions of which produced a limited 'constitutional' monarchy and the embryo of modern parliamentary government. Descartes had inaugurated a new style of thinking.

Rationality

John Locke (1632–1704) did much to set the style of liberal thinking as rational and undogmatic. He accepted some certainties like his own existence, God and mathematical logic but he always respected an area of doubt in relation to most propositions. He was inclined to accept differences of opinion as the natural consequences of free individual development. Liberal philosophers tended to give greater credence to facts established by scientific enquiry — the systematic testing of theories against reality — rather than to assertions accepted as fact purely on the basis of tradition.

Toleration

This lack of dogmatism was closely connected with a liberal prejudice in favour of toleration and compromise. Conflicts between Crown and Parliament, Catholicism and Protestantism had divided the country for too long, they felt: it was time to recognize that religious belief was a matter of personal conscience, not a concern of government.

Natural rights and the consent of the governed

Sir Robert Filmer argued in his *Patriacha* (1680) that the divine authority of monarchs could be traced back to Adam and Eve — from whom all monarchs were originally descended. John Locke would have none of this. In attacking Filmer he invoked the 'state of nature' argument (*Two Treatises on Government*, 1690). Unlike Thomas Hobbes, Locke did not believe that without the protecting framework of the state men would be at war: his view of human nature was much more optimistic. In their 'natural' context men would be generally well behaved: 'they are rational creatures and can see that when they deal with other creatures like themselves they ought to treat them as equals'. As 'equal and independent people' in this state of nature Locke believed they would decide whether or not 'by their own consent to make themselves members of some political society'.

In other words, governments originated when individuals freely entered into an agreement, or contract, with the state to abide by its laws. In exchange the state undertook to protect their rights. The two revolutionary ideas arising from this line of argument were as follows:

1. People everywhere had rights which were 'natural' and independent of the state.
2. The authority of government was dependent upon the consent of the governed.

Nearly a century later these ideas were neatly summarized in the American Declaration of Independence (1776).

> We hold these truths to be self evident, that all men are created equal, that they are endowed by their creator with certain inalienable rights, that among these are Life, Liberty and Happiness. That to secure these rights, Governments are instituted among men, deriving their just powers from the consent of the governed.

Individual liberty

The idea of natural rights was closely allied to the concept of individual liberty which had already been established by the eighteenth century.

> These liberties included the freedom from arbitrary arrest, arbitrary search and arbitrary taxation; equality before the law, the right to trial by jury; a degree of freedom of thought, speech and religious belief; and freedom to buy and sell.
>
> Gamble, p. 67

Such liberties in practice were protected by constitutional checks and balances, limited government and representation.

Constitutional checks and balances

Locke argued that to ensure that executive power was not exercised arbitrarily by the king the law making or legislative arm of government should be separate, independent and removable by the community. This doctrine of the 'separation of powers' informed the liberal enthusiasm for written constitutions — though ironically Britain has never had a written constitution nor indeed an effective separation of powers.

Limited government

Instead of the absolute power which Filmer argued the monarch was free to exercise, liberal philosophers sought to restrict the legitimacy of government to a protection

Elements of philosophical liberalism

> Rationality
>
> Toleration
>
> Natural rights and the consent of the governed
>
> Individual liberty
>
> Constitutional checks and balances
>
> Limited government
>
> Representation

of civil liberties. It was held to be especially important that government did not interfere with the right of property nor the exercise of economic activity.

Representation

It followed that if the legislature was to be removable then it needed to be representative. Many liberal Whigs in the eighteenth century believed that Parliament was generally representative of the nation even though the franchise was small and usually based upon a highly restrictive property qualification. Such positions were destined to be eroded, however, by the inherent logic of natural rights: *if everyone had equal rights then surely they should have an equal say in removing a government not of their liking?*

The influence of the liberal philosophers perhaps seems greater in retrospect than it was because they were often seeking to justify and accelerate political trends which were already well under way. Nevertheless, they were of key importance and provide ideas still used as touchstones in the present day.

Some commentators, like Eccleshall and Gamble, see liberalism as providing the philosophical rationale for modern capitalist society. Certainly the idea of individual freedom, property rights and limited government suited the emergent entrepreneurial middle classes destined to come of political age in the next century. Liberal views on government, however, have enjoyed a general acceptance not just in Britain but in the USA, Western Europe and elsewhere. They have provided the commonly accepted ground rules of democratic behaviour, the 'procedural values' of toleration, fair play and free speech which Bernard Crick argues should be positively reinforced in our classrooms. They have provided in one sense an 'enabling' ideology which all major parties have accepted. Indeed it is in some ways surprising that a creed originating in an agrarian, largely non-industrialized country should have provided a political framework which has survived so tenaciously into the present day.

Classical Liberalism

The American and French Revolutions applied liberal principles in a way which shocked many of their more moderate adherents. The Napoleonic interlude caused a period of reaction but during the mid- to late nineteenth century Classical Liberalism took shape. Claiming continuity with the early liberals this new school was based upon the economic ideas of Adam Smith and the radical philosophers Jeremy Bentham, James Mill and his son John Stuart Mill. Liberalism with a capital 'L' then took the stage in the form of the Liberal party, a grouping based upon the Whigs, disaffected Tories and the Manchester Radicals led by Richard Cobden and John Bright. Classical Liberalism was characterized by:

> **An acceptance of the liberal conception of the independent, rational and self-governing citizen as the basic unit of society.**

An *embrace* of the concept would be a better word in that it now represented a goal or vision to be worked for. Liberals hoped that through the erosion of aristocratic privilege and the moral transformation of the working class social differences would give way to a new society of equals.

Human nature

The Liberal view of human nature was fairly optimistic. John Stuart Mill, for example, doubted whether working for the common good would induce citizens to produce goods as efficiently as when self-interest was involved. He warned against too rapid a rate of social progress. At the heart of Liberal philosophy, however, was Locke's civilized reasonable human being, capable of being educated into responsible citizenship. Many Liberals felt such an education would take a great many years but that it was possible, especially through *direct* involvement in the economy and the political system.

Freedom

Classical Liberalism retained the emphasis on freedom. In his essay *On Liberty*, for example, Mill felt 'It was imperative that human beings should be free to form opinions and to express their opinions without reserve.' The only constraint should be that in the exercise of his freedom, an individual should not impinge upon the freedom of others.

Utilitarianism

Jeremy Bentham (1748—1832) took the rationality of liberal philosophy to new levels with his science of utilitarianism. His approach was based upon what now seems an extraordinarily simplistic view of human psychology. He argued that human beings were disposed to seek pleasure and avoid pain. While they sought what was best for themselves they frequently made mistakes. The role of government therefore was to assist individuals in making the correct choices thus achieving the greatest happiness for the greatest number. While Bentham embraced the *laissez-faire* economic system as highly utilitarian he believed that most laws and administrative arrangements reflected aristocratic privilege and therefore were in need of reform.

Minimal government

Bentham's influence paradoxically led to far-reaching legal and administrative reforms; for example, the regulatory framework for mines and factories. Other liberals, however, were strongly opposed to such regulation both as a violation of *laissez-faire* principles and as an interference in the moral education of the poor. Liberals like Herbert Spencer (1820−1903) argued that welfare provision was wrong in that it sheltered the poor from the consequences of their behaviour. 'Is it not manifest', he argued, 'that there must exist in our midst an immense amount of misery which is a normal result of misconduct and ought not to be dissociated from it?' State support for the poor was therefore a dangerous narcotic likely to prevent the right lessons being learnt. The stern lesson Classical Liberals wished to teach was that the poorer classes would face the penalties of poverty unless they adopted the values and lifestyles of their economic superiors: thrift, hard work, moderate indulgence and self-improving pastimes.

Representative government

Bentham and James Mill (1773−1836) introduced an alternative argument in favour of representative government. Bentham dismissed the natural rights argument as 'nonsense on stilts'. His own utilitarian reasoning was that such a form of government was the most effective safeguard for citizens against possibly rapacious rulers or powerful 'sinister interests'. As both men believed the individual to be the best judge of where his own interests lay they favoured universal franchise (though Mill sought to restrict it to men over 40.) His son, J.S. Mill (1806−73), is probably the best-known advocate of representative government. He urged adult male *and* female suffrage but to guard against a 'capricious and impulsive' House of Commons he advised a literacy qualification for voting and a system of plural voting whereby

'Democracy creates a morally better person because it forces people to develop their potentialities' — the Classical Liberalism of J.S. Mill.

educated professional people would be able to cast more votes than ill-educated workers. Mill also believed that a participatory democracy and the sense of responsibility it would imbue would contribute towards the moral education of society: 'Democracy creates a morally better person because it forces people to develop their potentialties'.

Laissez-faire economics

Laissez-faire economics was predicated upon the tenet of individual freedom: it asserted that the ability to act freely within the market place — to buy and sell property, employ workers and take profit — were central to any free society. Adam Smith's (1723−90) broadsides against the trade protection of the eighteenth-century mercantilist system provided the clearest possible statement of the case for economic activity free from political restrictions. According to Smith producers should be allowed to supply products at the price consumers are willing to pay. Provided that competition was fair the 'hidden hand' of the market would ensure that goods were produced at the lowest possible price commensurate with the quality consumers required. Producers would be motivated by selfish pursuit of profit but would also provide social 'goods', through providing employment, creating wealth and distributing it in accordance with the energy and ability of people active in the economic system. Smith believed government intervention and regulation would impede this potentially perfect self-adjusting system. Liberals were not especially worried by the inequalities thrown up by *laissez-faire* economics, nor did they waste any sleep over the socialists' claim that the wage labour system enabled the middle-class property owners to exploit their workers. Classical Liberals were opposed to inherited financial advantages but not so concerned with the differences created by different performances in relation to the market. They favoured the meritocracy of the market: they were the high priests of capitalism.

Peace through trade

Liberals, especially the so-called Manchester Radicals, also applied their free trade principles to foreign affairs. Richard Cobden, for example, regarded diplomacy and war as the dangerous pastimes of the aristocracy. His answer to these perennial problems was: 'to make diplomacy open and subject to parliamentary control'; eliminate trade barriers; and encourage free trade world-wide. Commerce, he argued was peaceful, beneficial and encouraged cooperation and contact between nations.

Elements of classical liberalism	Independent rational citizen as basic unit of society
	Cautiously optimistic view of human nature
	Individual liberty
	Utilitarianism
	Minimal government
	Laissez-faire economics
	Peace through trade

If the world were a completely open market, national economies would become more integrated and interdependent and governments would be less likely to engage in conflicts or war.

The New Liberalism

The emphasis of Classical Liberalism was upon *laissez-faire*, wealth production, toleration of inequality, minimal welfare, individual responsibility and moral education. Towards the end of the nineteenth century, however, Liberals themselves began to move away from their own ascetic economic doctrines. John Stuart Mill had argued that government was only justified in intervening in society in order to prevent injury to the life, property or freedom of others. To some Liberals it appeared that capitalist society had become so complex and repressive that the freedom of poor people to develop their potential was being restricted: even if they were inclined to emulate their middle-class betters their capacity to do so was held back by poverty, poor health and education, squalid living and working conditions. Liberal thinkers began to shift their emphasis away from 'negative' freedom — freedom from oppression — towards providing 'positive' freedom — the capacity of people to make real choices regarding education, employment, leisure and so on.

State responsibility for welfare

T.H. Green (1836—82) helped initiate this movement for positive action to assist the poor by calling for a tax upon inherited wealth. Alfred Marshall (1842—1924) believed capitalism now provided such material plenty that it had the capacity to redistribute some of its largesse to the disadvantaged so that they would be able genuinely to help themselves to become self reliant. But it was L.T. Hobhouse (1864—1929) who perhaps marked the key shift of Liberals towards paternalism.

> The state as over-parent is quite as truly liberal as socialistic. It is the basis of the rights of the child, of his protection against parental neglect, of the equality of opportunity which he may claim as a 'future citizen'.

Hobhouse insisted that his version of paternalism should not be oppressively imposed; he favoured a basic minimum standard of living which would provide 'equal opportunities of self development'. He followed Green in proposing taxation to finance such welfare innovations as health insurance and pensions. The great Liberal victory of 1906 enabled it to implement many of these new measures. Thereafter Liberals became firm advocates of welfarism; in 1942 the Liberal William Beveridge produced his famous blueprint for the post-war welfare state.

Elements of new liberalism	State responsibility for welfare
	Mixed economy: Hobsonian and Keynesian economics
	Internationalism
	Further development of democratic government

The mixed economy: Hobsonian and Keynesian economics

Government intervention of a different kind was proposed by J.A. Hobson (1858–1940). He was the first major Liberal economist (he later became a socialist) to argue that capitalism was fatally flawed. Its tendency to produce a rich minority who accumulated unspent profits and luxury goods meant that the full value of goods produced was not consumed by society. This created slumps and, indirectly, the phenomenon of economic imperialism. Capitalists were forced by such **underconsumption** to export their savings abroad, thus creating overseas interests with political and colonial consequences. Hobson argued that the state could solve this crisis with one Olympian move: redirect wealth from the rich to the poor via progressive taxation. The section of society most in need would then be able to unblock the mechanism which caused over production and unemployment: thus making moral as well as economic sense.

J.M. Keynes (1883–1946) completed this revolution in Liberal economic thought by arguing that demand could be stimulated not by redistribution of wealth to the poor but by government-directed investment into new economic activity. Confronted by a world recession and massive unemployment, he concentrated upon a different part of the economic cycle. He agreed that the retention of wealth by capitalists under a *laissez-faire* economic system lay at the heart of the problem but believed the key to be increased **investment**, not increased consumption. Instead of **saving** in a crisis governments should encourage businessmen to **invest** in new economic activity. Through the creation of new economic enterprises wealth would be generated,

The Mixed Economy: J.M. Keynes argued for stimulating demand by government-directed investment into new economic activity.

consumption increased, other economic activities stimulated and unemployment reduced. He envisaged a mixed economy in which the state would intervene with a whole range of economic controls to achieve full employment and planned economic growth. Keynes was not just concerned with the cold science of economics: his view of the mixed economy would serve social ends in the form of alleviated hardship and the extension of opportunity. But while Keynes was unhappy with capitalism in the 1930s he did not propose to replace it — merely to modify it. He was no egalitarian, unlike socialist economists, and disagreed with Hobsonian calls for wealth redistribution which he felt would adversely affect the incentives to achieve which human nature required: 'for my own part I believe there is social and psychological justification for significant inequalities of income and wealth' (Keynes, 1973, p. 374).

Internationalism

Radical Liberal intellectuals like J.A. Hobson, Norman Angel, E.D. Morel, C.R. Buxton, H.N. Brailsford, Lowes Dickenson and Charles Trevelyan produced an influential critique of the international system arguing that the practice of secret diplomacy, imperialist competition for markets, haphazard balance of power policies and the sinister role of arms manufacturers made war between nations tragically inevitable. The First World War appeared to vindicate their analysis and encouraged them to develop the idea of an overarching international authority: the League of Nations. The idea was picked up by political parties and world leaders including the US President, Woodrow Wilson, and through the catalyst of war was translated into The League of Nations by the Versailles Treaty. Most of the Radical Liberals joined the Labour party during and after the war but the Liberal party subsequently remained staunchly internationalist and in favour of disarmament proposals throughout the inter-war period.

Further development of democratic government

The New Liberals were no less interested than their predecessors in the development of representative democracy through extension of the franchise and the strengthening of the House of Commons. Lloyd George's device of including welfare proposals in his 1909 Budget — a measure which the House of Lords had traditionally passed 'on the nod' — precipitated a conflict between the two chambers which resulted in the House of Lords' power being reduced from one of absolute veto over legislation to one of delay only. In the early 1920s Liberals gave way to Labour as the chief opposition party returning 159 MPs in 1923, 59 in 1929 and only 21 in 1935. The dramatic decline in the party's fortunes coincided with support for a change in the electoral system from the 'first past the post' system, which favoured big parties, to alternatives which would provide fairer representation to smaller parties.

This chapter has sought to emphasize the centrality of the Liberal Tradition in the evolution of modern British political thought. In the eighteenth century it helped establish reason, toleration, liberty, natural rights and the consent of the governed in place of religious dogma, feudal allegiance and the divine right of monarchs to rule. In the nineteenth century it added representative, democratic government with power shared between various elements. Having provided key guidelines for our modern system of government Classical Liberalism argued for minimal government intervention in social policy and an economy run essentially in harmony with market forces.

The New Liberals, however, engineered a new intellectual revolution. They argued for government intervention to control an increasingly complex economy which distributed great rewards and terrible penalties with near-random unfairness. They also saw commerce not as the healing balm for international conflicts but as the source of the conflicts themselves. The irony is that the Liberals Keynes and Beveridge proved to be the chief architects of the post-war consensus between Labour and Conservatives while, as we shall see, Mrs Thatcher wrought her revolution not through application of traditional Conservatism but through a rediscovery of Classical Liberalism.

References and Further Reading

General

Eccleshall, R., *Political Ideologies* (Hutchinson, 1984).

Eysenck, H.J., *Sense and Nonsense about Psychology* (Penguin, 1964).

Gamble, A., *An Introduction to Modern Social and Political Thought* (Macmillan, 1981).

Greenleaf, W.H., *The British Political Tradition*, vol. 2. *The Ideological Heritage* (Methuen, 1983).

Keynes, J.M., *The General Theory of Employment, Interest and Money*, Vol. VII of his *Collected Writings* (Macmillan, 1973).

Plamenatz, J., *Man and Society* (Longman, 1963).

Russell, B., *History of Western Philosophy* (Unwin, 1965).

Tivey, L. and Wright, A., *Party Ideology in Britain* (Routledge, 1989).

Liberalism

Bentley, M., *The Climax of Liberal Politics* (Edward Arnold, 1987).

Eccleshall, R., *British Liberalism* (Longman, 1986).

Hobhouse, L.T., *Liberalism* (Oxford University Press, 1964).

Hobson, H.J., *The cisis of Liberalism* (Harvester Wheatsheaf, 1974).

Mill, J.S., *Principles of Political Economy* (Penguin, 1985).

Mill, J.S., *On Liberty* (Penguin, 1985).

Mill, J.S., *Representative Government* (Oxford University Press, 1975).

Stewart, M., *Keynes and After* (Penguin, 1972).

8 Conservatism

Bill Jones

**Until Mrs Thatcher, Conservatives traditionally disdained ideology in favour
of a judicious pragmatism. They, after all, were the survivors, the party which
would subtly assume as their own the political ideas of the age together with
the policies which circumstances required. This chapter argues, however, that
there has always been more to Conservatism than mere pragmatism and begins
by identifying the traditional tenets of Conservative belief. It then assesses the
extent to which the ideas associated with Mrs Thatcher have departed from
tradition and concludes by focusing on her economic ideas.**

The Tenets of Traditional Conservative Thought

Conservative thought has a long lineage, stretching back before the 1830s when the
term 'conservatism' replaced, or rather augmented, the term 'toryism'. Critics claim
that Conservatism lacks the status of a coherent philosophy, being merely the
rationalization of ruling elite interests through the ages. Conservatives themselves
would judge this unfair: it is possible to advocate changed policies while still adhering
to fundamental principles. For them there is no inalienable set of rights which all
men own, no immutable moral laws to govern their conduct. 'Conservatism is not
so much a philosophy', writes Lord Hailsham (1959, p. 16), 'as an attitude.' This
attitude, however, does rest upon certain core beliefs.

The purpose of politics: social harmony

For Conservatives the purpose of politics is to enable people to be what they are
or to become what they wish to be. They applaud the variety and diversity thus created
and the benefits which society receives from individuals who fully realize their talents
and potential. Politics should remain a means, not an end in itself. Once the politician
has done his job — created the conditions for self-fulfillment — he should humbly
bow out.

Conservatives have traditionally believed that politicians should aim for a balance,
a harmony in society. Thus, in the nineteenth century Conservatives opposed the
Liberals when they favoured an economic freedom which some were exploiting
unacceptably and in the present century have opposed what they perceive as an
unacceptably powerful socialist state. Conservatives have always been essentially
pragmatic: they avoid commitments to specific policies or courses of action but prefer
to keep open the optimum number of objectives. If policies fail they have tended

to abandon them and if opposed by an irresistible force they have usually compromised. They tend to agree with Edmund Burke that 'all government . . . is founded on compromise'.

Human nature: imperfect and corruptible

Conservatives believe that politics begins and ends with man's own nature, that the limits of political activity are set by what people desire and are capable of giving. They also believe people are more given to taking than giving, that human nature is imperfect and corruptible. Time and again Conservative arguments return to this premise and from it flows their approach to all political problems at home and abroad. They would agree with Hobbes that outside organized society men would exist in a state of brutish, warlike anarchy, pursuing their own selfish interests through 'force and fraud'. They doubt whether man's selflessness extends much beyond himself and his own family. Nor do they believe that human nature can be changed in any significant way. They believe in knowing the worst and formulating courses of action accordingly.

The rule of law: basis of all freedom

If so many of the dangers to man threaten from within himself then he must be protected from his own darker nature. Obviously law restricts freedom of action, but that freedom which would exist outside the law — the unregulated freedom of all to pursue their ends at the expense of others — would be excessive and destructive. By accepting the limitations of the law man can enjoy an infinitely greater freedom. The authority of the law is thus the precondition of liberty. This authority is based upon the law's efficacy over time, the degree of support for it within society and the overwhelming force exercised in its support by the state. To be effective the law must be administered impartially and everyone in society must accept a responsibility to obey the law upon pain of penalty.

Social institutions create sense of society and nation

If the law is the cornerstone of social order for Conservatives the multifarious social and political institutions of Britain perform a vital role in binding people together to form what we call 'society'. If his nature renders man potentially anarchic then it follows that social order is not easy to achieve or preserve. The ability to live peacefully and responsibly with others cannot be taught but only learnt through the trial and error of experience. It is an art. Traditional patterns of behaviour, forms of living together, are crucial constituent elements of social harmony and should be recognized and protected as such. At their heart lies the family, for Lord Hailsham 'the foundation of civilized society'. Marriage, private property and religion all have their part to play. At the apex of society the family is projected onto the national stage in the form of the Queen and the Royal Family: the monarchy is held to play a uniquely important symbolic unifying and moral role in the life of the nation.

If the family is the basic unit of society for Conservatives, then the nation state is the whole. As such it commands ultimate loyalty and is a cause worthy dying for.

Foreign policy: pursuit of state interests in an anarchic international environment

Conservatives tend to apply their analysis of political realities at home to the international plane: to them the world is a dangerous place. States exhibit all the faults of individual humans plus a few even more dangerous characteristics which occur when they are *en masse*. The best and safest mechanisms for survival are not to be found in speculative schemes to transform international politics, but in the judicious use of the balance of power system and the traditional tools of diplomacy.

Liberty: the highest political end

Conservatives regard liberty as the highest political end; it is also the means whereby individuals are enabled to pursue their own fulfilment. In the negative sense liberty entails freedom from opposition and arbitrary rule. In the positive sense Conservatives would broadly concur with Mill's idea that it is the ability to do as one pleases as far as is possible without encroaching unjustifiably upon the freedom of others. Conservatives strongly oppose, however, what they regard as the socialist fallacy that liberty is contingent upon social and economic equality. The necessary redistribution of wealth, they argue, could only be imposed upon a reluctant population through state power which of necessity would be dangerously concentrated. Conservatives agree emphatically with Lord Acton, that absolute power corrupts absolutely.

For freedom to be safe we should guard against the exercise of too much power by too few people. How can we achieve this? Through the dispersion of power. 'Political liberty', asserts Hailsham, 'is nothing else than the diffusion of power'. This is not to say that the Conservatives necessarily champion the old Liberal conception of a minimalist state or oppose the use of state power where necessary but they have tended to believe that all power should be limited or balanced by other centres of power. The essence of this approach is the creation of a tension or balance in society. As long as this tension exists liberty is safe; when it weakens or it is absent, liberty is in danger. This principle is also employed in Conservative approaches to government.

Government: checks and balances

Ever since the Civil War and the decline of the doctrine that monarchs rule by divine right, Tories have favoured a limited, 'constitutional' and latterly symbolic, ceremonial monarchy. The hereditary House of Lords performs limited though valuable functions and acts in part as a guardian of the constitution. The Commons is the more powerful chamber but Conservatives envisage for it a relatively passive watchdog role: MPs are not intended to govern directly but to question governments, to demand explanations from them and, *in extremis*, to dismiss them when unsatisfactory.

They support liberal democracy and believe that 'the public good is attained by the interplay of rival forces of which they recognize themselves to be but one' (Hailsham, 1959). This approach is an extension of the Conservative belief that freedom can be maintained through balancing mechanisms. They support the eighteenth century liberal idea that the different functions of government — legislative, judicial and executive — should be embodied in separate institutions which consequently have a degree of independence. In this way the different elements of government check or balance each other and our leaders are protected from the corrupting influence of excessive power.

Property rights: first principle of justice

Property for Conservatives is one more way of diffusing power in society through giving a degree of independence to the property owner and his family. This right begins with a person's ownership of his own body and capacities and extends to those goods and chattels which he or she may come to acquire, accumulate or exchange with others. For Hume, the right of property was the 'first principle of justice' upon which, together with the laws of trade and contract, 'that peace and security of human society entirely depended'. But 'property' as Norton and Aughey observed 'is not just possession. It is an education. It enlightens the citizens in the value of stability and shows that the security of small property depends upon the security of all property' (Norton and Aughey, p. 34). The Conservative policy of selling council homes to sitting tenants is a direct application of this doctrine: people learn social responsibility from valuing and cherishing their own property.

Equality of opportunity but not of result

Conservatives support the notion of equality before the law and equality of opportunity but they oppose what Friedman called 'equality of result': the achievement of social and political equality. Conservatives argue that people are motivated to effort chiefly through self interest and the promise of benefit to themselves, especially in terms of wealth. The resultant distribution of property is unequal but merely reflects the unequal distribution of ability in society. Conservatives justify these inequalities in three further ways.

First, they are products of the system of incentives which mobilizes effort, ingenuity and talent. If they were replaced by a system of equal rewards then those who strove hardest would be rewarded equally with those who did least. Secondly, equality of reward would deny society the achievements, the standards of excellence, which occur when men strive their utmost in competition with each other. Thirdly, Conservatives believe that equality of reward would deny the freedom of the individual to pursue and develop latent talents. To deny this function is to jeopardize all freedom.

The Conservative party, therefore, is fundamentally concerned with justifying social and economic inequality, with formulating a 'policy that conserves a hierarchy of wealth and power and making this intelligible to democracy' (Norton and Aughey, p. 47). As Conservatives see it, inequality is not only inevitable but desirable. Part of the Conservative defence of economic inequality is also used to justify a closely hierarchical political structure.

Rule by elite

While Conservatives believe in equal democratic rights they deny the efficacy of a democracy which gives the masses much of a role beyond the act of voting. They believe in rule by an elite. Why? To Conservatives it seems that men are unsure of what they need or want and even when they are sure are incapable of knowing how to achieve it. It follows from this that in their own best interests people need to be led and guided by those equipped for the task. Political leadership, moreover is a gift — again unequally distributed — and a skill learnt through a special kind of experience. The public schools and the ancient universities are tried and tested training grounds where the values and skills of leadership are nourished and developed.

Political change: when it can no longer be resisted

Conservative attitudes towards political change, naturally, reflect their analysis of human nature as anything but saintly; their view of society as a delicate, brittle structure resting on the subtly interlocking sinews of common history, attitudes and institutions; and their belief that the purpose of politics is the achievement of liberty and self fulfilment through balance and harmony. The Conservative disposition is to conserve, to be temperamentally against change.

Traditional Conservatism rejects the system-builder like Marx, the revolutionary like Lenin or Stalin, the root and branch reformer like Tony Benn. Their grand designs founder not only upon the perversities of the masses but also their own imperfections as political leaders.

But this is not to say that all change is anathema to Conservatives: according to their analysis it is, in any case, taking place all the time. There is a chemistry at work between people in society which, as the years pass, produces change often in surprising and unforeseen ways. The politicians' task is to recognize the results of this chemistry and to make the necessary formal adjustments — to the law or institutions — to reflect the changes which have already taken place.

When is change necessary? The Duke of Cambridge used to believe that 'the time for change is when it can no longer be resisted', but the most widely shared Conservative view is that it is a matter of judgement; 'the supreme function of a politician', argues Enoch Powell, 'is to judge the correct moment for reform.'

By this stage in the chapter readers may well be asking themselves whether the ideas of Mrs Thatcher — the epitome of Conservatism during the 1980s — can be reconciled with the key tenets of party beliefs so far identified. The fact is that on all of them Mrs Thatcher had her own singular and possibly un-Conservative views.

The Impact of Thatcherism

From the outset Mrs Thatcher would brush aside R.J. White's view that Conservatism is 'not so much a political doctrine than a habit of mind, a mode of feeling, a way

Tenets of traditional Conservative thought

The purpose of politics: social harmony
Human nature imperfect and corruptible
Rule of law basis of all freedom
Social institutions create sense of society and nation
Foreign policy: pursuit of state interests in anarchic world
Liberty: the highest political end
Government: checks and balances
Property rights: first principles of justice
Equality of opportunity but not of results
Political change: when it can no longer be resisted

of living'. She is a self-proclaimed 'conviction politician' who is not afraid to call herself a rebel or even a revolutionary within a party usually associated with conformism and defence of the status quo. Her response to the tenets listed above would be along the following lines.

She would agree emphatically with the traditional conservative line on the ***rule of law***, ***property***, ***liberty*** and for the most part, ***foreign policy***. But while she would go along with much described under the other headings there would be differences — some of them crucial.

1. Thatcherites would strongly agree that the ***purpose of politics*** is to reduce government powers and give people the freedom to be themselves and develop their talents. But they would point out that, perhaps paradoxically, strong government action is necessary to curb its own interferences and may be necessary from time to time even within a reduced sphere of government responsibility. For Mrs Thatcher less government did not mean weak government. It followed that she was flatly opposed to compromise and believed in creating a consensus around her own beliefs rather than following one created by others.
2. Mrs Thatcher would share a pessimistic view of ***human nature*** but her strong Anglican Christianity (she used to be a Methodist in her youth) provides some hope of man's salvation. Her belief, moreover, that a widespread acceptance of an enterprise culture was a prerequisite for national regeneration, indicated a faith in 'social engineering' more typical — as we shall see — of socialist thinking.
3. On the machinery of ***government*** Mrs Thatcher was no radical but was less troubled than her predecessors by the need for balance — she always sought to maximize her own power within the democratic process and saw no reason why she should not just defeat socialism but — as she proclaimed before the 1987 election — obliterate it completely.
4. Mrs Thatcher saw the need for unifying social mechanisms and, of course, identified passionately with the idea of nation but she played down the view of society as a cohesive unit, preferring to see it as no more than an aggregate of individuals and their families.
5. She was strongly opposed to measures aimed at reducing economic ***inequality***

and had long argued for better material incentives to effort — the corollary of which is more rather than less inequality.

6. The Thatcher position on *elites* is ambivalent. While she would accept the need for them as self-evident she would part company with the traditional view on their composition. Unlike Mr Heath, who came from a more socially deferential working-class background, Mrs Thatcher originates from the aspiring lower middle classes. Her father, Alderman Roberts, after all worked in harness with Lord Brownlow on Grantham's behalf. She has no automatic respect for the aristocracy or for the establishment and has shown a preference for the self-made and the upwardly socially mobile.

7. It will now be clear that on the subject of *political change* Mrs Thatcher was no traditionalist. Oakeshott's 'pursuit of intimations' are not for her. Hers was a crusade to 'change the heart and soul' of the nation.

The overwhelming thrust of Mrs Thatcher's politics places her outside the main Conservative tradition of the past 200 years or more. If it can be distilled into its major canons Mrs Thatcher could be seen to be advancing those of *freedom*, *property* and *nation*. However, for *balance*, *harmony* and *pragmatism* she substituted *conviction*, *resolution* and *strength*. The remainder of this chapter will concentrate upon Thatcherite ideas upon the economy.

The economy and Thatcherism

Conservatism has always been the political expression of the free enterprise system but controversy has always existed within the party over the extent of state control which is both necessary and desirable. It was Disraeli who exhorted his party to recognize as its major objective 'the elevation of the condition of the people' and thereby become a national party representing all classes. He introduced reforming welfare legislation and curbed the ability of capitalists to neglect the interests of their work-force in their pursuit of profits. Baldwin and Chamberlain, in the inter-war years, supplemented and extended this legislation and intruded government controls and incentives into the economy to encourage growth in desired directions. Harold Macmillan, as a young Conservative MP, had no doubts that the power of the state should be used to regulate the economy in order to alleviate the kind of unemployment suffered in his constituency of Stockon-on-Tees.

Writing in *The Middle Way* (1938) Macmillan believed that 'we must advance more rapidly and still further upon the road of conscious regulation'. His book was a plea for extensive long-term economic planning to remedy the shortcomings of capitalism and for some redistribution of wealth to the poor. He rejected as destructive policies which were merely 'the reflection of the money in our pockets'. Macmillan readily accepted the ideas of Keynes who, as we have seen in the previous chapter, argued that government intervention of the right kind could deliver the advantages of capitalism while avoiding its attendant disadvantages. The experience of the war legitimized Keynesian ideas which became the basis of the post-war Butskellite consensus.

In 1945 Margaret Roberts, the young president of the Oxford Conservative Association, did not demur but by the early 1970s she most definitely did. Under

Sir Keith Joseph

Sir Keith Joseph, born January 1918, was elected to Parliament in February 1956. He stood down from his Leeds North East seat at the 1987 general election, and he was made a life peer in July 1987.

Sir Keith Joseph was a key figure in the development of Thatcherism, and in a series of speeches between 1974 and 1977 he tried to map out a new agenda for the Conservative Party. In 1974 he made the extraordinary statement that it was only when he left office in February 1974 that he became a Conservative. He claimed that previous governments had tried to do too much; they were, in a word, 'overloaded' and therefore tended to do the essential tasks of government — notably maintaining law and order and providing a stable currency — badly. The Heath Government, in its pursuit of an anti-inflation policy, had ignored money supply, which was something governments could control.

Governments should also relinquish the goal of pursuing full employment at any cost. If workers and employers set their prices and wages at 'too high' a level, then they should pay the consequences in terms of loss of markets and loss of jobs. In 1974 Sir Keith Joseph established the Centre for Policy Studies with a brief to learn lessons from successful enterprise-oriented economies like Japan and West Germany. He was also personally close to Mrs Thatcher and she gave him overall responsibility for policy while the party was in opposition.

Source: Kavanagh, 1987b

the influence of Sir Keith Joseph she gained access to the ideas of Enoch Powell, Friedrich Hayek and Milton Friedman, who believed that high inflation was the central problem upon which all other problems depended. The Thatcherite view of the economy can be summed up in a number of simple propositions.

Control of the money supply will control inflation

Milton Friedman saw a causal link between the money supply (the amount of bank notes and credit available in the economy) and inflation. If governments borrow or in effect 'print money' businessmen receiving this will not increase production but will merely push up prices, thus generating demands for more wages from the workforce. Result? Inflation. 'Inflation occurs when the quantity of money rises appreciably more rapidly than output and the more rapid the rise and the quantity of money per unit of output the greater the rate of inflation' (Friedman, p. 299).

Friedman advises that money supply should not expand at a rate beyond that of production. Governments should state their objectives clearly and stick to them resolutely using high interest rates if necessary to restrict borrowing. Trade unions will then realize that if the money is not there wage increases unmatched by production will merely cause bankruptcy and unemployment. This fear of unemployment — 'economic realism' — will therefore keep wage demands and hence inflation down. At the same time workers will know that increased productivity will increase competitiveness and, therefore, ultimately wages. For their part, businessmen perceiving that the money is not present in the economy will not be tempted to push prices up. Prices and incomes policies which work in the short term but are overwhelmed in three or four years by pent-up demands are rendered unnecessary: the market is allowed to do its proper job in being the final arbiter of prices and incomes.

Individual freedom is inseparable from the free enterprise economy

Friedrich Hayek argued that the birth of individualism, or the primacy of personal freedom and personal development which occurred in Europe some four centuries ago, had helped wrest us away from feudalism and lay the foundations of free enterprise economies. Freedom to buy, sell and accumulate property were the crucial foundations upon which many other liberties were founded. Development of this new economic system had consequently further reinforced individual liberties but in the nineteenth century the drift towards 'collectivism', or the primacy of group interests, had presented grave threats. According to Hayek what the socialists promised as the 'road to freedom' was in fact the 'high road to servitude'.

Market forces work automatically for the benefit of all

Hayek and Friedman argued that through pursuing his own selfish economic interests, man directly contributed to the good of all. As long as suppliers (e.g. manufacturers, retailers) were allowed to meet demands for goods at the price the public were prepared to pay, an invisible hand would regulate economic activity in a beneficial way. Competition among suppliers would ensure that profits were not too high through the need to keep prices as low as possible and invest in more efficient means of production. Providing it was efficient, business would prosper, employment and wealth would be maximized for all and the consumer would benefit through having a wide variety of goods made freely available at minimum prices. To work properly the market system must offer substantial rewards and severe, sure sanctions. If he succeeds a businessman makes a profit, he and his workers live comfortably; if he fails he goes bankrupt, he suffers shame, ruin and his workers become unemployed.

The social corollary of this system is inequality: rich successful entrepreneurs at one end and the poor unemployed at the other. But, Thatcherites would argue, such inequalities are more beneficial than disadvantageous. Material inequality injects dynamism into the economy, gives it a buouyancy which raises minimum as well as maximum earnings.

**The freedom
of the
individual**

I believe the essential reason for our successes has been our determination to reinstate the *individual* to his and her rightful place in society. To offer him new incentives, and opportunities to use his initiative. To deploy his talents. To enable him to achieve something. And to control his own life.

That objective has been the inspiration of the Right to Buy policy, the trade union reforms and the continuing changes to the tax structure.

It guides our massive extension of share ownership. And it is the driving force behind our social agenda in this, our third term, encompassing housing, education, local government, and now health.

And *there is so much more to do.* We cannot be satisfied until we have an output like Japan's, living standards like Germany's and a dominant national will to mobilize against crime, grime and sloth.

How should we set about doing it? There are six questions we should ask ourselves whenever we consider a policy option.

Will it enlarge freedom and extend opportunity? Will it make producers more accountable to consumers? Will it help those who want to become less dependent to take more responsibility for their own lives? Will it improve life for the worst-off in society? Will its effects be environmentally sound?

And last, but not least, will it enable individuals to make the maximum contribution to society?

Source: **John Major**, in a speech to the Radical Society, 1989

Capitalism works: state intervention destroys freedom and efficiency

It follows from the above analysis that the economy works best if left alone by government except for rudimentary financial regulation and such matters as the prevention of monopolies. Government intervention in the economy merely produces the following effects.

1. Government distribution of consumer goods does inefficiently what consumers would do more efficiently for themselves. Only consumers can or should decide what they want in terms of goods and services.
2. Government takeovers in the economic sector through nationalization take power from the consumer and give it to officials. East European 'command' economies revealed how such power leads to over-privileged, inefficient, corrupt and ultimately oppressive bureaucracies.
3. Government measures to protect employment, though well-meaning, can only be temporary palliatives and ultimately create more unemployment, not less.
4. Measures to protect the consumer are unnecessary — most consumers are capable of exercising their own judgement.
5. Through a succession of gradual interventions the government's share of the economy after the war had become far too large. The wealth-producing private sector had been squeezed more and more to support a vast array of central and local bureaucrats, loss-making nationalized industries and social services we could ill afford. Public expenditure needed to be reduced.

Trade union power endangers national interests and should be curbed

Trade unions are generally perceived by Thatcherites as undemocratic, reactionary
vested interests, often led by political extremists who use unfair coercive methods
to extract wage rises way in advance of those justified by production. Mrs Thatcher
lost few opportunities to confront trade union power and overcame it either through
industrial battles like the miners' strike or through progressively restraining legislation
throughout the 1980s.

State welfare is excessive and inefficient

Thatcherite objections to the Welfare State are threefold.

1. It is expensive and absorbs a dangerously large share of public expenditure.
2. It is morally weakening in that it engenders a reliance upon the state rather than
   the self: the so-called 'dependency culture'.
3. The new state monopolies over welfare are inefficient and deny choice. The
   flourishing state of private education and private medicine reveal that people are
   prepared to pay for a superior service.

Readers might be forgiven for seeing parallels between Thatcherism and the classical
economics of nineteenth-century Liberals. The ideas of the New Right indeed bear
a striking resemblance to those of the nineteenth-century old left. David Marquand,
in his thoughtful study *The Unprincipled Society*, believes that Conservative leadership
'turned towards a new version of the classical market liberalism of the 19th Century'
and refers to this approach as 'neo-liberalism'. There is much truth in this. Sir Rhodes
Boyson explains that he became committed to his own brand of New Right
Conservatism through reading the works of Richard Cobden when studying for his
doctorate. Woodrow Wyatt, moreover, a close friend and advisor at No. 10, wrote
in 1979 'Mrs Thatcher may see herself as a Tory but I do not'. He prefers to see
her in the same camp as John Bright, the radical nineteenth-century Liberal from
Rochdale.

   Others would argue that the provenance of her ideas are less important than their
impact. *The Economist*, a journal which has been far from uncritical of Mrs Thatcher,
offered an assesment on 7 October 1989. After reviewing the far from satisfactory
state of the economy and identifying major errors it concluded:

> Mrs Thatcher's achievement — and it is a great one — has been to articulate a few
> simple but necessary rules for British politics, when all around her were speaking in
> the conditional. The rules include a commitment to an open, market economy; a
> recognition that wealth creation is more important than redistribution, because without
> it there is precious little to distribute; a clear-eyed understanding that the world is a
> risky place, where military defences remain necessary; a determination to challenge
> the corruption of vested interests; perhaps above all, the incessant repetition that people
> must bear the consequences of their actions.

But were the main tenets of Thatcherism after eleven years of government absorbed
by the British people? The evidence of poll data suggests not. Ivor Crewe's analysis
('Has the Electorate become Thatcherite?' in Skidelsky, 1988) shows that on the

Sources of Thatcherite ideas on the economy

The seminal figures of the old welfare collectivist consensus were people who were both 'in and outers', who combined a grasp of ideas with a talent for administration. They included the Webbs, Beveridge and Keynes. The heroes of the New Right in British politics — who have undermined the old Keynesian collectivism — are Hayek, Milton Friedman, and people associated with the Centre for Policy Studies and the Institute of Economic Affairs.

An influential critic of economic planning has been **Friedrich Hayek**, born in 1899, who gained a Nobel prize for economics in 1974. He claims that the free market allows voluntarism and experiment and that society is too complex for planning. He calls himself a Classic Liberal in his emphasis on limited government. He has also said that he is not a Conservative because Conservatives are too content to preside over the status quo and do not indicate another direction. His best known books are *The Road to Serfdom* (1949) and *The Constitution of Liberty* (1960).

Milton Friedman, born 1912, gained a Nobel prize for economics in 1976 and was the most prominent critic of Keynesian economics. He argues that there is a long-term equilibrium between supply and demand and that there is a natural wage level at which people can find jobs. The trade unions may distort this wage level by pushing for higher wages, but if the money supply is properly controlled the unions are liable to price their members out of work. His most popular works are *Capitalism and Freedom* (1962) and *Free to Choose* (1980).

The Institute of Economic Affairs was founded in 1957 to influence the climate of opinion. It is now the established home of markets, economic liberalism and monetarism in Britain. It has been particularly important in publicizing the ideas of Hayek and Friedman. It argues that the role of government should be limited where markets can supply goods; governments should supply essential public goods like clean air and defence. It also believes in the importance of competitive prices and wishes to privatize the health and education services. It is particularly critical of the public sector which, it argues, expands as a result of the ambitions of vote-seeking politicians, expansionist bureaucrats and selfish interests.

Also important in promoting free market ideas have been **The Adam Smith Institute** and **The Centre for Policy Studies**. In recent years, *The Times*, *Daily Telegraph* and *The Economist* have also provided weighty support.

But ideas alone were not sufficient. Conditions were changing to produce a more sympathetic environment for these ideas. Keynesian economics seemed to have no answer to inflation. Incomes policies only worked for a short time and had unacceptable political costs as well as creating complex bureaucracy and adding to economic difficulties — for example by squeezing differentials and bearing more heavily on the public sector. The attempts to gain trade union support also had costs in terms of demands for a high social wage, tolerance of restrictive practices and low productivity, and avoidance of legislation on industrial relations.

The slow-down of economic growth combined with inflation made it difficult to finance social programmes. A sense that the old policies were no longer working was seen in 1976 when the Labour Government resorted to the International Monetary Fund (IMF), which advanced a loan on condition that the Government cut planned public expenditure, continued incomes restraint, and accepted money targets: Denis Healey was the first monetarist.

Source: Kavanagh, 1987b

Thatcherism and the economy: the principal propositions

Control of the money supply will control inflation

Individual freedom inseparable from the free enterprise economy

Market forces work automatically for the benefit of all

Capitalism works: state intervention destroys freedom and efficiency

Trade union power endangers national interests and should be curbed

State welfare excessive and inefficient

whole on a whole raft of essentially Thatcherite issues including moral values, economic priorities and pride in Britain, the electorate became *less* Thatcherite during the 1980s rather than more so. The nationwide study undertaken by Jacobs and Worcester in 1989 confirmed these findings. The MORI pollsters asked respondents to indicate support for two sets of statements: five of them 'Thatcherist' and five 'socialist'. The results were clear:

If we define Thatcherists and socialists as people who endorse at least three of those rival sets of values then 54% of British adults can be called socialists and only 34% Thatcherists.

Jacobs and Worcester, p. 30.

Mrs Thatcher's astonishing electoral victories, therefore, were not matched by success in the battle for our hearts and minds. Indeed, the reverse seems to be the case. After more than a decade of Thatcherite individualism Jacobs and Worcester concluded that:

Any political party that seeks to tap Britain's deeper values would be wise to concentrate on collective solutions.

References and Further Reading

Beer, S.H., *Britain Against Itself* (Faber, 1982).
Blake, R., *The Conservative Party from Peel to Churchill* (Fontana, 1970).
Buck, P.W., *How Conservatives Think* (Penguin, 1975).
Burke, E., *Speeches and Letters in American Affairs* (Dent, 1908).
Friedman, M., *Free to Choose* (Secker & Warburg, 1980).
Gilmour, I., *Inside Right: A Study of Conservatism* (Quartet Books, 1978).
Hailsham, Viscount, *The Conservative Case* (Penguin, 1959).
Hayek, F.A., *On Liberty* (Routledge & Kegan Paul, 1976).
Hayek, R.A., *The Road to Serfdom* (Routledge & Kegan Paul, 1979).
Jacobs, E. and Worcester, R., *We British* (Weidenfeld & Nicholson, 1990).
Joseph, K. and Sumption, J., *Equality* (John Murray, 1979).

Kavanagh, D., *Thatcherism: The End of Consensus?* (Oxford University Press, 1987a).

Kavanagh, D., 'Mrs Thatcher's influence on British politics' *Social Studies Review* (November 1987b).

Layton-Henry, Z., *Conservative Party Politics* (Macmillan, 1980).

Macmillan, H., *The Middle Way* (Macmillan, 1938).

Marquand, D., *The Unprincipled Society* (Cape, 1988).

Norton, P. and Aughey, A., *Conservatives and Conservatism* (Temple Smith, 1981).

Oakeshott, M., *Rationalism in Politics* (Methuen, 1981).

Pym, F., *The Politics of Consent* (Hamish Hamilton, 1984).

Russell, T., *The Tory Party: Its Policies, Divisions and Future* (Penguin, 1978).

Skidelsky, R., *Thatcherism* (Chatto & Windus, 1988).

White, R.J., *The Conservative Tradition* (Kaye, 1950).

This chapter draws upon material used in Jones, B., 'The Anatomy of Conservative Thought' *Teaching Politics*, pp. 56–76 (January, 1985).

9 Socialism

Bill Jones

Socialism developed as a critique and alternative to capitalism and its political expression, Conservatism. It focused upon economics as the key activity but the full sweep of its ideology provided guidance on virtually all aspects of living. The problem with socialism, however, as so often with political alternatives, is that it takes many forms and is usually riven by disagreements on the best way of proceeding. This chapter starts with a classic definition of socialism and examines the main elements of its early form before moving on to its pre- and post-Second World War forms — both of the left and the right.

> 'Plenty of materials — Plenty of labour — Plenty of machinery — and nearly everybody going short of nearly everything! . . . Let us examine the details of this insane idiotic imbecile system.'

In this way 'Owen', the hero in Robert Tressell's *The Ragged Trousered Philanthropists*, introduces his analysis of early twentieth-century capitalist society. Alan Sillitoe recalls that the Glaswegian airforce wireless operator who gave him the book when out in Malaya told him that it was the 'book that won the 1945 election for Labour'. Mr Attlee and his colleagues might have been somewhat miffed to hear their own roles in this landslide victory so minimized but they would certainly have understood the point being made. Written by a working-class building worker it represents an eloquent statement of socialism which deeply influenced inter-war Britain.

Facing his sceptical, if not scornful, work-mates Owen begins his lecture by drawing a large oblong on a wall with a charred stick. This, he informs them, was to represent the adult population of the country — all those who 'help to consume the things produced by labour'. He then divides the oblong into five to represent five classes of people:

1. *Those who do nothing*, e.g. tramps, beggars and the aristocracy.
2. *Those who do mental work* which benefits themselves and harms other people, e.g. employers, thieves, bishops, capitalists.
3. *Those who do unnecessary work* 'producing or doing things which cannot be described as the necessaries of life or the benefits of civilization': the biggest section of all, e.g. shop assistants, advertising people, commercial travellers.
4. *Those engaged in necessary work* producing 'the necessaries, refinements and comforts of life'.
5. *The unemployed*.

Underneath the oblong he then draws a small square which, he explains, is to represent

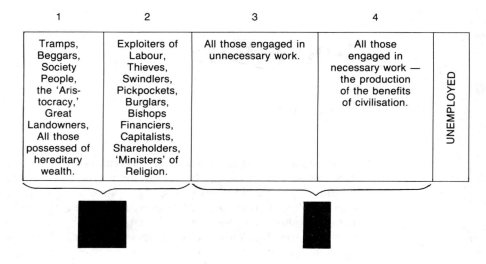

Figure 9.1 *How the things produced by people in division 4 are 'shared out' among the different classes of the population (Source: Tressell,* The Ragged Trousered Philanthropists*)*

all the goods produced by the producing class, group four. The crucial part comes next: how are these goods shared out under 'the present imbecile system'?

> As the people in divisions one and two are universally considered to be the most worthy and deserving we give them — two-thirds of the whole.
>   The remainder we give to be 'Shared Out' amongst the people represented by divisions three and four.
>   Tressell, p. 272

Owen then proceeds to point out that it is groups 3 and 4 which battle most ferociously for their third while 'most of the people who do nothing get the best of everything. More than three-quarters of the time of the working class is spent in producing the things used by the wealthy'.

Despite his eloquence Owen's workmates are reluctant to listen so, as Sillitoe observes (in his introduction to the 1965 Panther edition):

> he calls them philanthropists, benefactors in ragged trousers who willingly hand over the results of their labour to the employers and the rich. They think it the natural order of things that the rich should exploit them, that 'gentlemen' are the only people with the right to govern.

Towards the end of the book another character, Barrington, comes to Owen's assistance with his 'Great Oration'. This is his vision of a socialist society, or more precisely, Cooperative Commonwealth: nationalization of the land, railways and most forms of production and distribution; the establishment of community culture and leisure facilities; the ending of unemployment; the abolition of the police force (no need to protect the property of the rich in a socialist society); equal pay; good homes for all; automation and the reduction of the working day to 4–5 hours; free education to 21 and retirement at 45 at full pay; and the ending of military conflict world-wide.

This classic definition of socialism illustrates its distinctive elements. It issues from a fundamental set of assumptions; it provides a critique of capitalism and its related ideology; and it offers a superior form of society as an achievable alternative.

Robert Tressell (real name Noonan) wrote his book at the turn of the century having imbibed, no doubt, the main socialist ideas developed up to that time. In the early

Key dates in Marx's life

1818	Birth of Marx on 5 May in Trier, Germany
1841	Doctoral thesis on Greek philosophy approved
1842	Edits *Rheinische Zeitung*
1843	Marries Jenny in June. Writes critique of Hegel's *Philosophy of Right*
1844	Writes economic and philosophical manuscripts
1845	Drafts *The German Ideology* with Engels
1847	Joins the Communist League
1848	*Communist Manifesto* published in February in the Year of Revolutions
1848–9	Edits the *Neue Rheinische Zeitung*
1849	Moves to London in August
1852–62	London Correspondent of *New York Daily Tribune*
1864	Involved with the First International
1867	Publication of first volume of *Capital*
1871	Rise and fall of the Paris Commune
1872	Final congress of the First International
1875	Critique of the German socialist Gotha Programme
1882	Second Russian edition of *Communist Manifesto*
1883	Death of Marx in London on 13 March

Source: Hoffman (1985)

nineteenth century the doctrine was pitted against the Tories in their post-war reactionary phase. Thomas Hodgkins's justification of trade union power, *Labour Defended Against the Claims of Capital*, was an influential pamphlet. Robert Owen's experiments in cooperative industrial communities had given birth to the Cooperative Movement but socialism was embryonic at this time. It developed more muscle in matching the explicit unfettered capitalism of the early Liberals and later the One Nation Toryism of Disraeli and his successors. When Liberalism transformed into its paternalist form (see Chapter 7) socialism faced a powerful rival for the allegiance of the working classes.

The ideas of Karl Marx, William Morris, the Fabians and the Ethical Socialists were often in conflict but as Tressell's book reveals, a body of thought, called Socialism, had been assembled which had considerable coherence and force. The various elements of socialism at the turn of the century can still be perceived in more contemporary versions of the creed. Socialism begins with a critique of capitalism.

Exploitation. This notion owed much to the Labour Theory of Value — the essence of which was well expressed by Tressell. This was based on a development of Locke's Theory of Property which argued that the value of a product was the sum of the labour put into it. The person who created the value, however, the worker, received only subsistence wages and might well receive no bonus for increases in production. The owner of the means of the production, therefore, the capitalist, took a disproportionate share of the value in the form of profits, dividends, interest and rent. The workers were consequently denied what was rightfully theirs.

Inequality. As a result of the capitalist system vast differentials between rich and poor were created together with large destitute urban groups.

Personal gain and profit. Advocates of capitalism enthrone the profit motive and seek to make it a positive good through arguing that the poorest are best served by such a system. According to Marx this is part of the way in which the bourgeoisie subtly intrude their values into society, seeking to win support for the system from which they derive wealth, status and power. A complex web of mystifications are employed — patriotism, religion, economic 'commonsense' — and the worker will initially have no choice but to accept this 'false consciousness' (for fuller discussion see Concluding Comment to Part II).

Individualism. The defence of individual rights under capitalism is merely the cloak used by the ruling class to cover the exploitation of the weak by the strong.

Liberty. It follows that 'capitalist freedom' means crucially their ability to establish enterprises, employ and fire workers, extract profit and so forth.

Competition. The ruthlessness of capitalist economic processes set people against each other encouraging their darker natures.

Wage Labour. The introduction of wages as the sole reward for work:
(a) relieved the employer of historic obligations towards his workers and gave him a degree of power often amounting to tyranny;
(b) dehumanized workers into a mere economic commodity.

Appearance and reality in capitalism according to Karl Marx

In seeking employment, workers enter into a contract in which they exchange what Marx called their 'labour power' — their capacity to work — for a wage. According to market norms, this exchange is perfectly 'fair' and 'just', provided workers receive, as in all commodity exchanges, an exact equivalent for the sale of their labour power. Crucial for Marx, however, is the fact that workers of necessity receive less (why else employ them?) from the capitalist than the value of what they actually produce, and hence they are cheated of a surplus. They are exploited, but in a way which is perfectly 'fair'! (See below.) The point is that, strictly speaking, workers do not sell their 'labour' but their *labour power*, so that how much they in fact produce in the course of a contracted number of hours is none of their business. The wages they receive merely represent the value of their labour power which, as a commodity, is calculated in the same way as any other — according to the amount of labour time necessary to produce it. This means that workers are only entitled, in exchange for the sale of their labour power, to a wage which covers the cost of 'reproducing' them as human machines: the costs of food, shelter, clothing and training. The less skilled the worker, the lower this cost is deemed to be.

This is why Marx regarded the worker's freedom under capitalism as real in one sense and yet deceptive and paradoxical in another. Compelled by poverty to enter the labour market, workers are free to choose their own employer, but from a class which collectively enjoys a monopoly of capital (the kind of property which can be invested for a profit).

A fair and just process of exchange

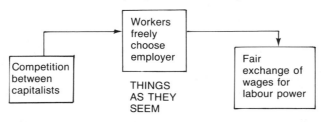

The exploitative character of capitalist production

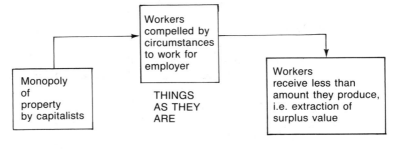

Source: Hoffman (1985)

Alienation. The urbanization associated with capitalism separates the individual from supportive family and community relationships and leaves him or her isolated and friendless.

Automation. Machinery extracts the craft from labour and turns men into mindless tenders of production lines. William Morris took this critique further arguing that mass production destroyed art and good design and created a vulgarized upper class.

Inefficiency. Capitalism, with its cyclical slumps, fluctuating levels of employment, creation of surpluses and its monopolistic tendencies, is an inefficient means of production.

Class conflict. Capitalism clearly created an owning class with its related professional groups and a working class. Karl Marx believed that all history is a story of class conflict, that conflict between classes is inevitable and *creative* in that it is the means whereby society progresses. Marx believed that capitalism would collapse when its internal contradictions reached crisis point. He argued that the process of capitalist competition would cause wages to be continually reduced, thus pauperizing the working classes and producing ever-increasing profits for the capitalist. Eventually the workers would realize the fact of their exploitation, develop a consciousness of their class interest and come together to overthrow the oppressive ruling class in some form of revolution. This doctrine of class conflict as both essential and inevitable has influenced British socialists to a degree but its appeal was limited and other schools of thought like the Fabians argued that socialism could be achieved via gradual parliamentary reform.

Principles Underlying Socialism

Leading from this critique it is possible to identify certain underlying principles.

1. *Human nature is fundamentally good.* It is the system of capitalism which distorts human consciousness and behaviour and destroys creativity.
2. *Environment creates consciousness.* It follows that the creation of a superior economic and social environment will create an improved type of human being.
3. *Fellowship.* Capitalism encourages suspicion, rivalry and conflict but under difficult conditions it is possible for men to cooperate happily together for the common good.
4. *Labour creates wealth.* The capitalists take in interest, dividends and profit, the value of which is in reality created by workers.
5. *Equality.* Men are born with equal rights; they will naturally develop in different ways but the strong should not be allowed to infringe upon the freedoms of the weak.
6. *Freedom.* In a capitalist society only the rich are free; material disadvantage prevents the poor from properly developing their potential or facing the opportunities and choices which are the essence of freedom.
7. *Collectivism.* Instead of everyone for themselves, an approach is required towards

the governance of society which recognizes the interdependence of all contributions in the productive process and recognizes the obligation of the strong to protect and support the weak, e.g. via welfare support and full employment.

8. *Happiness* is a positive good but does not consist merely of the acquisition of material goods.

9. *Efficiency.* A planned socialist economy would be more productive and efficient than capitalism.

Until the end of the First World War British Socialism remained inchoate: little more than a collection of similar but contrasting approaches. By the middle of the 1920s, however, Labour had already been in power for a brief period and took a more practical view. As G.D.H. Cole now observed, 'The ideal society that matters is not the utopia of our dreams but the best sort of society we can hope to help build out of the materials that lie ready to our hands' (Cole, 1929, p. 77). Divergent, idiosyncratic, philosophical schools of thought gave way to more pragmatic policy making as Labour measured itself for government. Socialist thinkers began to work in greater harmony, feeling their way towards what was destined to become Labour's programme of government in 1945 — a programme which has been described as 'Corporate Socialism'. It comprised the following major elements.

Keynesian economics

Keynes's emphasis on government intervention to inject investment into the economy, to manage demand through the control of taxation and other instruments appealed greatly to socialists like Ernest Bevin, Evan Durbin, Hugh Dalton and others. No matter that Keynes was a Liberal: British socialists made his most important ideas their own.

Centralized planning of the economy

Labour's Keynesian economists believed the ideas of their mentor could only be fully implemented within a planned socialist economy. In the early 1930s the Soviet Union's Five-Year Plans received enthusiastic support from the likes of Hugh Dalton — later Labour's post-war Chancellor. The idea was to create a national plan which would eliminate booms and slumps, distribute resources fairly, encourage social equality and achieve full employment.

Nationalization

The chief architect of this idea was Herbert Morrison (1888–1965) who, as Labour Minister of Transport in 1929, created a government-controlled authority to run London's transport. His idea was that government-appointed Boards should run selected areas of economic activity. They would be given considerable autonomy to run their enterprises in an efficient and business-like way, the objective being to serve the interests of ordinary working people.

Elements of corporate socialism

> Keynesian economics
>
> Centralized planning of the economy
>
> Nationalization
>
> A mixed economy
>
> Universal social services
>
> A Socialist foreign policy

Mixed economy

The precise extent of state control of the economy was not defined but most mainstream socialist theorists envisaged a mixed economy. Even the left-wing G.D.H. Cole did not believe it 'necessary to nationalize everything — heaven forbid!' (Cole, 1950, p. 53) The public sector should be large enough to be dominant, according to Cole, but he also envisaged a powerful private sector.

Social services

In his book *Equality*, R.H. Tawney had been concerned with inequalities caused by privilege in the areas of health and education. He called for state action to improve schools at all levels plus a national approach to health improvement. Most socialists welcomed the Beveridge proposals outlined in 1942.

A socialist foreign policy

Under the influence of radical Liberals who joined the Labour Party after the First World War, Labour based its foreign policy upon:

(a) collective security via the League of Nations;
(b) a pacifistic policy which supported disarmament. This led Labour to oppose rearmament under Conservative rule despite the threat posed by Hitler;
(c) support for alliances to curb the growth of Nazi Germany.

Left wing Dissent to this emergent programme was strident and continuous, especially during the 1930s. Neo-Marxists like Harold Laski could not believe that capitalism would meekly stand by while a transition to socialism took place. He urged socialists to prepare for strong opposition — even a counter-revolution. Nor did he believe the machinery of the state could be neutral, embedded as its servants were in the existing elite power structure. Left-wingers were worried by certain aspects of Keynesian socialism, especially its acceptance that wage labour and a substantial privately owned sector of the economy should continue. The left were also dismayed by the emphasis of 'corporate socialism' on centralized administrative efficiency rather than decentralized democratic workers control. Despite their vivid rhetoric, however, the left in the 1930s did not wield decisive strength: the block trade union votes at party conferences ensured that corporate socialism became official party policy.

The war also helped. The near-military efficiency of the war effort at home reinforced corporatists in that:

1. It vindicated centralized planning, government intervention in the economy and control of industry.
2. It demonstrated how resources, for example via rationing, could be consciously allocated on the basis of fairness.
3. Keynesian ideas became orthodoxy during the war and their leading Labour advocates — Morrison, Dalton, Bevin — gained enhanced prestige through their ministerial roles in the Coalition Government.

When Labour won its landslide victory in 1945 there was no real obstacle to the implementation of corporatist socialism: a mixed economy with extensive nationalization; universal social services with the health service at the centre; centralized management of the economy with full employment; and close involvement of the trade unions in the process of government.

Labour's experience of power had a profound effect upon its ideology. For some, theory had become almost irrelevant: Herbert Morrison is famous for saying that 'Socialism is what a Labour government does'. For many intellectuals within the Labour Party this ultimately cynical pragmatism was not acceptable. They preferred to redefine corporatism into what has commonly become known as 'Revisionism'.

Revisionism

Leading Revisionists both in theory and practice were Evan Durbin (before his tragic death in 1948), Douglas Jay, John Strachey (converted from neo-Communism during the war), Hugh Dalton, Hugh Gaitskell, Roy Jenkins, Harold Wilson, Dennis Healey and, most important of all, Anthony Crosland. Crosland's book *The Future of Socialism* (1956) suggested that the original focus of socialism, the economy, had radically changed and that the whole socialist strategy needed to be amended accordingly. The revisionist case was as follows.

Marxist predictions proved wrong

Far from collapsing as Marx had predicted, post-war capitalism appeared to be in robust health and enjoying an unprecedented period of growth. They also believed that Marx's prediction that the working classes would become increasingly 'immiserated' had been disproved: the working classes had become richer, sharing in the increased wealth.

Working class strengthened by full employment

A 'revolutionary change' according to Crosland had occurred, whereby workers now spoke to employers and government on an equal footing.

Business class weakened by a number of factors

These included: an expanding public sector as a result of Labour reform; far-reaching government controls over the economy, e.g. high taxation of incomes and profits; and the development of different, more cooperative attitudes by businessmen towards society. Crosland argued that capitalism had been changed and tamed — largely through Keynesian economic thought and a dominant public sector — into a more benevolent beast.

Ownership of the economy no longer relevant

Since the development of the Joint Stock Company, argued Crosland, financial ownership in the form of shareholders had been separated from day to day control. Business was now conducted by a new class of salaried managers for whom profits were not the sole objective. We did not really have a 'capitalist' economy any more; only 3 per cent of personal income was provided by dividend payments.

Nationalization not necessarily the most effective means of achieving socialist ends

The Scandinavian countries, argued Crosland, had shown that 'wholesale nationalization is not a necessary condition for greater equality'. Sweden had a privately owned economy but an open egalitarian society, while the Soviet Union had common ownership but a closed and in many ways inegalitarian society. Crosland believed that in any case there were many alternatives to public ownership, e.g. workers' control, local authority enterprises and so on.

Marxism an alien creed

Labour's close emotional support for the Soviet Union after 1917 and its concomitant sense of ideological affinity with a 'socialist' country was severely damaged by Stalin's perceived hegemonic policy in Eastern Europe after the war. This hardened Labour's traditional antipathy towards ideological approaches (see Jones 1977). Revisionists now made their opposition to this 'alien' and undemocratic creed loudly explicit.

Notions of a socialist foreign policy misconceived

The perceived hostility of the USSR post-war undermined socialist ideas that 'left can speak unto left' and that the great powers could introduce a workable world-wide collective security system. Some revisionists began to abandon completely any adherence to a distinctly socialist foreign policy and were joined by the Conservatives in supporting Ernest Bevin's (Labour Foreign Secretary 1945–50) mobilization of a US–European alliance against Stalin and his East European satellites.

A vigorous egalitarian social policy

The revisionist analysis of the economy and post-war society was fundamentally optimistic. It accepted a pluralist mixed economy and discerned a 'responsible' private sector. Crosland, however, believed that socialism should be more than 'Keynes-

Elements of revisionism	Marxist predictions proved wrong
	Working class strengthened by full employment
	Business class weakened
	Ownership of economy no longer relevant
	Nationalization not necessarily most effective means of achieving socialism
	Marxism an alien creed
	Notions of Socialist foreign policy misconceived
	A vigorous egalitarian social policy

plus-modified-capitalism-plus-welfare-state'. He laid great stress on the importance of welfare spending for the alleviation of distress and poverty but he called for a different kind of approach for the reduction of inequality in society: like Tawney he believed equality to be the foremost objective of socialism. Crosland was accordingly a trenchant critic of the British class system and believed it should be subverted from within via the educational system. He argued for the abolition of the 11-plus examination, the introduction of coeducational comprehensive schools and the expansion of university places. Though he did not use the term Crosland believed class could be abolished through 'social engineering': altering consciousness via institutional change.

Twenty years on the fatal flaw in Revisionism had been revealed: it was dependent upon continuing economic expansion. Crosland had felt confident in the 1950s that the problem of material plenty had been solved through Labour's mix of a dominant public sector and a vigorous private sector. Socialism, according to him, should henceforth concern itself with the achievement of social justice and equality through the mechanisms of social policy.

Britain's decline in the 1960s was cruelly exposed and accelerated by the rise in oil prices at the beginning of the next decade, precipitating a crisis which Labour could barely contain let alone solve. Cartwheeling inflation of prices and wages was tackled by an incomes policy whereby trade unions agreed to restrain wage demands within an annually agreed norm: the so-called 'Social Contract'. In 1976 Callaghan disavowed Keynesian economics when he informed the Party Conference that higher government spending in current conditions was more likely to produce inflation than higher output. In 1974 Crosland reviewed Labour's lack of progress (*Socialism Now*) but concluded that the original direction charted by him in the 1950s was fundamentally correct: what was needed were measures to achieve a higher level of production plus a firmer political resolve.

The Left

The post-war development of left-wing socialist thought is more complex than that of the centre right. As explained above, the corporate socialism of Attlee was merely refined by the Revisionists and applied in practice by both the Wilson and Callaghan governments. The left, however, moved through several phases and was subject to many influences — an historical approach is therefore appropriate.

1945—70

While the Attlee government set about its radical domestic programme left-wing Labour dissent in Parliament concentrated upon foreign policy. Ernest Bevin's desire to seek US support against Britain's 'socialist' former wartime ally was opposed by pacifists who disagreed with such power political manoeuvrings as likely to encourage further conflict; crypto-communists who believed Soviet intentions were being cruelly misjudged; and by the Keep Left group, led by Michael Foot, Richard Crossman and Ian Mikardo, who urged the creation of a neutral Third Force to preempt the creation of a bipolar world. Soviet actions in Eastern Europe, culminating in the Berlin Blockade, presaged the formation of NATO in 1949. By then some of the crypto-communists had been expelled, pacifist support depleted and Keep Left fatally split.

Foreign policy, however, provided a link with domestic policy for left-wingers in 1951. In that year Chancellor Gaitskell proposed a number of measures to help increase defence expenditure in the light of the Korean War. Aneurin Bevan, Harold Wilson and John Freeman resigned over the proposed introduction of national health charges for spectacles and false teeth. Once in opposition Bevan led the fundamentalist fight against emergent revisionist ideas in the Labour party. He disagreed that ownership was irrelevant and did not believe that capitalism had been tamed. He opposed complete state ownership but envisaged a mixed economy in which the state would control the 'commanding heights' of the economy. He argued, moreover, that Keynesian financial controls were no substitute for the direct control of nationalization. Accordingly, Bevan was not greatly taken with workers' control ideas, preferring centralized government boards. On foreign policy he favoured a neutral third force, in keeping with early Keep Left proposals, and until his famous *volte face* in 1957 he was opposed to Britain's nuclear deterrent.

Bevan's views then were closer to the corporate socialism of 1945 — before it became sullied by pragmatism, the compromises of office and revisionist dilutions. According to him there was nothing wrong with the strategy which a reassertion of political will could not put right. Maybe this was Bevan's key argument: his powerful charismatic personality commanded great loyalty and exuded the very political will for which he argued. The fact that Gaitskell too was a 'conviction politician' merely ensured several years of bitter intra-party dispute. The sudden disappearance of both personalities through untimely deaths left the field open for Harold Wilson in 1963.

The Bevanite revolt against revisionism	Ownership of economy not irrelevant Capitalism not tamed by changes to date Socialist control of the economy necessary More nationalization necessary Britain as a part of a neutral third force in international affairs

Wilson initially appeared to provide the dynamism which the left craved but his stirring emphases on socialist modernization and his attacks upon the independence of Britain's nuclear deterrent proved in office a cloak for continuity in revisionist form. The left suffered through lack of leadership but Bevan's critique was maintained by the Tribune group in Parliament and supplemented later in the decade by furious attacks upon Wilson's tacit support for US actions in Vietnam. The strength of the post-war consensus ensured that left-wing opposition was essentially a sideshow — albeit a noisy and colourful one — both in the 1950s and for much of the 1960s. The flagging economy, however, and industrial unrest created acute problems for Wilson in the late 1960s and promised to make the 1970s a turbulent decade.

1970—81

Labour's period of opposition (1970—4) and the continuing economic crisis ensured that the left for once received a sympathetic hearing within the trade union movement. Some left-wingers like Michael Foot sustained the Bevanite challenge but during the 1970s the mainstream of left-wing thinking was influenced by a number of new impulses. The result was not a coherent alternative to revisionism but rather a series of interacting critical theses.

Anti-corporatism

Rather like the Thatcherite right, left-wingers attacked what they believed to be the undemocratic and inefficient consequences of the post-war party political consensus. According to Tony Benn 'corporatism' is the system whereby leaders of the big power groups — trade unions, civil service, business and government — form a self-sustaining elite. Meeting in secret committees they reach agreements which are then imposed upon the rest of society, often backed up by legislation. Others like Ralph Miliband argued that by joining the corporatist political structure the Labour Party was in effect becoming the agent of capitalism: instead of articulating working-class interests and demands Labour was now managing them — drawing their sting.

Workers' control

The centralized bureaucracies of the nationalized industries came in for considerable criticism from the left. Benn conceded that they had been disappointing — merely recreating the old structures under state control. He called for a more imaginative approach to public ownership (not unlike Crosland's), for example, local councils, state shareholdings and worker cooperatives.

Socialist control via the state

This new emphasis on decentralized workers' control did not mean that the left had abandoned its belief in centralized state control: far from it. But the rationale and the favoured procedures had altered. Multi-national companies were now perceived as major threats to working-class interests and to national sovereignty. Responsible for a growing percentage of economic activity, multi-nationals owed loyalty only to the profit motive. In its pursuit they were prepared to drive unfair bargains with governments and scour the world for cheap quiescent labour-forces and minimum state controls. In his *Socialist Challenge* (1975) Stuart Holland argued that only governments had the financial and political clout to stand up to the skilful manipulations of multi-nationals and prevent these new juggernauts of international capitalism from extracting profits and siphoning off investment which should rightfully be used to regenerate the home economy. Holland played a part in drawing up Labour's 1973 programme which called for a controlling state interest in Britain's twenty-five largest companies and for 'a fundamental and irreversible shift in the balance of power and wealth in favour of working people and their families'.

Participatory democracy

A belief in and call for participatory democracy clearly underlies the notion of workers' control but for Tony Benn it provides the central focus of his philosophy. He believes it is morally right that people should be involved with decisions which affect them and that when they are, better decisions and more effective action ensues. Working people, he argues, have been led to believe that the 'educated' elite knows best: but in reality working people do know what is right for them and only need the opportunity to help shape their own destinies. Benn's belief in the curative powers of democracy applies to all levels of social and economic activity.

Extra-parliamentary activity

Along with Miliband, Heffer, Arthur Scargill and others Benn also argues that Labour needs to encourage extra-parliamentary activity to keep in touch with working people and help generate a mass popular political movement. This means supporting workers in their fight for better pay and conditions; mustering support among the network of single issue groups which sprang up during the 1970s; and seeking the support of groups of people struggling for justice. These last include:

1. **Women.** A number of radical women including Juliet Mitchell and Hilary Wainwright articulated the interests of women as a social group, challenging as shortsighted the established socialist view that social class was the most important division in society. Gender, they argued, was equally important and should be reflected in Labour policies.
2. **Minority groups.** Other sections of the Labour movement began to argue forcefully that black groups, recent immigrants and gay people were among the minorities most discriminated against and therefore deserving of special support.

Rejection of capitalist culture

Intellectuals associated with the journal *New Left Review* (founded in 1957) such as E.P. Thompson and Raymond Williams focused particular attention on values and culture. They were repelled by the emphasis on the accumulation of material goods, the achievement of individual success and the assimilation of selfish capitalist values to the exclusion of cooperation and sharing. They believed Labour had not changed the prevailing values of society but had been absorbed by them. The post-war consensus, in other words, preserved capitalism's values; Labour had been instrumental in this through helping to form the consensus. Won over by the material plenty of the post-war world workers were not inclined to challenge the axioms of the time.

Welfare state has not abolished poverty

A comfortable element in the post-war consensus, reflected in revisionism, was that poverty had been more or less eliminated in Britain. A series of empirical surveys in the 1960s by Richard Titmus, Brian Abel Smith, Peter Townsend and others suggested that this was far from the truth. Their evidence suggested that inequalities of income had actually increased during the 1950s and that the middle classes had benefited disproportionately from the state educational and health services. They also argued that the professionalized welfare bureaucracies were often exercising arbitrary power over society in an unaccountable fashion.

Unilaterialism and anti-Americanism

After its short-lived success in 1960 CND faded but made an astonishing comeback in the late 1970s and early 1980s in response to the escalation of the nuclear arms race. Many unilateralists also called for withdrawal from NATO and the adoption of a neutral policy independent of the two super-powers, but others argued that a non-nuclear defence policy is not inconsient with membership of NATO. Left-wing opposition to the Anglo−US alliance, however, was not matched — until the appearance of Gorbachev as leader in 1985 — by sympathy or support for the USSR; indeed most left-wingers (with some maverick exceptions) strongly condemned communist governments as brutal tyrannies.

Democratize Parliament

Some left-wing intellectuals like Ralph Miliband have criticized the deference accorded to Parliament by the Labour movement. According to him Parliament is part of the apparatus of a capitalist state and participation within it merely makes Labour a managing agent of capitalist interests. Tony Benn, however, tends to share Bevan's enthusiasm for the institution and his belief that it can be used as the instrument for a socialist transformation of Britain. But Benn is highly critical of the undemocratic nature of our parliamentary system. He points out that only the House of Commons is elected, while the other two elements of Parliament, the House of Lords and the Crown, are appointed on a hereditary basis. The Prime Minister,

Elements of Left-wing thinking in the 1970s	Anti-corporatism
	Workers' control
	Socialist control via the state
	A participatory democracy
	Extra-parliamentary activity
	Rejection of capitalist culture
	Welfare state has not abolished poverty
	Unilateralism and anti-Americanism
	Democraticize Parliament

moreover, has been able to inherit many powers from the monarch especially in foreign affairs and in appointments to a large number of important jobs. These powers, buttressed by a majority in the House of Commons, make the occupant in No. 10 Downing Street the equivalent of a medieval monarch.

Current Labour Party Thought

In the wake of Labour's 1979 defeat I remember talking to an old member of the Communist party who enthusiastically welcomed Mrs Thatcher. At last, he argued, the British people would have a chance of seeing capitalism in its true colours. Once they had fully appreciated how ruthless and cruel the system really was, the working class would at last see where its true interests lay: after a period of disillusion and hardship they would rally to the cause of genuine left-wing socialism. It did not quite work out that way.

The Labour party certainly swung to the left after 1979, radically altering its constitution in 1981 and electing Michael Foot as its leader. Its left-wing manifesto in 1983, however, was decisively rejected by the electorate. Neil Kinnock, fiery left-winger of the 1970s, now become leader, pledging that such a debacle would not happen again. Four years later it did. Kinnock resolved to shift Labour decisively towards the revisionist centre ground. *The Times* columnist, Ronald Butt, commented on the irony: 'So Mr. Kinnock, a child of the left, was blown to power on the wind of his socialist rhetoric only to find that after two election defeats he must offer

Meet the Challenge, Make the Change: The Labour Party under Neil Kinnock has shifted decisively towards the revisionist centre ground.

something different, representing a retreat from socialism, if he is to get power' (7 August 1988). In the wake of three election defeats Kinnock clearly believed that the Party's existing leftist programme had been decisively rejected. He opposed Benn and Scargill's insistence that the answer was even more socialist radicalism as 'ultra leftist Disneyland where insurrection and general strikes are supposed to bring capitalism crashing to the ground'. He announced a major review of all policy areas. In February 1988 he and Roy Hattersley published a 'statement on democratic socialist aims and values' which asserted the following:

1. *Liberty.* 'The true purpose of socialism . . . is the protection and extension of individual liberty.'
2. *Redistribution of power and wealth.* 'Unless we have the power to choose the right to choose has no value . . . Many, perhaps most of our citizens are deprived of the full right to choose because of the unequal distribution of power as well as wealth.' This point draws upon the central thesis of books by Roy Hattersley (*Choose Freedom*) and Bryan Gould (*Socialism and Freedom*).
3. *Change should benefit all.* 'Our task is to ensure that in our lifetime change brings benefits which are available to everyone.'
4. *Popular control.* 'Working men and women' should be 'offered the opportunity to achieve both a real stake in and real influence over the industries and services in which they are employed.'
5. *A degree of positive discrimination.* 'The full emancipation of both women and the ethnic minorities demands special measures to elevate their standing and status.'
6. *Individual rights.* 'Socialism is the gospel of individual rights but it is not the doctrine of callous individualism.'
7. *Power of state and freedom.* 'We do not believe in the intrusive state.'
8. *Centralized distribution opposed.* Centralized distribution of goods is held to be a denial of consumer rights in a free society.
9. *Control of markets.* The government needs to intervene to ensure genuine competition and fair wages and prevent defrauding of the consumer.

In May 1988 seven Labour party study groups produced papers on the productive and competitive economy; people at work; economic equality; consumers in the community; democracy for the individual; Britain and the world; and the physical and social environment. These papers, which fell within the framework of the statement on *Aims and Values*, were accepted by the NEC but attracted predictably strong criticism from the hard left who accused Kinnock of abandoning Clause IV and embracing the market economy.

A year later Labour produced its final version of its policy review for the 1990s: *Meet the Challenge, Make the Change*. This document reinforced the acceptance of market forces. 'The economic role of modern government is to help make the market system work properly where it can, will and should — and to replace or strengthen it where it can't, won't or shouldn't.' The emphasis was placed upon the consumer rather than the producer; Britain's future was seen to lie within the European Community — a contrast to earlier anti-EEC views; the House of Lords was to be reformed rather than abolished; protection of the environment was given priority; and defence policy was shifted decisively from unilateralism towards multilateral disarmament.

In May 1990 Labour produced a shorter manifesto-length document entitled *Looking to the Future* which nudged the party even more firmly into the centre ground: 'We welcome and endorse the efficiency and realism which markets can provide. The difference between ourselves and the Conservatives is not that they accept the market and we do not, but that we recognize the limits of the market and they do not . . . We will not spend, nor will we promise to spend more than Britain can afford.'

The history of the 1980s demonstrates an extraordinary ideological pilgrimage by the Labour party. First it moved sharply to the left, as my old Communist party friend had predicted. But when this failed to deliver electoral success in 1983 it slowly but surely moved into the centre ground, occupying positions more familiarly held by the Liberals and the much-reviled SDP. Mrs Thatcher once said that the only consensus in which she was interested was one built around her own views. The direction of Labour's policy rethink suggests that her wish was granted. After 1945 the Conservatives tacked into 'the middle ground' between their traditional views and the new dominant values of corporate socialism. Forty years later it is Labour which finds itself shifting towards a dominant Conservative position. The additional, uncomfortable irony for Labour is that upon his accession to power John Major set about 'stealing' some of Labour's hard-won new policy positions on education, Europe, the poll tax and other issues.

The hard left are right to argue that it was only when the Conservatives stopped tacking and reasserted their traditional ideology that they began to win the political battle. But Labour lacked an advocate with Mrs Thatcher's gifts and an economic crisis of a severity which invalidated the legitimacy of government policy. In 1979 it was the 'winter of discontent' which delivered victory to Mrs Thatcher. In 1983 it was the extraordinary circumstances of the Falklands War which saw her home but in 1987 it was a widespread feeling that Mrs Thatcher's recipe for the economy was finally beginning to work. As long as the Conservatives can convince the electorate that they've 'never had it so good' left-wing socialist alternatives will find little purchase within Labour's leadership, let alone the public mind.

References and Further Reading

Beer, M., *History of British Socialism* (Bell, 1929).
Benn, T., *Arguments for Socialism* (Penguin, 1979).
Callaghan, J., *Socialism in Britain since 1884* (Blackwell, 1990).
Cole, G.D.H., *The Next Ten Years* (Macmillan, 1929).
Cole, G.D.H., *Socialist Economics* (Gollancz, 1950).
Crick, B., *Socialism* (Oxford University Press, 1987).
Crosland, C.A.R., *The Future of Socialism* (Cape, 1956).
Crosland, C.A.R., *Socialism Now* (Cape, 1974).
Foote, G., *The Labour Party's Political Thought: A History* (Croom Helm, 1986).
Gould, B., *Socialism and Freedom* (Macmillan, 1985).
Hattersley, R., *Choose Freedom: the Future for Democratic Socialism* (Penguin, 1987).
Hodgkin, T., *Labour Defended Against the Claims of Capital* (Labour Publishing Co., 1922).
Hoffman, J., 'The life and ideas of Karl Marx', *Social Studies Review* (November 1985).

Holland, S., *The Socialist Challenge* (Quartet, 1975).

Jones, B., *The Russia Complex* (Manchester University Press, 1977).

Labour Party, *Labour's Programme* (1976).

Labour Party, *Labour Manifesto* (1979, 1983, 1987).

Labour Party, *Meet the Challenge, Make the Change* (1989).

Labour Party, *Looking to the Future* (1990).

Mackenzie, N., and Mackenzie, J. *The First Fabians* (Quartet, 1979).

Pimlott, B., *Fabian Essays in Socialist Thought* (Heinemann, 1984).

Seyd, P., *The Rise and Fall of the Labour Left* (Macmillan, 1987).

Tressell, R., *The Ragged Trousered Philanthropists* (Panther, 1965; first published 1914).

Wright, A., *British Socialism* (Longman, 1983).

10 The Centre Ground

Bill Jones

In the late 1980s the centre ground of British politics was crowded with the Liberal Democrats, the languishing but still extant Social Democratic Party (SDP) and the rightward-moving Labour party, seeking to find electorally favourable ground on which to fight. In addition 1989 saw the emergence of the Green party as a major player on the political stage, attracting support from right and left and the undecided centre. By the summer of 1990 Labour had managed to steal still more of the Liberal Democrats' clothes and the demise of the SDP in that year further boosted Labour's opinion poll recovery. This chapter covers the Liberal Democrats as the heirs of modern Liberalism, the nine-year history of the SDP as the development of revisionist socialism and investigates the surprisingly radical ideas of the Greens.

The SDP and Liberal Democrats

The Liberals and SDP fought much of the 1980s as the Alliance and in 1987 formally merged to form the Social and Liberal Democrats (later known as the Liberal Democrats), but the intellectual antecedants of their policy can only be found through examining the post-war Liberals and the SDP separately.

Post-war liberalism

The Liberal party applied to post-war conditions principles similar to those which underpinned the New Liberalism (discussed in Chapter 7).

Individual liberty

This remained at the heart of Liberal thinking. It explained their vehement opposition to what they regarded as the erosion of civil liberties and freedom of speech under Mrs Thatcher and also explains their enthusiasm for thoroughgoing *decentralization* in political and economic life as the best safeguard for the civilian against centralized bureaucratic control, whether by Conservatives or Labour.

The need for equality

In accordance with Liberal traditions Jo Grimond believed that 'given a decent minimum (Liberals) are not afraid of some resultant material inequality' but he also found 'something absolutely distasteful about too much inequality' and in the 1980s most Liberals believed that Mrs Thatcher's policies had created this state of affairs. The Liberal vision remained one of a classless society based around middle-class values. They do not wish to become identified with any class-based sectional interests like business or trade unions. The American writer Samuel Beer comments that for the Liberals 'the middle class was the class that would bring all classes, all hierarchy to an end' (Beer, p.37).

A mixed economy

Liberals favoured private enterprise 'unequivocally' as an 'important freedom and a protection for private liberties which will wither if the state takes too much power into its own hands' (Grimond, p.42). Liberals were in favour of a 'mixed' and not a state-owned economy in which economic criteria are the servants of human needs and liberties. They favoured progressive taxation, decentralization of large companies, profit-sharing schemes, workers' control, long-term incomes policies (possibly with a statutory basis), small businesses, especially cooperatives, and strong precautions against the growth of monopolies. Liberals argued that trust and cooperation between workers and management on the shop floor would help reduce the entrenched class differences which manifest themselves so intractably at the national level. Latterly some Liberals began to address themselves to the problems of a post-industrial society, experimenting with ideas of negative economic growth and the 'green' ideas of ecologists.

A developed welfare state

Post-war Liberals were in favour of an efficient welfare state providing a safe minimum for all, but they feared too much paternalism as a threat to liberty and their commitment to freedom and individualism prevented them from urging the outright abolition of private arrangements like public schools.

A democratized system of government

The Liberals continued to champion reforms to democratic institutions. They favoured reform but not abolition of the House of Lords and devolution of power from Westminster to a federal system of elected regional assemblies. They placed great emphasis on 'community politics', involving people in grass-roots issues and encouraging them to be active. Their major constitutional objective, however, was to introduce proportional representation, to break the undemocratic monopoly of Conservative and Labour and give themselves a chance to win power.

International and foreign policy

The failure of the League of Nations and of inter-war disarmament proposals did not dim Liberal enthusiasm for the United Nations after 1945 or for the ideas of a politically united Europe which they passionately advocated from the 1940s onwards and believed could be achieved through the evolution of the EEC. Liberals stressed the need for overseas aid, an echo of Cobden perhaps, and defended free trade as a way of protecting and nurturing Third World economies. Liberals preferred federal structures which dilute the strength of national frontiers but they favoured a strong defence policy with support for an independent nuclear deterrent for Britain.

One of the party's historians has written 'there is much of the atmosphere of a Greek tragedy. What failed was not Liberalism but Liberals' (Watkins, 1966). While political feuds and poor judgement robbed the party of political power its ideas on liberty, the economy, welfare and foreign affairs have been pillaged by other parties and have helped shape not just British politics but also international events. Keynes and Beveridge were the two pillars on which the post-war consensus was founded and yet their own political party derived no benefit from this. Liberals in the twentieth century consistently won the political arguments but consistently lost the political battles. Perhaps their lack of success can be attributed to an absence of obvious central themes in the way that socialism has common ownership and welfarism or conservatism has free enterprise and defence of private property. Eccleshall perceives a common thread running through Liberal thought from Locke onwards.

> The history of Liberalism reveals a succession of strategies to extend rights which, it is judged, will secure the economic and moral independence of individuals. Running through the varieties of liberalism, therefore, is a picture of a *one class society of self governing citizens*. The Liberal ideal is of a community where, despite inequalities of wealth, there exists a common morality of self discipline and mutual respect.
>
> Eccleshall, 1984, p. 49

Perhaps the crucial weakness of this position in modern times has been that appeals to values and morality are insufficient to attract votes if they are not obviously allied to sectional interests. The principal electoral advantages of Labour and Conservatives are that they can still rely upon the support of a fair proportion of their respective

Post-war Liberalism — a Greek tragedy? As Leader of the Liberal Party, David Steel presided over the Alliance with Dr David Owen's Social Democratic Party, only to call for separation after a less than successful 1987 General Election campaign.

Modern liberalism

> Individual liberty
>
> The need for equality
>
> A mixed economy
>
> A developed welfare state
>
> A democratized system of government
>
> International foreign policy

class constituencies. Liberals were not able to establish any heartlands of support and in consequence lost further credibility from not being perceived as a party which could conceivably win power.

It remains to be seen if Paddy Ashdown as the leader of the Liberal Democrats can confect a new and attractive version of the Liberal message.

The Social Democratic party

On 1 August, 1980, Shirley Williams, David Owen and William Rodgers published an open letter to the Labour party in *The Guardian*: the famous 'Gang of Three' statement. It followed in the wake of Roy Jenkins's Dimbleby Lecture in which he had suggested that a new Centre party might 'break the mould' of British politics. Such proposals had been floated from time to time, most notably by Dick Taverne who briefly sat as the 'Democratic Labour' MP for Lincoln in 1973. The Gang of Three opposed such an initiative on the grounds that a Centre party would 'lack roots and coherent philosophy', but they warned that if Labour's drift away from 'democratic and internationalist' principles continued they might have to reconsider their position.

After the Wembley Conference in January 1981, which pushed through measures strengthening the control of (predominantly) left-wing party activists over the election of the leadership and the reselection of MPs, the three ex-Cabinet ministers joined Jenkins in creating the Social Democratic Party. Over the ensuing months more than thirty centre-right Labour MPs joined plus a goodly number of peers and other figures — not forgetting one solitary Conservative MP. *The Guardian* article had called for a 'relevant programme offering a radical alternative to Tory policies, one that would take into account the changes in the world in recent years'. Such a programme was to be offered within the framework of a Labour party 'firmly committed to parliamentary democracy, rejecting the class war, accepting the mixed economy and the need to manage it efficiently and attaching importance to the ideals of freedom, equality and social justice.'

The SDP fought the 1983 election in alliance with the Liberals, gaining 26 per cent of the vote, but their high hopes were dashed in 1987 when they only mustered 22 per cent. The resultant merger negotiations split the SDP into 'Owenite' and 'Mergerite' camps and appeared to disperse finally the heady optimism which had attended its birth. During its brief life, did the SDP truly offer a 'radical alternative'? Certainly SDP members elaborated on *The Guardian* 'manifesto' in a spate of articles and books. Shirley Williams in *Politics is for People* drew heavily upon the ideas of Robert Owen and R.H. Tawney, while David Owen in *Face the Future* drew upon Mill, William Morris and G.D.H. Cole. Both authors fully acknowledged a debt to the Fabians and to Anthony Crosland. Despite the fact that Owen edited out of the paperback version some uses of the word 'socialism' which had appeared in the original hardback when Owen was still in the Labour Party, he still saw himself as a socialist in 1982. It is doubtful, however, if he would have sustained this claim in 1987 when his views on the 'social market' had been further developed.

The SDP's critique

As the SDP was born out of dissension it is hardly surprising that its critique of the existing political system should be a prominent, perhaps the most prominent, element in its thinking. Inevitably, Thatcherism was strongly opposed but much of the party's initial fire — predictably strongly reciprocated — was reserved for erstwhile colleagues.

Labour controlled by the Left

The Gang of Three bitterly attacked the attempt of the 'Bennite' hard left to commit Labour to 'inflexible policies based on bureaucratic centralism and state control, policies that offer no improvement in the quality of life in Britain and appeal only to a doctrinaire minority of party supporters'.

Two-party anachronistic system

An early advocate of a Centre party, Dick Taverne, believed the two-party system represented the politics of a vanished age and had 'no more relevance than the civil war between the Cavaliers and the Roundheads' (Taverne, p.171). Brian Magee, a later convert, condemned the system for being unrepresentative: 'maddened by persistent failure, parties have moved to the extremes, leaving nearly half the population unrepresented.'

Anti-Corporatism

According to David Owen (on this point echoing Tony Benn), Callaghan's minority government ran out of ideas and energy and resorted to elitist 'fixing' or 'corporatism'.

Values

Despite the fact that it is hard to find a clear statement on the topic the values of Social Democrats reflected their views on human nature. They appeared to believe that human beings are selfish, perverse, illogical, motivated by personal gain and advancement and capable of great evil. Shirley Williams quotes Kant: 'Out of the crooked timber of humanity, no straight thing can ever be made.' Yet she does not see this as necessarily a pessimistic assessment; human beings are also capable of great altruism and self-sacrifice. Social Democrats argued that this analysis was realistic and balanced: they were aware of the limitations imposed by human nature but believed that the right political approach could help realize the enormous potential for good in men and women. Such an approach needed to be founded on the following values.

Defence of liberty and pursuit of equality

Social Democrats recognised that liberty was to some extent a function of equality yet also potentially a victim of it. Individuals should be protected from the growing power of the bureaucratic centralized state and this freedom should not be sacrificed to state attempts to impose equality: 'The record of state controlled societies in overcoming inequality is not such as to make any thinking democrat change his or her disposition for liberty' (Owen, 1981 p.7). Williams quotes Tawney on this topic: 'The supreme goods of civil and political liberty' should not be 'part of the price' of achieving socialism (Williams, 1981 p.24). Social Democrats, therefore, were not so much in favour of equality as reducing inequality.

National unity through lessening of class differences

Peter Jenkins, one-time SDP sympathizer, expressed a characteristic belief when he wrote '. . . the British people remain, for the most part, pragmatic, moderate and reformist; by custom and instinct they are middle-of-the-roaders . . .' (*The Guardian*, 9 July 1980). This belief underpinned the SDP's critique of the excessively ideological nature of the two parties in the early 1980s, but it also informed the party's desire to reduce class differences. Roy Jenkins, for example, believed that the class war rhetoric of Parliament encouraged unnecessary conflicts between workers and management on the shop floor. By reviving the political centre the SDP hoped to attract the supporters from both major parties who were unhappy with the ideological polarizations of the time.

Realism and gradual change

Taverne argued that social democracy should not offer too much: 'No party has a monopoly of wisdom' (Taverne, p.171). He urged a pragmatic, open-minded approach to the political problems; a point of view which the politically experienced SDP leadership were inclined to endorse. They also favoured gradual change through consultation and agreement as opposed to the confrontation favoured by both Thatcher and Benn. Owen quotes Kolakowski's definition of social democracy in which no dazzling revelations are offered, 'no final victory over evil'. Rather, it 'needs an obstinate will to erode by inches the conditions which produce avoidable suffering'.

Decentralization

Dick Taverne had written in 1974 'when in doubt we should favour the small. Indeed, our guiding principle should be "small is beautiful"' (Taverne, p.147). His phrase was taken from the book of the same name by E.F. Schumacher which contributed so much to the intellectual climate of the 1970s and indeed provided the SDP with perhaps its most distinctive theme. Both Williams and Owen reached back for legitimacy for this theme to Robert Owen, Morris and Cole. All these writers had championed the rights of self-sustaining communities to make their own decisions and defend their interests against the potential tyrannies of the state and big business.

The mixed economy

The SDP proposed that instead of a constant war between the advocates of state socialism and a market economy the mixed economy should be accepted as a legitimate and effective arrangement. Roy Jenkins spoke of harnessing the 'innovating stimulus of the free market' yet avoiding the brutality of 'untramelled distribution of rewards' or 'indifference to unemployment'. At the same time he saw the role of the state in the economy as essential but stressed that it 'must know its place'. The SDP, therefore, argued for an acceptance of profits while also embracing a vigorous public sector. Owen soon left some of his colleagues behind by advocating a 'social market' approach which implied encouragement of the private sector through the easing of even more state regulations (for example on employment policy) and the further weakening of trade unions. But the distribution of wealth created by the market would be distributed according to standards of equity and fairness. Like Benn, the SDP favoured alternative forms of collective ownership such as worker cooperatives but parted company with both Benn and Croslandite revisionists in their enthusiasm for small firms and their potential contribution to economic revival.

Welfare spending a function of economic performance

SDP theorists were extremely supportive of welfare services but recognized that expenditure on them would have to be a function of economic performance. Theirs was consequently a less optimistic vision than Crosland's but Williams, who was impressed by the Adult Literacy Project, envisaged greater involvement of volunteers as one way of sustaining welfare growth. She and Owen were also in favour of breaking up the large welfare bureaucracies like the National Health Service and involving grass-roots citizen participation.

Democratize Parliament and devolve power

The SDP approach to government was characterized by a commitment to parliamentary democracy — which they had felt the Labour left were betraying — combined with decentralization of political power to the community and the individual. These twin concerns inspired a long list of constitutional reforms: reform of the House of Lords, open government, a reassertion of parliamentary control over special interests, proportional representation, devolution of power to the regions, greatly increased power for local government, liberal style 'community politics' with increased parental participation in schools.

Multilateral disarmament, pro-Europe, pro-NATO

The SDP's foreign policy reflected some traditional Labour and Liberal themes. Owen, Williams and Rodgers were committed Europeans — Jenkins, of course, had been President of the EEC during the 1970s. SDP support for closer political and economic integration in Europe was therefore predictable. Also predictable, given Owen's background, was their support for the Atlantic Alliance, a tough stance on defence and opposition to unilateralism. Support for the Third World was another important theme: the SDP opposed left-wing proposals for import controls as likely to harm the economies of developing and underdeveloped countries.

The ideas of the Social Democratic Party

> *The critique*
> Labour controlled by the left
> Two-party system anachronistic
> Anti-corporatist
>
> *Values*
> Defence of liberty and pursuit of equality
> National unity through lessening of class differences
> Realism and gradual change
> Decentralization
>
> *Policy themes*
> Mixed economy
> Welfare spending function of economic performance
> Democratize Parliament and devolve power
> Multilateral disarmament, pro-Europe, pro-NATO

The SDP was formed in a blaze of publicity and 'breaking the mould' rhetoric but was a genuine alternative philosophy ever offered? Probably not. In one sense it represented an amalgam of policies picked up across the political spectrum. Decentralization was close to the Liberal, Bennite and ecological position; SDP views on the market and trade unions were close to the Conservative position — Mrs Thatcher actually praised David Owen for being 'sound' on both; and on social policy and defence the SDP was close to the position of the Callaghan government to which the SDP leaders had once belonged.

This is not to say that the SDP lacked a carefully worked out and detailed programme; merely that it lacked a distinctive or even radical quality. History will judge the SDP as a party of protest with a limited appeal outside the middle classes. When its twelve-point plan was announced in March 1981 *The Times* concluded that this 'new beginning' was no more than 'a modern version of the Butskellism' which was 'seeking essentially to bring that consensus up to date'. In other words, the SDP was merely developing Labour revisionist policies free of the political and rhetorical restrictions caused through working within the Labour Party. In Samuel Beer's view:

> What had happened was quite simple: the Labour Party had been a socialist party. In recent years many of its adherents and leaders had ceased to believe in socialism.

In August 1980 the Gang of Three had written that 'a Centre Party ... would lack roots and a coherent philosophy'. The final irony of the SDP is that its leaders succeeded in writing its obituary well before they brought about their party's birth.

Green Thinking

> Today, in human society, we can perhaps hope to survive in all our prized diversity provided we can achieve an ultimate loyalty to our single, beautiful and vulnerable Planet Earth. Alone in space, alone in its life supporting systems, powered by inconceivable energies ... is this not a precious home for all us earthlings? Is this not worth our love? Does it not deserve all the inventiveness and courage and generosity

of which we are capable to preserve it from degradation and destruction and by doing so to secure our own survival?

This quotation concludes the classic work by Barbara Ward and René Dubos, *Only One Earth*, published in 1972 as the key document of the United Nations Conference on the Human Environment. Based upon evidence by a galaxy of distinguished international experts it was widely praised as authoritative, movingly written and a clarion call to action which even then might have been too late. The authors observed the irony that just when scientists were discovering the true extent of the earth's vulnerability to man's economic activity, an exponential increase in such damage was under way. The report placed a big question mark behind the notion of unrestricted economic growth and helped make the environment a mainstream rather than a peripheral issue. But while governments were willing to recognize concern for the environment as 'A Good Thing' they were not willing to do a great deal more.

Britain in particular lagged behind other nations in supporting and improving international initiatives to curb pollution. Despite the fact that the Greens had won seats at the local level, in most Western European legislatures and in the European Parliament, the simple majority voting system meant that the Greens had little chance of entering the House of Commons. Then in the autumn of 1988 came Mrs Thatcher's extraordinary *volte face*: her former indifference towards environmental issues was replaced by a ringing public endorsement. In the European election 17 June 1989 the Green's share of the British vote at 14.9 per cent was the biggest of any Green party in Europe. In July Mrs Thatcher replaced the anti-Green Secretary of State for the Environment, Nicholas Ridley, with Chris Patten — a young minister of relatively emerald hue. Why did Thatcher pay the Greens the compliment of stealing their clothes?

The answer is that she was responding to changes she perceived in British public opinion. In November 1988 a poll revealed that three-quarters of all voters were so concerned about pollution that they would accept higher prices for goods in exchange for a cleaner and healthier environment. The shift in public attitudes has been slow in coming. During the 1970s groups like Greenpeace, Friends of the Earth and the Ecology Party (forerunner of the Greens) had warned vainly of the armageddon soon awaiting a world obsessed with economic growth. During the 1980s, however, awareness grew of phenomena like acid rain; the dangerous plundering of equatorial rain forests; pollution of rivers and the North Sea (causing a much publicized epidemic among seals); the deleterious effects of man-made chlorofluorocarbons (CFCs) on the ozone layer of the earth's atmosphere (which filters out harmful radiation from the sun); and atmospheric warming or 'greenhouse effect' (caused by the build-up of carbon dioxide and other gases which absorb and hold the sun's heat).

The heavily populated south east of the country also began to question their quality of life: prosperity was very nice but should it be paid for in the coin of filthy streets, increasing air traffic and endless traffic jams? Well-publicized ecological disasters like Bhopal and the massive Exxon oil spill in Alaska also contributed to public awareness but the most widespread alarm was caused in 1986 when the nuclear power station at Chernobyl in the Soviet Ukraine exploded disastrously, scattering radioactive debris all over Europe via the action of the winds and the rain. Chernobyl was the most grimly effective propaganda which the Greens could have hoped for and was a message which penetrated deeply into the public consciousness.

Support for the Greens, however, tended to reflect specific fears about environmental pollution rather than their wider concern over the depletion of finite resources and their thinking on economic, social and foreign policy issues. Greens are quick to insist that theirs is not just a narrow environmental 'pressure group' concern: they maintain the 'ecological perspective' comprises an interlocking set of principles amounting to a comprehensive alternative political philosophy. Like any approach rooted in a profound dissatisfaction with the existing state of affairs, it begins with a critique of other political programmes.

The ecological perspective rejects philosophies of the right, left and centre as more similar than dissimilar. Jonathon Porrit characterizes them collectively as 'industrialism'. This 'super ideology' which is 'conditioned to thrive on the ruthless exploitation of both people and planet is itself the greatest threat we face.' Conservatives, socialists and centre politicians argue about rival economic approaches — individualism versus collectivism and how the cake of national income should be sliced up and distributed — but they all agree that the size of the national cake should be increased through vigorous economic growth. This is the central proposition which the Greens most emphatically reject. Industrialism, say the Greens, is predicated upon the continuous expansion of goods and services and upon the promotion of even more consumption through advertising and the discovery of an increasing range of 'needs'. It creates great inequalities whereby a rich and envied minority set the pace in lavish and unnecessary consumption while a substantial number (in many countries a majority) are either unemployed or live in relative poverty. Mrs Thatcher has presided over an increase in income differentials but has offered economic growth as the panacea: more for the rich and more for the poor. Porritt observes:

> If the system works, i.e. we achieve full employment, we basically destroy the planet; if it doesn't, i.e. we end up with mass unemployment, we destroy the lives of millions of people ... From an industrial point of view it is rational to ... promote wasteful consumption, to discount social costs, to destroy the environment. From the green point of view it is totally irrational, simply because we hold true to the most important political reality of all: that **all** wealth ultimately derives from the finite resources of our planet.
>
> Porritt, pp. 46–7.

The Green view goes on to adduce a number of basic principles:

1. *A world approach.* All human activity should reflect appreciation of the world's finite resources and easily damaged ecology.
2. *Respect for the rights of our descendants.* Our children have the right to inherit a beautiful and bountiful planet rather an exhausted and polluted one.
3. *Sufficiency.* We should be satisfied with 'enough' rather than constantly seeking 'more'.
4. *A conserver economy.* We must conserve what we have rather than squander it through pursuit of high growth strategies.
5. *Care and share.* Given that resources are limited we must shift our energies to sharing what we have and looking after all sections of society properly.

6. *Self reliance*. We should learn to provide for ourselves rather than surrendering responsibility to experts and specialized agencies.

7. *Decentralize and Democratize*. We must form smaller units of production, encourage cooperative enterprises and give people local power over their own affairs. At the same time international integration must move forward rapidly.

Porritt maintains this amounts to a wholly alternative view of rationality and mankind's existence. He contrasts the two world views of industrialism and ecology — summarized in Table 10.1.

Table 10.1   *Two world views: industrialism versus ecology*

Industrialism	Ecology
The Environment	
Domination over nature	Harmony with nature
Environment managed as a resource	Resources regarded as strictly finite
High energy, high consumption	Low energy, low consumption
Nuclear power	Renewable sources of energy
Values	
An ethos of aggressive individualism	Cooperatively based communitarian society with emphasis on personal autonomy
Pursuit of material goods	Move towards spiritual non-material values
Rationality and packaged knowledge	Intuition and understanding
Patriarchal values, hierarchical structure	Post-patriarchal feminist values, non-hierarchical structure
Unquestioning acceptance of technology	Discriminating use and development of science and technology
The Economy	
Economic growth and demand stimulation	Sustainability, quality of life and simplicity
Production for exchange and profit	Production for use
High income differentials	Low income differentials
A free market economy	Local production for local need
Ever-expanding world trade	Self-reliance
Employment as a means to an end	Work as an end in itself
Capital intensive production	Labour intensive production
Political Organization	
Centralization, economies of scale	Decentralization, human scale
Representative democracy	Direct democracy, participative involvement
Sovereignty of nation state	Internationalism and global solidarity
Institutionalized violence	Non-violence

Source: Adapted from Porritt, 1984, pp. 216–17

From these principles a radical programme of political action can be formed with which almost certainly only a small minority of Green voters were familiar in June 1989. The manifesto for the 1989 European Election can be summarized as follows:

1. *The regions*. The regions of Britain and other European countries should be given more autonomy while European institutions at the centre should be strengthened and made more accountable. Proportional representation should be introduced in all elections.

2. *Environmental protection*. The Greens want the 4th EEC Environmental Action

Programme to be fully implemented rather than becoming the object of lip-service. Britain in particular needs to implement its recommendations in order to lose the title of 'The Dirty Man of Europe'.

3. *Land.* Land represents 'everybody's "commonwealth" which is held in trust for future generations'. A land tax should be introduced 'to distribute land more fairly, stop land speculation and encourage ecologically sound use of land'.

4. *Agriculture.* Greens favour 'small organic mixed farms, rearing livestock humanely and naturally and rejecting the cruelty of factory farming'. Toxic pesticides will be banned.

5. *Energy.* A comprehensive energy conservation and energy efficiency policy needs to be followed. Greens encourage 'a move away from large-scale inefficient wasteful and polluting forms of energy production to smaller efficient, reliable sources of supply'. Nuclear power would be phased out.

6. *Transport.* Heavy investment is necessary in public transport especially waterways and railways as opposed to road and air travel. If regions become more self-sufficient transport requirements will lessen. The Channel Tunnel project should be discontinued.

7. *Water.* Greens want to improve the quality of drinking water and are opposed to privatization of water (though not in principle to private ownership itself).

8. *Air.* CFCs should be phased out and carbon dioxide output reduced by 50 per cent by 2015.

9. *Waste.* Unnecessary packaging would be outlawed and recycling introduced wherever possible. The transport of hazardous waste from one country to another would be banned.

10. *Technology.* Strict controls would be applied to technological development and a code of ethics drawn up.

11. *Social policy.* The Greens propose a 'basic income scheme' for the UK offering 'a tax-free non-means-tested income for all as a universal right from birth to death'.

12. *Women.* Women should be given the same freedom of choice as men and the opportunity 'to combine childcare with a full and fulfilling life outside the home'.

13. *Rich world–poor world.* Europe should introduce population control strategies of its own before enjoining poorer nations to do the same. The Europeans should learn to live more simply so that the poorer nations can have the chance to enjoy a fair share of the world's resources. Multi-national companies should be broken up.

14. *Peace.* The world should move away from out-dated military power blocs. Defence budgets should be turned into environmental protection budgets.

What are we to make of the Green philosophy? It has some points of contact with all the current major schools of thought: social democracy (e.g. acceptance of the mixed economy); liberalism (e.g. regional autonomy); left-wing socialism (e.g. a common basic income); and conservatism (e.g. self-reliance). But it is also unlike any other ideology in that it is posited upon a future way of life based upon static or shrinking resources and addresses the implications of such a state of affairs. While they all share the Greens' concern with pollution the established parties are equivocal on the rate at which the world's resources are being consumed and are flatly opposed to no-growth strategies. For example, the TUC report *Towards a Charter for the Environment* (August 1989) produced with Labour's environmental policy in mind, rejected 'simplistic notions that if only economic growth came to a halt the world would be a cleaner and safer place'. This strategy, argued the TUC, would create hardship in both the developed and Third Worlds.

With the exceptions indicated above the main political parties would reject most of the Greens' social and political programme as not necessarily connected to a concern with the environment. This is fair comment. There is no logical connection between caring about the environment or indeed a no growth economy and the sort of society which the Greens envisage and advocate. It would be perfectly possible, for example, for small scale self-reliant economic entities to be managed in an inegalitarian hierarchical fashion. So where does the Green vision of society come from?

The answer is found in the writings of certain anarchist and socialist utopian writers: Thomas Moore, Godwin, Thoreau, Kropotkin, Proudhon, Bakunin, Tolstoy and William Morris. Here we see the same conception of 'progress' as a reverse process, a retreat into simplicity; where men are freed from rigid bureaucracies and encouraged to become autonomous individuals; where the absence of luxury enables people to concentrate upon artistic pursuits and contemplate spiritual values. As Woodcock observes 'the anarchist sees progress not in terms of a steady increase in material wealth and complexity of living but rather in terms of the moralising of society by the abolition of authority, inequality and economic exploitation'. The Greens would be inclined to agree.

The nineteenth century anarchists were also passionately against state power and, like the Greens, argued for small scale, self-reliant, self-governing societies linked within a world-wide federal structure. Again, like the Greens, and contrary to their popular image, the anarchists were pacifistic: they abhorred war and favoured change through rational discussion and a peaceful transformation of society. William Morris's novel, *News From Nowhere*, envisaged a utopian world which both anarchists and

Denis Healey on 'Green' ideas

'You're quite right of course, but it's political suicide to say so'.

Denis Healey after listening to the 'Green' ideas of Sara Parkin, spokesperson for the Green party, in 1979.

Source: The Guardian. 18 September 1989.

Green issues and the public

An *Observer* Harris Poll (17 September 1989) revealed that Green voters were unaware of the party's more radical policies. 72 per cent knew that the Greens were in favour of cleaner air and 61 per cent believed their party wanted cleaner water, but only 12 per cent knew the Greens were opposed to economic growth and the same proportion that their party favoured withdrawal from the European Community.

Source: Data from an *Observer* Harris Poll, 17 September 1989)

Greens would applaud. Here mass production had been abolished, de-industrialization had taken place and pollution virtually ended. People lived in small settlements, sharing tasks and the products of their labour and developing their artistic proclivities. In effect the Greens have reached back into the past for a simple, non-materialistic, libertarian philosophy and have offered it as the formula for life in the post-industrial world.

Unfortunately, while the Greens share with Morris a comparable desired vision of the future they also share similar problems in relation to practical politics. While Morris's novel was much admired it was never taken seriously by early socialists as anything remotely like a serious political programme. Without its neo-anarchistic approach to social and political organization Green ideas would constitute a pressure group programme rather than a fully fledged political ideology. But during a fiercely fought election contest, with the Greens as major rather than peripheral players, these are the issues which would receive the closest scrutiny. A whole host of tricky questions queue up to be answered, e.g. how can distrust between nations be reduced to the point when old alliances can be dissolved and defence budgets reallocated? How will multi-national companies be broken up? As it stands at present it is unlikely that the Greens' political programme falls within the 'art of the possible'. But as Malcolm Muggeridge once pointed out 'utopias flourish in chaos' and if many respected scientists are to be believed, environmental chaos is what the future has in store for us. If there really *is* no alternative, then it is either the death of our planet or the Green Revolution, which is not too far away.

The government and environmental policy

• The Government should give a higher priority to environmental policy even if this means higher prices for some goods.

	ALL	1988	CON	LAB	SLD/SDP
Agree strongly (+2)	34	—	36	33	35
Agree slightly (+1)	36	—	39	35	33
No preference (0)	10	—	10	10	11
Disagree slightly (−1)	8	—	6	10	7
Disagree strongly (−2)	6	—	5	9	9
Don't know	5	—	4	4	5
Average response:	**0.88**	**—**	**0.99**	**0.76**	**0.84**

(Not asked last year.)
Public concern with the environment is still growing. In October 1987, a Marplan poll for *The Guardian* found 61 per cent in favour of this proposition and 19 per cent against. Now 70 per cent are in favour and only 14 per cent against. Support is strongest among voters under 35 and weakest among those over 65; strongest in social groups A and B and weakest in groups D and E.

Source: The Guardian, 18 September 1989

References and Further Reading

SDP and Liberal Democrats

Beer, S., *Britain Against Itself* (Faber, 1982).
Bogdanor, V., (ed.) *Liberal Party Politics* (Clarendon Press, 1983).
Bradley, I., *Breaking the Mould* (Martin Robertson, 1981).
Eccleshall, R., et al., *Political Ideologies* (Hutchinson, 1984).
Foote, G., *The Labour Party's Political Thought* (Croom Helm, 1985).
Grimond, J., *The Liberal Challenge* (Hollis & Carter, 1963).
Marquand, D., *The Unprincipled Society* (Jonathan Cape, 1988).
Mumford, L., *Pentagon of Power* (Secker & Warburg, 1976).
Owen, D., *Face the Future* (Jonathan Cape, 1981).
Owen, D., *A Future that will Work* (Penguin, 1984).
Owen, D., *The Social Market* (The Tawney Society, 1987).
Rodgers, W., *The Politics of Change* (Secker & Warburg, 1981).
Taverne, D., *The Future of the Left* (Cape, 1974).
Tivey, L. and Wright, A. (eds), *Party Ideology in Britain* (Routledge, 1989).
Watkins, A., *The Liberal Dilemma* (McGibbon and Kee, 1966).
Williams, S., *Politics is for People* (Penguin 1981).

The Greens

Green Party, *Don't Let your World Turn Grey* (The Green Party European Election Manifesto, 1989).
Icke, D., Irvine, S. and Ponton, A., *A Green Manifesto* (Optima, 1988).
Morris, W., *News from Nowhere* (first published 1890).
Porritt, J., *Seeing Green* (Blackwell, 1984).
Roszak, T., *Person/Planet* (Granada, 1981).
Shumacher, F., *Small is Beautiful* (Abacus, 1974).
Ward, B. and Dubos, R., *Only One Earth* (Pelican, 1972).
Woodcock, G., *Anarchism* (Pelican, 1962).

The section on Green Thinking was earlier published as an article in *Talking Politics*, Winter 1989—90, pp. 1—6.

Marquand and Politics as Mutual Learning

Friedrich Hayek, one of the high priests of the New Right, or neo-liberal thinking, placed the highest value upon the concept of individual liberty which he believed emerged with the Renaissance. English political philosophy went on to develop this theme with such force and vigour that its influence held sway in the civilized world for two hundred years, until leadership was lost in the nineteenth century to Germanic collectivist ideas. David Marquand, however, in his much-discussed *The Unprincipled Society* argues the opposite point of view.

Pre-Renaissance society, he observes, was characterized by a sense of community and mutual obligation between classes. All this was swept away after the Renaissance by an intellectual revolution which permeated British society more effectively than any other European country. According to this successor view,

> society is made up of separate sovereign atomistic individuals . . . The obligations which these individuals owe to their society derive ultimately from the fact that it can be shown that it is to their advantage to belong to it . . . Freedom means my freedom to choose my own good for myself and to pursue it in my own way, provided only that I leave others free to choose and pursue their good in their own way . . .

While this philosophy provided the perfect forcing ground for primitive industrialism it has outlived its usefulness, says Marquand. Ironically it is the communal ethic of the 'Old Society' which has turned out to be better adapted to the 'sophisticated, science based . . . capital and skill intensive industrialism of the twentieth century'. Indeed, it is in societies where the old ethic remains to some degree, argues Marquand, that sophisticated industrialism has been most successful. Marquand also apportions blame to the utilitarian individualism of Jeremy Bentham which asserted the doctrine which remains at the heart of British political institutions: the unlimited sovereignty of the Crown in Parliament. This has hindered the sharing of power either with supra-national organizations or with lower tiers of government or non-governmental organizations.

The result has been a failure of adjustment. Britain is not only poorer than other developed countries but her institutions face a crisis of confidence and she suffers from an 'intellectual and moral vacuum at the heart of her political economy'. Despite the development of a 'regulatory state and the transition from liberal to corporate capitalism' during the last two hundred years, the 'underlying intellectual and cultural hegemony of individualism' has hardly been shaken. The post-war Keynesian consensus was fine as far as it went. It helped raise living standards and make Britain a kinder and fairer society but attempts at direct government intervention to increase production (which Marquand dates 1958–74) failed because the major economic groups and the public at large did not trust the government sufficiently and preferred to pursue individual rather than communal objectives.

Labour abandoned Keynesianism after 1976 and the neo-socialist left-wing faction took over briefly in the early 1980s. This was founded on an outdated image of the class struggles of the 1920s and 1930s. The Conservatives, meanwhile, had fallen prey to Thatcherite neo-liberalism which relies upon the efficacy of market forces to bring about adjustment to modern conditions. This approach 'neglects the cultural, institutional or political factors which . . . make some societies more adaptable than others'. Most obviously it destroys the sense of mutual concern and communal togetherness. It also prevents the kind of firm agreements between employers and trade unions which have traditionally been reached by Scandinavian countries upon annual wage rounds and other forms of wealth distribution. Neo-liberalism is not the answer.

> Half a century of social change has, in short, invalidated the doctrines which are supposed to underpin the political order. This, in turn, has undermined public confidence in its equity, and made it more difficult for governments to mobilize consent for the changes without which economic adjustment is impossible.
>
> Marquand, p.10.

Marquand offers an approach to a new governing philosophy to take the place of the shattered post-war consensus. It is founded upon a richer and more generous view of human nature 'that men and women may learn if they are stretched; that they can discover how to govern themselves if they win self-government'. It concentrates upon Man as a persuasive and learning animal: 'politics as mutual education'.

He also draws upon the organizational studies of Schon and Argyris who make the distinction between 'single loop learning' which enables an organization to survive through detecting and correcting errors, and the more fundamental 'double loop learning', where members examine their fundamental values through a process of discussion and mutual education and try to re-shape them in accordance with the changed environment. Our political culture needs to acquire a similar facility, argues Marquand, so that citizens can 'listen to, argue with and persuade each other as "equal citizens" so as to find solutions to their common problems.'

For this to work we must become 'reflective and open minded', able to transcend our individual interests and make judgements which reflect the common good. According to this view all citizens become responsible, 'all citizens are politicians'. In such a world there is no distant '"they", government, or market there to blame for the mistakes we make in common. There is only us.' For this to work wider access to education would be needed and participatory experience in self-government gained at all levels. Rather like the Greens, Marquand is not keen on the nation state but wishes to see governmental power and functions shifted downwards to the regions and localities and upwards to supranational organizations. He also argues for functional representation, possibly through a reformed House of Lords and regional government.

Marquand's diagnosis is probably better than his prescription. Only a crude summary of his critique has been attempted here but as it is at once penetrating, and stimulating, it repays closer study. However, neo-Liberals and Socialists would reject Marquand's strictures as the jaundiced perspective of an SDP founder member. They would say that Marquand, himself an eminently rational man and a university

Mrs Thatcher and community

> 'There is no such thing as society, there are individual men and women and there are families.'
>
> **Margaret Thatcher**
>
> The community has been privatised. The home is the haven in a heartless world and families retreat into the home, not the community.
>
> Thatcherism is as much a product of this change as an agent. It appeals to self-interest and works against the grain of any sense of community. People only come together out of defensiveness, against a shared perception of threat, such as in Neighbourhood Watch.
>
> The modern form of community is to be found in sports clubs or special interest groups. It is regulated by 'what's in it for me' rather than by duty of obligation.
>
> *Source:* **Professor Howard Newby**, *The Guardian*, 6 September 1988

teacher of politics, is trying to recreate the world in his own image. Mrs Thatcher would argue that her 'active citizenship' emphasis and measures like more power to school governors and parents prove that she *is* striving to make individuals responsible as well as free. Left-wingers, moreover, would claim *their* perception of society is essentially mutually supportive and communal from the local to the national level.

The proposed way forward is also open to criticism as unrealistic and naive. James Reston commented, a little cynically no doubt, that 'all politics are based upon the indifference of the majority'. Marquand would appear to be fighting against a world-wide phenomenon: people are generally not interested in politics and are mostly happy to leave it to the interested few.

He is, therefore, not only asking for a major shift in our educational system but also a revolution in human thought and behaviour. But even supposing he should succeed is there any reasonable chance that agreements or consensus would emerge from his 'humdrum . . . collegial . . . conversational' process? Might not even more disagreements and conflict be the possible outcome? Might not his decentralized self-governing communities pursue infinitely divergent directions with even greater national fragmentation as the result?

On the other hand, Marquand is only indulging in the same kind of fundamental rethink of intellectual position reflected by many thoughtful people in the 1980s. Stuart Hall's work, for example, grapples with questions which 'take us to the root of things — to core values and commitments, to the outer limits of our capacities to reimagine the future'. The success of the Greens also reflects a wider searching by many people for an alternative, a better approach. Thatcherism has been so electorally and intellectually devastating to other political creeds that they have been thrown back upon the bedrock of their beliefs. In many cases, political thinkers have found their core ideas wanting and have offered reconstructions — convinced that Thatcherism would soon be overwhelmed by the convergence of technological, environmental and social forces beyond its narrow capacities.

PART IV The Representative Process

This section deals with the representative process in the British political system. In a democracy it is necessary to construct methods whereby the needs and demands of the people are expressed or **represented** to decision makers. In a small group of people this can be effected by each individual verbally at regular meetings. Universities, to take an example, involve much larger groups of people and devise various levels of representation and consultation rising from departmental board meetings to faculties and ultimately Senate — which typically comprises professors plus elected members — and meets several times a year. At the national level there are four major forms of representation: elections which occur at least once every five years — discussed in Chapter 11; the media which enables ideas to be represented and communication to circulate throughout the system at all times — discussed in Chapter 12; pressure groups which allow individuals and groups to represent their special interests between elections — discussed in Chapter 13; and political parties which provide a choice to voters at election times of different approaches to the government of the country — discussed in Chapter 14.

11 Elections and Voting Behaviour

Dennis Kavanagh

This chapter begins by discussing the framework in which elections are held. It then considers who is entitled to vote, the electoral system and the rules governing the nomination of candidates. It discusses the role of election campaigns and the factors which shape voting behaviour, particularly those which have produced changes in party allegiance in recent years. The final sections of the chapter assess the likely impact of the changes in voting behaviour on the relative strength of parties and on the making of the political system.

Elections lie at the heart of the democratic process; a crucial difference between democratic and non-democratic states is to be found in whether or not they hold competitive elections. The best indicator of such competition is the existence of a number of political parties at elections. In addition to choice there must also be participation. In Britain the entire adult population has the right to vote at least once every five years for candidates of different parties in the House of Commons.

Elections in Britain matter for other reasons. Firstly, they are the most common form of political participation; at general elections since 1945 an average of 75 per cent of adults on the electoral register have cast votes (Table 11.1). Secondly, these votes determine the composition of the House of Commons and therefore which party forms the government. Thirdly, elections are a peaceful way of resolving questions which in some other countries are settled by force; above all the question, who is to rule? They are also important in giving legitimacy to government. Election, by however narrow a margin, is how we decide who is to govern.

What are Elections?

Elections are a mechanism of social choice, a device by which people choose representatives to hold office and carry out particular functions. In a direct democracy, usually in small societies, people may of course do the tasks themselves or take turns (rotation) to carry them out. In large scale societies, however, the election of representatives is necessary.

Election is not the only method by which rulers are chosen. Leaders may emerge, for example, through heredity (e.g. monarchy) or force (e.g. the military). Indeed,

Table 11.1   *Election
turnouts 1945—87*

Date	Percentage
1945	73.3
1950	84.0
1951	82.5
1955	76.8
1959	78.7
1964	77.1
1966	75.8
1970	72.0
February 1974	78.1
October 1974	72.8
1979	76.0
1983	72.7
1987	75.4

appointments in many walks of life are made without elections: in the civil service and in many professions appointment is on merit (demonstrated, for example, by passing competitive examinations, serving an apprenticeship or gaining diplomas or other marks of competence). But today competitive elections are widely regarded as the symbol of legitimate and representative democracy.

In Britain competitive elections were well established in the eighteenth and nineteenth centuries, even though only small numbers of males had the vote. The suffrage, or right to vote, was steadily broadened during the nineteenth century. Britain effectively had mass suffrage by 1928, when the vote was extended to virtually all men and women over the age of 21 (see Table 11.2).

General elections for the House of Commons are called under two circumstances: either when the Parliament has run its full five years (until 1911 the permissable life-span of a Parliament was seven years) or when it is dissolved by the monarch on the advice of the Prime Minister of the day. In the exceptional conditions of war the elections due to be held by 1916 and by 1940 were delayed until the cessation of hostilities in 1918 and 1945, respectively. The USA has calendar elections prescribed by the constitution; even in wartime elections for the Congress and Presidency went ahead.

Some commentators have argued that the advent of opinion polls and the power to time economic booms for the run-up to an election give the incumbent too great an advantage (Hailsham, 1977). While the Thatcher victories of 1983 and 1987 may

Table 11.2   *Extension of the suffrage*

Date	Percentage of adult population with the vote
1832	5
1867	13
1884	25
1919	75
1928	99
1969	99

Opinion polling

By interviewing a sample of between one and two thousand voters drawn randomly from the electorate, surveys claim to be able to predict parties' share of the votes to within 3 per cent in 95 per cent of cases. The polls do have a good record of predicting winners, though they came unstuck in the 'upset' elections of 1970 and February 1974. The 1987 general election was the most exhaustively polled ever. In the month of the campaign seventy-three nation-wide opinion polls were conducted. The figure excludes polls in constituencies and regions. Often the newspapers and television broadcasts led with the latest results of the opinion poll. The main polling organizations are Gallup, NOP, MORI, Marplan and Harris. In the 1979, 1983 and 1987 elections the elections seemed to be a certain success for the Conservatives. As such the opinion polls did not have an exciting story to tell. In the 1987 election the eve of poll predictions by the main polling organizations overestimated the Conservative final share of the vote by 1 per cent, underestimated Labour's by 2 per cent and underestimated the Alliance by 1 per cent.

In addition the main parties conduct private polls during the election. These are designed to help the party leaders assess the progress of the campaign and to present issues in a more persuasive way for 'target' voters. Opinion polls have a demonstrated influence at by-elections. Voters are able to use the knowledge provided by the polls to vote tactically against the incumbent. By-election polls were extremely important in helping the Alliance gain some spectacular by-election victories in the 1983 Parliament.

support the Hailsham thesis, Mr Wilson's loss in 1970, Mr Heath's in 1974 and Mr Callaghan's in 1979 do not. With the exception of the 1970 and February 1974 elections most of the opinion polls have correctly predicted the winning party in the post-war period.

If the government is defeated on a major issue, or a vote of censure is carried against it in the Commons, it is expected to resign and recommend a dissolution. The only post-war case of a forced dissolution was in 1979, when the Callaghan government lost a vote of confidence following the failure of its Scottish and Welsh devolution plans to be carried by the necessary majorities in referendums in those two countries.

The other opportunity which British voters have for a nation-wide election of representatives is for members of the European Assembly every five years. To date elections have been held in 1979, 1984 and 1989 for eighty-one Euro-MPs (see Chapter 27). One might also note the introduction of referendums — over British membership of the European Community in 1975, and in Scotland and Wales over devolution in 1979.

Who votes?

To be entitled to vote a person must have his or her name on the electoral register of the constituency in which he or she resides. The register is a list compiled each year by the local Registration Officer. For inclusion on the register the person must

Referendums

> Referendums provide an opportunity for the electorate to vote on issues, and may be binding on Parliament or advisory. They have been held in Britain as a whole once (on whether Britain should remain in the European Community in 1975), in Northern Ireland once (on the Border in 1973) and in Scotland and Wales once (in 1979 on the proposals for assemblies in Scotland and Wales). Interestingly, each of these was held on a constitutional matter. The Scotland Act 1978 provided for a devolved assembly in Edinburgh but subject to approval by 40 per cent of the electorate in an advisory referendum. The Scottish voters approved by 33 per cent to 31 per cent; the proposal therefore failed. Only 12 per cent of Welsh voters supported a proposal for a Welsh assembly, compared to 47 per cent who voted against.

be resident in the constituency on the given date, be over eighteen years of age and be a British subject. Persons lacking a fixed address cannot be registered. One apparent anomaly is that citizens of the Irish Republic are also entitled to vote if they have had three months' continuous residence in the United Kingdom before the qualifying date. Peers, aliens, people judged insane in mental homes and people disqualified upon conviction of corrupt electoral practices and certain types of prison offenders are not eligible to vote.

Inaccuracies in the state of the register when it is compiled, combined with the greater mobility of people, mean that the register is often out of date when it is published. It becomes less accurate after publication, as voters die or change residence. A large part of the steady decline in election turnouts since 1951 is due to the growing inaccuracy of the register. A turnout of 75 per cent (as in 1987) may actually mean that some 80 per cent of eligible voters have cast a vote in the election. Not surprisingly, many of the non-voters are drawn from the unemployed, very old, young and poor. These people also tend to participate less in other social activities; many are poorly informed about politics and see little point in participating.

Constituency boundaries

The division of the country into constituencies is in the hands of permanent electoral ***Boundary Commissions***. There is a separate Commission for each of the four nations of the United Kingdom and each has the task of establishing an approximately equal size of constituency electorate. The Commissions periodically (between ten and fifteen years) review and make recommendations about the size of the constituency electorates. They arrive at a notional quota for each nation by dividing the total electorate by the available number of seats.

Notwithstanding the Commission's efforts, by the time allowances are made for such features as the existing boundaries of counties and London boroughs, sparsely populated constituencies and the sense of 'community' in an existing seat, there are many inequalities in the size of constituency electorates. In 1983 the average electorate per constituency was around 65,000, yet a third of seats varied from this figure by some 15,000. Recent boundary reviews have had to take account of the more rapid growth of electorates in the south of Britain and the suburbs compared to the north and cities and award relatively more seats to the former. These developments have helped the Conservative party at the expense of Labour. It was largely for this reason that the Labour government avoided implementing the recommendations of the 1969 Boundary Review which was calculated to be worth between five and twenty seats to the Conservative party. Scotland and Wales have long been given more seats in the House of Commons than the size of their populations strictly justifies, in part because both were guaranteed a minimum number of seats by the 1944 Redistribution of Seats Act. This works to the advantage of the Labour party, which in the 1987 election won twenty-four of the thirty-six Welsh seats and fifty of the seventy-two Scottish seats. The Boundary Commissions will complete their present work between 1993 and 1998. Once again Labour will lose out, perhaps to the extent of fifteen to thirty seats mostly in Greater London and the other major metropolitan conurbations. Some Labour MPs would like to change the rules which penalize their party for the shift of population into the suburbs.

The Electoral System

An electoral system is a set of rules governing the conduct of elections. A key feature prescribes how popular votes are translated into seats in the legislature. There are, broadly speaking, two types of electoral systems (Urwin, 1987). In *proportional* systems there is a close relationship between the distribution of votes between parties and the allocation of seats in the legislature. In *first-past-the-post majoritarian systems* the candidate who achieves a plurality of votes wins the seat. At the risk of over-simplifying one may say that proportional systems are found largely in West European states and majoritarian systems are found in Anglo—American societies (the United Kingdom, Canada, Australia, New Zealand and the USA). The two systems also broadly correlate with multi-party versus two-party systems, respectively.

The different types of electoral systems do seem to reflect national outlooks about government and politics. Proportional systems are often adopted in divided societies and emphasize the importance of the legislature being broadly representative of society. Plurality systems are defended on the grounds that they help to provide a more stable government and, where there is one party in government, allow the voters to hold the government responsible for its record at the next election. Their disproportionality also means that a party often has a majority of seats for a minority of the vote. In October 1974 Labour won a majority of seats with only 39.2 per cent of the vote and in 1983 the Conservatives amassed 61 per cent of seats for 42 per cent of the vote.

Until recently the British public and much of the elite assumed that the electoral system was satisfactory. Undoubtedly it enjoyed the virtues of familiarity and clarity; in the post-war period, only in February 1974 has one party failed to gain an overall majority of seats. This assumption also accompanied the belief that the British system of government was superior to that of many West European states. For much of the twentieth century Britain was an economic and industrial power of the first rank. Her record in resisting Hitler's military aggression, avoiding political extremism (of both the left- and right-wing varieties) and maintaining political stability was superior to that of many West European states which had various forms of proportional representation.

In recent years, however, that complacency has been challenged. In part this has reflected the more general dissatisfaction with Britain's economic performance and international standing. The electoral system, like so much else, has come in for criticism. It is not clear, however, how much responsibility for the country's poor economic performance rests with the political system in general, with the electoral and party systems in particular, or with other factors.

Britain is also unusual in not having any form of proportional representation (PR) for direct elections to the European Parliament. The leaders of the two main parties have not wished to set a precedent for the introduction of PR for Westminster elections. After all, the Parliamentary strength of the Labour and especially Conservative parties would be substantially reduced under PR. In 1973 the Royal Commission on the Constitution proposed PR for elections to the recommended Scottish and Welsh assemblies.

One has only to look at Northern Ireland to see the shortcomings of the British electoral system when it operates in a bitterly divided society. The use of the first-past-the-post-system there means that, as long as religion dictates voting, the Catholics will be in a permanent minority in the twentieth century. Northern Ireland politics is different from Great Britain in that the elections for local elections and for its three seats to the European Parliament use PR.

Among the criticisms of the electoral system in Britain are the following:

1. The system does not invariably produce secure majorities for one party. In three of the last eight general elections (1964, February 1974 and October 1974) the winning party did not have a majority sufficient to last for a full Parliament. Many commentators felt that in the era of three-party politics in the 1980s the chances of an indecisive outcome are greatly increased (Butler, 1983).
2. Because some three-quarters of seats are safe for the incumbent party many voters are denied an effective choice in most seats. It produces a House of Commons and government which do not fairly represent the political opinions of the nation.
3. As the Liberal and Social Democratic Alliance parties gained significant support (over 20 per cent) in the 1980s, so the disproportional effects of the electoral system became more glaring (Table 11.3). It can be argued that when the Liberals were gaining less than 10 per cent of the vote this disproportionality was not too objectionable; but when a party gains over 25 or 23 per cent of the vote and gets only 3.5 per cent of the seats (as in 1983 and 1987) the distortion is less acceptable. It is worth noting that the British system does not discriminate against all minor political parties. Where a party can consolidate its votes in a region, e.g. the Nationalists in Scotland or the Unionists in Northern Ireland, then it can collect a representative number of seats. The system penalizes those parties which spread their votes widely, as did the Liberals and the Alliance.
4. Critics of the adversary party system (in which the opposition routinely attacks what the government does and promises to do) complain that the all-or-nothing nature of the British system encourages abrupt discontinuity in policy when one party replaces the other in government. Frequent reversals in policy in such fields as education, regional policy, housing, finance, incomes restraints and the economy may be highly damaging.
5. As the two main parties have become more regionally based between the north

Table 11.3 *Third party seats in House of Commons*

Date	Number of Seats	
1945	34	
1950	11	
1951	9	
1955	8	
1959	7	
1964	9	
1966	14	
1970	12	
February 1974	37	
October 1974	39	
1979	27	
1983	44	
1987	44	Average 21

and south and between urban and suburban/rural areas, so they may become less national in their outlooks. It is certainly true that in recent elections the south of Britain and the midlands have cumulatively become more Conservative while the north and Scotland have become more solidly Labour; the 1987 election was no exception (Table 11.4).

In 1987 there was much opposition criticism of the Conservatives gaining 57 per cent of the seats for only 43 per cent of the votes. But in Scotland Labour gained 70 per cent of the seats for 42 per cent of the votes and in Wales, 63 per cent of seats for 45 per cent of the votes. There is now a sharp disparity between shares of votes and of seats in Britain as a whole and in different regions; the effect is to 'over-represent' Labour in north Britain and the Conservatives in south Britain. Only a handful of Labour MPs sit for the affluent and growing population in the south east of Britain; Conservatives are hardly represented in the major cities and have no representation at all in Liverpool, Manchester, Glasgow, Bradford, Stoke, Newcastle upon Tyne or Leicester; and only one Conservative MP is found in the hundred constituencies which suffer the worst unemployment.

One may point to shortcomings in most schemes of proportional representation. For example, it would be difficult for the voters to assign responsibility to any one party for a government's record if there are coalition or minority governments. If

Table 11.4 *Conservative–Labour swing in regions 1983–7*

	Con–Lab swing (per cent)
London and South England	(−0.1)
Midlands	(0.1)
Wales	(4.5)
North England	(3.6)
Scotland	(5.9)

a coalition government is formed then its programme will very likely be a result of post-election bargaining between the party leaders. Critics also argue that, apart from wartime — when the overriding goal is national survival — coalitions are likely to be weak and lack coherence.

It is also likely that if a party list system is used (as in many West European states) and the party headquarters draws up the list of candidates in multi-member seats, then the direct link between an MP and his constituents will be weakened. One form of PR — the additional member system in West Germany — retains the link between constituency and MP. In this system half the MPs are elected for single-member constituencies while the remaining half are allocated on a proportional basis to correct distortions from the first round of voting. Finally, if a party is short of a working majority by a few seats in the House of Commons the bargaining power of a small party will be greatly increased.

The close relationship between geography, economic prosperity and party strength (i.e. a prosperous Tory south versus a less prosperous Labour north) means that fewer seats are now politically 'marginal'. This means that fewer seats are likely to change hands between the major parties. After 1959, when the Conservatives had a majority of 101 seats (as in 1987) eight seats were held by majorities of 100 votes or less and forty-three by 1,000 votes or less. After 1987 the numbers of seats in each category were two and twenty-four.

Prospects for electoral reform

A poll by ITN Harris on election day 1987 found that the public was evenly divided between supporting the present electoral system and a more proportional system. Liberals and SDP supporters overwhelmingly preferred a change, Conservatives preferred the present system and Labour voters were evenly divided. But it needs emphasizing that electoral reform is not considered to be an important issue compared with the economy, the health service and so on, except for centre party activitists. There has been talk of electing a reformed second chamber on a proportional basis — but while Labour has shown some belated interest the Conservatives have not. If there was a deadlock (or a 'balanced Parliament', as the centre parties like to call it) it is extremely unlikely that either a minority Labour or Conservative government would agree to introduce PR. Each would be more likely to soldier on for a while and dissolve Parliament in the hope of gaining a working majority — as Harold Wilson did in the general election in October 1974. However, if there were a series of deadlocked elections and it seemed that minority Parliaments were here to stay then a coalition or a form of power-sharing — which involved at least two parties — might seem to be the only way of ensuring stable government.

In such a situation the Alliance, in 1987, argued that it would insist on a free vote in the House of Commons on the introduction of proportional representation. No doubt the centre parties will do the same in the future. Since 1987 a number of Labour MPs and trade union leaders, largely frustrated by the Thatcher government's landslide victories on a minority of votes, have supported the principle of PR. Results similar to the 1983 and 1987 elections are likely to strengthen such calls. The introduction of coalitions and/or a proportional system would be likely to alter radically the conduct of British government and politics. At present, however, electoral reform is not a practical political issue. But if Labour decisively loses another general election then the party may turn to it out of desperation.

Nomination

For election to the House of Commons it is virtually necessary to be nominated as a candidate by a *major* political party. Each constituency party nominates a candidate and, if approved by the party headquarters, he or she becomes the constituency's prospective Parliamentary candidate. Each major party maintains a list of approved candidates from which local parties may select. If a candidate is not already on the party list then he or she has to be approved by party headquarters.

This power has been important in the Labour party. In the 1950s the party's National Executive Committee (NEC) turned down a number of left-wing nominations by constituencies. In 1986 the NEC, as part of its drive against Militant on Merseyside, made clear to the Liverpool (Knowsley North) constituency that it would not accept left-wing Euro-MP Les Huckfield as Labour candidate for a by-election. In the end the NEC imposed its own candidate, George Howarth, who won the by-election in November 1986.

To be nominated, a parliamentary candidate must himself be eligible to vote, nominated by ten local voters and pay a deposit of £500 to the returning officer which is forfeited if he or she fails to gain 5 per cent of the vote. Two points are interesting about nominations in Britain.

Because many seats are safe for the incumbent party, nomination is often tantamount to election

Yet very few people participate in the process; the numbers range from a few dozen in some Labour general management committees to a few hundred in some Conservative associations. The small number of active members in some Labour inner city parties has allowed 'entryism' by some left-wing groups. Neil Kinnock advocates the selection of candidates by a vote of all members, in the hope that Labour candidates will become more representative of the membership.

Nomination is assured for many MPs

In the late 1970s, however, Labour left-wingers, as part of their campaign to extend democracy in the party, changed the party rules so that all Labour MPs were subject to mandatory re-selection in the lifetime of Parliament. This was widely regarded as a device to make MPs more beholden to left-wing activists in the constituencies than to the party whips in Westminster. Some (ten) Labour MPs were de-selected for the 1983 election, and some of the MPs who departed for the Social Democratic Party would probably not have been re-selected by their local parties. For the 1987 election six were de-selected. To date, the rule change has not proved to be the major force once expected for the advance of the left in the party — on the contrary, in some cases left-wingers have been threatened with de-selection — and a number of constituency parties confine themselves to renominating the sitting MP.

Expenditure

British constituency elections are cheap in comparison to those in many other Western states largely because expenditure by local candidates is strictly limited by law. Each candidate is required to appoint an election agent who is responsible for seeing that the limits on expenses are not broken. The legal limits are usually raised before each election in line with inflation. The maximum permitted in constituencies ranged between £5,000 and £6,000 in 1987. On average candidates for the main three parties spent under £4,000 each, with Conservatives usually spending the most. The bulk of this goes on printing a candidate's election leaflets and addresses. Local candidates also have free postage for their election leaflets and free hire of school halls for meetings.

In sharp contrast there is no legal limit on the spending by national party organizations and no legal obligation for them to publish their election budgets. Most national spending goes on advertising, opinion polling, financing the leaders' tours and meetings and providing grants to constituency parties. Centrally, the parties in 1987 spent £15 million compared to just over £7 million in 1983. According to estimates by Michael Pinto-Duschinsky Labour's spending over the 1987 campaign amounted to nearly £4 million. Of this over half went on advertising. The Conservative's central spending was nearly £9 million, with two-thirds of this being spent on posters and advertisements. The Alliance spent nearly £2 million centrally (Butler and Kavanagh, 1988).

One important difference between election campaigns in Britain and the USA is that British parties are precluded from purchasing time on the broadcasting media although they can buy advertising in the press. In the USA there is little doubt that the opportunities for advertising have made elections very expensive and heightened the importance of personalities and the wealth of candidates. Some $100 million was spent by candidates in the 1988 US presidential campaign on television commercials alone.

Campaigns

There is a ritual element to British election campaigns. This is particularly so at the constituency level with candidates and helpers pursuing their time-worn techniques of canvassing, addressing meetings and delivering election addresses to electors' homes. At the national level the party leaders address public meetings in the major cities, attend morning press conferences and prepare for national election broadcasts. Elections today are effectively fought on a national scale through the mass media, particularly television. The activities of the party leaders — visiting party committee rooms, factories, and old people's homes, speaking at evening rallies and making statements at morning press conferences — are conducted with an eye to gaining such coverage. If activities are not covered by peak-time television they are largely wasted as a means of communicating with the public. One of the most famous images of the 1979 election was Mrs Thatcher on a Norfolk farm, cuddling a new-born calf. This had little to do with discussion of political issues but the bonus for the Conservatives was that photographs of the event were carried in almost every national newspaper and on the television screens. There is some Americanization of campaigning in Britain; local face to face meetings have declined in importance, while the national parties employ their own opinion pollsters and advertising agencies.

Recent elections have shown the limits of issues as an influence on voting. In fact, people rarely vote on the basis of one issue alone. Even when they prefer one party's position on an issue they may doubt that party's ability to carry out the policy or fear its damaging consequences for other desirable goals, e.g. on inflation. In 1983 and 1987, voters overwhelmingly mentioned unemployment as the most important issue and a large majority regarded Labour as the better party on the issue. Yet in both elections Labour was trounced.

Voters had doubts about Labour's ability to deliver, were worried that Labour policies would have damaging consequences on the inflation rate and above all doubted Labour's 'competence to govern'. Yet there is no doubt that the voter's calculations about the effects of a policy on himself and his family is likely to shape his vote. In 1987 defence and taxation were vote-losers for the Labour party. Issues are also important in contributing to the overall image of the political party; perhaps the most important aspect of a party's image is its ability to provide effective government, strong leadership and persuade voters that it has a clear sense of purpose. On these criteria the Conservatives ran far ahead of Labour in the 1983 and 1987 elections.

It is difficult to prove that election campaigns make much difference to the final result. One party's good campaign in a constituency may fail to show a marked improvement because the opposition parties have also made strenuous efforts in the seat. There is some evidence that an active new MP, perhaps using local radio and television over the lifetime of a Parliament, can gain up to 700 'personal' votes at the following general election. For many voters, however, the choice of who to support on polling day is a product of a lifetime of influences, rather than the four weeks of an election campaign. Most observers agreed that in 1983 the Conservative campaign was vastly superior to Labour's, which was something of a disaster. Yet, according to the average score of the opinion polls, the fall in support for both Labour and Conservatives between the first week of the campaign and polling day was identical (4 per cent). In 1987 many observers were critical of the Conservatives' campaign but on polling day they had preserved the eleven-point lead over Labour enjoyed at the outset of the campaign. Compared to the disaster of 1983 Labour's campaign was admired for its smooth organization and professionalism. But for all this, and Neil Kinnock's campaigning superiority to Michael Foot, Labour added just 3 per cent to its 1983 record low vote. Packaging and presentation can only do so much.

Voting behaviour

For most of the post-war period it has been comparatively easy to provide broad explanations of voting behaviour in Britain. Three guidelines simplified analysis. The *first* was that people were regarded as being either middle or working class on the basis of their occupations. Although there were divisions within these groupings, notably between the skilled and unskilled working class, there was a strong correlation between class and vote: the vast majority of the working class voted Labour and most of the middle class voted Tory. *Secondly*, an average of about 90 per cent of voters supported either Labour or Conservative in general elections

Issue voting

During the 1960s it was generally believed by psephologists that British people tended to vote according to traditional associations of class and party. By the 1980s, however, such loyalties had waned. The work of Särlvik and Crewe (1983) and that of Mark Franklin (1985) suggest that these days the British vote to a much greater degree upon the basis of issues. According to this view we are now in an era of 'partisan dealignment' where citizens no longer vote blindly for the party of their parents or workmates but, in the true spirit of pluralist democracy, listen to what the parties have to say on issues and react accordingly — sometimes in a volatile fashion.

Crewe distinguishes between 'salience', the extent to which people are aware of an issue, and 'party preferred' in terms of policies on that issue. The table below reveals how issues have waxed and waned in importance over the last two decades.

Issues in elections, 1974–87

	October 1974		1979	
	Salience	Preferred party lead	Salience	Preferred party lead
Prices	82	Lab. +11	42	Lab. +13
Unemployment	12	Lab. +19	27	Lab. +15
Trade unions/strikes	15	Lab. +33	20	Con. +15
Common Market	11	Con. +3	—	—
Taxes	—	—	21	Con. +61
Law and order	—	—	11	Con: +27

	1983		1987	
	Salience	Preferred party lead	Salience	Preferred party lead
Prices	20	Con. +40	—	—
Unemployment	72	Lab. +16	49	Lab. +34
Defence	38	Con. +54	35	Con. +63
NHS	11	Lab. +46	33	Lab. +49
Education	—	—	19	Lab. +15

Note: The table reports issues mentioned by more than 10 per cent of voters at any of the four elections. The preferred party's lead is the percentage saying the party most preferred on the issue overall had the best policy minus the percentage saying the same of the next most preferred party.

Source: Denver, 1989.

'Prices' were stated by respondents as being of key importance in the 1974 election but less than 10 per cent identified this issue in 1987 — an election, of course, which followed an extended period of low inflation. Defence was not mentioned in 1974 or 1979 but was of considerable importance in the post-Falklands election of 1983. Crewe believes the Conservative emphasis on taxes, law and order and trade union reform won the 1979 election for them, and the table seems to support this view. In 1987, however, Labour led the Conservatives on three of the most salient issues — unemployment, the health service and education — yet lost the election. Crewe's explanation was that despite their identification of issues and their preferences for Labour prescriptions voters reacted to a key personal consideration when it came to the crunch. People were happy to identify issues upon which they felt that action should be taken but they chose to vote for the party which they thought delivered the highest degree of personal prosperity.

Crewe's work on issues has been the subject of controversy and has been criticized by Heath *et al.* (1985) and by Rose and McAllister (1986) who both offer contrasting explanations of voting behaviour.

---

between 1945 and 1970. *Finally*, most (over 80 per cent) of voters were partisans or identifiers with one or other of the above parties. Surveys indicated that for most people party allegiance hardened over time so that they were unlikely to turn to a new party. Identifiers are also more likely than other voters to agree with *their* party's policies and leaders.

For most of the post-war period, therefore, social class and partisanship (and, as noted earlier, the electoral system) interacted to buttress the Labour/Conservative party system. There were only small margins of change in the parties' share of the votes between elections. Between 1950 and 1970, for example, the Conservative share of the vote ranged from 49.7 per cent (1959) to 41.9 per cent (1945) and Labour's from 48.8 per cent (1951) to 43.8 per cent (1959). Stability was the order of the day and it was difficult to envisage a change in the system.

The above description needs some qualification, of course. The most important is that between a quarter and a third of the working class usually voted Conservative. Without this 'deviant' vote there would not have been a competitive two-party system and the Conservatives would hardly have been the 'normal' party of government in the twentieth century. Another is that class distribution was gradually changing as the proportion of the work-force engaged in manufacturing fell and the proportion employed in service and white-collar occupations grew.

Yet in recent years that old two-party two-class model explains a diminishing part of British election behaviour. First, consider *partisanship*: between 1964 and 1983 the proportion of the electorate identifying with the Labour and Conservative parties fell from 81 per cent to 70 per cent and *strong identifiers* from 38 per cent to 23 per cent over the same period. Since an increasing number of voters have weak ties to parties, more votes are 'up for grabs' at elections.

Secondly, consider *social class*. The relationship between class and voting was fairly strong until the mid-1970s. Yet even in the 1960s surveys suggested that class loyalty was weakening in its intensity for many voters (Butler and Stokes, 1970, 1974). In general elections since 1970, Labour's normal two-thirds share of the working-class vote has fallen to less than a half (and as low as 38 per cent in 1983). Over the same period the Conservatives' normal four-fifths share of the middle-class vote has fallen to three-fifths. Quite separate from these trends has been the shift in the balance between the classes in the electorate. From a rough 40–60 split between the middle class and working class, the distribution today is nearer 50–50. In other words, Labour has been gaining a diminishing share of a smaller working-class constituency.

Social changes moreover have weakened the old class bases of the party system. Over 60 per cent of homes are now privately owned; since 1979 the proportion of council tenants has fallen from 45 per cent to 27 per cent. Jobs in services and white-collar professional and managerial occupations have increased, those in manufacturing have fallen. As a proportion of the work-force trade unionists have fallen from 30 to 22 per cent, and are now outnumbered by holders of shares. Although many people are now in 'mixed' social class groups, e.g. working-class home-owners, Britain is increasingly becoming a middle-class society.

Finally, consider the *level of support* for the two main parties. The Labour and Conservative parties' combined average of 90 per cent of the vote in general elections between 1945 and 1970 has fallen to around 75 per cent in the elections since then. Electoral stability has been replaced by fluidity and the two-party, two-class model by three-party less-class-based voting in 1983 and 1987. As the moorings of class and partisanship have declined, so volatility has increased. The election campaigns (and the personalities, issues and events associated with them) may have more influence.

The February 1974 election campaign was overshadowed by the sense of economic (and, for some, constitutional) crisis occasioned by the energy shortage and the miners' strike against the government's statutory incomes policy. Labour's campaign in 1979 foundered on the preceding 'winter of discontent', when many public sector workers took industrial action to break the government's incomes policies. Labour's claims to have an 'understanding' with the trade unions and to be uniquely placed to gain their consent were shattered. In October 1978 the opinion polls showed Labour ahead of the Conservatives, yet in February 1979 the Conservatives were ahead by 20 per cent, according to Gallup. In the early months of 1982 the three parties were pretty level according to the opinion polls and some Conservatives were even talking of the need to replace Mrs Thatcher as party leader. Yet after the Falklands victory the government shot into an overwhelming lead which they held for the next two years. In September 1986 Labour had a clear lead in the opinion polls but by March 1987 they were twelve points adrift of the Conservatives.

As the electorate has become more volatile so the campaigns may have more impact. Ivor Crewe (1987) has measured the change in the main parties' share of the vote according to changes between the average of opinion polls at the end of the first week and on polling day in recent election campaigns. In 1970 the change was 2 per cent, in February 1974 2.8 per cent, in 1979 3.9 per cent and in 1983 5.3 per cent. In 1987 the trend was reversed and the change was only 1 per cent.

British voting behaviour	**British voting behaviour** has become less predictable for the following reasons:
	Partisanship: strong identifiers with parties have reduced in number
	Social class: class loyalties have weakened and the working class is diminishing in size
	Social changes: housing and occupational patterns have changed
	Level of support for the two parties: reduced from 90 per cent in 1945 to 75 per cent during the 1980s

Social class

There are several different approaches to defining social class. Most researchers have relied on the six-category scheme of the British Market Research Society (BMRS): A, B, C1, C2, D and E. The first three (professional, managerial and clerical) are conventionally termed 'middle class', and the final three (skilled and unskilled manual workers, and a residual group of old age pensioners, widows and their families) are 'working class'. This scheme relies on occupation combined with life-style and incomes as the bases for differentiating classes and splits the population 40–60 per cent between the middle and working class (Table 11.5c).

Another approach to social class has been developed by researchers at Oxford University in their study into social mobility. This focuses more on the conditions in which incomes are earned and a person's degree of autonomy and authority at work. *How Britain Votes* (Heath *et al.* 1985), uses this approach. Its middle class broadly corresponds with the ABC1 groups of the BRMS and the proportions are broadly similar. The most dramatic change is the reduction in the size of the **working class** of manual workers to 34 per cent (Table 11.5a). They also create other non-manual groups, including the **intermediate** class, of clerical and sales workers and foremen (24 per cent) and the **salariat** of managers, executives and professionals (27 per cent). In addition they have a **petit bourgeoisie** of self-employed and **small employed** which the BMRS allocate to the skilled working class.

Other researchers, writing from a neo-Marxist perspective, are more concerned with dividing classes according to whether individuals do or do not own the means of production, i.e. control of labour (Table 11.5b). The study of electoral behaviour by Patrick Dunleavy and Chris Husbands, *British Democracy at the Crossroads* (1985), also takes account of what it calls 'consumption' or 'production' classes. This is based on a person's 'location on a system of production and exchange and

Table 11.5   *Different definitions of social class*

(a) Social class categories (Heath *et al.*) (%)	
Salariat	27
Routine non-manuals	24
Petit bourgeoisie	8
Foremen, technicians	7
Working class	34

(b) Social class categories (Dunleavy and Husbands) (%)	
Manual workers	45
Non-manual	25
Controllers of labour	22
Employees/petit bourgeoisie	8

(c) Social class categories (British Market Research Society) (%)	
A Upper middle	2
B Middle	13
C1 Lower middle	24
C2 Skilled workers	31
D Semi-skilled and unskilled workers	18
E Poor	2

the level of power people can exert over their own tasks'. For example, people in manual work may differ according to whether they are primarily dependent on private or collective provision of services. Do they own or rent their houses privately or from the local council; do they have children in private or state schools; do they use private health care or the national health service?

One may also make a similar division among manual and non-manual workers according to whether people are employed in the public or private sector. Studies have found some 'sectoral' effects; workers in the public sector, for example, are more likely to vote Labour compared with similar groups in the private sector. The effects, however, are rather modest. Similarly a large part of the explanation of the 'two Britains' — a Tory south and Labour north is because the south contains middle-class home-owning households.

Parties and their support

What are the sources of electoral support for the three major political parties in Britain?

Conservative

The Conservatives have clearly been the dominant party in Britain in the twentieth century. As of 1990 they have been in office, alone or in coalition, for over two-thirds of the period. They have also been in office for more than half the period since 1945. Indeed, in the past century the only three occasions in which the non-Conservative parties have had clear majorities were: the 1906—10 Liberal government, the 1945—50 Labour government; and the 1966—70 Labour government. In recent years a significant part of the Conservative success has been due to the effects of the first-past-the-post electoral system and the divided opposition (Table 11.6). In 1979, 1983 and 1987, 42 per cent of the vote has been enough to produce Conservative landslides as the Alliance (Table 11.7), and the Labour parties divided the non-Conservative vote between them. The Conservatives have also been the beneficiary of Labour's internal divisions and unpopular policies.

Yet in the 1980s the party also identified itself firmly with economic prosperity. In spite of presiding over a return to levels of mass unemployment the party under Mrs Thatcher managed to fashion a large constituency which had an interest in the continuation of Conservative rule. People who have done well since 1979 include many who live in the affluent south and suburbs, home-owners, share-owners (who expanded from 7 per cent in 1979 to over 20 per cent in 1987), and most of those in work.

Table 11.6 *How the nation voted*

	June 1987 (%)	June 1983 (%)
Conservative	42.2	42.3
Labour	30.8	27.6
Alliance	22.6	25.4
Others	3.4	4.7

Table 11.7 *Government
parliamentary majorities 1945–87*

	(Overall majority)
1945	Lab 147
1950	Lab 6
1951	Con 16
1955	Con 59
1959	Con 99
1964	Lab 5
1966	Lab 97
1970	Con 31
1974 (February)	None
1974 (October)	Lab 4
1979	Con 44
1983	Con 144
1987	Con 102

Labour

As partisanship and class are weakening so the long-term future for the Labour party has become less secure. The party's share of the vote has fallen below 40 per cent in all general elections since 1970. Its 1983 share of 27.6 per cent was its lowest since 1918 (when Labour was still a new party and fighting its first nation-wide election). The recovery in 1987 was modest, to 31 per cent.

Optimists may claim that Labour lost so badly in 1979 largely because of the public's hostile reaction to the trade unions and Labour government in the 'winter of discontent'. They may also point out that before the 1983 election, the party had suffered damaging internal rows over Militant, constitutional changes — and the associated breakaway of the Social Democrats — the weakness of Michael Foot as leader and the bitter battle between Healey and Benn for the deputy leadership. These explanations are plausible and it is generally admitted that Labour's campaign in 1983 was disastrous. But it is difficult to produce special circumstances as an explanation of Labour's poor result in 1987, its second worst performance in seats and votes since 1945.

The faster growth of population in the south compared to the north, spread of home-ownership and decline of council tenancy, contraction of public sector employment (through the privatization of British Gas, British Airways, British Telecom, etc.), reduction of heavy manufacturing and growth of service industries and fall in membership of unions have all weakened the traditional institutional supports for Labour. The working class today is increasingly divided between home-owners and council tenants, skilled versus unskilled workers and members of strong or weak trade unions. The old working class — members of trade unions, engaged in heavy industrial work, renting property from a council and employed in the public sector — is a steadily diminishing electoral minority. Labour has to look outside the manufacturing working class for votes.

The 'new working class', as Crewe (1987) describes it, is increasingly home-owning, living in south Britain, car-owning, not in a union and employed in the private sector. In 1983 and 1987 it decisively preferred the Conservatives to Labour (see Table 11.8).

Table 11.8   *How the working class voted in 1987 (%)*

	The new working class				The traditional working class			
	Lives in south (40%)[1]	Owner-occupier (57%)[1]	Non-union (66%)[1]	Works in private sector	Lives in Scotland/North	Council tenant	Union member	Works in public sector
Con.	46	44	40	38	29	25	30	32
Lab.	28	32	38	39	57	57	48	49
Lib./SDP	26	24	22	23	15	18	22	19
Con./Lab.	Con.	Con.	Con.	Lab.	Lab.	Lab.	Lab.	Lab.
maj. 1987	+18	+12	+2	+1	+32	+17	+28	+18
Con./Lab.	Con.	Con.	Con.	Lab.	Lab.	Lab.	Lab.	Lab.
maj. 1983	+16	+22	+6	+1	+38	+17	+10	+21
Change from 1983	+4	+3	+7	+2	−1	−4	−7	−2

Note: 1% of all manual workers
Source: Crewe, *The Guardian*, 15 June 1987

Third party voting

The growth of 'other' parties — or decline of aggregate support for the two main parties — may mean different things. Among the electorate over 95 per cent of votes are cast for three parties (accepting the Alliance as one party in 1983 and 1987). In the House of Commons, however, nearly 95 per cent of seats are in the hands of the Labour and Conservative parties. The disproportional effects of the first-past-the-post electoral system 'wasted' much Alliance electoral support.

In the House of Commons the third force is particularly heterogeneous. Apart from the Liberal Democrats and SDP MPs it also includes Welsh Nationalists, Scottish Nationalists and the members from the various Northern Ireland parties. One reason for the growth of these 'other' MPs from 1974 onwards had less to do with the Liberal and then Alliance upsurge in the country than with the fragmentation of the Ulster Unionists after 1974.

Much of the popular support to date for 'other' parties outside Northern Ireland has not been translated into a sufficient number of seats to threaten the two main parties. In the 1974 elections the growth in Liberal support (to 19 per cent of the vote in the February election) and the rise of the Nationalists in Scotland (to 30 per cent of the Scottish vote in October 1974) represented a potential threat. But these advances were not consolidated and both parties actually retreated in seats and votes in 1979. The referendum in March 1979 showed weak support for national devolution (let alone independence) in Scotland and Wales (only 11.9 per cent of Welsh votes supported it). In the 1983 and 1987 elections Nationalist support averaged 13 per cent in Scotland and 7.5 per cent in Wales.

The most formidable threat yet to the dominance of the Labour–Conservative party system developed in 1981. Following the breakaway of a number of leading right-wingers from Labour to form the Social Democratic party, its alliance with the Liberals enabled the new force to gain greatly from the unpopularity and the divisions within the two major parties. Between March 1981 and March 1982 the Alliance was regularly first or second in the opinion polls and had a remarkable string of by-election successes. It failed to maintain its support after the recapture of the Falklands in April 1982. In 1987 the Alliance party was disappointed with its 23 per cent share of the vote and twenty-one seats. The two party leaders quarrelled in the aftermath of the election over whether or not to merge. The SDP split into a faction headed by David Owen, which preferred independence, and a majority under Robert MacLennon, which supported merger with the Liberals in the new Social and Liberal Democratic party (Liberal Democrats).

The relative lack of an electoral following based upon issues or social groups has meant that the centre parties' support has depended largely on the fortunes of the other two major parties. The even spread of Alliance support over the country in 1983 and 1987 also meant that even with 30 per cent of the vote it would only have got some fifty seats. It has no regional strongholds, like Labour in the north and Conservatives in the south. With more than 40 per cent of the vote, however, a centre party could profit from the first-past-the-post electoral system and even get a majority of seats.

Until the 1987 election there was talk of *realignment in the British party system*, largely based on the fortunes of the Alliance. Realignment may come about in one of two forms.

1. The Liberal Democrats may replace Labour as the main alternative to the Conservative party. This was certainly in the minds of those who were behind the original SDP break away from the Labour party. Yet in the wake of the 1987 election this looks a remote possibility; the SDP finally wound itself up in May 1990.
2. The Liberal Democrats may become a significant third party (in terms of seats). Either development could have profound consequences for electoral choice. There is, however, a paradox. Liberals have traditionally done better under Conservative governments, attracting disillusioned Tory voters; in addition, the Social Democratic party was originally anti-Labour. Yet of the 100 seats which were most likely to fall to the Alliance if it broke through in 1983 and 1987 three-quarters were held by the Conservative party. In the short term at least a Liberal Democrat breakthrough is more likely to reduce the number of Conservative seats.

The party system and the party attachments of voters were particularly fluid in the 1970s and the 1980s.

The new electoral pattern means that the three main parties fight on two fronts. For example, Conservatives have had to worry not only about Labour, which is the main opposition in Parliament, but the Alliance, particularly in the south where that party was often runner-up in Conservative seats in the 1983 and 1987 elections. Some commentators often suggest that nearly 55 per cent of the electorate (i.e. combined Labour and centre support) was anti-Thatcherite. But since as many centre party supporters prefer the Conservatives as prefer Labour, one might just as well claim that some 70–75 per cent of voters are anti-Labour or anti-centre.

The next general election (to be held no later than June 1992) may have several possible outcomes. If the old two-party Labour/Conservative dominance reasserts itself among the electorate (for instance, if the two parties get over 85 per cent of the vote between them) this will mark another turning point. In the last five general elections 'other' parties in aggregate have averaged 25 per cent of the votes cast and multi-partyism became the new electoral 'norm'. Presumably, for a recovery of the two-party system Labour will have to do considerably better than it has done in recent general elections.

If the Conservatives were to win a fourth successive election it would be the only time such a sequence has occurred in the twentieth century. If they win in 1991–2 and remain in office until 1996–7 they would have been in office for 67 of the 97 years in the twentieth century. They would also have had the opportunities to shape the political agenda and promote significant social and economic policy changes — (e.g. in cutting direct taxes, reshaping education, housing and welfare, extending privatization and weakening local government) — which might be difficult to reverse.

If Labour lost a fourth successive election — and decisively once more — what might its reaction be? Might it promote full-blooded measures of socialism on the grounds that radical socialism had not been tried in the past? Or might it adjust to a change of electoral mood (particularly the changes made under Mrs Thatcher) and/or join forces with other parties in an anti-Conservative coalition?

If there were to be a series of deadlocked Parliaments and coalition or minority governments ensued, **and** there was continued large support for a third party, pressure would almost certainly increase for a new set of rules of the game. There is little historical evidence about how voters might react to political and constitutional uncertainties. Might they prefer a clear choice of a government with a majority, or might a substantial number vote in the hope of actually preventing a majority for one party? Multi-party politics provides voters with the opportunity to vote tactically — against the party they most dislike. In 1987, the ITN Harris poll found that 17 per cent claimed to have voted tactically. At present surveys suggest that potential deadlocked Parliaments are not popular.

If we turn to voting behaviour, many of the old guidelines have also lost their usefulness. Because fewer voters are party loyalists the forces of habit or tradition are weaker. The old divide between the middle and working class is also less useful because:

(a) a substantial third party vote obviously weakens the link between class and party vote;

(b) changes in the classes themselves. Both the middle and working class now divide their vote between the three parties and no one party had a majority in either class in 1983.

Some social class-related features are still important, however. Among both classes trade union membership increases a person's likelihood of voting Labour and home-ownership, regardless of class, is substantially more likely to increase Conservative tendencies.

For a discussion of the 1992 General Election campaign and results, see Chapter 29.

References and Further Reading

Butler, D., *Governing without a Majority* (Collins, 1983).
Butler, D. and Kavanagh, D., *The British General Election of 1987* (Macmillan, 1988).

Butler, D. and Stokes, D., *Political Change in Britain* (Macmillan, 1970, 1974).

Crewe, I., 'Why Mrs Thatcher was returned with a landslide', *Social Studies Review* (September 1987).

Denver, D., *Elections and Voting Behaviour in Britain* (Philip Allan, 1989).

Dunleavy, P. and Husbands, C., *British Democracy at the Crossroads* (Longman, 1985).

Franklin, M., *The Decline of Class Voting in Britain* (Oxford University Press, 1985).

Hailsham, Lord, *Dilemma of Democracy* (Collins, 1977).

Heath, A., Jowell, R. and Curtice, J., *How Britain Votes* (Pergamon Press, 1985).

Rose, R. and McAllister, I., *Voters Begin to Choose* (Sage, 1986).

Sarlvik, B. and Crewe, I., *Decade of Dealignment* (Cambridge Univeristy Press, 1983).

Urwin, D., 'The mechanics and effects of various political systems', *Social Studies Review* (March 1987).

12 The Mass Media and Politics

Bill Jones

**Without newspapers, radio and pre-eminently television, the present political
system could not work. The media are so omnipresent and all-pervasive we are
often unaware of the addictive hold they exert over our attention and the
messages they implant in our consciousness on a whole range of matters —
including politics. This chapter assesses the impact of the mass media upon the
working of our political system and different theories of how they work.**

During the wedding of Prince Andrew and Sarah Ferguson in 1986, ITN newcaster
Martyn Lewis was moving about among the crowds with a camera crew. 'What
for you has been the highlight of the day?' he asked a young man. 'Oh, being
interviewed by you, definitely Martyn' was his instant reply. This episode helps
illustrate the point made by Canadian writer Marshall McLuhan that the principal
means of communication in modern society, television, has become more important
than the messages it carries; to some extent the medium *has* become the message.
The impact of the mass media upon society has been so recent and so profound it
is difficult as yet for us to gauge its impact with any precision.

The term 'mass media' embraces books, pamphlets and film but is usually
understood to refer to newspapers, radio and television; since the 1950s television
has eclipsed newspapers and radio as the key medium. Surveys indicate over 60
per cent of people identify television as the most important single source of
information about politics (see Table 12.1). On average British people now watch
over twenty hours of television per week and given that 20 per cent of television
output covers news and current affairs, a fair political content is being imbibed.
Indeed, the audience for *News at Ten* (ITN) and the *Nine O'Clock News* (BBC)
regularly exceeds 20 million. Surveys also show that the majority of viewers trust
television news as fair and accurate.

Television is now such a dominant medium it is easy to forget its provenance has
been so recent. During the seventeenth and early eighteenth centuries political
communication was mainly verbal: between members of the relatively small political
elite, within a broader public at election times, within political groups like the
seventeenth-century Diggers and Levellers and occasionally from the pulpit. Given
their scarcity, books and broadsheets had a limited though important role to play.

The agricultural and industrial revolutions in the eighteenth century revolutionized
work and settlement patterns. Agricultural village workers gave way to vast

Table 12.1 *Voters' major sources of political information in the 1983 election*

Media source	% citing as most important media source	In top two sources cited
TV	63	88
Newspapers	29	73
Radio	4	14
Personal contacts	3	12
Other	1	3

Source: Adapted from Dunleavy and Husbands, 1985, p.111

conglomerations of urban industrial workers who proved responsive to the libertarian and democratic values propagated by the American and French political revolutions. Orator Hunt was able to address meetings of up to 100,000 people (the famous Peterloo meeting has been estimated at 150,000) which he did purely (and in retrospect, astonishingly) through the power of his own lungs. Later in the nineteenth century the Chartists and the Anti-Corn Law League employed teams of speakers supplementing their efforts with pamphlets — which could now be disseminated by the postal system.

The Press

By the end of the nineteenth century newspaper editorials and articles had become increasingly important: *The Times* and weekly journals for the political elite and the popular press — the *Mail, Mirror* and *Express* — for the newly enfranchised masses. Press barons like Northcliffe, Rothermere and Beaverbrook became major national political figures, wooed and feared by politicians for the power which the press had delivered to them within a democratic political system. Britain currently has eleven daily newspapers and some three-quarters of the adult population read one. Two dailies, the tabloids *Daily Mirror* and *Sun*, have circulations in excess of three million (Table 12.2). There is a smaller but growing aggregate circulation for the 'qualities' like *The Guardian, The Times, The Independent* and *Daily Telegraph*. The two tabloids have a predominantly working-class readership, the 'qualities' a more middle-class and well-educated one. The *Daily Express* and *Daily Mail* are more up-market tabloids and have a socially more representative readership.

There is certainly a pro-Conservative bias in the newspapers (see Table 12.3). In the 1987 general election seven of the eleven supported a Conservative victory and only the *Mirror* and *The Guardian* (with about a fifth of the total circulation) favoured Labour. Of the two relatively new newspapers, *The Independent* (founded 1986) refused to endorse any party and *Today* (also founded 1986) supported the Alliance. From 1945 to 1970 the total circulation of pro-Conservative newspapers

Table 12.2 *Party choice by daily newspaper read, sales and readers' assessments of their newspapers' party support*

	Sales (millions)	Vote of readers (%)			Readers' assessments of their newspapers' party support (%)			
		Conservative	Labour	Alliance	Cons	Lab	Alliance	None/ Don't Know
Tory press								
Sun	4.0	41	31	19	63	12	7	18
Daily Mail	1.8	60	13	19	78	2	5	15
Daily Express	1.7	70	9	18	87	0	4	9
Daily Star	1.3	28	46	18	23	16	7	54
Daily Telegraph	1.2	80	5	10	85	0	3	12
The Times	0.4	56	12	27	61	0	33	6
Labour Press								
Daily Mirror	3.1	20	55	21	2	84	8	6
Guardian	0.5	22	54	19	13	30	43	14
Non-Tory press								
Today	0.3	43	17	40	11	4	18	67
Independent	0.3	34	34	27	12	6	20	62

Source: Butler and Kavanagh, 1988, p.187; *Social Studies Review*, September 1987, p.60)

Table 12.3 *Press bias: reports on the March for Jobs rally, June 1981*

Newspaper	Estimate of number attending	Comment in news report
Guardian	Police: 15–20,000 Organizers: 130,000	None
Daily Telegraph	About 10,000	Ended in chaos and confusion
The Times	15–20,000	Low turnout will be seen as blow to the labour movement
Daily Express	Police estimate fewer than 20,000 but *Daily Express* count suggests fewer still. Union leaders say at least 15,000	Soggy anti-climax
Daily Mail	20,000	Ended with allegations of violence
Daily Mirror	Thousands flocked in on 200 coaches and 11 special trains	Defiant end to 'gissa job' march
Daily Star	More than 150,000	Huge rally
Sun	Little more than 5,000	Pathetic, rain-soaked end
Morning Star	100,000	Shook the conscience of the nation
Scotsman	About 150,000	Huge rally

Source: Butler and Kavanagh, 1984, p.20

Neil Kinnock
and the
tabloids

> During the 1987 election campaign Neil Kinnock was interviewed by
> David Frost and spoke in terms which suggested that, under a Labour
> government, there would not be military resistance to a Russian
> invasion. The *Daily Express* led on the issue three times during the
> week: 'IF THE ENEMY COMES, BY NEIL'; 'WHITE FLAG, KINNOCK
> ACCUSED', 'MAGGIE NUKES KINNOCK'. Other Conservative
> supporting tabloids also made front page headlines on the story.
>
> The *Sun* in the election tried to associate Labour politicians with
> sexual minorities. 'LABOUR USES GAY JIMI TO WIN OVER YOUNG
> VOTERS', 'LABOUR PICKS RENT BOY AS SCHOOL BOSS'. The
> paper also launched a 'SPECIAL NIGHTMARE ISSUES — LIFE
> UNDER THE SOCIALISTS. See p.5, 6, 8, 9 and 13'. John Benyon took
> up the story in *Social Studies Review*, November 1987:
>
> > The *Sun* even carried 'interviews', via 'a medium and psychic
> > investigator', with figures such as Stalin (Labour supporter) and Henry VIII
> > and Lord Nelson (both Conservative)! Boadicea, who died over 1900
> > years ago, stated in the *Sun*: 'When I hear the words of Kinnock and his
> > treacherous ilk I feel ashamed for England'. Keir Hardie, a Founder of
> > the Labour Party, was now a Social Democrat, while Genghis Khan
> > wouldn't vote, although he admired Mrs Thatcher.

was not substantially above that of the pro-Labour newspapers. The Conservative
lead has grown in recent years, however, in large part because of the switch of the
Sun (formerly the Labour-supporting *Daily Herald*) to the Conservative party in
1974, and the relative decline of the *Mirror*'s circulation.

In recent elections some of the tabloids have become more partisan against Labour.
Some observers detected a close correlation between the issues 'run' by the
Conservatives and the lead stories of the tabloids: it was known that editors of some
of the tabloids had frequent contacts with Conservative Central Office. In the 1987
general election the *Sun, Star* and the *News of the World* chose to publish lurid front-
page stories about the private (i.e. sex) lives of Labour and Liberal leaders (David
Steel successfully sued the *Sun* and the *Star* over their stories).

Broadcasting

Adolf Hitler was the first politician fully to exploit the potential of radio for overtly
propaganda purposes; Franklin D. Roosevelt with his fireside chats and Stanley
Baldwin with his similar, relaxed, confidential style introduced the medium more
gently to US and British political cultures. Some politicians like Neville Chamberlain
were quite skilled at addressing cinema audiences via *Pathé News* films, but others
like (surprisingly) the Fascist leader Oswald Mosely proved to be wooden and
ineffective. During the war radio became the major and much-used medium for
political opinion — Churchill's broadcasts were crucial — and news while film drama
was used extensively to reinforce values such as patriotism and resistance.

It was in 1952, however, that the television revolution began in earnest with Richard
Nixon's embattled 'Checkers' broadcast, made to clear his name of financial
wrongdoing. Offering himself as a hard-working honest person of humble origins

**Richard Nixon
— the
'Checkers
Speech'**

> I should say this: Pat doesn't have a mink coat, but she does have a
> respectable Republican cloth coat ... One other thing I should
> probably tell you, because if I don't they'll be saying this about me
> too. We did get something, a gift, after the election ... a little cocker
> spaniel in a crate, all the way from Texas ... And our little girl,
> Trisha, the six-year-old, named it Checkers. And you know, the kids
> love that dog, and I just want to say this right now, that regardless of
> what they say about it, we're gonna keep it!
>
> **Richard Nixon,** US vice-president, in the 'Checkers Speech', after he
> had been accused of using campaign funds for his personal gain,
> 1952.
>
> *Source*: J. Green 1982.

he finished his talk by telling viewers how his daughter had received a puppy as
a present: he didn't care what anyone said, he wasn't going to give 'Checkers' back.
This blatant appeal to sentiment proved spectacularly successful and confirmed
Nixon's Vice-Presidential place on the Eisenhower ticket. Later on, television
ironically contributed to Nixon's undoing through the famous televised debates with
Kennedy during the 1960 Presidential election contest. Despite an assured verbal
performance, Nixon, the favourite, looked shifty with his five o'clock shadow and
slightly crumpled appearance. Kennedy's good looks and strong profile gave him
the edge. Politicians the world over looked, listened and learned that how you appear
on television counts for as much as why you say.

The British Broadcasting Corporation (BBC) was established as a monopolistic
public corporation in 1926, a monopoly that was defended on the grounds that the
BBC provided a public service. Commercial television (ITV) began broadcasting
in 1955, and commercial radio in 1973. The BBC was granted a second television
channel (BBC 2) in 1964 and a second ITV channel (Channel 4) began broadcasting
in 1982. Although the Prime Minister appoints the Chairman of the BBC and its
Board of Governors and the government of the day reviews and renews the BBC's
charter, its governors are supposed to act in an independent fashion. The creation
of the independent television network under the IBA in 1954 ended the BBC's
monopoly in television broadcasting. Independent Television's Chairman, like the
BBC's, is appointed by the government. However, since ITV is financed out of
advertising revenues it enjoys more financial independence from the government
of the day. Broadcasting — especially television — has had a transforming impact
on political processes.

Media organizations are now major actors in the political process

Two minutes of exposure at peak time television enables politicians to reach more
people than they could meet in a lifetime of canvassing, hand-wringing or addressing
public meetings. Alternatively, speaking on BBC Radio Four's early morning *Today*
programme gains access to an 'upmarket' audience of opinion formers and decision
makers. In consequence, broadcasting organizations have become potent players in

the political game:

1. The regularity and nature of access to television and radio has become a key political issue.
2. Interviewers like Brian Walden, David Dimbleby and Brian Redhead have become important national figures.
3. Investigative current affairs programmes like *World in Action* and *This Week* have become the source of bitter political controversy.

Television has influenced the form of political communication

In the nineteenth century it was commonplace for political meetings to entail formal addresses from great orators like Gladstone or Lloyd George lasting an hour or more. Television has transformed this process. To command attention in our living rooms politicians have to be relaxed, friendly, confidential — they have to talk to us as individuals rather than as members of a crowd. Long speeches are out: political messages have to be compressed into spaces of 2−3 minutes — often less. Slogans and key phrases have become so important that speech writers are employed to think them up. The playwright Ronald Millar was thus employed and helped produce Mrs Thatcher's memorable 'The Lady's not for Turning' speech at the 1981 Conservative Party Conference.

Broadcasters have usurped the role of certain political institutions

Local party organization is less important now that television can gain access to people's homes so easily and effectively. The message, however, is a more centralized national one, concentrating upon the party leadership rather than local issues and local people. The phenomenon of the SDP, moreover, has shown that a national party can now be created through media coverage without any substantial branch network. It also reveals how quickly such parties can decline once media interest wanes.

The House of Commons has lost some of its informing and educative function to the media. Ministers often prefer to give statements to the media rather than to Parliament and interviewers gain much more exclusive access to politicians than the House of Commons can ever hope for. Even public discussion and debate is now purveyed via radio and television programmes like the BBC's *Today*, *Newsnight* and *Question Time*. Some hope that televising the House of Commons will win back some of these lost functions but others worry that the 'cure' will have damaging side effects upon the seriousness and efficacy of Parliamentary procedures.

The appointment of party leaders

In 1951 Attlee was asked by a *Pathé News* reporter how the general election campaign was going. 'Very well', he replied. When it became obvious that the Prime Minister was not prepared to elaborate the interviewer broke the silence by asking him if he wished to say anything else. 'No' was the reply. Such behaviour did not survive the 1960s. Sir Alec Douglas Home's lack of televisual skills was believed to have helped Labour win the 1964 election: he was smartly replaced by Edward Heath — himself not much better on television, as it turned out. The success of Wilson and to a lesser extent Callaghan as television communicators made media skills an essential element of any aspiring premier's curriculum vitae. This is what made the choice of Michael Foot as Labour's leader in 1981 such a risky venture. A powerful public speaker, Foot was ill at ease on television, tending to address the camera like a public meeting and to give long rambling replies. Worse, he tended to appear with ill-chosen clothes and on one occasion with spectacles held together with sticking plaster. These shortcomings may seem trivial, but they are not. Research shows that viewers make up their minds about people on television within seconds; manner and appearance are crucial in determining whether the reaction is positive or negative. Neil Kinnock was elected substantially as the televisual antidote to Foot. His style is confidential, warm and friendly but he tends to lose points by being too vague and verbose.

Unsurprisingly, the media and politics have become more closely interrelated with media professionals like David Steel, Tony Benn, Brian Gould, Austin Mitchell and Tim Brinton going into politics, while Robert Kilroy-Silk, Brian Walden and Mathew Parris moved out of politics and into the media. The apotheosis of this tendency was represented by Ronald Reagan who used his actor's ability to speak lines to the camera to compensate for other political inadequacies. His astonishing political success is testimony to the prime importance of media skills in the current age. Professional help has become commonplace with many ambitious politicians attending television training courses.

The government uses the media more extensively to convey its messages

On 31 January 1989 Kenneth Clark and other sundry Ministers participated in a £1.25 million nation-wide television link-up to sell the government's White Paper, *Working for Patients*. The Conservative government in the 1980s embraced the media as the key vehicle for favourable presentations of its policies and programmes to the public. In the autumn of 1989 it was revealed that spending on government advertising had risen from £35 million to £200 million between 1979 and 1989. This made the government one of the country's ten biggest advertisers. Critics pointed out that a government which had passed legislation to prevent Labour local authorities using ratepayers' money to advance partisan policies seemed to be doing precisely the same at a national level — but on a vastly increased scale.

Public relations hype had been used extensively to sell early privatizations but, allegedly at the instigation of Lord Young (former Trade Secretary), had subsequently been used for party political purposes. This is clearly a grey area in that any government has to spend money to explain new laws and regulations to the public at large and it is inevitable that such publicity will often reflect party political values. But clear Cabinet rules do exist on this topic: in using advertising governments should exercise restraint, should not proselytize party policy and, most importantly, should not advertise programmes which have not yet been enacted into law.

The controversy over government advertising

Water privatization

On 4 September 1989 a BBC *Panorama* programme produced evidence to suggest that rules had been broken in respect of water privatization. The programme revealed that over £21 million had already been spent by the water boards on a publicity campaign. Had substantial public funds been used to persuade the public on a party political issue before legislation had been passed? The government replied that this campaign was nothing to do with them but was part of an 'awareness-raising' programme by the water boards of a kind regularly employed by large enterprises to enhance their images. But why bother to raise awareness of a monopoly service? Was the timing of the campaign purely a coincidence? The programme revealed leaked documents from the public relations firm commissioned to handle water privatization in which the awareness campaign was clearly designed as the first part of a coherent plan to sell the privatization policy. The response of the minister concerned, Michael Howard, was singularly unconvincing.

Action for jobs

The *Panorama* programme also focused attention on the Action for Jobs campaign run just before the 1987 general election. This campaign was allegedly aimed at the unemployed but a London firm of public relations consultants testified that it had all the hallmarks of something completely different. The advertisements seemed to be designed with a more upmarket audience in mind (158 television advertising spots were taken out during 'upmarket' *News at Ten* time slots while only thirty-eight were taken out during *Coronation Street*), and the campaign was run most heavily in the south east rather than in the north where unemployment was highest. It was hard to resist the conclusion that this campaign, ostensibly aimed at the unemployed, had in reality spent £9 million of taxpayers' money beaming reassuring messages on unemployment to people in work in marginal south east constituencies in the run-up to a general election. When Action for Jobs started Labour had been substantially ahead in the polls as the party best equipped to deal with the problem of unemployment; at the end of the campaign Conservative ratings had doubled to virtually equal Labour's.

The Public Accounts Committee examined the issue but its report in June 1990 judged that the Department of Employment's campaign had not breached the conventions over political advertising. The Committee did say, however, that government departments need to take greater care that their campaigns do not have the appearance of being politically inspired. It noted in passing that, as the rules involved are conventions (rather than the statutes which regulate local government actions in this area) ministers are ultimately responsible for advertising content.

The televising of Parliament

The proposal that the proceedings of Parliament be televised was first formally proposed in 1966: it was heavily defeated. While other legislative chambers, including the House of Lords, introduced the cameras with no discernible ill effects, the House of Common resolutely refused chiefly on the grounds that such an intrusion would rob the House of its distinctive intimate atmosphere. By the late 1970s, however, the majorities in favour of exclusion were wafer-thin and the case would have been lost in the 1980s but for the stance of Mrs Thatcher. In November 1985 it had been rumoured she had changed her mind but at the last minute she decided to vote true to form and a number of Conservative MPs, about to vote for the televising of the House, instead rushed to join their leader in the 'No' lobby.

Even after the vote in favour of a limited experiment the introduction of the cameras was substantially delayed and the Select Committee on Procedure introduced severe restrictions on what the cameras could show: for example, only the head and shoulders of speakers could be featured, reaction shots of previous speakers were not allowed and in the event of a disturbance the cameras were to focus immediately on the dignified person of the speaker. Finally, however, on 21 November 1989 the House appeared on television, debating the Queen's Speech. Mrs Thatcher reflected on the experience as follows:

> I was really glad when it was over because it is ordeal enough when you are speaking in the Commons or for Question Time without television, but when you have got television there, if you are not careful, you freeze — you just do ... It is going to be a different House of Commons, but that is that.
>
> *The Times*, 24 November 1989

How different only time will tell. In January 1990 some of the broadcasting restrictions were relaxed: reaction shots of an MP clearly being referred to were allowed together with 'medium range' shots of the chamber some four rows behind the MP speaking or from the benches opposite. By the summer of 1990 it was obvious even to critical MPs that civilization as we know it had not come to an end. On 19 July the Commons voted 131−32 to make televising of the chamber permanent. David Amess MP opined that the cameras had managed to 'trivialize our proceedings and we have spoilt that very special atmosphere we had here'. His was a lone voice.

Television has transformed the electoral process

Since the 1950s television has become the most important media element in general elections. Unlike the USA political advertising is not allowed on British television but party political broadcasts are allocated on the basis of party strength. These have become important during elections, have become increasingly sophisticated and some — like the famous Hugh Hudson-produced party political broadcast on Neil Kinnock in 1987 — can have a substantial impact on voter perceptions. More important, however, is the extensive news and current affairs coverage and here US practice is increasingly being followed:

1. Professional media managers — like the Labour Party's Peter Mandelson (now a parliamentary candidate) — have become increasingly important. The

Television cameras hover overhead Labour Party MPs in November 1989. Will the televising of Parliament influence the role of Britain's legislative chamber?

Conservatives employ professional public relations agencies, the most famous of which was Saatchi and Saatchi. Political management of media dominated elections can cause major internal rows — like that between Norman Tebbit and Lord Young during the 1987 election.

2. Political meetings have declined. Political leaders now follow their US counterparts in planning their activities in the light of likely media coverage. The 'hustings' — open meetings in which debates and heckling occurs — have given way to stage-managed rallies to which only party members have access. Entries, exits and ecstatic applause are all carefully planned with the audience as willing accomplices. Critics argue that this development has helped to reduce the amount of free public debate during elections and has shifted the emphasis from key issues to marketing hype. Defenders of the media answer that its discussion programmes provide plenty of debate; since 1974 Granada TV has run a television version of the hustings, whereby a representative five hundred people from the north west regularly question panels of politicians and experts on the important issues.

3. Given television's requirements for short easily packaged messages political leaders insert pithy, memorable passages into their daily election utterances — the so-called 'sound-bite' — in the knowledge that this is what television wants and will show in their news broadcasts and summaries throughout the day.

Leading on from this next section assesses the impact of the media upon how people vote in general elections.

The Mass Media and Voting Behaviour

Jay Blumler wrote in 1978 that 'modern election campaigns have to a considerable extent become fully and truly television campaigns'. But what impact do the mass media have on the way in which citizens cast their votes? Does the form which different media give to political messages make any major difference? Substantial research on this topic has been undertaken, though with little definite outcome. One school of thought favours the view that the media does very little to influence voting directly but merely *reinforces* existing preferences.

Blumler and McQuail (1967) argued that people do not blandly receive and react to political media messages but apply a *filter* effect. Denver (1989, p.98) summarizes this effect under the headings of selective exposure, selective perception and selective retention.

Selective exposure

Many people avoid politics altogether when on television or in the press while those who are interested favour those newspapers or television programmes which support rather than challenge their views.

Selective perception

The views and values which people have serve to 'edit' incoming information so that they tend to accept what they want to believe and ignore what they do not.

Selective retention

The same editing process is applied to what people choose to remember of what they have read or viewed.

This mechanism is most likely to be at work when people read newspapers. As was noted in Table 12.1 most people — some readers excepted — read a newspaper which coincides with their own political allegiances. Harrop's studies produce the verdict that newspapers exert 'at most a small direct influence on changes in voting behaviour among their readers' (quoted in Negrine, 1989, p.206). Election results in 1983 and 1987 have given support for the reinforcement-via-filter-effect argument. Both these media-dominated election campaigns had little apparent impact upon the result. Over 80 per cent questioned in one poll claimed they had voted in accordance with preferences established before the campaign began and the party's eventual share of the vote accorded quite closely with pre-campaign poll ratings. In 1983 the Conservatives kicked off with a 15.8 per cent lead over Labour and finished with a 15.2 per cent advantage. Some weeks before the election in 1987 the average of five major polls gave Conservatives 42 per cent, Labour 30.5 per cent and Alliance 25.5 per cent; the final figures were 43, 32 and 23 per cent respectively — and this despite a Labour television campaign which was widely described as brilliant and admired even by their opponents. Perhaps people had 'turned off' in the face of excessive media coverage? Certainly, viewing figures declined and polls reflected a big majority who felt coverage had been either 'too much' or 'far too much'.

The filter—reinforcement thesis, however, seems to accord too minor a role to such an all-pervasive element. It does not seem to make sense. In an age when party preferences have weakened and people are voting much more instrumentally, according to issues, then surely the more objective television coverage has a role to play in switching votes? Is it reasonable to suppose the filter effect negates all information which challenges or conflicts established positions? If so, then why do parties persist in spending large sums on party political broadcasts? Some empirical data supports a *direct* influence thesis, especially in respect of television.

1. Ivor Crewe's research reveals that 20—30 per cent of the electorate *do* switch their votes during election campaigns, so despite the surface calm in 1983 and 1987 there was considerable movement beneath the surface. The 1987 election may have been unusual in any case: the before and after campaign variations were much larger in 1979, 1974 and 1970.
2. Many studies reveal that the four weeks of an election campaign provide too short a time over which to judge the impact of the media. Major shifts in voting preference take place between elections and it is quite possible that media coverage plays a significant role.
3. Crewe's research also suggests that the Alliance's television broadcasts did have a significant impact in 1983 and to a lesser extent in 1987 in influencing late deciders.
4. Following the Hugh Hudson-produced party political broadcast in 1987 Kinnock's personal rating leapt sixteen points in polls taken shortly afterwards. It could also be that *without* their professional television campaign Labour might have fared much worse.
5. Other research suggests that the impact of television messages will vary according to the group which is receiving them. 'A change in attitude is more likely to occur amongst those whose exposure to the media is moderate, who have limited knowledge of the issues and who rarely discuss politics with friends and colleagues' (McIlroy, 1989, p.114). This may help explain the pro-Alliance switchers and the responses recorded in Table 12.4. Here the question posed

Table 12.4 *Impact of television on voters: response to question 'Has television coverage helped you in deciding who to vote for in the election?'*

	Same as 1979 (%)	Stability of vote Different from 1979 (%)	'New' voters (%)
Yes	13	25	31
No	85	73	63
Don't know	1	2	6

Source: Negrine, 1989, p.190

in 1983 was: 'Has television coverage helped you in deciding about who to vote for in the election?' The table shows that people who voted for the *same* party as in 1979 were less likely to answer 'yes' than those who voted for a *different* party. It also shows that young people, voting for the first time, were much more likely to attribute a decisive influence to television.

Judging the effect of the media on voting behaviour is very difficult, because it is so hard to disentangle it from myriad factors like family, work, region, class and so forth which play a determining role. It seems fair to say, however, that firstly, the media does reinforce political attitudes. This is very important when the degree of commitment to a party can prove crucial when events between elections, as they always do, put loyalties to the test. Secondly, the media help to set the agenda of debate. During election campaigns party press conferences attempt to achieve this but the media do not always conform and between elections the media plays a much more important agenda-setting role. Thirdly, it is clear that media reportage has some direct impact upon persuading voters to change sides but research has not yet made clear whether this effect is major or marginal.

The political impact of the media: the process

Given the ubiquity of media influence, Seymour-Ure is more than justified in judging that 'the mass media are so deeply embedded in the (political) system that without them political activity in its contemporary form could hardly carry on at all' (Seymour-Ure, 1974, p.62). He directs attention to the factors which determine the political effects of media messages and which will naturally have a bearing upon the way in which politicians attempt to manipulate it.

The *timing* of a news item 'can make all the difference to its significance' (p.28). For example, Sir Alan Walters, Mrs Thatcher's part-time economic adviser in 1988 wrote an article in which he described as 'half-baked' the European Monetary System which Chancellor Nigel Lawson wanted Britain to join. Had it appeared immediately it might have caused some temporary embarrassment but coming out as it did eighteen months later, in the middle of a highly publicized row over this very issue between Mrs Thatcher and her Chancellor, it contributed importantly to Nigel Lawson's eventual resignation on 26 October 1989.

The *frequency* with which items are featured in the mass media will influence their impact. The unfolding nature of the Westland revelations, for example, kept Mrs Thatcher's political style on top of the political agenda for several damaging weeks in January and February 1986. By comparison the Lawson resignation, though a major cataclysm and one which touched on much more important policy issues, was relatively straightforward and after little more than a week the fuss had subsided.

The *intensity* with which media messages are communicated is also a key element. The Westland crisis and the Lawson resignation were so damaging to Mrs Thatcher because every daily and Sunday newspaper — serious and tabloid — and every radio and television news editor found these crises irresistible. The Lawson resignation story made the front page for over a week while two successive Brian Walden interviews with Mrs Thatcher and Lawson (29 October and 5 November, respectively) were themselves widely reported news events.

The mass media and the theory of pluralist democracy

If the mass media have such a transforming impact upon politics then how have they affected the fabric of British democracy? It all depends upon what one means by democracy. The popular and indeed 'official' view is that our elected legislature exerts watchdog control over the executive and allows a large degree of citizen participation in the process of government. This *pluralist* system provides a free market of ideas and a shifting, open competition for power between political parties, pressure groups and various other groups in society. Supporters of the present system claim that is not only how the system ought to work (a *normative* theory of government) but is, to a large extent, how it works in practice.

According to this view the media plays a vital political role:

1. It reports and represents popular views to those invested with decision making powers.
2. It informs society about the actions of government, educating voters in the issues of the day. The range of newspapers available provides a variety of interpretations and advice.
3. It acts as a watchdog of the public interest, defending the ordinary person against a possibly overmighty government through its powers of exposure, investigation and interrogation. To fulfill this neutral disinterested role it follows that the media need to be given extensive freedom to question and publish.

This pluralist view of the media's role, once again both normative and descriptive, has been criticized along the following lines.

Ownership and control influences media messages

Excluding the BBC, the media organizations are substantially part of the business world and embrace profit making as a central objective. This fact alone severely prejudices media claims to objectivity in reporting the news and reflecting popular feeling. In recent years ownership has concentrated markedly. About 80 per cent of newspaper circulation is in the hands of three conglomerates: Maxwell Communications Corporation, United Newspapers and News International. Robert Maxwell owns the *Daily Mirror, Sunday Mirror* and *Sunday People*; Rupert Murdoch's News International owns the *Sun, News of the World, The Times, Sunday Times* and, since 1987, the *Today* newspaper as well. Both of these latter-day press barons also have strong television interests: Murdoch owns Sky Television and Maxwell has an interest in Central TV.

Bilton *et al.* (see Table 12.5) demonstrate how newspaper and television ownership is closely interlinked and have become part of vast conglomerates with world-wide interests. Does it seem likely that such organizations will fairly represent and give a fair hearing to political viewpoints hostile to the capitalist system of which they are such an important part?

True, Maxwell's newspapers support the Labour Party but not anything which could be called a coherent socialist ideology. Murdoch's newspapers, on the other hand, all loudly and openly support the Conservative Party. In the case of the *Observer* and *The Guardian* it can be argued that ownership is separate from control but this

Table 12.5 *Ownership of British press and related economic interests*

	Main British press interests	**Selected other media interests**	**Selected non-media interests**
Pergamon (Maxwell)	*Daily Mirror* *Sunday Mirror* *Sunday People* *Daily Record* *Sunday Mail* (Total circulation: 11.7 million)	Central Independent TV Rediffusion cablevision Pergamon Press International Learning Systems British Printing and Communications Corporations	E.J. Arnold (furniture) Hollis Plastics Paulton Investments Jet Ferry International (Panama) Mares Australes (Chile)
News Corporation (Murdoch)	*Sun* *News of the World* *The Times* *Sunday Times* *Times Educational Supplement* (Total circulation: 10.2 million)	Satellite TV Collins (Fontana) News Group Productions (New York) Channel Ten — 10 (Sydney) *Daily Sun* (Brisbane)	Ansett Transport (Australia) Santos (Natural gas—Australia) News-Eagle (Offshore oil — Australia) Snodland Fibres Whitefriars Investment
Fleet Holdings (Matthews)	*Daily Express* *Sunday Express* *Daily Star* *The Standard* Morgan-Grampian Magazines (Total circulation: 7.1 million)	TV-AM Asian Business Press (Singapore) Specialist Publications (Hong Kong) Capital Radio	JBS Properties M G Insurance Lefpalm Ltd David McKay Inc. (USA) (Trafalgar House)

is not true of Maxwell and Murdoch, who exert strong personal editorial controls.

Nor is the press especially ***accountable***: the Press Council used to be a powerful and respected watchdog on newspaper editors but in recent years it has meekly acquiesced in the concentration of ownership on the grounds that the danger of monopoly control is less unacceptable than the bankruptcy of familiar national titles. Moreover, since the *Sun* has regularly flouted its rulings the Council has lost even more respect and has been unable, for example, to prevent the private lives of public figures being invaded by tabloid journalists to an alarming degree.

Television evinces a much clearer distinction between ownership and control and fits more easily into the pluralist model. The BBC, of course, is government-owned and in theory at least its Board of Governors exercises independent control. Independent television is privately owned and this ownership is becoming more concentrated — five of the companies serve three-quarters of the national audience — but the Independent Broadcasting Authority (IBA) has used its considerable legal powers under the 1981 Broadcasting Act to ensure 'balance' and 'due accuracy and impartiality' on sensitive political issues. This is not to say that television can be

Table 12.5 *Ownership of British press and related economic interests*

	Main British press interests	**Selected other media interests**	**Selected non-media interests**
Reed Group	IPC Magazines IPB Business Press Berrows Newspapers (Total circulation: approx. 12 million)	Fleetway Publications (USA) Hamlyn Books Anglia TV A&W Publishers Inc. (USA) Européenne de Publications SA (France)	Crown Paints Maybank/Krever International (Bahamas) Reed Finance (South Africa) Reed Consolidated Industries (Australia) Consolidated Industries Holdings
Associated Newspapers (Rothermere)	*Daily Mail* *Mail on Sunday* *Weekend* Northcliffe Newspapers Associated South Eastern Newspapers (Total circulation: 5.3 million)	London Broadcasting Company Herald-Sun TV (Australia) Plymouth Sound Wyndham Theatres Harmsworth House Pub. (USA)	Blackfriars Oil (North Sea) Bouverie Investments (Canada) Burton Reproduction GmbH (W. Germany) Transport Group Holdings Jetlink Ferries
Pearson Longman (Cowdray)	Westminster Press Group *Financial Times* *The Economist* *Northern Echo* (Total circulation: 1.8 million)	Longman Penguin Goldcrest Films Yorkshire TV Viking (USA) Morie Channel	Midhurst Corporation (USA) Whitehall Mining (Canada) Lazard Bros Royal Doulton Tableware Camco Inc. (USA)

Source: adapted from Bilton *et al.*, 1987, pp. 435–7

acquitted of the charge of bias — as we shall see below — but merely that television controllers are forbidden by law to display open partisanship and that those people who own their companies cannot insist upon particular editorial lines.

News values are at odds with the requirements of a pluralist system

In order to create profits media organizations compete for their audiences with the consequent pursuit of the lowest common denominator in public taste. In the case of the tabloids this means the relegation of hard news to inside pages and the promotion to the front page of trivial stories such as sex scandals, royal family gossip and the comings and goings of soap opera stars. On television the same tendency has been apparent with the reduction of current affairs programmes, their demotion from peak viewing times and the dilution of news programmes with more human interest stories. As a result of this tendency it can be argued the media's educative role in a pluralist democracy is being diminished. Some would go further, however, and maintain that the dominant *news values* adopted by the media are in any case inappropriate for this role.

The experience of successful newspapers has helped to create a set of criteria for judging newsworthiness which news editors in all branches of the media automatically accept and apply more or less intuitively. The themes to which the public are believed to respond include:

1. *Personalities*: people quickly become bored with statistics and carefully marshalled arguments and relate to stories which involve disagreement, personality conflicts or interesting personal details. Westland and the Lawson resignation demonstrated this tendency in action when the clashes between Mrs Thatcher and her Cabinet colleagues were given prominence over the important European questions which underlay them.
2. *Revelations*: journalist Nicholas Tomalin once defined news as the making public of something someone wished to keep secret. Leaked documents, financial malpractice and sexual pecadilloes are assiduously reported and eagerly read.
3. *Disasters*: the public has both a natural and a somewhat macabre interest in such matters.
4. *Visual backup*: stories which can be supported by good photographs or film footage will often take precedence over those which cannot be so supported.

It is commonly believed that newspapers which ignore these ground rules will fail commercially and that current affairs television which tries too hard to be serious will be largely ignored and described, fatally, as 'boring'. There is much evidence to suggest these news values *are* based on fact: these are the themes to which we most readily respond. It does mean, however, that the vast media industry is engaged in providing a distorted view of the world via its concentration upon limited and relatively unimportant aspects of social reality.

The lobby system favours the government of the day

The pluralist model requires that the media report news in a truthful and neutral way. We have already seen that ownership heavily influences the partisanship of the press but other critics argue that the *lobby system* of political reporting introduces a distortion of a different kind. Some 150 political journalists at Westminster are known collectively as 'the lobby'. In effect they belong to a club with strict rules whereby they receive special briefings from government spokesmen in exchange for keeping quiet about their sources. Supporters claim this is an important means of obtaining information which the public would not otherwise receive, but critics disagree. Anthony Howard of the *Observer* has written that lobby correspondents, rather like prostitutes, become 'clients' or otherwise 'instruments for a politician's gratification' (Hennessy, p.9). The charge is that journalists become lazy, uncritical and incurious, preferring to derive their copy from bland government briefings — often delivered at dictation speed. Peter Hennessy believes that this system 'comes nowhere near to providing the daily intelligence system a mature democracy has the right to expect ... as it enables Downing Street to dominate the agenda of mainstream political discussion week by week' (ibid., pp.10–11). The *Sun, The Guardian* and *The Independent* are so opposed to the system that they have withdrawn from it.

Television companies are vulnerable to political pressure

Ever since the broadcasting media became an integral part of the political process during the 1950s governments of all complexions have had uneasy relationships with the BBC, an organization with a world-wide reputation for excellence and for accurate, objective current affairs coverage. Mrs Thatcher, however, took government hostility to new lengths, indeed 'abhorrence of the BBC appeared for a while to be a litmus test for the Conservativeness of MPs' (Negrine, 1989, p.123). Governments seek to influence the BBC in three major ways. First, they have the power of appointment to the corporation's Board of Governors. The post of Chairman is especially important; Duke Hussey's appointment in 1986 was believed to be a response to perceived left-wing tendencies. Secondly, governments can threaten to alter the licence system: Mrs Thatcher was known to favour the introduction of advertising to finance the BBC but the Peacock Commission on the financing of television refused to endorse this approach. Thirdly, governments attempt to exert pressure in relation to particular programmes — often citing security reasons. The range of disputes between the Thatcher governments and the BBC is unparalleled in recent history. In part this was a consequence of a dominant, long established and relatively unchallenged Prime Minister as well as Mrs Thatcher's determination to challenge the old consensus — she long suspected that it resided tenaciously within the top echelons of the BBC. During the Falklands War some Conservative MPs actually accused BBC reports of being 'treasonable' because they questioned government accounts of the progress of the war. On such occasions, they claimed, the media should support the national effort. In 1985 the government leaned heavily on the BBC to withdraw the *Real Lives* programme, which featured coverage of IRA operations, even though the Home Secretary, Leon Brittan, had not seen it. Other disputes involved a programme on the Zircon spy satellite (the police actually raided the Glasgow studios and seized film); the revelations that MI5 had been vetting BBC staff; and the government's injunction in December 1987 to prevent the broadcast of the Radio 4 series *My Country Right or Wrong*. In 1986 a monitoring unit was set up in Conservative Central Office and in the summer a highly critical report on the BBC's coverage of the US bombing of Libya was submitted together with a fusillade of accusations from party chairman, Norman Tebbit. The BBC rejected the accusations and complained of 'political intimidation' in the run-up to a general election. The pressure almost certainly had some effect upon the BBC's subsequent news and current affairs presentation — supporting those who claim that the pluralist analysis of the media's role is inappropriate.

Television news coverage tends to reinforce the status quo

The argument here is that television news cannot accurately reflect events in the real world because it is, to use Richard Hoggart's phrase, 'artificially shaped' (Glasgow University Media Group, 1978, p.lx). ITN's editor, David Nicholas, says that '90 per cent of the time we are trying to tell people what we think they will want to know' (Tyne Tees TV, April 1986). It is what he and his colleagues think people want to know which attracts the fire of media critics. Faced with an infinitely multi-faceted social reality television news editors apply the selectivity of news values, serving up reports under severe time constraints in a particular abbreviated form. According to this critical line of argument television news reports can never be objective but are merely versions of reality constructed by news staff.

Reports will be formulated, furthermore, within the context of thousands of assumptions regarding how newsmen think the public already perceive the world. Inevitably they will refer to widely shared consensus values and perceptions and will reflect these in their reports, thus reinforcing them and marginalizing minority or radical alternatives. So television, for example, tends to present the parliamentary system as the only legitimate means of reaching decisions and tends to present society as basically unified without fundamental class conflicts and cleavages. Because alternative analyses are squeezed out and made to seem odd or alien, television — so it is argued — tends to reinforce status quo values and institutions and hence protect the interests of those groups in society which are powerful or dominant. The Greens offer an interesting case study in that for many years they fell outside the consensus. Towards the end of the 1980s, however, it suddenly became apparent even to the main party leaders that the Greens had earned a place for themselves within rather than outside the mainstream of political culture.

The Glasgow University Media Group take this argument further. On the basis of their extensive programme analyses they suggest that television coverage of economic news tends to place the 'blame for society's industrial and economic problems at the door of the workforce. This is done in the face of contradictory evidence, which when it appears is either ignored (or) smothered' (*Bad News*, p.267—8). Reports on industrial relations were 'clearly skewed against the interests of the working class and organised labour . . . in favour of the managers of industry'. The Glasgow research provoked a storm of criticism. David Nicholas dismissed it as a set of conclusions supported by selective evidence (Tyne Tees TV, April 1986). In 1985 an academic counterblast was provided by Martin Harrison (*TV News — Whose Bias?*) which criticized the slender basis of the Glasgow research and adduced new evidence which contradicted its conclusions.

Marxist theories of class dominance

The Glasgow research is often cited in support of more general theories on how the media reinforces, protects and advances dominant class interests in society. Variations on the theme were produced by Gramsci, in the 1930s by the Frankfurt School of Social Theorists and in the 1970s by the social—cultural approach of Professor Stuart Hall (for detailed analysis see McQuail, 1983, pp. 57—70) but the essence of their case is summed up in Marx's proposition that 'the ideas of the ruling class are in every epoch the ruling ideas'. He argued that those people who own and control the economic means of production — the ruling class — will seek to persuade everyone else that preserving status quo values and institutions is in the interests of society as a whole.

The means employed are infinitely subtle and indirect via religious ideas, support for the institution of the family, the monarchy and much else. Inevitably the role of the mass media, according to this analysis, is crucial. Marxists totally reject the pluralist model of the media as independent and neutral, as the servant rather than the master of society. They see it merely as the instrument of class domination, owned by the ruling class and carrying their messages into every home in the land. It is in moments of crisis, Marxists would claim, that the fundamental bias of state institutions is made clear. In 1926, during the General Strike, Lord Reith, the first Director-General of the BBC, provided some evidence for this view when he confided to his diary, 'they want us to be able to say they did not commandeer us, but they know they can trust us not to be really impartial'. Marxists believe the media obscures the fact of economic exploitation by ignoring radical critiques and disseminating entertainments and new interpretations which subtly reinforce the status quo and help to sustain a 'false consciousness' of the world based on ruling class values. For Marxists, therefore, the media provides a crucial role in persuading the working classes to accept their servitude and to support the system which causes it. Table 12.6 usefully contrasts the pluralist with the class dominance model.

Which of the two models best describes the role of the media in British society? From the discussion so far the pluralist model would appear inadequate in a number of respects. Its ability to act as a fair and accurate channel of communication between government and society is distorted by the political bias of the press, the lobby system, news values and the tendency of television to reflect consensual values. The media, moreover, is far from being truly independent: the press is largely owned by capitalist enterprises and television is vulnerable to government pressures of various kinds. Does this mean that the dominance model is closer to the truth? Not really.

While the dominance model quite accurately describes a number of media systems operating under oppressive regimes, it greatly exaggerates government control of the media in Britain.

Table 12.6 *Dominance and pluralism models compared*

	Dominance	Pluralism
Societal source	Ruling class or dominant elite	Competing political, social, cultural interests and groups
Media	Under concentrated ownership and of uniform type	Many and independent of each other
Production	Standardized, routinized, controlled	Creative, free, original
Content and world view	Selective and coherent; decided from 'above'	Diverse and competing views; responsive to audience demand
Audience	Dependent, passive, organized on large scale	Fragmented, selective, reactive and active
Effects	Strong and confirmative of established social order	Numerous, without consistency or predictability of direction, but often 'no effect'

Source: McQuail, 1983, p. 68

The media and general elections: a chronology

1918 Representation of the People Act increased the electorate to 277 per cent of its 1910 level. Also the Act reduced the amount a candidate in a constituency campaign could legally spend.

1918 The use of motor cars became more and more common.

1924 The first party election broadcasts on the wireless.

1934 National Publicity Bureau established under Joseph Ball to service the propaganda needs of the National Government.

1935 The last general election before 1945. Though some changes in electioneering practice could be attributed to wartime research, other developments were retarded by the war's intervention.

1945 The parties' radio broadcasts set the tone for the election. They were listened to by nearly 45 per cent of the adult population nightly.

1948 Representation of the People Act regularized the postal vote as an alternative to the proxy and made it available to civilians. Legal restrictions were imposed on the number of cars that could be used by a party on polling day; these lasted until 1958. The Act also reduced the amount that a candidate in a constituency campaign could legally spend.

1950 The BBC transmitted its first general election results programme on the television. 10 per cent of British households had a television set.

1951 The first party election broadcasts on the television. Each of the three national parties received one broadcast of 15 minutes.

1952 Tronoh-Malayan judgement opened the way for political press advertising.

1958 End of the Fourteen-Day Rule.

1958 The Conservatives put on a major image building campaign in the press in advance of the 1959 election. Conservative experiments in the use of direct mail to opinion formers.

1958 Rochdale by-election of 12 February reported on TV by ITN.

1959 Limited news coverage of the election was introduced on television. The parties' own election broadcasts became more sophisticated. 75 per cent of households had a television.

1959 The parties' national, daily press conferences changed from routine briefings into the centre-pieces of their campaigns.

1964 Excerpts of the parties' morning press conferences were televised; some regularly scheduled political programmes were kept on the air and discussed election issues.

1966 Much more frequent use of front-bench spokesmen in ministerial confrontations etc., following the courts' rejection of a petition to unseat Sir Alec Douglas-Home after the 1964 election. 90 per cent of households had a television.

1969 Representation of the People Act lowered the age of voting to eighteen, and allowed party leaders to appear on ballot papers for the first time.

1970 Heath's itinerary for election was planned with scrupulous attention to the filming and timing of TV news bulletins.

1974 Liberal Party used an advertising campaign in the press during the February election without legal repercussions.

1979 Extensive use of press advertising during the election by Labour and Conservatives. Also, advertisements for the Conservative Party were screened in cinemas.

1981 Launch of the SDP, with its computerized national membership register.

1983 The SDP started direct mailing non-members for fund-raising purposes.

1985 Representation of the People Act made postal votes more widely available and enfranchised British subjects living overseas. Act also obliged local authorities to make the electoral register available to political parties on computer tape.

1985 Brecon and Radnor by-election of 4 July, a significant watershed in the use of computers as a tool of constituency electioneering. Each subsequent by-election of the parliament was also a technical landmark in this respect.

1986 Launch of the Amstrad PC1512 personal computer brought the cost of computing down to a level local parties could afford.

1987 General election. The role of computers was exaggerated in press accounts, but they were nonetheless one of the most significant innovations in the practice of constituency electioneering for many years.

Source: Contemporary Record, Winter 1988.

1. As David Nicholas observes, 'trying to manipulate the news is as natural an instinct to a politician as breathing oxygen', but because politicians try does not mean that they always succeed. People who work in the media jealously guard their freedom and vigorously resist government interference. The *This Week* 'Death on the Rock' programme on the SAS killings in Gibraltar *was* after all shown in 1988 despite Sir Geoffrey Howe's attempts to pressure the IBA. And Lord Windlesham's subsequent enquiry further embarrassed the government by completely exonerating the Thames TV programme.

2. The media may tend to reflect consensual views but this does not prevent radical messages regularly breaking into the news — sometimes because they accord with news values themselves. Television also features drama productions which challenge and criticize the status quo: for example, at the humorous level in the form of *Spitting Image*; and at the serious level in the form of BBC's excellent 1988 legal series *Blind Justice*. Even soap operas like *Eastenders* often challenge and criticize the status quo.

3. Programmes like *Rough Justice* and *First Tuesday* have shown that persistent and highly professional research can shame a reluctant establishment into action to reverse injustices — as in the case of the Guildford Four, released in 1989 after 15 years of wrongful imprisonment. Consumer programmes like Esther Rantzen's *That's Life* and the radio series *Face The Facts* do champion the individual, as do regular newspaper campaigns.

4. News values do not invariably serve ruling-class interests, otherwise governments would not try so hard to manipulate them. Mrs Thatcher, for example, cannot have welcomed the explosion of critical publicity which surrounded Westland, her July 1989 reshuffle or the Lawson resignation. And it was Rupert Murdoch's *The Times* which took the lead in breaking the story about Cecil Parkinson's affair with his secretary, Sarah Keays, in 1983.

Each model then contains elements of the truth but neither comes near the whole truth. Which is the nearest? The reader must decide but despite all its inadequacies and distortions the pluralist model probably offers the better framework for understanding how the mass media impacts upon the British political system.

The Media and Politics: Future Developments

Since the war the British may have lost an Empire but have — or so we like to think — gained a television service which is the envy of the world. All this may change, say critics of the Conservative attempts to introduce market forces into the organization of British broadcasting. The 'deregulators' formerly led by Mrs Thatcher want to replace the BBC's licence fee with revenue derived from advertising, weaken the degree of regulation exercised over independent television and open up the latter's franchises to the highest bidder. While the first objective has been delayed for the time being following the Peacock Commission's lukewarm response the latter two measures are, at the time of writing, approaching the implementation stage.

Many broadcasters view these proposed changes with horror and predict the end of civilization as we know it. The government has replied that broadcasters have always made such protests in the face of change. In 1957 they objected strongly to the introduction of commercial television but in retrospect have accepted that this measure did nothing but good to the health of British broadcasting. What eventually happens will depend upon the detail and pace of changes already under way so it remains to be seen if market forces will, as some predict, destroy the Reithian tradition and inflict damage on our culture and civic education.

Lord Reith, the first Director-General of the BBC, was an unashamed elitist who believed the BBC should lead public taste by offering high intellectual and moral standards. Many argue that the introduction of commercial television introduced different values and the consequent ratings battle with the IBA has lowered certain intellectual standards and diluted the 'public service' broadcasting ideals. The subsequent consensus has been that the regulatory role of the IBA has protected the public service tradition to a satisfactory degree and that by making the BBC more conscious of consumer demands commercial television has provided a useful corrective to complacent high-mindedness. The Conservatives, however, should not, in the minds of present critics, cite this example in defence of current proposals which are qualitatively of a different kind. Firstly, the finite amount of money available for television advertising would eventually cause a deterioration in quality. Secondly, the pursuit of mass audiences to give advertisers a return for their money would lead to a fall in standards and the proliferation of low budget bad taste productions. Thirdly, the selling of franchises to the highest bidder will effectively hand over commercial television to media moguls like Rupert Murdoch, who will then proceed to do for television what the *Sun* has done for the British newspaper industry. Fourthly, news and current affairs programmes will move 'down market' while expensive investigative programmes — like those which regularly embarrass the government in power — will virtually disappear. Finally, the weakening of regulatory mechanisms for commercial television will make it easier for business ethics to permeate television output.

In other words, according to the critics, British broadcasting will become more like the American system: infinitely diverse yet unremittingly mediocre. At the time of writing the political process is still in progress over the future of the media. Time alone will tell whether status quo loyalists have either been fair to the American model or whether the British system will come to replicate it.

References and Further Reading

Bilton, A. *et al.*, *Introductory Sociology* (Macmillan, 1987).

Blumler, J.G. and McQuail, D., *Television in Politics* (Faber & Faber, 1967).

Blumler, J.G., Gurevitch, M. and Ives, J., *The Challenge of Election Broadcasting* (Leeds University Press, 1978).

Cockerall, M., *Live from Number 10* (Faber & Faber, 1988).

Cockerall, M., *et al., Sources Close to the Prime Minister* (Macmillan, 1984).

Crewe, I., 'How to win a landslide without really trying; why the Conservatives won in 1983', *Essex Papers in Politics and Government*, Essex, **1**, April 1984.

Curran, J. and Seaton, J., *Power without Responsibility: The Press and Broadcasting in Britain* (Routledge, 1988).

Denver, D., *Elections and Voting Behaviour in Britain* (Philip Allan, 1989).

Dunleavy, P. and Husbands, C.T., *British Democracy at the Crossroads* (Allen & Unwin, 1985).

Glasgow University Media Group, *Bad News* (1976); *More Bad News* (1980) (Routledge and Kegan Paul).

Green, J., *Book of Political Quotes* (Angus & Robertson, 1982).

Harrison, M., *TV News: Whose Bias?* (Hermitage, Policy Journals, 1985).

Harrop, M., 'The Press and post-war elections', in Crewe, I. and Harrop, M. (eds), *Political Communications: the 1987 Election Campaign* (Cambridge).

Harrop, M., 'Voters', in Seaton, J. and Pimlott, B. (eds), *The Media in British Politics* (Avebury, 1987).

Hennessy, P., *What the Papers Never Said* (Political Education Press, 1985).

McIlroy, J., 'Television today . . . and tomorrow', in Jones, B. *Political Issues in Britain Today* (Manchester University Press, 1989, pp. 109–34).

McLuhan, H.M., and Fiore, Q., *The Medium is the Message* (Penguin, 1971).

McQuail, D., *Mass Communications Theory: An Introduction* (Sage, 1983).

Negrine, R., *Politics and the Mass Media in Britain* (Routledge, 1989).

Seymour-Ure, C., *The Political Impact of the Mass Media* (Constable, 1974).

Treneman, J. and McQuail, D., *Television and the Political Image* (Methuen, 1961).

Tunstall, J., *The Media in Britain* (Constable, 1983).

Whale, J., *The Politics of the Mass Media* (Fontana, 1978).

13 Pressure Groups

Dennis Kavanagh and Bill Jones

This chapter considers some of the ways in which ordinary citizens impress their views on the country's rulers. Democratic government is supposed to be government *of* the people, and politicians often claim to be speaking on behalf of public opinion. But how do rulers learn about what people want? Elections provide a significant but infrequent opportunity for people to participate in politics. These are usually held every four years or so, but pressure groups provide continuous opportunities for such involvement.

Interest or pressure groups are formed by people to protect or advance a shared interest. Like political parties, groups may be mass campaigning bodies, but whereas parties have policies for many issues and, usually, wish to form a government, groups are sectional and wish to influence government.

The term 'pressure group' is relatively recent but organized groups tried to influence government long before the age of representative democracy. The Abolition Society was founded in 1787 and under the leadership of William Wilberforce and Thomas Clarkson succeeded in abolishing the slave trade in 1807. In 1839 the Anti-Corn Law League was established, providing a model for how a pressure group can influence government. It successfully mobilized popular and elite opinion against legislation which benefited landowners at the expense of the rest of society and in 1846 achieved its objective after converting to its cause the Prime Minister of the day, Sir Robert Peel. In the twentieth century the scope of government has grown immensely and impinges upon the lives of many different groups in society. After 1945 the development of the mixed economy and the welfare state drew even more people into the orbit of governmental activity. Groups developed to defend and promote interests likely to be affected by particular government policies. For its own part government came to see pressure groups as valuable sources of information and potential support. The variety of modern pressure groups therefore reflects the infinite diversity of interests in society. A distinction is usually drawn between the following:

1. *Sectional or interest groups,* most of which are motivated by the particular economic interests of their members. Classic examples of these are trade unions, professional bodies (e.g. the British Medical Association) and employers' organizations — the Anti-Corn Law League would also have fallen under this heading.

2. *Cause groups,* which exist to promote an idea not directly related to the personal

interests of its members. The Abolition Society was such a group and in modern times the Campaign for Nuclear Disarmament (CND), Child Poverty Action Group (CPAG) or the Society for the Protection of the Unborn Child (SPUC) can be identified. Of the environmental groups, the Ramblers Association, Greenpeace and Friends of the Earth are perhaps the best-known.

Membership of the former category is limited to those who possess the specific interest, for example coal miners or doctors. In contrast support for a cause like nuclear disarmament or anti-smoking can potentially embrace all adults. The two types of groups are not, however, mutually exclusive. Some trade unions take a stand on many political causes, for example apartheid in South Africa or sexual equality, and some members of cause groups may have a material interest in promoting the cause, e.g. teachers in the Campaign for the Advancement for State Education. It should be noted that pressure groups regularly seek to influence each other to maximize impact and often find themselves in direct conflict over certain issues. Baggot has shown how pressure groups lined up over the issue of longer drinking hours (see Figure 13.1).

The lobby in favour of longer drinking hours	*Opposed to such changes*
Brewers Society (brewery companies)	Action on Alcohol Abuse (a campaigning body set up by the Royal Colleges of Medicine)
Campaign for Real Ale (beer drinkers)	Alcohol Concern (a semi-official body responsible for co-ordinating services for alcoholics)
British Hotels, Restaurants and Caterers Association	
British Tourist Authority (a semi-official body which promotes tourism)	UK Temperance (a moral pressure group concerned about alcohol abuse)
NULV and NALHM (the pub landlords' associations)	The Campaign Against Drink Driving
	The Royal Colleges of Medicine (e.g. Royal College of Physicians)
	The British Medical Association

Figure 13.1 *Pressure groups and the licensing laws (Source: Baggott, 1988)*

Pressure Groups and Government

The relationship between interest groups and government is not always or even usually adversarial. Groups may be useful to government. Ministers and civil servants often lack the information or expertise necessary to make wise policies, or indeed the authority to ensure that they are implemented effectively. They frequently turn to the relevant representative organizations to find out defects in an existing line of policy and seek suggestions as to how things might be improved. They sound out

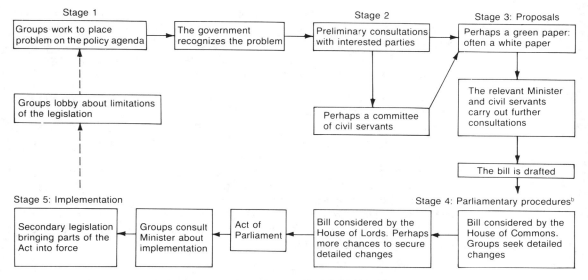

Figure 13.2 *Pressure groups and the policy process (Source: Grant, 1988)*

Notes: (a) Not all the stages will necessarily occur in any particular policy initiative.
(b) Many policy changes do not require new legislation; they may, for example, depend upon ministerial action.
(c) Bills may of course be introduced in the House of Lords.

groups leaders about likely resistance to a new line of policy. Groups may also be helpful in administering policies, e.g. teachers in schools or trade unions and employers in a prices and incomes policy. Moreover, an interest group's support, or at least acceptance, for a policy can help to 'legitimize' it.

In the several stages of the policy process groups have opportunities to play an important role. At the initial stage they may get an issue on the policy agenda (e.g. environmental groups have promoted awareness of the dangers to the ozone layer caused by many products and forced government to act). When governments issue *Green Papers* (setting out policy options for discussion) and *White Papers* (proposals for legislation), groups may lobby back-benchers or civil servants. In Parliament groups may influence the final form of legislation. As we can see from Figure 13.2, groups are involved at virtually every stage of the policy process.

Insider–outsider groups

Groups are usually most concerned to gain access to ministers and civil servants — the key policy makers. Pressure group techniques are usually a means to that end. When government departments are formulating policies there are certain groups which they consult. The Ministry of Agriculture, Fisheries and Food is in continuous and close contact with the Farmers' Union. Indeed in 1989, in the wake of the salmonella food poisoning scandal, it was alleged by some that the ministry neglected the interests of consumers compared to that of the producers. Wyn Grant (1985)

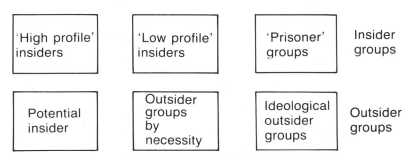

Figure 13.3 *Grant's typology of pressure groups (Source: Grant, 1985)*

has described groups which are regularly consulted as ***insider*** groups. He distinguishes between 'high profile' insider groups, discreet 'low profile' ones, and 'prisoner groups', which are wholly dependent on government funding.

On the other hand, the Campaign for Nuclear Disarmament, for example, mounts public campaigns largely because it has no access to Whitehall; according to Grant's classification, it is an 'ideological' ***outsider***. 'Potential insider' groups will try to establish themselves through sustained lobbying activity. Most outsider groups will be excluded from real influence through lack of skills and resources (see Figure 13.3).

To gain access groups usually have to demonstrate that they possess at least some of the following features:

1. *Authority,* which may be demonstrated in the group's ability to organize virtually all its potential members. The National Union of Mineworkers spoke for nearly 100 per cent of miners for a number of years, but its authority was weakened by the formation in 1985 of the breakaway Union of Democratic Miners. Similarly, the authority of the teachers' unions has been weakened because of the divisions between so many different groups. Overwhelming support by members for the group's policies is another indicator of authority.

2. *Information:* Groups like the British Medical Association or the Howard League for Penal Reform command an audience among decision makers because of their expertise and information.

3. The *compatibility* of a group's objectives with those of the government. For example, trade unions traditionally received a more friendly hearing when pressing for favourable trade union legislation or state intervention in industry from a Labour than a Conservative government. Groups seeking access should not put forward demands which the government regards as unreasonable.

4. Possession of *powerful sanctions*. Some groups of workers are able to disrupt society through the withdrawal of their services. The bargaining power of coal miners, for example, was very strong in the mid-1970s when Middle East oil was in short supply and expensive but much weaker a decade later, when cheaper oil was more available as a source of energy.

But becoming and remaining an ***insider*** group requires the acceptance of

The conditions for group access to government

Authority

Information

Compatability

Sanctions

constraints. Group leaders, for example, should respect confidences, be willing to compromise, back up demands with evidence and avoid threats (Grant, 1989 and 1990).

Among some of the *activities of groups* in the political process are the following:

1. They may try to influence the policies of a party in the areas which concern them, e.g. trade unions or CND in the Labour party. On the whole, however, groups concentrate their efforts on the government of the day.
2. They try to educate the public's opinion to their point of view through such activities as rallies, advertising and petitions.
3. They continually lobby government, particularly Whitehall, about the working of legislation or details of impending legislation. Many government ministries grant representation to groups on their departmental inquiries and advisory committees. In recent years the House of Lords has become a popular focus for pressure groups as its unreliable Conservative majority has improved Opposition chances.
4. Some try to seek pledges from candidates at elections. This strategy is used by both the pro- and anti-abortion groups.
5. Some may pay MPs a retainer to represent the views of the group in Parliament. Most MPs have such an interest (which they are expected to declare before speaking on the issue). More than a third of Labour MPs are sponsored by trade unions and a majority of Tory MPs are paid retainers by business groups. Sir Giles Shaw MP is employed by Hill and Knowlton, an example of the new breed of professional lobbying organizations which offer their contacts and knowledge of the corridors of power to organizations wishing to influence specific policies. (See concluding comment to Part V.)

Pressure group methods include the following:

Violence, unconstitutional action, illegality (e.g. violent demonstrations, bombings).
Denial of function (e.g. strikes).
Publicity-seeking techniques (e.g. petitions, advertisements, leaflets, marches, use of media).
Expansion of membership, mobilization and training.

Target groups include all elements in the political system:

The public at large.
Other pressure group members.
Political parties.
Parliament — especially the House of Commons, but in recent years increasingly the House of Lords.

Ministers.

Civil servants.

The media — as an additional means of reaching all the above groups.

Factors affecting effectiveness

Baggot points out that the effectiveness of pressure groups is also a function of organizational factors: they need a coherent organizational structure; high-quality and efficient staff; adequate financial resources; good leadership; and a clear strategy. Economic interest groups are usually well financed but cause groups can often compensate for shoestring resources by attracting high-quality committed leadership; for example, Jonathon Porrit (Friends of the Earth), Frank Field (CPAG), Mike Daube (ASH) and perhaps the most effective popular campaigner of them all, Des Wilson of Shelter and many other causes.

The American political scientist, Robert Downs, has suggested that the media and the public's receptivity to pressure group messages is another potent factor influencing effectiveness. He pointed out that the new cause groups must run the gauntlet of the 'issue—attention' cycle (see Figure 13.4).

The pre-problem stage is followed by alarmed discovery coupled with the feeling that something could and should be done. When it becomes clear, as it usually does, that progress will not be easy, interest declines and this is when the pressure group faces its toughest tests. This has certainly been true of environmental, nuclear disarmament and AIDS campaigns but all three of these reveal that with new discoveries and fresh events the issue—attention cycle can be re-run — possibly frequently over time.

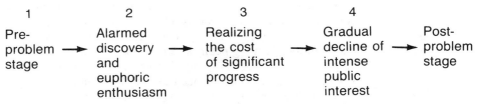

Figure 13.4 *The 'Issue-attention cycle' (Source: McCulloch, 1988)*

Economic interest groups

The policies of the government in such areas as interest rates, trading policy and industrial relations are important in providing the context for the economy. Two of the most powerful interest groups which try to influence these policies are *business* and *trade unions*.

Business

Business is naturally deeply affected by government economic policies and it is understandable that its representatives will seek to exert influence. Many firms depend on government handouts, subsidies and orders and will seek to influence the awarding of contracts. This is particularly true of shipbuilding, highway construction, housebuilding and defence. Others will be more interested in policy matters like interest rates, taxation levels and so forth.

In one sense any sizeable business organization acts like a pressure group. Multi-national companies — many with turnovers larger than those of small countries — make their own regular and usually confidential representations to government. Particular industries often form federations like the Society of Motor Manufacturers or the Engineering Employers Federation and seek strength in unity. The Confederation of British Industry (CBI) was formed in 1965 and since that date has provided an overall 'peak' organization to provide a forum for discussion — it holds an annual conference — and to represent the views of members to government. It has a membership of 15,000, employs several hundred staff and has an annual budget approaching £5 million. The CBI is dominated by big companies and this helps to explain the 1971 breakaway Small Business Association. For much of Mrs Thatcher's first term of office her policies of high interest and exchange rates damaged manufacturing industry and the CBI criticized the government. It blamed the government for not spending enough on infra-structure, it complained that the high exchange rate made exporting difficult and that high interest rates were discouraging investment. On one famous occasion the then Director General of the CBI, Sir Terence Beckett, called for a 'bare knuckle' fight to make Mrs Thatcher change her deflationary policies — but his violent rhetoric abated after a stormy confrontation with the Prime Minister. In recent years the CBI has been more supportive of the Conservative government: John Banham lined up against the European Social Charter in November 1989, for example, but disagreed over the European Monetary System, which the CBI believed Britain should join.

The Institute of Directors is a more Thatcherite and political campaigning body. It opposed the prices and incomes restraints, which the CBI was prepared to support in the 1970s, and has vigorously supported the Conservative government's policies of privatization, cutting public spending and encouraging free market economics. The Institute also welcomed the Thatcher government's measures to lower direct taxation, reform the trade unions and limit minimum wage regulations and would like the policies to go further. Other organizations such as Aims of Industry are used as means of raising support and indirectly revenue for the Conservative Party. Although no business group has a formal association with the Conservative Party a number of major firms do make financial contributions (for more details see Chapter 14).

Trade unions

The trade unions have two distinct roles. The first is **party-political**. Since they helped to form the Labour party in 1900 they have played, and still play, a decisive role in the internal politics of that party. About half of all trade unions are affiliated to the party, providing seven-eighths of the party's membership and votes at the annual conference. They also provide, through the political levy on trade union members, some three-quarters of the party's funds. In addition they elect eighteen of the twenty-nine members to the National Executive Committee and have 40 per cent of the vote in the electoral college which, since 1981, elects the party's leader and deputy leader. Thus, trade unions are more deeply involved in party politics than any other interest group.

The second role of individual trade unions is ***industrial bargaining***, to represent the interests of their members on pay and working conditions in negotiations with employers. Some three-quarters of unions are affiliated to the Trades Union Congress (TUC), which speaks for the trade union movement as a whole. The outstanding case of trade unions concerting their policies with the government of the day was the 'Social Contract', which operated in the first years of the 1974 Labour government. Under this the trade unions promised restraint in wage settlements in return for favourable government policies covering food subsidies, old age pensions, action on low pay and repeal of the Heath government's industrial relations legislation which they found objectionable. From the government's point of view the policy was a failure and within a year wage settlements and inflation were running at an annual rate of nearly 30 per cent.

Since 1964 governments of both parties have had periods of cooperation and conflict with trade unions over ***incomes policies***, or attempts to restrain the level of incomes settlements. As part of a strategy to slow down the rate of inflation, governments have regularly turned to statutory or informal incomes policies. These often lasted for two or three years but usually ended in confrontation. The Heath government's statutory incomes policy collapsed during the coal miners' strike in February 1974 and in 1979 the Callaghan government's voluntary incomes policy ended in the 'winter of discontent'. In both cases the confrontations spelt the ruin of the government's anti-inflation policy and helped to unseat the government at the next general election. After 1979 the Thatcher governments deliberately abstained from any kind of formal incomes policy, though they leaned more heavily on wage settlements in parts of the public sector.

The decade 1969–79 probably saw the height of union power in the post-war period. The unions used their muscle in the Labour party to prevent the Wilson government from legislating to deal with unofficial strikes in 1969. Wilson felt obliged in 1968 to declare 'The TUC has arrived. It is an estate of the realm, as real, as potent, as essentially part of the fabric of our national life as any of the historic estates.' Mr Heath's government brought in the Industrial Relations Act in 1971 which, among other things, imposed penalties on unofficial strikes. The unions opposed the measure, refused to consult with the government over it and made it unworkable when they refused to register under it. The miners broke Mr Heath's incomes policy, the 1974 Labour government repealed the Industrial Relations Act and provided other favourable legislation for the unions.

Under Mrs Thatcher the economic and political influence of trade unions declined. The unions made themselves deeply unpopular by their excesses in the 'winter of discontent' in 1979 and there was strong support for moves to limit the unions' legal immunities from damages during certain types of strikes. The idea of incomes policies as an answer to inflation was discredited; members refused to go along with agreements made by leaders. The Thatcher government claimed that it would rely on its monetarist policy to squeeze inflation out of the system even if this resulted in higher unemployment. Some of the post-1979 changes in the unions' position include the following.

Table 13.1 *Union membership, earnings, strikes and unemployment in the UK, 1978—87*

	Union members (000)	Density (%)	Change in real earnings (%)	Strikes	Strike-days (000)	Registered unemployment (%)
1978	13,112	54:1	+4.6	2,498	9,405	5.7
1979	13,289	54.4	+2.0	2,125	29,474	5.3
1980	12,947	52.6	+3.8	1,348	11,964	6.8
1981	12,106	49.3	−0.7	1,344	4,266	10.4
1982	11,593	48.0	+2.3	1,538	5,313	12.1
1983	11,236	46.8	+2.5	1,364	3,754	12.9
1984	10,994	45.4	+1.9	1,221	27,135	13.1
1985	10,716	43.3	+3.0	903	6,402	13.5
1986	10,333	41.6	+3.4	1,074	1,920	11.7§
1987	10,200*	41.1*	+4.8	1,016	3,546	10.7

* Estimate
§ Change in method of compilation explains 1985—6 decline
Source: Hyman, 1989, p.147

Membership has fallen by over three million, approximately 25 per cent, from 1979 to 1987. In part the fall has been a consequence of the rise in unemployment in manufacturing industry, as in the case of the Transport and General Workers Union (TGWU), the National Union of Mineworkers (NUM) and engineering unions. Moreover, there has been an expansion in employment of part-timers and women, two groups which are weakly unionized. It is worth noting, however, that unions still represent over 40 per cent of the work-force — high by international comparison.

Industrial action by unions has been defeated. The action by print workers at Wapping in 1985 and the coal miners' year-long strike between March 1984 and March 1985 both ended in defeat for the unions. The government also succeeded in banning union membership among workers at GCHQ, the military intelligence centre at Cheltenham.

Legislation hostile to the trade unions has proved popular and effective. After 1979 Conservative governments passed Employment Acts (1980, 1982) and a Trade Union Act (1984). These have made unions liable for the actions of their members which break the law; limited sympathy action and secondary picketing; imposed mandatory ballots before strikes; and required the regular election of union officials. In 1984—5 the NUM's funds were sequestrated because it did not hold a pre-strike ballot and at Wapping, Rupert Murdoch's News International Corporation created separate organizations which were therefore protected from secondary picketing action.

The ***government has refused to consult with the trade unions*** over many issues and ***downgraded the role of the National Economic Development Council (NEDC)***. In July 1987 the Chancellor announced that the Council would henceforth meet only four instead of the usual ten times a year.

The government's claims that ***union leaders are often out of touch with their members*** have been confirmed in some pre-strike ballots. On a number of occasions many union leaders have failed to get the support for strikes in ballots and in the 1983 and 1987 elections over a third of trade union members voted Conservative.

The Conservative legislation on trade unions

The three foundation pieces of legislation, the *Employment Acts*, 1980 and 1982 and the *Trade Union Act*, 1984, contain the following provisions:

(1) **Individual and union rights are limited**: it is harder to claim unfair dismissal or maternity leave, and the procedures for seeking union recognition and extending the terms of collective agreements have been abolished. The Fair Wages Resolution has been rescinded.

(2) **The closed shop is weakened**. For employers to be protected against unfair dismissal proceedings the closed shop agreement must have been sanctioned by 80 per cent of those covered by it in a secret ballot. Ballots must be held every five years. Existing employees are not bound by the ballot while even those employed later have a right not to be members if they can show genuine grounds of conscience. Compensation for those unfairly sacked in closed shop situations is dramatically increased and can total well over £20,000. Unions can be liable for damages if they seek dismissal of non-unionists.

(3) **Union members are given new rights** to claim unreasonable exclusion or expulson from the union even if the rules are followed, if they work in a closed shop.

(4) **Industrial action is curtailed** by giving the courts new powers to strike down secondary boycotts and sympathy strikes, unless certain complicated and stringent conditions are met, and by removing immunities from those picketing at any work-place other than their own.

(5) **Union-labour-only contracts are made unlawful** by outlawing all agreements, tenders, lists of suppliers which require union membership as a condition of award.

(6) **Elections of union executives and executive officers must meet stringent balloting requirements** or they can be struck down by the courts.

(7) **Union immunities are removed** if industrial action is called without a majority vote in a secret ballot.

(8) **Ballots on whether a union can maintain a fund for political expenditure** must be held every ten years commencing in 1986. Unions will find it more difficult to use their ordinary funds for political campaigning.

(9) **The Taff Vale doctrine is re-enacted** so that unions as organizations are made responsible where members or officials commit civil wrongs unless the union denounces the action in question and polices the membership. Union funds are therefore at risk.

Source: J. McIlroy, 1988, pp.98–9.

The union movement has also been divided, as some unions, notably the engineers and electricians, have been prepared to make no-strike deals and single union agreements with employers in defiance of TUC policy. This culminated in 1988 in the expulsion of the electricians' union from the TUC. During the miners' strike in 1984 a breakaway group from the NUM formed the Union of Democratic Miners.

Britain's twelve largest Unions

Union		Membership 1987
TGWU	Transport and General Workers' Unon	1,337,944
AEU/AUEW	Amalgamated Engineering Union/Amalgamated Union of Engineering Workers	857,599
GMWU/GMBATU	General and Municipal Workers' Union	814,084
NALGO	National and Local Government Officers' Association	750,430
NUPE	National Union of Public Employees	657,633
ASTMS	Association of Scientific, Technical and Managerial Staffs	390,000
USDAW	Union of Shop, Distributive and Allied Workers	381,984
ETU/EETPU	Electrical Trades Union/Electrical, Electronic, Telecommunications and Plumbing Union	336,155
UCATT	Union of Construction Allied Trades and Technicians	249,485
NUT	National Union of Teachers	184,455
NUR	National Union of Railwaymen	125,000
NUM	National Union of Mineworkers	104,941

It is worth noting the dilemma which still faces the unions in their relations with a potential future Labour government. *Industrially*, trade union leaders seek free collective bargaining; negotiating with employers to improve their members' wages and working conditions is the primary reason for their existence. But *politically*, the goals of the unions (and the Labour party) — e.g. help for the low paid, more spending on public services, low inflation, economic planning and an expanding public sector (with the government as paymaster) — almost inevitably requires the government to have a view about matters like wages and salaries and therefore about the economic and social consequences of free collective bargaining.

Yet it is not only trade unions which have been shaken up by the government. Local government, traditionally a strong pressure group on Whitehall, has been much weakened since 1979 and its policy making role in housing and education reduced. Some of the professions have lost a number of their privileges and been exposed to market forces. Solicitors have lost the monopoly on conveyancing, opticians on the sale of spectacles and university lecturers on tenure. In 1989 proposals were made to shake up the legal profession and alter the work practices of doctors.

Tripartism

Like political parties pressure groups want to influence the policies of government. In 1961 the government created the National Economic Development Council (NEDC), a forum in which the government, employers and trade unions could meet regularly to consider ways of promoting economic growth. The activities of NEDC, together with periods of prices and incomes policies and the 1974 Labour government's Social Contract with the unions, were seen at the time as evidence that Britain was moving to a *form of corporatism or tripartism* in economic policy. Governments would negotiate economic policy with the major producer interest.

Ministers were increasingly aware of the power of producer groups and of how they could frustrate a government's economic policies. They therefore sought the cooperation of leaders of business', employers' and trade union organizations. In spite of objections that such negotiations — notably on prices and incomes policies — bypassed Parliament, this was the path pursued by government in the 1970s.

In 1972 Mr Heath offered the unions a voice in policy making in return for wage moderation. That offer was not accepted, but there were closer relations between the 1974 Labour government and the unions.

Tripartite forms of policy making and the Social Contract have not been successful. Neither the TUC nor CBI have sufficient control over their members to make their deals stick. Incomes policies broke down after two or three years. And after 1979 Mrs Thatcher set her face against such tripartism and relied more on market forces. Before 1979 governments usually tried to pursue consensus policies and their policies (e.g. on regional aid, incomes and price controls) required consultation with the producer groups. After 1979 Mrs Thatcher's determination to break with the consensus and her pursuit of different economic policies shut the groups (particularly the unions) out of the decision making process.

Pressure Groups and Pluralist Democracy

Do pressure groups contribute towards a more healthy democracy? As in the debate over the media in the Chapter 12 it depends upon what you mean by democracy. The commonly accepted version of British representative or pluralist democracy accords them a respected if not vital role. According to this view:

1. They provide an *essential freedom* for citizens, especially minorities, to organize with like-minded individuals so that their views can be heard by others and taken into account by government.
2. They help to *disperse power* downwards from the central institutions and provide important checks against possibly over-powerful legislatures and executives.
3. They provide *functional* representation according to occupation and belief.
4. They allow for *continuity* of representation between elections, thus enhancing the degree of participation in the democratic system.

Some claim, however, that groups operate very differently in practice. They claim the following:

1. The freedom to organize and influence is exploited by the rich and powerful groups in society; the poor and weak have to rely often on poorly financed cause groups and charitable bodies;
2. Much influence is applied informally and secretly behind the closed doors of ministerial meetings, joint civil service advisory committees or informal meetings in London clubs. This mode of operating suits the powerful insider groups while the weaker groups are left outside and have to resort to ineffective means like influencing public opinion;

3. By enmeshing pressure groups into government policy making processes a kind of **corporatism** has been established which 'fixes' decisions with ministers and civil servants before Parliament has had a chance to make an input on behalf of the electorate as a whole;

4. Pressure groups are often not representative of their members and in many cases do not have democratic appointment procedures for senior staff;

5. Pressure groups are essentially sectional - they apply influence from a partial point of view rather than in the interests of the country as a whole. This tendency led some political scientists to claim that in the 1970s Britain had become harder to govern (King, 1975).

The Marxist critique of pressure groups

Marxists would argue that the whole idea of pluralist democracy is merely part of the democratic window dressing which the ruling economic group uses to disguise its hegemonic control; the distortions identified above would provide partial confirmation. Naturally, according to this view the most potent pressure groups will be the ones representing business while trade unions for the most part will be given a marginal role and will in any case act as agents of the capitalist system to a substantial extent. Marxists would also argue that most members of elite decision making groups implicitly accept the dominant values whereby inequality and exploitation are perpetuated. In consequence most pressure group activity will be concerned with the detailed management of inequality rather than the processes of genuine democracy.

Are pressure groups becoming less effective?

The decline of tripartism has led some commentators to answer the question in the affirmative. Certainly trade unions have been virtually excluded from important policy making processes and almost certainly other pressure groups will have been cold-shouldered by ministers and Whitehall. Mrs Thatcher asserted a powerful self-confident message: she did not need advice. After many years in office this message and *modus operandi* spread downwards to ministers and outwards through the civil service network.

But what of the pressure groups which are in sympathy: intellectual think tanks like the Institute for Economic Affairs, business groups like the Institute of Directors or media barons like Rupert Murdoch? There is much evidence that **their** advice **is** well received and it follows that their 'pull' in the highest quarters has been enhanced rather than diminished in recent years. It also needs to be remembered that pressure group activity at the popular level has grown apace during the 1970s and 1980s. In Chapter 6 this feature was noted as a major new element in the pattern of participation in British politics. Inglehart (1977) has sought to explain this as a feature of affluent societies where people are less concerned with economic questions but more with quality of life. Other explanations can be found in the decline of class as the basis of party political activity in Britain. As support for the two big class-based parties has diminished so cause-based pressure group activity has won popular support. As Moran (1985) notes,

The importance of citizen campaigning

Des Wilson is probably the best known popular campaigner in the country. On a Tyne Tees TV programme in 1986 he explained his own philosophy on citizen campaigning and suggested ten guidelines for people wishing to become involved in such campaigns.

It is very important to remember that the very existence of campaigners, the fact that people are standing up and saying 'No, we don't want this, this is what we want instead', is terribly important because it makes it impossible for the political system to claim that there is no alternative to what they are suggesting.

Citizen organizations are about imposing citizen priorities on a system which we have set up which doesn't always act as well for us as it should. The more we can impose human values by maintaining surveillance, getting involved in organizations, being prepared to stand up and be counted, the better. Even if we are beaten the important thing is that the case has been made, the voice has been heard, a different set of priorities has been set on the table.

Our movement is, if you like, the *real* opposition to the political system because I believe all the political parties are actually one political system which runs this country. If we are not satisfied, it's no use just switching our vote around and it's no use complaining, 'They're all the same, those politicians'. We can create our own effective opposition through our own lives by standing up and making demands on our own behalf.

Guidelines for Campaigners

1. **Identify objectives** — always be absolutely clear on what you are seeking to do. It is fatal to become side-tracked and waste energy on peripheral issues.
2. **Learn the decision making process** — Find out how decisions are made and who makes them.
3. **Formulate a strategy** — try to identify those tactics which will best advance your cause and draw up a plan of campaign.
4. **Research** — always be well briefed and work out alternative proposals to the last detail.
5. **Mobilize support** — widespread support means more political clout and more activists to whom tasks can be delegated.
6. **Use the media** — the media is run by ordinary people who have papers or news bulletins to fill. They need good copy. It helps to develop an awareness of what makes a good story and how it can be presented attractively.
7. **Attitude** — try to be positive, but also maintain a sense of perspective. Decision makers will be less likely to respond to an excessively strident or narrow approach.
8. **Be professional** — even amateurs can acquire professional research media and presentational skills.
9. **Confidence** — there is no need to be apologetic about exercising a democratic right.
10. **Perseverence** — campaigning on local issues is hard work: this should not be underestimated. Few campaigns achieve their objectives immediately. Rebuffs and reverses must be expected and the necessary resilience developed for what might prove to be a long campaign.

Source: Is Democracy Working? (Tyne Tees Television 1986).

> Once established class and party identification weakens, citizens are free to enter politics in an almost infinite variety of social roles. If we are no longer 'working class' we can define our social identity and political demands in numerous ways: so groups emerge catering for nuclear pacifists, radical feminists, homosexuals, real ale drinkers, single parents and any combination of these.
> (Moran, 1985)

Some of the upsurge in pressure group activity has been in direct response to the policies of Thatcherism and its style of exclusion — CND provides the best example here — but much of it has been in support of cross-party issues, particularly those relating to the environment. A letter to Greenpeace members in November 1989 reports on activities during the year and comments on the organization's increased effectiveness.

> This has been the fastest growing year in Greenpeace history. With 300,000 fellow supporters in the UK and millions more worldwide, you can now count yourself part of one of the most successful campaigning organisations in British history.
>
> And we have campaigned accordingly. Barely a week has gone by without Greenpeace pressing its arguments in the papers, on radio and television and on the streets. The continuing seal crisis, nuclear reactors, pollution of all kinds, sewage sludge, toxic waste shipments, the Greenhouse Effect . . . on issue after issue we have taken the initiative, reported the half-concealed facts, presented the alternative case.
>
> The results are obvious. The environment is now a fixed item on the social agenda — not just a fashion item but a core anxiety of millions of people who see the world getting worse and are looking for ways that can prevent us sliding into global catastrophe. The politicians and the industrialists are having to listen and to react. Five years ago this would have been unthinkable.
>
> Greenpeace hasn't done this single-handed. But we have emerged as a respected, radical voice, authoritative as well as provocative. We have, after all, been proved right on issue after issue. It is a long time since we could be dismissed as a bunch of fanciful troublemakers.

Pressure group activity is therefore more widespread and more intense. Much of this is 'outsider' activity, attempting to raise public consciousness, but environmental groups have shown that, with the occasional help of events like the Chernobyl explosion, decision makers can be influenced.

On balance, pressure groups are probably more effective now than they were at the start of the 1970s. While the power of some of the most important groups like trade unions has fallen in recent years, pressure groups remain one of the most important means by which citizens can take part in politics. In this chapter we have given special attention to unions and business because they have been at the centre of policy processes in Britain in recent decades. But it is important to realize that the range of groups is much wider than the two sides of industry. Important groups can be found in the professions (medicine, law), among the churches and in the wide spectrum of organizations — sporting, charity, artistic — in the community. Virtually everybody is a member of a group that tries to exercise influence on policy because virtually everybody is a member of some organization or other; and sooner or later every organization, even the most unworldly, tries to influence an item of public policy.

References and Further Reading

Alderman, G. (ed.), *Pressure Groups and British Government* (Longman, 1984).

Baggot, R., 'Pressure Groups', *Talking Politics*, (Autumn 1988).

Coates, K. and Topham, T., *Trade Unions in Britain* (Spokesman, 1988).

Grant, W., 'Pressure groups and the policy process', *Social Studies Review* (1988).

Grant, W., *Pressure Groups, Politics and Democracy in Britain* (Philip Allan, 1989).

Grant, W., 'Insider and outsider pressure groups', *Social Studies Review*, (September 1985 and January 1990).

Grant, W. and Marsh, D., *The CBI* (Hodder & Stoughton, 1977).

Hyman, R., 'What is happening to the unions?' *Social Studies Review*, (March 1989).

Inglehart, R., *The Silent Revolution: Changing Values and Political Styles among Western Publics* (Princeton University Press, 1977).

King, A., 'Overload: Problems of governing in the 1970s' *Political Studies* (1975).

Marsh, D. (ed.), *Pressure Politics* (Junction Books, 1983).

McCulloch, A., 'Politics and the environment', *Talking Politics*, (Autumn 1988).

McCulloch, A., 'Parties and the environment', *Social Studies Review* (1988).

McIlroy, J., *Trade Unions in Britain Today* (Manchester University Press, 1988).

Moran, M., 'The changing world of British pressure groups', *Teaching Politics* (September 1985).

14 Political Parties

Dennis Kavanagh and Bill Jones

In the British political system parties are of central importance. They involve and educate their members who also provide the key personnel for democratic control of central and local government. The party winning a majority in the Commons, providing it can maintain cohesion and strict discipline, has virtually unrestricted access to the legislative system and the commanding heights of the executive machine. The second largest party forms the official opposition and, through criticism of the party in power and the shadowing of major policy areas, offers itself as the alternative government. To be effective, political parties need well financed, well staffed and well supported administrative machinery throughout the country. This chapter examines the functions and major characteristics of the party system together with leadership and organization features. Inevitably the major focus is on the Conservative and Labour parties but some attention is also paid to centre parties and the new player on the national scene, the Green Party.

While pressure groups are concerned to influence specific policies, political parties set themselves more ambitious objectives. They aim to originate rather than merely influence policy; they address the whole gamut of government policies; and they seek to win control of the representative institutions. They do not wish to *influence* the government so much as *become* the government (see Figure 14.1). Political parties are often criticized on a number of grounds: they impose a uniformity upon members which can be interpreted as inimical to true democracy; they help to perpetuate social divisions and arguments which are arguably out of date; and in combination with the first-past-the-post voting system, the old parties marginalize and squeeze out new influences. Marxists, of course, criticize parties in capitalist democracies as the likely agents of ruling class interests rather than the vehicles of genuine democracy. According to the dominant pluralist theory of democracy, however, political parties perform a vital series of functions.

1. *Reconciling conflicting interests.* Political parties represent coalitions of different groups in society. They provide a means whereby the *conflicting elements of similar interests are reconciled, harmonized and then fed into the political system.* At general elections it is the party which people vote for rather than the candidate.

2. *Participation.* As permanent bodies *parties provide opportunities for citizens to participate in politics,* e.g. in choosing candidates for local and parliamentary elections, campaigning during elections and influencing policy at party conferences.

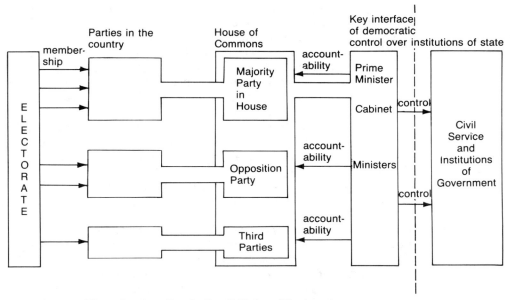

Figure 14.1   *The role of parties in the British political system*

3. **Recruitment.** Parties are the principal means whereby ***democratic leaders are recruited*** and trained for service in local councils, Parliament, ministerial and Cabinet office and the premiership itself.

4. **Democratic control.** It is the democratically elected members of political parties who as ministers are placed in charge of the day to day running of the vast government apparatus — employing millions of people and spending over £200 billion per annum.

5. **Choice.** By presenting programmes and taking stands on issues ***parties allow voters to choose between rival policy packages.*** The existence of ***parties*** rather than just one party within a political system is widely held to be the crucial test of a genuine democracy — hence the calls for multi-party free elections in Eastern Europe during the break-up of Communist hegemony in 1989.

6. **Representation.** According to the strictly constitutional interpretation elected candidates represent geographical regions of the country — constituencies — but they also serve to represent in the national legislature a range of socio-economic groups.

7. **Communication.** Parties provide sounding boards for governments and channels of communication between them and society, e.g. when MPs return to their constituencies at weekends to hold surgeries and attend functions.

8. **Accountability.** At election times the party (or parties) forming the government is held accountable for what it has done during its period of office.

Parties, or groups of like-minded MPs, have existed in the House of Commons for centuries. But they emerged in their recognizably modern form of ***being disciplined, policy orientated, possessing a formal organization in the country and*** *appealing to a large electorate* after the second Reform Act (1867). Indeed, the growth of a large electorate required the parties to develop constituency associations in the country. At that time the two main parties were the Conservatives and Liberals. But with the presence of about eighty Irish Nationalists between 1880 and 1918 and then some thirty Labour MPs between 1906 and 1918, Britain had a multi-party system in the early years of this century. After 1918 the Irish Nationalists withdrew from the British Parliament and the Liberals declined. The new post-1918 party system pitted the rising Labour party against the established power of the Conservatives and Liberals though the latter still gained substantial support until 1929. The inter-war years were a period of Conservative dominance of government. Since 1945 the Labour and Conservative parties have together always gained over 90 per cent of the seats in the House of Commons (Table 14.1).

To a large extent this two-party dominance of Parliament is a consequence of the first-past-the-post electoral system. As noted in Chapter 11 the decline in support for the two main parties in recent years has largely been at the expense of the Labour party. Yet the three-quarters of the total votes which the Conservative and Labour parties received still translates into 95 per cent of the seats in the House of Commons. In 1981 the Social Democratic Party broke away from the Labour Party and entered into an alliance with the Liberal Party. For a few heady months, with Alliance poll ratings close to 50 per cent, it seemed as if the mould of two-party policies was about to be broken but at the 1983 election this level of support, as Enoch Powell predicted, had dispersed like 'mist in the morning sun'. Nevertheless, the Alliance's 26 per cent of the vote created if not a three-party system between 1983 and 1987, then at least a 'two-and-a-half' party system. The 1987 election, however, saw the Alliance's vote dip to 23 per cent and the reassertion of two-party politics. The botched negotiations in 1987 which resulted in a new merged party, the Liberal Democrats,

Table 14.1 *British election results 1945–87: Seats in the House of Commons and percentage of votes cast*

Elections	Conservative		Labour		Liberals		Others		Total number of MPs
	Seats	%	Seats	%	Seats	%	Seats	%	
1945	213	39.8	393	47.8	12	9.0	22	3.4	640
1950	298	43.5	315	46.1	9	9.1	3	0.7	625
1951	321	48.0	295	48.8	6	2.5	3	0.7	625
1955	344	49.7	277	46.4	6	2.7	3	1.2	630
1959	365	49.4	258	43.8	6	5.9	1	0.9	630
1964	304	43.4	317	44.1	9	11.2	0	1.3	630
1966	253	41.9	363	47.9	12	8.5	2	1.7	630
1970	330	46.4	287	43.0	6	7.5	7	3.1	630
1974 (Feb.)	297	37.9	301	37.1	14	19.3	23*	5.7	635
1974 (Oct.)	277	35.8	319	39.2	13	18.3	26	6.7	635
1979	339	43.9	269	36.9	11	13.8	16	5.4	635
1983	397	42.4	209	27.6	23†	25.4	21	4.6	650
1987	375	42.3	229	30.8	22	22.6	24	4.3	650

* Northern Irish MPs are counted as 'others' from 1974
† In 1983 and 1987 Liberal figures cover the results for the SDP/Liberal Alliance

and the defiant rump of the SDP postponed indefinitely the break-up of the dominant post-war two-party system (see section on Centre Parties below). The dramatic entry of the Green Party into British politics when it won 15 per cent of the votes cast in the European elections in June 1989 provided another false dawn for those who hoped for the demise of two-party politics; by the end of that year poll support for the Greens had fallen to a disappointing (but still not insignificant) 5 per cent.

The Conservative Party

Principles

The Conservative party is famous for its pragmatism and opportunism, qualities which have helped the party to survive and thrive (see Chapter 8). It is worth noting that the party has been in office alone or in coalition for some two-thirds of the twentieth century. Each party leader has had the opportunity to re-define the Conservative policies, but there are some abiding ideas.

The *rejection of class divisions* and an *emphasis on the importance of national unity.* The Conservatives portray themselves as the party of 'one nation'.

The authority of government: this is reflected in the importance attached to strong defence and law and order. On the other hand, the party opposes economic planning and is less sympathetic than Labour to state intervention in the economy or state ownership of industry. Yet until Mrs Thatcher Conservative leaders accepted many of the nationalization measures of Labour.

Social reform: Disraeli, the Conservative Prime Minister between 1874 and 1880, is often regarded as the founder of 'One Nation' Toryism and pledged the party to improve the 'condition of the people'.

Freedom and liberty, defined largely as the absence of state coercion and intervention. The party believes that individuals should make choices for themselves and as such it encourages private education and health care, lower taxes, and indirect rather than direct taxation.

The party suffered a shattering defeat in the 1945 election. In that year the electorate was clearly in favour of full employment and the welfare measures, greater conciliation of trade unions and probably supported an extension of public ownership in the basic industries. The Conservative party promised to go some way in accepting these, except for public ownership. But the electorate voted for the party that believed in them more fully.

Thus, after 1945 the Conservative party faced a problem similar to that which the Labour party faced in the 1980s. Should it carry on clinging to the policies that the electorate had repudiated or should it try and come to terms with what that government had done? On the whole it favoured the latter. R.A. Butler and Macmillan played an important role in re-defining Conservative policies, accepting many of the main planks of the Labour government's programme. If one looks at the record between 1951 and 1964 the Conservative government largely accepted the above four ideas. It accepted the greater role of the trade unions and the mixed economy (though it reversed the nationalization of iron and steel), it acquiesced in and continued the passage of many countries from colonial status to independence. It protected the welfare state and maintained a high level of public spending. Finally, it had also adopted economic planning by the early 1960s. Much of the above was a social democratic consensus and it prevailed regardless of whether Labour or Conservative were in office (see Chapter 3).

Leadership

The modern Conservative Party emerged in the middle of the nineteenth century as the new democratic form of the old Tory Party. From its parliamentary base it extended itself organizationally downwards into the electorate as the franchise grew in the nineteenth century. Its role in representing the established order gave it a hierarchical culture in which the leader is given considerable power and accorded automatic loyalty.

Conservative leaders Churchill, Eden and Macmillan were careful to position themselves on the centre left, (or 'One Nation' strand, of the party — see below). They did this for two reasons. They believed, first, that maintaining the post-war consensus was the only way to run the country. In other words one had to maintain full employment, consult with the main economic interests and intervene in the economy (in the interests of boosting employment, helping exports and assisting the more depressed regions). Secondly, they believed that such policies were necessary to win that crucial portion of working-class support upon which Conservative electoral success depended.

Yet there have been tensions in the Conservative party. Historians often distinguish two strands. One is the Tory or *One Nation* Conservatism. This accepts a positive role for the state in providing welfare, full employment and taking care of the poor in society. The second is the *neo-liberal* strand which upholds the role of the free market and sees much government activity as unnecessary, and even a hindrance, to the good working of society and the economy. It prefers a regime of low taxes and low public spending so that people are left to spend their own money as they see fit. But until the election of Mrs Thatcher as party leader in 1975 the Conservative party was always led by people from the former tradition.

The authority of the Conservative party leader has already been mentioned. However, this does not mean that the party leader has a completely free hand. A Conservative party leader has to keep his leadership team reasonably united and also maintain the morale of the party. When choosing the Cabinet or shadow Cabinet, a leader has to make sure that people are drawn in from different wings of the party. Mrs Thatcher, for example, gave office to many leading 'wets', people who, particularly in her first government, had doubts about her economic policies. In addition the party leader may have to compromise over policy. Mrs Thatcher was unable to get the public spending cuts that she wished in her first Cabinet and was not able to move as far as she wished in matters such as the introduction of education vouchers, because many Conservatives had doubts about such measures.

The power of the party leader usually differs according to whether the party is in office or not. In government, the party leader is the Prime Minister with all the authority that goes with that office. For much of the past century the Conservative party has been in government, either alone or in coalition, and this has tended to reinforce the authority of the leader. Conservative MPs have also expected to be in office and have been troublesome when leaders have lost general elections. It is interesting that A.J. Balfour (having lost three successive general elections) had to resign in 1911, Sir Alec Douglas Home (after the 1964 election defeat) stood down in 1965 and Mr Heath (having lost the two 1974 elections) was defeated by Mrs Thatcher in 1975. On each of these occasions the party had recently lost a general election. Thus, a Tory leader's authority and the loyalty he or she can command tends to vary in direct relation to his or her ability to win elections.

It would be a mistake to think that Conservative leaders have always been 'conservative'. This has certainly been true of some, like Lord Salisbury, but many, like Robert Peel, Disraeli, Macmillan and Mrs Thatcher, have been vigorous reformers. During the Thatcher reign two types of reformism came into conflict: the orthodox 'wet' reformism of Macmillan and the post-war consensus and the neo-Liberal reformism of the leader herself. Because of the Conservative tradition of maintaining external unity internal debates took place in a peculiar way. Instead of the spectacular open leadership conflicts of the Labour Party (e.g. the Bevanite challenge to Gaitskell) Conservative struggles were couched in a gentlemanly code. For example, instead of calling for a return to consensus politics senior 'wets' would issue apparently academic lectures on the value of Disraeli's 'One Nation' Toryism.

Until 1965 the leader 'emerged' when the party was in office (which was usually the case), as the monarch invited a prominent Conservative Minister to form a government after consulting senior party figures. (In 1957 the Queen sent for Macmillan rather than Butler to succeed Eden, and in 1963 she sent for Lord Home over the luckless Butler. Both choices angered some Conservative MPs and so involved the monarchy in controversy.) In 1965 the party adopted a system by which MPs elected the leader and Mr Heath was the first leader to be so elected.

The contest has a maximum of three ballots. To win on the first a candidate needs 50 per cent of the votes of the parliamentary party and in addition, according to the rules, '15 per cent more of the votes . . . than any other candidates'. If these conditions are not met more candidates can join a second ballot and if an overall majority still proves elusive a third ballot can be held involving the top three candidates and using the alternative vote method. In 1975 a new provision was introduced, the annual re-election of the leader, principally to ensure that election-losers like Heath could be disposed of efficiently.

In that year Mrs Thatcher was brave enough to challenge the 'loyalty culture' of the Conservatives by standing against Heath and was rewarded — wholly unexpectedly at the time — by a narrow majority in the first ballot. Julian Critchley called this 'the Peasants' Revolt'. By the time the heavyweights like Whitelaw joined in the second ballot it was too late and the Grantham grocer's daughter increased her momentum to romp home.

For fifteen years the mechanism lay unused until Sir Anthony Meyer chose to challenge Mrs Thatcher in December 1989. Sir Anthony's was not a serious personal challenge; he had hoped a more credible candidate would come forward to join in the first ballot. This did not happen and, in the event, he received thirty-three votes while twenty-seven others abstained. Thatcher loyalists rightly claimed an overwhelming victory. The outcome was to be very different when Mrs Thatcher was challenged again in November 1990 (see Chapter 29).

Party Organization

1922 Committee

The Conservative leader is at the apex of party organization, in charge of front-bench appointments (whether in or out of office) and of the party bureaucracy. But the leader's writ does not extend to the 1922 Committee, the name given to the Conservative MPs' own organization. The name dates back to the Carlton Club meeting in that year when Conservative MPs prevailed upon Austen Chamberlain to pull out of the coalition with the Liberals: the name symbolizes Conservative back-bench power. The Committee jealously guards its influence, electing its own officers and executive committee and only giving audiences to the leader by invitation.

Usually the Committee provides solid support for the leadership but behind the scenes discreet influence is often applied and its officers supplement the information flow on party feeling and morale provided by the Chief Whip and his cohorts — a nominated whip, incidentally, always attends Committee meetings. The 1922 Committee, therefore, is far from being the leader's poodle. After Lawson's resignation in October 1989 a feeling grew among Conservative MPs that Mrs Thatcher's management of her senior colleagues had been at fault. A deputation of the 1922 Committee went to meet her and in the words of the Party Chairman, Kenneth Baker, told her to 'get her act together' (she subsequently hotly denied that any such words had been used to her). Conservative leaders, if they are wise, take care never to ignore the advice of the 1922 Committee: ultimately it decides upon their political life or death.

Party committees

The parliamentary party has also established a network of twenty-four specialist committees of policy matters and seven regional groupings. In opposition Shadow Ministers chair the relevant policy groups but in government the Minister does not attend except by invitation. When in government these committees can have considerable influence, often on the detail of policy; individual MPs, for example, might well use them to promote or defend constituency interests. Conservative MPs are also represented on the considerable number of ***all-party committees*** which exist on a wide range of policy issues.

The National Union of Conservative Associations

This body was set up in 1867 to coordinate local constituency associations in England and Wales: there are separate bodies for Scotland and Northern Ireland. The central council of the National Union, comprising Conservative peers, MEPs, prospective MPs and representatives of regional bodies and advisory committees meets once a year to elect officers; a smaller executive committee itself appoints a General Purposes Committee. Perhaps the most important function of the National Union is to organize the party conference.

Conference

The role of conference is formally advisory but in practice it has become important as an annual rallying of the faithful and a public relations exercise in which the leader receives a standing ovation (a regulation ten minutes for Mrs Thatcher in the 1980s) and an impression of euphoric unity is assiduously cultivated for public consumption. As a result of extensive television coverage leading figures in the party seek to secure their positions and new ones to make their mark. A poor showing by a front bench spokesman can impede progress or, as in the case of Reginald Maudling in 1965, prejudice their leadership chances. A measure of the conference's importance is that since the late 1960s the leader has attended throughout instead of descending like royalty for the final day. Indeed, Mrs Thatcher used to dominate proceedings by sitting close to the rostrum and fixing each speaker with an intent appraising gaze. It is rumoured by one ex-Cabinet member that at conference only Mrs Thatcher was allowed the use the invisible autocue which enables speakers apparently to 'orate' without notes.

As a policy making body the Conference has traditionally been dismissed — Balfour said he would rather take advice from his valet. Richard Kelly (1989, p. 3), however, argues otherwise. He claims that the consensual conference culture masks an important form of communication: that of 'mood'. Party leaders, he maintains, listen to (or decode?) the messages which underlie the polite contributions from grass roots members and act, or even legislate accordingly. He also points out that a substantial network of regional and national conferences take place every year involving related sections like Conservative Women, Conservative Trade Unionists and the Federation of Young Conservatives. At least 5,000 activists attend two or more conferences each year: 'Why should so many people bother to attend supposedly worthless conferences?' Kelly pertinently asks. He also points out that activists are now less deferential: they are 'increasingly convinced that theirs is the new vox pop and are much more impatient with Tory leaders who do not heed their advice'. They also

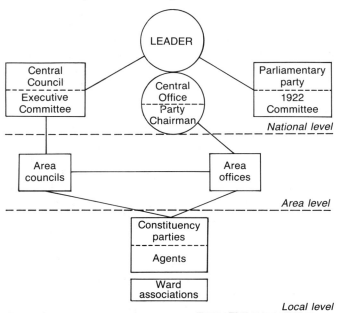

Figure 14.2 *Conservative party organization (Source: Derbyshire, 1987)*

knew in the 1980s that in Mrs Thatcher they had a leader who was often closer to their own views than many of her senior colleagues and advisers. The fact is that the leadership does listen to the party in such gatherings — though how important an input they provide into the policy process is difficult to gauge precisely.

Constituency associations

One of the main aims of conference is to send party workers home buoyed up with new enthusiasm for their constituency tasks: recruiting members, attending committees, organizing social and fund-raising events, leafletting, exploiting issues at the local level and most important of all, seeking victory in local and national elections. About half of the local Conservative associations employ full-time agents who provide professional assistance. The fact is that despite a nominal membership of 1.5 million the active membership of the Conservative Party is probably around one-fifth of that number.

To win elections parties must have good candidates and local associations do their best to select them. Candidatures for local elections seldom generate a great deal of heat but parliamentary candidatures, especially in safe seats, can attract hundreds of applicants from all over the country. Before 1948 rich candidates willing to donate party funds had an advantage but in that year the Maxwell Fyfe report put a limit to such contributions. Some research suggests policy stance in the Conservative Party is less important than personality qualities — not just the candidate but his wife as well. In the case of women candidates it is unclear if their husbands are similarly appraised — in 1987 only seventeen Conservative women MPs were elected.

The Central Office

Central Office is the organizational core of the Conservative Party. In common with the hierarchical nature of the party it comes under the direct control of the party leader who appoints the Party Chairman and Vice Chairman, the two officers in charge on a day to day basis. Mrs Thatcher tended to make caretaker appointments for the first half of her administrations — John Selwyn Gummer in 1985, Peter Brooke in 1987 — and then heavyweights in the run-up to the election — for example Norman Tebbit for the last one.

Central Office represents an important nexus between party activists in the country and MPs at Westminster, providing advice on small businesses, community groups, trade unions and political education as well as training for professional constituency agents. The Research Department was set up in 1925, becoming a power base for R.A. Butler — who was its head for two decades after the war — and a springboard for able young politicians like Iain Macleod, Enoch Powell and most recently Chris Patten. The Research Department lays on secretarial support for the shadow cabinet when the party is in opposition, supports policy groups, briefs the parliamentary party (with officers providing secretarial backup for subject committees) and produces a range of publications, notably the journal *Politics Today* and the pre-election *Campaign Guides*.

The Department naturally plays an important role in policy formulation and it was not surprising that one of Mrs Thatcher's first acts in 1975 was to replace the 'wet' Sir Ian Gilmour as Chairman of the Department with the austerely dry Sir Angus

Maude; the wettish Patten, however, survived as Director until he became MP for Bath in 1979. At the same time and in the same spirit she appointed Sir Keith Joseph as Chairman of the Advisory Committee on Policy. This important forum meets once a month in opposition to help formulate policy along with the shadow cabinet, and in government to provide a sounding board of party opinion. This body acts as an access point to expert advice in the academic and business worlds.

Sir Keith was not content with merely being in charge of policy initiation. He also set up, with Mrs Thatcher's support, the Centre for Policy Studies, which together with the Institute for Economic Affairs (established 1957) provided 'think tank' advice and policy ideas throughout the period of Conservative opposition and thereafter to the Thatcher governments. Conservative leaders, however, have never wanted for advice from groups within the party.

Party groupings

Perhaps the oldest group is the ***Primrose League***, set up in 1883 by Lord Randolph Churchill to advance the liberal conservatism of Disraeli and encourage social contact among the grass-roots membership. By 1951 the latter function was in the ascendant and it fell to the ***Bow Group***, founded in that year, to urge the party's acceptance of the post-war consensus. The Group has a national membership including thirty or so MPs, a number of policy groups and publishes a journal, *Crossbow*.

The ***Monday Club*** was set up in 1961 in the wake of Macmillan's 'wind of change' African policy and has always concerned itself with defence, external and immigration policies on which it has invariably taken a strong right-wing line — so much so that it has sometimes been accused of being an entry point for National Front influence.

The ***Selsdon Group*** formed in 1973 was more concerned to champion the neo-liberal economic policies which Heath's 1972 policy U-turns had appeared to abandon. The ***Salisbury Group*** is another right-wing intellectual ginger group which exerts influence through its journal *The Salisbury Review*.

Membership of the Advisory Committee on Policy		
Parliamentary party:	two from the House of Lords and five (appointed by the 1922 Committee) from the House of Commons;	
National Union:	eight, of whom four are ex-officio, including, invariably, the chairman of the Young Conservatives, and four elected;	
Five ex-officio members:	the chairman and deputy chairmen of the party, the director of the Research Department, and the director of the Conservative Political Centre:	
Up to six co-opted members:	who include, by tradition, the chairman of the Federation of Conservative Students	
The secretary of the Advisory Committee on Policy:	who has always been a member of the Conservative Research Department	

Source: Chris Patten in Layton-Henry (1979).

The *Tory Reform Group* was set up in 1975 to defend the beleaguered Disraelian tradition; it has some thirty MP members, the most prominent of whom is Peter Walker.

In addition to the above from time to time the parliamentary party establishes policy groupings, some of which prove ephemeral, like the Blue Chip group to which Chris Patten belonged in the early 1980s, and Centre Forward, the group of twenty-plus MPs formed by Francis Pym in 1983. The anti-European Bruges Group may prove more lasting and more influential.

Funding

The central organization of the party receives about one-third of its funding via a quota system levied on local constituency organizations. The balance is provided by individual and company donations which flow in directly and often indirectly through what could be called 'front organizations' like British United Industrialists, the Aims of Industry and a number of companies especially set up for the purpose and named after rivers in the United Kingdom. The party is relatively wealthy: it spent £9 million in the 1987 election compared with Labour's £4 million and the Alliance's £2 million. In 1974 when submitting evidence to the Houghton Committee the party opposed the idea of state aid to political parties.

The Labour Party

The Labour party is so different from the Conservative party it requires a completely different approach. The major contrasts are as follows:

1. Unlike the Conservative Party, which developed from within Parliament, Labour developed as a grass-roots popular movement *outside* the legislature. In 1900 the trade unions, cooperative and socialist societies formed the Labour Representation Committee (LRC) to represent interests of trade unions and assist the entry of working men into Parliament. In 1906 the LRC changed its name to the Labour party.
2. The Conservatives have been in power — either alone or as the dominant coalition partner — for two-thirds of the years since 1918, Labour for less than a third.
3. Conservatives have traditionally been the party of the status quo, Labour the party dedicated to its overthrow. Conservatives attracted sober members of the ruling elite who, with some justification, were expecting to preside over an unquestioned existing order. Labour, on the other hand, attracted people whose political style had developed through years of opposition to such an order, who spoke in fiery rhetorical terms and were skilled in manipulating democratic procedures — skills used by members both against the Conservative enemy and against party comrades with whom they disagreed. And there was much to disagree about. There is only one status quo while there are an infinite number of theoretical alternatives. In practice the key differences were reduced to those between the gradual and the root and branch reformers: Ramsay MacDonald and John Wheatley in the 1920s; Attlee and Stafford Cripps in the 1930s; Gaitskell and Bevan in the 1950s; Foot

and Wilson in the 1960s; Callaghan and Benn in the 1970s; and Kinnock and Benn in the 1980s.

4. Labour was originally a federation rather than a unified party like the Conservatives, comprising trade unions and intellectual socialist societies each with their own self-governing mechanisms. Despite the formation of a single party in 1918 a similar coalition still underlies Labour party politics.

5. The written constitution which the party gained in 1918 committed it to certain ideological objectives and laid down procedures for elections, appointments and decision making. While more democratic than the autocratic Conservative party organization, the constitution precludes some of the flexible adaptation to changing circumstances which the latter enjoys and when in government offers an alternative source of authority which has on occasions caused Labour embarrassment.

The various stresses which the coalition of interests causes in the Labour party, further compounded by the wide ideological spectrum which it covers, creates a fascinating bundle of contradictions. Labour is at once more bureaucratic than the Conservatives yet more democratic; more fraternal yet more fractricidal; more iconoclastic yet more traditional; more outspoken and open yet often more hypocritical and devious.

Labour's constitution and the power of the unions

The contrasting 'top down' and 'bottom up' provenance of the two big parties explains why the Conservative party in the country is organizationally separate and subservient to the parliamentary party while for Labour the situation is — at least in theory — reversed. This proviso is important because the relationship between the Parliamentary Labour Party (PLP) and the other party organs is complex and has changed over time. The 1918 constitution aimed to provide a happy marriage between the different elements of Labour's coalition: the trade unions, socialist societies, local constituency parties, party officials and Labour MPs. Institutionally the marriage — which has not been an easy one — expressed itself in the form of the leadership and the Parliamentary Labour Party (PLP), the National Executive Committee (NEC) constituency parties and the Conference (Figure 14.3). The absence of trade unions from this list is misleading because in practice they play a leading role:

1. About half of the country's trade union membership affiliate to the Labour Party; the political levy paid by members as part of their subscriptions provide over 80 per cent of Labour's annual finance. During the 1980s the Trade Unions for Labour (TUFL) was set up to raise additional finance for the party, especially for general election campaigns.

2. At Conference trade union leaders are empowered to cast a block vote representing those members paying the political levy. There has been criticism of some unions for misrepresenting these figures. As votes are allocated on the basis of each 1,000 members or part thereof the numerically small socialist societies and the 300,000 or so individual constituency members are easily outvoted by the trade union big battalions. This means that decisive power is given to the leaders of the five largest unions who control well over half the vote: the Transport and

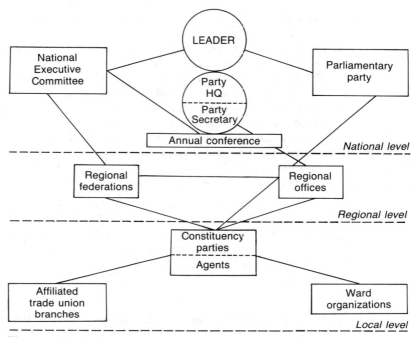

Figure 14.3 *Labour party organization (Source: Derbyshire, 1987)*

General Workers (TGWU), the Amalgamated Engineering Union (AUEW), the General and Municipal Workers (GMBATU), the National Union of Public Employees (NUPE) and the Union of Shop Distributive and Allied Workers (USDAW). During the 1970s when union power over the Labour Party was at its height the leaders of the two largest unions, Jack Jones of the TGWU and Hugh Scanlon of the AUEW were sometimes described as the two most powerful men in Britain.

3. The National Executive Committee (NEC) which is responsible for running the party's organization is elected at Conference. Five members are elected by the constituency parties only and twelve members are elected by the trade unions only. In addition five women and the party Treasurer are elected by the entire conference. This means the unions effectively elect eighteen of the twenty-nine NEC members. The socialist associations vote for one representative and the leader of the Young Socialists; the party leader and deputy leader are *ex-officio*.

4. The trade unions also sponsor (i.e. pay up to 80 per cent of election expenses and often a contribution to the full-time agent's salary) 150–200 parliamentary candidates: over twenty Labour MPs are currently sponsored by the TGWU alone.

Power and leadership in the Labour party

Unlike the Conservatives who stress loyalty, hierarchy and strong leadership Labour's ethos was founded in democracy, egalitarianism and collective decision making. As Minkin observes 'Leadership was an organizational function — a set of roles to be performed'. In harmony with trade union traditions 'Every member via their constituent unit had the right to submit resolutions (to the Annual Conference) and it was from the agenda formed by these resolutions that decisions would ultimately be made.' While this ethos was clearly important it has been questioned as an accurate description of how leadership and policy making has been carried out in practice. The sociologist Robert Michels questioned whether mass labour organizations can ever achieve genuine democracy. Given the indifference and poor knowledge of most members he argued that a small group would inevitably come to control real power. This 'iron law of oligarchy' theory was reinforced by Robert McKenzie in a classic 1950s study of Britain's political parties in which he claimed that appearances notwithstanding, both major parties reflected similar concentrations of power and authority in the party leadership with the external party organizations playing a merely supportive role. Such analyses make nonsense of Labour's official constitution and the widespread notion that conference constitutes the 'parliament' of the Labour movement.

McKenzie argued that 'By the time the Labour Party had taken office in 1924, its transformation was almost complete. By accepting all the conventions with respect to the office of the Prime Minister and of Cabinet government it ensured that effective power within the party would be concentrated in the hands of the leadership of the PLP' (McKenzie, p.639). There is much in this argument. Once elected to Westminster Labour MPs become subject to a different set of forces: they become responsible for all their constituents and not just Labour supporters; they often need to consider their re-election in terms of what non-Labour voters want or will accept; and they become influenced by the dominant Burkean notion that within the House of Commons MPs are not delegates of some outside organization but individuals elected to use their judgement on behalf of the nation as a whole. The constitution of the Labour Party, therefore, becomes challenged by the constitution of the country. In government this challenge is greatly strengthened. With a legislative programme before it and a possibly full term of government Labour leaders have not wanted their hands tied by the external party. They have also felt it necessary, possibly for electoral considerations, to disavow such pressures; for example, Ramsay MacDonald to the 1928 Conference: 'As long as I hold any position in the Parliamentary Party — and I know I can speak for my colleagues also — we are not going to take instructions from any outside body unless we agree with them' (Minkin, 1980, p. 14). When first Prime Minister in 1924 MacDonald had followed traditional precedents and appointed his own Cabinet without any internal party consultation. It was MacDonald, moreover, who challenged the low key traditions of Labour leadership. His platform oratory, commanding presence and the immense prestige of prime ministerial office won him a most inegalitarian degree of adulation from the party's rank and file. During much of his period as leader the party organization acted in a secondary supportive or to use Minkin's term 'handmaiden' role. Much later in 1960 party leader Hugh Gaitskell refused to accept a conference resolution embracing unilateralism and succeeded in reversing it the following year. Harold Wilson as Prime Minister, moreover, ignored a series of conference decisions in the late 1960s and survived while James Callaghan did much the same when Prime Minister in the 1970s. To dismiss Labour's intra-party democracy as unimportant, however, would be foolish.

From the 1930s onwards the party leadership became less assertive

In 1930 MacDonald was quoted as saying, 'If God were to come to me and say "Ramsay, would you rather be a country gentleman than a prime minister" I should reply, "Please God, a country gentleman".' The following year he was expelled from the party he had led for so many years when he formed, with minimal consultation, a coalition government with Conservatives and Liberals. After the ensuing election Labour entered a long period of opposition. A strong reaction set in against the MacDonald conception of leadership which expressed itself in the modest and exceedingly uncharismatic person of Clement Attlee, who in 1935 took over as leader from George Lansbury. To use the terminology of Francis Williams a 'pathfinder—visionary' leader had been replaced by a 'stabilizer' — from then on the preferred leadership type in the Labour Party (Ingle, 1987, pp.48–9).

In opposition Labour's internal democracy asserts itself

Unlike the Conservative party leader who is effectively in charge of the party organization the Labour leader has to deal with individuals and committees elected from the grass-roots upwards. When in opposition Labour leaders must select their Shadow Cabinet from the Parliamentary Committee which is elected by the PLP. It followed that without the prestige of office, and after 1931 reduced to a rump of four dozen or so MPs, the PLP was unable to dominate the party during the 1930s as it had in the 1920s. The NEC and the TUC played a leading role in policy formulation. The annual conference became a crucial gathering in which policy was debated and then confirmed. In 1937 Attlee recognized its authority:

> The Labour Party Conference lays down the policy of the party and issues instructions which must be carried out by the Executive, the affiliated organisations and its representatives in parliament and on the local authorities.

After 1945 Attlee was in office but was able to sustain this doctrine largely through the willingness of trade union leaders to cast their block votes at conference in support of policies generated in practice by the PLP leadership.

Labour leaders who flout party democracy pay a price in lost support

Minkin points out that while Wilson was defying conference resolutions and pursuing foreign, economic and industrial policies deeply offensive to the party's left wing he was also losing the loyalty and hence control of crucial elements in the party. Little by little the constituency parties, the NEC and the trade unions turned against him. 'Though the party had only a limited effect on immediate government policy, the government in turn had decreasing control over the policy output of the party.' The NEC's control over forward policy formulation subsequently created problems for Wilson and his successor Callaghan in the 1970s. Similar problems were created by the rule that a resolution carried by a two-thirds majority at conference automatically becomes part of the party's election programme.

Indeed, the 1960s witnessed the splintering of Labour Party unity. Disillusioned with the revisionism of the Wilson government the next generation of important trade union leaders found common cause with the left wing of the parliamentary party. In opposition after 1970 conference shifted sharply to the left and by 1974 most constituency parties and the NEC were also firmly in the left wing camp. The result was that Labour governments of Wilson and Callaghan (1974—9) were 'obviously at odds with the party machine . . . as if there were two Labour parties, one with the voice of the NEC and the conference and the other with that of the parliamentary leadership' (Butler and Kavanagh, 1980). Disillusion with revisionist policies caused an exodus of party supporters leaving 'shell' constituency parties vulnerable to take overs by far left activists, especially members of the Militant Tendency. Parliamentary candidates face a selection procedure similar to the Conservatives. A shortlist is compiled by the local party executive from candidates nominated by affiliated groups and the general management committee (GMC) makes the final choice. During the 1970s GMCs in many parts of the country were taken over by the left, inevitably giving rise to an increasing number of left-wing candidates.

Michels and McKenzie therefore overstate the authority which the parliamentary leadership exercises within the Labour party. When in opposition the extra-parliamentary party plays an important part in policy formulation and when in government the leadership can only ignore the extra-parliamentary party at the subsequent cost of party unity. This tendency was dramatically manifested when Labour again became the opposition party in 1979.

The 1981 constitutional changes

Internal party divisions reached a new degree of bitterness in 1979 in the wake of the so-called 'winter of discontent' when the collapse of Labour's incomes policy produced industrial paralysis. On 28 March Callaghan's minority government lost a vote of confidence and a general election was called. The party manifesto is decided jointly by the parliamentary leaders and the NEC but by this time the gulf between the two was immense. When Callaghan vetoed measures which the left wished to include in the manifesto — including the abolition of the House of Lords — he alienated the left still further and set the battle lines for a fratricidal fight over the reform of the party's constitution.

The party's left wing pressed for radical changes in the rules of the party and in particular they wished to introduce greater 'democracy' into the party. The left insisted that the party leader be elected by an electoral college and not by MPs alone. In 1981 the Wembley conference agreed to set up an electoral college in which the trade unions would have 40 per cent of the vote, constituency parties 30 per cent and MPs 30 per cent. A second aim was for mandatory reselection of MPs within the lifetime of a Parliament. They succeeded in this. But they failed in their third goal, which was to give control of the party's manifesto to the National Executive Committee. The central thrust of all of these reforms was to increase the power of the extra-parliamentary elements of the party over MPs. Mandatory re-selection was a factor which persuaded some threatened MPs to 'jump' into the SDP in 1981 and 1982. The re-selections have on balance favoured the left.

The new machinery for electing the deputy leader was first tried in 1981 when Tony Benn challenged Denis Healey and came within a whisker of toppling him. But the election was time-consuming, bitterly divisive and left many scars. Neil Kinnock and Roy Hattersley contested the leadership in October 1983; Kinnock won easily, while Hattersley decisively won the deputy's post. Yet, if the left managed to overturn the constitution and help drive some disillusioned right-wing MPs to the SDP, its victories have been short-lived. Mr Kinnock has managed to impose his authority on the party machine, particularly the NEC. The *Militant* leaders have been expelled from the party, and the party's aims and principles are being restated in a less left-wing form.

Labour principles

While most members of the Labour party agree that it is a socialist party, they disagree about what 'socialism' is (see Chapter 9). According to the famous Clause 4 of the party constitution the party's object is 'the common ownership of the means of production and the best obtainable system of popular administration and control of each industry and service . . .'. The Labour party therefore worked for the nationalization or public ownership of major industries and utilities. Its rhetoric has been hostile to the capitalist ideas of competition and private profit emphasizing the values of fellowship, and advocating production for use. Workers' control has made little advance in the party. If Clause 4 is taken literally, a Labour government would work for the economy to be wholly owned by the state. In fact the leadership has never espoused such a goal.

Instead the leaders have emphasized socialism as the promotion of greater equality of opportunity, notably through programmes of progressive taxation, and through state rather than private provision of social services.

The party's left and right wings have frequently been bitterly divided over the above goals. The party's right wing has been pragmatic about public ownership and state intervention in the economy, whereas the left has regarded it as a litmus test of socialism. The right has been more interested in promoting equality of opportunity, whereas the left has been more wedded to promoting the equality of outcome. Finally, the right has advocated a strong role for Britain in NATO, supported the Anglo—US alliance, and defended Britain's retention of nuclear weapons. The left has disagreed with all three of these principles. From 1982 Labour's official defence policy was non-nuclear, substantially a consequence of left and CND influence.

In 1989, however, this commitment was dropped at the insistence of a leadership determined to shift the party into the 'electable' centre ground. Since being elected as a left-wing candidate for the leadership in 1983 Kinnock has persuaded his party to accept British membership of the European Community, sale of council houses to tenants, some of the industrial relations measures of the Thatcher government and the abandonment of unilateral nuclear disarmament. The decision of Tony Benn and Eric Heffer to stand for the leadership and deputy leadership in 1988 represented a last throw of the dice by the defeated fundamentalist left wing: both were heavily defeated.

Kinnock's successful redirection of party policy stemmed from his control over the NEC. In the 1970s and early 1980s Tony Benn was able to exert a major influence over policy through his chairmanship of the Home Policy Committee. Over the years since 1983 Kinnock's strength on the NEC improved. In the wake of the 1987 election defeat he authorized a comprehensive review of policy to be undertaken not by the Home Policy Committee but by seven specialist groups involving MPs and outside experts. The resultant reports were endorsed in 1989 by an NEC which was now solidly Kinnockite. He has also used his power to prune drastically the NEC's shambling committee system, to establish four centralized directorates of which two, Policy and Communications, have become dominant. Indeed, Peter Mandelson as the Director of Communications had a major impact on Labour's image and the policy shift to the centre ground.

Kinnock's determined campaign to reform internal party democracy has been less successful to date. He has urged the adoption of one man one vote arrangements for the selection of candidates and re-selection of sitting members and has urged the abandonment of the trade union block vote at conference. Such hallowed rules, in a party immersed in its own traditions, are inevitably more difficult to change than mere policy positions. In June 1990, however, the NEC voted by a big majority in favour of a paper recommending the reduction of the unions' vote at conference from 90 to 70 per cent and over the longer term to a mere 40 per cent.

Neil Kinnock would probably agree that leading the Labour Party in opposition is one of the toughest political jobs in Britain. In addition to the usual tribulations of being in opposition the present Labour leader has had to overcome the anti-leadership culture inherited from the trade unions and the unhappy MacDonald experience; his lack of direct authority over the party organization and the need to negotiate constantly with the shifting elements of the Labour coalition; and the wide ideological differences between Marxists on the left and liberal socialists on the right. The ultimate test of the Labour leader is whether he can display to the electorate an image of a united confident party, sure of where it wishes to go and with the necessary agreed policies. The experience of the 1980s is that the electorate will punish a party which lacks these characteristics. As Lloyd George commented, 'You can't make a policy out of an argument.' In government the Labour leader has an easier time but it sometimes seems — as in the case of Harold Wilson — that Labour prime ministers are forced to spend time and energy on managing the party which could more profitably be spent on pursuing party objectives and exercising good government.

Groups in the Labour party

Given its ideological breadth it is not surprising that Labour has been even more prone to internal groupings than the Conservatives. The best-known group is the *Fabian Society*, established in 1884 and a founder partner of the Labour Representation Committee in 1900. It has declined in relative terms since the days when Sidney and Beatrice Webb used to influence the tone and content of Labour policies, but it still boasts a national membership of several thousand and over one half of the PLP (which also provides a fair proportion of the Fabian executive). The Society still performs its traditional roles of initiating debate, gathering information and issuing tracts, many of which contain important policy proposals. As the Fabians favour a gradual reformist path to socialism they are usually perceived as centre right in the party.

Organized right wing factions, however, did not appear in the Labour party until the Campaign for Democratic Socialism in 1960, inspired by a group of Gaitskellite MPs and with a degree of nation-wide support. This faded away in 1964 but *Manifesto*, a PLP grouping, was set up in 1974 to resist the policies of the left and to press for 'one member one vote' in the selection and re-selection of parliamentary candidates. The right was further strengthened in 1981 by the 150 MPs who joined Roy Hattersley and Peter Shore in forming *Solidarity* in response to the sweeping left-wing constitutional changes of that year.

Unsurprisingly, left wing groups have also been active. During the 1930s a number thrived, some of them related to the Communist party as part of the agitation for a Popular Front against fascism. After 1945 the *Keep Left Group* led by Michael Foot, Richard Crossman and Ian Mikardo was established involving some twenty MPs, urging a more independent and less pro-US foreign policy. During the 1950s elements of this defunct group joined the fifty or so MPs who supported Aneuran Bevan's bid for leadership. *Victory for Socialism*, though founded in 1944, became prominent after 1958 as a Bevanite faction with a national organization. In the early 1960s this was superceded by the *Unity Group* and in 1966 the *Tribune Group* was born, named after the left-wing journal founded in 1937. This group attracted considerable support in the 1970s when the left was vehemently urging alternative policies on Europe, nuclear weapons and state intervention. During the 1980s Tribune's role as a left-wing ginger discussion group began to alter when one of its leading members, Michael Foot (also an ex-editor of *Tribune*) became leader. A proportion of the group's membership began to shift towards the centre in support of Foot's efforts to formulate an agreed consensus within the party. During the 1982 deputy leadership election a crucial twenty Tribunite MPs either voted for Healey or abstained, thus denying Tony Benn the victory he craved. Left-winger Bob Cryer accused the group of possessing 'establishment symptoms of anaemia' and urged the creation of another 'harder' left-wing parliamentary grouping: the *Campaign Group* duly appeared. When another left-wing Tribunite, Neil Kinnock, succeeded Foot, Tribune became even 'softer' left; it proceeded to support Kinnock's policy drive towards the centre and has now become, arguably, a leadership support group rather than a critical faction. Its officers tend to be youngish, recently elected MPs like Chris Smith, Ian McCartney and Keith Bradley. The presence of so many Tribunites in the Shadow Cabinet suggests that many MPs join — it currently boasts 110 members — and attend meetings because they are ambitious for similar preferment. Moves are afoot within the current leadership of Tribune, however, to remedy its anaemic tendencies and to infuse some red blood of genuine debate and criticism into its proceedings.

The *Campaign Group* itself was set up in 1982 by twenty-three MPs; it soon attracted a membership of over forty. While Tribune moved to the centre Campaign has insisted on a more muscular version of familiar left-wing themes but has added two more important elements. Firstly, Campaign is unusual in advocating sweeping constitutional changes like the abolition of the House of Lords and the Royal Prerogatives exercised by proxy by the Prime Minister. These concerns reflect the ideas of Campaign's chief inspiration, Tony Benn. Secondly, Campaign believes the PLP should strengthen links with extra-parliamentary organizations and establish close links with constituency activists. Accordingly, some of the Tribune constituency groups have declined while Campaign groups have increased in number. The socialist conferences held in Chesterfield (Tony Benn's constituency) have provided a rallying point for the extra-parliamentary left but none of this activity has been able to halt the party's decisive shift away from left-wing fundamentalism. The Campaign Group became somewhat isolated in the party in the late 1980s and in consequence Alan Roberts, the late MP for Bootle, attempted to establish a bridge between the two groupings. He initiated a series of discussions, mostly involving new MPs, on a wide range of issues in the hope that the gulf between the hard and the soft lefts could be reduced. Because the meetings took place in pubs and involved the consumption of buffet meals they were dubbed *The Supper Club*.

The position of *Militant Tendency* has also been exposed by Labour's shift towards the centre. This is a Trotskyist group which successfully moved into constituency parties depleted by the exodus of the disillusioned following the Wilson and Callaghan years. Their first major success came in 1970 when they won control of the Young Socialists. Some constituency parties were captured and a position of dominance established in Merseyside where Derek Hatton, though nominally Deputy Leader, became the frontman for Militant's control. By the 1980s three Militant supporters were also in Parliament — Terry Fields, Dave Nellist and Pat Wall — closely associated with the Campaign group. Militant was a major force by the middle of the decade with 4—5,000 members, a staff of over 200 workers (more than the Labour Party itself) and a newspaper, *Militant*, within an estimated circulation of 40,000. The Labour leadership had first become alerted to Militant by the Underhill Report in 1975; this was followed by the Hayward Report in 1982 which advised the establishment of 'a register of recognised groups allowed to operate within the party' on the grounds that this would isolate Militant members. This measure had little practical impact and the most Kinnock could do in 1983 was to effect the expulsion of five members of Militant's editorial board.

The 1985 Whitty Report on the Liverpool Party was much tougher and urged specific expulsions. After a spectacular confrontation with Neil Kinnock at the 1986 Party Conference Hatton and others were purged in 1987. Expulsions increased in subsequent years but while isolated at the highest levels Militant strength remains a problem in many constituency parties. In December 1989 it was widely asserted that Militant influence was responsible for the de-selection of Frank Field as Birkenhead's Labour MP; after Field submitted evidence of Militant infiltration the NEC authorized an investigation.

Other extra-parliamentary groups like the *Labour Coordinating Committee* (LCC) and the *Campaign for Labour Party Democracy* (CLPD), which helped the left to win such an ascendancy in the early 1980s, have either become isolated or have joined the Kinnock-led move into the centre. These groups still exert some strength in constituency parties and at conference but their ability to influence the new direction of party policy is now minimal.

Within the PLP the influence of party groups has also declined and lost sharpness of definition. This is partly because the party's search for electoral success has inspired a desire for internal unity and partly because Tribune has moved so far to the right that it has virtually stolen the clothes of Solidarity and Manifesto. The groups are now less likely to produce regular policy statements on a wide range of issues while membership and attendance has become closely bound up with the ambitions of individual MPs. Each of the major groups have traditionally produced lists of candidates or 'slates' for Shadow Cabinet and other important PLP elections: association with one group or another — or combinations of them — can consequently help build up support. Solidarity and Manifesto no longer offer comprehensive slates but it is rumoured that unofficially their endorsements still apply. Tribune has also ceased to offer a slate in the hope that membership will reflect genuine interest and commitment rather than mere ambition. It should not be forgotten that other groups within the parliamentary party like regional meetings, the women's caucus, the black caucus as well as closely knit working groups like the shadow policy teams can also contribute to policy and can provide power bases for ambitious MPs — for example, Gordon Brown commands great support in the fifty-strong Scottish group of Labour MPs.

'Other' Parties

The centre parties

The main third party after 1918 was the *Liberal party*. It was one of the two parties of government between 1867 and 1918. However, it steadily declined during the inter-war years and attracted only miniscule support for much of the post-war period. In the 1970s it improved its share of the vote, in February 1974 garnering 19 per cent of the poll. However, the first-past-the-post electoral system has been a barrier and prevented it from receiving a proportional share of seats in the House of Commons. Its most distinctive policies in recent years have been political decentralization and constitutional reform (more open government, proportional representation and a Bill of Rights).

An opportunity for a realignment of the party system came in 1981 when Labour right-wingers broke away to form the Social Democratic Party. In 1983 its twenty-nine MPs (all but one of whom came from Labour) formed a partnership with the Liberals. The two parties had a common programme, a joint leader (the SDP leader Roy Jenkins was Prime Minister designate of an Alliance government), an electoral pact and fought under the label of the Alliance. As noted earlier in the chapter the Alliance gained 26 per cent of the vote in 1983, but only 3.5 per cent of seats. In 1987 the two parties again formed an electoral Alliance and gained 23 per cent of the vote but few seats. In 1988 the Liberals and a majority of the SDP merged in a Social Liberal Democratic Party known initially as the 'Democrats' and then after 1989 as the 'Liberal Democrats'.

From over one-fifth of the vote in the 1987 election, centre party poll ratings plummeted to less than one-tenth at the beginning of 1990. The SDP's dream of a new centre party displacing Labour as the major opposition party — just as Labour replaced the Liberals in the 1920s — had seemed close to reality in the early years of the decade. By the end of it Labour had bounced back remarkably, in the process surreptitiously taking over centrist policies, while the centre parties themselves appeared to shrivel away. In retrospect the decision of David Steel to propose a merger in the wake of the 1987 reverses was a major error. Taken without consultation with Dr David Owen the initiative was probably an attempt to pre-empt his known opposition to the idea. In the event it merely provoked an extraordinary long-running public row and led to a half-hearted merger which impressed few and caused many SDP members to fade back into the political wilderness from whence they had emerged. Instead of consolidating the centre ground David Steel and David Owen

The saga of the Centre Parties

1981	Jan.	Formation of 'The Council for Social Democracy' inside the Labour Party.
	March	*Social Democratic Party* group established in the House of Commons.
	Sept.	The SPD and the Liberals formed the *Alliance*: they remained separate parties, but cooperated at election times to ensure that SDP and Liberal candidates did not stand against each other.
1983	June	The Alliance fought election with joint manifesto, and with Roy Jenkins (SDP) as Prime Minister designate, and David Steel (Lib.) as campaign leader.
1987	June	The Alliance fought the election on joint manifesto, and under joint leadership of David Steel (Lib.) and David Owen (SDP). Following the disappointing result, David Steel called for a full merger of the two parties. David Owen rejected the suggestion.
	July–Aug.	Ballots among members of both parties on merger proposal. Both resulted in majority for merger.
	Sept.	SDP conference. Majority accepts formation of new party.
	Nov.	David Owen formed 'Campaign for Social Democracy' as splinter group within the SDP.
1988	Jan.	Formation of new party: *The Social and Liberal Democratic Party* (SLD or The Democrats). David Owen continued as leader of separate SDP.
	Aug.	Paddy Ashdown (formerly Lib.) elected as leader of the SLD.
1989	May	After disappointing results at by-elections and county council elections, the SDP leader David Owen announced that the SDP would cease to operate as a national party. It would only field a few candidates in selected constituencies for parliamentary elections.
	Sept.	SLD agrees to change its name to 'Liberal Democrats'.
1990	Jan.	SDP poll ratings down to 2 per cent. LD's to 5 per cent.
	June	SDP formally winds itself up.

Source: J. Lundskaer-Nielsen *et al.* (1989), p. 116.

had succeeded in fragmenting it into a new party which had lost the Liberals' old distinctive profile and a small SDP party sustained by its three surviving MPs — notably the charismatic Owen. To make matters worse a former Liberal MP, Michael Meadowcroft, tried to attract old Liberals with a revived version of the Liberal party in 1988.

Party organization

The Liberal Democrats' leader, Paddy Ashdown, faces daunting problems in establishing his party's credibility but at least he has the framework and support

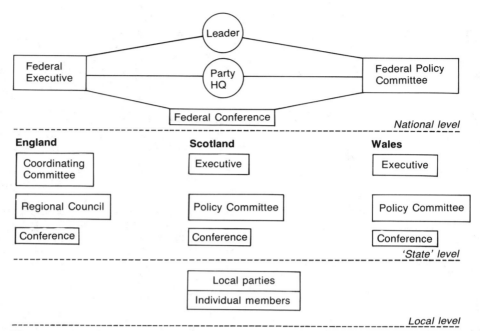

Figure 14.4 *Liberal Democrats party organization*

of the old Liberal Party to help him. His party (see Figure 14.4) has a federal structure comprising three 'state' parties for Scotland, Wales and England plus a federal organization. The Federal Policy Committee (FPC) is in charge of policy formulation and comprises the leader, the president, four MPs, one peer, three councillors, two Scottish and two Welsh representatives plus thirteen members elected by the twice-yearly conference. 'Green' policy papers are produced and circulated for consultation throughout the party and the FPC prepares election manifestos in consultation with the parliamentary party. Each state party has responsibility for organizational matters, finance, selection of local candidates and so forth. The Federal Executive runs the national organization and comprises the President, three Vice-Presidents, the leader, two MPs, one peer, two councillors and fourteen other members elected by conference. The party leader must be an MP but is elected by ballot by all individual members. Ballots can also be called by the FPC 'on any fundamental question where, in its judgement, the values and objectives of the party are at issue or it is otherwise in the essential interests of the party'. The policy declaration, 'Democracy of Conscience', states the initial policy position of the party.

The exodus of SDP members into the Liberal Democrats reduced the party's national organization to something of a shell. The local branch network was never especially strong, even in the heyday of the party, and many wound up altogether when it was reduced to a rump. The party struggled to survive financially despite the loyal support of millionaire businessman, David Sainsbury.

In June 1990 the SDP gave up the unequal struggle and formally wound itself up. Its three MPs, David Owen, Rosie Barnes and John Cartwright, continued as independent MPs. From being a potential prime minister, David Owen was reduced to a political lone wolf, respected but not liked or wanted by any party, including Labour, the one he was disposed to rejoin. SDP members comforted themselves with the notion that their party had forced Labour to abandon its left-wing adventures and adopt a programme more in keeping with the expectations of the ordinary voter — a programme in fact very close in essentials to that offered by the SDP throughout its nine-year history. Unsurprisingly, most Labour activists disagree.

The Green party

The British Green party originated bizarrely out of reactions to an article in *Playboy* magazine by Paul Erlich. In 1973 under the name 'People' it began life as an environmental pressure group. It quickly began to develop policies across a broad spectrum and changed its name to the Ecology party. It committed itself to 'Policies which preserve the planet and its people; decentralised decision making in all areas of government, industry and commerce; a recognition that the human spirit is integral to a political system; and the realisation that all our policies are connected and none can be designed in isolation'. This means 'a whole hearted commitment to an end to overall economic growth so the economy is designed to run at a stable size — meaning in practice that some economic activities will be reduced, while others expand' (Green party statement: for an elaboration of Green ideas see Chapter 9).

In 1985 the party changed its name to the Green party and thus came into line with environmental parties internationally. During the 1980s Green support grew apace: candidates were elected to eleven national parliaments around the world. In Britain, however, the Greens are shut out by the electoral system. In 1983, 108 candidates mustered barely 1 per cent of the votes (55,000). In the May 1989 local elections, however, Greens won 8.6 per cent of the vote in seats fought by four or more candidates and Green councillors were elected in Stroud, Woodspring, Avon, Malvern Hills and elsewhere. In June 1989 the Greens took an astonishing 15 per cent of the vote in the elections to the European Parliament.

In accordance with its philosophy of decentralization the Green party stresses that the 250 local parties provide the most important level of organization. The Greens insist that theirs is a grass-roots democratic movement (see Figure 14.5). Party conferences, which are held twice a year, elect a party council which administers the party nation-wide. Conference also elects three co-chairpersons and six speakers whose job it is to speak for the party in meetings, conference, contacts with the media and so forth. The party is also non-hierarchical: 'it needs to be stressed that neither party council nor its co-chairs are "leaders" in any form. Our leaders are the members of the local party, for it is they who make the decisions' (Green party statement, June 1989). It follows that party policy bubbles up from the local parties and from policy working groups; proposals are circulated around members and discussed at conference before being referred to a second conference for decision.

The party's amateurish organizational approach, however, has caused problems. Its staff of three-and-a-half in 1989 doubled during the Euro-elections but fell back to four by the beginning of 1990. Despite a successful year with a burgeoning membership of 18,000 the party finished 1989 with a £32,000 debt. *The Guardian* (14 February 1990) quotes the party's press office:

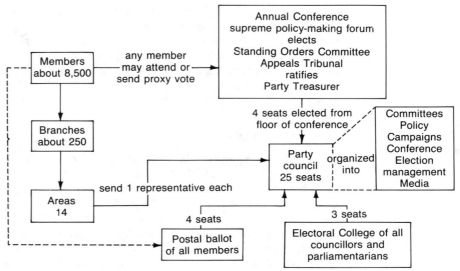

Figure 14.5 *Organogram: Green party (Source: Parkin, 1989)*

We used to draw up strategies for the day every morning, but then the phone started ringing and we never got to do any of it. Our members are always complaining we are not in the news any more, but quite honestly if we are going to react to events as Britain's third biggest party, we've got to have some money ... Glasnost has brought East European diplomats beating a path down to Balham to find out how Europe's most successful green party is organised. But often they have left bewildered. How on earth, they keep asking, can the party survive on a full-time staff of four and a phone? 'I feel so awful giving them coffee in this chipped mug,' says a volunteer helping out in the office.

Nationalist Parties

Party politics in **Northern Ireland** is different from that on the mainland. In part this is because of the dominance of issues regarding the border, religious rivalries between Protestants and Catholics and because no mainland party contests any Ulster seat. The two main Protestant parties are the Official Unionists and Democratic Unionists (led by Dr Ian Paisley). They oppose power-sharing with the Catholic community in any Northern Ireland legislature and also oppose the Anglo–Irish agreement (1985) which gives the Irish government a voice in Northern Ireland's affairs. The main Catholic party is the Social Democratic and Labour party (SDLP) which favours power-sharing. Sinn Fein, the parliamentary wing of the IRA, won one seat in 1983 and 1987 but the MP refused to take his seat.

In **Scotland** and **Wales Nationalist** parties want independence for their countries and each has three MPs in the present Westminster Parliament. For all the talk of the strength of nationalism in Wales and Scotland it is worth noting that overwhelmingly Scottish and Welsh MPs are drawn from parties which are pro-union. Indeed, the 'national' party in both nations is Labour; in Scotland it has fifty of seventy-two seats and in Wales it has twenty-four of thirty-eight seats.

Support for 'Other' parties

The growth of support for 'other' parties — a consequence of the decline in aggregate support for the two main parties — is heterogeneous. In the Commons it covers the Liberal Democrats, Welsh Nationalists, Scottish Nationalists and the members from the various Northern Ireland parties. One reason for the growth of these 'other' MPs from 1974 onwards has less to do with the Liberal and then Alliance upsurge in the country than the fragmentation of the Ulster Unionists after 1974.

Much of the popular support to date for 'other' parties, outside of Northern Ireland, has not been translated into a sufficient number of seats to threaten the two main parties. In the 1974 elections the growth in Liberal support (to 19 per cent of the vote in February) and the rise of the Nationalists in Scotland (to 30 per cent of the vote in Scotland in October 1974) represented a potential threat to the two main parties. But these advances were not consolidated and both parties actually retreated in seats and votes in 1979. The referendum in March 1979 showed weak support for national devolution (let alone independence) in Scotland and Wales (only 11.9 per cent of Welsh voters supported it). In the 1983 and 1987 elections 13 per cent of voters in Scotland and 7.5 per cent of voters in Wales voted for Nationalist candidates.

The Effect of Parties

For all the formal strength of British governments in the House of Commons their performance has been much criticized. The failures of most post-war governments, notably in the economic sphere, weaknesses in the face of organized labour (particularly in 1974 and 1979) and the frequent reversals of policies both during and between governments, have been seen by many as signs of weak government. According to Professor Richard Rose, in *Do Parties Make a Difference?* (1975, 1984), British parties are ill-equipped to direct government. Rose argues that they are poorly prepared in opposition and that counter-pressures from other groups like the civil service, the City, business, and trade unions are strong. Rose points in particular to the failure of governments pre-1979 to improve macro-economic conditions, like inflation, unemployment, economic growth and interest rates to show that parties do not make much difference in shifting the trend of these indicators. The continuity is regarded by Rose as proof of the relative weakness of the parties.

Against this some argue that the parties in government may have too much power. The relative ease with which they get their legislation through Parliament, for example, has enabled them to alter the framework of policy quite easily in education, industrial relations, housing, public or private ownership of industry, etc. Adversary party politics, according to these critics (Finer, 1975), has produced frequent and damaging reversals of policy in Britain in recent years. Such critics advocate the introduction of a proportional electoral system, partly on the grounds of fairness (since to have a majority of seats in the Commons, governments would also need the support of a majority of the electorate), and partly on the grounds that coalitions would slow down the damaging reversals of policy resulting from competing party ideologies. Figure 14.6 shows the overlapping allegiances and viewpoints within the parties.

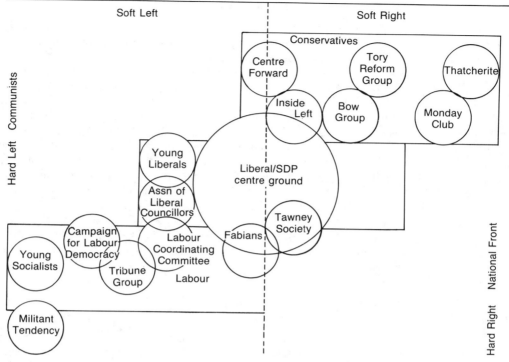

Figure 14.6   *The British party playing field (Source: Derbyshire, 1987)*

On the whole, the experience since 1979 supports one line of the adversary politics analysis. There have been significant discontinuities in the fields of industrial relations, abandonment of formal incomes policy and tripartite style of decision making, privatization of state industries and services. Moreover, the Thatcher record shows that parties can make a difference, particularly when they have a determined leader, have a clear case of political strategy and are in office for a lengthy period (Kavanagh, 1990).

References and Further Reading

Attlee, C., *The Labour Party in Perspective* (Gollancz, 1937).
Baker, B., *The Far Left* (Wiedenfield & Nicholson, 1982).
Butler, D. and Kavanagh, D., *The British General Election of 1979* (Macmillan, 1980).
Callaghan, J., *The Far Left in English Politics* (Basil Blackwell, 1987).
Crewe, I., 'The campaign confusion', *New Society* (8 May 1987).
Crick, M., *Militant* (Faber & Faber, 1984).
Derbyshire, J.D., *The Business of Government* (Chambers, 1987).
Finer, S., *Adversary Politics and Electoral Reform* (Wigram, 1975).
Ingle, S., *The British Party System* (Basil Blackwell, 1987).
Kavanagh, D., 'The rise of Thatcherism', *Social Studies Review* (1987a).

Kavanagh, D., *Thatcherism and British Politics* 2nd edn. (Oxford University Press, 1990).

Kelly, R.N., 'The Tory Conference: A Misunderstood Occasion', Politics Association Resources Bank Paper, 1988.

Kelly, R.N., *Conservative Party Conferences* (Manchester University Press, 1989).

Lundskaer-Nielsen, J., *et al.*, *Contemporary British Society* (Akademisk Forlag, 1989).

Layton-Henry, Z., *Conservative Party Politics* (Macmillan, 1979).

McKenzie, R.T., *British Political Parties* (Heinemann, 1963).

McCulloch, A., 'Shades of Green ideas in the British Green Movement', *Teaching Politics* (May 1988).

Michels, R., *Political Parties* (Doner Publications, 1959).

Minkin, L., *The Labour Party Conference* (Manchester University Press, 1980).

Norton, P. and Aughey, A., *Conservatives and Conservatism* (Temple Smith, 1981).

Parkin, S., *Green Parties* (Heretic Books, 1989).

Pelling, H., *A History of the British Communist Party* (Adam and Charles Black, 1985).

Rose, R., *Do Parties Make a Difference?*, 2nd edn. (MacMillan, 1984).

Seyd, P., *The Rise and Fall of the Labour Left* (Macmillan, 1987).

Taylor, S., *The National Front in English Politics* (Macmillan, 1982).

The Underclass and the Governance of Britain

In December 1987 a memorable *Weekend World* programme entitled 'The Underclass' investigated a disturbing new feature of Britain in the 1980s: the development of a distinctive social grouping below the working class and conforming to an alternative system of values. The problems thrown up by this group — perhaps 6–8 per cent of the population — represented in the words of Professor Ralph Dahrendorf 'the greatest single challenge to civilized existence' in Britain. Since then the term 'underclass' has become part of common parlance: in 1989 Labour MP Frank Field produced a book, *Losing Out: The Emergence of Britain's Underclass* and in November of that year the *Sunday Times* ran a major feature by a well-known American political scientist, Charles Murray, apocalyptically entitled 'Underclass: A Disaster in the Making'.

Many of the commentators agree on the provenance, nature and significance of this development for the governance of Britain but there is less agreement on how it can be combated. Field identifies the causes as fourfold:

1. Mass unemployment caused by government economic policies in the early 1980s and the widespread introduction of automated forms of production.
2. The widening of class divisions on a large number of indices including income, wealth, housing, infant and adult mortality (in relative terms poverty, by any measure, has increased markedly during the 1980s as Figures A, B and C and Table I reveal. A further report from the DHSS in July 1990 revealed that average incomes for the poorest 10 per cent of the population fell by 5.7 per cent between 1979 and 1987 while average income levels increased by 23 per cent).
3. The linking of benefits to rising prices rather than wages, therefore excluding the poor from the general rise in prosperity which the nation enjoyed during the last decade.
4. The increasing replacement of working-class solidarity as a widespread sentiment by a 'drawbridge mentality' whereby the upwardly mobile working class have lost any sense of obligation to their less fortunate peers.

The result of these forces has been the creation, in Field's view, of a 'subtle form of political, social and economic apartheid'. Those in work share a common faith in the maintenance and improvement of prosperity while those in the underclass have been isolated even from the working class itself. Murray comments that 'Britain does have an underclass, still largely out of sight and still smaller than the one in the United States. But it is growing rapidly.'

The three principal groups affected are the long-term unemployed, both youngsters and adults; single-parent families and their children; and elderly people wholly dependent on their state pension. Murray points out that the first and second groups

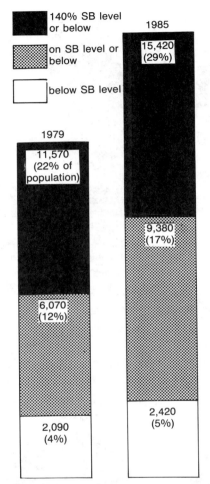

In 1979 the population numbered 52,660,000
In 1985 the population numbered 54,140.000

Figure A. *Numbers of people living in or on the margins of poverty in Britain in 1979 and 1985 (Source:* Social Studies Review, *January 1990) Note:* SB = Supplementary Benefit

are concentrated in Occupational Class V and can be found predominantly in inner city areas. All these causal factors interact to produce a number of distinctive features, according to Dahrendorf:

> a lifestyle of laid back sloppiness, association in changing groups or gangs, congregation around discos or the like, hostility to middle class society, particular habits of dress, hairstyle, often drugs or at least alcohol — a style in other words which has little in common with the values of the work society around.
>
> *New Statesman,* 12 June 1987

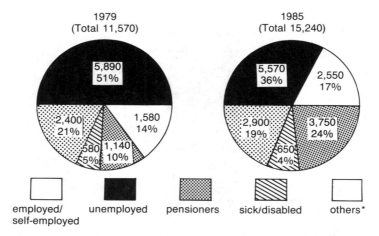

*Others consists largely of single parents, full-time students, full-time workers temporarily away from work on part or no pay, carers and any others under pension age not working or seeking work

Figure B.   *Numbers of people living in or on the margins of poverty in Britain in 1979 and 1985 by employment status (000s) (Source:* Social Studies Review, *January 1990)*

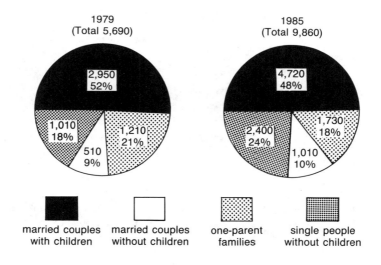

Figure C.   *Numbers of people under pension age living in or on the margins of poverty in Britain in 1979 and 1985 by family status (Source:* Social Studies Review, *January 1990)*

Table I   *Top directors' pay*

Company (financial year ending)	Recipient	Salary £
Walsham Brothers (December 1987)	William Brown	2,015,083
Barings & Co (December 1987)	Christopher Heath	1,339,219
Hanson (September 1988)	Lord Hanson	1,239,000
Robert Fleming Hldgs (March 1988)	Highest paid director	1,238,000
IMO Precision Controls (March 1988)	Maurice Hatter	1,232,700
Lonrho (September 1988)	'Tiny' Rowland	1,015,051
Burton Group (September 1988)	Sir Ralph Halpern	966,000
Blue Arrow (October 1988)	Mitchell Fromstein	970,000
Lazard Brothers (December 1988)	Sir John Nott	885,235
Littlewoods Organization (December 1987)	Desmond Pitcher	863,334

Note: A Labour Research Department Report in August 1989 recorded that 10 per cent of major British companies have directors on their payroll earning over £100,000 per year. The average pay increase for top executives in the financial year ending 1989 was 28 per cent.

Source: The Guardian, 3 August 1989

Murray comments

> it is an irretrievable disaster for young men to grow up without being socialised to the world of work . . . by remaining out of the workforce during the crucial formative years, young men aren't just losing a few years of job experience. They are missing out on the time in which they need to have been acquiring skills and the network of friends and experiences that enable them to establish a place for themselves — not only in the workplace but a vantage point from which they can make sense of themselves and their lives.
>
> *Sunday Times*, 26 November 1989

The *Weekend World* programme interviewed several young Liverpudlians who testified that crime was accepted as an everyday necessity. 'Some people have got jobs', said one, 'they can go out and buy things they want. But we're on the dole, we haven't got the money so we go out robbing to get the money'. Often drugs are an additional element, providing both a reason for crime and a catalyst to it. Young people in these circumstances do not admire the normal models of social achievement but those of crime and delinquency. Murray cites the explosion of crime in the 1980s, especially violent crime, as disturbing evidence of this criminal culture in practice.

Another salient feature of the underclass is the high rate of illegitimacy which, like crime, has increased exponentially during the last decade from 10.6 per cent of live births to single women in 1979 to 25.6 per cent in 1988. Once again illegitimacy is concentrated in inner city areas and reveals a worrying breakdown of family life in these areas. It is now quite common for girls to become pregnant in their teens partly in order to claim the higher level of benefit. They then go on to have children by other men and tend not to live in nuclear families. Unemployed husbands cannot become effective breadwinners; 'In this world', *Weekend World* commented, 'men don't form families'. According to Murray, 'The indispendable civilising force' of 'taking responsibility for a wife and children' is therefore denied young men in these circumstances and 'men who do not support families find other ways to prove that they are men which tend to take various destructive forms'.

Some commentators now believe the forces at work have created a vicious circle in which a substantial proportion of underclass children will themselves be educational failures who will become socialized into a criminal rather than a work culture and who will go on perpetuating themselves in deteriorating inner city ghettos. What dangers does this emergent underclass pose for British society?

Dahrendorf's fear is for the moral health of any society which might choose to abandon such a large proportion of its citizens and for the long-term subversive effects on society of harbouring an alienated minority in its midst:

> Any group which does not have a stake in the values of a society tends to undermine that society quite systematically.

Certain inner city communities are already close to collapse or have already done so, imploding into riots and looting. Theft and violence are inflicted indiscriminately on fellow underclass members, including the weak and the elderly. As far as the rest of society is concerned these are virtually 'no go' areas. The danger is that over time these areas will multiply and expand. But the threat already extends far beyond the inner cities. In search of richer pickings underclass criminals travel further afield. Criminal and deliquency role models are also attractive to youngsters in work — football hooliganism, for example, is by no means restricted to the underclass. Casual violence and callousness towards others can spread throughout society, lowering overall standards of behaviour and reducing the quality of life for everyone.

The political system is also threatened. Dahrendorf does not detect any revolutionary threat from the underclass and those of their political views which can be discerned tend to be to the right rather than the left. The threat is rather to the efficacy of our democratic system in inner city areas. To function effectively representative democracy requires a citizenry which fulfils the following conditions:

1. Some basic awareness of the major issues and of how the system works.
2. Regular participation in the system, at least to the minimal extent of casting their votes.
3. What Bernard Crick calls *procedural values* or the ground rules of democracy: freedom of speech and discussion; respect for truth and reason; the peaceful resolution of conflict and the toleration of opposing political views.

There can be no confidence that any of these conditions are being met by inner city underclass members. No precise data exists on political awareness in the inner cities but we know it correlates positively with educational level and the lowest educational levels are to be found in such areas. One anecdote illustrates the problem. During the 1981 Toxteth riots a television news report featured Michael Heseltine asking a group of Liverpudlian youths whether they ever took their problems to their local councillor. 'What's a councillor?' asked one of the youths. Turnout figures in the inner cities on the other hand reveal a disturbing degree of abstention: in some areas barely over 50 per cent at general elections and in local elections some wards show figures of 20 per cent and lower. Procedural values must also be undermined by the proliferation of criminal values which entail personal gain at others' expense (most of the criminal activity occurs *within* the inner city areas), routine deceit to avoid being caught and the regular use or threat of violence. The growth of the Militant Tendency in Merseyside suggests that the inner cities provide fertile ground for political creeds of questionable tolerance. One ESRC survey reported that support for the National Front and the British Movement increased from just under 7 per cent in 1979 to 14 per cent in 1982, the chief causal factors appearing to be increasing unemployment combined with immigrant groups on the labour market (though no evidence was provided on whether such support was localized in inner city areas).

But perhaps apathy and lack of faith in any political creed or system are the distinguishing characteristics of the new underclass. The riots in Toxteth, Liverpool; St Paul's, Bristol; Handsworth, Birmingham; and Brixton and the Broadwater Farm Estate, Tottenham reveal that the fragile political and legal frameworks in such areas can be swept away in orgies of petrol bombs and looting.

Immediately after her 1987 election victory Mrs Thatcher publicly resolved to solve the problems of the inner cities yet the ***Action for Cities*** initiative launched in March 1988 was credited by the National Audit Office Report (in January 1990) with only 'piecemeal' success. Part IV of this book has analysed the major ways whereby individuals and groups can represent their views to government. For a number of interrelated and intractable reasons it seems a substantial section of the community are either unable or disinclined to represent their views or indeed to participate in the representative process. As society becomes more prosperous, production techniques are automated and work more skills-based, the gap between the underclass and the rest of society will grow. How can the problem be solved?

The right-wing approach is to tighten the screw: the underclass are seen as the undeserving poor who have chosen to live a feckless life beyond the pale of society. The right wing has urged an increase in penalties for crime and the reduction in benefits so that the underclass will be forced to work even for very low wages. The US experience, however, suggests that this approach does not work: prisons become ever more overcrowded and very low wages still leave the underclass poor, embittered and likely to turn to crime.

The left-wing approach is to see the underclass as the victims of circumstances beyond their control. Frank Field argues that the deviant culture and political abstentionism is a reaction to the loss of citizenship caused by Thatcherite policies. He believes the problem needs to be tackled on a wide number of fronts including employment, education, training, tax reforms, social and sex education.

Dahrendorf also centres his solutions on the concept of citizenship:

> We must insist on a principle, one which has underlain British social policy the last fifty years: every citizen should have certain basic rights that cannot be taken away and include more than just the right to vote. They must include a certain minimal social position as part of a modern society of citizens.

The American Charles Murray, however, does not blame Thatcher. He detects the growth of the underclass phenomenon as far back as the 1950s and 1960s and believes greater expenditure on welfare will be wasted if the US experience is anything to go by. His novel solution is a 'massive dose of self government' with vastly greater responsibility being given to inner city areas in respect of criminal justice, education, housing and benefit systems. His premise is that 'it is unnatural for a neighbourhood to tolerate high levels of crime or illegitimacy or voluntary idleness amongst its youth' and that given the chance 'communities will run affairs so that such things happen infrequently'. He concludes: 'Money isn't the key. Authentic self-government is.'

References and Further Reading

Butler, D. and Kavanagh, D., *The British General Election of 1979* (Macmillan, 1980).

Church of England, *Living Faith in the City* (Church House 1990).

Dahrendorf, R. 'The Erosion of Citizenship and the Consequences for us all', *New Statesman* (12th June 1987).

Field, F., *Losing Out: The Emergence of Britain's Underclass* (Basil Blackwell, 1990).

McGurk, Professor H., *What Next?* (ESRC, 1988).

Murray, C., 'Underclass: A Disaster in the Making', *Sunday Times* Colour Magazine, 26 November 1989.

'Counting up the poor', *Social Studies Review*, (January 1990).

'The Underclass', *Weekend World*, London Weekend Television, 13 December 1987.

PART V The Legislative Process

During the late medieval period of British history the aristocracy and the gentry, through the House of Lords and the House of Commons, asserted their right to check the arbitrary power of the king to make new laws and determine the level of taxation. Neither chamber wished at that time to challenge the king's right to run the country from day to day, but they wished to exercise control over the guidelines within which he operated: they wished to exert *legislative* control over the *executive*. After the Civil War and the Bloodless Revolution of 1688 Parliament confirmed its supremacy. Parliament, destined to be copied in countries all over the world, had come of age and the monarchy began its slow decline towards constitutional ceremonialism. Parliament remains the fulcrum of the constitution though the massive growth in the extent and power of the executive arm of government has shifted it away from the centre of effective political power.

This section begins by examining Britain's peculiar unwritten constitution (Chapter 15) and considers whether reform is not now in order. The evolution of parliament and the monarchy into its present role is analysed in Chapter 16 while Chapter 17 takes an in-depth look at the House of Commons and its workings. Chapter 18 concludes the section by covering the House of Lords and the subject of parliamentary reform. The Concluding Comment examines the topical controversy over MPs' private financial interests.

15 The Constitution in Flux*

Philip Norton

In a debate in the House of Commons early in 1986, one MP referred to the Westland affair as providing 'nuggets of gold for students of the British Constitution'. The mine from which such nuggets are drawn has not been well explored. Over the past twenty years, the Constitution has become a topic of political debate. It is a debate conducted with little clarity. What precisely is a Constitution? Why has Britain's become a topic of debate? What changes has it undergone? What further changes are advocated? And can such changes be seen within the framework of different approaches to constitutional change? Neglect of such questions has denied students a clear picture of the Constitution and of the nature of constitutional debate in the 1990s: this chapter seeks to redress the balance.

The Constitution: Definition and Sources

What is a Constitution? It can be defined as the system of laws, customs and conventions which defines the composition and powers of organs of the state, and regulates the relations of the various state organs to one another and to the private citizen. In short, it stipulates the structures and powers of government and the relationship between the several parts of government and between government and the citizen.

From what sources is a Constitution drawn? As the definition reveals, the sources are several. In some countries, the main provisions are drawn up in one binding document (a written Constitution) supplemented by statute law, judicial interpretation and precedent. The British Constitution has four principal sources (Figure 15.1):

Statute law, comprising Acts of Parliament and subordinate legislation made under the authority of the parent Act.

Common law, encompassing rules of custom, the royal prerogative and judicial decisions.

Conventions, constituting rules of constitutional behaviour which are considered binding by and upon those who operate the Constitution but which are not enforced by the courts nor by the presiding officers in the Houses of Parliament.

*This chapter has been adapted from an article which appeared originally in *Social Studies Review*, September 1986.

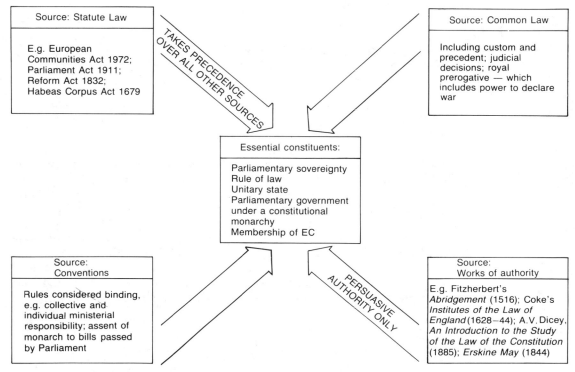

Figure 15.1   *The British constitution: sources and constituents (Source: Norton, 1986)*

Works of authority, comprising various written works — often but not always accorded authority by reason of their age — which provide guidance and interpretation on uncertain aspects of the Constitution; such works have persuasive authority only.

Statute law is the pre-eminent of the four sources and occupies such a position because of the main constituent of the Constitution: the doctrine of Parliamentary Sovereignty. Under this judicially self-imposed concept, Parliament (formally the Queen-in-Parliament) can pass law — Acts of Parliament — and the courts will enforce such law, recognizing the authority of no body other than Parliament to set it aside. Statute law, then, can be utilized to override common law or judicial decisions. No extraordinary procedures are laid down in Parliament for the passage of measures of constitutional significance. Constitutional law can be passed by a simple majority in both Houses.

Its most distinctive feature?

Unlike many other countries, the Constitution is not drawn up in one authoritative, binding document. Hence, it has often been described as 'unwritten' and this has often been lauded as its most distinctive feature. Such a characterization is misleading.

Parliamentary sovereignty

> Parliamentary sovereignty is . . . complete both on its positive and on its negative side. Parliament can legally legislate on any topic whatever which, in the judgement of Parliament, is a fit subject for legislation. There is no power which, under the English constitution, can come into rivalry with the legislative sovereignty of Parliament. Not one of the limitations alleged to be imposed by law on the absolute authority of Parliament has any real existence, or receives any countenance, either from the statute book or from the practice of the courts. This doctrine of the legislative supremacy of Parliament is the very keystone of the constitution.
>
> Source: A.V. Dicey, 1885.

The Constitution is not 'unwritten'. Part of it is written, primarily that embodied in statute law, but it is not codified in one single document. Thus, what we have is a part-written but uncodified Constitution. In that we are not unique. What, then, is the most distinctive feature of the Constitution? Its most noteworthy feature, I would suggest, has derived not from its form or content but rather from perceptions of it. Until recently, it was distinctive for being taken for granted.

In the 1950s and most of the 1960s it was not something that was much discussed, either in academic or in political circles. On those occasions when it was mentioned, it was in order only to praise it, not to explain and certainly not to question it. The reasons for such uncritical acceptance are not difficult to discern. Constitutions cannot be considered in isolation from the political and economic environment. In Britain, that environment provided the basis for adulation.

Support in the 1950s and 1960s

Thirty years ago Britain was a relatively prosperous nation. It had a political system which appeared to be working well. Government was seen to be delivering the goods expected of it. Spending on the National Health Service was being increased; taxes were being cut. Politicians were content with the structures of government and the 'rules of the game' that accompanied them. Not surprisingly, there was little pressure to question the Constitution that provided such a framework of government. Any mention of it was usually in order to extol its virtues. It was seen as embodying the accumulated wisdom of generations; it was flexible; and it appeared to work — unlike a great many written Constitutions which new nations rushed to adopt. Indeed, it was often contrasted with the US Constitution. The British Constitution appeared to facilitate effective government; the US one did not. Any British Government, secure in a majority in the House of Commons, could ensure the speedy passage of its measures, secure in the knowledge that such measures could not then be struck down by any authoritative body. In the USA a President could not count on a majority in Congress to enact his measures nor could he assume that, even if enacted, they would not then be challenged in the courts and struck down as conflicting with the provisions of the Constitution. On the basis of such a comparison, the British system was viewed with envy by many US observers.

So, until the 1970s, the British Constitution was taken largely for granted. There was an element of self-satisfaction about it. We had succeeded where foreigners had failed. It was, in the words of one Conservative MP, 'the envy of the world'.

All this was to change and to change significantly as the 1970s progressed. The Constitution ceased to be taken for granted. It ceased to be an object of unqualified praise. Proposals for constitutional change came on to the agenda of political debate. Why?

The challenges of the 1970s and 1980s

The reason for the change, primarily, was that the political system appeared unable to deliver the goods. Government appeared unable to cope with the problems of rising unemployment and spiralling inflation. The British economy ceased to expand at the rate it had previously; indeed, at times it was static. Government was, in consequence, denied the resources to meet increasing demands. The economic pie ceased to expand, while citizens maintained their desire for a greater share of that pie.

Government thus had difficulty in raising resources to meet its commitments to public policy. And at times when *government* appears unable to cope then the *system* of government itself starts to be questioned. If government cannot cope, is it sufficient to change the composition of government (that is, replace one party in office with another)? Or is more fundamental change necessary, changing not only the personnel but also the very powers and structures of government?

The growing tendency to ask such questions was exacerbated by political pressures of the same period. Nationalist parties became significant forces in Scotland and Wales; the Scottish National Party, in particular, emerged as a significant threat to Labour support. The 'troubles' in Northern Ireland raised questions about the unique constitutional position of the province. And the indeterminate results of the two 1974 general elections called into question the claimed capacity of the existing electoral system to provide strong, popular government.

A consequence of these developments was to be the enactment of *some* major constitutional reforms, attempts to implement others, and pressure for more. Yet the changes implemented, and those proposed, were notable for being disparate, a response to *specific* problems. And that, in many respects, was because the Constitution had been taken for granted. There was little familiarity with discussing the Constitution in broad conceptual terms. Constitutional change was a useful tool to deal with particular problems; it was not perceived as a vehicle for comprehensive reform, supplanting the existing Constitution with a new, carefully crafted one. There was no blueprint for reform.

Only as constitutional change began to be discussed did more coherent schools of thought emerge, adopting distinctive and coherent stances in relation to the Constitution; but these schools of thought, also, were disparate. The old consensus had collapsed.

What, then, were the main changes implemented, attempted or proposed in the 1970s? And what were the different schools of thought, the different approaches to constitutional change, that emerged?

Constitutional Changes and Challenges

Of the changes to have taken place during the past twenty years, they can be characterized under the headings of ***additions*** and ***amendments***.

Additions

The additions constitute the most radical changes, introducing new dimensions to the Constitution. They constitute the grafting on of new structures or procedures to the existing framework. Foremost among them have been British membership of the European Communities and the use of referendums. As a response to Britain's economic (and, to some extent, its political) problems, successive Governments sought membership of the European Community. Agreement on the terms of membership was reached in 1972. The European Communities Act of that year provided the legal 'nuts and bolts' necessary for membership and Britain became a member of the Communities on 1 January 1973. As a consequence of membership, Britain accepted a supranational decision making body, allowing decisions affecting Britain to be made by bodies on which Britain was represented but on which its representatives were in a minority; decisions, furthermore, that under the terms of the 1972 Act were to have legal force, automatically, in the United Kingdom.

In order to overcome serious internal divisions the Labour Party in 1974 committed itself to re-negotiating the terms of British membership of the European Community and then to submit those re-negotiated terms to the British people. The medium chosen for submitting those terms to the people was that of a referendum. The device was employed, on a UK-wide basis, in 1975. Later in the same Parliament, in order to reduce opposition to its devolution proposals, the Government conceded referendums in Scotland and Wales on those proposals. The referendums took place on 1 March 1979.

Referendums constituted novel constitutional devices, which called into question the legitimizing function of Parliament. Hitherto, the final assent to major constitutional proposals (as on all legislation) had been given by Parliament. Now that final assent was being given, in effect (the referendums were advisory), by the electorate — not by its elected representatives.

Both additions significantly affected the Constitution, adding new dimensions and altering in many respects existing constitutional relationships. Many critics of membership of the European Communities and the use of referendums attacked them as undermining, in particular, the position of Parliament.

Amendments

It was not just these novel and radical developments that were to have an effect upon constitutional structures and relationships. The period witnessed also disparate changes in ***existing*** structures and relationships; that is, there were various amendments to the existing framework. These amendments, listed in Figure 15.2, follow no neat pattern.

THE CHANGES
ADDITIONS
British membership of the European Communities (EC) **The use of referendums**
AMENDMENTS:
Executive–legislative relations *(strengthening of Parliament)* **Centre–local relations** *(strengthening of the centre)* **Minister–civil service relations** *(weakening of the convention of* *individual ministerial responsibility)* **Cabinet–Minister relations** *(weakening of the convention of* *collective ministerial responsibility)* **Government–group relations** *(greater cooption of groups in policy making)* **State**–citizen relations (Amendment, limitation and extension of civil liberties) **Government–party relations (Labour Party)** *(strengthening of the party)*
THE CHALLENGES
Written Constitution **A Bill of Rights** **Electoral reform** **Devolution** **Reform/abolition of the House of Lords**

Figure 15.2 *Constitutional changes and challenges (Source: Norton, 1986)*

Recognition of the fact that the relationship between Parliament and the executive was becoming too heavily orientated in favour of the executive led to various structural and procedural changes in Parliament. The House of Commons established fourteen departmentally related Select Committees; these are supplemented by other changes, including Special Standing Committees, Estimates Days and two statutory bodies: the House of Commons Commission and the Public Accounts Commission. Such changes were made possible by a growth of back-bench assertiveness. Similar changes were witnessed in the House of Lords. Peers displayed greater independence of government and utilized more regularly Select Committees, especially for the scrutiny of European Communities legislation.

The perceived need of the Government to enforce limits on public expenditure has led to greater controls of local government. This has encompassed not only legislation abolishing the Greater London Council and the metropolitan counties, but also the replacement of domestic rates by a 'community charge' (payable by every adult resident) and by business rates, levied and collected centrally and then distributed uniformly to local authorities. The effect of the changes is redistributive and makes local councils more subject to the centre.

The reactions of a number of civil servants to governmental secrecy (and, in some cases, disagreement with policy) has led to cases which constitute, in effect, challenges to the long-standing convention of individual ministerial responsibility. Under the convention, civil servants act solely in the name of their minister and exist to carry out their minister's wishes. The most notable challenge to the convention arose in the Ponting case (see also Chapter 6). Clive Ponting, a senior official in the Ministry of Defence, was prosecuted under Section II of the extant Official Secrets Act for leaking material that his Minister wished not to be disclosed. The civil servant's defence, that his action was in the 'interests of the State' (referred to but not defined in the Act) was successful. The case suggests that civil servants may not be answerable to a *single* higher authority.

The convention of collective ministerial responsibility has also been challenged in recent years by semi-public and sometimes public disputes between ministers over Cabinet decisions. Under the convention ministers are required to abide by and publicly support such decisions. In the 1970s, Harold Wilson and James Callaghan had to issue reminders to ministers to abide by the convention. In 1975, ministers were so divided on the issue of continued British membership of the European Communities that the convention was actually suspended to allow ministers to speak against the Government's policy. At the beginning of 1986, Defence Secretary Michael Heseltine pursued a public stance on the Westland issue that conflicted with his colleagues. Many observers were surprised that the Minister was allowed to express his public disagreement without being dismissed from office. When an attempt was made to impose the convention, he resigned.

The increasing dependence of government upon outside groups for advice, information and cooperation in implementing policy has also resulted in such groups acquiring a significant role in the shaping of public policy. On occasion this has been at the expense of the formal legitimizing role ascribed to Parliament. The most notable instance occurred in 1976 when the Chancellor of the Exchequer, Denis Healey, announced that a reduction in income tax was to be dependent upon the Trades Union Congress agreeing to wage restraint. The decision was denounced by critics, including David Steel, as handing over to the trade unions the veto power that formally resided with Parliament. Since the return of a Conservative Government in 1979, there has been a marked, and deliberate, rejection of group cooption in policy making, especially at the level of high, usually economic, policy. Government has been concerned to achieve autonomy of group activity in order to impose its economic policy.

Relations between the state and the individual have also been variously modified as a result of a range of disparate measures. Civil liberties, in particular, have been variously amended, limited and extended. The measures have encompassed the franchise, data protection, public demonstrations, trade union powers, immigration and deportation, police powers, the activities of the security services and broadcasting. In many of these measures, and in various actions against present and past civil servants (banning union membership at the government communication headquarters in Cheltenham; prosecution of Sarah Tisdall and Clive Ponting), the broadcasting authorities (trying to prevent the broadcasting of certain programmes, including a BBC programme on the Zircon satellite) and miners (restricting free movement during the 1984–5 miners' strike), various civil libertarians have claimed to detect a very clear and strong trend in favour of restricting civil liberty in Britain, though the evidence is not necessarily that clear-cut. One of the most important measures of recent years, the Police and Criminal Evidence Act of 1984, extends police powers of search and seizure while at the same time extending the rights of suspects. Under pressure from back-benchers, the government accepted an amendment to the 1988 Local Government Bill (now Section 28 of the Act) that prohibited the 'deliberate promotion' of homosexuality by local authorities. Several years earlier, in order to comply with its international obligations, the government extended the provisions of the 1967 Sexual Offences Act (allowing homosexual relations between consenting adults) to Northern Ireland. The changes are notable for their extent rather than their direction.

Finally, developments within the Labour Party — notably the use of an electoral college for the election of the party leader and the policy of compulsory reselection for all Labour MPs — have raised doubts about the representative nature of Members of Parliament and the presumed constitutional necessity of the Prime Minister to command the confidence of a majority in the House of Commons. Compulsory reselection has been criticized on the ground that it shifts further power from the electorate to the party's electorate. And it is now possible, under Labour's internal electoral arrangements, for a Labour leader to be elected who does not enjoy the support of a majority of Labour MPs. That possibility, if realized when the party was in power, would entail a departure from an existing maxim of the Constitution.

In combination, these changes — the additions and the amendments — are significant. The British Constitution in 1991 is much changed from what it was in 1960. The framework of debate is also different in that there is pressure for further, radical change.

Proposals for further change

The most important and far-reaching reforms that have been advocated, but not yet achieved, can be simply stated: a written constitution, an entrenched Bill of Rights, devolution, electoral reform and abolition or reform of the House of Lords. Each now has its advocates in political debate.

To some observers, Parliament is no longer capable of withstanding the excesses of the executive. Recent structural and procedural changes in the House of Commons are regarded as irrelevant tinkering. A Government elected with a parliamentary majority is free to do what it wants. Because of the doctrine of parliamentary sovereignty, there is little that the courts or any other authoritative body can do about it. Britain, according to Lord Hailsham, is faced by the prospect of an 'elective dictatorship'. To combat the dangers of an over-mighty executive, he proposed in his 1976 Dimbleby Lecture both a written constitution and an entrenched Bill of Rights. A written constitution, according to its advocates, would allow the powers of the different institutions of government to be authoritatively delineated, preventing the unchecked flow of power to the Prime Minister; and an entrenched Bill of Rights would put fundamental rights beyond the reach of an ordinary majority in the two Houses of Parliament.

Other, sometimes the same, reformers have also come up with other proposals designed to limit an over-mighty executive (as well as other perceived faults of the structure of government); most notable among these is that of a new electoral system.

A written constitution? Lord Hailsham, one-time opponent of 'elective dictatorship' and the sovereignty of Parliament.

The excesses of one-party government, they argue, include parties which out-promise one another at general elections and which, when in office, lack the resources to fulfil those promises. The present system is characterized by adversary politics and policy discontinuity, the former being politically harmful and the latter economically harmful. When one party succeeds another in office, it reverses the policies of its predecessor. If in office for any period of time (as with the Conservative Government returned in 1979), the adversary nature of politics prevents Government from being able to mobilize popular support in order to implement policy; instead, it has to resort to taking more and more formal powers. Hence the centralization of power. The solution, so the argument runs, lies in a reform of the electoral system, most reformers favouring the replacement of the existing first-past-the-post method of election with one based on PR. Such a system, reformers contend, would produce not only a fairer but also a more consensual (almost certainly a coalition) government that would be able to engage popular support for its policies.

A further group of reformers are those who argue for devolution, that is for certain executive and/or legislative powers to be devolved from central government to elected assemblies in Scotland, Wales and the English regions. Such a system of devolved government, they believe, would be both politically and economically desirable: by being closer to the people who elected it, devolved government would attract greater popular support and participation; by being closer to the region, economic decisions would be better informed and more appropriate to the particular region.

All these proposals have important supporters. The House of Lords has twice actually passed a Bill of Rights, introduced by Liberal peer Lord Wade. Devolution came within a hair's breadth of being implemented in 1979, failing only at the last hurdle of the referendums. (Parliament stipulated that 40 per cent of registered voters had to vote 'Yes' in each referendum, otherwise an order to repeal the devolution provisions was to be laid; in neither referendum was the limit met.) All the main political parties, with the exception of the Conservative Party, are committed to a policy of devolution. And electoral reform enjoys the support of the SLD, as well as substantial elements of the Conservative and Labour Parliamentary parties; it is likely to form a condition of any centre party participation in any future coalition government.

Finally, there is reform or abolition of the House of Lords. Schemes of reform for the Upper House are not new, but the issue came on the political agenda with renewed vigour in the late 1960s. The then Labour government sought to reform the House and introduced the Parliament (No. 2) Bill to achieve that goal; the Bill sought essentially to phase out the hereditary element of the House and ensure a working majority for the government of the day. The Bill fell because of opposition in the Commons led by the 'unholy alliance' of Enoch Powell and Michael Foot. Powell felt that the Bill went too far; Foot believed that it did not go far enough. The issue then lost much of its appeal (at least to government) but reappeared in the latter half of the 1970s, especially after a number of confrontations with the 1974–9 Labour Government. The Labour party committed itself to abolition. Various Conservative committees set up to study the problem recommended reform, favouring the retention of the Upper House but with some element of election. A small number of writers advocated a functional second chamber, members being chosen to represent the interests of particular designated interest groups. (See also Chapter 18.)

All these issues remain on the agenda of political debate. As we have seen, each has its supporters. But each also has its opponents, which explains why they remain *proposals* for reform. And it is in looking at the configuration of support and opposition that leads to our final section: the identification of different approaches to constitutional reform. As different items of constitutional change began to be discussed in the 1970s so different, identifiable schools of thought began to emerge.

Approaches to Constitutional Reform

Writing in 1982, in *The Constitution in Flux*, I delineated six approaches to constitutional reform. This delineation, I believe, has stood the test of time. The six approaches, listed in Figure 15.3, remain central to an understanding of the contemporary debate on the British Constitution.

First, the *High Tory* approach. This is an approach not much in evidence today, represented essentially by what may be termed the Old Right in the Conservative Party. It takes the view that the Constitution has evolved organically and that change, artificial change, is neither necessary nor desirable. In its pure form, it is opposed not only to radical additions to the Constitution but also to the various amendments. Hence, it opposes not only a written Constitution, referendums, a Bill of Rights, electoral reform, membership of the European Communities (in most cases) and reform of the Upper House, but also the introduction of such modest structures as Select Committees in the House of Commons. The House, it argues, works well, like other elements of the Constitution, and is in no need of mechanical tinkering. A motion introduced to the House in April 1981 by (now Sir) John Stokes expressed this view extravagantly well:

Figure 15.3 *Approaches to constitutional change (Source: Norton, 1986)*

> That this House believes in preserving the unity of the United Kingdom and all the great institutions of the realm, namely the Monarchy, the Church, the Houses of Parliament, the judiciary, the Armed Services of the Crown and the police; and deplores the attacks on these institutions by those who ought to know better.
>
> Quoted in Norton, 1986

Secondly, we have the *Socialist* approach. This does favour reform but a particular type of reform. It seeks strong government, but a *party*-dominated strong government, with adherence to intra-party democracy and the concept of the mandate. A party government would be elected to carry out a particular radical policy and the internal structures of the party would ensure that the party's leaders carried out that policy. In essence, it is an approach that seeks a shift from the existing form of 'top down' leadership in Britain, power resting with government leaders such as the Prime Minister, to a 'bottom up' form of leadership, with power lying with party activists.

This approach thus favours the use of the electoral college in the Labour party along with compulsory re-selection procedures. Of the major constitutional additions implemented or proposed, it favours only the abolition of the House of Lords, viewing the Upper House as a potential brake upon socialist legislation. It opposes membership of the European Communities, seeing the EC as a capitalist mechanism for restricting a future socialist government; it opposes a Bill of Rights for similar reasons. It also fears that electoral reform would deny the opportunity for a reforming socialist government to be returned to power with a parliamentary majority. Thus, what it seeks is not a change in constitutional structures but rather a change in constitutional relationships, with party playing a dominant role.

Thirdly, there is the *Marxist* approach. This does not advocate constitutional change. Instead, it tends to stand aloof and to see reform as reflecting the crisis of capitalist society. It contends that government, any government, in Britain is forced to defend the interests of capital and in times of crisis will seek to alter the formal constitutional structure in order to achieve that end. Thus, Marxists expect constitutional change but do not advocate it. Such change is taken as demonstrating the weakening of the capitalist state.

Fourthly, we have the *group*, or functionalist, approach. This, quite simply, seeks the greater incorporation of groups into the formal structures of government. As

**A written
constitution**

In 1976 Lord Hailsham delivered a scathing attack upon the British constitution in the BBC's Dimbleby Lecture. His central argument was that the fundamental tenet of the constitution — the sovereignty of Parliament — made it vulnerable to capture by political movements wholly out of tune with majority opinion. All that was needed was for a party to win a majority in the Commons and it had vast executive authority at its disposal. The absence of a bill of rights and a written constitution, the existence of a weak second chamber and a subservient local government meant that governments were restrained by nothing more than a sense of decency — surely a flimsy foundation upon which to base the governance of Britain?

> I have . . . reached the conclusion that our constitution is wearing out. Its central defects are gradually coming to outweigh its merits . . . I envisage nothing less than a written constitution for the United Kingdom
> Lord Hailsham (1976)

Lord Hailsham's target of course had been the allegedly far left Labour government elected in 1974 on barely 40 per cent of votes cast. When the Conservatives achieved power, however, in 1979, Hailsham (who became Lord Chancellor) became strangely quiet on the subject of 'elective dictatorship' — despite the fact that during the 1980s his party was implementing the most radical political programme since 1945 on just over 40 per cent of the vote. After the 1987 Conservative victory a number of anti-Thatcher intellectuals took up the argument for a written constitution with an enthusiasm born possibly of desperation at the thought of unlimited one-party, one-woman government. Labour disagrees with Charter 88's espousal of a full Bill of Rights as too dependent upon rightward-leaning judges. Its solution, unveiled by Roy Hattersley in early December 1989, is to introduce a Charter of Rights with specific liberties guaranteed by law.

Laws against Discrimination on the basis of race, sex or sexual orientation would be strengthened.

A Freedom of Information Act would oblige the government of the day to declare secret only that information which they can demonstrate must be restricted in the national interest.

A Security Services Act would give a Commons Standing Committee powers of scrutiny over MI5 and MI6.

A state-funded Press Council would be given powers to adjudicate complaints.

In addition a ***Right to Privacy Act*** was being considered to protect non-public people from media prying. Mr Hattersley rejected a ***Right to Work*** law as something which was too dependent on economic circumstances.

Below the arguments for and against a written constitution are summarized.

A Written Constitution?

The arguments for:

1. The Constitutional Settlement of 1688/9, designed to restrict one over-mighty executive (the Crown), created the means (the doctrine of parliamentary sovereignty) for the emergence of another.

2. There has been a growing centralization of power in government; there are no constitutional barriers to further centralization.
3. There has been a growing erosion of the rights of individuals and minority groups. In any challenge to these erosions, the government can use its power, through Parliament, to over-rule the courts.
4. A written constitution would delineate and constrain the particular powers of each organ of the state. The limits would be both created and known.
5. A written constitution, as with the US Constitution, could embody a Bill of Rights, thus providing protection to fundamental rights, putting them beyond the easy reach of the government of the day.
6. A written constitution would ensure that people know their rights, thus increasing public confidence in the nation's constitutional arrangements.

The arguments against:

1. A written constitution is unnecessary. British government is not omnipotent. Political constraints operate; one of the problems of the political system is the fragmentation of power (to groups, to civil servants, to the European Community), not its centralization.
2. A written constitution is undesirable. It would, in effect, put tremendous power in the hands of an unelected, unrepresentative elite (the judges) and would make the resolution of essentially political issues more difficult. Confidence in the political system would be undermined, not strengthened, if judicial interpretation runs counter to prevailing norms.
3. A written constitution is unachievable. There is no way under the existing system by which a written constitution and an entrenched Bill of Rights can be implemented. There is also no agreement on the provisions of any such constitution and Bill of Rights. In practical terms, it is a non-starter.

we have seen, groups play a greater role in influencing public policy, but that role — though politically significant — is not recognized formally. Groups have no formal right to be consulted by government or to be part of the policy making machinery.

What is advocated by those who adhere to this approach is a change in constitutional structures and relationships. Some would like government consultation with outside groups to be encompassed by a convention of the Constitution; that is, that it be a convention that groups affected by a proposed government policy have a right to be consulted on that policy. Others would like to see a more formal cooption of groups into government, with wider and more extensive representation on government committees and advisory bodies. Some would also like to see the House of Lords reformed in order to constitute a functional second chamber.

This group approach thus seeks some change, but it opposes some of the constitutional changes implemented or advocated. It opposes referendums fearing that they could constitute a populist weapon to be used against particular groups (such as trade unions); it also regards a Bill of Rights as likely to interfere with the free interplay between groups and government. On electoral reform and devolution it is more ambivalent. Devolution, for example, could be useful in that it would provide another layer of government at which well-organized groups would be able to exert considerable influence. As a rule, though, it does not seek *major* constitutional change, but rather amendments to the existing framework and relationships.

Of the various approaches the one that favours most reform is the penultimate one listed, the *liberal* approach, which emphasizes the centrality of the individual, government acting as an arbiter and within the rule of law. It views with horror the growth of group power, of executive dominance within the formal constitutional structures and of adversary politics, with party squabbles being harmful to the search for consensus. In order to counter these developments, it seeks a major reformulation of the Constitution.

It favours a new constitutional settlement, including electoral reform, a Bill of Rights and devolution for the reasons already given. These measures, basically, would shift power from government and groups back to the individual citizen. This approach is vehemently opposed to greater centralization of government. Favouring greater participation and opposing privilege, it favours an elected Upper House.

The only major reform about which it is ambivalent is the use of referendums, fearing that a referendum could be used by a majority to oppress a minority. Otherwise, it is the major proponent of the major changes discussed. In terms of political debate it tended to make much of the running in the latter half of the 1970s. In debate, it remains the most prominent of the approaches and has achieved a new impetus since 1987.

Finally, there is the *traditionalist* approach: this used to be dominant but is now challenged by the others. It is a very British approach: it adheres to the Westminster model of government; it stresses strong government, but one subject to parliamentary scrutiny and limitation. That is both what *should* be and to a large extent *what has been*. In other words, it is a part prescriptive, part descriptive approach. It favours the existing relationships. But, unlike the High Tory approach, it accepts the need for some change. If the system fails to work some modification is accepted as necessary; but it must be modification, not wholesale reform. It thus favours amendments to the Constitution, not additions.

A written constitution and an entrenched Bill of Rights, it believes, constitute a challenge to parliamentary sovereignty; electoral reform could deny the country strong government; referendums derogate from the functions and power of Parliament; and devolution could weaken both central government and Parliament. Instead, if there is to be change, it should be more of an incremental nature; hence, reform of the committee system in the House of Commons is favoured, along with a number of similar amendments to existing structures. Within the Conservative government and within Parliament this traditionalist approach retains predominant support.

Identification of the different approaches to constitutional change helps give some shape to the debate of the past two decades. The old consensus on the Constitution has disappeared. The Constitution is now part of political debate. In the 1970s, as we have noted, advocates of the liberal approach tended to be to the fore. In the first half of the 1980s the debate became less prominent, in part because some of the advocates of reform (notably Lord Hailsham) became members of the government, in part because of a recognition that reform of the Constitution was not likely to

Charter '88

The time has come to demand political, civil and human rights in the United Kingdom. The first step is to establish them in constitutional form, so that they are no longer subject to the arbitrary diktat of Westminster and Whitehall.

We call, therefore, for a new constitutional settlement which would:

1 Enshrine, by means of a Bill of Rights, such civil liberties as the right to peaceful assembly, to freedom of association, to freedom from discrimination, to freedom from detention without trial, to trial by jury, to privacy and to freedom of expression.

2 Subject executive powers and prerogatives, by whomsoever exercised, to the rule of law.

3 Establish freedom of information and open government.

4 Create a fair electoral system of proportional representation.

5 Reform the upper house to establish a democratic, non-hereditary second chamber.

6 Place the executive under the power of a democratically renewed parliament and all agencies of the state under the rule of law.

7 Ensure the independence of a reformed judiciary.

8 Provide legal remedies for all abuses of power by the state and the officials of central and local government.

9 Guarantee an equitable distribution of power between local, regional and national government.

10 Draw up a written constitution, anchored in the idea of universal citizenship, that incorporates these reforms.

Our central concern is the law. No country can be considered free in which the government is above the law. No democracy can be considered safe whose freedoms are not encoded in a basic constitution.

We, the undersigned, have called this document Charter 88. First, to mark our rejection of the complacency with which the tercentenary of the Revolution of 1688 has been celebrated. Second, to reassert a tradition of demands for constitutional rights in Britain, which stretches from the barons who forced the Magna Carta on King John, to the working men who drew up the People's Charter in 1838, to the women at the beginning of this century who demanded universal suffrage. Third, to salute the courage of those in Eastern Europe who still fight for their fundamental freedoms.

emanate from a Conservative government under Margaret Thatcher. However, the debate became more pronounced following the 1987 general election. More than a decade of Conservative government encouraged many on the left of the political spectrum to toy with the idea of a new system of government. The Labour party was suffering under the existing system; why not, then, contemplate a new system? Perceptions of a growing centralization of power and of growing alienation in the UK periphery (especially in Scotland) helped swell the ranks of liberal advocates. Consequently, the socialist approach receded somewhat in significance. The Labour party began to move more towards the liberal approach. The signatories of 'Charter

'88' included not only prominent figures in centre parties but also some well-known left-wing writers, including Bernard Crick, Ralph Miliband and Martin Jacques. Advocates of the traditionalist approach remained where it mattered — in power. Advocating major reform of the Constitution remains a particular prerogative of the 'outs' in British politics.

References and Further Reading

Brazier, R., *Constitutional Practice* (Oxford University Press, 1988).

Dicey, A.V., *Introduction to the Study of the Law of the Constitution* (first pub. 1885; Macmillan, 1950).

Graham, C. and Prosser, T. (eds), *Waiving the Rules* (Open University Press, 1988).

Hailsham, Lord, *Elective Dictatorship* (BBC Publications, 1976).

Holme, R. and Elliott, M. (eds), *1688–1988: Time for a New Constitution* (Macmillan, 1988).

Johnson, N., *In Search of the Constitution* (Methuen, 1980).

Jowell, J. and Oliver, D. (eds), *The Changing Constitution*, 2nd edn (Oxford University Press, 1989).

Norton, P., *The Constitution in Flux* (Basil Blackwell, 1982).

Norton, P., (ed.), *Parliament in the 1980s* (Basil Blackwell, 1985).

Norton, P., *Social Studies Review* (September 1986).

16 Crown and Parliament

Philip Norton

It is an extraordinary fact, often overlooked, that Britain's representative democracy evolved over a thousand years out of an absolute monarchy underpinned by the religious notion of the divine right of kings. The monarchical shell remains intact but the inner workings have been taken over by party political leaders and civil servants. This chapter analyses the emergence of the modern monarchy and considers its still important functions together with the arguments of its critics.

A.H. Birch, in his seminal work *Representative and Responsible Government*, identified two theories of representation that were current before 1832: those of Tory and Whig. The Tory approach emphasized the need for a strong executive (in those days, the monarch); the Whig approach emphasized the importance of Parliament (Birch, 1964, pp. 23–31). For several centuries, the political culture in England, if not the rest of Britain, has facilitated what may be seen as a blend of the two theories: that is, a strong executive bounded by limits set by Parliament. That relationship pre-dates by several centuries the emergence of the concept of representation.

The term 'representation' entered the English language through French derivatives of the Latin *repraesentare*, and did not assume a political meaning until the sixteenth century (Beard and Lewis, 1959). It permits of at least four separate usages (see Birch, 1964; Pitkin 1967):

1. It may denote acting on behalf of some individual or group, seeking to defend and promote the interests of the person or persons 'represented'.
2. It may denote persons or assemblies that have been freely elected. Though it is not always the case that persons so elected will act to defend and pursue the interests of electors, they will normally be expected to do so.
3. It may be used to signify a person or persons typical of a particular class or group of persons. It is in this sense in which it is used when opinion pollsters identify a representative sample. A representative assembly, under this definition, would be one in which the members reflected proportionally the socio-economic and other characteristics of the population as a whole.
4. It may be used in a symbolic sense. Thus, individuals or objects may 'stand for' something: for example, a flag symbolizing the unity of the nation.

The House of Commons can claim to be a representative assembly under the first two usages of the term, the first having greater applicability historically than the second. Under both the Tory and Whig theories of representation, Members of Parliament were returned to defend and pursue the interests of different classes or groups within the realm, but neither recognized the need for Members to be elected by those bodies on whose behalf they expressed themselves. This concept of 'virtual representation' was well expressed by Edmund Burke. It was a form of representation, he wrote, 'in which there is a communion of interests, and a sympathy in feelings and desires, between those who act in the name of any description of people, and the people in whose name they act, though the trustees are not actually chosen by them'. A corollary of this view was that Members offered their judgements on behalf of those they represented and were not in any sense 'delegates'.

In the nineteenth century this view of representation was challenged by radical interpretations (popular participation, concept of the mandate) and by liberal ones (free elections, representation of the individual *qua* individual); their influence was such that by the end of the century, with the extension of the franchise and changes in the system of election (secret ballots, for example), the House of Commons could claim to be a freely elected assembly, though the mode of election — and those entitled to participate in it — was far from being problem-free. Only in the twentieth century has the franchise been extended to women (by Acts of 1918 and 1928) and to eighteen-year-olds (1969); the first-past-the-post method of election — which does not necessarily produce seats for parties in proportion to the number of votes cast — constitutes a contemporary issue of controversy (see Chapter 11). The twentieth century has witnessed the growth of more collectivist theories of representation, with emphasis on parties and the representation of groups and classes; hence the relevance of the dispute over the method of election.

None of these views of representation, though, has served to displace completely the blend of Tory and Whig views. The emphasis on a strong executive remains; so too does an emphasis on Parliament as the body vested with responsibility for setting the limits within which that executive may operate. Indeed, given the relevance of the House of Commons now as a freely elected assembly — in other words, being representative under the second and not just the first definition of the term — the greater the legitimacy of the House to fulfil that role. Formally, Members of Parliament continue to be returned to represent individuals living in defined geographical areas (constituencies) and are not bound by the concept of the mandate. The constraints upon their parliamentary behaviour are political; in that, historically, there is nothing new.

What has changed significantly has been the relationship between the two Houses of Parliament and the relationship of the monarch to the political system. As the concept of representation as acting on behalf of some individual or group gained currency, so the House of Commons — as the representative chamber — gradually gained political ascendancy over the House of Lords. (The House of Lords is not a representative chamber under any of the usages of the term. Though peers may claim to speak on behalf of others, their writs of summons are personal.) This ascendancy was embodied in statute in the Parliament Acts of 1911 and 1949, the acceptance of the concept of representation as entailing election serving to relegate the unelected Upper House to a recognizably inferior role to that of the elected chamber.

The most significant change historically has been that of the role of the monarch.

The political culture favours a strong executive and that initially meant the monarch. Following the emergence of a recognizable Parliament, the king was constrained from exercising unfettered powers; attempts to do so — under Charles I and James II — resulted in the monarch being displaced. Following the Glorious Revolution of 1688, the relationship between Crown and Parliament was asserted in the Bill of Rights of 1689: the dispensing or executing of laws without the authority of Parliament was declared to be illegal, as was the levying of money without the consent of Parliament. Even so, those responsible for a Bill of Rights still wanted a 'real, working, governing king, a king with a policy' (Maitland, quoted in Wiseman, 1964, p.5). However, the contradictions between an executive which could claim to be representative only in the symbolic sense and an occasionally assertive elective assembly with powers to deny supply could not be long maintained and gradually the executive power passed, in practice, to the King's ministers. The period between the reigns of Queens Anne and Victoria saw the transfer of power from monarch to ministers and the emergence of Prime Minister and Cabinet. Ministers remained, as they still are, legally responsible to the Crown; politically, they became — and remain — responsible to Parliament.

Over the past 150 years Parliament — or rather one chamber of it — can claim to have become a more representative chamber under the first two usages of the term, though operating as a reactive body to government (it is not, and never has been, the governing body itself); while, ironically, by withdrawing from partisan activity, the monarch can claim to be more representative under the fourth usage of the term: that is, better able to symbolize the unity of the nation.

The Monarch

The monarchy is the oldest secular institution in England, dating back at least to the ninth century. Only once has the continuity of the institution been broken, during the period of rule by the Council of State and Oliver Cromwell (1642–60), though the line of succession was restored with the accession of Charles II. The principle of heredity has been preserved since at least the eleventh century; despite various breaks in the direct line of succession, the present monarch can trace her descent from King Egbert, who united England under his rule in 829 AD. The succession is now governed by statute and common law, the throne descending to the eldest son or, in the absence of a son, the eldest daughter. If the monarch is under eighteen years of age, a Regent is appointed.

The terms monarch and Crown are often used interchangeably. In fact, they are distinct. The Crown symbolizes supreme executive authority. It is conferred on the monarch, hence the constitutional significance of whoever occupies the throne. In Anglo-Saxon and Norman times, the executive power that the Crown conferred was exercised personally by the monarch. However, it was never an absolute power. In the coronation oath, the king promised to 'forbid all rapine and injustice to men of all conditions', and he was expected to consult with the leading men of the realm, both lay and clerical, in order to discover and declare the law and also before the levying of any extraordinary measures of taxation. Such an expectation was to find documented expression in Magna Carta, to which King John affixed his seal in 1215 and which is now recognized as a document of critical constitutional significance: at the time, it was seen by the barons as an expression of existing rights, not a novel departure from them.

The expectation that the King would consult with the leading men of the realm gradually expanded to encompass knights and burgesses, summoned to assent on behalf of local communities (***communes***) to the raising of more money to meet the king's growing expenses. From the summoning of these representatives, there emerged a Parliament: the term was first used in the thirteenth century. At various times in the fourteenth century, the knights and burgesses deliberated separately from the leading lords and churchmen and so there emerged two Houses: the former constituting a lower house, the House of Commons, the latter forming an upper house, the House of Lords.

From that time on, there was a struggle between the monarch and Parliament. Though formally the king's Parliament, the king depended upon the institution for the grant of supply (taxes) and increasingly for assent to law. Parliament made the grant of supply dependent upon the king granting a redress of grievances. Tudor monarchs turned to Parliament for support and usually got it; but the effect of their actions was to acknowledge the growing importance of the body. Stuart kings were less appreciative. James I and his successor, Charles I, upheld the theory of the divine right of kings (that is, that the position and powers of the king are given by God and the position and privileges of Parliament derive therefore from the king's grace); Charles's pursuit of the doctrine led to an attempt to rule without the assent of Parliament and ultimately to civil war and the beheading of the king in 1649. The period of republican government that followed was a failure and consequently short-lived. The monarchy was restored in 1660, only to produce another clash a few years later. James II believed in both the divine right of kings and the Roman Catholic faith; both produced a clash with Parliament and James attempted to rule by prerogative instead. A second civil war was averted when James fled the country following the arrival of William of Orange (James's son-in-law), who had been invited by leading politicians and churchmen. At the invitation of a new Parliament, William and his wife Mary (James II's daughter) jointly assumed the throne. In so doing, they also accepted the Declaration of Right — embodied in statute as the 1689 Bill of Rights — which declared the suspending of laws and the levying of taxation without the approval of Parliament to be illegal. As the historian G.M. Trevelyan observed, James II had forced the country to choose between royal absolutism and parliamentary government (Trevelyan, 1938, p.245). It chose parliamentary government.

The dependence of the monarch on Parliament was thus established and the years since have witnessed the gradual withdrawal of the sovereign from the personal exercise of the executive authority. Increasingly, the monarch became dependent on ministers, both for the exercise of executive duties and in order to manage parliamentary business. This dependence was all the greater when Queen Anne died in 1714 without an heir and yet another monarch was imported from Europe — this time George, Elector of Hanover. George I of Britain was not especially interested in politics and in any case did not speak English so the task of chairing Cabinet — traditionally the King's job — fell to the First Lord of the Treasury. Under Robert Walpole, this role was assiduously developed so that he became indisputably the most important of the king's ministers: he became 'Prime Minister'. It is perhaps ironic to reflect that Anne's inability to produce an heir and George's poor language skills were responsible for the early development of the office currently held by John Major.

George III succeeded in winning back some of the monarchy's power later on in the eighteenth century. It was still the king, after all, who appointed ministers and by skilfully using his patronage, he could influence representation in Parliament. These successes, however, were destined to be shortlived. In 1832 the Great Reform Act introduced a uniform electoral system and subsequent reform acts in 1867 and 1884 extended the right to vote to millions of people. The age of representative democracy had arrived. The monarch had no place in it. To win votes groups in Parliament organized themselves into disciplined parties and the leader of the majority party following a general election now became automatically the Prime Minister with, effectively, rights of appointment previously held by the Crown.

Queen Victoria was the last monarch to consider seriously vetoing legislation (the last monarch to actually do so was Queen Anne who withheld the Royal Assent from the Scottish Militia Bill in 1707). 1834 was the last occasion that a ministry fell for want of the sovereign's confidence; thereafter it was the confidence of the House of Commons that counted. She was also the last monarch to exercise a personal preference in the choice of Prime Minister (later monarchs, where a choice existed, acted under advice), the last to attempt with some measure of success to veto Cabinet appointments and the last to be instrumental in pushing successfully for the enactment of particular legislative measures (Hardie, 1970, p.67). By the end of her reign, it was clear that the monarch, whatever the formal powers vested by the constitution, was constrained politically by a representative assembly elected by the adult male population, the government being carried on by ministers drawn from that assembly. Prior to Victoria's reign, what Walter Bagehot referred to in 1867 as the elective power (the power to choose a government) was exercised by the monarch; during her reign the power shifted, first to the House of Commons and then to the electorate.

The monarch now sat on the sidelines of the political system, unable to control Parliament, unable to appoint ministers, unable to appoint judges. The absolute power once exercised by the king had now passed to the people. However, this sovereign power was only exercised on election day: in between elections it was the PM who exercised many of the powers relinquished by the monarch. By controlling government appointments, the PM was able to dominate the executive side of government. And as long as he could command the support of the majority party in Parliament he was able to dominate the legislative side of government as well. Here we have an even greater irony: hundreds of years of development towards Parliamentary government could have destroyed the power of the Crown but merely replaced it with a lay figure exercising similar powers.

The shift to a position above the partisan fray of politics, and above the actual exercise of executive power, has been confirmed in the twentieth century. 'Since 1901 the trend towards a real political neutrality, not merely a matter of appearances, has been steady, reign by reign' (Hardie, 1970, p.188). The transition has been facilitated by no great constitutional act. Several statutes have impinged upon the prerogative power but many of the legal powers remain. There is nothing in law that prevents the monarch from vetoing a bill or from exercising personal choice in the invitation to form a government. The monarch is instead bound by conventions

The development of a constitutional monarchy

A thousand years ago, most of the functions of government were exercised by the King. He was the strongest single influence on: the making of laws or the 'legislative' function; the implementing of laws — the 'executive' function; and the interpreting of laws — the 'judicial' function.

As government became more complex these functions began to be performed by separate institutions which built up their own traditions and sense of identity. But the king kept pretty close control over all of them. It was he who appointed the great officers of state like the Chancellor or Lord Privy Seal and other members of what in medieval times was called his Privy Council.

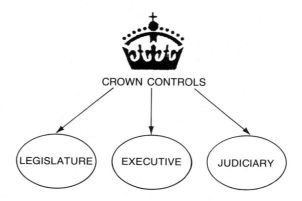

The Civil War, however, broke the power of the Crown and by the end of the seventeeth century Parliament had confirmed its right to have the last word. By the end of the nineteenth century the monarch had been relegated to a ceremonial role with a legislature (Lords and Commons) and executive (ministers and civil servants) linked by an increasingly powerful Prime Minister and Cabinet.

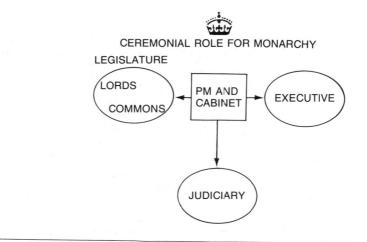

of the constitution, unwritten rules (unwritten in a legal sense) that are accepted as binding by those at whom they are directed in order to make the constitution work. They constitute, in effect, the oil in the machinery of the constitution. They have helped ease the passage of the monarch from one important constitutional position to another.

The monarch in the 1990s

What, then, is the contemporary role of the monarch? Two primary tasks can be identified. One is essentially a representative task: that is, to symbolize the unity and the traditional standards of the nation. The second is to fulfil certain political functions. The weakness of the monarch in being able to exercise independent decisions in the latter task has ensured the strength of the monarchy in fulfilling the former.

The functions fulfilled by the monarch under the first heading are several. The most central, those to which citizens attach most importance, are revealed in Table 16.1. This reproduces the findings of a Gallup Poll conducted in December 1988 in which respondents were asked to assess the importance of a number of functions usually ascribed to the Royal Family. A majority of respondents considered six functions to be 'very' or 'quite' important.

Table 16.1   *Principal functions of the Royal Family, percentage of responses*

Function	Very	Quite	Importance Not very	Not at all	Don't know
Represent the UK at home and abroad	67	25	4	2	1
Set standards of citizenship and family life	59	26	8	4	3
Unite people despite differences	52	30	8	6	4
Ensure armed forces owe allegiance to the Crown rather than government	52	24	10	7	7
Maintain continuity of British traditions	51	34	9	3	2
Preserve a Christian morality	43	26	17	10	4
Preserve the class system	13	16	23	43	5
Distract people from problems affecting country	9	16	25	42	7

Note: Poll conducted 9–14 December 1988 among representative quota sample of 918 adults interviewed in more than 95 districts in Britain
Respondents were asked to assess the importance of functions ascribed to the Royal Family

Source: results of *Daily Telegraph* poll, 28 December 1988

Pomp or politics? What is the contemporary role of the monarchy?

Representing the UK at home or abroad

More than 90 per cent of respondents in the Gallup Poll considered this to be very or quite important. As a symbolic function, it is a task normally ascribed to any head of state. In the British context, the Queen is seen as especially well suited to the task. Because no partisan connotations attach to her activities, she is able to engage the public commitment of citizens in a way that politicians cannot. When the President of the United States travels within the USA or goes abroad he does so both as head of state and as head of government; as head of government he is a practising politician. The problems that this dual role may generate were highlighted in 1973 and 1974 during the Watergate crisis: crowds who turned out to watch and cheer President Nixon as head of state also expressed support for his impeachment. By now being above the partisan fray, the monarch in Britain avoids such a conflict. By attending a major conference or international gathering — or even opening a new hospital or attending a major domestic sporting event — the Queen is able to appear on behalf of the nation, a living symbol of its unity and pride, without inviting controversy or opposition. A similar invitation to the Prime Minister or Leader of the Opposition would rarely be free of partisan objection.

At least two practical benefits are also believed to derive from this symbolic role, one political, the other economic. By virtue of the number of years the Queen has spent on the throne (heads of government, in contrast, come and go with greater regularity, both in Britain and most other countries) and her neutral position, she is accorded a significant degree of international respect. This respect constitutes a bonus for Britain on the international stage, and especially in the context of the Commonwealth, of which the Queen is titular Head. During the 1980s, when relations between the British and a number of Commonwealth governments were sometimes acrimonious (on the issue of South African sanctions, for example), various Commonwealth heads attested to the unifying influence of the Queen. Economically, the Queen and other leading members of the Royal Family (notably the Prince and Princess of Wales) are often judged to be good for British trade. The symbolism, the history and the pageantry that surrounds the monarchy serves to make the Queen and her immediate family a potent source of media and public interest abroad. Royal visits are often geared to export promotions, media interest being used to focus on particular British goods.

Setting standards of citizenship and family life

This, as the Gallup Poll revealed, remains an important task in the eyes of all but a small percentage of those questioned. The Queen in particular, and members of the Royal Family in general, are expected to lead by example in maintaining standards of citizenship and family life. As head of state and as secular head of the Established Church, the Queen is expected to be above criticism. She applies herself assiduously to her duties; even her most ardent critics concede that she is diligent (Wilson, 1989, p.190). She lends her name to charities and voluntary organizations, variously patronizing their meetings, as do other members of the Royal Family. The Prince of Wales is an active sponsor of several charitable trusts. Princess Anne, the Princess Royal, is President of the Save the Children Fund. As the mother of Britain's most public family, the Queen is held to epitomize family life in a way that others can both empathize with and seek to emulate. (Queen Elizabeth, the Queen Mother — widow of George VI — is also now popularly portrayed as epitomizing 'the ideal grandmother'.) Significantly, during the national miners' strike in 1984, it was the Queen that miners' wives petitioned for help. If anything, this task has assumed greater significance during the reign of the present monarch, as the Royal Family has achieved greater public visibility through the medium of television and the daily activities of the Queen and her family become more accessible to the public gaze.

Uniting people despite differences

The monarch symbolizes the unity of the nation. The Queen is head of state. Various public functions are carried out in the name of the Crown, notably public prosecutions, and as the person in whom the Crown vests the monarch's name attaches to the various organs of the state: the government, the courts and the armed services. The Government is Her Majesty's Government; even the Opposition is Her Majesty's Opposition. Members of the armed services are in the service of the Crown. The Crown, in effect, substitutes for the concept of the State (a concept not well understood or utilized in Britain) and the monarch serves as the personification of the Crown. Nowhere is the extent of this personification better demonstrated than on British postage stamps. They are unique: British stamps alone carry the monarch's head instead of the name of the nation. The monarch provides a clear, animate focal point for the expression of national unity, national pride and, if necessary, national grief.

The effectiveness of this uniting role is made possible now by the monarch transcending political activity. Executive actions are carried out in the name of the Crown, but no personal responsibility for these actions attaches to the monarch. Twentieth-century monarchs have abjured the public expression of any personal or partisan preferences in the affairs of state. Separating the roles of head of state and head of government, coupled with the absence of election, avoids the tainting of the monarch with partisanship. Citizens' loyalties may thus flow to the Crown without being hindered by political considerations.

Allegiance of the armed forces

Ensuring that the armed forces give their allegiance to the Crown rather than to the government is an important function, though it is interesting — and possibly surprising — that respondents to the 1988 Gallup Poll accorded it the importance they did; more than 75 per cent judged it to be very or quite important, ahead of maintaining continuity of tradition and preserving a Christian morality. The armed services, as we have noted, are in the service of the Crown. Loyalty is owed to the Crown. Indeed, there is a history of close association between the armed services and the Royal Family, members of the Royal Family either serving in (usually) the Navy or the Army or holding ceremonial rank as Colonel-in-Chief of a particular regiment. The Queen takes a particular interest in military matters, including awards for service. 'With the outbreak of the troubles in Ulster in the late 1960s she was a moving force in getting a medal created for services there, and she read personally all the citations for gallantry there — as she had always done for medals of any sort' (Lacey, 1977, p.222). Such a relationship helps emphasize the apolitical role of the military and also provides a barrier should the military, or more likely a section of it, seek to overthrow or threaten the elected government. (In the 1970s there were rumours — retailed in the press and on a number of television programmes — that a number of retired officers favoured a coup to topple the Labour Government returned in 1974; Peter Wright's *Spycatcher* later added a certain credence to plots in military intelligence.) In the event of an attempted military coup, the prevailing wisdom is that the monarch would serve as the most effective bulwark to its realization, the Queen being in a position to exercise the same role as that of King Juan Carlos of Spain in 1981, when he forestalled a right-wing military takeover by making a public appeal to the loyalty of his army commanders.

Maintaining continuity of British traditions

Change is a feature of British governments, both in terms of personnel and policy. Continuity in the polity is provided by the civil service and by the monarch, the civil service in terms of administration, the monarch in terms of more public traditions. Some of these traditions have a symbolic relevance: for example, the State Opening of Parliament and — in the context of the previous point — the annual Trooping of the Colour. Other traditions serve a psychological function, helping maintain a sense of belonging to the nation, and a social one. The awarding of honours and Buckingham Palace garden parties are viewed by critics as socially elitist but by supporters as helping break down social barriers, rewarding those — regardless of class — who have contributed significantly to the community. Hierarchy of awards, on this argument, is deemed less important than the effect on those receiving the awards. The award of an MBE to a local health worker may mean far more to the recipient, who may never have expected it, than the award of a knighthood to a senior civil servant who may have come to regard such an honour as a natural perk of the job. Investiture is often as important as the actual award. 'To some it is a rather tiresome ordeal but to most a moving and memorable occasion. A Fire Brigade officer, who was presented with the British Empire Medal, spoke for many when he said: "I thought it would be just another ceremony. But now that I've been, it's something I'll remember for the rest of my days" ' (Hibbert, 1979, p.205). Each year 30,000 people are invited to royal garden parties. Few decline the invitation.

Preserving a Christian morality

The Queen is supreme Governor of the Church of England and the links between the monarch and the Church are close and visible. After the monarch, the most significant participant in a coronation ceremony is the Archbishop of Canterbury, who both crowns and anoints the new sovereign. Bishops are appointed by the Crown, albeit acting on advice. National celebrations led by the Queen will usually entail a religious service, as for instance on the occasion of the Queen's Silver Jubilee in 1977. The Queen is known to take seriously her religious duties. Though the British are not an ardent Church-going race (fewer than one in twenty of the adult population are members of the Church of England), moral values are nonetheless deemed important. The Queen, largely by way of example, is looked to as a symbol of a basically Christian morality. Morality has assumed greater relative importance as emphasis on the Protestant religion has declined. Though the monarch is required by the Act of Settlement of 1701 to 'joyn in communion with the Church of England as by law established', recent monarchs have managed to reduce or dispense with oaths and ceremonies that may offend members of other faiths.

Preserving what are deemed to be high standards of Christian morality is probably of most importance in the twentieth century — earlier monarchs were keener to protect the Church of England than they were to practice its morality — and has forced some notable instances of self-sacrifice by certain members of the Royal Family. The most obvious example came in 1955 when the Queen's sister, Princess Margaret, decided not to marry Group Captain Peter Townsend because he was a divorcee. News of their romance produced negative comments from the press — 'It is quite unthinkable that a royal princess ... should ever contemplate a marriage with a man who has been through the Divorce Courts', declared the *People* — and on 31 October 1955 the Princess announced that 'mindful of the Church's teaching that Christian marriage is indissoluble, and conscious of my duty to the Commonwealth, I have resolved to put these considerations before others'. Twenty-one years later, with attitudes towards divorce more relaxed, the Princess was to separate from her husband of fifteen years, the Earl of Snowdon, and the two subsequently divorced.

Powers and duties of the monarch

Underpinning the monarch's capacity to fulfil a unifying role, and indeed underpinning the other functions deemed important, is the fact that she stands above and beyond the arena of partisan debate. This also affects significantly the monarch's other primary task: that of fulfilling certain political duties, perhaps best described as duties of state. Major powers still remain within the royal prerogative: the choice of Prime Minister, the assent to legislation, the dispensing of ministerial portfolios, the dissolution of Parliament, the making of treaties and the declaring of war being among the most obvious. All such prerogative powers are now, as far as possible, governed by convention. By convention, the monarch assents to all legislation passed by the two Houses of Parliament. By convention, the leader of the party with an overall majority of seats in the House of Commons is invited to form a government (the position, as we shall see, is less clearly governed by convention when there is no majority); when a Prime Minister retires, the leader elected by the governing party as his or her successor is then invited to 'kiss hands' (form a government). When there is no governing convention, the monarch seeks to act in accordance with precedent. In the exercise of prerogative powers where choice exists (for example, the power to grant a pardon) the Queen acts on the advice of her ministers. By thus avoiding any personal choice — and being seen not to exercise any personal choice — in the exercise of the powers vested in the Crown, the monarch is able to remain 'above politics'. Hence the characterization of the monarch as enjoying 'strength through weakness' (Norton, 1990, pp.328–40). The denial of personal discretion in the exercise of political powers strengthens the capacity of the monarch to fulfil a representative — that is, symbolic — role.

Could it not be argued that the exercise of prerogative powers is, by virtue of the absence of personal discretion, a waste of time and something of which the monarch should be shorn? (Why not, for example, vest the power of dissolution in the Speaker of the House of Commons?) There are two principal reasons why the powers remain vested in the sovereign.

Firstly, the combination of the symbolic role and the powers vested in the Crown enable the monarch to stand as a constitutional safeguard. A similar role is often ascribed to the House of Lords, but that is in a situation where a government seeks to extend its own life without recourse to an election. What if a government sought to dispense with Parliament? To return to an earlier example, what if there was an attempted military coup? The House of Lords could not act effectively to prevent it. It is doubtful if a Speaker vested with formal powers could do much to prevent it. The monarch could. By engaging the loyalty of the nation, including the armed services, the sovereign could deny both legitimacy and support to the insurgents. Thus, ironically, the monarchy serves as the ultimate protector of the political institutions which have displaced it as the governing authority.

Secondly, retention of prerogative powers serves as a reminder to ministers and other servants of the Crown that they owe a responsibility to a higher authority than a transient politician. Ministers are Her Majesty's Ministers: the Prime Minister is invited to form a Government by the sovereign. The responsibility may, on the face of it, appear purely formal. However, though the monarch is precluded by calling the Prime Minister (or any minister) to public account, she is able to require a private explanation. In *The English Constitution*, Walter Bagehot offered his classic definition of the monarch's power as being 'the right to be consulted, the right to encourage, the right to warn'. The Prime Minister has a weekly audience with the Queen (usually on Tuesday evenings when the Queen is in London). The Queen is reputed to be an assiduous reader of her official papers — she receives all Cabinet papers and Foreign Office telegrams — and is known often to closely question the Prime Minister and, on other occasions, the relevant Departmental ministers. Harold Wilson recorded when in his early days as Prime Minister he was caught on the hop as a result of the Queen having read Cabinet papers which he had not yet got round to reading. 'Very interesting, this idea of a new town in the Bletchley area', commented the Queen. It was the first the Prime Minister knew of the idea.

The relationship between the monarch and her Prime Minister, derived from the Queen's formal status and powers, serves both as a potential limitation and also a more realizable strength for the Prime Minister. It is a limitation in that the Queen may subject her first minister to rigorous questioning and, in certain circumstances, make her displeasure known. In 1986, for example, it was reported — though not confirmed — that the Queen was distressed at the strain which Margaret Thatcher's refusal to endorse sanctions against South Africa was placing on the Commonwealth; she was also reported to have expressed her displeasure in 1983 following the US invasion of Grenada (Cannon and Griffiths, 1988, p.620). Indeed, relations between the Queen and her first female Prime Minister were rumoured to have been correct rather than close. The same was said of her relations with Mrs Thatcher's Conservative predecessor, Edward Heath (Hibbert, 1979, pp.151–2). Her rapport with Labour Prime Ministers Harold Wilson and James Callaghan was believed to be much closer — Wilson paying warm testimony to the relationship in his memoirs — as it was with earlier Conservative Prime Ministers such as Harold Macmillan and Winston Churchill.

The advantages to the Prime Minister are twofold. First, the Queen provides a unique source of advice. She has extensive experience, not least of the Commonwealth. She is well read in terms of government papers and she provides the premier with a private opportunity to discuss issues with someone who has no political axe to grind. The Queen is neither a political opponent nor a ministerial colleague plotting for future preferment. Successive Prime Ministers have attested to the value of the Queen's advice. Macmillan referred to it on a number of occasions in his diaries. He wrote of 'the most complete co-operation and confidence'. To his successor, Sir Alec Douglas-Home, the fruits of her experience were 'invaluable' (Hibbert, 1979, p.149). Secondly, the monarch relieves the head of government of many ceremonial duties. Where heads of state serve also as heads of government, much time is taken up with ceremonial duties — presenting honours, receiving ambassadors, formal public appearances, opening public buildings and so on. The British Prime Minister is relieved of much of that ceremonial burden. It is carried out instead by the Queen and other members of the Royal Family. The head of government is thus enabled to get on with the work of government; the head of state is able to be closer to the people.

Criticisms of the monarchy

Various advantages thus derive from the nature and operation of the monarchy. Are there any problems associated with or criticisms levelled at the monarchy? And if so, what responses have been offered to them? There is essentially one problem: the potential for political involvement. And there are criticisms which can be levelled under three heads: namely that the monarchy is unrepresentative, overly expensive, and unnecessary.

The Queen and the selection of a Prime Minister

Prior to 1965, Leaders of the Conservative Party became such by a process of 'emergence'. A successor to the incumbent Leader normally became apparent before the resignation of the incumbent. If the party was in office, it was this ***heir apparent*** who was summoned to Buckingham Palace and invited by the monarch to become Prime Minister. Thus, for example, in 1955 when Sir Winston Churchill retired from office, the automatic successor was Sir Anthony Eden who had been recognized within the party for several years as Churchill's natural successor. However, no leader had obviously emerged in 1957 following Eden's medically enforced resignation. There were two leading contenders for the succession: R.A. ('Rab') Butler and Harold Macmillan. There was no formal means by which the party could make a clear choice and, Eden having resigned, time was of the essence. The choice thus fell to the Queen. After consulting senior statesmen (notably Churchill and the Marquess of Salisbury) she sent for Macmillan instead of — as many assumed she would — the more senior figure of Butler.

A similar dilemma faced the Queen in 1963 when Macmillan himself resigned, again unexpectedly following hospitalization for an emergency operation. There was no heir apparent and several senior figures made clear their willingness to succeed to the office. Again the Queen found herself having to make a choice. After seeing Macmillan, who reported various soundings that had been taken in the party, she summoned the Foreign Secretary, Lord Home, to form a government. (Lord Home immediately renounced his title and entered the House of Commons at a by-election.) In so doing, the Queen was drawn into political controversy. Various allegations were subsequently made that Macmillan had given advice in a way designed to prevent Butler becoming Prime Minister. Two Cabinet ministers refused to serve under Home (Sir Alec Douglas-Home as he became). Supporters of Butler — and of other contenders for the leadership — were unhappy at the way in which the new Prime Minister had been chosen. There was also clear embarrassment in the party at the way in which the Queen had been drawn, without any choice, into the party's difficulties.

The problem was resolved in 1964 when the party accepted a new method of choosing the leader, this time by election by the parliamentary party. Thus, when a party leader retired the choice of a new leader would be made by the party's MPs under an agreed procedure. If the party was in office, that leader could then be summoned to the Palace. The new process ensured that the Queen would no longer face the problem of having to choose from competing candidates.

Potential for political involvement

The monarch is seen not to be engaged in taking partisan decisions by virtue of the fact that her actions are governed by convention and hence predictable; no personal choice is involved. However, a problem arises from the fact that not all the actions that she may be called upon to take are governed by convention. This is most notably the case in respect of the power to appoint a Prime Minister and to dissolve

Parliament. Usually, there is not a problem. If a party is returned at a general election with an overall majority, the Queen by convention summons the leader of that party. However, if a 'hung Parliament' was returned, no one party enjoying an overall majority, and the leader of the largest party in the House accepted the Queen's invitation to form a government, met the House and was defeated on a vote of confidence, would the Queen then be obliged to grant the Prime Minister's request for a dissolution? Or should she summon the leader of the second largest party to see if he or she could command a majority in the House? There is no clear convention to determine the Queen's response and the opinion of constitutional experts on what she should do is divided. Similarly, if a Prime Minister was isolated in Cabinet and requested a dissolution, with the majority of the Cabinet making clear that it was opposed to such a move, would the Queen be obliged to grant her Prime Minister's request? These are instances of problems to which there is no obvious solution and they pose a threat to the value that currently derives from the sovereign being, and being seen to be, 'above politics'. She is dependent upon circumstance and the good sense of politicians (that is, acting to avoid putting her in a situation where she has to act without benefit of convention) to avoid such a situation: when she was drawn into partisan controversy in 1957 and 1963 in the choice of a new Conservative Prime Minister, the obvious embarrassment to the monarchy was such that the Conservative Party subsequently changed its method of selecting a leader. There is always the danger that circumstances may conspire again to make involvement in actual — as opposed to formal — political decision making unavoidable.

Unrepresentative

The monarchy is deemed to be unrepresentative in the second sense of the term; in other words, it is not a freely elected institution. The monarch is also variously criticized for being unrepresentative in the third sense of the term: that is, not socially typical. The monarchy, as we have seen, is a hereditary institution, based on the principle of primogeniture: that is, the Crown passes to the eldest son. By the nature of the position, and what is expected of the monarch, it is of necessity socially atypical. Critics contend that social hierarchy is reinforced by virtue of the monarch's personal wealth. The Queen is believed to be among the world's richest women and may possibly be the richest; though details of her wealth are not made public, *Fortune* magazine in 1987 estimated it to be in the region of £4.5 billion; in 1990 the *Sunday Times* estimated it at £6.7 billion. No tax is paid on this personal fortune. Many of the functions patronized by the Queen and members of the Royal Family, from formal functions to sporting activities, are also criticized for being socially elitist. Those who surround the Royal Family in official positions (the Lord Chamberlain, Ladies-in-Waiting and other senior members of the Royal Household), and those with whom members of the Royal Family choose to surround themselves in positions of friendship, are also notably if not exclusively drawn from a social elite. In the 1950s, Lord Altrincham criticized the Queen's entourage for constituting 'a tight little enclave of British "ladies and gentlemen" ' (Altrincham, 1958, p.115). Various changes were made in the wake of such criticism — the Royal Family became more publicly visible, the presentation of debutantes to the monarch at society balls was abolished — but pressures continue for the institution to be more open in terms of the social background of the Queen's entourage and, indeed, in terms of the activities and background of members of the Royal Family itself. The 1988 Gallup Poll found that 64 per cent of respondents believed that royal children should spend at least part of their education in the state system; 49 per cent believed that the Prince of Wales should have a job and 68 per cent believed other members of the Royal Family should also have one. Various critics, including a substantial number of Labour MPs, have also argued for the Queen's private wealth to be subject to taxation. In 1975, this view influenced many Labour Members who voted against the proposed increase in the Civil List, the money granted by Parliament to the Crown for the expenses incurred in meeting official duties. Among the ninety-one Labour MPs voting against the increase was the then back-bencher Neil Kinnock.

In recent years criticism has come from the radical free market right. One of its aspiring political researchers Brian Oxley typically claims: 'If there is no need for the state to mine coal there is clearly no need for the state to keep palaces. The monarchy should be privatised' (*Sunday Times*, 21 January 1990). The centre right Radical Society — which includes Norman Tebbitt and Lord Chalfont among its members — has also called for the monarchy to adapt 'itself to the democratic instincts of a modern society' (ibid.).

Overly expensive

The expenses met from the Civil List include staff costs, upkeep of royal residences, the cost of functions and of transportation. Provision is also made to meet the cost of public duties undertaken by other members of the Royal Family. (This excludes the Prince of Wales, whose income derives from the Duchy of Cornwall; among other titles, the Prince is Duke of Cornwall and the Duchy includes several income-generating estates.) The expense is criticized because it includes money paid to some members of the Royal Family considered by critics to be peripheral, or 'hangers on', not providing a public service sufficient to justify their inclusion on the Civil List. Of respondents in a 1989 MORI poll asked to identify members of the Royal Family who they thought represented 'the worst value for money to the British taxpayer', 37 per cent said Sarah, Duchess of York; 23 per cent said Andrew, Duke of York; and 14 per cent said Princess Margaret, the Queen's sister. The expense is criticized also because of its sheer size. In the 1980s it ran at about £5 million per year but in July 1990 a new arrangement was made whereby the Queen will receive £7.9 million for each of ten years. When other costs, such as the maintenance of royal castles and the royal yacht *Britannia* and aircraft of the Queen's Flight (the cost being met by Government Departments) are taken into account, the annual upkeep of the monarchy may exceed £20 million. Critics, such as former Labour MP William Hamilton, assert that this is too costly, both in absolute terms and relative to the costs of a presidency, which would entail less ceremony and splendour. They would like to see members of the Royal Family — described by Hamilton in the House of Commons in 1975 as no more 'than glorified civil servants' — either taking up paid posts and receiving no money from the Civil List or being paid on a more modest, and productivity related, basis; and for some expenses of the monarchy to be met from the Queen's personal wealth. A MORI poll in the *Sunday Times* (21 January 1990) revealed that three out of four people questioned believed the Queen 'should pay poll tax like everyone else'; the same proportion believed she should pay income tax; and half those interviewed believed the Royal Family was receiving too much money from the taxpayer.

Unnecessary

Those who criticize the monarchy on grounds of its unrepresentative nature and its cost are not necessarily opposed to the institution of the monarchy itself. A more open and less costly monarchy would be acceptable to various critics. The criticisms levelled by Lord Altrincham in the 1950s, for example, were designed to strengthen the institution. 'It has been suggested that I was attacking the Monarchy, whereas my sole object was to help an institution in which I am a fervent believer' (Altrincham, 1958, p.116). Others, however, take an opposite view. They see the monarchy as an unnecessary institution; the cost and social elitism of the monarchy are seen merely as illustrative of the nature of that institution. The most recent advocates of this view have been Tom Nairn in *The Enchanted Glass — Britain and its Monarchy* (1988) and Edgar Wilson in *The Myth of the British Monarchy* (1989). Wilson contends that the various arguments advanced in favour of the monarchy — its popularity, impartiality, productivity, capacity to unite, to protect the democratic institutions of state, and its ability to generate trade — are all myths, generated in order to justify the existing order. To him and Nairn, the monarchy forms part of a conservative establishment that has little rationale in a democratic society. They, like a number of critics, would prefer to see the monarchy abolished. 'The constitutional case for abolishing the Monarchy is based mainly on the facts that it is arbitrary, unrepresentative, unaccountable, partial, socially divisive, and exercises a pernicious influence and privileged prerogative powers' (Wilson, 1989, p.178). Necessary functions presently fulfilled by the Queen could be equally well fulfilled, so critics contend, by an elected President. Most countries in the world have a non-hereditary head of state. So why not Britain?

How, then, do defenders of the monarchy respond to such criticism? The response may be said to lie essentially in the argument that the Royal Family is cost effective, popular and fulfils functions that could not be carried out by an elected head of state.

The monarchy is considered to be *cost effective* in that the nation derives substantial income (approximately £45 million in 1980) from Crown Lands (surrendered to the state in 1761 in return for an annual income from the Civil List) and that further income derives from intangibles such as tourism and trade generated by royal influence abroad. When these assets are offset against the Civil List, the monarchy is less demanding on the public revenue than critics suppose. The contention that the monarchy is socially elitist is partially acknowledged in that it would be difficult for the sovereign to be anything other than that; the very nature of the job — as with elected or appointed heads of state — imposes such a position. In so far as it can be avoided, the Queen and other members of the Royal Family have moved substantially in the past two decades to be more publicly visible and closer to the people. The Prince of Wales has made a particular point of visiting inner city areas and areas of urban decay; he has been active in promoting the need to improve the environment. Furthermore, the closeness of the monarchy to the people is deemed to be more important than perceptions of elitism. Survey evidence — as in the 1988

The case for abolition of the monarchy: Tom Nairn

(1) The main reason for wanting an end to monarchy in Great Britain is a simple one: to set us free.

Yet to say so still invites derision, because 'freedom' has for so long been the greatest boast of the old British Constitution — the most important of those customary rights all Britishers (or at least, Englishmen) are supposedly born into. 'Our traditional liberties' is the resonant phrase for this: the British way, guaranteed by laws announced in a Queen's Speech and forever defended in her crown courts.

(2) When defenders of the monarchy claim that the Crown holds together this 300-year-old system, they are perfectly right. Equally correctly they say that today — in an age of mass media — the massive popularity of Royalty acts like a cement for that system's foundations. To an astonishing degree the British have built monarchy into their national identity — their sense of 'who they are' and what they stand for as a national community.

Republicans don't dispute these historical facts. Nor are they really very concerned about 'how much it all costs', the garish antics of the younger royals, or the bees in Prince Charles's bonnet. The argument is a deeper one than that.

Wanted: a new Constitution

(3) What they maintain is simply that the British 'freedom' won and maintained in that way was always ambiguous and partial, and has now — in the rapidly changing conditions of the 1980s — become hopelessly and dangerously defective. So dangerous that we urgently need a new constitution, a redesigned political and legal order where our rights are written down (rather than prescribed by tradition or 'convention') and democracy is more secure.

(4) This can be put in another way: people often speak loosely about the United Kingdom as 'a constitutional monarchy' similar to Denmark, Holland or Spain. This is a mistake. What we do have is a **monarchic constitution** which bestows almost absolute authority upon the government (in effect, upon the Prime Minister) of the day — a secretive and mounting power ever less restrained by the old unwritten conventions of 'decency' and 'fair play'.

It was a **comparatively** good political system as long as such customs were upheld by a liberal ruling elite. After all, until the 1950s constitutional democracy remained either insecure or simply unknown in most parts of the world (including Europe), so that our archaic compromises continued to appear quite tolerable, even progressive.

Britain's backwardness

(5) Such circumstances have now completely altered. We no longer have a 'gentlemanly' elite devoted to the old spirit of customary rule. And the rest of the world has moved on — as far as Western Europe is concerned, it has moved far ahead of us politically and we have turned into the recalcitrant, 'backward' member of a union of stable, modernized democracies.

(6) While the required radical reform of the Crown Constitution could (theoretically) be carried out through the existing parliamentary system, leaving monarchy in place as a decoration, in practice that would be difficult. The very popularity of Royalty, its special place 'in our hearts' as the most emotive symbol of our past history, has made it a great psychological obstacle to real change. That's why all radical reformers — both on the left and the right of the party-political spectrum — currently find themselves being pushed towards some kind of republicanism.

Changing the national identity

(7) It is, in fact, the only honest position reformers can now adopt. We need to become a different sort of people: more democratic, more equal, less poisoned by those 'class' distinctions which propped the Old Regime up (and were consecrated by royalty). But this means changing our identity as a nation — the symbol-system and cultural assumptions we employ to stay united. And just because monarchy has been so influential on that level — the national Holy Family which used to make us feel 'like one big family' — it's extremely difficult to develop the new attitudes and customs which a constitutional overhaul requires.

(8) In short: the limited, old-fashioned democracy we had is disintegrating and must be replaced; but this demands a new social culture as well as a proper written constitution; and monarchy was such a central feature of the old British social culture that it is bound to perish with it. Indeed it is already perishing with it — and that's really why it has returned to being a subject for debates like this.

The old outlook: source of our problems

(9) Incidentally, it's also why the heir to the throne, Prince Charles, is trying so hard to restore the old outlook with his speeches and films. But we shouldn't be deceived by that: the old family customs he is so keen to keep going are those out of which all our present problems have sprung. It's useless to try and wriggle back into them when we badly need to make a more decided break with our past and go forward — forward, that is, to the safer, more rational freedom which only our own form of republicanism can secure.

Source: Tom Nairn, *Social Studies Review*, January 1989.

Gallup Poll — reveals a popular perception that the monarchy serves to unite the nation and, more generally, reveals the ***popularity*** of the institution. The Queen is recognized as both popular and hardworking. A Gallup Poll in 1983 found that 93 per cent of respondents thought that the Queen did 'a good job'; only 5 per cent disagreed. There is little support for the abolition of the monarchy. A Gallup Survey in 1973 found that 80 per cent of respondents would prefer to retain a king or queen as head of state, with only 11 per cent indicating a preference for a president. The 1988 Gallup Poll elicited a similar response, 82 per cent of those asked being in favour of the monarchy in its present form. A 1989 MORI poll found a decline in the number of respondents who believed that Britain would be 'worse off' if the monarchy was abolished. However, a majority (58 per cent, down from 77 per cent in 1984) still believed the country would be worse off in such a situation and the proportion who believed Britain would be 'better off' if the monarchy was abolished had increased from only 5 per cent in 1984 to 7 per cent in 1989; the difference was explained by the increase in those believing it would make no difference. However, believing abolition would make no difference is not the same as supporting such a move.

The monarchy is also believed to be ***distinctive*** by virtue of the ***functions*** it is able to fulfil. It is considered doubtful that an appointed or elected head of state would be able to fulfil to the same extent the symbolic role, representing the unity of the nation. For a head of state not involved in the partisan operation of government, it is this role (representative in the fourth sense of the term) that is more important than that of being an elected leader. Indeed, election could jeopardize the head of state's claim to be representative in the first sense of the term (acting on behalf of a particular body or group of individuals). The monarch has a duty to represent all

The Royal Prerogative

The most contentious hangover from the age of absolute monarchy is the Royal Prerogative, surrendered by the Crown in 1688 and given not to Parliament, but to ministers and Whitehall. It has left Parliament weaker than it was before the 'Glorious Revolution' for although monarchs had more power and authority before, they still had to go to Parliament for money for their secret services, for example, or for funds to make war. Professor John Griffith, Emeritus Professor of Public Law at the London School of Economics, has said:

> 'Despite the great constitutional changes that have taken place between the period of the first Elizabeth and today, the struggle is so far from ended that it may be said the executive today has more control over the Commons than Charles I had at any period of his reign.'

Prerogative powers enable the Government to exercise powers — to make war, declare peace, ratify treaties, recognize foreign governments, make appointments, for example — without Parliament having any say. They also enable the Government to bypass Parliament by making 'Orders in Council', a useful device and a reference to the monarch's Privy Council. The hallmark of the Privy Council is secrecy. When its members are briefed by ministers 'on Privy Council terms' it means that they were given 'state secrets' that they must not divulge, especially not to ordinary Members of Parliament. The Privy Councillor's oath, drawn up in about 1250, is the earliest weapon in the Government's formidable armoury defending official secrecy. 'You will,' it states, 'keep secret all Matters committed and revealed unto you.'

In 1867, Walter Bagehot noted that Queen Victoria 'has a hundred (prerogative) powers which waver between reality and desuetude.' He added: 'A secret prerogative is an anomaly — perhaps the greatest of anomalies. That secrecy is however, essential to the utility of English royalty as it now is. Above all things our royalty is to be reverenced, and if you begin to poke about it you cannot reverence it.' Since the present Queen does not have the prerogative powers of her predecessors — and Bagehot was already out of date — we are left with the mystique of secrecy.

Source: Richard Norton Taylor, *The Guardian*, 31 January 1990.

subjects; an elected head may have a bias, subconscious or otherwise, in favour of those who voted for him or her or in favour of those responsible for arranging the nomination. By virtue of being non-partisan, the Queen is able to fulfil the functions deemed important by respondents in the 1988 Gallup Poll in a way that a president could not; by virtue of the aura surrounding the monarchy and the popular attachment to it, the Queen can engage the loyalty of the armed services; by virtue of her longevity in office, she can assist the government in a way not possible by a person appointed or elected for a limited term. Hence, by virtue of these assets particular to the Queen, the monarch is deemed unique and not capable of emulation by an elected or appointed president.

The monarchy remains, as it has been for several centuries, a core institution in the life of the nation. The monarch's transition from directing the affairs of state to a neutral non-executive role has been a gradual and not always smooth one, but a move necessary to justify the monarchy's continuing existence. Transcending partisan activity is a necessary condition for fulfilling the monarch's symbolic ('standing for') role and hence a necessary condition for the strength and continuity of the monarchy. The dedication of the present Queen in fulfilling her duties has served also to elevate the monarchy — in a way not necessarily achieved by all her predecessors — to the position of the country's most popular institution of state.

References and Further Reading

Adams, G.B., *Constitutional History of England* (Jonathan Cape, 1935).

Altrincham, Lord *et al., Is the Monarchy Perfect?* (John Calder, 1958).

Beard, C.A. and Lewis, J.D., 'Representative government in evolution', in J.C. Wahlke and H. Eulau (eds), *Legislative Behaviour: A Reader in Theory and Research* (Free Press, 1959).

Birch, A.H., *Representative and Responsible Government* (Allen & Unwin, 1964).

Cannon, J. and Griffiths, R., *The Oxford Illustrated History of the British Monarchy* (Oxford University Press, 1988).

Crossman, R.H.S., 'Introduction', in W. Bagehot, *The English Constitution* (Fontana, 1963).

Hardie, F., *The Political Influence of the British Monarchy, 1868–1952* (Batsford, 1970).

Hibbert, C., *The Court of St James* (Weidenfeld & Nicolson, 1979).

Keir, D.L., *The Constitutional History of Modern England, 1485–1937* (A & C Black, 1943).

Lacey, R., *Majesty* (Hutchinson, 1977).

Lowell, A.L., *The Government of England*, Vol. II (The Macmillan Co., 1924).

Morton, A., *Theirs is the Kingdom: The Wealth of the Windsors* (Michael O'Hara, 1990).

Nairn, T., *The Enchanted Glass — Britain and its Monarchy* (Century Hutchinson Radius, 1988).

Nairn, T., 'Should Britain abolish its monarchy?' *Social Studies Review* (January 1989).

Norton, P., *The British Polity*, 2nd edition (Longman, 1990).

Pitkin, H.G., *The Concept of Representation* (University of California Press, 1967).

Sedgemore, B., *The Secret Constitution* (Hodder & Stoughton, 1980).

Trevelyan, G.M., *The English Revolution, 1688–9* (Thornton Butterworth, 1938).

White, A.B., *The Making of the English Constitution 1449–1485* (G.P. Putnam, 1989).

Wilson, E., *The Myth of the British Monarchy* (Journeyman/Republic, 1989).

Wiseman, H.V. (ed.), *Parliament and the Executive* (Routledge and Kegan Paul, 1964).

17 Parliament I — The House of Commons

Philip Norton

In the mid-nineteenth century the House of Commons could alter bills, sack ministers and defeat governments. Since then the growth of disciplined parties, pressure groups and a powerful civil service have siphoned away much of its power but it still remains a chamber of considerable potency. Here the executive is challenged regularly, disrespectfully and noisily in a legislative chamber which sits twice as long as any other in the world. Once party leaders lose their grip on party loyalty on any major issue their position is at risk and legislative control over the executive begins to be exerted. No single chapter can fully cover the myriad facets of this great institution: this one concentrates upon parliamentary developments over the last century, current functions performed by the Commons, the legislative process, scrutiny of the executive and recent developments.

Origins of Parliament

Parliament has its origins in the thirteenth century. It was derived not from first principles or some grand constitutional design but from the king's need to raise more money. Its subsequent development may be ascribed to the actions and philosophies of different monarchs, the ambitions and attitudes of its members, external political pressures and prevailing assumptions as to the most appropriate form of government. Its functions and political significance have been moulded, though not in any consistent manner, over several hundred years.

Despite the rich and varied history of the institution, two broad generalizations are possible. The first concerns Parliament's position in relation to the executive. The political culture has, at least since Norman times, favoured a strong executive. Parliament is not, and never has been on any continuous basis, a part of that executive. Though the Glorious Revolution may have confirmed the form of government as that of 'parliamentary government', the phrase meant — and means — government through Parliament and not by Parliament. There have been periods when Parliament has been an important actor in the making of public policy, not least for a period in the nineteenth century, but its essential and historically established position has been that of a reactive, or *policy influencing*, assembly (Mezey, 1979; Norton, 1984); that is, public policy is formulated by the executive and then presented to Parliament for discussion and approval. Parliament has the power to amend or reject that which is placed before it, but it has not the capacity to substitute a policy of its own. Historically, Parliament has looked to the executive to take the initiative in the formulation of public policy; it continues to do so.

The second generalization concerns Parliament's functions. Formally, it retains the functions that it acquired in the first two centuries of its development. Though others have been variously acquired and dispensed with, its original functions form the base of its constitutional significance and underpin the various functions — or tasks — ascribed to the contemporary institution.

Original functions of Parliament

The original functions can be identified as three in number, though their nature and the distinction between them were not necessarily well understood by those responsible for their creative development.

1. *Assenting to supply*. The knights and burgesses were summoned initially to vote taxes. At the time, this was not taken to imply a power to refuse the king the taxes he sought; indeed, they were summoned to confirm assent already given in the localities they came from. Nor was Parliament a body summoned in order to assent to all forms of money raised by the king. Not until a statute of 1341 did the king agree that the people should not 'be from henceforth charged nor grieved to make common aid or to sustain charge' without the assent of Parliament. Henceforth the principle, if not the practice, of parliamentary control of taxation was deemed to have been conceded.

2. *Legislation*. Every citizen had a right to petition the king for a redress of grievances. Parliament presented such petitions and in the fourteenth century it was willing to use its powers over taxation to ensure such petitions were accepted; the granting of supply was delayed until grievances had been redressed. From these petitions there developed measures which had the assent of king, Lords and Commons. These came to be known as statutes and were distinct from ordinances promulgated by the king alone. Gradually, statute law became the most frequent form of law, ordinances declining in number. The fifteenth century witnessed the introduction of bills (draft statutes) introduced to prevent the king interfering with Parliament's will in drawing up statutes in written legal form (the wording, once petitions had been approved, was previously done by judges, subject to royal interference). The king nonetheless retained power to dispense with or suspend statutes. Parliament variously objected to the use of this power. Not until the Bill of Rights of 1689 was it finally dispensed with.

3. *Scrutiny of administrative actions*. As the business of Parliament was to grant money, it was concerned to ensure that the money was collected honestly; it also developed an interest in its expenditure. In 1340, parliamentary commissioners were appointed to audit the accounts of the collectors of recent subsidies. Actions by government affected citizens and where these resulted in abuses Parliament started to take an interest in remedying those abuses. In exercising scrutiny it acquired an important power, that of impeachment for public offences (the Commons voting impeachment and the Lords trying the case); the first occasion

it was employed was in 1376. It was a weapon to be used against public officials. During the fourteenth century, Parliament thus became, in a rather haphazard manner, a body for the critical scrutiny of government,.

The role and functions of the institution were not defined in any single, authoritative document and were not always conceded by the king. Clashes occurred and, as we saw in Chapter 16, not until the Bill of Rights of 1689 was Parliament's place in the polity confirmed. Henceforth, legislative supremacy was enjoyed by the King-in-Parliament (in legal terms the entity that constitutes Parliament), with the courts accepting that no body had authority to set aside Acts of Parliament. Though scholars have argued that the concept of parliamentary sovereignty pre-dated 1689, it has been the central pillar of the Constitution since that time.

Parliament's power as a legitimizing body was assured: its assent was required to legislation and to the raising of supply. However, that assent was usually given. Historically, that had been the case before 1689. It continued to be the case afterwards. In the eighteenth century, Parliament was not assertive, operating largely under the sway of royal patronage. Royal influence was employed, either directly or through the aristocratic patrons of 'rotten boroughs', to ensure the return of a House favourable to the ministry. Only in the nineteenth century did the picture change and even then only for a relatively short period — the so-called 'Golden Age' of Parliament. Pressure from a growing and politically dispossessed non-landed middle class produced parliamentary reform, initially in the form of the Reform Act of 1832. That Act enlarged the electorate by 49 per cent and abolished many, but not all, 'rotten boroughs'. The effect of the measure was to loosen the grip of the aristocracy on the House of Commons; seats could no longer be bought to the same extent as they had before. The size of the electorate was such as to encourage the embryonic development of political organizations, but these organizations were not sufficiently widespread or powerful to make Members of Parliament overly beholden to them. The consequence was to be a House of Commons enjoying a greater degree of political independence than before and, to the extent that it was returned under a new franchise, a greater political legitimacy.

The 'Golden Age' of Parliament and its demise

The consequence of these developments was threefold. First, a ministry no longer fell for want of the confidence of the monarch; the 'elective function', as we have already noted, passed to the House of Commons. Secondly, within Parliament, the superiority of the elected House was established, though not until the 1911 Parliament Act was the House of Lords forced to accept its diminished status. Thirdly, it generated a House of Commons that was willing and able to assert itself in the affairs of government. For a period of about forty years, the House of Commons was to display the characteristics of an active, or policy making, legislature. It could, and did, replace one government with another without suffering a dissolution (as, for example, in 1852, 1855, 1858 and 1866); it could, and did, remove ministers who had erred (Lord John Russell, for instance, in 1855); and legislation was variously amended or rejected. The government was variously forced to divulge information and private Members could and sometimes did initiate measures. The House still looked to the government to govern, but it was prepared to create the conditions under which it did so. Except for the years from 1841 to 1846, party voting was virtually unknown. The period was historically atypical, but it is a period with which subsequent Parliaments — including those in post-war years — have been compared and judged.

The 'Golden Age' was to disappear as a consequence of the effects of the Reform Act of 1867. The measure enlarged the electorate by 88 per cent; in the boroughs the increase was one of 140 per cent. Other measures followed in the 1880s, further enlarging the electorate, creating more equal electoral districts and significantly reducing corrupt practices. Extensive organization was now necessary to reach the new voters. Promises were increasingly necessary to attract the votes of the new electors. For promises made by political parties to be carried out, a cohesive party organization in Parliament was necessary and by the end of the century such cohesion was a feature of parliamentary life.

The effect on Parliament of the rise of a mass electorate was profound. Governments came to be chosen not by the House of Commons but by the electorate. Legislation ceased to be a shared function. Policy making became a function of the Cabinet, a body enjoying majority — and cohesive — support in the House of Commons. By the turn of the century, Parliament lacked both the political will and the resources necessary to subject increasingly extensive and complex government bills to sustained and effective scrutiny. The 'Golden Age' of Parliament was dead. Albeit in a somewhat different form to earlier centuries, executive dominance had returned.

Twentieth-century developments

Government dominance was to be confirmed by the developments of the twentieth century. The electorate was further enlarged, government responsibilities — and consequently powers — increased, policy making began to seep downwards — to civil servants — and outwards, to interest groups. Parliament failed to keep pace with these developments. What changes did take place in Parliament were designed to facilitate government business, not increase the capacity of the institution to scrutinize and influence that business. The use of standing committees became standard in 1907. Private members' time was progressively diminished. Writing shortly after the turn of the century, Josef Redlich was able to assert that in the previous quarter of a century, three tendencies had stood out in bold relief: the strengthening of the disciplinary powers of the Speaker, the continuous extension of the rights of the Government over the direction of all parliamentary action in the House and, lastly, the complete suppression of the private Member. 'Not one of the three is a consequence of any intentional effort; they have all arisen out of the hard necessity of political requirements' (Redlich, 1908, p.206).

What, then, is the position of Parliament in the twentieth century? What functions does it retain? How well has it been able to fulfil them? And to what extent have developments of the past ten to twenty years strengthened or weakened its capacity to fulfil those functions? Given the significant difference between the two Houses, it is appropriate to separate the two in addressing these questions: the rest of this chapter deals with the House of Commons while the House of Lords is addressed in Chapter 18.

The House of Commons

The House of Commons now has 650 Members. The number has varied, ranging in the twentieth century from a high of 707 (1918—22) to a low of 615 (1922—45). The number was reduced in 1922 because of the loss of (most) Irish seats; it has varied in post-war years and from 1955 until 1974 stood at 630; because of the increase in the size of the population, it was increased in 1974 to 635 and in 1983 to 650.

The atmosphere of the House

Anyone entering the gothic splendour of the Houses of Parliament begins to experience its special atmosphere. The Speaker's procession which opens every day's proceedings at 2.25 p.m. (the House only sits in the morning on Fridays) is almost a parody of solemnity. The peculiar archaic forms of address also amuse foreign visitors: MPs must not refer to others by name but as 'honourable members' for the constituencies they represent. But the atmosphere is anything but formal on other occasions. Ministers sometimes lounge on the benches with feet resting on the table in front of the Speaker's Chair. Members do not by convention applaud but they often cheer loudly or wave their order papers: conversely they can heckle relentlessly and when roused make so much noise the Speaker's calls of 'order, order' often resemble the feeble cries of a schoolmaster who has completely lost control of his class.

The former Speaker, George Thomas, defended this behaviour as evidence of the House's life and vigour: a quiet legislature, he suggested, is invariably a lifeless one. Others argue that the noisy barracking of speakers is a necessary test of the person and their arguments: if MPs cannot defend their arguments in the face of such pressure they lack the mettle for higher office. This adversarial atmosphere is enhanced by two factors: the Chamber of the House of Commons is very small — on big occasions MPs crowd onto the benches and many spill over into the galleries — and its rectangular shape encourages confrontation between government and opposition (Figure 17.1). Unlike many legislatures the government of the day is obliged to explain its actions continually and open itself to constant criticism. The US president does not face a critical Congress and can even hide away from the press if he so chooses. The British Prime Minister, however, has to face the Leader of the Opposition twice a week over the Despatch Box. The tension of such occasions and their theatricality imparts a drama to certain debates which compels interest and often gives birth to genuine oratory. British politicians, trained in the House of Commons, are often excellent debators, used to thinking on their feet and experts in the use of wit to decorate their own arguments or demolish those of their opponents.

The special atmosphere of the House is therefore a product of its intimate geography combined with its robust debating traditions. This is what causes new members to quail as they stand to deliver their maiden speeches and which often exerts such an addictive hold upon MPs that election defeat assumes for them the status of tragedy.

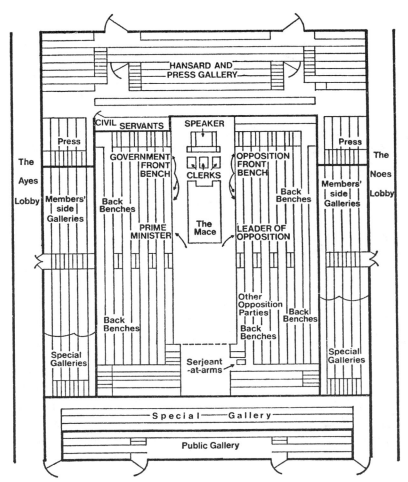

Figure 17.1 *House of Commons seating plan (Source: Padfield, 1972)*

Elections

Members (MPs) are returned for single-member constituencies. These have been the norm since the Reform Act of 1885, though twelve double-member constituencies survived until the General Election of 1950. The method of election employed is the 'first-past-the-post' system with the candidate receiving the largest number of votes being declared the winner. This again has been the norm since 1885 though not until the 1950 General Election (with the abolition of University seats, for which a system of proportional representation was employed) did it become universal. The post-war practice has been for all seats to be contested; in elections before 1945 a significant fraction of Members — an average of 13 per cent — had been returned unopposed. (As late as the 1951 election, four Ulster Unionist MPs were returned unopposed.) Each constituency comprises a defined geographical area and the Member is returned to represent all citizens living within that area. (University seats were exceptional: the constituencies comprised graduates who were geographically scattered.) Constituency boundaries are drawn up and regularly revised by independent Boundary Commissions (one covering each country — England, Scotland, Wales and Northern Ireland); each Commission is chaired by the Speaker of the Commons, with a judge as deputy chairman. Under existing legislation, boundary reviews are required every ten to fifteen years, the last major boundary redistribution taking effect at the General Election of 1983. The maximum life of a Parliament is five years and has been since 1911; between 1715 and 1911 it was seven years and prior to the Septennial Act of 1715 there had been no statutory limit.

Backgrounds of MPs

The Members returned to the House are generally male, middle class and white. These characteristics have been marked throughout the twentieth century, with only slight variations. The middle-class nature of the House has, in fact, become somewhat more pronounced in post-war years. Before 1945, and especially in the early years of the century, the Conservative ranks contained a significant proportion of upper and upper-middle class men of private means, while the Parliamentary Labour Party (PLP) was notable for the number of Members from manual backgrounds; they comprised a little over half of the PLP from 1922 to 1935 and before then had been in the overwhelming majority (Rush, 1979, pp.69−123). Since 1945, the number of businessmen on the Conservative benches has increased, as has the number of graduates, often journalists and lecturers, on the Labour benches (Mellors, 1978).

Table 17.1(a−d) is drawn from work by Burch and Moran in 1985 and provides interesting perspectives on shifts in the social composition of MPs by party since the War. Table 17.1a reveals the stability of the social backgrounds of Conservative MPs until 1974: the public school educated proportion averaged about 70 per cent, while Oxbridge graduates averaged just over 50 per cent. Some small declines are noticeable in old Etonians and increases in state educated and red-brick university educated MPs, together with a marked increase in MPs with local government experience. Figures for 1979 and 1983, however, in Table 17.1b display quite marked discontinuities among new MPs: much lower percentages from Eton, other public schools and Oxbridge, with much higher percentages from red-brick universities and people with local government experience. Data for Labour in Table 17.1c reveal a decline in MPs with working-class backgrounds from 27.6 per cent in 1945 to 15.3 per cent in 1983 — though rising to 20 per cent among new MPs in 1979 and 1983. Those with public school backgrounds, apart from a dip in the 1970s, have averaged around 20 per cent; the Oxbridge figure has remained stable in the higher teens; state school/non-Oxbridge figures have increased markedly from the higher teens in 1945 to almost 40 per cent in the 1980s; the percentage of teachers and lecturers has increased too, though declined among recent new entrants. As with Conservative MPs the proportion of Labour MPs with local government experience has increased steadily since the war and markedly among new entrants. The background and education of MPs returned in 1987 is given in Tables 17.2 and 17.3.

Women only became eligible to sit in the House in 1918. The number elected

Table 17.1(a) *Background of all Conservative MPs, 1945–83 (%)*

	1945	1950	1951	1955	1959	1964	1966	1970	Feb. 1974	Oct. 1974	1979	1983
All public schools	83.2	83.1	70.2	79.7	75.8	77.9	78.9	74.2	75.0	74.6	73.0	64.1
Eton	27.1	26.7	23.7	23.1	19.4	22.2	21.8	19.0	18.2	17.0	15.0	12.4
Oxbridge	53.3	54.0	54.3	53.7	50.6	54.3	57.1	51.3	55.7	55.1	49.2	45.7
Public/Oxbridge	50.3	51.9	51.0	51.3	46.5	49.3	51.6	44.7	48.3	47.5	37.4	37.1
Elem/sec only	3.7	5.3	6.4	7.2	7.9	8.2	5.1	7.5	7.7	7.2	8.2	8.8
State sec/univ	7.0	6.0	6.8	6.6	8.2	7.8	9.0	10.0	11.4	11.9	16.2	17.9
All universities	64.7	64.7	64.6	65.9	60.7	63.8	67.0	63.5	66.9	67.4	68.0	71.7
Local government	14.1	16.8	16.6	20.7	25.5	27.2	28.9	30.4	32.0	31.0	35.0	38.1
Numbers	213	298	321	344	365	304	253	330	297	277	339	396

(b) *Background of new Conservative MPs, 1945–83 (%)*

	1945	1950	1951	1955	1959	1964	1966	1970	Feb. 1974	Oct. 1974	1979	1983
All public schools	81.2	76.5	68.7	70.5	73.1	82.9	84.5	67.0	85.6	87.5	53.2	47.0
Eton	26.1	21.4	25.0	20.5	16.3	21.9	15.4	12.1	14.5	—	13.2	6.0
Oxbridge	42.1	46.9	53.1	50.0	45.2	56.3	46.1	40.7	59.7	62.5	36.0	35.0
Public/Oxbridge	43.5	44.9	43.8	47.4	39.4	50.0	46.1	34.1	53.2	62.5	30.4	25.0
Elem/sec only	6.9	9.8	11.7	10.3	5.7	3.1	7.6	11.1	1.6	12.5	16.0	12.0
State sec/univ	2.7	8.8	11.7	7.7	9.6	9.3	—	13.3	11.2	—	22.6	30.0
All universities	50.8	61.3	56.3	66.3	53.8	70.4	62.0	57.2	72.6	75.0	73.2	72.0
Local government	10.8	22.5	22.1	35.9	36.5	34.4	38.7	32.5	27.4	25.0	41.2	52.0
Numbers	72	102	34	77	104	64	13	90	62	8	75	100

(c) *Background of all Labour MPs 1945–83 (%)*

	1945	1950	1951	1955	1959	1964	1966	1970	Feb. 1974	Oct. 1974	1979	1983
All public schools	19.4	22.2	23.4	23.5	24.6	24.0	22.8	19.4	15.7	16.4	17.0	13.4
Oxbridge	14.5	15.4	16.8	16.4	17.2	17.7	19.3	20.4	19.3	20.8	20.4	14.4
Public/Oxbridge	10.4	14.5	13.7	13.1	12.9	12.9	12.7	12.8	9.7	10.4	11.2	9.1
State sec/univ	18.7	18.6	18.8	18.6	20.3	24.6	29.8	35.0	39.0	40.3	37.1	38.2
Elem/sec. only	52.4	49.2	36.9	59.9	47.2	39.4	35.5	31.0	26.5	24.4	28.9	21.5
All universities	34.2	37.7	38.7	38.2	39.5	43.9	48.5	51.2	53.0	55.7	57.0	54.1
Manual workers	27.6	27.6	26.2	25.3	21.1	18.4	16.6	13.2	12.3	12.0	19.8	15.3
Teachers/lecturers	12.1	13.9	14.8	14.3	14.9	16.5	20.1	20.9	25.8	28.1	24.2	25.8
Local government	43.5	41.4	40.8	40.8	39.3	42.9	43.7	41.3	46.6	46.4	37.6	47.8
Numbers	393	315	295	277	258	317	363	287	301	319	269	209

(d) *Background of new Labour MPs 1945–83 (%)*

	1945	1950	1951	1955	1959	1964	1966	1970	Feb. 1974	Oct. 1974	1979	1983
All public schools	21.5	27.4	13.3	15.4	11.9	19.8	15.3	12.5	6.5	18.2	18.0	22.5
Oxbridge	17.7	19.4	13.3	7.7	4.8	17.9	23.6	18.8	15.2	22.7	5.0	11.8
Public/Oxbridge	12.2	16.1	6.7	7.7	2.4	11.3	8.3	9.4	6.5	9.1	2.5	11.8
State sec./univ.	19.4	19.4	26.7	26.9	26.2	29.2	48.6	43.7	41.3	50.0	52.5	38.2
Elem./sec.	51.9	38.7	46.6	50.0	59.5	32.3	22.2	23.4	26.0	13.6	40.0	20.6
All universities	37.6	43.6	40.0	34.6	31.0	45.3	63.9	56.2	47.8	72.2	52.2	55.9
Manual workers	19.7	17.6	20.0	19.2	23.8	18.9	12.5	6.2	19.6	4.6	20.0	20.6
Teachers/lecturers	13.3	17.7	20.0	23.1	9.5	18.9	34.7	29.7	19.9	50.0	15.0	17.6
Local government	42.2	45.2	40.0	53.0	54.7	51.9	43.1	39.1	56.5	45.4	62.5	64.7
Numbers	227	62	15	24	42	105	72	64	46	22	40	34

Source: Burch and Moran, 1985

Table 17.2 *Background of MPs 1987*
(a) *Occupations of MPs elected in 1987*

Occupation	Conservative (%)	Labour (%)	Alliance (%)	Other (%)	Total (%)
Professions	33.3 (125)	41.0 (94)	12	13	37.5 (244)
Business	51.5 (193)	4.8 (11)	5	9	33.5 (218)
Workers	0.8 (3)	29.7 (68)	—	2	11.2 (73)
Miscellaneous	14.4 (54)	24.5 (56)	5	—	17.7 (115)
Total	100.0 (375)	100.0 (229)	22	24	99.9 (650)

Definitions: Professions: lawyers, doctors, dentists, school, university, and adult education teachers, retired officers of the regular forces, and all recognized professions
Business: all employers, directors of public and private companies, business executives, stockbrokers, farmers and landowners, and small businessmen
Workers: self-explanatory, but including all employed manual and non-manual (or 'white-collar') workers and full-time trade-union officials
Miscellaneous: housewives, professional politicians, welfare workers, journalists, professional party organizers, and miscellaneous administrators

(b) *Analysis of the occupations of MPs elected in 1987 according to the Hall-Jones scale of occupational prestige*

Class	Conservative (%)	Labour (%)	Alliance (%)	Other (%)	Total (%)
Class 1	40.5 (152)	24.0 (55)	12	7	34.8 (226)
Class 2	44.5 (167)	31.9 (73)	5	12	39.5 (257)
Class 3	12.8 (48)	17.0 (39)	3	3	14.3 (93)
Class 4	1.9 (7)	5.7 (13)	2	—	3.4 (22)
Class 5a	—	3.5 (8)	—	—	1.2 (8)
Class 5b	0.3 (1)	10.9 (25)	—	1	4.2 (27)
Class 6	—	7.0 (16)	—	—	2.5 (16)
Class 7	—	—	—	1	0.1 (1)
Total	100.0 (375)	100.0 (229)	22	24	100.0 (650)

Notes: Short definitions of the classes on the scale are as follows:
Class 1: professionally-qualified and high administrative
Class 2: managerial and executive (with some responsibility for directing and initiating policy)
Class 3: inspectional, supervisory and other non-manual (higher grade)
Class 4: inspectional, supervisory and other non-manual (lower grade)
Class 5a: routine grades of non-manual work
Class 5b: routine grades of non-manual work
Class 6: manual, semi-skilled
Class 7: manual, routine

Source: Rush, in Ryle and Richards, 1988

since then has been small: indeed, the total number to sit in the House between 1918 and 1974 was only 112 (including Countess Markievicz, the first women elected but who did not take her seat). At the General Election of 1983, twenty-three women MPs were returned; in 1987 the figure was forty-one, the highest number to be returned at a single election (Table 17.4). Table 17.5 reveals that Britain lags behind most developed countries in terms of female representation. The number of non-white MPs has been miniscule: though one or two MPs of Indian origin were elected to pre-war parliaments, no MP of Afro-Asian origin had ever been returned prior

Table 17.3 *Education of Labour and Conservative MPs 1987*

	Labour (%)		Conservative (%)	
School				
Eton	2	1	43	11
All public schools	32	14	256	68
State secondary school	197	86	120	32
University				
Oxford and Cambridge	34	15	166	44
Other	95	41	97	26
All universities	129	56	263	70

Source: Adonis, 1990, p.40

Table 17.4 *Women candidates and MPs in the 1987 election*

Party	Candidates won (%)			MPs won (%)			Success rate (%)	
		Men	Women		Men	Women	Men	Women
Con.	633	46	7	375	17	5	61	37
Lab.	633	92	15	229	21	9	38	23
Lib.	327	45	14	17	1	6	6	2
SDP	306	60	20	5	1	20	2	2
Other	426	84	20	24	1	4	7	1
Total	2,325	327	14	650	41	6	31	13

Source: Adonis, 1990, p.40

to 1987. In the 1987 election, four non-white MPs were elected, all four sitting on the Labour benches.

Sittings of the House

The House to which the Members are returned meets annually, each parliamentary session running usually from October to October (or early November). There is a long summer adjournment, but the session is not prorogued (ended) until shortly after the House returns in the autumn; that allows the House to meet and transact any urgent business should the need arise during the summer, something which it could not do if it had been prorogued. The effect of prorogation is to kill off all unfinished public business; any bills which have not received the Royal Assent have to be reintroduced and go through all their stages again in the new session.

The House usually sits for more than 150 days a year, a not unusual number compared with other legislatures such as those of the USA, Canada and France (though considerably more than, say the legislatures of Germany and Australia). What makes it distinctive is the number of hours for which it sits: on average, more than 1,500 hours a year (see Table 17.6), many more than any of the other legislatures mentioned. (The House meets from 2.30 p.m. until at least 10.30 p.m. Mondays to Thursdays and from 9.30 a.m. to 3.00 p.m. on Fridays.) Relative to members

Table 17.5   *Percentage of women MPs in selected countries in 1975 and 1985*

	1975	1985
United Kingdom	4.2	3.8 (6.3 in 1987)
Council of European Countries	7.0	11.5
France	1.8	4.3
West Germany	5.8	9.8
Italy	2.8	6.7
Australia	3.1	10.2
Canada	3.3	9.8
India	5.1	8.7
New Zealand	4.6	12.6
USA	3.3	4.5
Albania	33.2	30.4
Bulgaria	18.7	21.7
China	22.6	21.2
Czechoslovakia	25.5	28.3
East Germany	31.8	32.4
Hungary	28.7	23.3
Poland	15.8	23.0
Romania	15.2	34.4
USSR	31.3	32.8
Denmark	15.6	25.7
Finland	23.0	30.5
Iceland	5.0	15.0
Norway	15.5	23.0
Sweden	21.4	28.9

Source: Kennon, 1987

Table 17.6   *The House of Commons: length of sittings 1984–8*

Session	Number of sitting days	Number of hours sat	Average length of sitting day
1984–5	172	1,566	9 h 6 min
1985–6	172	1,536	8 h 57 min
1986–7*	109	930	8 h 32 min
1987–8*	218	1,978	9 h 0 min

* The 1987 General Election resulted in the 1986–7 session being a short one and the subsequent session of 1987–8 a long one

Source: HMSO, pp.1–2

of other Western legislatures, MPs are modestly paid (an annual salary of £26,701 from 1 January 1990 with a secretarial and research allowance of £20,140). Legislators in comparable institutions enjoy a far better package of pay, allowances, research facilities and pensions. They also have fewer constituents to represent: that is, there are more legislators per capita. The result, as Austin Mitchell observed, is that 'British MPs get less money for more work and greater responsibility than in any comparable system' (Mitchell, 1982, p.19).

Functions

The essential functions, or tasks, of the House have been subject to modification over the centuries but those it retains can mostly be seen to have their origins in the first two centuries of parliamentary development. There are three principal functions: those of legitimization, debate, and scrutiny. A number of other functions may also now be identified. One — the provision of the personnel of government — has been acquired by virtue of the need of the executive to enjoy the confidence of the House; the others have in effect flowed from the existing functions.

Legitimization

The primary purpose for which the representatives of the **communes** were summoned was to assent to the king's demand for additional aids. Subsequently, as we have seen, its assent also came to be necessary for legislation. It has thus been, since its inception, a legitimizing body. Indeed, it now fulfils three forms of legitimizaton. It fulfils what Packenham has termed the function of 'latent legitimization'; this derives from the fact that 'simply by meeting regularly and uninterruptedly, the legislature produces, among the relevant populace and elites, a wider and deeper sense of the government's moral right to rule than would otherwise have obtained' (Packenham, 1970, pp.527—8). Given that Parliament not only sits regularly and without interruption but has done so since the seventeenth century, it is arguably a much stronger agent of latent legitimization than many other legislatures; it would seem plausible to hypothesize that the function is weaker in a political system in which the legislature is a recent and conscious creation of resuscitation by the prevailing regime. In Britain, legitimization may also be considered to be reinforced by the fact that government is derived from, and governs through, Parliament — Ministers remaining and fulfilling functions as Members of Parliament.

The House also fulfils the task of manifest legitimization, that is the overt, conscious giving of assent. This encompasses not only the giving of assent to measures introduced by government but also (the third form of legitimization) to the government itself: government by convention depends for its continuance in office upon the confidence of the House of Commons. Assent is given by vote: for the assent of the House to be given, a simple majority is all that is necessary. (That is subject to forty Members — a quorum of the House — being shown by the division to be present and to one hundred Members having voted in favour in the case of closure motions.) It is this accepted need for assent that constitutes the basic power of the House in relation to government. Initially, the knights and burgesses summoned to the king's court, the **curia**, were called to give assent, with no recognition of any capacity to deny that assent; gradually members came to realize they could, as a body, deny assent both to supply and later to legislation. This formed the basis on which they could ensure the effective fulfilment of other functions. It remains the basis of the power of the Commons. The contemporary point of contention is the extent to which it is prepared to use it: critics contend that the effect of the growth of party and hence party cohesion has largely nullified the capacity of the House to employ it.

Scrutiny and influence

Though called initially to assent to the king's demands, knights and burgesses were later summoned to confer with the nobles and prelates concerning the affairs of the kingdom. Members, as already noted, increasingly began to give voice to the grievances of citizens, delaying the granting of supply until grievances were redressed. In order to ensure that money was expended properly it also began to undertake some measure of administrative oversight. Hence, there developed what may be termed a scrutinizing role for the House, scrutiny that was undertaken on the Floor of the House or in committee; at various times, committees of enquiry were frequently utilized. Scrutiny was not undertaken for its own sake. If problems were identified, the government was expected to attend to them; committees would often make specific recommendations. Hence, the House came to exercise what has been characterized as a function of scrutiny and influence (Norton, 1981, pp.69–74).

This function is fulfilled at two levels: at what may be termed the general, or policy, level and at the specific level. The former encompasses scrutiny of the merits of government policy and its legislative proposals. The latter, specific scrutiny, encompasses scrutiny of the effects of policy, undertaken on behalf of particular interests, primarily constituencies and constituents. The general scrutiny is now largely undertaken via the medium of party, the Opposition utilizing the opportunities available to it to ensure that the government is publicly subject to its scrutiny. The specific representation is undertaken by Members occasionally acting in concert but more often than not operating separately as constituency Members.

This function — of scrutiny and influence — may be deemed to be the one most central to the activities of the House. It is the function that absorbs most of the time of the House. (Giving legitimization in manifest form — that is, voting — takes a relatively small amount of time; latent legitimization is essentially a passive function.) It is also the most contentious. Critics contend that the stranglehold of party prevents the House from fulfilling it adequately. Through its party majority, the Government ensures that its measures are carried; it also uses that majority to ensure that the House is denied adequate facilities to undertake sustained and effective scrutiny. The concentration on the general level of scrutiny — the House being dominated by the partisan clash between Government and Opposition — serves also to squeeze out and limit the opportunities for Members to undertake the task of specific scrutiny on behalf of their constituents.

The results of a survey, reported in early 1990, provide interesting evidence of the similarities and differences between issues on which MPs receive representations from the public and the views of MPs themselves (see Table 17.7).

'Tension release'

By engaging in debate and scrutiny, the House is in a position to fulfil what Bagehot referred to as the 'expressive' function and what today is termed tension release: that is, allowing the views and especially the worries of citizens to be expressed. In regimes where no representative assembly exists (that is, where there is no assembly at all or one where members are unwilling or unable to speak and act on behalf of citizens) the only recourse citizens have to express any significant political dissent is by taking to the streets; in Britain, such dissent is partially expressed through

Table 17.7 *MPs' opinions and those in their postbags*

Issue	MPs' views[a] (%)	MPs' postbag/ other approaches[b] (%)
National Health Service	41	68
Inflation	40	2
Law and order	33	12
Interest rates	30	5
Britain's competitiveness	29	0
Housing	23	46
Unemployment	18	6
The environment	17	12
Poll tax/rates	17	16
Pollution	14	3
Public transport	12	6
Education	11	8
Social security	10	35
Pensions	4	14
Animal testing	2	20
Sunday shop opening	2	10

Notes: (a) The question was: 'Could you please look at this list and tell me the three or four you think are the biggest problems in Britain today?'; consequently, MPs could choose three or four answers. (b) The question was: 'Which of these subjects do you receive most letters about in your postbag, or receive most approach from individuals in surgeries or other ways?'; MPs could select more than one topic.

Source: MORI poll, April–June 1989; a random sample of 202 MPs was approached of whom 125 were interviewed. Taken from *Social Studies Review*, September 1990.

the medium of Members of Parliament. This function can be fulfilled both at the level of the individual citizen, hence the relevance of the MP as constituency Member, and at the level of particular groups in society (Table 17.4a). This shades into the functions of both conflict resolution and integration. By allowing the views of competing groups to be expressed, the House offers an opportunity for conflict to be resolved, or at least for its sharp edges to be softened. By allowing different groups to be represented and to speak, it may enable disaffected groups to be integrated in the polity. This has as a prior condition the return of MPs from, or willing to speak on behalf of, these groups. As a means of facilitating the integration of the Scots and the Welsh into the British polity, they are provided with a disproportionate number of seats in the House (that is, more than the population of Scotland and Wales would strictly justify); the return of four black MPs in the 1987 general election was also seen as serving a valuable integrative role, the MPs enhancing that role by their activities in the House.

Critics maintain nonetheless that the House fails badly in fulfilling these integrative tasks. The dominance of party in the House results in an adversary relationship between the two main parties, debate focusing upon the issues which divide them and which they consider to be politically salient; fundamental issues in British society, to which the parties have no answers, tend to be shoved to one side and ignored. The ability of the House to help integrate different groups is also limited by the mode of election, members of a group who are not geographically concentrated having little chance of being able to get elected a supporter of their cause.

'Support mobilization'

This function has been identified by Samuel Beer (1966, pp.30–48) and involves the raising of public support for the specific programmes formulated by government in between elections. It is arguably a particularly important function at times of economic crisis when government has difficulty in raising resources to meet commitments of public policy. Where the government is able to pursue a distributive policy (everyone getting a share of the economic pie) it has little difficulty in mobilizing support for its policy. Where it has to pursue a redistributive policy (taking part of the economic pie from one group to give to another) it has difficulty in mobilizing support. By meeting and debating in open session, it can be contended that the House can help increase public awareness of government policy. However, its capacity to mobilize support is extremely limited. Because of the dominance of the executive in policy making, Parliament is viewed — and treated — as marginal; hence the attention it receives by the press and broadcast media has been limited. Government tends to be secretive and for most of the twentieth century has taken its parliamentary support for granted. It has been unwilling to allow the House to equip itself with the procedures that would allow it to inform itself more thoroughly of government policies and by so doing create the potential for fulfilling a support mobilization role. Government, ironically, has thus allowed itself to be hoisted by its own petard. Only in recent years, as we shall see, has the House itself acted to give itself a greater capacity for scrutiny and, potentially, for mobilizing support for particular measures of public policy.

Providing the personnel of government

The last but by no means least function can be identified as that of providing the personnel of government. This, as we have seen, has arisen from the changes in the nature of the political system and the relationship between the House and the executive. By convention, ministers are now drawn from Parliament and, by convention, predominantly from the House of Commons. (It has been accepted as a convention since 1922 that the Prime Minister must be in the Lower House.) By virtue of the convention of individual ministerial responsibility, each minister is answerable to the House for his or her actions and departmental policy; by the convention of collective ministerial responsibility, the Cabinet is answerable to the House for government policy as a whole.

The convention that ministers be drawn from and remain within Parliament is a strong one inasmuch as virtually all ministers are MPs or peers. It is extremely rare for a minister to be appointed who is not in either House; it is even more rare for that person to then remain outside Parliament. What has usually happened when a minister has been appointed who is not in either House is for that person then to be ennobled or else found a safe seat. (Occasionally things go wrong. In 1964 Labour politician Patrick Gordon Walker lost his seat, but was nonetheless appointed Foreign Secretary; he was then found a seat to fight at a by-election — he lost that too and so resigned.) Occasionally, one of the Scottish law officers serves in neither House (in 1987, for example, the Solicitor General for Scotland, Peter Fraser, lost his seat in the Commons but was nonetheless appointed by the Prime Minister to continue in the post); it is, though, the exception which tends to prove the rule.

Having ministers as Members of the House obviously facilitates the House in fulfilling the function of scrutiny and influence. However, providing the personnel of government may be described as a limited and in some respects a passive function. The House provides an arena in which potential ministers may make their mark but the Prime Minister operates under certain political and practical limitations in the choice of ministers: being an MP or peer is merely a starting point for consideration and, in any event, the House does not create the pool itself — that is done by the party selection committees and the electorate. The presence of ministers in the House, along with their unpaid parliamentary private secretaries, also provides the government with a minimum vote in the division lobbies — the so-called 'payroll vote' — of at least one hundred. It has also been argued that, as ministers are drawn from the House, back-benchers keen for promotion to ministerial office are thus encouraged not to disagree too frequently or too vocally with government policy.

These are the most important functions that may be ascribed to the House of Commons. The list is not an exhaustive one. Other relatively minor tasks may also be ascribed to the House. These include a disciplinary role (punishing breaches of privilege and contempt) and a small quasi-judicial role, primarily in the treatment of Private legislation (legislation affecting private interests and not to be confused with Private Members' legislation). Two other major functions it has effectively lost. One is the 'elective' function — that is, choosing the government — which, as we have seen, it held briefly only for part of the nineteenth century; previously it resided with the monarch, now it rests with the electorate. (Through a vote of no confidence the House can still turn a government out, but it cannot choose its successor.) The other one is that of legislation. Initially, the need for the House to assent to legislation was transformed by Members into the power to initiate measures; this, as we have seen, was done through presenting petitions and later through the introduction of bills. This initiating power was especially important during the 'Golden Age' of Parliament. Today it remains only in very limited form, confined to Private Members' bills for which there is usually time in any one session to discuss a very small number.

The functions that the House retains can be described as modest, but appropriate to a reactive legislature. They are largely consistent with the functions fulfilled by the House since the fourteenth or fifteenth centuries. They have been modified over time but are still largely recognizable. The question then arises as to how well the contemporary House fulfils them. Can it scrutinize and influence government and, consequently, fulfil the other system maintenance functions ascribed to it? Or is it, as some critics maintain, a largely malfunctional or dysfunctional body in need of reform?

Traditional means of scrutiny and influence

The scrutiny of government undertaken by the House can be divided into that of legislative scrutiny and that of the scrutiny of executive actions. Legislative scrutiny is undertaken by a well established process involving debate and consideration in committee. Scrutiny of executive actions is undertaken by debate on the floor of the House, Questions, and increasingly by committee. Both forms of scrutiny are supplemented by official and unofficial channels available off the floor of the House.

Legislative scrutiny

When a Bill is introduced it has to go through three 'readings' plus a committee and report stage (see Table 17.8). ***The First Reading*** is the formal introduction. ***The Second Reading*** constitutes a debate on the principle of the measure. Most Government Bills will be allocated a half or a full day's debate for Second Reading. The debate itself follows a standard pattern: the minister responsible for the Bill opens the debate, his opposite number on the Opposition Front Bench responds, back-benchers from alternate sides of the House are then called (usually including a spokesman from one of the minor parties in the House) and then an Opposition Front Bench spokesman and another minister wind up the debate; if the Bill is contested, a vote ensues. Debates are usually though not always predictable, usually in content and almost always in outcome: only three times this century, for example, has a government lost a vote on Second Reading (in 1924, 1977 and 1986). Speeches on occasion may influence votes, even whole debates, but they are exceptional. Once approved in principle, a Bill is then committed to a ***committee*** for detailed scrutiny.

Some Bills, because of their constitutional significance or because of the need to pass them quickly, will have their committee stage on the Floor of the House. The majority will be sent instead to standing committees, the standard practice since 1907. The name 'standing committee' is a misnomer: the committees do not have a permanent, or standing, membership. They are appointed afresh for each bill and are identified by letters of the alphabet: Standing Committee A, Standing Committee

Table 17.8 *Legislative stages in the House of Commons*

Stage	Where taken	Comments
First reading	On floor of the House	Formal introduction only. No debate
Second Reading	On floor of the House (non-contentious Bills may be referred to a Second Reading Committee)	Debate on the principle of the measure
(Money resolution)	(On floor of the House)	
Committee	Standing Committee (constitutional and certain other measures may be taken in Committee of the Whole House)	Considered clause by clause. Amendments can be made
Report	On floor of the House (no Report stage if Bill reported unamended from Committee of the Whole House)	Reported to the House by the Committee. Amendments can be made
Third Reading	On floor of House	Final approval of the Bill. Debate confined to its content
Lords amendments	On floor of the House	Any amendments made by the House of Lords considered, usually on motion to agree or disagree with them

**The
Exceptional
Debates**

'In this House I have heard many a speech that has moved men to tears — but never one that has turned a vote': **Cobden**.

Speeches very rarely influence how MPs vote in the House of Commons. In the 1950s and 1960s — and into the 1970s — MPs would often go into the chamber to listen to particular speakers, especially Labour MP Michael Foot and Conservative (later Ulster Unionist) MP Enoch Powell, but they went to listen and be impressed, not to be persuaded of how to vote. Ironically, in the 1970s independence in voting increased as MPs complained both of a decline in oratory and of attendance in the chamber.

Occasions when MPs have been influenced by what has been said in a debate are thus exceptional; occasions when this has affected the outcome of a vote even rarer. In the second Reading debate on the European Communities Bill in 1972, some Conservative waverers were prepared to listen to the debate before finally casting their votes. The Government survived with a majority of only eight after fifteen Conservatives voted with the Opposition; other potential dissenters were persuaded to vote with the Government after a partisan speech by the Leader of the Opposition.

Occasions when the outcome of a debate *has* been influenced by what has been said during debate include the following:

1. **The Immigration rules 1972**. Many Conservative MPs were opposed to the immigration rules introduced by the government, contending that they gave preferential treatment to EC citizens over Commonwealth subjects. The speeches of the Home and Foreign Secretaries were designed to win over the doubters. Several Conservative MPs spoke against the rules 'and it was clear from their speeches that unless the Foreign Secretary was to announce some new concession, or provide some assurances of substance, they would be unable to support the Government in the Lobby' (Norton, 1976, p.410). The Foreign Secretary failed to satisfy them. Seven Conservatives voted against the Government, a further forty-nine abstained from voting. The Government was defeated by thirty-five votes.

2. **The Shops Bill 1986.** Many Conservatives were opposed to the Bill which was designed to liberalize the laws on Sunday trading. However, it was expected to receive a Second Reading on 14 April 1986. No Government with an overall majority had lost a Second Reading vote in the twentieth century. The debate, though, went badly for the Government and the speeches of ministers appeared to have the opposite effect to that intended. A promise by the Home Secretary not to try to guillotine (time-limit) the Bill at any stage encouraged waverers to actually vote against the Bill. 'They realised that, with no time limit, the committee stage of the bill would be long and painful and that only if the bill was not given a second reading would they be spared a "long hot summer of Parliamentary activity"' (Regan, 1988, p.230). Seventy-two Conservatives voted against the Bill and the Second Reading defeated by 296 votes to 282.

   Such occasions are infrequent but help maintain the relevance of the Floor of the House.

B and so on. One committee will normally deal with Private Members' Bills, the rest with government bills. Each committee comprises between sixteen and fifty members, reflecting proportionally party strength in the House as a whole. The purpose of committee scrutiny is to render a Bill more 'generally acceptable' through scrutinizing it and, if necessary, amending it (without rejecting it or running counter to the principle approved on Second Reading). Each Bill is considered clause by clause, the committee discussing any amendments tabled to a clause before discussing the motion 'that the clause stand part of the Bill'.

Committee stage constitutes one of the most criticized stages of the legislative process. Discussion in committee tends to follow the adversary lines adopted in the Second Reading debate and a Government whip is appointed as a member and ensures that government-tabled amendments, or those supported by the government, are carried and all others are defeated; occasional cross-voting produces a different result to that intended by the government, but usually the outcome is predictable. To encourage the swift passage of measures, government supporters are encouraged to say as little as possible. (If committee stage drags on, the government may resort to introducing a guillotine, that is, a timetable motion.) Consequently, service on committees is not particularly popular. Various reforms have been proposed. In 1980 the House approved the referral of certain Bills to special standing committees with power to interview witnesses prior to commencing detailed scrutiny; such committees have proved useful when used, but have been rarely employed. Other schemes of reform, including automatic timetabling of controversial Bills, have not been implemented.

After committee stage, a Bill returns to the House for *report stage*. This provides an opportunity for the House to decide whether it wishes to make any further amendments and is often used by the government to introduce changes promised during committee. (There is, though, no report stage if a bill has had its committee stage on the Floor of the House and not been amended.) This is then followed by the Bill's *Third Reading*, when the House gives its final approval to the measure. In 1967 a procedure was introduced whereby the Third Reading was taken formally unless six Members tabled a motion to force a debate; on most Bills such motions were tabled and so after nearly twenty years the procedure was abandoned and all Third Reading motions are now debatable.

After Third Reading a Bill is sent to the Lords and, if the Upper House makes any amendments, it then returns and the House debates *the Lords' amendments*. In most cases, such amendments are accepted; if the House refuses to accept them, the Lords usually gives way. Once both Houses have agreed the Bill, it receives the Royal Assent.

All Bills, with certain exceptions, go through this procedure. There are some variations: some uncontentious Bills, for example, can be sent to a Second Reading Committee, thus avoiding taking up valuable debating time on the Floor of the House; Private Members' Bills are also treated somewhat differently to government Bills, especially in terms of timetabling. It does not, though, constitute the only form of legislative scrutiny. Bills will often contain powers for regulations to be made under authority of the measure once enacted. This delegated legislation may be made subject to approval by the House, it may be required solely to be laid before the House with no action necessary, or it may not have to be laid at all. Given the growth of

Private Members legislation

The Case of Alf Morris, MP and his Chronically Sick and Disabled Persons Act 1970.

Timetable of Events

1.	6 November 1969	Alf Morris comes first in ballot for Private Members' Bills which are debated on twenty Fridays during the parliamentary session. 450 organizations immediately make proposals to him but he decides to help the disabled.
2.	First week of December 1969	The Bill receives its first and second readings.
3.	Third week in December	The Bill negotiates committee stage. Alf has to do his own drafting of clauses but receives voluntary help from Sir John Fiennes, the First Parliamentary Counsel, in this complex task.
4.	February 1970	Treasury support is crucially obtained and a Money Resolution passed in support of the Bill.
5.	May 1970	The Bill passes through the House of Lords. On 29 May the Chronically Sick and Disabled Persons Bill, which amended thirty-nine other Acts and which legislated in fields where previously there was no legislation of any kind was signed by the Queen.

Alf Morris comments:

The whole process took up six busy months and I must confess there were times when I thought my bill would fail through lack of time or government support. Even if your name comes first in the ballot, there are many obstacles on the course to be surmounted. I tend to agree with Roy Jenkins whose own Private Member's Bill became the Obscene Publications Act in 1959. He believes that the rare event of a successful Private Member's Bill needs the following combination of circumstances: 'First, a certain amount of luck; second, a great deal of time and even more patience: third, some all-party support; fourth, a minister who will be personally sympathetic at crucial times; fifth, some well organised and determined allies both inside and outside the House of Commons; and sixth, an articulate and impressive body of extra-parliamentary support.' Since my Bill needed *twelve* ministers to be 'personally sympathetic at crucial times', I sometimes think that I must have been about the luckiest Private Member of them all.

Alf Morris (1982)

Private Members' Bills can be introduced in four other ways — see Table 17.8.

delegated legislation in post-war years, the House has sought to undertake scrutiny of it. Detailed, and essentially technical, scrutiny is undertaken now by a joint committee of both Houses, chaired by an Opposition MP, but the task is a daunting one and there is no requirement that the government wait until the committee has reported on a particular piece of delegated legislation before bringing it before the House for approval. Time for debate is also extremely limited and much of the legislation is hived off for discussion in the standing committee on delegated legislation. Overall, the procedure for scrutiny is limited and subject to much criticism (see Norton, 1981, pp.95–9).

Scrutiny of executive actions

The House spends about one-third of its time debating government Bills and less than five per cent of its time considering Private Members' Bills (see Tables 17.9 and 17.10). Most but not all of the rest of its time is spent debating the actions of government (see Figure 17.2). Such **debate** may either be on a specific motion (for example, congratulating or condemning the government on a particular policy) or, where the government wishes to allow discussion of a topic for which it has no direct responsibility or on which a wide-ranging debate is considered beneficial, on an adjournment motion. On twenty days, termed **Opposition Days**, the topic for debate is selected by opposition leaders: the Leader of the Opposition can choose the subject on seventeen of them, the remaining three now being in the control of the leader of the third largest party in the House (currently the Social and Liberal Democratic Party). On three days, termed **Estimates Days**, when the House can debate specific estimates, those estimates are selected by the Liaison Select Committee (comprising select committee chairmen); it has adopted the practice of choosing estimates on which select committees have issued reports. There are thus more than twenty days on which the Government does not control the subject for debate. Also, supplementing full-scale debates, there is a **half-hour adjournment debate** at the end of each day's sitting and a series of mini-debates before each recess (recess adjournment debates) and after the Second Reading — taken formally — of the Consolidated Fund Bill. These are occasions when back-benchers can raise issues of particular and usually non-partisan interest to them, notably constituency matters: a Member outlines the problem for about fifteen minutes and then the appropriate junior minister replies for fifteen minutes. Though poorly attended, these debates provide Members with a valuable opportunity to air constituency grievances.

Table 17.9 *Private Members' Bills 1983–7 Parliament*

	Ballot	10-minute rule	Standing Order 58	Private peers	Total
Total introduced	79	195	107	60	441
Not printed	3	78	11	0	92
One Reading	13	111	77	9	210
Second Reading lost/adjourned	18	3	4	8	33
Royal Assent	39	2	13	14	68
Success rate (%)	49	1	12	23	15

Source: Adonis, 1990, p.77

Table 17.10 *House of Commons: time spent on the floor of the House 1985–6*

Business	Percentage of time spent in the sitting
Government Bills	
Second Reading debates	9.8
Remaining stages	18.6
Private Members' Bills	3.7
Private Members' Motions	4.5
Private Business	2.7
Opposition Days	6.9
Adjournment debates	
Government motions	6.2
Daily half-hour adjournment debates	5.3
Other (recess adjournment, etc.)	4.6
Delegated legislation	6.9
(including prayers to annul instruments)	
Estimates Days	1.1
Substantive Motions	4.8
European documents	2.7
Questions	8.3
Other	13.2
Total	99.3

Note: Total less than 100 per cent as a result of rounding percentages

Source: Calculated from data in House of Commons *Sessional Information Digest 1984/85* (HMSO, 1987)

Full-scale debates are similar in format to Second Reading debates with opening and winding-up speeches from the two front benches and the intervening gap filled by contributions from the back benches. The term debate itself is something of a misnomer: Members rarely debate but rather deliver prepared speeches which often fail to take up the points made by preceding speakers; there is also a growing tendency for Members not to stay for the whole debate after having spoken. Attendance at

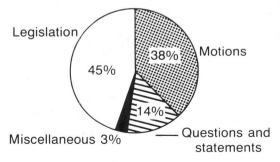

Figure 17.2 *How the Commons' time is spent (Source:* The Economist, *18 November 1989)*

debates generally is also considered to be falling nowadays, a consequence largely of most Members now having their own offices (in the 1960s, most did not). The outcome is also usually predictable: as long as the government has an overall majority in the House it will triumph in the division lobbies.

Debates nonetheless fulfil a number of useful purposes. They force the government to defend itself and to do so in an open forum. They allow different views to be expressed; any embarrassment or difficulties on the part of the government will attract media interest. Criticism from government back-benchers, regardless of the outcome of the vote, will cause particular embarrassment and the government will go to some lengths to avoid it, especially if it is likely to emanate from a large number of its supporters. There is also the potential now on particularly important occasions for debates to be broadcast live on radio (as happened when the House met extraordinarily on a Saturday morning in April 1982 to discuss the Argentinian invasion of the Falkland Islands and during the Westland crisis in January 1986) or since November 1989 on television (as with the debate on an Opposition motion of no confidence in November 1990). Debates, however inadequately, provide a means of helping keep the government on its toes and alert to critical though not always opposing views.

Question Time

The act of scrutinizing government is also carried on through the medium of **Question Time**. This is held at the beginning of each day's sitting from Monday to Thursday and occupies a maximum of fifty-five minutes (2.35 p.m. to 3.30 p.m.). Historically, it is of relatively recent origin. The first record of a parliamentary question being asked in the Lords was in 1721 and the first printed notice of questions to minsters was issued in 1835 (Bradshaw, 1954, pp.317−26). The use of a question time developed significantly in the nineteenth century and more especially in the twentieth. For most of the century, the demand to ask questions has exceeded the supply of time available. Members are now restricted in the number they can table: no more than eight by one Member in ten sitting days and no more than two on any one day. (If two are tabled for the same day, they must not be to the same minister.) Questions must be that (i.e. questions — statements or expressions of opinion are inadmissable) and must cover a matter for which a minister has responsibility; there is also an extensive list of topics (including, for example, arms sales, Sterling balances, budgetary forecasts, discipline in schools, telephone tapping and purchasing contracts in the Department of Health and Social Security) on which the government will not

Table 17.11   *Questions in the House of Commons 1985−8*

Session	Number of Questions tabled for	
	Oral answer	Written answer
1985−6	18,139	31,808
1986−7 (short session)	12,766	21,331
1987−8 (long session)	24,940	47,726

answer questions (see Sedgemore, 1980, pp.184−7). Despite this, many but by no means all Members are active in tabling questions for oral answer (see Table 17.11, which makes clear that they are also active in tabling questions for written answer, for which there is no limit on the number that can be tabled). Of these, approximately one-quarter receive an answer by the minister at the despatch box; the rest — for which time is not available — receive written answers.

Question Time provides an opportunity for Members to raise a whole range of topics. It has generally been looked upon as a valuable weapon for back-benchers and especially useful for raising constituency problems. Increasingly, though, it has been dominated by front-benchers, Opposition front-benchers jumping up to ask supplementary (that is, follow-up) questions once the minister has answered. Concomitantly, it has become more adversarial in nature, opposition Members seeking to catch out the government. A number of Members use Question Time

---

An example of the first page of a House of Commons Order Paper

| No. 58 | **MONDAY 27TH FEBRUARY 1989** | 2103 |

ORDER PAPER

QUESTIONS FOR ORAL ANSWER

Questions to the Minister for the Arts will begin not later than 3.10 p.m.

Questions to the Minister for the Civil Service will begin not later than 3.20 p.m.

★1 **Mr Ian McCartney** (Makerfield):　To ask the Secretary of State for Energy, when he next expects to meet the Director General of Gas Supply to discuss the code of rights for the domestic gas consumer.

★2 **Mr David Atkinson** (Bournemouth East):　To ask the Secretary of State for Energy, what information he has on the extent of oil deposits in Poole Bay and the Solent; and what special measures he expects to be taken to protect this coast line when these fields are developed.

★3 **Mr Irvine Patnick** (Sheffield, Hallam):　To ask the Secretary of State for Energy, how many low income households have been insulated under programmes initiated by the Energy Efficiency Office; and how many more are expected to be insulated in the current year.

★4 **Mr Martin Redmond** (Don Valley):　To ask the Secretary of State for Energy, when he expects to announce a reconstruction of British Coal's balance sheet and to write off its debt.

★5 **Mrs Teresa Gorman** (Billericay):　To ask the Secretary of State for Energy, what will be the cost for the Central Electricity Generating Board to comply with the European Community directives on emissions of carbon dioxide and sulphur dioxide.

★6 **Mr Dennis Skinner** (Bolsover):　To ask the Secretary of State for Energy, further to his Answer of 30th January, Official Report, column 5, if he will now indicate what measures he will take to resolve the problems for redundant mineworkers created by the Restart programme; and if he will make a statement.

extensively. During the 1988—9 session Mr Ron Davies (Caerphilly) asked an astonishing 775 questions, Mr Dafydd Elis Thomas (Merrionydd Nant Conwy) 717. Other MPs make little use of questions and usually more than one hundred Members do not table any questions at all for oral answer. Some consider it a farce. It does, though, retain its uses: it helps seek out information, it helps keep ministers on their toes (figuratively and literally) and it may help bring an issue to a minister's attention that otherwise he or she may not be aware of. *Prime Minister's Questions* take place from 3.15 p.m. to 3.30 p.m. on Tuesdays and Thursdays.

Select Committees

Supplementing debates and Question Time, the House has increasingly had recourse to *committees* as agents of scrutiny. Historically, the use of scrutinizing, or investigative, committees by the House is well established and they were frequently employed during Tudor and Stuart Parliaments. Their use declined in the latter half of the nineteenth century, the government bolstered by its party majority not looking favourably on the prospect of critical scrutiny. For most of the twentieth century, the use of such investigative committees — select committees — has been extremely limited. For most of the period before the 1960s there were only two major committees: the *Public Accounts Committee* (PAC) and the *Estimates Committees*. Founded in 1861, the PAC remains in existence and is the doyen of investigative select committees. It undertakes *post hoc* scrutiny of public expenditure, seeking to ensure that it has been properly incurred for the purpose for which it was voted. The Estimates Committee was first appointed in 1912 with the purpose of examining ways in which policies could be carried out more cost-effectively. In abeyance from 1914 to 1921 and during the Second World War, it fulfilled a useful but limited role (see Johnson, 1966). It was abolished in 1971 and replaced by an Expenditure Committee with wider terms of reference.

The PAC and Estimates Committees were supplemented in the 1950s by a Select Committee on the Nationalized Industries (Mikardo, 1970; Norton, 1981, p.129) and in the 1960s, as part of a package of procedural reform initiated by Leader of the House Richard Crossman in the new Labour Government returned in 1964, by Select Committees on Agriculture and Science and Technology; these were later joined by committees covering education and science, overseas development, race relations and immigration and Scottish affairs. (One was also appointed with responsibility for the Parliamentary Commissioner for Administration.) The agriculture committee had an altercation with the Department of Agriculture and the Foreign Office and was soon wound up; another two were wound up after the creation of the Expenditure Committee, their areas of interest being covered by the Committee's sub-committees. Overall, the experience of the committees failed to live up to the expectations of their supporters (Johnson, 1979). They suffered from limited resources, from doubts about their role, from a lack of interest (on the part of back-benchers as well as government), from the absence of an effective linkage between their activities and the Floor of the House, from limited powers (they could only send for 'persons, papers and records') and from the lack of a coherent approach to, and coverage of, government policy.

Recognition of these problems led to the appointment of a Select Committee on

Procedure, which reported in 1978. It recommended the appointment of a series of select committees, covering all the main departments of state, with wide terms of reference and the power to appoint specialist advisers as the committees deemed appropriate. It also recommended that committee members be selected independently of the whips, the task to be undertaken by the Committee of Selection, the body formally responsible for nominating members. Though opposed by the then Leader of the House, Michael Foot, Members on both sides pressed for the implementation of the Procedure Committee's recommendations and early in the new Parliament returned in 1979 they were given an opportunity to vote on the proposals: by a vote of 248 votes to twelve, the House approved the creation of the new committees. Twelve were initially appointed, soon joined by two covering Scottish and Welsh affairs. In the light of their appointment, various existing committees were wound up. The PAC and the Committee on the Parliamentary Commissioner were retained. In 1980 a Liaison Committee, comprising predominantly select committee chairmen, was appointed to coordinate the work of the committees.

The fourteen new committees effectively began operating in 1980. Appointed for the lifetime of the Parliament, they were re-appointed (with one exception) in the 1983 and 1987 Parliaments. (The one exception was Scottish Affairs which was not re-appointed in 1987 because of a failure to obtain a sufficient number of Conservative MPs to serve on it.) Each committee has eleven members (except for the abeyant Scottish Affairs Committee, which has power to appoint thirteen; before 1983, some committees had only nine members); three have power to appoint sub-committees — Foreign Affairs, Home Affairs and Treasury and Civil Service — but in the 1987 Parliament only the Treasury and Civil Service Committee exercised this power. The chairmanships are shared between the parties: in the 1979–83 Parliament, seven were chaired by Conservative MPs and seven by Labour Members; in the 1983–7 Parliament the distribution was nine Conservative and five Labour and in the Parliament returned in 1987 nine Conservative and four Labour (see Table 17.12). The committees are appointed to 'examine the expenditure, administration and policy of the principal Government Departments' and each has power to appoint specialist

Table 17.12 *Departmental Select Committees in the House of Commons 1989*

Committee	Chairman
Agriculture	Jerry Wiggin (Con)
Defence	Michael Mates (Con)
Education, Science and Arts	Rt Hon.Timothy Raison (Con)
Employment	Ron Leighton (Lab)
Energy	Sir Ian Lloyd (Con)
Environment	Sir Hugh Rossi (Con)
Foreign Affairs	Rt Hon. David Howell (Con)
Home Affairs	John Wheeler (Con)
Scottish Affairs — not appointed	
Social Services	Frank Field (Lab)
Trade and Industry	Kenneth Warren (Con)
Transport	David Marshall (Lab)
Treasury and Civil Service	Rt Hon. Terence Higgins (Con)
(sub-committee on the Civil Service	Giles Radice (Lab))
Welsh Affairs	Gareth Wardell (Lab)

advisers for as long as deemed necessary (and not just for a specific enquiry) as well as the traditional power to send for persons, papers and records.

The practices adopted by the committees have varied considerably (see Drewry, 1989); some have examined expenditure, others have not; some favour long-term enquiries, some short-term, some a combination of the two. Some have looked at administrative problems rather than questions of high policy; others have looked at more contentious issues. In so far as generalization is possible, the committees have attracted greater interest than their predecessors (both among Members and attentive outside publics), greater commitment by members, and have been extremely active in meeting and examining witnesses and prolific in issuing reports (Table 17.13). In the 1979−83 Parliament they issued 197 reports; in the 1983−7 Parliament they issued 306. At least fifty reports will now normally be issued each session. By calling evidence from interested groups, the committees have demonstrated a capacity to fulfil a tension release function; they provide an authoritative parliamentary forum in which outside groups can make their views known. Previously such groups were denied such a forum; the Floor of the House did not provide that opportunity, and the timetable was controlled by the government — select committees determine their own agenda. The committees also fulfil a support mobilization function, their reports having the potential to mobilize support among affected groups. (Committee reports are fairly well reported in the relevant trade and professional journals.) Their main role, though, is that of scrutiny and influence. They constitute a major addition to the House's scrutinizing capacity, providing it with a degree of specialization which it previously lacked. Their reports have served to help educate Members and they have had some input in debates; the use of Estimates Days now allows for some reports to be debated directly. Reports have also served to influence government. Though the extent of influence cannot be assessed quantitatively (the government may not concede the impact of a report or it may use a report to justify action it had already decided upon; some reports may also have delayed impact, influencing future rather than existing ministers), nonetheless various instances of influence have been identified both by the committee chairmen in their reports to the Liaison Committee and also by ministers. In 1986, in a parliamentary written question, the Prime Minister was asked to list the recommendations made by select committees in the period from March 1985 to March 1986 which the government had accepted: her answer ran to several pages of *Hansard* and in total listed 150 recommendations. Though the committees continue to labour under significant limitations — they have limited powers and their linkage with the Floor of the House is still not well developed — they constitute a major advance on what existed before 1979.

MPs and Ministers

Members also have a number of other opportunities to undertake a limited degree of scrutiny and influence. Of formal channels available, the most used for the pursuit of constituency casework is that of *corresponding with ministers*. Letter writing constitutes a major part of most MPs' work. Apart from replying to letters from constituents, they write letters to ministers on behalf of constituents. Approximately 10,000 letters a month are written to ministers by MPs (see Norton, 1982; Mitchell, 1982). For a Member, writing to a minister is one of the most cost-effective ways

Table 17.13 *Select Committees 1987–8 Session*

Committee	Members	Former ministers	Party of chairman	Attendance record of members (%)	Meetings	Reports	Witnesses: Civil servants	Witnesses: Ministers	Witnesses: Others	Special advisers	Committee votes	Sessional costs (£000)
Agriculture	11	0	Con	68	24	5	30	3	66	3	0	24
Defence	11	1	Con	76	33	12	24	2	17	13	0	40
Education	11	1	Con	75	30	3	21	2	85	5	0	21
Employment	11	1	Lab	76	36	4	19	2	79	4	0	28
Energy	11	0	Con	75	33	8	9	3	70	7	4	16
Environment	11	1	Con	73	28	7	15	1	54	4	0	32
Foreign Affairs	11	4#	Con	81	46	4	23	4	30	6	5	22
Home Affairs	11	0	Con	73	28	7	21	1	47	0	0	11
Scotland	—	1	—	—	—	—	—	—	—	—	—	—
Social Services	11	1	Lab	81	29	7	22	4	42	11	0	18
Trade & Industry	11	2	Con	75	40	4	18	4	96	3	0	61
Transport	11	0	Lab	69	33	5	26	1	72	7	0	49
Treasury & Civil Service*	11	0	Con**	73	43	12	41	5	26	9	3	17
Welsh Affairs	11	1	Lab	76	20	3	7	1	40	6	0	16

Notes: * Including one (civil service) sub-committee.
 ** Labour chairman of sub-committee.
 # Including two former Cabinet ministers, one of them (David Howell) the chairman.

Source: Adonis, 1990, p.108

of pursuing constituency casework. A letter invites a considered response, usually free of the constraints of party consideration and free of the partisan environment of the House; by being a private communication it also avoids putting a minister publicly on the defensive. Ministers are thus more likely to exercise discretion, where that is possible, in response to a Member's letter than they are if faced with a demand made publicly on the Floor of the House or in the press. Though not much studied, corresponding with Ministers is important not only as a means of redressing grievances but also as a means of tension release, constituents being able to air their views via their Member of Parliament (Norton, 1982).

If a letter to a minister fails to evoke the desired response, a Member then has the option of raising the matter on the Floor of the House, via a Question or a half-hour adjournment debate, or — if it involves alleged maladministration on the part of a government department — referring it to the ***Parliamentary Commissioner for Administration*** (the Ombudsman). Appointed in 1967, the Parliamentary Commissioner deals with cases of maladministration referred to him solely by MPs (citizens cannot refer a case directly). He labours under a number of limitations: limited resources, limited access to files, and no formal powers of enforcement. If he reports that officials have acted improperly or unjustly in the exercise of their administrative duties (he has no power to consider policy), it is then up to the government to decide what action to take in response; if it fails to act, the only remaining means available to achieve action is through parliamentary pressure. The Commissioner constitutes something of a limited last resort for most Members. Whereas all MPs will use the technique of writing to ministers in order to obtain a redress of grievances 'often' or 'always', less than ten per cent 'often' resort to the Parliamentary Commissioner; indeed, in the early 1970s a little over ten per cent of MPs admitted that they 'never' referred cases to him (Gregory and Alexander, 1973; Marsh 1985).

Early Day Motions

One other official device that Members may use to draw attention to a particular issue is the ***Early Day Motion***. A Member may table a motion for debate 'on an early day'. In practice, there is invariably no time to debate such motions but they are printed and other Members may add their names to them. Consequently, they act as something of a noticeboard of Members' feelings on particular issues. If a motion on a contentious issue attracts several hundred signatures, it acts as an important warning to the government. Most motions, though, do not fall into that category. Each year Members table EDMs on a wide range of subjects, expressing support or approval for a particular policy or action, congratulating a football team or national team on winning a particular trophy, or expressing an opinion on a topical issue. The range of topics is excessively broad and the number tabled is an increasingly large one: in the 1989–90 session, for example, 1,400 were tabled. The consequence is that their use as a means of indicating strength of opinion on an issue of political significance is devalued. Their utility, which was always limited, is thus marginal.

Opportunities for back-bench participation

Andrew Kennon, a Senior Clerk in the Table Office of the House of Commons has helpfully described all the opportunities available to back-benchers for participation in House of Commons proceedings. They are summarized below.

Pressing for ministerial action

Exchange of letters with minister.

Tabling of Questions for written answers — some 30,000 tabled each year.

Raise issues on the Adjournment of the House (30-minute debate at close of each day's business, ballot used to select lucky MPs).

Private Members' Bills: *three options*

1) Enter annual ballot — top twenty can introduce bills.
2) Ten Minute Rule (Standing Order No. 15). At start of public business on Tuesday and Wednesdays.
3) Standing Order No. 58: Member may present a Bill for first Reading — no speeches or vote allowed.

Airing issues at greater length

Introduce Private Members Motion: ten Fridays each session (five hours each) and four Mondays (three hours each); ballots used.

Debates following proceedings on the Consolidated Fund. Three all-night debates each sesson — ten topics discussed in each debate. Ballot used.

Adjournment debates on the Recess. Four times a year — thirty-plus topics usually debated. Ballot used.

Questions for oral answer

Questions for oral answer — some eighty tabled every day for fifty-five minute Question Time; 15,000 each year.

Early Day motions: MP allowed 250 words. About 1,000 tabled each session.

Private Notice questions: by special arrangement with Speaker at 3.30 p.m.: about one allowed per week.

Emergency debate *under Standing Order No. 10*

Usually two or three allowed each year by the Speaker. When applying, however, MPs allowed to make a 3-minute speech. MPs use this opportunity to make their points.

Other opportunities

Supplementaries at PM's Question Time.

Pressing Leader of House for debate during his weekly Answers to Business Questions.

Arguing that the House should **not** adjourn.

Applying for a second Adjournment Debate.

In total back-bench MPs use up one-fifth of the total business time of the House of Commons.

Source: A. Kennon, 1987.

These examples
of Early Day
Motions show
how MPs use
this device to
draw attention to
particular issues.

No. 69	Notices of Motions: 14th March 1989	3125

501 *RETIRED MINEWORKERS AND WIDOWS*

Mr John Cummings
Mr Jack Thompson
Mr Ronnie Campbell
Mr Eric Illsley
Mr Terry Patchett
Mr Frank Cook

★ 53

Mr Martyn Jones   Mrs Ann Taylor

That this House continues to note with concern the severe financial hardship experienced by retired mineworkers and widows of mineworkers whose housing benefits are reduced owing to the cash in lieu allowance being reckonable against housing benefit; and further, in acknowledging the invaluable service rendered by retired mineworkers to their nation and industry, calls upon Her Majesty's Government to amend housing legislation so as to remove this anomaly.

504 *GREEN TOP MILK*

Mr Gary Waller
Mr John Greenway
Mr Timothy Kirkhope
Mr William Hague
Mr Graham Riddick
Sir Marcus Fox

★ 28

Mr A. J. Beith

That this House, recognising that informed choice is preferable to prohibition, supports the continuing availability of untreated green top milk, combined with effective labelling and widespread distribution of information to consumers.

Parliamentary parties

Over and above the official avenues available to Members, there remains one important unofficial avenue, that of the ***parliamentary parties***. Both the Conservative and Labour parliamentary parties have well developed internal structures. Apart from the weekly meetings of the parliamentary parties, each has a series of back-bench committees (Norton, 1979). These cover the main sectors of government responsibility, the Conservatives currently boasting twenty-five such committees (see Table 17.14) and the Labour Parliamentary Party fourteen (Table 17.15). Each committee has elected officers and meets regularly; on the Conservative side most committees meet weekly, on the Labour side not always as frequently. The committees will usually discuss relevant parliamentary business (for example, a bill within their area of interest), consider topics of interest and listen to invited experts; most committees invite outside authorities on the subject to speak to them. A number will also go on occasional fact-finding tours. On the Conservative side, committees have no fixed membership — any interested Conservative MP can attend — and so attendance can reflect growing concern about an issue. Most meetings will attract a handful of Members, usually less than twenty; if an issue suddenly becomes contentious, attendance may swell to nearer one hundred. Meetings are confidential and provide Members with a means of expressing their views fully to their leaders; a whip attends each meeting and will report any disquiet to the Chief Whip and

Table 17.14 *Conservative committees, 1987–8*

Committee	Chairman
Agriculture, Fisheries and Food (sub-committees on: fisheries; food and drinks; forestry; horticulture and markets)	Ralph Howell
Arts and Heritage	Toby Jessel
Aviation	Michael Colvin
Constitutional affairs	Ivor Stanbrook
Defence	Sir Antony Buck
Education	James Pawsey
Employment	James Lester
Energy	John Hannam
Environment (sub-committee on housing improvement)	John Heddle
European affairs	Eric Forth
Finance	Sir William Clark
Foreign and Commonwealth affairs	Sir Peter Blaker
Health and Social Services	Dame Jill Knight
Home affairs	Michael Mates
Legal	Ivan Lawrence
Media	John Gorst
Northern Ireland	Sir John Biggs-Davison
Party organization	Robert Jones
Smaller businesses	Graham Bright
Sports	*
Tourism	David Gilroy Bevan
Trade and Industry (sub-committees on: shipping and shipbuilding; space)	Michael Grylls
Transport	Terence Higgins
Unpaired Members	Michael Stern
Urban and New Town affairs	Anthony Steen

Notes: In addition, there are eight regional groups: East Midlands, Greater London, North West, Northern, Scotland, Wales, West Country, and Yorkshire
 * There was a tied vote for chairman in the elections held in July 1987

Table 17.15 *Labour Committees 1987–8*

Committee	Chairman
Agriculture	Dr Gavin Strang
Defence	Harry Cohen
Education, Science and Arts	Ann Taylor
Employment	Bob Cryer
Energy	Peter Hardy
Environment	Allan Roberts
Foreign affairs	Tony Lloyd
Health and Social Security	Ann Clwyd
Home affairs	Chris Smith
Northern Ireland	Martin Flannery
Parliamentary affairs	Brynmor John
Trade and Industry	Doug Hoyle
Transport	David Marshall
Treasury and Civil Service	Austin Mitchell

Note: In addition there are eight regional groups: East Midlands, Greater London, North West, Northern, Scotland, Wales, West Midlands, and Yorkshire

relevant minister or front-bencher. They thus provide valuable channels of communication and also fulfil an educative role for Members, allowing interested Members to specialize in and learn about a particular sector of government responsibility. Prior to the creation of the departmentally related select committees in 1979, the party committees provided the only form of organized specialization within the Palace of Westminster. They still provide the only form of voluntary specialization in that a back-bencher may join a committee of his or her choice; select committees are limited in the number of members they have and those members are not self-appointed.

In combination, then, there are a variety of means available to Members to scrutinize and influence government. The means vary in effectiveness and viewed in isolation may appear of little use. Most, though, are not mutually exclusive and an MP will have recourse to a number of them in pursuing a particular issue. He or she may write to the relevant minister, raise the issue at a party committee meeting, table a question (or — as sometimes happens — table a great many for written answer, one way of drawing attention to an issue), seek a half-hour adjournment debate, table an EDM, threaten to speak critically in a debate or even vote against one's own side in the lobbies. The most effective Members are those who know how to deploy these various techniques. Collectively, Members tend to have most effect when grouped in committees, either party committees or, at a more cross-party level, select committees, and ultimately — on the government side — by voting against the government, or threatening to. In recent years, this has become a potent weapon in the hands of government back-benchers and reflects significant changes in Parliament over the past twenty years.

Recent developments

By the early 1970s the House was seen by many observers as being in a weak and essentially peripheral position within the nation's political framework. As a result of the developments of the latter half of the nineteenth century it no longer played a role in policy making and the growth of government in the twentieth made it increasingly difficult to exert effective scrutiny. The House was seen as a largely unspecialized and under-resourced body relying on debate and questions in plenary session to scrutinize and influence an ever-growing administrative machine.

Not only was it no longer a partner in the making of policy, the place at which policy was made was moving further and further away from it, thus making it more difficult to undertake critical scrutiny: the process of sectorization was shifting day to day incremental policy decisions down from ministers to small policy communities (Jordan and Richardson, 1982) while membership of the European Communities moved certain policy making from Whitehall up to supranational bodies in Brussels. The effect was that a large proportion of public policy was being formulated by bodies that were at one further remove from the House of Commons. The House, it was argued, was unable to keep pace with these developments and what small changes it made to its own procedures, such as the 'Crossman reforms' of the 1960s, were inadequate to meet the challenge.

The criticisms levelled against the House in the 1960s and 1970s have continued to be levelled (see, for example, Walkland, 1981, 1983). However, they tend to overlook significant changes which have taken place within the House since 1970. Though the changes have not altered the relationship of the House to the executive, they have served to enhance the capacity of the House to fulfil the functions ascribed to it. The changes themselves fall under three headings, behavioural and attitudinal, structural and procedural and representational.

Behavioural and attitudinal

Party cohesion in the Commons' division lobbies was, as we have noted, well established by the turn of the century. It remained a significant feature of parliamentary life, so much so that by 1965 Samuel Beer wrote that it was so close to 100 per cent that there was little point in measuring it (Beer, 1965, p.350). This, though, was to change significantly in the 1970s. In the first Parliament of the decade, that of 1970−4 when the Conservative Government of Edward Heath was in office, Conservative back-benchers voted against their own side on more occasions, in greater numbers and with more effect than ever before (Norton, 1975). Two-thirds of all Conservative back-benchers voted against the whips on one or more occasions; one back-bencher — Enoch Powell — voted against on no less than 113 occasions. There were 204 divisions (more than 20 per cent of the total) in which back-benchers entered the Opposition lobby and in only a small minority of cases (thirty-five) was the cross-voting done by a single Member. The extent of the dissension was such that on six occasions the government — despite a clear overall majority in the House — was defeated, three of the defeats taking place on three-line whips. It was saved from defeat in a number of divisions (probably as many as seventeen) on the European Communities Bill because of Liberal votes and some Labour abstentions. Fifteen Conservatives actually voted against the Government in a vote that was made one of confidence. The Government could clearly no longer take its supporters for granted in the way that it had done before 1970.

To the six defeats of the 1970−4 Parliament were added seventeen during the short 1974 Parliament, the result of opposition parties combining against the minority Labour Government. The most numerous — and significant — defeats were to occur, though, in the subsequent Parliament. In the 1974−9 Parliament, the Labour Government suffered a total of forty-two defeats. The majority of these (twenty-three) were the result of Labour back-benchers voting, sometimes in quite considerable numbers, with the Opposition. The rest were the consequence of opposition parties combining against the Government after it had slipped into a minority in the House in April 1976. The defeats were important not only quantitatively but also qualitatively. They took place on important issues, including economic policy and the government's main constitutional measure of the Parliament, the Scotland and Wales Bill; the government itself was to be brought down when it lost a motion of confidence on 28 March 1979. The defeats also served to bring about a change of attitude on the part of many MPs.

As the decade progressed and Members continued voting against their own side, so they began to realize that they could influence a change in government policy (most defeats were accepted by the government) without themselves incurring any hideous retribution. They realized that the presumed powers of the whips were largely based on bluff; as one Member observed, they were 'not so much whips as feather dusters'. The essential power of the whips was that of persuasion. Members also came to realize that a defeat, even on an important issue, raised no wider constitutional questions about the capacity of the government to continue in office; a government was constitutionally required to resign or request a dissolution only in the event of losing a vote of confidence (see Norton, 1978b). Consequently, MPs began to shed their old deferential attitude toward government, adopting instead a more participant one (Beer, 1982, p.190). They now wanted to be more involved in scrutinizing and influencing government and were prepared to use their basic power — that of the vote — to achieve that involvement.

This independence on the part of MPs was maintained in the 1979 and subsequent Parliaments (Norton, 1985). The return of a government with an overall majority reduced the extent of the effectiveness of cross-voting but it did not reduce its incidence (if anything, it facilitated it as Members knew there was often little chance of defeating the government); it thus received less public notice. Nevertheless, Members were able to exert influence, not so much through defeating the government but through threatening to defeat it. Given the experience of the 1970s, the government took such threats seriously and withdrew or modified measures when it thought it may lose a vote. In the 1979—83 Parliament, for example, two government Bills were withdrawn and various measures modified under threat of defeat. In the subsequent Parliament, despite an overall majority in excess of 140, the government was forced to bow to back-bench pressure on at least two issues (student grants and the sale of parts of the car producer British Leyland); indeed, on the issue of student grants it looked as if a majority of its own parliamentary party was prepared to vote against it. On occasion, the government has ploughed ahead with a measure and risked defeat. In 1982, it suffered a defeat on the immigration rules and, most remarkably of all, it lost the Second Reading of the Shops Bill in 1986. Seventy-two Conservative MPs voted with the Opposition in order to defeat the Bill, the first time this century that a government with a clear overall majority has lost a Second Reading vote. The government has also suffered defeats on traditional House of Commons matters (procedure and Members' allowances in particular), including in the Parliament returned in 1987. In April 1988 alone, dissent by Conservative back-benchers on nurses' pay, the community charge and housing induced Government concessions totalling £240 million.

The House, then, has witnessed a greater degree of independence by its Members than hitherto. What caused this new independence? And does it have the potential to fulfil the House's function as a body of continuous scrutiny and influence? Various explanations have been offered for the sudden increase in intra-party dissent in the 1970s (see Franklin, *et al.*, 1986; Norton 1987) including ideology and a 'new breed' of MP, but the most plausible is that of the *poor leadership hypothesis*. This contends that the leadership style of Edward Heath precipitated supporters to enter the lobbies against the government (Norton, 1978a); the Prime Minister insisted upon the expeditious and unamended passage of measures and was not prepared to listen to, or encourage support among, his back-benchers, with the consequence that they found they had little alternative but to express their disagreement in the division lobbies. When this produced a defeat for the government, Members began to realize what they could achieve. As one dissenter (later a Cabinet minister) put it, 'once you have defeated the government, it is much easier to do it a second time'. The defeats of the Heath Government provided precedents for later Parliaments and the independence of behaviour developed a momentum which then continued after Edward Heath had ceased to occupy the premiership.

But will this independence prove a lasting feature of parliamentary behaviour? It has already existed for nearly two decades and, even should it peter out (itself unlikely given the disappearance of the constraints previously operating on Members' voting behaviour), it has helped generate structures and new procedures which have the capability — and purpose — of subjecting government to continuous scrutiny. Towards the end of the 1970s, MPs began to comprehend what they could achieve by flexing their political muscles and utilized their new-found power to force the creation of the new select committees; they also used it to introduce other new tools of scrutiny. Hence the behavioural changes have helped generate significant structural and procedural changes.

Structural and procedural

The period since 1979 has witnessed the introduction of a number of structures and procedures in the House which have enhanced its capacity to fulfil its functions. The most significant, certainly the most well known, of the changes has been the introduction of the departmentally related select committees. Whereas previous committees were brought in on the initiative of government, these were the product of pressure from back-benchers; indeed, most members of the Cabinet were agnostic or hostile to their introduction. Members proved willing not only to force their introduction but also to sustain them: this is reflected in the work done by committee members. The committees, as already outlined, are active in meeting and prolific in issuing reports. They have provided the House with a specialized scrutinizing capability which it never had before. The range of government activity that they can subject to investigation is limited, but their strength in relation to government lies in what they can do as much as in what they actually do. The potential to undertake subjects of their choice gives the committees an important deterrent effect.

The House has also introduced several other reforms. In 1983 the House passed the National Audit Bill; it had been given a Second Reading against the wishes of the government. The measure created a National Audit Office to undertake efficiency reviews of departments, made the Comptroller and Auditor General (who assists the Public Accounts Committee) clearly an officer of Parliament, and created a Public Accounts Commission comprising nine MPs to be responsible for the accounts of the Office (Norton, 1986, pp. 73−5, 85−6). The previous year, following widespread dissatisfaction within the House over the inability to debate the estimates (ironic given the genesis of the House and the basis of its power), the House approved the introduction of three Estimates Days a session for the discussion of specific estimates; the choice of estimates was, as already noted, put in the hands of the Liaison Committee, the first time that control of part of the parliamentary timetable was put in the hands of a committee of the House. The new procedure was first employed in 1983 and has provided a modest but useful opportunity to debate select committee reports. The reports debated in the 1987−88 session are listed in Table 17.16.

Changes were also made to the legislative process. In 1980, the House approved the creation of special standing committees (SSCs) to which certain Bills could be referred. The committees were empowered to each hold four meetings prior to the

**The
Comptroller
and Auditor
General**

The Comptroller and Auditor General (C&AG) is one of the most powerful public officials in British government. Set up by the Exchequer and Audit Department Act in 1866 the C&AG's primary job is to ensure money raised through taxation is spent on the purposes which Parliament intended. During the twentieth century the C&AG's staff has grown to almost 900 and he has focused more sharply on value for money and efficiency. As a more truly independent force since 1983 the National Audit Office's (NAO) reports have ranged widely.

The current C&AG is Dr John Bourn, a career civil servant. He has interpreted his brief widely and has not been afraid to tackle politically sensitive areas. Dr Bourn's name regularly appears in the press as his department's investigations unearth incompetence, inefficiency or worse. In 1989, for example, National Health Service operating theatres were examined. It was discovered that despite the huge waiting list for operations, theatres were not used for 28 per cent of the time for which they were scheduled and for 23 per cent of the time lay idle through cancelled operations. The NAO came up with three explanations for this under-utilization of public assets: hospitals were poor at managing waiting lists and exploiting the advantages of new technology, operational research and statistical analysis; shortage of suitably qualified staff; and the right of doctors under existing contracts to cancel operations even at short notice.

On the basis of this report the Public Accounts Committee (PAC) questioned the Chief Executive of the NHS and submitted a report to the government suggesting ways in which theatres could be used more efficiently. Such reports are inevitably controversial (the BMA dismissed this one as 'amateur') but they regularly focus an unflattering eye upon activities funded by public money. As such they are a formidable reinforcement of the legislature's power in relation to the Executive.

Perhaps the most politically damaging report in recent years was that on the government's sale of the state-owned Rover Group to British Aerospace (BAe) in July 1988 — described at the time by Lord Young, then Trade and Industry Secretary, as the 'deal of the decade'. Seventeen months later the NAO report to the Public Accounts Committee revealed that the £150 million paid by BAe fell short of the real market value of the company by between fifty and four hundred million pounds. These revelations caused a political storm but the plot thickened when confidential memos to the PAC were leaked to the press. These indicated that £38 million was paid to BAe by the government as 'sweeteners' to expedite the sale of the then ailing car company. These payments breached European Commission regulations and in June 1990 the Commission demanded that BAe repay these illegal inducements — much to the embarrassment of Lord Young and his successor Nicholas Ridley.

In 1987–8 the NAO made 174 recommendations for improvements to achieve value for money. The PAC endorsed 161 of them and passed them on to the government, who in turn accepted 153. The C&AG is strictly forbidden from commenting on policy but it is inevitable that many recommendations have clear policy implications.

Table 17.16 *Estimates Days in the House of Commons, Session 1987—8*

Date	Estimate class number and vote discussed	Principal subjects
8 March 1988 (Day 1)	Class IV, vote 3	Storm damage of October 1987
	Class VI, vote 11	Coal industry
7 July 1988 (Day 2)	Class I, vote 1	Merchant shipping and civil aviation
21 July 1988 (Day 3)	Class XIV, vote 1	NHS pay awards
	Class VII, vote 5	Adult employment and youth training

normal standing committee stage, three of which were to be public sessions for examining witnesses. The procedure was not much used — only five Bills were referred in four years — but when employed the SSCs proved useful scrutinizing tools. The first Bill considered by an SSC — the Criminal Attempts Bill — was variously amended as a result of the evidence taken by the committee. The value of the committees was recognized by many Members and by the Select Committee on Procedure, which in 1985 recommended that it be more frequently employed. The committee recommended that any Member be entitled to move that a Bill be referred to a special standing committee instead of, as was the procedure, only on the motion of a minister. The government opposed the recommendation, but in 1986 the House approved it.

One final, and significant, reform approved by the House in the 1980s was that of televising its proceedings. Previously, the House had voted against the introduction of the television cameras. However, in 1978 both Houses agreed to the commencement of sound broadcasting and in 1985 regular television broadcasts began of the House of Lords. The televising of the Lords, and the realization that sound broadcasting exacerbated the noise in the chamber, added to the pressure for proceedings in the Commons to be televised. On 9 February 1988, the Commons — by a vote of 318 to 264 — agreed in principle to the televising of proceedings on an experimental basis. A Select Committee on Televising of Proceedings of the House was established and in 1989 recommended that the proceedings of Select and Standing Committees be included in the experiment. By televising the work of the Commons, supporters believed it would raise knowledge and appreciation of the House among the public and provide the House with additional leverage in influencing government. Broadcasts began in November 1989 with a minimum of fuss and have subsequently been well received (see Chapter 12). In 1990, the House voted to make the presence of cameras permanent.

These various changes added usefully to the means available to the House to scrutinize and influence government. However, for Members to make use of them they needed to be well resourced themselves. Since 1979, the House has forced an increase in Members' pay over and above what the government considered desirable. In July, 1987, the House approved a 20 per cent increase in pay, the government making it clear it was deferring to the wishes of the House because it could do little else. The previous year the government had opposed a 50 per cent increase in Members' secretarial and research allowance: the House voted for it. Members have also acquired greater office space and the building of a hundred new offices in Bridge Street, opposite Big Ben, was begun in 1987.

By themselves, each of these changes may not seem significant. In combination, they constitute the biggest enhancement of the House's capacity to scrutinize and influence government in the twentieth century.

Representational

Less often commented upon, in part because less directly observable, there have been notable changes in the fulfilment of the specific task of representation: that is, in the pursuit of constituency interests. In the 1950s and before, constituents did not make great demands of their Members of Parliament. Some Members could deal with constituency correspondence without secretarial help, replying to letters in longhand. All this has changed significantly over the past twenty to thirty years.

Constituents now make greater demands of MPs, in part attributable to the greater involvement of the government in the social and economic life of the nation. When a constituent has a problem concerning a government department, such as the Department of Social Security, or one concerning any public body (notably local authorities), the first port of call for help is that of the local MP (Marsh, 1985). The MP is contacted in preference to councillors (even where the problem concerns local government), citizens' advice bureaux or other such agencies. On average, an MP is estimated to receive now between twenty-five and one hundred letters a day from constituents. Dealing with this correspondence occupies roughly two to three hours a day, the Members not only having to reply to the writers but also having to pass on their letters to ministers for their response; if a minister's reply is unsatisfactory, several more letters may need to be written. Constituents may also see the Member in person, either at the Commons (relatively easy for London citizens, less so for those in Scotland), or more likely in the constituency itself. Virtually all Members now hold constituency surgeries, publicly advertised meetings at which constituents can come to see the Member to discuss their problems privately. Such surgeries have been the norm since at least the mid-1960s.

The value of such constituency casework we have noted already. It provides an opportunity for citizens to make their views known and for their grievances to be redressed. It serves also to enhance the legitimacy of the House as a representative assembly. 'It symbolises the availability of "them" to "us"; it is the area where the individual, actually or in theory, has a direct line to where the action is' (Dinnage, 1972, p.393). It is a role with which constituents generally appear satisfied. A survey in 1978 found that of those who contacted their MP, 75 per cent reported a 'good' or 'very good' response (Cain *et al.*, 1979, pp.6–7). It thus adds an important dimension to the work of Members of Parliament. There are also signs that MPs are beginning to come to terms with their European equivalents.

Europe and Westminster

> The 1986 Single European Act could help end the isolation of MEPs from Westminster, according to *The Economist*, 16 December 1989.
>
> Traditionally most MPs have agreed with Mr Denis Healey, who in his memoirs said of members of the European parliament (MEPs) that, 'because they are cut off from their national parliaments, they lack influence where it really matters'. MEPs have been derided and shunned by the 'real MPs': although they have recently been allowed into limited areas of Westminster unescorted, they still cannot wander into the bars, restaurants, libraries, lobbies and corridors where most the Commons day is played out.
>
> This is now changing. Both the 1922 committee of Tory backbenchers and the Parliamentary Labour Party have recently voted to allow their respective MEPs to attend their private meetings. More significantly, a report by the Commons procedure committee has recommended a wide-ranging series of changes to the way MPs deal with European legislation. The more radical suggestions, which included coopting MEPs onto committees and forming a grand European committee, were rejected by the procedure committee.
>
> But many of its ideas are likely to be given the go-ahead by the government, which is still considering the report. Sir Geoffrey says he finds it 'a very professional, sensible, well-balanced analysis'. He senses a 'significant shift' in Westminster's awareness of the need for closer contact with the European institutions. Asked about the proposal for Commons debates before each EC summit, he praises it as 'the kind of change that will respond to that [new awareness] quite effectively.' He also lauds the specialist, wide-ranging House of Lords committee on the EC, adding, 'you will find this developing increasingly within the Commons'.
>
> What is happening is that behind the choruses of 'we shall not be moved' by those in love with the mystique of the Commons and the Lords, Westminster is quietly adapting itself to a new world, ruled increasingly from Brussels. Indeed, Britain's Parliament is entering a curious constitutional race: if it does not learn, along with the other national parliaments, to exercise effective scrutiny over the European institutions, then the Strasbourg parliament will get the job.
>
> Nobody should be surprised. The 1986 Single European Act accelerated the European project in a way which made discussion of Europe-wide democracy inevitable. At the time, the Commons select committee on foreign affairs huffily warned that it might mean a covert step in the direction of greater power for the EC institutions at the expense of the national ones. Many believe Mrs Thatcher herself did not fully understand — or was not told — what she was committing herself to. A grand conspiracy? Not necessarily. Sir Geoffrey, the then foreign secretary, argues that when any important institution is changed, 'no one ever fully foresees the implications of what you're doing because of the evolutionary change of human institutions.'
>
> Source: *The Economist* 16 December 1989

Recent years have thus witnessed important changes which have affected the capacity of the House of Commons to fulfil the functions ascribed to it. These changes have to be seen in perspective. They have not affected the place of the House in the policy cycle: it remains, as it has been for most of its history, a reactive or policy influencing legislature. Nor, according to some critics, have they been sufficient to make the House the effective scrutinizing body that it could and should be. Hence, reform of the House remains on the agenda of political debate.

References and Further Reading

Adonis, A., *Parliament Today* (Manchester University Press, 1990).

Beer, S.H., *Modern British Politics* (Faber & Faber, 1965).

Beer, S.H., 'The British legislature and the problem of mobilising consent', in E. Frank (ed.), *Lawmakers in a Changing World* (Prentice Hall, 1966).

Beer, S.H., *Britain Against Itself* (Faber & Faber, 1982).

Bradshaw, K.A., 'Parliamentary questions: A historical note', *Parliamentary Affairs*, **7**(3), 317–26 (1954).

Burch, M. and Moran, M., *A Reader in British Politics* (Manchester University Press, 1985).

Cain, B.E., Ferejohn, J.A. and Fiorina, M.P., 'The Roots of Legislator Popularity in Great Britain and the United States', *California Institute of Technology: Working Paper 288* (California Institute of Technology, 1979).

Dinnage, R., 'Parliamentary Advice Bureau', *New Society* (24 February 1972).

Drewry, G. (ed.), *The New Select Committees*, revised edition (Oxford University Press, 1989).

Franklin, M., Baxter, A. and Jordan, M., 'Who were the Rebels? Dissent in the House of Commons 1970–1974', *Legislative Studies Quarterly*, **11**, 143–59 (1987).

Gregory, R. and Alexander, A., 'Our parliamentary ombudsman, Part 2: Development and the problem of identity', *Public Administration*, **51**(1) (1973). See also Part 1 (1972).

Griffith, J.A.G. and Ryle, M., *Parliament: Functions, Practice and Procedures* (Sweet and Maxwell, 1989).

House of Commons, *Sessional Information Digest 1985/6* (HMSO, 1986, 1987, 1988, 1989).

Hanham, H.J., *Elections and Party Management* (Harvester Wheatsheaf, 1978).

Johnson, N., *Parliament and Administration* (Allen & Unwin, 1966).

Johnson, N., 'Select committees and administration', in S.A. Walkland (ed.), *The House of Commons in the Twentieth Century* (Oxford University Press, 1979).

Jordan, G. and Richardson, J.J., 'The British policy style or the logic of negotiation?', in J.J. Richardson (ed.), *Policy Styles in Western Europe* (Allen & Unwin, 1982).

Kennon, A., 'Opportunities for Back-benchers', *Social Studies Review* (January 1987).

Marsh, J.W., 'The House of Commons: Representational changes', in P. Norton (ed.), *Parliament in the 1980s* (Basil Blackwell, 1985).

Mellors, C., *The British MP* (Saxon House, 1978).

Mezey, M., *Comparative Legislatures* (Duke University Press, 1979).

Mikardo, I., 'The Select Committee on Nationalised Industries', in A. Morris (ed.), *The Growth of Parliamentary Scrutiny by Committee* (Pergamon Press, 1970).

Mitchell, A., *Westminster Man* (Thames Methuen, 1982).

Morris, A., 'The Chronically Sick and Disabled Persons Act 1970', in L. Robins, *Topics in British Politics* (The Politics Association, 1982).

Norton, P., *Dissension in the House of Commons* 1945–74 (Macmillan, 1975).

Norton, P., 'Intra-party dissent in the House of Commons. A case study: The immigration rules 1972', *Parliamentary Affairs*, **29**(4), 404–20 (1976).

Norton, P., *Conservative Dissidents* (Temple Smith, 1978a).

Norton, P., 'Government defeats in the House of Commons: Myth and Reality', *Public Law*, 360–78 (1978b).

Norton, P., 'The Organisation of parliamentary parties', in S.A. Walkland (ed.), *The House of Commons in the Twentieth Century* (Oxford University Press, 1979), pp. 7–68.

Norton, P., *The Commons in Perspective* (Basil Blackwell, 1981).

Norton, P., '"Dear Minister ..." The Importance of MP–to–Minister Correspondence', *Parliamentary Affairs*, 35 (1) (1982), 59–72.

Norton, P., 'Parliament and policy in Britain: The House of Commons as a policy influencer', *Teaching Politics,* **13**(12), 198–221 (1984).

Norton, P. (ed.), *Parliament in the 1980s* (Basil Blackwell, 1985).

Norton, P., 'Independence, scrutiny and rationalisation: A decade of changes in the House of Commons', *Teaching Politics,* **15**(1), 69–98 (1986).

Norton, P., *Parliament in Perspective* (Hull University Press, 1987).

Norton, P. (ed.), *Parliaments in Western Europe* (Frank Cass, 1990).

Packenham, R.A., 'Legislatures and political development', in A. Kornberg and L.D. Musolf (eds), *Legislatures in Developmental Perspective* (Duke University Press, 1970).

Redlich, J., *The Procedure of the House of Commons*, vol. 1 (Constable, 1908).

Regan, P., 'The 1986 Shops Bill', *Parliamentary Affairs*, **41**(2), 218–35 (1988).

Richards, P.G., *Parliament and Conscience* (Allen & Unwin, 1970).

Rush, M., 'The Member of Parliament', in S.A. Walkland (ed.), *The House of Commons in the Twentieth Century* (Oxford University Press, 1979).

Ryle, M. and Richards, P.G. (eds), *The Commons Under Scrutiny* (Routledge, 1988).

Sedgemore, B., *The Secret Constitution* (Hodder & Soughton, 1980).

Silk, P., *How Parliament Works*, 2nd edn (Longman, 1989).

Walkland, S.A. (ed.), *The House of Commons in the Twentieth Century* (Oxford University Press, 1979).

Walkland, S.A., 'Whither the Commons?', in S.A. Walkland and M. Ryle (eds), *The Commons Today* (Fontana, 1981).

Walkland, S.A., 'Parliamentary reform, party realignment and electoral reform', in D. Judge (ed.), *The Politics of Parliamentary Reform* (Heinemann, 1983).

18 Parliament II — The House of Lords and Parliamentary Reform

Philip Norton

In the 1980s one-party domination of the House of Commons shifted attention to the House of Lords where changes in its political complexion made Conservative victories by no means assured. Between 1979 and 1990 the Lords voted down Mrs Thatcher's legislation over 150 times — most of them minor but in some cases major items. The House of Lords, therefore, is no longer a political afterthought: even the Labour Party has abandoned plans for its abolition and now takes the question of its reform seriously. The first part of the chapter examines the nature and functions of the Lords, while the second addresses the subject of parliamentary reform of both chambers.

The House of Lords is generally viewed by historians as having its origins in the *Witenagemot* and more especially its successor the Norman *Curia Regis*. Indeed, two basic features of the House in the twentieth century are to be found in the king's *Curia* of the twelfth and thirteenth centuries. One is the basic composition, comprising the Lords Spiritual and the Lords Temporal (at the time of Magna Carta the *Curia* was made up of archbishops, bishops, abbots, earls and chief barons); historically, the main change has been the shift in the balance between the two. The other significant feature is the basis on which members were — and are — summoned. The *Curia* comprised the king's tenants-in-chief who attended by virtue of their position and minor barons whom the king wished to attend. 'From the beginning the will of the king was an element in determining its make up' (White, 1908, p.299). If a baron regularly received a summons to court the presumption grew that the summons would be issued to his heir. There thus grew a body which peers attended on the basis of a strictly hereditary dignity without reference to tenure. The result was to be a House of Lords based on the hereditary principle, with writs of summons being personal to the recipients. In other words, the House could — and can — make no claim to being a representative assembly. Members of the House have never been subject to election; nor have they been summoned to defend or pursue the interests of any other individuals or bodies.

The lack of any representative capacity has led to the House coming to occupy a position of political — and now legal — inferiority to the House of Commons.

As early as the fifteenth century, the privilege of initiating measures of taxation was conceded to the Lower House. The most significant shift took place, though, in the nineteenth century: as we have seen, the effect of the Reform Acts was to consign the Lords to a recognizably subordinate role to that of the Commons, though not until the passage of the Parliament Act of 1911 was that role confirmed by statute. Under the terms of the Act, the House could delay a non-money Bill for no more than two sessions (reduced to one session by the Parliament Act of 1949), and money Bills were to become law one month after leaving the Commons whether approved by the House of Lords or not. Bills to prolong the life of a Parliament (along with delegated legislation and provisional order Bills) were excluded from the Act's provisions.

What, then, constitutes the contemporary House of Lords? What role does it have? And how well does it fulfil it?

Nature of the Lords

The House of Lords in the 1990s boasts over one thousand members, making it the largest legislative assembly in the world. Its size is hardly surprizing given the number of peers created over the centuries by the nation's monarchs, although the largest increase has been in the twentieth century. In 1906 the House had a membership of 602. Of the 1,190 members existing in 1984, 793 were hereditary peers. The remainder comprised 351 life peers, twenty law lords (a category of peer created by the Appellate Jurisdiction Act of 1876) and the Lords Spiritual: the two Archbishops, the bishops of London, Durham and Winchester, and twenty-one other bishops according to their seniority of appointment. Life peerages were an innovation introduced in 1958 and have been the main form of creation since that time. No hereditary peerages were created in the period from 1964 until 1983; two were created in 1983 and one in 1984.

In the 1950s, the House met at a leisurely pace and was poorly attended. Peers have never been paid a salary and many members, like the minor barons in the thirteenth century, found attending to be a chore, sometimes an expensive one; the practice, as in the thirteenth century, was to stay away. The House rarely met for more than three days a week and each sitting was usually no more than three or four hours in length. For most of the decade, the average daily attendance did not reach three figures.

This was to change significantly in the 1960s and 1970s (see Table 18.1). Peers began to attend in greater numbers and the House sat for longer. In the 1970s, average attendance climbed, reached 275 by 1976, and each sitting usually lasted more than five hours. In the 1980s the House became especially active. The average daily attendance exceeded 300. Almost 800 peers attended one or more sittings each session. Late-night sittings became a regular feature. In the session of 1985—6 the House sat after ten o'clock on almost one hundred occasions. The House also became a more visible body, having admitted — as we have noted — the television cameras in 1985. The reasons for these changes we shall consider shortly.

Politically, the House remains — as it has been since the end of the eighteenth century — a predominantly Conservative assembly (see Table 18.2). Of peers with

Table 18.1   *Increased activity of the House of Lords 1959–86*

Session (at approximately 4-yearly intervals)	Total number of peers on roll	Total number who attended	Total number who spoke	Average daily attendance	Number of days House sat	Total number of hours House sat	Average length of sittings in House (h)	Number of sittings after 10 p.m.
1959–60	907	542	283	136	113	450	4	1
1963–4	1,012	525	289	151	110	534	4¾	3
1967–8	1,061	679	424	225	139	803	5¾	31
1971–2	1,073	698	419	250	141	813	5¾	28
1975–6	1,139	752	486	275	155	969	6¼	39
1981–2	1,174	790	503	284	147	930	6¼	41
1985–6	1,171	798	529	317	165	1,213	7¼	93

Note: Calculated from information supplied by House of Lords Information Office and from the sessional index to *Hansard*

Source: Shell, 1988

a known political affiliation, Conservative peers outnumber Labour peers by more than three to one. In terms of peers who are regular attenders, the Conservative dominance is less marked. There has been a notable growth in the number of peers sitting on the cross benches. This, coupled with a greater independence on the part of peers generally, has made the House far less predictable than it was before 1970.

The House differs significantly from the Commons not only in its size and composition but also in its procedures. Though the Lord Chancellor (or, more often, a deputy) sits on the Woolsack, he has no powers to call peers to speak, nor to enforce order. The maintenance of the rules of the House is the responsibility of the House itself, though peers usually look to the Leader of the House to give a lead. Peers

Table 18.2   *Political affiliation of Peers 1970–88*

Party/group	1970		June 1984			November 1988	
	n	(%)	n	(%)		n	(%)
Conservative	468	43.4	460	38.6		538	45.4
Labour	120	11.1	133	11.2		117	9.9
Liberal	38	3.5	39	3.3	SLD	60	5.1
Social Democrat	—	—	38	3.2		25	2.1
Communist	2	0.2	2	0.2		1	0.1
Independents — cross-bench*	110	10.2	209	17.6		220	18.6
— non-party†	51	4.8	50	4.2		54	4.5
No declared political affiliation‡	289	26.8	259	21.7		168	14.2§
Total	1,078	100.0	1,190	100.0		1,185	100.0

* Those in receipt of the independent cross-bench whip or 'notification of business'
† Law lords, archbishops, bishops and (some) royal dukes
‡ Those peers about whose party allegiance no information available
§ Includes twenty-seven peers who declare themselves to be 'Independent' but who are not in receipt of the cross-bench whip

Source: Baldwin, in Norton, 1985; for 1988, Baldwin

wishing to speak usually indicate so in advance and a list of speakers for a debate is then circulated. If two Lords rise at the same time to speak, one is expected to give way. There are also far fewer divisions in the Lords than in the Commons. In part, this reflects the recognition by peers of the political predominance of the elected chamber. By agreement reached between the two Front Benches in the 1945—50 Parliament, the House does not divide on the Second Reading of any Bill promised in the government's election manifesto.

Functions

The functions of the House are similar but not identical to those of the Commons. The extent to which they are different derives from the fact that politically the house is no longer co-equal with the Commons.

Latent legitimization

By virtue of being one of the two chambers of the legislature and of meeting regularly and uninterruptedly, the House may have a marginal claim to fulfil a function of latent legitimization: such a claim is largely offset, however, by the House having no claim to being a representative assembly and by its limited legislative authority. It is called upon to give its seal of approval to non-money Bills; if it fails to do so, there is provision for the measure to be enacted later without its assent. Though not quite falling into the realms of a formal function (that is, the House not being prepared to deny its assent to a measure), the limited political legitimacy of the House itself acts as a considerable restraint. Legitimization of the government is a function solely of the House of Commons.

Scrutiny and influence

This is the most important function of the House. It does not encompass the specific task of scrutiny on behalf of constituents, as peers have none. Rather, it takes the form of general scrutiny by debate and legislative scrutiny through detailed consideration in committee. The House provides an important forum for debate of general issues of public policy, especially those which are not regularly considered in the Lower House. By virtue of its composition — many of the leading figures in the spheres of industry, education, science, arts and the like having been elevated to the peerage — it is assumed especially appropriate that the House concentrate on such topics for which it is likely to be able to draw upon unrivalled expertise. By virtue of its lack of political legitimacy, it is also considered an appropriate body to undertake detailed revision of Bills emanating from the Commons. The Commons approves the principle of a measure, debates its principal and contentious clauses and then sends it (with many clauses sometimes left unconsidered) to the Lords. The task of the Upper House is seen as ensuring that the Bill is internally coherent and well drafted and to suggest any amendments that would help improve the measure. In terms of legislative scrutiny, the House is thus expected to play a role complementary to, rather than one competing with (or identical to), that of the Commons.

Tension release

By virtue of having a less crowded timetable and a membership more varied and independent than that of the Commons, the House may serve to fulfil something of a limited tension release function. It can debate issues which are causing concern to particular groups in society. Formally, it is not a function that the House can be expected to fulfil. Peers are under no obligation to give voice to outside interests and groups; indeed, Erskine May's seminal work on parliamentary procedure makes clear that Lords speak for themselves and not on behalf of outside interests, 'and while they may indicate that an outside body agrees with the substance of the views that they are expressing, they should avoid creating an impression that they are speaking as a representative of outside interests' (1983, p.485). (Thus, not only is the House not a representative assembly, members should not give the impression of being one.) In practice, disquiet on a particular issue outside the House may lead members to raise it as a subject of debate. Indeed, the House may serve to give voice to issues which are squeezed out by the partisan battle in the Lower House.

Support mobilization

Again, there is a potential for the House to fulfil this function. However, the basis for mobilizing support is extraordinarily restricted. The House of Lords *qua* House of Lords has little political legitimacy with which to rally support. It attracts relatively little attention, that is relative to the Lower House, and it has enjoyed little specialization through committees. The scope to fulfil the function has increased slightly as a result of the introduction of television cameras (greater visibility with which to mobilize support via debate) and the limited use of committees (issuing reports that may mobilize support among affected groups), but nonetheless the opportunities are limited and the basis on which support may be mobilized is likely to derive from the authority of the individuals speaking in debate, or comprising a committee, rather than the authority of the body itself.

Providing the personnel of government

The House does provide some of the personnel of government, for which there are practical and political reasons. The government needs to get its legislation through the House, hence the need for spokesmen to explain it and whips to marshall support to see it through. Also, the House provides a pool from which the Prime Minister can draw in order to supplement ministers drawn from the Commons; the advantage offered by peers is that, with no constituency responsibilities, they are likely to be able to devote more time to ministerial duties than ministers in the Commons. However, the supply is a limited one. Usually a minimum of two and rarely more than four peers sit in the Cabinet. About ten junior ministers are normally drawn from the Lords, supplemented by seven whips. Indeed, the number of ministers is normally fewer than the number of ministerial portfolios. Consequently, the whips serve as spokesmen for particular departments.

To these may be added a number of other functions, some of which are peculiar to the Upper House. Foremost among these is a ***judicial function***. The House constitutes the highest court of appeal within the United Kingdom. However, the function is exercised by a judicial committee comprising the Lord Chancellor, ex-Lords Chancellor, the law lords and peers who have held high judicial office. By convention, other peers do not take part in the proceedings. Cases are heard in a committee room, though the decisions are announced in the chamber. The House, like the Commons, still retains a small *legislative role*, primarily in the form of Private Members' legislation and much of the social reform legislation of the latter half of the 1960s was first introduced, or was first discussed, in the Upper House; the House was particularly important in the passage of legislation liberalizing the law on homosexuality (see Richards, 1970, pp.76–7).

The Lords is also ascribed a distinct role, that of a *constitutional safeguard*. This is reflected in the provisions of the Parliament Acts. The House, as we have noted, retains a veto over Bills to extend the life of a Parliament. It is considered a potential brake upon a government that seeks to act in a dictatorial or generally unacceptable manner; hence it may use its limited power to deny assent to a particular piece of legislation or, failing that, to amend it. In practice, the House has been willing to use its powers since 1970 in order to act as such a brake, but when it does so it encounters accusations that it is acting contrary to the wishes of an elected assembly. To be effective, it is a power that can only be utilized on rare occasions.

In combination, the functions render the House a useful body — especially for debating issues on which members are well informed and for revising legislation — but one that is clearly subordinate to the elected chamber. The fact that the House is not elected explains its limited functions; it is also the reason why it is considered particularly well-suited to fulfil the functions it does retain.

Traditional means of scrutiny and influence

The scrutiny of government undertaken by the House can be divided, like that undertaken by the Commons, into legislative scrutiny and scrutiny of executive actions. What is distinctive about the Lords is that, until relatively recently, both forms of scrutiny were undertaken predominantly, indeed almost exclusively, on the Floor of the House.

Legislative scrutiny

In the Upper House, Bills have to go through stages analagous to those in the House of Commons. There are, though, differences in procedure. First Readings are normally taken formally but there have been rare occasions when they have been debated; on four occasions (in 1888, 1933, 1943 and 1969) First Readings were actually opposed. Second Readings, as in the Commons, constitute debates on the principle of the measure. The significant differences occur at committee stage. For some Bills, this stage is dispensed with. After Second Reading, a notice may be moved 'That this Bill be not committed' and, if the motion is agreed to, the Bill then awaits Third Reading. This procedure is usually employed for supply and money Bills when there is no desire to present amendments (Erskine May, 1983, p.502). For those Bills that do receive a committee stage, it is taken usually on the Floor of the House. Furthermore, all amendments tabled are debated. The less crowded timetable of the House allows such a procedure. It has the advantage of allowing all peers with an interest or expertise in a measure to take part and ensures consideration of any amendments they believe to be relevant. There is thus the potential for a more thorough consideration than may be possible in the Commons. At this stage, as already noted, the emphasis is on ensuring that the Bill is well drafted and coherent and most Lords' amendments are accepted by the Commons. Many of the amendments introduced are government amendments though, as we shall see, the House has proved increasingly willing to carry amendments moved by back-benchers.

The House has, since 1968, been able to refer Bills for committee consideration in the equivalent of standing committees, known as public Bill committees, but the procedure has not been much utilized. More long-standing is its power to refer a Bill, or indeed any proposal, to a select committee for more detailed investigation. 'Since 1976 . . . these *ad hoc* committees have formed a much greater part of the Lords' work and have helped to improve the reputation of the House significantly' (Grantham and Moore Hodgson, 1985, p.115). At least one such committee has been appointed each session. They are utilized primarily when it is considered necessary or desirable to examine witnesses and evidence from outside bodies. As such they can and do fulfil an important tension release function as well as one of scrutiny. The extent to which one of these committees can achieve this is reflected in the experience of the Committee on Laboratory Animals Protection. It invited comments from members of the public and interested bodies and received in response some 900 letters and memoranda.

Scrutiny of executive actions

This takes place predominantly through the media of general debates and questions. **Debates** may, as in the Commons, take place on substantive motions, with the House being asked to reach a definite conclusion on a particular matter. They may also take place on 'take note' motions, in which the House is asked to consider usually a particular document or report without reaching a decision on it, or on a motion calling for papers. The former are employed particularly to debate reports from select committees or topics which the government wish discussed (ministers do not table motions calling for papers as they are responsible for supplying the papers being called for) and the latter are used by back-benchers to call attention to a particular topic; at the end of the debate it is customary to withdraw the motion, the purpose for which it was tabled — that is, to ensure a debate — having been achieved. In such debates, all peers who wish to speak do so and there is a somewhat greater likelihood than in the Commons that the proceedings will constitute what they purport to be: a 'debate'. Party ties are less rigid than in the Commons and if a division is to follow (it often does not) peers may be influenced by those who have spoken. Within the context of the chamber, the chances of one's speech having an impact are considerably greater than in the somewhat more predictable Lower House.

These debates are also supplemented by short debates. One day each month, usually a Wednesday, is set aside for two short debates, each of up to two-and-a-half hours in length. These are occasions for issues to be raised by back-benchers on either side of the House or by cross-benchers, and the choice of subjects is made by ballot. The purpose of each short debate is to allow for peers to discuss a particular topic rather than to come to a conclusion about it. Topics discussed in these debates tend to be non-partisan and the range is broad. Thus, for example, on 11 February 1987 Lord Stallard, a Labour peer, raised the problems associated with maintaining and conserving an adequate and efficient level of heating, while Lord Campbell of Croy, a Conservative, called attention to the case for further improvement in the national schemes for the parking of vehicles used by handicapped people. Both motions provided an opportunity for interested peers to offer their views and for ministers to explain the government's position and to reveal what proposals were under consideration by the relevant department.

Questions

These various debates are also supplemented by **questions**. These are of two types: starred and unstarred. However, whereas in the Commons the terminology of 'starred' and 'unstarred' questions refers to oral and written questions, the distinction in the Lords is between a non-debatable and a debatable question. (Lords may table questions for written answer, though the number tabled is not numerous, rarely more than half-a-dozen on any particular day.) At the beginning of each day's sitting, up to four 'starred' questions may be asked. These are questions similar to those tabled for oral answer in the Commons. A peer rises to ask the question appearing in his or her name on the Order Paper, the relevant minister (or whip) replies for the government, and then supplementary questions — confined to the subject of the original question — follow. This procedure, assuming as many as four questions are tabled (they usually are), is expected to last no more than twenty minutes. This allows for perhaps as many as four or five supplementaries on each question to be asked, the peer who tabled the question by tradition being allowed to ask the first supplementary. Hence, though a shorter question time than in the Commons, the concentration on a particular question is much greater and allows for more probing.

At the end of the day's sitting, there is also usually an unstarred question: that is one which may be debated. Peers who wish to do so rise to speak on the subject and, when all peers who wish to take part have done so, the relevant minister rises to respond. Thus, for example, on 18 February 1987 the Earl of Longford rose 'to ask Her Majesty's Government whether they are satisfied with the moral condition of the tabloid press'. His Lordship spoke for twenty-four minutes on the subject and was followed by seven other peers before the Minister rose to respond. The advantages of such unstarred questions are similar to those of the half-hour adjournment debates in the Commons, except that in this case there is a much greater opportunity for other members to participate; in the instance of Lord Longford's question discussion occupied nearly two hours.

Committees

These traditional floor-bound methods of scrutiny have been supplemented recently by the **use of committees**. Apart from the appointment of *ad hoc* select committees to consider the desirability of legislation on particular topics, the House has made use of its power to create sessional select committees, i.e. committees appointed regularly from session to session rather than for the purpose of one particular inquiry.

Three such committees have been appointed since 1974. (The House also has a number of long-standing select committees dealing with procedure, its judicial function and privilege.) Of the three, two remain in existence.

The most prominent is the **European Communities Committee**. Established in 1974, it undertakes scrutiny of European Community proposals, seeking to identify those which raise important questions of principle or policy and which deserve consideration by the House. Working through seven sub-committees (one of which considers the legal implications of each EC proposal), the committee utilizes the services of ninety-six peers. Each sub-committee, after having had EC documents referred to it by the main committee, calls in evidence from government departments and outside bodies; written evidence may be supplemented by oral evidence and, on occasion (though not often), a minister may be invited to give evidence in person. The sub-committees prepare reports for the House, including recommendations as to whether the documents should be debated by the House. (About 4 per cent of the time of the House is taken up debating EC documents, usually on 'take note' motions.) The EC Committee has built up, in a relatively short space of time, an impressive reputation as a scrutinizing body, providing reports which are more objective, frank and extensive than its counterpart committee in the Commons (Grantham and Moore Hodgson, 1985, p.127) and which are regarded as influential both within Whitehall and in Brussels.

The **Select Committee on Science and Technology** was appointed in 1979 following the demise of the equivalent select committee in the Commons. The remit of the committee — 'to consider science and technology' — is wide and it works through two sub-committees. The Committee benefits from the number of peers with an interest in the subject and its reports — about two a year — are often highly detailed and complex. The Committee has been used to raise issues which otherwise might have been neglected in government and a number of its reports have proved influential. Thus, for example, its 1986 Report on Civil Research and Development led to the Prime Minister taking charge of the government's consideration of priorities on science and technology and the appointment of a council to advise the premier.

The **Select Committee on Unemployment** was in existence from 1979 to 1982. Set up 'to consider and make recommendations on long-term remedies for unemployment', it collected evidence from sixty-eight sources and, after two-and-a-half years, issued a 205-page report. It figured notably, though not dominantly, in a subsequent Commons debate, the government indicating that it would not be ruling out any of the committee's ideas. It was nonetheless apparent that the committee's recommendations went far beyond (to the sum probably of £5 billion) what the government was prepared to accept.

The use of committees thus constitutes a modest but, especially in the case of the EC Committee, a valuable supplement to the work undertaken on the floor of the House. It is also indicative of a modest revitalization of the Upper House.

Recent developments

The House has witnessed changes since 1970 which largely parallel those of the House of Commons. Though precluded by its very nature from experiencing any 'representational' changes, it has undergone changes in attitude, behaviour and structures.

In the 1950s, as we have seen, the House met at a leisurely pace and with few peers being actively involved in daily business. All this was soon to change. Peers became more active: they began to attend in greater numbers, sit for more days and spend more time on each day's sitting. They also became far more independent in their voting behaviour. Given the preponderance of Conservative peers, a period of quiescence during Conservative governments and of opposition during Labour governments might be expected. What has been surprising since 1970 has been the willingness of the House to disagree with Conservative administrations. During the Heath administration, the government suffered twenty-four defeats at the hands of their Lordships. The Thatcher administration was defeated more than one hundred times, several of the defeats taking place on contentious political issues, including the 1980 Education (No. 2) Bill and the 1984 Paving Bill for the abolition of the Greater London Council. The extent of the defeats has been such that the government's business managers are now far more inclined to anticipate reaction in the Lords before proceeding with measures. 'There is clear evidence that Conservative government concern over not being able to secure the passage of particular items of legislation in a particular session has been at least a factor in persuading ministers to accept unpalatable amendments and to reach compromises on a number of occasions during the post-1979 period' (Baldwin, 1985, p.101). Ironically, as a result of their Lordships' greater independence, at times the House has appeared to be more responsive to public disquiet and has become a greater target for lobbying by outside groups, providing a better channel for some interests to make their views known than the House of Commons.

The reasons for this significant behavioural change have been identified by Nicholas Baldwin as twofold: a combination of a change in attitude and an influx of life peers (Baldwin, 1985, pp.96–113). Following the collapse of the 1969 Parliament (No. 2) Bill, peers began to realize that their House was not likely to be reformed in the foreseeable future; hence they may as well get on with the task of scrutinizing government — no one was likely to take their place to do it. They were also more able (as well as willing) to undertake the task as a result of the influx of the new life peers. Life peers are proportionately more active in the daily business of the House than are hereditary peers and provide more than two-thirds of the members of the sub-committees of the EC Committee. From the point of view of the House, the juxtaposition of these two developments has been a fortunate one, transforming it into a more prominent and effective body of scrutiny. The introduction of television cameras has probably also served to reinforce peers' willingness to be involved in the business of the House, though the initial novelty has worn off. The cameras have helped increase the public visibility of the House, to the benefit of the body.

This change in behaviour and attitudes has also made possible the structural changes outlined above, with peers being willing and able to sustain the sessional committees (particularly the EC Committee) and the *ad hoc* investigative committees. Though the creation of the committees may seem a modest development, relative to what existed before it constitutes a significant advance. It has also proved a cost-effective change, the select committees having allowed the Lords to mobilize considerable expertise at virtually no expense to investigate and report on matters of parliamentary concern (Shell, 1983, p.102). The fact that the matters have also been of wider concern has helped enhance the reputation of the House among a wide range of affected groups. The work of the committees has also helped concentrate minds in Whitehall on topics that otherwise might be neglected.

The committees of the House have thus provided an important channel for the new professionalism and independence exhibited by peers and, in combination, these developments have equipped the House with a new facility to scrutinize and influence government. The extent to which it is able to do so is limited but nonetheless significant; and some members of the House would like to see its scrutinizing capacity further extended. Compared to thirty years ago, the contemporary House of Lords is physically and politically a much more active body, far better able to fulfil the functions ascribed to it.

Parliamentary Reform

The developments in both Houses in the years since 1970 have helped craft a Parliament that is a more effective reactive, or policy influencing, body in the policy cycle than it has been since the latter half of the nineteenth century. However, such changes have not freed the institution from pressures for further reforms and, indeed, in some cases for a radical transformation. Those pressing for further change may be categorized as 'internal' and 'external' reformers. The former focus upon changes within the two Houses that would enable them to fulfil more effectively their existing functions. The latter — 'external' — reformers concentrate upon the extent to which neither House can claim fully to be a representative chamber, arguing consequently for radical reforms that would help create a greater basis of legitimacy for the two Houses.

Internal reformers largely accept the relationship of Parliament to the executive that has existed for most of the institution's history. There is an acceptance of the balance inherent in the blend of Tory and Whig views of representation: that is, acceptance of the need for government to govern, but operating under the effective scrutiny of Parliament. There is an awareness that the balance in the relationship has shifted heavily toward government in the period since 1867. The need therefore is seen as one to help restore the balance, Parliament being enabled to fulfil its essential functions.

Consequently, such reformers have argued for the development of existing procedures in both Houses and for the introduction of new ones. It was pressure from internal reformers in the 1960s that helped generate the 'Crossman reforms'. It was pressure from internal reformers (in some cases, the same as those in the 1960s) that helped realize the creation of the departmentally related Select Committees in the 1970s. While applauding the changes that have been achieved in the past decade, there is a recognition nonetheless that more can and should be done in order to strengthen Parliament as a scrutinizing and influencing body. As a result, such reformers have argued for the use and extension of investigative select committees, better pay and facilities for members (both individually as well as collectively in the form of library and other support services), the use and extension of special standing committees (SSCs), the availability of more time to consider estimates, a more rational timetable and — in the House of Lords — a greater use of committees, including possibly a series of committees analagous to the departmentally related committees in the House of Commons. More ambitious recommendations have included the merging of select and standing committees and a limit on the amount of legislation that can be passed in a session.

These various schemes, it is argued, would enable parliamentarians to undertake more effective scrutiny of government and, coupled with the willingness of Members to use their basic power of the vote, to exert greater influence on public policy; by so doing, and by building up its channel of communication with the public generally and with attentive publics (notably but not exclusively through committees), Parliament would be better able to fulfil the tasks of tension release and support mobilization, hence enhancing its own legitimacy.

What support, then, does internal reform enjoy? And how likely is it to be achieved? Support has come predominantly from within Parliament itself, from individual Members and — providing the catalysts for change — from Procedure Committees of both Houses. Significant reform has been achieved usually as a result of three variables coming together at the same time: a large number of back-benchers restless at the apparent inability of the House to exert itself effectively in the scrutiny of government, a reform-minded Leader of the House, and a Procedure Committee Report recommending specific changes. All three variables came together in 1979 to produce the departmentally related select committees when, as we have seen, back-benchers from both sides of the House — aided by a new Leader of the House, Norman St John-Stevas — forced the acceptance of the 1978 Report from the Procedure Committee. In the 1980s, one of the three variables was missing (a reform-minded Leader of the House), though this did not prevent the House from going against the advice of the government or the Prime Minister in order to achieve further reforms, from the creation of the National Audit Office in 1983 to the decison to approve televising of the House in 1988. However, the Parliament of 1979 to 1983 proved the high point of internal reform. The remainder of the decade was, in the words of one long-serving MP, 'a period of consolidation'. A number of Members on both sides of the House continued to press for reform and formed an All-Party Commons Reform Group. Attendance at Group meetings, though, rarely exceeded thirty or forty. Some observers also began to doubt whether the behavioural and attitudinal changes of the 1970s could be sustained.

However, what appeared to be little prospect of further significant reforms in the mid- to late 1980s began, as the decade closed, to give way to renewed optimism. Expectations of wide-ranging changes increased, and those expectations were the product of two independent events:

1. The passage of the European Communities (Amendment) Act of 1986. This gave effect to the Single European Act, an amendment to the Treaty of Rome which effected a shift in power relationships between the institutions of the Community and the institutions of the member states. It enhanced the independent decision making capacity of the EC Council of Ministers, as well as strengthening the position of the EC Parliament in Community law making. Only in 1988, following a speech by the Prime Minister in Bruges, did MPs begin to become concerned

about the implications of the Single European Act for Parliament and its capacity to scrutinize and influence what was happening in an EC context. Significant pressure for change began to build. Former Leader of the House John Biffen, an opponent of major reform when he was in office, was in the forefront of advocating change.

2. The decision to televise the House. After some delay, agreement was reached in 1989 on the actual details of televising the House. There was also a growing realization of the wider implications of televising proceedings for the House's own procedures. How long will some of the existing procedures be maintained in the glare of public scrutiny? Will not the watching public expect, and be entitled to expect, an efficient House of Commons, free of unnecessary procedural frills? (Rather like the House of Lords which, having always had simple procedures, had to make little change to accommodate the cameras?) And will not the public also expect to see greater independence on the part of MPs, hence reinforcing the behavioural changes of the 1970s?

By 1990, internal reformers were thus in a position of some strength to press the case for significant changes within the existing framework of Parliament. Procedural changes, they contended, were both desirable and achievable. The 1970s and early 1980s had demonstrated what could be achieved. There was no going back on those changes: they were substantial and permanent. What was needed now was to build on them. Essentially an incrementalist approach, but one deemed to be sufficient — and practical — to meet the needs of Parliament.

The argument against this approach is that it is insufficient to keep pace with developments taking place outside Parliament. Increasingly, low level, day to day policy making has passed downward from ministers to small, fluid policy communities, comprising civil servants and representatives of affected groups (see Jordan and Richardson, 1982). The making of high policy has been centralized within government — the 'elective dictatorship' thesis advanced by Lord Hailsham in 1976 — or, in some cases, transferred upwards to the institutions of the European Community. Parliament, it is argued, lacks the power and resources to know and to influence what is going on in the mass of policy communities or in Brussels, and it lacks both the political will and the resources to influence what is going on in Downing Street, be it No. 10 or No. 11. The influences that determine economic policy are essentially global and, in so far as they are domestic, include the institutions of the City of London, the Institute of Directors, and various think tanks, including the Prime Minister's own policy unit. Parliament is deemed marginal to these influences. It has failed to keep pace with what has been happening and the procedural reforms of recent years are dismissed as nothing more than tinkering, the equivalent of the band playing while the *Titanic* sinks. Further procedural reform is considered incapable of restoring political vigour and legitimacy to Parliament. For that, more radical change — external to the institution — is needed. Without it, so its advocates contend, Parliament will atrophy, in danger of ceasing to be a policy influencing legislature, returning instead to the days of being no more than a 'rubber-stamping' body for the measures of government.

External reformers, in essence, seek a reformulation of the constitution in order that Parliament may acquire both greater power and legitimacy to become more centrally involved in decision making. At the heart of the reforms proposed is reform of the electoral system (see especially Walkland, 1983). The House of Commons is criticized on the grounds that, by virtue of the method of election, it cannot be truly representative in the second sense of the term and that, by virtue of the stranglehold enjoyed by party, it cannot be properly representative in the first sense (defending and promoting the interests of others). The existing electoral system allows a party to win a majority of seats with only a minority of the votes cast in the country. Enjoying a parliamentary majority, that party may then pursue whatever policy it wishes. The House, on this analysis, lacks both the legitimacy and the political capacity to fulfil the functions ascribed to it and, it is argued, no amount of internal reform will alter that. Consequently, reformers advocate a new electoral system — most favour a system of proportional representation based on the Single Transferable Vote (STV) or the West German-style Additional Member System — as a means of restoring legitimacy and political influence. By virtue of introducing a fairer electoral system, reformers believe the House will enjoy greater legitimacy in the eyes of electors. Introducing a system in which electors can choose different candidates within the same party — they are not confined to one party candidate — will allow more independent-minded Members to be elected; and, furthermore, if current voting patterns are repeated, no one party will be returned with an overall majority, thus destroying the one-party stranglehold on power that the present system favours. On this analysis, party in Parliament will be weakened, allowing Members greater scope to influence and shape public policy. This will help create a new balance between Parliament and government, the old balance having swung too far to be correctable. A revitalized House of Commons will be achieved, prominent rather than marginal in the policy cycle.

For many if not most external reformers, a new electoral system constitutes part of a package of desirable constitutional reform. Among other reforms sought is one of the Upper House. The House of Lords, as presently constituted, is seen as inherently incapable of being anything more than peripheral in the making of public policy. Lacking any claim to be a representative assembly, under any of the definitions of the term, it has no effective political clout to employ. Procedural reforms within the House will have no effect upon that basic problem. Hence, reformers argue, what is needed is a major reform of the composition of the House of Lords or a new second chamber altogether. The Parliament (No. 2) Bill in 1969 sought to reform the Lords, phasing out the hereditary principle and distinguishing between voting peers (life peers) and non-voting peers (existing peers by succession). The Bill failed in the Commons in the face of sustained opposition led by Enoch Powell and Michael Foot: the former felt the Bill went too far, the latter — an abolitionist — felt that it did not go far enough. Since then, various schemes have been put forward for an elected or part-elected chamber (a Senate) and, most radically of all, for the abolition of the second chamber (see Norton, 1982, Chapter 6). In 1977, the Labour Party Conference voted in favour of 'an efficient single-chamber legislating body', reaffirming its vote in 1980, though in a policy review in 1989 the party reverted to supporting bi-cameralism and an elected second chamber. Various Conservative bodies have also advocated introducing an element of election. An elected unicameral or bicameral legislature would, it is argued, have a greater claim to legitimacy than the existing institution and, as such, provide the basis for a truly representative and more politically assertive body.

Just how much support, then, does external reform enjoy? And how likely is it to come about? Pressure for external reform grew especially in the 1970s. S.E. Finer's edited volume, *Adversary Politics and Electoral Reform*, published in 1975, was especially influential in advancing the case for a new electoral system. It appeared as a wider debate was developing on Britain's constitutional arrangements. There was growing pressure for a Bill of Rights and for devolution of legislative and executive powers to elected assemblies in Scotland and Wales. Though achieving prominence towards the end of the 1970s, the return of a Conservative government in 1979 and succeeding years of Conservative dominance appeared to push the issue from the forefront of debate. However, in the late 1980s it began to reappear, motivated especially by the third consecutive Conservative election victory in the 1987 General Election. Politicians on the left began to find the prospect of constitutional change attractive. Some observers began to argue that ten years in office had given added weight to Hailsham's thesis of an elective dictatorship. The movement for reform began to gather pace and to attract new support from different parts of the political spectrum.

Support for electoral reform — and for other measures of constitutional change — had been a long-standing feature of the Liberal party and was taken up with equal vigour by its successor, the Social and Liberal Democratic party. In the 1970s, it found some support for change among small numbers of Conservative and Labour MPs (most Labour supporters subsequently defecting in 1981 to the newly formed Social Democratic party) and, in advocating a Bill of Rights, among Conservative peers. Other support came especially from academics and writers, especially those associated with the political centre. In the late 1980s, the support widened. More Labour politicians, including some members of the Shadow Cabinet, began to toy with the proposal for electoral reform. Intellectuals on the left also began to move in that direction. In 1988, a new body, 'Charter '88', was formed in order to press for a new constitutional settlement, three hundred years after the previous one. It published a manifesto signed by leading figures of the political centre (such as Lord Jenkins of Hillhead) and a significant array of left-wing writers, including Bernard Crick (leader of the movement for internal reform in the 1960s), Ralph Miliband, Bruce Kent and Martin Jacques. Among the proposals contained in the Charter were a system of proportional representation, a Bill of Rights, 'a democratic, non-hereditary second chamber', and the placing of the executive 'under the power of a democratically renewed Parliament' (see also Chapter 15).

Though achieving by 1990 a much higher public and political profile than before, the movement for external reform remained a minority one within the political system — the Conservative Government of Mrs Thatcher being especially opposed — and did not, and does not, go unchallenged. Opponents contend that the reformers' analysis is flawed, exaggerating the extent to which Parliament has been weakened in relation to the executive. They also argue that internal reform may not only be sufficient to achieve a redress of the balance between executive and legislature but may also constitute the only reform actually achievable. External reform is considered difficult if not impossible to achieve as well as undesirable, threatening (in the case of electoral reform) the capacity of government to govern, no one party being returned with an overall majority and (in the case of a Bill of Rights) transferring political questions for resolution by an unrepresentative (that is, non-elected) body, namely the judiciary. If government was unable to govern, it would destroy any advantage that may be gained by Parliament. If government was so incapacitated, with a consequent decline in support for the political system that that would necessarily engender, then Parliament's role in the policy cycle — and its capacity to mobilize support — would be far more marginal than it is under the present system. And even if the end results could be achieved without jeopardizing support for the political system, the effect on government would be undesirable, encouraging delay and stalemate in reaching decisions at a time when government needs to be able to respond quickly to crises. Thus, for internal reformers, external reform is not only not necessary, it is also potentially highly dangerous.

Dangers are also seen in the proposals to reform radically the House of Lords. Opponents draw attention to the fact that few of the reform schemes advanced for the Upper House envisage changing the provisions of the Parliament Acts. Hence, though an elected second chamber may be more representative in the second sense of the term (freely elected) it would not accrue any more power by which to fulfil a representative role under the first definition of the term (defending and pursuing the interests of others). Furthermore, there would be the danger that an elected second chamber would merely replicate the partisan configuration of the House of Commons and — if it did not — offer instead the opportunity for stalemate between the two chambers. And getting rid of the chamber altogether would offer the danger of producing a legislative overload for the House of Commons that would make it impossible to function effectively, if at all.

There is thus a fundamental divide between those favouring reform internal to Parliament and those favouring a wider reformulation of the constitution. In this, historically, there is nothing new. Arguments about Parliament's place in the political system have scattered the historical landscape. Schemes of reform have been variously advanced and the debate of the 1970s and 1980s was and remains remarkably similar to that of the 1920s and 1930s. The debate is hardly likely to abate. Those who seek to strengthen Parliament as a reactive, or policy influencing, legislature will continue to press for different forms of change within both Houses. Those who posit a more ambitious role for Parliament, akin to that which it played briefly in the period between the two Reform Acts of the nineteenth century, will maintain their pressure for major constitutional change. Those who have written off Parliament as a body to restrain government will do likewise.

References and Further Reading

Baldwin, N. 'The House of Lords: behavioural changes', in P. Norton (ed.), *Parliament in the 1980s* (Basil Blackwell, 1985).

Beavan, J., 'At bay in the Lords', *Political Quarterly* (Autumn 1985), 375–81.

Bell, S., *How to Abolish the Lords* (Fabian Tract No. 476, Fabian Society, 1981).

Finer, S.E. (ed.), *Adversary Politics and Electoral Reform* (Wigram, 1975).

Grantham, C. and Moore Hodgson, C., 'The House of Lords: Structural changes', in P. Norton (ed.), *Parliament in the 1980s* (Blackwell, 1985).

House of Lords, *Report by the Group on the Working of the House*, HL Paper 9, 1987/88, (HMSO, 1988).

Jordan, G. and Richardson, J., 'The British Policy Style or the Logic of Negotiation?' in

J. Richardson (ed.), *Policy Styles in Western Europe*, George Allen & Unwin (1982).

Judge, D. (ed.), *The Politics of Parliamentary Reform* (Heinemann, 1983).

Morgan, J., *The House of Lords and the Labour Government, 1964–70* (Oxford University Press, 1975).

May, Erskine, *Treatise on the Law, Privileges, Proceedings and Usage of Parliament*, 20th edn, ed. Sir Charles Gordon (Butterworth, 1983).

Norton, P., *The Constitution in Flux* (Martin Robertson, 1982).

Richards, P.G., *Parliament and Conscience* (Allen & Unwin, 1970).

Shell, D., 'The House of Lords', in D. Judge (ed.), *The Politics of Parliamentary Reform* (Heinemann, 1983).

Shell, D., *The House of Lords* (Philip Allan, 1988).

Shell, D. 'The evolving House of Lords', *Social Studies Review*, **5**(4), (March 1990), 128–33.

Walkland, S.A., 'Parliamentary Reform, Party Realignment and Electoral Reform' in D. Judge (ed.), *The Politics of Parliamentary Reform* (Heinemann, 1983).

Wheeler-Booth, M.A.J., 'The House of Lords', in J.A.G. Griffith and M. Ryle, *Parliament: Functions, Practice and Procedures* (Sweet and Maxwell, 1989).

White, A.B., *The Making of the English Constitution 1449–1485* (G.P. Putnam, 1908).

Members of Parliament: Public Role and Private Interests

> Being an MP is a vast subsidized ego trip. It is a job which needs no qualifications, that has no compulsory hours of work, no performance standards and provides a warm room and subsidized meals to a bunch of self opinionated windbags and busy bodies.

This view of our elected members, expressed by Jim Hacker, the ministerial character in BBC's *Yes Minister* series, would probably find considerable resonance in the public mind. The British as a nation take unusual pleasure in making fun of their politicians and do not hold them in deferentially high esteem. While they are elected to serve the community it is widely felt that politicians as a species are more interested in personal advancement of various kinds.

The public is right to be sceptical of politicians when, as the revelations about Eastern European rulers in 1989 made only too clear, human nature exhibits frail defences against the twin lures of ambition and corruption. However, we hope that our political leaders appreciate the prime importance of resisting such temptations and will act in ways which allay rather than arouse suspicion. For this reason recent controversy over the private interests of MPs causes particular concern.

Granada's *World in Action* on 15 January 1990 was one of several television programmes in recent years to investigate this topic. The programme revealed that 385 MPs had declared commercial interests while thirty-seven are paid consultants, directors or owners of lobbying companies. While MPs are often approached by companies it seems that others are keen to sell their services. Richard Alexander MP, for example, placed an advertisement in a House of Commons magazine as follows: 'Hard working backbench Tory MP of ten years standing seeks consultancy in order to widen his range of activities'. Members of the House of Lords are also involved. An article in the *Observer*, 21 January 1990, revealed that the former Prime Minister, Lord Wilson of Rievaulx, was closely involved with a company called Rindalbourne which specialized in Anglo—Rumanian trade. At the firm's request he sent congratulatory telegrams to Ceausescu and in 1985 joined a Rindalbourne-financed visit to Rumania to meet the subsequently disgraced dictator. Included in that visit were Lord Whaddon and a number of MPs including the aforementioned entrepreneurial Richard Alexander. Is such activity necessarily wrong? There are a number of arguments adduced in support.

1. MPs have always had outside interests — and this has not impaired the working of the system in the past. Indeed, the absence of morning sittings has often been defended in terms of the opportunities such a timescale provides for those wishing to sustain a career in for example, the law, journalism or business.

2. Some MPs claim that £26,000 per annum is insufficient reward for able people who face higher than normal expenses, for example, through having to run London and constituency homes. To make ends meet, they argue, they need to take additional work.

3. Safeguards exist in the form of a Register of Interests in which MPs are obliged to record their commercial interests together with any 'payments or any material benefits or advantages received on behalf of foreign governments, organisations or persons'. If speaking in a debate MPs must first declare any financial interests which might have a bearing on the issue under discussion. If they become ministers the rules are even stricter: they must sever any direct connection with prior outside financial interests.

Critics are unconvinced by these arguments and put forward the following points.

1. *MPs should be full-time politicians.* In the nineteenth century MPs might legitimately have had time to pursue other interests but now government is so complex and all embracing their full-time energies are required. Many MPs argue that attending debates and committees, researching issues and dealing with constituency problems should fill up virtually every waking hour: anyone who spends time as company directors or consultants must by definition be neglecting their duties. Who, for example, represents the constituents of Blaby when Nigel Lawson is putting in his two days each week at the bank? Contact with 'the real world', it can be argued, is readily available to all MPs in the form of their constituents whom they should visit regularly at weekends. Left-wing Labour MPs are quick to point out that the majority of MPs with substantial private interests belong to the Conservative party. They argue that the parliamentary salary is quite adequate: indeed Terry Fields MP accepts only a skilled worker's pay and gives the balance to the Labour movement. Another left-wing MP so suspects the blandishments of outside interests that he is rumoured to refuse even the offer of a free cup of tea!

2. *MPs should not compromise themselves on any issue.* Constitutionally MPs are obliged to use their energies and their judgement on behalf of their constituents and their country. In the *World in Action* programme Graham Zellick, Professor of Public Law at London University, was emphatic: 'An MP has complete freedom to act as he sees fit and his own judgement must not be compromised by anybody . . . or be fettered by any arrangements he has . . . MPs should not be for sale.'

3. *MPs who work for lobbying organizations exploit their privileged position.* In recent years a number of specialist lobbying organizations have sprung up offering their skills and contacts to organizations — usually big companies or multi-nationals — wishing to influence government decisions in particular ways, for example the awarding of business contracts. Some of them have established an impressive record of effectiveness. MPs are natural targets for such lobbying organizations and some have been recruited onto their payrolls; others actively canvass for such work while others, like Sir Peter Emery and Michael Forsyth (before he became a minister) have been involved in setting up lobbying organizations. Bob Cryer, the Labour MP, accepted lobbying as a perfectly legitimate activity in a democratic system but condemned MPs who used their privileged positions to enable big companies to gain access to ministers and other

groups in Parliament and thereby 'buy influence'. *World in Action* also revealed how it is possible for non-elected people who work for MPs or ministers to exploit their privileged access to decision makers for financial advantage.

4. ***The safeguards are not effective.*** *World in Action* illustrated how weak the safeguards are and how often they are breached.

   (a) The Register of Interests is voluntary: MPs can withhold information if they choose. One MP, Enoch Powell, boycotted it on principle but others, it has been alleged, conceal their interests on purpose. Others declare their involvement in companies but are not obliged to list the clients served even when they are — on some occasions — unsavoury foreign governments or companies with an interest in the award of contracts arising from current legislation, for example privatization of cleaning contracts in NHS hospitals.

   (b) Some MPs neglect to declare their interests before speaking in the debate but even when they do they have complete freedom subsequently to speak on all aspects of the issue. This contrasts with local government where councillors with an interest are disqualified from any involvement including speaking. Sir Geoffrey Johnson-Smith MP, Chairman of the Select Committee on Members' Interests, explained that local councillors are in a different position in that they have ***executive*** responsibility for their actions while MPs have not.

   (c) MPs do not have to declare an interest when they ask questions. *World in Action* alleged that one MP who asked no less than fifty-eight parliamentary questions on details of government computer contracts was helping his client, the accountancy firm Price Waterhouse, to draw up a business plan on this matter.

US Congressmen and Lobbyists

Last week's Commons register of members' interests showed another big increase in paid consultancies taken on by MPs (mostly Tory back-benchers) last year. This is a highly controversial area.

Britons are keen critics of the political action committee (PAC) system in Washington whereby senators and congressmen can accept $5,000 (£3,100) for each election campaign from any number of lobbies — cancer, sugar, guns, abortion, you name it. If the politician then fails to vote the way the lobby wants, he is unlikely to get another $5,000 for his next campaign. And it takes a lot of moola to buy televison time when you're running for office.

'Honorariums' of $1,000 are handed out to politicians at the drop of a hat. I sat in on a private breakfast given by a firm of Washington 'consultants' (nicer word than 'lobbyist', don't you agree?), and it was attended by defence contractors and some defence chaps from the British embassy. The guest of honour was a congressman who sits on a defence committee.

The information he smoothly imparted for his $1,000 was nothing more than we could have learned from studying the congressional record. But everybody present ended up with a cosier relationship.

It would be interesting to know how our British legislators earn the money they are paid for their mushrooming consultancies.

Source: **Susan Crosland**, *Sunday Times*, 28 January 1990.

The Register of Members' Interests

The Register was introduced in 1975 on the basis of a parliamentary resolution: MPs are not therefore required by law to make declarations. MPs are asked to provide information under nine headings: paid directorships; paid employment; trades or professions; clients; financial sponsorship or gifts; overseas visits; payment from abroad; land and property, and shareholding. Below are some extracts from the annual publication of the Register in February 1990.

AITKEN, JONATHAN (Con, South Thanet) — Chairman, Aitken Hume International plc, directorships of group's principal subsidiary and associate companies. Director, Al Bilad (UK), Beaverbrook Investments, British Manufacturer and Research Co. Ltd.

ASHDOWN, PADDY (Dem, Yeovil) — Shareholder, Westland plc (less than £100).

ASHLEY, JACK (Lab, Stoke-on-Trent S) — Consultant, Society of Telecom Executives. Sponsor: GMB. Research assistant paid by Royal Association for Disability and Rehabilitation.

ATKINSON, DAVID (Con, Bournemouth E) — Partner, Exponential, Parliamentary Advisers. New Clients: Mood Media, £250 received from both the Association of Estonians and the Lithuanian Association in Great Britain, £120 research contribution from the Byelorussion Liberation Front.

BLUNKETT, DAVID (Lab, Sheffield Brightside) — Adviser, Chartered Society of Physiotherapists (unpaid). Sponsored by NUPE (constituency party). Sheffield City Council provides rent-free premises for use as Parliamentary Office in Sheffield. UCW contributes to costs of a volunteer.

BRAINE, SIR BERNARD (Con, Castle Point) — Consultant, Police Superintendents' Association of England and Wales; visiting professor, Baylor University,

Texas (receives professorial stipend).

FAULDS, ANDREW (Lab, Warley W) — Actor, occasional voice-overs for TV, occasional filming.

FRY, PETER (Con, Wellingborough) — Director, CBA Public Affairs Ltd. Consultant, Country Political Communications Ltd, British Leather Confederation, Hamblin Group of Companies. Client: Bingo Association of Gt. Britain, London Country (North West) Ltd. Shareholder: PMS Ltd.

GRANT, BERNIE (Lab, Tottenham) — Gift: Donation from Afro Caribbean Trust for admin help because of extra commitment falling on his shoulders arising out of problems of the black community.

HATTERSLEY, ROY (Lab, Birmingham Sparkbrook) — Writer, broadcaster, occasional lecturer. Sponsored by USDAW.

HEATH, EDWARD (Con, Old Bexley and Sidcup) — Director and shareholder, Dumpton Gap Co. Member, Public Review Board, Arthur Andersen and Co. Writer, lecturer, TV, radio broadcasts on behalf Dumpton Gap Co. Lloyd's member.

HESELTINE, MICHAEL (Con, Henley) — Consultant, Haymarket Publishing Group. Owns houses in London and Northamptonshire. Shareholder, Haymarket Group and subsidiaries, J. Pridmore (Swansea) Ltd, Yoka Developments Ltd, Kensington Freeholds Ltd. London offices of Haymarket group mostly

owned by Lancaster Gate Properties Ltd; Teddington Properties Ltd; Ansdel Street Properties Ltd.
(Mr Heseltine has a private fortune of some £60 million and is ranked as one of the UK's richest 100 people).

HOWELL, DENIS (Lab, Birmingham Small Heath) — Director, Wembley Stadium Co. Ltd, Birmingham Cable Co, Buzz FM, Birmingham Radio Broadcasting, Denis Howell Consultants. Sponsored by APEX (£50 towards secretarial costs).

MEACHER, MICHAEL (Lab, Oldham West) — Sponsored by COHSE, £650 pa to constituency party.

MELLOR, DAVID (Con, Putney) — Non-practising barrister.

MEYER, Sir ANTHONY (Con, NW Clwyd) — Lloyd's underwriter (non-active).

HURD, DOUGLAS (Con, Witney) — Novelist.

TEBBIT, NORMAN (Con, Chingford) — Director BET plc, Blue Arrow plc, British Telecom plc, Sears plc, JCB Excavators Ltd (all non-executive). Adviser to chairman of British Aerospace plc. New: Director, Spectator (1828) Ltd, Golden Globe plc, charity (both unpaid). Programme presenter Sky News, contributor, *The Times, Evening Standard*.

WEATHERILL, BERNARD (Con, Croydon NE) — The Speaker, Election expenses contribution from Federation of Merchant Tailors.

(d) The rules relating to ministers and financial interests are for some extraordinary reason kept secret. The Treasury has confirmed in addition that there are no rules limiting former ministers going to work for City institutions — not even a minimum period of grace before they take up employment, as in the case of civil servants. Should ex-Chancellor Nigel Lawson's unrivalled knowledge of government economic policy be made available to a private sector institution?

US experience is relevant here. While Political Action Committees provide millions in campaign funds for US legislations, rules regarding personal remuneration have been recently tightened up. Senators are allowed to earn no more than 30 per cent of their salary in 'honoraria' while members of the House of Representatives have recently decided to forego any extra earnings at all in exchange for a hefty salary increase. New rules also forbid Cabinet Secretaries, White House Staff or Congressmen setting up shop as lobbyists for one year after leaving their posts.

Professor Zellick argues that 'the public would be appalled if it knew how much MPs were in the pockets of those who were able to buy them' and that the present situation is 'an affront to any parliamentary system of democracy'. His concern is also shared within Parliament. Sir Geoffrey Johnson-Smith's committee is currently investigating the whole area of directorships, consultancies, the role of lobbying organizations and the efficacy of existing regulations. In 1977 an earlier select committee roundly criticized three MPs who had had dealings with the corrupt architect, John Poulson. The current debate reveals that suspicions linger on. There seems little doubt that a tension exists between the public role of MPs we elect to tend our democratic institutions and their pursuit of private pecuniary interests. It would also seem that this is an area which is not only grey, but murky into the bargain.

Reference

Doig, A., *Westminster Babylon* (Allison and Busby, 1990).

PART VI The Executive Process

The American political scientist, Arthur Okun, once wrote 'Nobody comes out of graduate school with a Ph.D. in priority setting or applied ideology. And yet these are major tasks in the Executive's policy making.' Perhaps this is why so much of what the Executive branch of government seeks to do falls lamentably short of intentions. And yet is there any good reason to suppose that highly qualified political scientists would do any better? The conclusion that policy making is an imperfect art rather than a science is difficult to avoid after studying — as this section does — those agencies of government tasked with the formulation and implementation of policy. Chapter 19 begins with an analysis of the nerve centre of government, Prime Minister and Cabinet; Chapter 20 moves on to consider the workings of the central government machine, controlled by ministers but staffed essentially by Whitehall civil servants. Chapter 21 addresses an area of government which has been in retreat from the mid-1970s onwards: local government.

19 The Cabinet and Prime Minister

Dennis Kavanagh

This chapter examines the work of the Cabinet. It discusses the factors which influence its size and composition, then analyzes the structure of the Cabinet and its committees and evaluates proposals for improving the coordination of policies. It also examines the role of Prime Minister and assesses the impact of Mrs Thatcher on the office. The Cabinet system, like much of the political system, has been subject to much discussion in recent years. The final section reviews some of these criticisms and suggestions which have been made for reform.

Cabinet

The modern Cabinet is able to trace its origins back to the Middle Ages and the Privy Council, a group chosen by the monarch to give him advice on affairs of state. In the course of the eighteenth century the Cabinet gradually freed itself from the domination of the monarchy. After 1832 it was increasingly chosen to reflect the preferences registered at general elections and the mood of the House of Commons; in effect, elections rather than the wishes of the monarch decided the government of the day. The parties developed organizations so that they could win votes among the expanding electorate. In turn, the parties became more disciplined. During the nineteenth century the rise of organized political parties and the emergence of a dominant Prime Minister influenced the character of the Cabinet. As the Cabinet was drawn from the majority party, or a group which could command a majority in the House of Commons, so it was more easily able to arrive at unanimous decisions. In addition, as party discipline increased it was increasingly seen as the Cabinet of the Prime Minister of the day. The leader of the second largest party became the official leader of the opposition — a kind of PM in waiting.

The Cabinet is a committee which has both political and executive functions. The functions derive from the fact that Cabinet ministers are usually the heads of the major government departments as well as being political heavyweights. Although they are united by membership of a political party, some at least are rivals of the Prime Minister for the leadership. References to British government being an elective dictatorship (Hailsham, 1977) pay tribute to the dominant position of the Cabinet and Prime Minister today. The sovereignty of the House of Commons is in fact vested in the majority party and its leadership, i.e. the Cabinet. The manner of its work has been organized in a more formal way since Lloyd George's creation of a Cabinet Secretariat in 1916. Peter Hennessy, in his book *Cabinet* (1986, p.8ff), has reprinted the confidential *Questions on Procedure for Ministers; A Guide for Cabinet Ministers*. Some of the relevant parts are:

> 'Cabinet Procedure: Preparation of Business for the Cabinet'.
> 1. The business of the Cabinet consists, in the main, of the following points:
>   (a) questions which engage the collective responsibility of the Government, either because they raise major issues of policy or because they are likely to occasion public comment or criticism;
>   (b) questions on which there is an unresolved conflict of interest between Departments.
> 2. Proposals which involve expenditure or affect general financial or economic policy should be discussed with the Treasury.
> 3. Matters which fall wholly within the Departmental responsibility of a single Minister and do not engage the collective responsibility of a government need not be brought to Cabinet at all. A precise definition of such matters cannot be given, and in borderline cases a Minister is well advised to bring the matter before his colleagues.
> 4. These rules do not limit the right of Ministers to submit to the Cabinet memoranda setting out their views on general issues of policy.
> 5. When a Minister wishes to raise a matter at the Cabinet, the Prime Minister's consent should be sought through the Secretary of the Cabinet.

The work of the Cabinet is affected by two outstanding conventions of the British constitution; ministerial responsibility and collective responsibility.

Ministerial responsibility

According to this doctrine, each Minister is responsible to Parliament for his own personal conduct, the general conduct of his Department, and the policy related actions or omissions of his civil servants. The most important consequence of the convention is that the Minister is answerable to Parliament for the work of his department. Another interpretation is that Parliament can actually force the resignation of a Minister who has been thought to be negligent. The outstanding resignation on grounds of policy in recent years was that of the Foreign Secretary, Lord Carrington (and two other Ministers) in April 1982, following the widespread criticism of his Department's policy when Argentina captured the Falklands. There are, however, two difficulties in the way of the Commons forcing the dismissal of a Minister. One is that MPs in the majority party can usually be counted upon to support a Minister under pressure. In addition, the Cabinet is also responsible for policy and a Prime Minister knows that a Minister's resignation often reflects badly on the work of the government. Collective responsibility may therefore weaken a minister's individual responsibility (for a longer discussion see Chapter 20).

Collective responsibility

According to the convention of collective responsibility Cabinet Ministers assume responsibility for all Cabinet decisions and a Minister who refuses to accept, or opposes, a decision is expected to resign. In more recent years the convention of collective responsibility has been extended to incorporate all junior government ministers, including even the unpaid and unofficial Parliamentary secretaries. The doctrine is supported by the secrecy of the Cabinet proceedings: the refusal to make public the differences of opinion which precede or follow a Cabinet decision assists the presentation of a united front to Parliament and the country. Another aspect of the convention is that the government is expected to resign or seek a dissolution if it is defeated on a vote of confidence in the House of Commons. In other words the Cabinet is collectively responsible for policy to the Commons. (See Chapter 20 on individual accountability of ministers.)

In recent years, however, both aspects of the convention have come under pressure. The 1974—9 Labour government relaxed the principle of collective responsibility over the referendum on Britain's membership of the EEC in 1975 and the vote on the European Assembly Elections Bill in 1977. On both issues the Cabinet was divided. The myth of Cabinet unity has also been exploded by the increase in the leaks to the news media of Cabinet proceedings in recent years. In 1969 the opposition of James Callaghan, then Home Secretary, to the Labour Cabinet's decision to proceed with an industrial relations bill was widely known because of his leaks to the media and his open vote against the government's policy on the party's National Executive Committee. Mr Wilson responded by reminding all Cabinet Ministers that acceptance of collective responsibility applied at all times and in all places. He did not, however, dismiss Mr Callaghan, presumably because of the latter's powerful political backing from the unions. In 1974 some Ministers voted against the Labour government policies on the party's National Executive Committee and similar warnings were given.

There was also a good deal of leaking of Cabinet proceedings under Mrs Thatcher. In 1981 a number of Cabinet Ministers made known their disagreement with the Chancellor's budget strategy and the Leader of the House, Francis Pym, disagreed publicly with the Chancellor over economic policy. Mrs Thatcher herself, however, also publicly indicated her disagreement with Cabinet dissenters from the Chancellor's strategy. In January 1986, the disagreements between Mr Heseltine and Mr Brittan over plans for the rescue of the Westland Helicopter Company were freely reported in the mass media, as was the long-running row over exchange rates and membership of the European Monetary System between Mrs Thatcher and Nigel Lawson.

The functions of the Cabinet may be considered under various headings.

1. Although it does not actually decide many policies (though all ministers may be collectively responsible for the policies of the government), *it is the arena in which most important decisions are taken*. Often the Cabinet receives reports or ratifies recommendations from its committees (see page 390); with the annual budget — an important influence on the economic policy of the government — Cabinet ministers merely hear the Chancellor of the Exchequer's main

Functions of the Cabinet

> 1. Arena in which most important decisions are taken
> 2. Plans for business of Parliament
> 3. Arbitrates between Departments
> 4. Oversight and coordination in government
> 5. Political leadership

recommendations shortly before his statement to the House of Commons.

2. *It plans the business of Parliament*, usually a week or so in advance, making decisions about the timetabling of legislation and choosing major government speakers.

3. *It arbitrates in cases of disputes between departments*. A Cabinet adjudication is regularly occasioned when some departments fail to agree with the Treasury about their spending totals. A more dramatic case was the confrontation between Michael Heseltine, the Defence Secretary, and Leon Brittan, the Minister at the Department of Trade and Industry. The two Ministers (with Mrs Thatcher supporting Mr Brittan) favoured rival rescue bids for the Westland Helicopter Company. In the end Mr Heseltine objected to Mrs Thatcher's style of dealing with the issue and resigned in January 1986.

4. *It provides for oversight and coordination in government policies* (for further discussion of this, see below).

5. *It provides political leadership for the party* in Parliament and in the country.

The Cabinet meets weekly on Thursdays for three hours or so and at other times when summoned by the Prime Minister. A good part of its business is fairly predictable. Regular items concern the review of foreign and Commonwealth affairs and a parliamentary business report from the Leader of the House of Commons. In addition issues which are politically sensitive or topical are usually considered.

An item is usually introduced by the responsible departmental Minister. In chairing the Cabinet the Prime Minister may wish to promote a particular line but more often wants to establish how much agreement there is about a proposed course of action. At the end of the discussion the Prime Minister sums up the mood of the meeting. Once the summary is written in the minutes it becomes a decision of the Cabinet. Votes are rarely taken; they advertise divisions, may fail to reflect the different political weight and experience of Ministers and detract from its role as a deliberative body.

The Cabinet occupies a central position in the political system, *vis-à-vis* Parliament, the civil service and the public. Government Ministers and whips have to ensure they have a majority in the House of Commons for it is the Commons which sustains and may unseat them as a government. The decisions of Cabinet are instructions for civil servants to translate into laws and policies. Finally, the Cabinet has to gain the consent of the public, represented by interest groups and public opinion. Peter Hennessy describes this mix of pressures:

> Ministers must look constantly in three directions: inward to the civil service machine, across Whitehall to Parliament, and outward to the party beyond Westminster, to institutions, professions, the country as a whole and to other nations.
>
> Hennessy, 1985

If the work of Ministers varies with the Department, so Minister—civil servant relationships also vary according to personalities, departments and the nature of issues. Bruce Headey (1974) in his study of Cabinet Ministers has usefully distinguished three broad types of ministerial role.

1. **The ambassador**, who sells the policies of the government to bodies outside Westminster and Whitehall and even abroad. In particular this describes the case of a Foreign Secretary who spends a good deal of time representing the position of the British government to other states.
2. **The executive**, who is concerned to promote legislation and take decisions. He thus focuses on winning Cabinet battles (for approval of policy, legislation, or money) and getting Parliamentary time for his legislation. For example, in 1988, Mr Baker's education bill (the Education Reform Act) covered a large number of educational issues and dominated the parliamentary agenda.
3. **The key issues Minister** who selects a few policy areas and tries to initiate policy. This means that he has to delegate much of his other work to junior ministers and departmental officials.

A surprising amount of time is spent on public relations activities by Ministers, including the Prime Minister. A typical Minister will spend a good deal of time attending functions, making speeches and making official visits and inspections (see Table 19.1).

A good example of such demands on the Prime Minister came in the second week of December 1973, a particularly difficult period for the British government. The Arab oil producers had quadrupled the price of oil and Britain's coal miners were working to rule in their attempt to break the Conservative government's statutory prices and incomes policy. The government's economic policy lay in ruins, the pay negotiations were extremely difficult and many ministers and senior civil servants were on the point of physical and nervous exhaustion. Yet at the height of the

Table 19.1 *Cabinet Minister's working week*

Activity	Time (h)
Cabinet	4
Cabinet Committees	4
Parliament	14
Party meetings	3
Visits, inspections	6
Inverviews, deputations, the press, MPs with constituency problems, pressure group representatives, etc.	5
Formal receptions, lunches, meetings with ministers from abroad etc.	8
Constituency matters	2
Paperwork, office meetings	15
Total	61

Source: Headey, 1974, p. 36

negotiations with the miners, Mr Heath entertained visiting heads of states from Italy and Zaïre, presided over the Sunningdale Conference on the future of Northern Ireland and then attended the European Summit in Copenhagen. Douglas Hurd (Mr Heath's political secretary at the time) ruefully observed of these meetings:

> They all involved talks, travel, long meals, extensive briefing beforehand; yet none of them had anything to do with the crisis which was swallowing us up.
>
> Hurd, 1979, p. 121

Who serves in the Cabinet?

In a 1985 article (*Parliamentary Affairs Vol. 38, no. 1*) Martin Burch and Michael Moran examined Cabinet personnel from 1916 onwards. Their findings (see Table 19.2) challenged the widely held view that grammar school educated meritocrats like Heath and Thatcher have come to the fore in Conservative Cabinets. During the period 1955–84 a *higher* percentage of public school-educated Cabinet members served than during the 1916–55 period, together with a higher percentage of Oxbridge graduates and people from working-class backgrounds. However, the proportion of Eton and Harrow-educated Cabinet Ministers has fallen from nearly half to a (still quite remarkable) third and those with aristocratic origins from just under a third to less than one-fifth.

Examination of the years 1970–84 reveals the maintenance of public school and Oxbridge percentages at former levels and a continuing decline of aristocrats, Etonians and Harrovians. Heath and Thatcher therefore represent no revolution: they are the exceptions rather than the rule.

The Labour pattern is rather more complex. Their small number of aristocrats has virtually disappeared but big increases were registered in university- and especially Oxbridge-educated members. Ex-public school boys also increased from just over one quarter in the earlier period to about one-third in the later period. But these increases are put into a different perspective when class origins are examined: over 60 per cent of Labour Cabinet Ministers were working class in the later period and of the nineteen new entrants between 1974 and 1979 no less than eight were from

Table 19.2   *Background of Cabinet Ministers (per cent)*

	1916–55		1955–84	
	Conservative	Labour	Conservative	Labour
All public schools	76.5	26.1	87.1	32.1
Eton/Harrow	45.9	7.6	36.3	3.5
Oxbridge	63.2	27.6	72.8	42.8
Elem./Sec. only	4.0	50.7	2.5	37.5
All universities	71.4	44.6	81.6	62.5
Aristocrat	31.6	6.1	18.1	1.8
Middle class	65.3	38.4	74.0	44.6
Working class	3.0	55.3	2.6	41.0
No data	—	—	4.0	12.6
Number	98	65	77	56

Source: Burch and Moran, 1985

manual working backgrounds. In the later period it is clear that working class recruitment to Labour Cabinets was still substantial but improved educational opportunities explained why an increased proportion had enjoyed a university education. The Labour party has experienced an embourgeoisement process to some extent, but on the basis of these figures Burch and Moran argue that it is less than is widely supposed.

Size

Peacetime Cabinets in the twentieth century have varied in size between sixteen (Bonar Law in 1922) and twenty-four (Wilson in 1964). The average size of Cabinets in the twentieth century has been twenty. The wartime Cabinets of Lloyd George and Winston Churchill have been much praised and both contained fewer than ten members. It is important to note, however, that in war very different considerations operate from peacetime politics.

Decisions about the Cabinet size and composition have to balance the needs of decision making and deliberation against those of representativeness. The Cabinet is a committee which has to be small enough to allow Ministers the opportunities to discuss, deliberate and coordinate policies. Yet at the same time it must be large enough to include heads of major departments and accommodate different political groups in the party. Lobbies for different interests, e.g. education, Scotland or health, expect to have 'their' Minister represented in Cabinet.

Prime Ministers have frequently expressed their wish for small or smaller Cabinets. Some commentators have advocated a Cabinet of six non-departmental Ministers, which would concentrate on strategy and coordination and be supported by standing and *ad hoc* committees of other departmental Ministers. The growing burden of work on Ministers and the tendencies for some Ministers gradually to acquire a departmental perspective do pose problems of oversight and strategy in the Cabinet. On his return to 10 Downing Street in 1951 Winston Churchill appointed a number of so-called 'overlords', Ministers who sat in the House of Lords, were free from departmental and constituency duties, and were charged with coordinating policies in related departments. The experiment was not, however, a success. It was difficult to separate the coordinating responsibilities of the 'overlords' in the Lords from the ministerial duties of Ministers who were formally answerable to the House of Commons. More generally it is difficult to separate the tasks of coordination and strategy from those of the day to day running of a department. Separating policy from administration is easier in theory than in practice. In opposition before 1964 Harold Wilson implied that the large size (twenty-three) of Sir Alec Douglas Home's Cabinet (1963–4) reflected the weakness of Sir Alec as Prime Minister. He was implying that he would have had a much smaller one. In the event he ended up with one of twenty-four, the largest of the century. Mrs Thatcher's Cabinets in 1983 and 1987 had twenty-two members.

Appointments

If the size of the Cabinet has hardly grown in the twentieth century that of the government certainly has. The major increase since 1900 has been in government appointments outside the Cabinet — non-Cabinet ministers, junior ministers and parliamentary private secretaries (PPSs) in the House of Commons. In 1900 forty-two MPs were involved in government; today, *the number is around a hundred, or nearly a third of government MPs*. Although the PPSs are unpaid they are still bound by the doctrine of collective responsibility.

The increase in patronage is obviously an advantage for Prime Ministers. They can use it to reward or punish colleagues and perhaps to promote policies. It is, however, a power which is exercised subject to several administrative and political limitations, including the following.

1. *Ministers must sit in Parliament and most of them must be members of the House of Commons.* A few Cabinet Ministers have been appointed shortly after their election to the House of Commons. The trade union leader, Ernest Bevin, at the Ministry of Labour in 1940, was a success but another trade unionist, Frank Cousins, Minister of Technology (1964–7) and a businessman, Sir John Davies, at Trade and Industry (1970–4) were less effective. A Cabinet must also contain at least two peers, the Lord Chancellor and the Leader of the House of Lords. The parliamentary background increases the likelihood that ministers will be skilled in debate and able to handle parliamentary questions competently. Mrs Thatcher has been willing to reach out and appoint to the Cabinet peers who have had a short party political career, for example Lord Young of Graffham, Secretary of State for Employment (1985–7) and then at Trade and Industry (1987–9), and Lord Cockfield (Trade and then Duchy of Lancaster) before becoming a Commissioner with the European Economic Community. Elevating laymen to the peerage and then giving them office is a useful way of utilizing extra parliamentary talent but it can cause resentments in the government's parliamentary party.

2. *Appointments also need to take account of a person's political skill and administrative competence.* In any Cabinet there are at least half a dozen Ministers whose seniority and reputation are such that it is unthinkable to exclude them. In 1964 Harold Wilson 'had' to give senior posts to James Callaghan and George Brown, his rivals for the leadership. In 1974 there was little doubt that posts would be found for Barbara Castle, Roy Jenkins, Anthony Crosland, Denis Healey, Tony Benn and Jim Callaghan. Margaret Thatcher's Cabinet in 1979 contained hardly any surprises: Sir Keith Joseph, William Whitelaw, James Prior and Lord Carrington were all expected to hold senior posts.

The qualifications appropriate for particular posts are not always obvious and this is suggested by the apparently haphazard movement of Ministers between departments — from Environment to Defence (1981), in the case of Mr Heseltine; from the Scottish Office to Defence (1986) in the case of Mr Younger; or from the Home Office to Industry (1984) in the case of Leon Brittan. On the other hand, appointments to legal offices (Lord Chancellor, Attorney General and Solicitor General) must be made from lawyers in the party. The Chancellor of the Exchequer is expected to be competent in economic matters; Nigel Lawson (Mrs Thatcher's Chancellor for the five years before he resigned in October 1989) took a degree in Politics, Philosophy and Economics and was a financial journalist before he went into politics. The Secretaries of State for Scotland and Wales are expected to sit for Scottish and Welsh seats, respectively, and if possible be nationals of the country concerned.

In general, however, Ministers are expected to have skills in managing Parliament and coordinating meetings, reading papers quickly, and making decisions. If one excludes as effectively 'ineligible' for office MPs who are very young or inexperienced, too old or suffer from political or personal deficiencies, the Prime Minister may actually be giving government appointments to about one half of 'eligible' MPs in his party.

3. *Prime Ministers use some appointments to reward loyalty and limit dissent or outright opposition.* Mrs Thatcher pointedly excluded Mr Heath from her Cabinet in 1979 and Mr Heath excluded Mr Powell in 1970. Both were powerful figures but had been at odds with so many aspects of the party's policies and with the party leader personally that their presence would have made the Cabinet a divisive body. The Cabinets of Mr Wilson in 1964 and Mrs Thatcher in 1979 contained majorities who had almost certainly voted against them at the first stage of the leadership elections in 1963 and 1975, respectively, but both Prime Ministers had to take account of administrative talent and political weight. Mr Benn was a prominent left-wing dissenter from the Labour leadership in the 1970s but both Mr Wilson and Mr Callaghan thought it safer to keep him in the Cabinet rather than act as a focus for opposition on the backbenches. In November 1990 the new Prime Minister John Major gave the difficult job of Environment Secretary to the man who had precipitated Mrs Thatcher's downfall, Michael Heseltine. The appointment both recognised Heseltine's strength in the party and promised to keep him absorbed with fulfilling his claims over reforming the Poll Tax.

4. *Prime Ministers also want their Cabinets to be representative of the main elements in the party.* This is particularly the case with the Labour party which has had well defined left- and right-wing factions. Mrs Thatcher was less tolerant of the Wets in her early Cabinets and set about weeding them out one by one and breaking their influence in the party.

There is no adequate preparation for being a Cabinet Minister. The British tradition has been to rely on a form of on-the-job learning in which Ministers, like civil servants, pick up the skills as they settle into the job. Three background features which most Ministers have and which probably shape the way they work are:

1. *Lengthy tenure in the House of Commons.* Since 1945 the average length of time spent in the House of Commons, prior to becoming a Cabinet minister, is fourteen years, a sufficient period of time to acquire parliamentary skills.

2. *Experience on the ladder of promotion*, or ministerial hierarchy, which most politicians ascend. In an ideal world they would start off as parliamentary private secretaries and move through the ranks of junior minister, minister outside the Cabinet, and then through some of the Cabinet positions, ending with the most senior ones like Chancellor of the Exchequer or Foreign Secretary and then perhaps Prime Minister.

3. *Preparation in opposition.* In 1955 the Labour leader Clement Attlee formalized the arrangements of a Shadow Cabinet in opposition, in which a front-bench spokesman 'shadows' a Cabinet minister. Both Mr Heath and Mrs Thatcher used

| Considera-
tions affecting
Cabinet
appointments | 1. Must be members of Parliament
2. Political skill and administrative competence
3. Reward of loyalty and limitation of dissent
4. Representation of main elements in the party

Usual background qualifications
1. Lengthy tenure in the House of Commons
2. Experience on the ladder of promotion
3. Preparation in Opposition |

the opportunity of making appointments in opposition in order to prepare for office. For example, all but two of Mr Heath's appointments in the Consultative Committee (the Conservative front-bench team in opposition) in 1969 went to similar Cabinet postings. Over 80 per cent of Mrs Thatcher's opposition front-bench appointments went directly to similar Cabinet postings in 1979.

Cabinet committees

The system of Cabinet committees is a practical response to the overload of Cabinet and the need for some specialization in considering issues. In line with the concentration of Cabinet responsibility it is conventional that the names and members of most of the committees are not made public. As part of the Cabinet system, the committees are bound by secrecy and served by the Cabinet secretaries. There are various types of Cabinet committee. *Standing Committees* are permanent for the duration of the Prime Minister's term of office, while miscellaneous or *ad hoc committees* are set up to deal with particular issues. An example of an *ad hoc* body is the so-called Star Chamber which meets each Autumn to reconcile disputes between spending departments and the Treasury. A third category is *ministerial committees*, which consist only of civil servants.

A number of critics have seen the development of the committee system as a means for the Prime Minister to bypass the full Cabinet and expand his own power. It is the Prime Minister who decides to set up committees and appoint their members, chairmen and terms of reference. Scope for prime ministerial influence is enhanced by the *ad hoc* committees, since the PM has more discretion to define their terms of reference than those of the standing committees, such as Defence and Foreign Affairs.

Ministers can appeal against a committee's conclusion to the full Cabinet but only with the approval of the committee chairman. Mr Heath commented in 1975 'In my experience too many decisions came up from committees rather than too few, and there were too many cases where a chairman ought to have reached agreement but did not do so.' Even where a committee is in agreement it may want to have the decision referred to the Cabinet because of broader political considerations. During negotiations for the IMF loan in 1976 Mr Callaghan actually held twenty-six full Cabinet meetings to ensure that the issues were fully discussed and the Cabinet kept united.

Mrs Thatcher was more reluctant than her predecessors to set up Cabinet committees. She preferred to hold 'bilateral' meetings with the Minister and officials in a Department. She chaired a number of important committees, including: M15, on military intelligence and security; OD, on overseas and defence matters; EA, on economic strategy; and E (N1) on public sector strategy and oversight of the nationalized industries. A number of important decisions were taken at committee level under Mrs Thatcher. She was also careful to ensure that key economic committees contained majorities which supported her policies. For example, the decision to prohibit trade union membership for workers at the military surveillance centre GCHQ at Cheltenham was taken by a small group of ministers and then reported to the Cabinet. The decision to replace Polaris with Trident in 1980 was taken by an *ad hoc* committee consisting of Mrs Thatcher, Francis Pym (Defence Secretary), Lord Carrington (Foreign Secretary), Sir Geoffrey Howe (Chancellor of the Exchequer) and William Whitelaw (Home Secretary).

The Cabinet machine

Until 1916 there were no formal procedures for keeping minutes of Cabinet meetings or records of decisions. In that year, however, the Cabinet Secretariat was established by Lloyd George. Today the Cabinet Office is at the heart of the government machine. Its main task in relation to Cabinet and the committees are: to prepare the agenda of the Cabinet by circulating relevant papers to Ministers beforehand, record Cabinet proceedings and decisions and to follow up and coordinate the decisions by informing the departments of decisions and checking that appropriate action has been taken. The Cabinet Secretary is also the Prime Minister's secretary. Sir Robert Armstrong, a previous Cabinet Secretary, was sent by Mrs Thatcher to answer questions by the House of Commons Select Committee in 1986 when it investigated Westland, and he also answered for the government in the Australian courts when the government tried to prevent publication of the *Spycatcher* memoirs of an ex-M15 officer.

The Prime Minister also has a ***private office*** consisting of half a dozen middle-ranking civil servants as well as a press office. The former helps the Prime Minister prepare for parliamentary business and parliamentary questions and assists with correspondence and advice about the work of other departments. Some of Mrs Thatcher's advisers achieved a high profile. For example, her press officer, Bernard Ingham, presented the government's version of events in daily briefings to the press lobby. When the press and broadcasting commentators stated, 'According to sources close to the Prime Minister', or 'The view from Number 10 is . . . ', they were usually reporting the views of Mr Ingham. Some Cabinet Ministers complained that he was too closely identified with Mrs Thatcher and sometimes gave briefings which undermined other Ministers. For example, in 1986 Mr Biffen, the Leader of the Commons, and a critic of Mrs Thatcher's style, was dismissed by Number 10 as 'a semi-detached member of the government'. The dismissals in 1985 of Patrick Jenkin and Peter Rees from Cabinet were widely leaked in the media for weeks beforehand.

In 1974 Mr Wilson created a small ***Policy Unit*** to provide himself with political advice and this has been retained by his successors. Its members are political appointees and they help the Prime Minister with speech-writing, advice on politics, liaison with the party and comment on papers from other departments. They are particularly interested in the party and political consequences of existing policies.

**Cabinet
Committees**

These are supposed to be secret but over the years Peter Hennessy has published regular lists in *The Times* and elsewhere. Mrs Thatcher was frank in admitting that most ministerial business is carried out by such committees. Below is a list of some of the committees known to have been set up in the 1980s.

Economic and industrial

Committee Initials	Function
EA*	Economic strategy, energy policy, changes in labour law, the most important EEC matters
E(EX)*	Exports policy
E(NI)*	Public-sector strategy and oversight of the nationalized industries
E(NF)	Nationalized industry finance
E(PSP)	Public-sector and public services pay policy
E(DL)	Disposal and privatization of state assets
E(CS)	Civil Service pay and contingency plans for Civil Service strikes
PESC	Committee of finance officers handling the annual public expenditure survey
E(ST)	Science and Technology Policy

Overseas and defence

OD*	Foreign affairs, defence and Northern Ireland
OD(E)	EEC policy
EQ(O)	Official committee on routine EEC business
OD(SA)*	Committee on the South Atlantic, the so-called 'War Cabinet' of 1982
OD(FOF)*	Committee on the future of the Falklands
Northern Ireland	Preparation of future initiatives

Home, legislation and information

QL	Preparation of the Queen's Speech
H	Home affairs and social policy, including education
H(HL)	Reform of the House of Lords
HD	Home (i.e. Civil) defence
HD(O)	Official committee shadowing HD

Mrs Thatcher perhaps made greater use of the Policy Unit to pursue policies than any other Prime Minister. Dr Bernard Donoughue, an academic, headed the Policy Unit between 1974 and 1979, working for Mr Wilson and then Mr Callaghan. Under Mrs Thatcher there was a rapid turnover of heads of the Unit. At first it was led by Sir John Hoskyns, a businessman, then by Ferdinand Mount, a political journalist, then John Redwood, a merchant banker, and after 1985 by Professor Bryan Griffiths.

Some commentators have advocated the creation of a Prime Minister's Department. In 1981 Sir Keith Berrill, a former head of the Central Policy Review Staff (CPRS), argued for such a development on the grounds that the centre of government needed strengthening. He claimed that the Prime Minister was increasingly called upon to

HD(P)	Updating of central and local government civil defence plans
TWC	Transition to War Committee which updates the 'War Book' for the mobilization of Whitehall and the Armed Forces in a period of international tension
EOM	Monthly meeting of Whitehall establishment offices on industrial and personnel policy
MIO(E)	Special group for handling economic information. Now meets infrequently

Intelligence and security

MIS*	Ministerial steering committee on intelligence which supervises MI5, MI6 and GCHQ and fixes budget priorities
PSIS	Permanent secretaries' steering group on intelligence: prepares briefs for ministerial group
JIC(EA)	Economic intelligence assessments
SPM	Security and policy methods in the Civil Service
Official Committee on Security Personnel Security Committee	Official group supervising the working of positive vetting, polygraphs, etc.

Ad hoc

MISC 3	Public records policy
MISC 7*	Replacement of the Polaris force with Trident
MISC 15	Official group for briefing MISC 14
MISC 32	Deployment of the Armed Forces outside the NATO area
MISC 42	Military assistance (e.g. training of personnel) for the armed services of friendly powers

* Chaired by Prime Minister

Source: Peter Hennessy, 'The Secret World of Cabinet Committees', *Social Studies Review*, November 1985.

speak for the British government on a range of domestic and international issues and that other national leaders had stronger support. In 1982 Mrs Thatcher appeared to be taking steps to create such a department when she appointed personal political advisers on foreign affairs and defence. After the 1983 election she abolished the CPRS, or 'Think Tank' as it was called, strengthened her Policy Unit and made no secret of her impatience with many of the established procedures in Whitehall. She was increasingly a figure apart from her Cabinet, at times pursuing her own policies and was given to making brusque comments on some colleagues. But she subsequently disavowed any intention of creating a Prime Minister's Department.

It is possible to envisage a revamped Cabinet Office providing the basis of a Prime

Machine Minders

> The six secretariats in the Cabinet office which service the Cabinet and its Committees.
>
> Sir Robin Butler: **Cabinet Secretary**
>
> **The economic secretariat**
> Deals with economic, industrial and energy policy
>
> **The overseas and defence secretariat**
> Blends foreign and defence policy making with the output of the intelligence agencies
>
> **The European secretariat**
> EEC business has become so bulky across a wide span of Whitehall departments that it merits a secretariat of its own, separate from the rest of foreign and economic policy
>
> **Home affairs secretariat**
> This covers social policy, law and order, environment, education, housing and local government. The planning of the Government's legislative programme also falls to Home Affairs
>
> **Science and technology secretariat**
> This is the newest of the secretariats. The job used to be done by the Economic Secretariat and the Central Policy Review Staff, the now disbanded think tank. Mrs Thatcher, the first British Prime Minister to have a science degree, took a close interest in its work
>
> **Security and intelligence secretariat**
> This is the most sensitive secretariat of all. It is headed by an officer usually with the rank of permanent secretary
>
> Source: Adapted from Hennessy, 1985

Minister's Department, but there are many obstacles in the way of such a development. It is difficult to reconcile with the doctrine of collective responsibility and the principle of collegial decision making. Some Cabinet Ministers would also be concerned that their positions in their Departments might be undermined by the Prime Minister having access to independent assessments of their policies. The case for a Prime Minister's Department may be more pressing if the PM clearly has different political interests and a different political agenda from that of the Cabinet. But if he or she feels blocked then it would be simpler to change the Cabinet, as Mrs Thatcher did in 1981. It is still the case that Prime Ministers who are thought to ride roughshod over Cabinet colleagues or ignore them take political risks and generally get a bad press. This aspect of Mrs Thatcher's political style was devastatingly criticised in Sir Geoffrey Howe's resignation speech in November 1990 and was a major factor in her subsequent downfall.

Coordination

Some observers have suggested that British government resembles a medieval system in which the departments operate as relatively independent fiefdoms. Bruce Headey

(1974) interviewed a number of former and present Cabinet ministers and found that most of them regarded themselves primarily as ***representatives*** of or spokesmen for the department *vis-à-vis* Parliament, the Cabinet and the public. Others emphasized the internal aspect of their work, ***managing*** and organizing the department. Only one in six regarded themselves as ***initiators*** of policies, in the sense of defining the department's policy options. The departmental pressures on many Ministers tended to limit their opportunities to contribute to the formation of government policy making in general. Thus Headey argued that ***Britain had departmental rather than Cabinet government***.

How, therefore, is government policy coordinated? Do Ministers have a sense of strategy, a sense of ***where***, collectively, they are going? On a financial level Treasury control of public spending and the annual spending reviews obviously provide the opportunity for some oversight. Informal consultations between senior officials of departments and the formal interdepartmental meetings also provide the opportunity for coordination. The role of the Cabinet Office in servicing the Cabinet and its committees, preparing and circulating papers and following up Cabinet decisions is also relevant. Finally, there is the system of Cabinet committees itself to coordinate policy.

Yet many argue that the Cabinet does not coordinate very efficiently. In part, this is a problem of sheer overload of work which results in Ministers lacking sufficient time to read and digest papers on many matters outside their departmental responsibilities. The Cabinet does many things other than coordinating policy (see above). In part it is also a consequence of so much of Ministers' time being spent on running and representing their own Departments. A number of Ministers have remarked upon how rare it was for them to comment on other issues before the Cabinet. Many illustrations of these pressures are to be found in the published diaries of Richard Crossman and Barbara Castle: Ministers, for example, arrived at Cabinets having only glanced at papers which did not concern their own Departments.

It is worth considering the views of two experienced observers on the 'overload' problem. Sir Frank Cooper, a senior civil servant under Attlee until shortly before the end of the first Thatcher administration, commented:

> I think the whole idea of collective responsibility, in relation to twenty-odd people has had diminished force, quite frankly, over the years, coupled with the fact that to deal with the modern world . . . with the very, very complex problems that government have to deal with, it's inevitable that they should move into a situation where four or five are gathered together.
>
> cited in Hennessy, 1986, p.164

David Howell, who served as a Minister under Mr Heath and Mrs Thatcher, commented:

> The Cabinet is not a place where decisions can be formulated. It's bound to be a place where decisions that have been formulated by smaller groups, maybe of ministers, and party people together, or may be parliamentary groups outside and then put to ministers or maybe the Prime Minister and her advisers quite separately, are then tested and validated and argued about.
>
> cited in Hennessy, 1986, p.164

Steps to improve coordination

1. Small Cabinets
2. Small groups or 'Inner' Cabinets
3. Amalgamation of departments
4. Central analytical body
5. Prime Minister's department

There are a number of steps which might promote coordination, including the following.

1. The creation of a *small Cabinet*, including some *non-departmental ministers*. The model often advanced is that of the wartime Cabinets of Lloyd George (1916—18), Winston Churchill (1940—5), or even Margaret Thatcher during the Falklands War. But many are not convinced that the wartime model is suitable for peacetime and there are political and administrative problems involved in divorcing coordination from policy making.

2. The creation of *small groups, or 'Inner' Cabinets*, of senior figures, to impart a greater sense of direction to Cabinet. After 1945 Clement Attlee regularly consulted with the senior Ministers, Morrison, Bevin and Cripps. In 1968 Harold Wilson created a parliamentary committee which was supposed to operate like an inner Cabinet. In fact, Crossman's diaries confirm that Mr Wilson was not keen on developing a strategy and the group never played such a role. Most Prime Ministers have had groups of colleagues with whom they informally discussed matters before they reached the full Cabinet. But such behaviour may be more a recognition that ministers are not equal in political weight and experience than evidence of attempts to develop an inner Cabinet.

3. *The amalgamation of Departments*. Of major Departments today those of Defence, Foreign and Commonwealth Office, Environment, Health and Social Security and Trade and Industry have all resulted from amalgamations in the past twenty years of previously autonomous Departments. It has been argued that the creation of giant Departments provides the opportunity for coordination of policies within the enlarged Departments and allows for the creation of a smaller Cabinet. Mr Heath introduced two of the giant Departments, Environment and Trade and Industry, and also had the smallest (eighteen) post-war Cabinet.

4. The creation of *a central analytical body*, not attached to a Department but serving the Cabinet as a whole. Mr Heath had this in mind in 1970 when he set up the Central Policy Review Staff, or 'think tank' as it was called, located in the Cabinet Office. Its task was to present briefing papers on issues, free from any departmental perspective, and to undertake research and suggest ideas which did not fall within the responsibility of any particular department. It also provided periodic reviews on how the government and departments were performing in relation to the strategies set out in the party's 1970 manifesto. (As already mentioned, Mrs Thatcher had less use for the CPRS and abolished it in 1983.)

5. The creation of *a Prime Minister's Department*. In spite of the Prime Minister's private office and Policy Unit it is doubtful that he or she has sufficient resources to monitor and coordinate the policies of departments. The development of a strong Prime Ministerial Office would probably move Britain into a more presidential style of leadership and might face resistance in departments.

Classifying
Prime
Ministers

Francis Williams (Attlee's Press Secretary) classified leaders either as **pathfinders**, **problem solvers** or **stabilizers**: Gladstone, Lloyd George and Baldwin were cited respectively as exemplars of each type. Philip Norton suggests an interesting alternative classification:

Innovators seek power in order to achieve a future goal and are prepared, if necessary, to bring their party kicking and screaming in their wake in order to achieve that goal. **Reformers** seek power in order to achieve implementation of a particular programme, but one drawn up by party rather than by the premier. **Egoists** seek power for the sake of power; they are concerned with enjoying the here and now of office rather than with future goals. **Balancers** can be divided into two categories: those that seek power in order to achieve balance within society and within party, and those that, though having the same aim, do not seek power, but rather have it thrust upon them, usually as a compromise choice for party leader.

The categories are not mutually exclusive but designed rather to identify preponderant tendencies. An individual may display some elements of each category, but with one preponderant. It would be unusual, for example, for a Prime Minister not to display some egoist tendencies, even though his or her primary purpose may be to achieve some philosophically dictated future goal.

Norton uses his classification to categorize the eighteen twentieth-century (to 1990) Prime Ministers as follows:

Innovators		**Reformers**
Churchill		Campbell-Bannerman
(wartime)		Asquith
Heath		Chamberlain
Thatcher		Attlee

Egoists		**Balancers**
Lloyd George?	Salisbury	Bonar Law
MacDonald?	Balfour?	Douglas-Home
Eden	Baldwin	
Wilson	Churchill	
	(peacetime)	
	Macmillan	
	Callaghan	

Source: Norton, 1988

The Office of Prime Minister

Chapter 16 on 'Crown and Parliament' traced the evolution of Britain's political system from an absolute monarchy to a representative democracy in which the Prime Minister has come to exercise many of the executive powers wrested from the Monarch. During the twentieth century the office has increased in power.

Study of the style and impact of the Prime Minister is almost inevitably an analysis of what particular premiers have done. There are certain statutes and conventions which affect the premier's institutional position but the lack of a formal written constitution means that there is considerable scope for each incumbent to make what he will of the office. As Sir William Harcourt noted,

'In practice the thing depends very much upon the character of the man. The office of Prime Minister is what its holder chooses and is able to make of it.'

Two features are noteworthy about the political background of those who make it to 10 Downing Street.

1. They have already served a lengthy apprenticeship in the House of Commons; on average, twenty-four years in the twentieth century up to the accession of John Major.
2. They have usually already occupied a number of Cabinet offices, often senior ones. Table 19.4 shows that of the Prime Ministers who have held office in the twentieth century all but seven had already occupied one of the three great offices as Home Secretary, Foreign Secretary or Chancellor of the Exchequer. The Foreign Office had been held by six, the Home Office by three and the Treasury by nine. Mr Callaghan had occupied all three offices. It is also interesting to note that Lloyd George, Baldwin, Churchill, Heath and Wilson had all served as Presidents of the Board of Trade (now part of the Department of Trade and Industry) before becoming Prime Minister. Only Ramsay MacDonald in 1924 had no prior Cabinet experience. Both Mr Wilson and Mrs Thatcher had some

Table 19.3   *Prime Ministers during the twentieth century*

Prime Minister	Party	Took office
The Marquess of Salisbury	Unionist (Conservative)	25 June 1895
Arthur James Balfour	Unionist (Conservative)	12 July 1902
Sir Henry Campbell-Bannerman	Liberal	5 December 1905
Herbert Henry Asquith	Liberal*	8 April 1908
David Lloyd George	Liberal†	7 December 1916
Andrew Bonar Law	Unionist (Conservative)	23 October 1922
Stanley Baldwin	Unionist (Conservative)	22 May 1923
J. Ramsay MacDonald	Labour	22 January 1924
Stanley Baldwin	Conservative	4 November 1924
J. Ramsay MacDonald	Labour	5 June 1929
J. Ramsay MacDonald	National Labour‡	24 August 1931
Stanley Baldwin	Conservative‡	7 June 1935
Neville Chamberlain	Conservative‡	28 May 1937
Winston S. Churchill	Conservative§	10 May 1940
Clement Attlee	Labour	26 July 1945
Sir Winston Churchill	Conservative	26 October 1951
Sir Anthony Eden	Conservative	6 April 1955
Harold Macmillan	Conservative	10 January 1957
Sir Alec Douglas-Home	Conservative	19 October 1963
Harold Wilson	Labour	16 October 1964
Edward Heath	Conservative	19 June 1970
Harold Wilson	Labour	4 March 1974
L. James Callaghan	Labour	5 April 1976
Margaret Thatcher	Conservative	4 May 1979
John Major	Conservative	28 November 1990

Notes: * Coalition government from May 1915; † coalition government; ‡ national government; § coalition government from May 1940 until May 1945; national government from May 1945 until July 1945

Source: Norton, 1988

Table 19.4 *Ministerial backgrounds of Prime Ministers, 1900—90*

	Foreign Office	Home Office	Treasury
Salisbury	✓		
Balfour			
Campbell-Bannerman			
Asquith		✓	✓
Lloyd-George			✓
Bonar Law			✓
Baldwin			✓
MacDonald			
Chamberlain			✓
Churchill		✓	✓
Attlee			
Eden	✓		
Macmillan	✓		✓
Home	✓		
Wilson			
Heath			
Callaghan	✓	✓	✓
Thatcher			
Major	✓		✓
Total	6	3	9

experience in two relatively junior departments — the Board of Trade for Mr Wilson and the Department of Education and Science for Mrs Thatcher.

This background ensures that party leaders and Prime Ministers have had the opportunity to acquire parliamentary skills, gain experience in running departments and become familiar through proximity with the premier's role. It also ensures that they are well known to colleagues who are able to judge their suitability for leading the party. John Major is unusual in that he became Prime Minister after only eleven years as an MP, although he had held the offices of Foreign Secretary (if only briefly) and Chancellor of the Exchequer.

Prime Ministerial power

Controversy about whether the expansion of Prime Minister's power has now effectively displaced Cabinet government is one of the perennial subjects of debate in the study of British politics. The old textbook model portrayed the premier as *primus inter pares* and the government as collective, even though commentators admitted that such leaders as Gladstone, Lloyd George and Neville Chamberlain acted independently of the Cabinet. Richard Crossman (1963) and John Mackintosh (1962) are the major proponents of the view that the Prime Minister has become so dominant in the post-war period that the Cabinet has been almost relegated to a side-show. Both were academics as well as Labour politicians. Walter Bagehot's *English Constitution* (1867) drew a distinction between the dignified and the efficient parts of the British constitution. He claimed that although many people thought that the monarchy had effective power the reality was that it only had ceremonial importance and the less glamorous Cabinet was the effective source of power.

In his 1963 *Introduction* to Bagehot's book Crossman extended the image and argued that the Cabinet had now joined the dignified part of the constitution. John Mackintosh in his *The British Cabinet* (1962) had also argued that the Prime Minister had become more dominant during the course of the twentieth century. Both men point to such features as the rise in disciplined political parties which deliver assured majorities and which have a vested electoral interest in preserving unity; the emergence of a Cabinet Secretariat which gives the Prime Minister something akin to a department of his own; the unification of the civil service with the Head responsible directly to No. 10; and the development of the Cabinet committee system which enables the Prime Minister to 'divide and rule' through personally chairing key committees and bringing the resultant decisions to Cabinet for confirmation. Other students of government point to the concentrated media spotlight within which the modern premier works. Whatever he does is instant news and with clever media management — especially when playing the prestigious globe-trotting role of world leader — the PM can project an attractive, impressive and vote-winning image. The sheer pace of modern politics also delivers power to the premier: many things have to be decided quickly by small groups over which the PM can exert decisive control.

According to Crossman (1963, p.51) the post-war epoch has seen the final transformation of Cabinet Government into Prime Ministerial Government. Against this, a number of points can be made:

1. One has to be cautious in talking of prime ministerial versus Cabinet power; the temptation is to see the power relationships as zero sum, i.e. what the Cabinet gains the Prime Minister loses, and vice versa. But a Prime Minister should benefit, both politically and administratively, from having able Cabinet colleagues, and could certainly be undermined by a weak cabinet.
2. There are political costs if the Prime Minister is seen to defeat Cabinet colleagues. If such actions are reported — as they usually are — they will tend to weaken loyalty and collegiality within the Cabinet and undermine the public and parliamentary standing of defeated ministers.
3. A Prime Minister may get his way in Cabinet largely because he has few policy preferences distinct from those of the majority in Cabinet. Some Prime Ministers are careful not to push a line unless they are sure that it will command the greatest acceptance of Cabinet. Mr Wilson was virtually isolated in Cabinet over trade union reform in 1969 and this undoubtedly had a chastening effect on his subsequent behaviour as Prime Minister. Mrs Thatcher won many Cabinet battles but she also suffered many defeats (e.g. the sale of Land Rover to General Motors in 1986 and numerous cases between 1979 and 1981). The crucial point is that very little is decided without the Prime Minister's approval. Peter Madgwick (1986, p. 32) expressed this well when he said that, although very little may be decided by the Prime Minister alone, 'the Prime Minister is always consulted — not so the Cabinet'. There is such a thing as a *central executive territory* and the important point is the centrality in it of the Prime Minister.

The Prime Minister is certainly more than 'first among equals'. Formal powers (see below) are important in distinguishing him from Cabinet colleagues. He also has many more opportunities to present himself as the spokesman of the government

— in the Commons at Question Time, in interviews with the mass media and at international conferences he speaks for the government.

Much of the discussion about 'the power' of the Prime Minister, however, suffers from being too general and static. Power varies according to the interplay of the broad political situation, the personality and skills of the Prime Minister and the particular issue. One also needs to distinguish between opportunities for exercising power and power itself. Does it refer to a Prime Minister's resources, e.g. the right to appoint to Cabinet and many other posts, chair the Cabinet or seek a dissolution of Parliament — which may be used to exercise power — or the achievement of intended policies?

Fixed and variable powers

A useful way to proceed is perhaps to distinguish between the *fixed* and *variable* powers of the Prime Minister.

Fixed

Many of these are prerogatives which have been gained from the Crown. They include, for example, the right to appoint and dismiss Cabinet Ministers, seek a dissolution of Parliament and summon and chair Cabinet meetings. These powers are fixed regardless of who the Prime Minister is.

However, each of the above powers is qualified.

1. The *power of appointment* to ministerial positions and dismissal is a very considerable power but it is subject to many limitations (see above). A Prime Minister may have to make concessions to Ministers to keep the Cabinet united and avoid damaging resignations. Mrs Thatcher tried very hard to dissuade Lord Carrington in 1982 and Leon Brittan in 1986 from resigning, and Mr Callaghan relied heavily on the loyalty of Michael Foot between 1976 and 1979 to keep Labour's left wing in check.

2. Similarly, the right to *dissolve Parliament* is not a 'big stick' to use against dissenting colleagues, but an opportunity to choose the most favourable time to the government for holding an election. Yet it is worth noting that five of the eleven post-war dissolutions have been lost by the defending party (1951, 1964, 1970, February 1974, 1979). Prime Ministers are also careful to consult widely among influential figures in the party before selecting a date. Mr Callaghan in 1979 and Mr Heath in 1974 found that choosing 'wrongly' and losing an election fatally weakens a leader's position. In other words, the power to seek a dissolution is a two-edged sword.

3. The power to *set the agenda* for Cabinet and summarize discussions is not unlimited. It is difficult for a Prime Minister to exclude controversial items from the agenda when an existing line of policy is unpopular and/or is thought to be failing, and a sufficient number of colleagues wish to discuss it. Both Mr Wilson and Mrs Thatcher had to give way to sustained pressure from Cabinet colleagues and discuss issues, the first over devaluation in 1966, the latter over economic strategy in 1981. Both Prime Ministers had previously confined discussion of

Britain's first woman Prime Minister

Margaret Hilda Roberts was born in Grantham on 13 October, 1925. She was brought up in a flat above her father's grocer shop, with an outside toilet and without a bath or running hot water. Every Sunday the family went to the local Methodist Church. At the age of eleven she won a scholarship to the local girls' high school and from there she went to Somerville College, Oxford, where she read Chemistry.

Following her defeat, in 1950, in the Labour seat of Dartford, she qualified as a barrister and married Major Denis Thatcher. Her political career did not falter with the birth of twins, and in 1954 Margaret Thatcher became MP for Barnet. She held a junior post in the Macmillan government and her star continued to rise during the 1960s. In 1970 Edward Heath made her Secretary of State for Education, and she fought hard and successfully for large increases in her Department's budget.

It was clear after the Conservatives' two election defeats in 1974 that Mr Heath's days as Leader of the Party were numbered, and in early 1975 he was forced to seek re-election. Sir Keith Joseph was not a contender — ruled out after an extraordinary speech in which he lamented the high rates of birth among the 'lower social groupings' and advocated birth-control to control poverty, for which he was dubbed 'Sir Sheath' by *Private Eye*. He later explained that the speech 'led to my precipitate withdrawal from any pretensions and made way for Margaret Thatcher with her infinitely larger political capacities'.

None of the leading figures in the Cabinet would run against Mr Heath, so Margaret Thatcher was the only real alternative for whom anti-Heath MPs could vote. In the first ballot, on 4 February 1975, she received 130 votes against Mr Heath's 119 (Sir Hugh Fraser received sixteen and eleven votes were not cast). In the second ballot a week later after Heath's withdrawal, it was too late for William Whitelaw (seventy-nine votes), Sir Geoffrey Howe (nineteen), James Prior (nineteen) or John Peyton (eleven) to prevent Mrs Thatcher (146 votes) from being elected. In June 1974, she had told the *Liverpool Daily Post*: 'It will be years before a woman either leads the Party or becomes Prime Minister. I don't see it happening in my time'. Only nine months later, to the surprise of most people, Margaret Thatcher became Leader of the Conservative Party — to some extent by accident. After winning three general elections in 1978, 1983 and 1987 she became the longest-serving Prime Minister in the twentieth century. She resigned in November 1990.

the issues to a small number of ministers and kept it away from full Cabinet.

4. A Prime Minister's freedom from departmental responsibilities does leave him with some opportunities to survey the whole scene and perhaps busy himself in the affairs of another department. But the scale and complexity of modern government means that most business is inevitably left to the departments. Prime ministerial interventions in departmental matters represent opportunity costs, including a Prime Minister's opportunity to do other things. Such interventions may be counterproductive because the Prime Minister is inevitably absent from the germinating stage of many policies in the department. Prime Ministers are almost invariably involved in issues of international diplomacy and the economy, and their tight schedules limit the issues with which they can involve themselves.

Variable

1. Power over colleagues does not necessarily extend to decisive power over events. As Hugo Young points out, 'The Prime Minister exists on a diet of insoluble dilemmas. All the most difficult problems in the end finish up with the PM and very few of them have an obvious answer. So that, at least, is a very great limitation on their power.' (Jones 1986, p.14).

2. Back-benchers, or Cabinet Ministers who have substantial back-bench support, can challenge a Prime Minister and reduce their room for manœuvre. As Lord Home has remarked, 'if the Prime Minister cannot command the House of Commons then he's done'. Effectively this means the ability of the PM to retain the loyalty of his own party. The PM's control over appointments and the confirment of honours can hold a goodly proportion of the governing party in thrall but there are limits to this power. Within his own Cabinet Mr Wilson found this to his cost with his Industrial Relations Bill in 1969. Mr Callaghan was a prominent opponent, and a key stage in the collapse of Mr Wilson's plans was when the Chief Whip reported to Cabinet that he would not guarantee the passage of the Bill. According to Gordon Walker (1970, p. 93), Mr Wilson and his Foreign Secretary were also overruled by the Cabinet over a proposal to send ships to the Gulf of Akaba in a effort to forestall the six-day war between Israel and Egypt.

In 1975 the Wilson Cabinet was so divided over Britain's membership of the European Community, and in 1977 over the type of electoral system to be used for elections to the European Parliament, that collective responsibility was abandoned.

Mrs Thatcher was also forced to bow to back-bench pressure. Often this was exercised discreetly via the Whip's Office or the 1922 Committee but on other occasions revolts broke out on the floor of the House; in April 1986 Mrs Thatcher was severely embarrassed when the Shops Bill was defeated following a major revolt by Conservative MPs.

**James
Callaghan**

James Callaghan was born in Portsmouth in 1912 of working-class parents; leaving school at 16 he joined the Inland Revenue and became active in trade union work. From 1937 to 1947 he was Assistant Secretary of the Inland Revenue Staff Federation. During the war he became a junior officer in the navy and in 1945 won South Cardiff for Labour and later South East Cardiff. He began his ministerial career in 1947 as the parliamentary secretary to the Minister of Transport. During the 1950s he steadily climbed the ladder of seniority in the party, somewhat to the left of its revisionist wing.

In 1963 Callaghan stood for election as Labour leader and finished third behind Harold Wilson and George Brown. In 1964 he became Chancellor of the Exchequer but after devaluation of the pound in 1967 moved to the Home Office where he stayed until 1970. At first it was thought he had suffered a demotion but he managed to rehabilitate himself. His powerful trade union backing helped him to sabotage Wilson's *In Place of Strife* plans for reforming the trade unions. From 1974 to 1976 Callaghan served in his third great office of state, the Foreign Office, before replacing Wilson as party leader — but only after the third ballot.

Callaghan's main objective was to keep the Labour movement together. He was a centrist in ideology, appealing to many members of the left and right wings of the party. His public image was one of smiling geniality but this disguised a toughness which he showed in private dealings. At PM's questions he regularly saw off the new Leader of the Opposition, Mrs Thatcher, through the employment of his own brand of humorous condescension.

In October 1978 his decision not to hold a general election proved a calamitous mistake. The ensuing 'winter of discontent' scarred the public image of Labour as a party of industrial chaos. After losing the 1979 election he resigned as Leader in 1980. He left the House of Commons in 1983 to tend his farm but he accepted a peerage and still speaks — often on foreign affairs — in the House of Lords.

Margaret Thatcher as Prime Minister

In spite of the persistent role requirements, each office holder has the opportunity to write a fresh page of prime ministerial history. Some have been political *mobilizers*, concerned to achieve significant changes (e.g. Gladstone over Home Rule for Ireland, or Attlee on social and economic change in 1945, or more recently, Mrs Thatcher). Other Prime Ministers operate more as *stabilizers* or *conciliators*, not wishing to disturb the status quo.

Mrs Thatcher's premiership shows how a Prime Minister's 'score' on these two criteria may change over time. Until 1982 her Cabinet was very divided on economic policy and this was widely reported in the mass media. So-called 'wets' (who favoured more public spending and more government action to reverse the rise in unemployment) and 'drys' (who agreed with Mrs Thatcher in regarding the conquest of inflation as the main task) leaked their own selective version of events to the media. By contrast, there were very few leaks from Mr Heath's Cabinet. Frequent leaking of rows is a sign of poor Cabinet morale. Mrs Thatcher (and her Chancellor, Sir Geoffrey Howe) had their way on economic policy but only after bitter Cabinet rows. After 1982, as the Thatcher government came to be regarded as more successful, and many dissenting 'wets' were replaced, so there were fewer reports of divisions. Mrs Thatcher was widely seen as a dominant and successful Prime Minister. She was prepared to lead the Cabinet from the front rather than be a collector of voices. On several issues — abolishing domestic rates, ending the metropolitan authorities, tackling trade union powers, prohibiting trade union membership for workers at GCHQ and promoting privatization — she made an important difference to government policy.

The reasons why Mrs Thatcher became more dominant provide important insights into the source of prime ministerial power. They seem to be as follows.

1. Her *successful use of Cabinet reshuffles* — or the power to hire and fire — over time to produce a more loyal team. She had originally appointed her supporters to the key economic departments in 1979. During 1981 she gradually dismissed a number of dissenters from her Cabinet, including Soames, Gilmour, Carlisle and St John Stevas, and moved James Prior to the office of Northern Ireland. Later she dismissed Francis Pym from the Foreign Office and David Howell. She appointed newcomers like Parkinson, Brittan, King, Lord Young and Lawson, who were more supportive of her policies and owed their promotion to her.
2. She gained from *policy successes*, particularly the down-turn in inflation in 1982 then, decisively, the recapture of the Falklands, the steady rise in the living standards of those in work and, of course, from general election victories in 1983 and 1987.
3. She simply held fewer Cabinet meetings — Peter Hennessy suggests half as many as her Labour predecessors. Ex-Defence Minister John Nott reckoned full Cabinet meetings were more often occasions when decisions reached elsewhere were formally endorsed.

4. She ***bypassed the Cabinet*** on occasions, relying heavily upon her Policy Unit and making decisions either in Cabinet committees (see above), bilateral meetings between herself and her advisers and the departmental minister, or high powered inter-departmental task forces of able Civil Servants reporting direct to No. 10. Peter Hennessy describes a typical example of this way of working:

> Mrs Thatcher will ask a particular Cabinet colleague to prepare a paper on a particular issue just for her, not for the Cabinet or her Cabinet Committee. The Minister is summoned to Number Ten with his back-up team. He sits across the table from Mrs Thatcher and her team which can be a blend of people from the Downing Street Private Office, the Policy Unit, the Cabinet Office and one or two personal advisers. She then, in the words of one Minister, proceeds to 'act as judge and jury in her own cause'.
>
> Hennessy, 1986, p. 289

4. She also ***interfered energetically in departments***, following up initiatives and taking an unprecedentedly close interest in the promotion of senior civil servants.

It is difficult to generalize from the Thatcher experience. She did not change the office of Prime Minister. She did not, for example, as we have seen, create a Prime Minister's Department or other major new institutions. She pushed her powers to the limit and may have demonstrated to successors what can be done by a Prime Minister who is determined, energetic and knows what he or she wants.

The fixed powers in the office are formidable when they are exercised by a skilled and determined Prime Minister, such as Lloyd George, Winston Churchill and Margaret Thatcher — especially when the incumbent has been in the office for some time (see Figure 19.1). An economic or military crisis usually produces a speeding up and concentration of decision making. But wars and crises do not necessarily produce heroic premiers — think of Asquith, Lloyd George's predecessor, or Neville Chamberlain who preceded Churchill. Finally, the power of the Prime Minister who is popular, and whose party is in a commanding position is likely to be more influential in Cabinet than one who is dogged by unpopularity and economic or other failures.

Longest consecutive spell in office, months

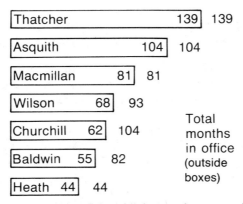

Figure 19.1   *Prime Ministers: time served*

Success tends to build on success and failure upon failure. Mr Wilson, for example, was a less dominant figure in his Cabinet after the devaluation of the pound in 1967 than he had been before. Mrs Thatcher was more powerful after Falklands and after her 1983 and 1987 election successes.

Mrs Thatcher has often been described as 'presidential' but it is inappropriate to compare the Prime Minister as Presidential with the President. Three significant institutional differences between the two political systems preclude us from doing so.

1. The President is directly elected by the voters, separate from his party. The British premier is essentially the leader of the majority party in the Commons returned by a single election.
2. The President is not necessarily in control of his party in Congress and in recent years has not enjoyed an assured majority in Congress: the Republican George Bush faces a Democratic majority on Capitol Hill. This is the separation of powers in action. In Britain, the Cabinet's existence derives from its being backed by a majority in the House of Commons.
3. The Cabinet in the USA is weak, infrequently convened and in no sense a decision making body. The constitution, after all, vests the executive power in the President; he is constitutionally responsible for exercising it. In Britain, as noted, the executive is collective, and the Cabinet at times has overridden the Prime Minister. Mrs Thatcher may appear to have been presidential but that is only because she so dominated her own party and hence the whole political system. Such a command of events does not come with the job; it has to be earned through persuasion, leadership and successful policies.

Nor can it be said that Mrs Thatcher destroyed Cabinet government. Certainly she bypassed and weakened it and certainly she dominated it. Hennessy relates the occasion in January 1984 when Geoffrey Howe began to introduce a paper to the Cabinet's Overseas and Defence Committee on the need for exploratory talks with the Argentine Government on the sovereignty of the Falkland Islands: 'Mrs Thatcher cuts in "Geoffrey, I know what you're going to recommend. And the answer is 'no'! End of item. Nobody argues with the boss." But according to senior officials close to the centre of power, "Cabinet government is largely intact." ' Mrs Thatcher has been regularly bested in Cabinet and during the Falklands War as one Cabinet Member testified, 'she had to carry us on every major decision'. (Hennessy, 1986, p. 111.) Hugo Young agreed. 'Cabinet government undoubtedly still exists despite rumours sometimes heard to the contrary.' He perceived 'a collective mood of those who are in Cabinet which acts, may be often, as an explicit veto on what Prime Minsters may want to do' (Jones, 1986, p.14).

Nevertheless, it is probably true that the system is not performing as efficiently as it ought to.

The problem of Prime Ministerial overload

During the nineteenth century Disraeli was able to find time to sustain his position as one of the country's most popular novelists — despite being Prime Minister of a country with the largest empire in history. During the twentieth century pressures became more acute but Asquith still had time to pursue scholarly interests; Churchill used to paint, lay bricks, take afternoon naps and enjoy more than just the occasional drink; Macmillan used to consume great draughts of Trollope even during crises; and Edward Heath had his music and his yacht to help him relax. The amount of time available to perform prime ministerial tasks, let alone unwind, has been cruelly squeezed.

Bernard Donoughue worked as a No. 10 adviser in the 1970s and has analysed the diary arrangements of Wilson and Callaghan between 1974 and 1979:

650	Cabinets and Cabinet Committees
120	audiences with the Monarch
300	meetings with individual ministers
200	meetings with individual MPs
1000s	of meetings with officials
130	meetings of the Parliamentary Labour party
400	Question Times
50	major Commons speeches and statements
200	meetings with party committees and officials
120	visits to party constituencies and organizations
1000	appointments and 150 formal meals with British visitors and hosts
160	meetings and 120 formal meals with visiting representatives of foreign countries
35	official visits overseas (taking some 75 days)
15	weeks of general elections, referenda and party conferences.

Donoughue, 1988

Cabinet and party affairs clearly take up major slabs of available time while appearances in the House and meetings with overseas visits take up most of the rest. Donoughue comments, 'A PM needs to be both lark and owl. The early mornings are disturbed by telephone calls about urgent political or government business. Yet he is still often at the Commons or at a State banquet until midnight. It is a pounding, physical and nervously stressful regime.'

Each premier is different, of course:

Callaghan's life was more 'regular' and structured than Wilson's because their personalities differed in that way. Callaghan needed more sleep and disliked late nights. He did not drink alcohol whereas Wilson liked to spend hours sharing a beer or a brandy with those around him. Callaghan preferred to see his personal staff on a pre-arranged basis, whereas Wilson enjoyed calling impromptu meetings for both serious policy discussions and frivolous gossip; the former also spent more time with his wife and family than did Wilson.

ibid.

It is generally accepted that, when she was Prime Minister, Mrs Thatcher had virtually no known relaxations, survived on five hours' sleep or often less, and chose to work around the clock, seven days a week. She was even known to have become bored when on holiday, cut it short, and return to work. Francis Pym once claimed that she would have liked to run every department herself: by any standards an unrealistic ambition.

Quality of Cabinet Government

Dissatisfaction with the structure and performance of Cabinet government is not surprising in view of the criticisms of Britain's economic performance in the post-war period. Among criticisms which have been advanced are the following.

1. Ministers are too frequently *generalists* and appointed to posts for reasons which may have little to do with their presumed expertise. For example, Richard Crossman, having shadowed education in opposition before 1964, was surprised to learn that he would become Minister of Housing and Local Government in the new Labour government. In the 1979 Conservative government Francis Pym started off in Defence, moved to the leadership of the House of Commons and then became Foreign Secretary, all in the period of three years. In cases of routine policy making it is perhaps not surprising that civil servants may often determine policy and the principle of ministerial responsibility may provide a shield behind which the civil service dominate the policy process.

2. *The frequent turnover of Ministers*, who last an average of some two years in each Department, a rate of change exceeding that in most other western states. Such turnover means that at any one time a number of Ministers are actually learning their jobs. Under Harold Wilson (1964—70) the average ministerial tenure was less than two years. In his 1966—70 government only Denis Healey at Defence, Lord Gardiner as Lord Chancellor, William Ross, Minister of State for Scotland and Mr Wilson himself held the same office for the duration of the government, and in the lifetime of Mrs Thatcher's 1979 government only six Ministers held the same office. Some commentators have claimed that Ministers need a period of two years or so to actually master a Department. On the other hand, it is often claimed that if a Minister spends too long in a Department he may 'go native' and perhaps become too closely identified with its interests. The case for introducing a new Minister is that he is likely to provide a stimulus to the policy routine. But many reshuffles of Ministers are made for reasons which have little to do with policy.

3. *Ministers are often overloaded with work*. Richard Crossman's diary portrays a Minister frequently reading his briefs for Cabinet at the last moment, rushing about from meeting to meeting and complaining about the lack of time or opportunity for thinking about political strategy. In his revealing book *Inside the Treasury* (1982), the former Labour Minister Joel Barnett commented on how 'the system' can defeat ministers:

> The sheer volume of decisions, many of them extremely complex, means that by the time even a fairly modest analysis of a problem is done, and the various options considered, you find yourself coming up against time constraints. Consequently ministers often find themselves making hasty decisions, either late at night or at an odd moment during a day full of meetings
>
> p.20.

4. *Decisions are taken for short-term political gain*, as instanced in Barnett's book,

as well as in the Castle and Crossman diaries. Barnett (p.17) criticized the ways in which decisions were taken by his 1974–9 Cabinet colleagues 'for some other reason which has nothing to do with the merits of the case'. About priorities in public expenditure he commented:

> expenditure priorities were generally decided on often outdated, and ill-considered plans made in Opposition, barely thought through as to their real value, and never as to their relative priority in social, socialist, industrial or economic terms. More often they were decided on the strength of a particular spending minister and the extent of the support he or she could get from the Prime Minister'.
>
> ibid., p. 59

Reform

Among reforms of the Cabinet which have been canvassed in recent years are the following.

1. ***The creation of a body which can help the Cabinet deal with strategy***. This may include the re-creation of something along the lines of the CPRS which existed between 1970 and 1983. A number of observers claim that even if the original CPRS did not fill the need there is still scope for a body which can brief the Cabinet as a collective body.
2. ***The creation of a Prime Minister's Department*** (see above).
3. ***An increase in the number of political aides or advisers for Ministers***. Since 1974 between twenty and thirty political advisers have worked in Whitehall. It is often argued that this system should be extended and strengthened, as in France and the USA. This is urged on the grounds of strengthening ministerial influence in the Department rather than enhancing the collective role of the Cabinet.
4. ***A reduction in the power of the Prime Minister***, so developing what Tony Benn, in 1979, called a constitutional premiership. Benn objected to the scale of the Prime Minister's patronage as well as other fixed powers. He advocated the election of Cabinet Ministers and allocation of their duties by Labour MPs and the confirmation of public appointments by Parliament.
5. Taking steps to ***improve the quality of policy making in opposition***. It is striking how total the divorce between government and opposition is in the British system. It is possible for a government to take office with many of its members having little or no executive experience. This was largely the case with Ramsay MacDonald's first Labour government in 1924 and Wilson's 1964 government. Neil Kinnock has not held even a junior ministerial post. In the first post-war Labour government a Minister, Emmanuel Shinwell, confessed that for many years he had talked about nationalizing the coal industry but when he came to implement the manifesto pledged in 1945 he found no plans existed.

According to Peter Hennessy (1986) a number of measures might improve the transition between opposition and government, including the following.

1. Relaxation of secrecy so that the documents and options considered by Ministers and civil servants are opened to public discussion.

2. The temporary appointment of a few high-flying civil servants to the opposition to assist the policy making process.
3. An increase in the budgets and research expenses of political parties. At present the two major parties get £440,000 per annum for 'parliamentary work' with about £150,000 given to the SLD.
4. Greater use of the Douglas Home rules (1963) which allow opposition spokesmen to have contacts with senior civil servants in the relevant departments. The Conservatives made some use of this facility before 1979 but Labour did not before 1983.

References and Further Reading

Bagehot, W., *The English Constitution* (1867; Fontana, 1963).
Barnett, J., *Inside the Treasury* (Deutsch, 1982).
Burch, M. and Moran, M., *British Politics: A Reader* (Manchester University Press, 1987).
Burch, M. and Moran, M., 'The Changing British Parliamentary Elite', *Parliamentary Affairs*, **38**(1), (1985).
Crossman, R., 'Introduction to W. Bagehot', in *The English Constitution* (Fontana, 1963).
Donoughue, B., *Prime Minister* (Cape, 1987).
Donoughue, B., 'The Prime Minister's Day', *Contemporary Record* (Summer 1988).
Gordon Walker, P., *The Cabinet* (Collins, 1970).
Hailsham, Lord, *Dilemma of Democracy* (Collins, 1977).
Headey, B., *British Cabinet Ministers* (Allen & Unwin, 1974).
Heath, E., 'Mr Heath and Lord Trend on the art of Cabinet government', *The Listener* (April 22 1976).
Hennessy, P., 'The Secret World of Cabinet Committees', *Social Studies Review*, (November 1985).
Hennessy, P., *Cabinet* (Blackwell, 1986).
Hurd, D., *An End to Promises* (Collins, 1979).
Jones, B., *Is Democracy Working?* (Tyne Tees TV, 1986).
Jones, B., 'Mrs Thatcher's political style', in B. Jones (ed.), *Political Issues in Britain Today* (Manchester University Press, 3rd edn 1989).
Mackintosh, J., *The British Cabinet* (Stevens, 1962).
Madgwick, P., 'Prime Ministerial power revisited', *Social Studies Review* (1986).
Norton, P., 'Prime Ministerial Power', *Social Studies Review*, (January 1988).

20 Administering Central Government

Andrew Gray and Bill Jenkins

A friend once told me that an intelligent Italian asked him about the principal English officers (civil servants) and that he was very puzzled to explain their duties, and especially to explain the relation of their duties to their titles . . . The Italian could not comprehend why the First Lord of the 'Treasury' had as a rule nothing to do with the Treasury, or why the 'Woods and Forests' looked after the sewerage of towns . . .
. . . the unsystematic and casual arrangement of our public offices is not more striking than their difference of arrangement for the one purpose they all have in common (serving ministers) . . . Yet there are almost no two offices which are exactly alike in the defined relations of the permanent official to the Parliamentary chief.

Bagehot, (1867, p.210)

Bagehot's comments still apply more than a century later. Indeed, they have become more pertinent as state services have expanded and administrative arrangements have become more complex. In central government there is now not only a variety of Departments and Ministries, headed by secretaries of state or Ministers, but also public corporations and special purpose bodies, usually headed by chief executives or chairmen who report to Ministers. Moreover, the relationships between the political masters and the executive organizations differ widely. As with much else in British government, all this has developed rather haphazardly over the years and is not governed by any single set of principles, let alone a body of law. This chapter sets out to describe this world of administering central government by emphasizing two features: first, its *organizational* dimension, i.e. the way the administration of central government is the product of its organizations, and secondly, its *political* dimension, i.e. the relationship in theory and practice between politics and administration. In the following section, we shall outline the principal functions of the central administrative system and identify the elements of the organizational and political dimensions. These will then be explored in turn: the organizational dimension by investigating the structure and processes of the central administrative organizations, and the political dimension by examining the way that the various operations of representative and responsible government affect central administration. The chapter will conclude with a discussion of some current issues and trends, especially those which bring out the political nature of central administration and the shift in it towards a new managerialism.

Functions, Organizations and Politics

The functions of the administrative process

'Well,' said Owl, 'the customary procedure in such cases is as follows.'

'What does Crustimoney Proseedcake mean?' said Pooh. 'For I am a Bear of Very Little Brain, and long words Bother me.'

'It means the Thing to Do'.

'As long as it means that, I don't mind', said Pooh humbly.

Winnie the Pooh, A.A. Milne (1958)

Many would regard administration as about customary procedures and thus 'the Thing to Do'. But these procedures serve a variety of functions, so much so that Pooh might well have got a little bothered if he realized how contentious some of these can become. For ease of reference we can distinguish between those activities which arise from, first, the managerial function of government in society; secondly, the different roles played by organizations in the policy making process; and thirdly, the services and benefits which such organizations provide directly to the public (see Table 20.1).

Despite the attempts since 1979 to reduce the role of the state, any government in the UK provides three *managerial functions for society:* those of economic management, political management and national integration. In *economic management* the executive process helps to provide the structure to support the development of the economy. This is less extensive now than a decade ago but it has always been a function of government to facilitate trade. Similarly, the executive provides a machinery whereby government can assimilate and satisfy political forces. Pressure group representations, for example, are made directly to administrative organizations. To the extent that these organizations help to register and manage these represented interests, they serve the function of *political management* and thereby contribute to *national integration*.

Policy management conceals a host of different functions, from those providing supporting services for policy making and implementation, through research and advisory tasks, to promotional or even obstructive roles. Much of this is hidden from public view (although it has been given popular enactment in the television shows

Table 20.1 *Functions of the administrative process*

Managerial function for society	Policy management function	Service-providing function
Economic management	Support function	Scope of service
Political management	Research function	Technical complexity
Management of national integration	Advisory function	Resource requirements
	Promotional function	Client groups
	Obstructive function	

Source: Gray, 1975

Yes Minister and its successor *Yes Prime Minister*). To the citizen, however, administrative organizations are important because they provide a wide range of *services* to society. Each has its own scope, technical complexity, resource requirements and client group which give it its character.

Many of those who seek to join the higher ranks of the civil service are aware of something of these functions. Almost all recognize the potential power and influence which arises from such proximity to the centre of government. Few, at least until recently, however, have made much of the managerial scope which is offered by participation in the organizations which comprise central government. Yet their scope and scale of operations means that in government there are some of the most rewarding challenges offered by the organizational world. It is this combination of the organizational and the political which gives central administration its character and significance. The next few pages will introduce what is meant by these organizational and political dimensions.

The organizational dimension of the administrative process

'Off with her head!' said the Queen at the top of her voice. Nobody moved.
Alice in Wonderland, Lewis Carroll (1865)

The state has been a pioneer in using organization as the principal mechanism by which its decisions and orders are translated into effects; the epithet 'bureaucratic' is still (if mistakenly) associated more with government than with private business. Thus, we cannot account for the administration of government without an examination of those of its features which derive from the existence of organizations within it. It is this which constitutes the *organizational dimension* of the administrative process (see Table 20.2).

The importance of this dimension has been recognized increasingly over the past twenty years as more attention has been paid in government to its structure and processes. Structure refers to the allocation of authority, the division of labour, formalization and different aspects of size and complexity of organizations. Processes are the dynamic mechanisms by which the executive organizations maintain themselves (e.g. staffing, decision making, implementation and control). Moreover, organizations do not exist in a vacuum but relate to the world outside (i.e. their environments). The forces in the environment can push and pull organizations or in turn be influenced by them. The environment and the organization are thus always in a state of change. Managing this changing relationship is a vital part of administration in government (Table 20.2).

Table 20.2 *Organizational dimension of administration*

	Environment	
Organizational structure	**Organizational process**	**Organizational behaviour**
Organization of authority, division of labour, etc.	Staffing, decision making, implementation, control, etc.	Loyalty, compliance, morale, etc.

Source: Gray, 1975

The political dimension of the administrative process

Sir Humphrey Appleby: 'I am merely a civil servant, I just do as I am instructed by my master' (i.e. the minister).

Yes Minister, J. Lynn and A. Jay (1981)

References to the political dimension are legion in books on public administration. However, these references are rarely elaborate, sufficing with a few passing remarks on the public interest or political accountability. So, what does it involve? We should begin by examining the relationship between politics and administration.

The quotation above highlights what political scientists call a descriptive/normative problem. What the distinction between politics and administration *should* be (i.e. the normative part of the problem) varies with writers and contexts. However, in general it seeks a separation of adminstration from politics often with a view to preventing a type of pollution of the former by the latter. The spirit of this distinction is captured by the fictional civil servant, Sir Humphrey Appleby, in the above quotation. The premise is, of course, that politicians make policy and officials implement it. In practice (i.e. the descriptive part of the problem), the distinction is not as simple as this. Despite the way textbooks on British government have implied that only politicians engage in politics, the latter are found wherever differences between people affect their interests. Something of the practical as well as semantic difficulties of the distinction may be seen from the first box.

Another practical distinction implied is that between the *making* and the *taking* of decisions. Ministers often like to think that they take decisions; here not only constitutional doctrine but the practical reality suggests that they do. On the other hand, the basis on which they so take them and the extent of their choice may be severely constrained not least by the crucial factor of time. Events themselves may seem to suggest a particular course of action. So too might the way a decision comes to be presented. In these ways the administrative processes may have a very real influence on the construction of options and thus of the choices themselves.

Politics and administration: fact or fiction?

Mrs Betty Oldham (MP on Select Committee):
'Look, Sir Humphrey. Whatever we ask the Minister, he says is an administrative question for you. And whatever we ask you, you say is a policy question for the Minister. How do you suggest we find out what is going on?'

Sir Humphrey Appleby (Permanent Secretary, Department of Administrative Affairs):
'Yes, I do think there is a real dilemma here, in that while it has been governmental policy to regard policy as the responsibility of Ministers and administration as the responsibility of officials, questions of administrative policy can cause confusion between the administration of policy and the policy of administration, especially where the responsibility for the administration of the policy of administration conflicts or overlaps with the responsibility for the policy of the administration of policy.'

Source: Lynn and Jay, 1982, p. 176

What is here called the political dimension of the administrative process derives in part from the wider political system and in part from within the process itself. It comprises both attitudes towards the fundamentals of the political system as well as the activities that make up the workings of government. ***Political attitudes***, e.g. those toward the system of representative democracy, the role of the state or the conduct of the individual in government, provide a climate in which the process operates. During the past ten years there has been a more persistent questioning of these underlying political values than for some decades previously, and this has necessarily affected central administration. Similarly, the actual ***working of the wider political system*** provides a context to which administration must necessarily adapt. These workings have been described as *Representative and Responsible Government* (Birch, 1964). 'Representative' here refers to the patterns of participation in the system, the elective method of selection to office and to the sense in which government reflects the population over which it rules. 'Responsible' means responsive, rational or considered government, and accountable government.

The character of representative and responsible government in the UK is important for the administation of central government. Ours is a system which relies on the elective principle for members of the legislature and indirectly the executive branch, but not for other appointments in government. That administrative organizations may be representative of the wider population to only a limited extent was recognized by the Fulton Committee in 1968 (Cmnd 3638) in its remarks on the way the Civil Service was too parochial and out of contact with the population it served.

Similar observations may be made about the importance of responsible government. In relatively open systems, governments like to show their responsiveness to public pressure and events. The nature of the response is significant for the character of the administration. Some governments, including that of Edward Heath, 1970–4, have had a tendency to establish new agencies, thereby demonstrating their activity but creating a certain amount of organizational upheaval and fragmentation in the process. Other governments, including those of Mrs Thatcher, 1979–90, have eschewed structural responses in favour of changes to working methods and personnel and a reliance on the government information machine.

The interpretation of responsible government as rational or considered implies that decisions are taken by a process of consultation and deliberative judgements. In turn this implies an elaborate machinery by which different branches of administration are involved, not only in implementing and reporting on the results of past decisions but in the formulation of choices and strategies for new ones. The forms of responsibility or accountability for these decisions vary widely, some involving the legal process or the judgements of professionals, as well as the wider parliamentary and political process.

We shall describe later some of the ways in which these modes of accountability matter in the executive process. But it is important to note that these political aspects are not restricted to the wider political system of which the executive process is a part but also comprise the political character of activity within it. Politics is about accommodating interests. Agencies and sub-agencies have interests (perhaps reflecting clients, professional values or simply budgetary desires) which they wish to pursue. These also form part of the political dimension of central administration (see Figure 20.1).

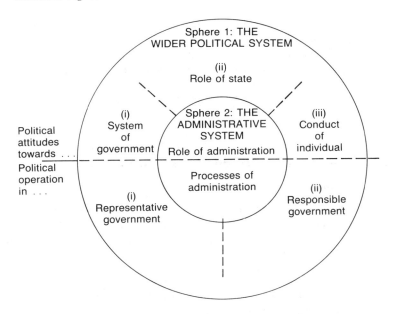

Figure 20.1 *The political dimension of the administrative process*
(Source: Gray 1975)

Organization and Central Administration

In the early 1970s an obscure government agency, the Crown Agents, found itself at the centre of a controversy. Originally this organization acted as the London representative of colonial governments in such matters as recruitment, financial borrowing and supplies. As these governments gained their independence, the Agents' role lost its validity but many of the new Commonwealth governments continued to use them. This meant considerable sums of money flowing through the organization. The temptation to speculate with these funds proved too great and over three or four years the Agents amassed losses of £180 million and were prevented from bankruptcy only by an urgent rescue operation by the Treasury. It was not an auspicious illustration of what in 1968 the Fulton Committee on the Civil Service had advocated, i.e. the quasi-independent government agency (Cmnd 3638). Not surprisingly, there were not many new agencies established in the 1970s, despite the support given to the idea by Mr Heath's Conservative Government of 1970–4.

In February 1988, after eight years of paying little attention to the machinery of government, the Prime Minister announced to the House of Commons that the government was to separate from departments a number of agencies which, while still accountable to Parliament through Ministers, would have considerable discretion in the discharge of their affairs. Progress since 1988 suggests that this is a potentially far-reaching reform subjecting substantial parts of government operations to the rigours of more professional management and the disciplines of the market.

This turnaround suggests that not only is the machinery and management of central government subject to fashion but in general its overall development has lacked a set of guiding principles. In fact, it is not so much the shortage of underlying principles as their inconsistent use which explains this. This is not simply the fault of those responsible for the structures and processes which have evolved; for the *differentiation of tasks, functions, and contexts* is both a cause as well as an effect of administering central government.

The structure of central administration

A variety of organizations

The principal organization of central government is the ministry or (much more commonly these days) **Department**. Each is responsible for providing a service or function and is headed by or directly accountable to a Minister or secretary of state in the Cabinet. This link between the Department and Parliament is crucial. Through it policies are formulated, decisions taken, programmes and services implemented and accountability exercised. Among these Departments are the great offices of state (the Foreign and Commonwealth office, the Home Office and the Treasury) and others still retaining the title of office (e.g. Northern Ireland, Scottish and Welsh) and ministry (as in Defence and Agriculture). Of those now called Departments, many are well known because of the services they provide directly to the public (e.g. the Departments of Health, Social Security and Employment). Some Departments, however, are very small and hardly impose themselves on the public in a visible way. These include the Land Registry (with which a house buyer registers his entitlement) and the Lord Chancellor's Department (which administers the system of justice through the courts).

Although the Conservative governments since 1979 have made few changes to the responsibilities of these departments (they separated Social Security and Health, but resisted the temptation to split up the Ministry of Agriculture after the epidemic of food scares in 1988 and 1989), they have adopted a consistent policy of reducing the *size of the civil service*. Figure 20.2 traces the changes since the Second World War. The Conservative government achieved a reduction of over 100,000 between 1979 and 1984, almost a fifth of the total it inherited. Official statistics suggest that about a third of the reduction was due to the transfer of functions to non-civil service or private sector organizations or the ending of services and about a half due to increases in efficiency.

The civil service departments have been the mainstay of central administration for centuries. Over the past forty years, however, some of their functions have been delegated to semi-independent *departmental agencies*. These bodies are responsible for clearly defined executive operations without a significant public policy implication. The Property Services Agency in the Department of the Environment, for example, provides accommodation and related services for other government bodies, the National Health Service Management Board in the Department of Health oversees the various regional and district health authorities through which the National Health Service is provided, and the Training Agency in the Department of Employment

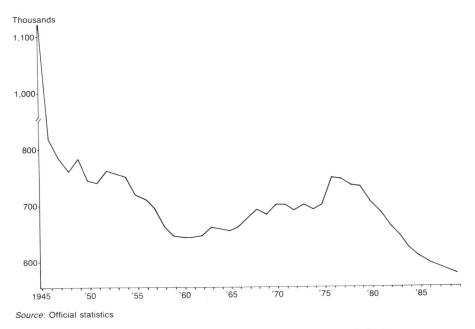

Source: Official statistics

Figure 20.2 *Civil service numbers (Source: Government statistics)*

is responsible for government training programmes. Each agency has a director or chief executive responsible to the permanent secretary of the parent department or directly to the minister. Their advantage lies in the way day to day management is relatively free from ministerial interference and the flexibility which they can provide in government (including in their creation and dissolution).

In early 1988 the Government published a report entitled *Improving Management in Central Government: the Next Steps*, which became instrumental in extending the use of agencies in central government. The Report itself was written by members of the Efficiency Unit, part of the Cabinet Office (Efficiency Unit 1988). It proposed the establishment of agencies wherever the execution of services could be feasibly separated from policy work. The Government endorsed the proposal and set up a project team to implement the programme.

The intention is to eventually reorganize about three-quarters of the central administration into agencies, leaving small cores of headquarters staff in each Department. From the middle of 1988 a succession of new agencies was established, each with its own framework of policy and resources agreed with its parent Department and the Treasury. There are now over fifty agencies comprising half of the civil service.

Table 20.3 contains examples of both old and new agencies classified by their principal function. This development is potentially the most significant of all the Conservative government's reforms of the civil service. It has implications for the accountability of Ministers and their officials because it seems to separate responsibility for administration and management from that for policy. It will also

Table 20.3   *Some examples of departmental agencies*

Common service agencies for Central Government	Promotional agencies	Regulatory agencies
Civil Service College* Her Majesty's Stationery Office Property Services Agency	Research Councils (science, medical, etc.) Housing corporation	Commission for Racial Equality Monopolies Commission Companies House* Vehicle Inspectorate* Training Agency DSS Resettlement Units*

*Set up under the agency programme from 1988

affect the way in which government services are provided, not least in the emphasis placed on serving customer needs.

Another development which has been a feature of the period since the Second World War, and associated particularly with the Labour government of 1945–51, is the development of nationalized industries. These take organizational form in **public corporations**. They are accountable to Parliament through their Ministers, who set policy for standards of service, pricing and financial targets, but their day to day operations are the responsibility of their managements.

The purpose of such corporations is to ensure that industries which contribute strategically to the national infrastructure should be guided by the public interest while still operating on a commercial basis. Some of these corporations survive within the government machine (e.g. British Coal and British Rail). Others have been **privatized**, i.e. sold to private owners through the issue of shares, and are now public limited companies (plcs) (for a list of the major companies involved see Table 20.4). Some of the one-time public corporations have had very varied histories. What is now British Telecom plc, for example, began life as a government department (part of the old General Post Office), was then established as part of the Post Office public corporation, and later set up separately as a public corporation before being sold to the private sector.

Why are there these different central government organizations and how are functions allocated between them? As we have seen already, there is no golden rule by which these matters are regulated. Rather, different factors are influential in different times and contexts. However, this does not mean that there cannot be any underlying principles. The justification for having different types of central organization, for example, lies in the fact that government tasks and functions vary and thus one form would not be suitable for all of them. Some may be essentially commercial in nature (and are subject to the discipline of the market), while others are intrinsically political and require ministerial involvement. Similarly, dividing up functions helps to develop specialization in the performance of tasks, while encouraging discipline and quality in the provision of services. Yet these advantages also bring their problems; each separation of function brings a potential for those who work in them to identify with their functional interests rather than with the general interest of government as a whole.

Table 20.4 *Principal privatizations 1979–89*

Company	Date and Value of Sale (£millions)	
British Petroleum	November 1979	290
British Aerospace	February 1981	150
British Petroleum	June 1981	293
Cable and Wireless	October 1981	224
Amersham International	February 1982	71
Britoil	November 1982	549
Associated British Ports	February 1983	22
British Petroleum	September 1983	566
Cable and Wireless	December 1983	275
Associated British Ports	April 1984	52
Enterprise Oil	June 1984	392
Jaguar	July 1984	294
British Telecom	November 1984	3,916
British Aerospace	May 1985	551
Britoil	August 1985	449
Cable and Wireless	December 1985	933
British Gas	December 1986	5,434
British Airways	February 1987	900
Rolls Royce	May 1987	1,363
British Airports Authority	July 1987	1,225
British Petroleum	October 1987	7,240
British Steel	December 1988	2,500
Water	November 1989	5,240

Objectives

These issues arise notably in the central government Departments themselves, not least in the extent to which they have *objectives*. In practice there are many problems with the idea of government Departments having objectives (e.g. they can be multiple and conflicting). Yet the obvious appeal of Departments with purposive activities has led to an increasing emphasis on objectives and their achievement in the management of government Departments. Most recently this has come in the Conservative government's Financial Management Initiative (FMI) which since 1982 has sought to provide departmental managers with 'a clear view of objectives and performance' (Cmnd 8616, Appendix 3, para 5).

As part of the FMI, departments had to specify their goals. It is notable that Departments actually find it hard to articulate their intended achievements; they are better at telling us what they do. This may be because the Departments are themselves federations of divisions and sections all with their purposes and goals. They also show how varied these activities are.

Authority

Government organizations are designed to serve Ministers and their authority. This authority comes from their position within the government and in turn from Parliament. Each organization may be seen as a bureaucracy, that is, an organization

> **Department of Education and Science**
> Its role is to secure the effective provision of services and the
> execution of national policy by local authorities and others by the
> exercise of regulatory and other powers and through discussion,
> explanation and persuasion
>
> **Department of Transport**
> The main functions of the Department of Transport are:
> (a) development and management of the national road system;
> (b) sponsorship and regulation of, and financial assistance to, inland
> surface public transport; and sponsorship and regulation of road
> haulage;
> (c) sponsorship and regulation of the shipping and ports industries;
> sponsorship of the civil aviation industry and, mainly through the Civil
> Aviation Authority, its regulation on safety and economic grounds;
> (d) allocation of resources and guidance to local authorities for their
> transport functions;
> (e) conduct of international relations and negotiations in respect of
> international civil aviation and shipping;
> (f) road safety, including regulation and licensing of vehicles and
> drivers, and marine safety, including the coastguard;
> (g) prevention of pollution of the sea by ships and cleaning up
> pollution of the sea caused by ships and oil installations
>
> **Treasury**
> The core of the Treasury is a policy orientated central organization
> concerned with financial and economic policies and the control of
> public expenditure
>
> Source: Cmnd 9058, 1983

in which there are fixed areas of jurisdiction, activities governed by rules, and authority allocated through a hierarchy of positions; in short an organization governed by office. But Departments are also organizations in which other authorities are exercised. To be effective in the discharge of their functions they require expertise, which comes to be an authority in its own right. Thus lawyers, accountants, doctors, engineers and others in government are recognized as holding their own authority based on professionalism and expertise.

Government organizations are therefore characterized by many authorities, often reflected in the structures which separate the responsibilities of generalist administrators (i.e. those representing the main line of ministerial authority) and specialist professionals. Nowadays this distinction is less obvious in the formal structures of Departments but is still important for day to day operations. Thus professional authority can challenge the main ministerial authority of the organization.

Allocation of functions

Government organizations are not, however, simply structures of authority; they are also mechanisms by which functions in government are allocated and provided for. Here, at last, are some principles which we can identify as being usable. Faced with the multiplicity of functions of modern government, an administration can allocate them in at least four distinct ways: by purpose, by process, by client group or by territory.

An allocation by *purpose* takes us back to goals or objectives. Traditional governmental tasks such as law and order, defence and foreign relations and the facilitating of trade are supplemented in modern government by a range of welfare and related services such as social security, health, housing and education. Departments and other agencies based on allocation by purpose will be organized around these services.

Often these services or purposes depend on particular working methods or *process* and the skills which they call for. Where these processes (e.g. medicine, finance, engineering) have distinctive characteristics requiring separate organizational forms we can expect to find organizations based on them.

Departments or agencies based on purpose or process may well contribute beneficially to the development of specialized service provision by integrating effort around a particular purpose or skill. There is a danger in such an arrangement, however, which lies in the way that the needs of the *clients* of these services rarely if ever neatly coincide with these purposes or skills themselves. Indeed, clients tend to have conditions which require integrated treatments, not separate ones. This can apply especially to those who are socially disadvantaged as one condition can often be associated with another; the poorly housed, for example, tend to suffer more sickness. Over the past hundred years or so this has led to demands for services to be provided by organizations which bring together the needs of clients rather than the needs of the service or process. In principle, this could mean agencies dealing with the elderly, the young, the unemployed or any other client group with an identifiable set of interrelated needs.

It is also possible to see an integration of services or processes in relation to the needs of *territories* as well as clients. If different areas of the country have their own topographical, cultural, economic or political characteristics, it may be advantageous to bring services together to serve the resulting distinctive needs. In the recession which began in the mid-1970s, for example, it was noticeable how the traditional heavy industries were hit hardest. These tended to be in a few parts of the UK (the north east, Clydeside and Northern Ireland, for example). Where such characteristics are reinforced by the need to acknowledge distinctive political traditions (as in the case of Scotland, Wales or Northern Ireland) this makes an even stronger case for agencies based on these territories so that their development can be tackled in a coherent way consistent with their character and local wishes.

It is clear that these principles are not mutually consistent, which implies a problem for British central government because, as Table 20.5 shows, it uses all of them simultaneously. But the problem goes deeper, for even these Departments represent

Table 20.5 *Allocation of functions: some examples by Departments*

Purpose principle	Process principle	Client principle	Territory principle
Health and Social Security Education and Science Environment	Foreign and Commonwealth Office Board of Inland Revenue Lord Chancellor's Office	Employment	Northern Ireland Office Scottish Office Welsh Office

combinations of these principles. In practice, however, the ***purpose principle*** has been the most persistent influence, even if other factors have been important enough to have been frequently overruled. The explanation of the variety (or you may think it an inconsistency) is of course that circumstances and political pressures change. Thus, at one moment an economic recession may lead a government to attend (or wish to show it is attending) to hardship in certain areas, at another to a particular client group's needs and at another to the development of a particular service. We must also remember that a government has to accommodate a number of political forces represented often by particular Ministers all using the machinery of government as the means of advancing their own careers. Thus all these factors exert competing pressures on the allocation of functions to government organizations.

A structure of disintegration?

One of the major problems arising from all these separated structures is the ***integration of government organizations***. Governments can overcome this by coordinating institutional arrangements. These include some of the central departments and other agencies which have functions across central government (e.g. the Treasury through its management of public expenditure and the economy, and the Office of the Minister for the Civil Service through its responsibility for personnel matters). There are also Cabinet and interdepartmental committees which work to coordinate activities in areas covered by more than one department. But in the past decade a number of these integrative arrangements have been dismantled, including the Civil Service Department (which was the personnel department for the civil service) and the Central Policy Review Staff (a corporate policy planning unit). As a result, more coordinating responsibility has fallen on the Cabinet Office and especially on the Prime Minister's own staff. Episodes such as the Westland helicopter affair (of which more later) suggest that this responsibility is difficult to discharge effectively. This may mean an increasing integrating burden on the processes of central administration.

The processes of central administration

The processes of central administration are those systematic activities designed to help facilitate the delivery of government. This section will examine only a few of the main processes but from them you should be able to understand not only how they operate but also the contribution they make to the effectiveness of government. These are the systems which give government its management style.

The increasing recognition since 1979 of the importance of the management of central Departments has led to a more systematic approach to the definition of problems, the setting of goals, the making of choices and the implementation and control of programmes of activity. The following sections will explore some of these aspects to see whether they represent a shift to a more coherent ***management*** of central government.

Staffing

The previous section spoke of the danger of a disintegration of government and how administrative mechanisms could alleviate this. Of central importance here is ***staffing***,

Table 20.6 *Senior grades in the Civil Service: the open structure*

Senior grades in the Civil Service	
Grade 1	First Permanent Secretary
Grade 1A	Second Permanent Secretary
Grade 2	Deputy Secretary
Grade 3	Under Secretary
Grade 4	Executive Directing Bands
Grade 5	Assistant Secretary
Grade 6	Senior Principal
Grade 7	Principal

i.e. those processes of recruitment, training and personnel review which can promote a social and technical homogeneity in the management of government. Because central government is a massive undertaking, much of the responsibility for the content and design of staffing processes rests with the government organizations themselves. However, in the central Departments and associated agencies there is a common policy and, especially at senior levels (the open structure, see Table 20.6), a central implementation as well. The principal organization responsible for civil service recruitment, for example, is the Civil Service Commission. Its primary role is in the selection of entrants into the higher grades of the Service, i.e. the administrative and professional trainees and more senior entrants.

The main qualifications for selection include certain minimum academic attributes and personality characteristics all of which are assessed by the Civil Service Selection Board (CSSB) in a series of tests combining simulations, analytical exercises and interviews. In the past some criticism has been made of the validity of the tests employed for the way successful candidates came very largely from arts-based subjects studied at Oxford and Cambridge. Over the years this pattern has become gradually less marked, but still few scientists and technologists come through the procedures. Of course, this may be as much the result of the predisposition of persons from these disciplines towards civil service work as a reflection of any distortion in the selection process itself.

Training in central government is carried out largely by the organizations themselves. Especially in the big Departments, there are extensive training divisions which cater for the varied, usually technical, needs of functional performance. One such departmental training establishment is that which was shared by the Departments of the Environment and Transport with the Property Services Agency (which in the early 1970s were all one department). A boxed profile of the training programme provided is shown. Programmes such as these are very important in maintaining the quality of personnel and thus performance.

Top peoples' pay in the Civil Service

(as at 1 January 1991)	
Head of Civil Service	£95,756
Permanent Secretary (Treasury)	89,500
Permanent Secretary	77,000
Deputy Secretary	64,300
Under Secretary	52,100

**Internal
training
programmes**

Reception and new entrant training
General management
Financial management
People, skills and office techniques
Information technology
Computer-based training
Department procedures
Contracts
Accommodation management
Building and civil engineering
Professional training
Mechanical and electrical engineering
Programmes for particular groups:
    Driver vehicle license officials
    Coastguards
    Vehicle inspectorate, etc.

Source: Departments of Environment and Transport, 1988–9

There is also, however, an important central training facility for central government as a whole in the Civil Service College. Part of the original intention in 1970 was to develop a staff college on similar if not quite such developed lines as the Military Staff College at Sandhurst. Under such a scheme officials would undergo regular training programmes, some of which would be required for promotion. However, there has never been the Government commitment to the training function nor to the College itself necessary to give this idea any chance of being realized. Indeed, paradoxically the College has gained a reputation for considerable competence in routine training programmes at the same time as its capacity for innovation and development has been reduced. The recent introduction of the Top Management Programme, a three-week course with which the College is associated and which is designed for ascending under-secretaries, is one of very few programmes which fits the original conception. However, this development and one or two recent appointments suggest a revival of its central role, even a recognition that training too has to be managed. The College's re-establishment in July 1989 as an executive agency (still within the Office of the Minister for the Civil Service (OMCS)), confirms this.

Departmental management

Since 1979 the Government has initiated a number of management reforms designed to promote economy, efficiency and effectiveness. Although these terms are often confused by Ministers, they represent a rallying call to the new managers and, more significantly, a philosophy for decision making and control. What are its elements?

The theory of decision making points to the need to *identify problems, specify objectives, search for* and *select options, implement choices* and *review effects*. In reality decisions are never as straightforward as this rational exposition implies. Objectives and means tend to become merged in government, especially where there is a need to move forward on an agreed basis. However, Mrs Thatcher's governments attempted to edge closer to the theoretical model, in particular by seeking to separate the choice of values and objectives from the management of means. The former, the Conservatives believe, are the preserve of Ministers and they are supposed to have some very clear ideas about what these are. It is the job of civil servants to manage the implementation of the chosen policies.

There have been two principal developments in the government's programme, the Efficiency Strategy and the Financial Management Initiative. The former was originally established in 1979 under Sir Derek Rayner, who until 1983 was Mrs Thatcher's adviser on efficiency. Sir Derek was a well-respected businessman from Marks and Spencer who had worked in the Ministry of Defence in the early 1970s. From the outset his scheme sought to combine attempts to reduce operating costs with the identification of more deeply seated obstacles to good management in government. Thus, it identified problems with the collection of government statistics, systems for paying benefits and those caused to members of the public and managers alike by unwieldy and incomprehensible forms. Over the years the reviews of efficiency which were undertaken led to considerable savings in the costs of services, even if some would argue that there was also a deterioration in their effectiveness.

The second development was established in 1982 as the Financial Management Initiative (FMI). Compared with the Efficiency Strategy, the FMI is a more comprehensive undertaking embracing all the central Departments and agencies. It is intended to make managers responsible for specific blocks of resources and activities, give them the means for executing those responsibilities and then hold them to account for their discharge. The emphasis has been on formalizing top management structures and information systems, installing procedures for measuring performance of activities and developing management accounting systems that stress the delegated management of resources. There has been considerable progress in these respects. Most departments, driven by their own senior managements, have put a great deal of effort into institutionalizing this reform so that its elements become established as part of the normal way of managing. Officials in Whitehall as well as in the operational outposts of central Departments (which have always been more managerially minded) talk now of budgets, cost centres, financial responsibility and performance indicators.

Undoubtedly, the emphasis given to the new management of government has developed a whole new vocabulary in central administration. The Government itself began by introducing the three 'E's of *economy, efficiency*, and *effectiveness* and subsequent debate about public sector management has revealed at least five more 'E' principles, i.e. *efficacy, equity, excellence, enterprise* and, perhaps most important of all, *electability*. From the definitions given in Table 20.7 it is clear that these concepts tend to contradict each other, mainly because, as with other management principles, it is not clear what weights should be allocated to each in different circumstances. This may be less important, however, than the way the ideas represented have come to influence the style and content of administrative activity. The signs are that all this is more than simply a new way of talking. It represents a new way of administering. Mrs Thatcher did more than any Prime Minister to promote the new culture. The next few years will test the long term effects.

Table 20.7 *Principles of Departmental management*

Principles of departmental management

Economy	Minimization of resource consumption
Efficiency	Ratio of resources consumed to outputs gained
Effectiveness	Maximization of outputs
Efficacy	Maximization of beneficial impacts for community
Equity	Equality of treatment for equal cases
Excellence	Maximization of quality of process and product
Enterprise	Maximization of profit making initiative
Electability	Maximization of electoral gain

Politics and Central Administration

> Don't confuse me with the facts; my mind's made up already.
>
> Sign on the desk of Junior Employment Minister

At the beginning of this chapter we saw that although there might be a theoretical distinction between politics and administration it is very difficult to sustain in practice. Politics arise when differences affect interests. Administration necessarily has political implications because it raises issues which affect interested parties. Thus, politics can be found in administration not only at the ministerial or parliamentary level (more on this in a moment), but within the administrative process itself.

Political interests within administration

These internal politics come principally from the way administrative structures divide up functions and responsibilities and help to form interests and loyalties. One of the reasons often given for moving civil servants from post to post is to prevent the officers identifying themselves too closely with the activity they are responsible for. Nevertheless, it is human nature to develop such attachments. But administration also involves the interaction of people and groups with different views about how things should be achieved and, perhaps above all, it makes demands especially on resources which are in short supply. Thus, the administrative process, even in some of its very practical and mundane activities, comes to be permeated by political activity.

Quite apart from their views about major policy directions Ministers also have views about administration and management. Often these arise from the implications of administrative developments for wider government policy. A good illustration of this has affected the character of the management changes which were described in the previous section. A number of Departments have been very active in developing these reforms, so much so that senior managers come to conceive of their operations largely in managerial terms. This can mean that, when faced with problems or opportunities, their preferences are guided by what constitutes good management rather than, say, good politics. Thus, for example, a manager of a tax district might well be able to show that the cost of employing two more inspectors would be recovered perhaps ten times by the extra revenue gained. In a private business such an economic argument would lead to extra recruitment. But if there is a government, or just a Minister, committed to a reduction rather than an expansion of the civil

We had a most extraordinary meeting today . . . with the Under-Secretaries from the Department of Transport . . . one from Air, one from Road and one from Rail. It was extraordinarily acrimonious . . . The positive suggestions were somewhat predictable. Richard (from Rail) promptly suggested a firm commitment to rail transport, Graham (from Road) a significant investment in motorway construction, and Piers (from Air) a meaningful expansion of air freight capacity!

Source: Lynn and Jay, 1983, pp.95–6.

service, what seems to make sense administratively may not make sense politically. Thus the political comes to constrain the administrative.

Individual accountability of Ministers

Much of the political character of administration arises, as we saw above, from the principles of our representative and responsible system of government. One of the most significant of these is the doctrine of individual ministerial accountability. This governs the way individual Ministers are held to account by Parliament for the policy and conduct of themselves as Ministers and of their departments (though not their actions as individuals, however unsuitable these may render them for office, nor for their share of the collective responsibility of the government as a whole). Some have seen a sinister development in the way the FMI and executive agencies are undermining this chain of responsibility by separating out the accountability of officials from that of ministers (and thus exposing the former who have previously remained anonymous and impartial).

The constitutional doctrine which holds that a Minister is accountable for all the

Mr Leon Brittan and the Westland affair 1986
During a dispute between Mr Brittan, Secretary of State for Trade and Industry, and Mr Michael Heseltine, Secretary of State for Defence, Mr Brittan arranged for one of his officials to leak to the press extracts unfavourable to Mr Heseltine of a letter from one of the government law officers. Mr Brittan resigned when it became clear that he had lost the confidence of the House of Commons not only over his account of this affair, but also the impropriety of his actions.

Mr John Davies and the Vehicle and General affair 1971
The V and G was an insurance company which went bankrupt after a history of financial problems. A subsequent enquiry found that the Department of Trade and Industry had acted negligently in monitoring and acting on the company. The section and officials involved were identified and the Secretary of State, although giving an account of the situation and the remedial action, faced no censure.

Sir Thomas Dugdale and Crichel Down 1954
As Minister for Agriculture, Sir Thomas resigned when an enquiry into his and other departments' handling of the failure to resell land requisitioned in wartime found negligence by some of his officials.

actions of a Department has now, however, passed into disuse. Effectively Ministers have to answer for their own conduct but are not deemed to be held responsible for that of their officials unless this was in the name and cogniscance of the Minister. Thus Mr Leon Brittan was forced to resign as Secretary of State for Trade and Industry during the Westland affair of 1985–6 because of his own conduct and that of his officials acting under his instructions. But Mr John Davies, a previous Secretary of State for that Department, did not have to resign in 1971 when some of his officials were found to have been negligent in the course of their regulatory duties.

There has developed, however, some ambiguity over the precise *responsibility of Ministers and officials*. This became evident during the trial in 1985 of Clive Ponting (see Chapters 6 and 15). Confusion was emerging over exactly what the obligations of a civil servant were to a Minister, particularly whether obedience should extend to matters of doubtful legality or propriety. In what some saw as an attempt to restrict the implications of the acquittal (i.e. that an official might be able to disclose confidential information in the public interest), Sir Robert Armstrong, then Cabinet Secretary and Head of the Civil Service, issued a note reasserting the responsibilities of civil servants to their Ministers.

Despite the Armstrong memorandum the nature of ministerial accountability is changing. This is realistic. The business of central administration is now so vast, complex and professionalized that a Minister cannot effectively be held ultimately responsible for it. But the process of accountability is itself more complex than this.

Sir Robert Armstrong Cabinet Secretary, 1979–88

> I would like to see more open government and I've made no secret of that in a variety of respects. But I don't think that's government-in-a-goldfish-bowl. And I think it would be very difficult to conduct the business of government in a reasonably orderly fashion if you were conducting it . . . in a goldfish bowl, particularly where the onlookers could throw stones in all the time. So though . . . I believe that governments ought to explain the decisions which they take as fully as possible to Parliament and the public, and, if possible, more fully than they do now, I don't think that that means the process of reaching the decision should be completely open.
>
> Whether it's as Principal Private Secretary at No. 10, or now as Secretary to the Cabinet, there you are at the centre where these discussions are being taken, and it's very hard work, and the hours are very long, and you can use almost any epithet you like to describe the activity except 'boring'. It's fascinating and sometimes it's infuriating. Sometimes it's frantic. A lot of it is tremendous fun from the sense that Edward Bridges, my predecessor, used to say that things were fun because they were very stimulating and exciting to do.

Armstrong was sometimes portrayed as a Thatcherite. This was wrong. It stemmed from his traditional and genuine conviction that a permanent secretary must, having given his advice plainly, fearlessly and privately, do the bidding of his minister and, as he once put it in a television interview, in his job he was 'as near as we came in the British system to a permanent secretary to the Prime Minister'. But, in so far as he ever let his own political views slip to his friends, they were old-fashioned 'One Nation' Conservatism, of the kind that prevailed when he was a young Treasury assistant principal.

Source: Extracted from Hennessy, 1988

The duties and responsibilities of civil servants in relation to ministers

Civil Servants are servants of the Crown. For all practical purposes the Crown in this context means and is represented by the Government of the day . . . The duty of the individual civil servant is first and foremost to the Minister of the Crown who is in charge of the Department in which he or she is serving . . . The determination of policy is the responsibility of the Minister . . . In the determination of policy the civil servant has no constitutional responsibility or role, distinct from that of the Minister . . . When, having given all the relevant information and advice, the Minister has taken the decision, it is the duty of civil servants loyally to carry out that decision . . . Civil servants are under an obligation to keep the confidences to which they become privy in the course of their official duties . . .

Source: Note by the Head of the Home Civil Service, the Cabinet Office, 25 February 1985

It implies an obligation on the Minister first to give accounts of his Departmental activities, second to answer questions on this account, and only third to be judged on these accounts. If the FMI becomes institutionalized, government managers themselves will be increasingly obliged inside their organizations to present accounts of and answer to the discharge of their responsibilities. From this it may be only a small step to a Minister's being able to avoid this accountability himself (Gray, 1989).

External control of administration

Any system of government needs ways in which it can learn about the relative success or failure of its activities. In a democracy much of this knowledge comes through machinery which makes it possible for citizens or their representatives to put right general or particular errors. Of course, one general control of this sort is through the ballot box, but this is necessarily a clumsy instrument. More significant, but within the same tradition, is the development of *select committees*, especially those of the House of Commons since 1979, which in watching over the activities of the central administration can see files and papers and interview witnesses. Their investigations can be uncomfortable for the agencies concerned and their reports can publicize errors in embarrassing ways. Sometimes they can even be innovative.

This helps the individual only in general ways. So what of the opportunities for the citizen to gain redress for wrongs done to him personally? One possibility is to take the offending agency or Minister to *court* (often so expensive as to be out of reach of ordinary mortals). He can also take a similar action by appealing to a *tribunal* (e.g. Supplementary Benefits Appeal Tribunal or Commissioners for the Inland Revenue). In practice, however, a citizen is more likely to seek help in the first instance from an *MP* who may write letters and seek interviews on the constituent's behalf. But of particular significance over the past twenty years has been the way an MP can also refer matters to one of the *Parliamentary Commissioners for Administration*, or 'Ombudsmen', as they are called after their Scandinavian antecedents. There is now not only the original Parliamentary Commissioner for Administration (set up under the Parliamentary Commissioner

Act of 1967), but also commissioners for Health and for Northern Ireland (as well as a whole Commission for Local Administration).

The principle is straightforward: every citizen who feels he has been the victim of an administrative error and who has not been able to gain redress by direct appeals to the agency concerned has the right of access to these commissioners (sometimes through an MP, sometimes directly). The commissioners in turn have the power to inspect files and other papers and interview officials and then to express their conclusions. In many cases these powers are sufficient to bring redress, but as the commissioners have no power to enforce their judgements on offending agencies, there is still an obvious weakness. Moreover, some areas are outside their jurisdiction. They are empowered, for example, only to investigate cases of maladministration. This may be defined as to include 'bias, neglect, inattention, delay, incompetence, perversity, turpitude, arbitrariness and so on' (Richard Crossman, Leader of the House of Commons introducing the Bill in 1967) but not matters of policy judgement. Further, they may not investigate where there are other established procedures for gaining a remedy (such as through the courts or tribunals), nor matters such as security, foreign affairs, defence and nationalized industries.

The Commissioners regularly find against those departments which by the sheer volume of their transactions with the public are liable to make mistakes, e.g. the Departments of Health and Social Security and Inland Revenue. As a result of investigations, these Departments have been able to remedy not only individual cases but also their operating procedures. Further, these investigations and their findings have been carried through without upsetting the general principle of individual ministerial responsibility. Indeed, they have tended to reinforce the development of the current practice by establishing a distinction between the acts and omissions of the Minister and those of the official acting in an administrative capacity.

It would be misleading to claim, however, that the introduction of the ombudsman principle into the control of central administration has revolutionized it. That would not be in the British tradition. But it has undoubtedly added a significant new avenue of redress which has become accepted and extended.

Secrecy and freedom of information

All the matters discussed so far in this section on the politics of the administrative process share a requirement for information. The extent to which this is freely available in a form to genuinely inform choices, accountability or redress, will determine the extent to which the administrative process can function effectively. 1988 was the year of the tri-centenary of the Bill of Rights, yet in May of that year, in the shadowy studio of Channel 4's *After Dark* programme, a group of former British (and US) intelligence officers discussed the qualities of the Conservative government's new legislative proposals for official secrets. (Now that the legislation has been enacted such a gathering is illegal!)

A variety of incidents led to the government's reform. They included two prosecutions of Ministry of Defence officials brought by the government in 1984. The first was of a junior official who was convicted for passing to *The Guardian* documents about the installation of cruise missiles in the UK. The second was of a senior official (Clive Ponting) who passed to an MP documents about the sinking of the Argentinian battleship *General Belgrano* during the Falklands war in 1982. As we saw above, this acquittal led to the then Head of the Home Civil Service issuing a note on the duties and obligations of civil servants. This note became relevant in the subsequent Westland affair of 1985—6 in which Ministers, their press officers and regular civil servants were involved in a good deal of underhand activity. Even the Prime Minister and the Head of the Civil Service themselves appear to have been guilty of misjudgements in the manipulation of disclosure of information. At the centre of events was Mr Leon Brittan, Secretary of State for Trade and Industry, who ordered the disclosure of part of a letter from the Solicitor-General which questioned the validity of arguments used by Mr Heseltine (then Secretary of State for Defence) in an inter-ministerial dispute over the future of the Westland Helicopter Company. Apart from the impropriety of using a law officer's letter in this way, the case demonstrated the very fine dividing line between official and unofficial disclosure.

These events turn on fundamental qualities of the administrative process much in need of serious examination and reform. In practice, the Government came to devote its attention to the matter only after the more recent events involving *Spycatcher*, the published memoirs of a former intelligence officer, Mr Peter Wright. Mr Wright held a grievance against his employers over his pension rights. Publication was intended to compensate him. He succeeded admirably thanks to the free publicity generated by the British government's single-minded attempts to prevent publication. The government's argument was very properly based on the need to maintain the oath of confidentiality of its MI5 employees. The argument, which should have been about what was fit for disclosure, became diverted by a series of steamy civil court cases in Britain and overseas featuring government witnesses later found, by the admission of one of them, to have been 'economical with the truth'.

Realizing (after Ponting) that the Official Secrets Acts were probably unworkable and alarmed by the support for a liberalizing measure introduced by one of its own back-benchers (Richard Shepherd), the government introduced its own reforms. The aim of the new legislation is to clarify the grounds for non-disclosure to include defence, security, intelligence (including international cooperation) and information relating to criminal investigations. Some important former classifications have been liberalized, including Cabinet minutes and advice to Ministers, unless they are covered by the restricted topics. However, it will not be a defence to argue that information needed to be disclosed in the public interest, nor that it was already available abroad.

These are important changes for the conduct of the administrative process. Information is the fuel of that process, serving both the activity and its proper audit. However, the Government's changes have been introduced as a result (so it seems) of a fear of embarrassment. While some aspects of the changes will have beneficial effects on the administrative process (e.g. in the information relating to decision making), we still await a proper examination of the information required for policy making, accountability and individual rights.

Some General Issues

Throughout the preceding sections a number of references have been made to underlying trends and problems. In this final section we shall bring one or two of these into sharper focus. For a discussion of Mrs Thatcher's impact on the civil service see the concluding comment to this section.

Centralization of the administrative process

We begin on Thursday 9 January 1986 when Michael Heseltine, Secretary of State for Defence, walked out of a Cabinet meeting after tendering his resignation. Later that day he read out a statement relating a series of events involving the Government, the Westland Helicopter Company and various other parties, and attacking the demise of collective Cabinet government, a theme he returned to in his 1990 Tory leadership campaign.

The Westland affair was essentially a dispute between two central government Departments and their Ministers over the future of a helicopter company which wished to restore its financial stability by linking up with one of its US competitors. As such it demonstrated how structures in administration can shape politics: the Ministry of Defence sought to promote the interests of the defence community, the Department of Trade and Industry those of industrial competition. The story escalated into two resignations (the other, as we have seen, was that of Mr Leon Brittan, the Secretary of State for Trade and Industry) and questions about the direction of the government itself.

On the role of Cabinet Mr Heseltine argued that government had become more centralized and that Ministers need support if they are to restore their constitutional roles. This argument was taken up by a range of commentators. Sir John Hoskyns, once Mrs Thatcher's policy adviser, saw Whitehall and Westminister as an 'embattled culture' which could only be improved by serious attention to the machinery of government (*Financial Times*, 11 April 1986). Two books and a series of television documentaries by one of the most respected of Whitehall commentators, Peter Hennessy, also postulated that Cabinet government was overloaded and the civil service incapacitated (Hennessy, 1986, 1989). Both these critiques came to similar conclusions, i.e. that Ministers needed their own cabinets in their Departments in order to restore some balance at the centre of government.

Meanwhile, the Treasury and Civil Service Committee (perhaps now the most prestigious of the new select committees of the House of Commons) pursued more detailed issues (HC 92i, 1985−6). Of particular interest were the roles of the Cabinet Secretary as Head of the Civil Service; the problem lies in the way that the duties of the former to a Prime Minister and Cabinet may conflict with the responsibilities of the latter to the civil service as a whole. Further concern lay with the way that officials were being forced into political roles as more responsibility and power were taken on by the centre, specifically through the Prime Minister and a few trusted official aides.

These worries over centralization and confusion in the roles at the centre of government organizations and process were treated with scepticism in the government's reply (Cmnd 9841). But the issue continued to cause concern and perhaps contributed to Mrs Thatcher's downfall. Such a centralizing tendency has been observed in other aspects of central administration, including within departmental management and in the relations between central and local government (see Chapter 21). Despite the explicit decentralizing ethic of the Financial Management Initiative and executive agencies, the frameworks which govern the new arrangements appear to replace one type of centralization with another. Removed certainly are the detailed controls over individual activities, but in their place have appeared systemic mechanisms which so regulate and constrain operations as to prevent much freedom of manœuvre for managers (what one senior official described to the authors as 'a little bit of freedom but a lot of grief').

Perhaps these illustrations of a centralizing force in the administrative process are coincidental. After all, we would not expect a government committed to a reduced role for the state to be party to such a contradictory tendency. On the other hand, perhaps the government is itself trapped by deeper and more powerful centralizing forces. The causes and the issues remain.

Privatization: private ownership of public goods?

One clear decentralizing policy in central administration has been the privatization of nationalized industries, utilities and related activities. For some, this policy's rationale is simply to provide revenue for the Exchequer to offset its spending and tax reductions. The former Prime Minister, the late Harold Macmillan, likened this to 'selling off the family silver'. This conceals, however, a more fundamental effect, for the theory behind the public ownership of what economists call public goods is to prevent private ownership encouraging its development in partial ways inconsistent with the requirements of society as a whole. Thus, power supplies, communication services and other contributions to the infrastructure of the country are critical to our progress as a nation. The issue, therefore, is how to secure them.

In fact, privatization has been about more than just selling off state industries: it has encapsulated the wider issue of de-regulation (e.g. of the buses), contracting out of services (e.g. in the Health Service) and the opening up of the public sector generally to market forces. The whole debate raises questions about whether there exist natural monopolies which should not be in private hands, how to measure the efficiency of nationalized undertakings and how these should be managed and regulated to promote the public interest.

The civil service, management, and morale

Privatization is, of course, just part of a long-running debate over the structure and function of the civil service and the appropriate roles of civil servants in the business of management. The issues involved have been invigorated by a squeeze on civil service manpower and pay since 1979 and a succession of reforms designed to managerialize the service. The issues are brought together in the story of one official. We referred earlier to Clive Ponting who, as a civil servant in the Ministry of Defence, fell foul of the Official Secrets Act. Prior to that however he came to prominence within Whitehall as a champion of the new managerial style. Indeed, he was honoured for his efforts in bringing the disciplines of good management practice to his Ministry. Yet in 1985 Mr Ponting found hiself in the dock of the Old Bailey on a charge under the Official Secrets Acts. That he came to be in this position reflected his view that his minister misled Parliament over the sinking of an Argentinian cruiser, *General Belgrano*, during the Falklands War of 1982. Mr Ponting sought to complete the picture for MPs by providing the missing information himself . . . anonymously in a plain brown envelope and to one of the Government's keenest critics, Mr Tam Dalyell MP. That he was acquitted owed more to the gut feelings of the jury and the confused constitutional theory of the judge than to the technically legal aspects of the case.

Many issues in the current debate over pay, motivation and morale concern all levels of the service. But as with Clive Ponting the focus is on the senior officials in Whitehall. Here themes such as politicization, neutrality and the new managerialism link up. Part of the concern arises from what is seen as the decline of consensus politics in government which has gradually resulted in the erosion of service neutrality. This was taken up by a Treasury and Civil Service Committee enquiry in 1986—7 into the roles and responsibilities of civil servants and Ministers (HC 92i, 1985—6). With the memorandum from the Cabinet Secretary to guide it, the Committee sought to define the accountability of senior officials. It recognized that the civil service's prime loyalty to the government of the day was not infinite, that the new management systems were beginning to delegate more responsibility to them, and that existing conventions could be construed as convenient fictions designed to protect the status quo.

Behind the new management style is the question of what constitutes appropriate structures and processes for achieving both policy and management objectives within the constraints of parliamentary accountability and the requirements of good government. Governments have not generally been willing or capable of addressing these systematically and, with the extra pressures imposed since 1979, it is steadily losing the support of the service. The exit from Whitehall to companies in the private sector, many of which gain an advantage in their dealings with government by their employment of such ex-officials, have included senior civil servants from the Treasury's privatization programme, the Efficiency Unit and the Inner Cities Directorate. These are the very competent managers which the government should hope to retain.

Perhaps they may indeed be attracted by the development of executive agencies which can offer senior managers the opportunity to run services like small (and in some cases very large) businesses. There is great merit in freeing government services from unnecessary procedural and other constraints and in promoting a climate of management in which customer service is the priority. Early developments in the agency programme are encouraging in this respect. But progress is inevitably linked to the wider climate of management and morale, in particular that relating to pay and conditions.

The latter are important. Many of those in private industry are appalled by the conditions and facilities which many public officials have to contend with: outdated, ill-equipped and under-maintained offices and public reception areas designed to do anything but make clients feel at ease. The irony of the development of agencies may well be that managers will be given the chance to run services like businesses but, having proved that they can, will expect to be rewarded accordingly . . . in the private sector.

Such departures could be seen as beneficial if they were part of an orchestrated interchange of staff between government and the outside world. But they are not. Rather, they are symptomatic of a wider loss of morale associated not only with politicization but with general conditions including pay and the attitude of the government to its officials. This is not to say that the changes which the government has been making since 1979 are wrong: rather it is to observe that as in all successful organizations change needs to be planned and managed through comprehensive, coherent and properly resourced programmes. The government's implicit assumption that change is intrinsically cost-free has caused it many problems with the civil service. It is a difficulty which Mr Major's government will have to address.

Who governs: ministers or civil servants?

We end with a popular question. Much energy has been expended on it by students of politics in their examinations while Anthony Jay and Jonathan Lynn, of course, founded an internationally successful comedy series upon it. The silken-voiced Sir Humphrey Appleby was regularly portrayed as outwitting and outflanking his 'master', the Minister, Jim Hacker. It is possible, however, that the subject has so much comic potential because it is in fact so important. This, after all, is the crucial interface between the elected representative, democratic side of the political system and the full-time appointed bureaucracy. It really does matter who the master is because if it is Sir Humphrey then our democracy is elaborate but irrelevant: mere window-dressing.

On the face of it Sir Humphrey's real-life equivalent has a strong hand. He is permanent, professional, full-time and usually formidably clever while his Ministers are temporary (usually shifted after two years), often inexperienced, of necessity part-time and not always especially able. The Minister has the constitutional power backed by a general election, but the senior civil servant can manage the Minister's life, control the flow of information and advice and use his extensive knowledge of the Whitehall machine to get his own way.

Sir Humphrey's potential power is therefore considerable but does his real life counterpart exercise it? Labour cabinet ministers Richard Crossman, Barbara Castle and Tony Benn have claimed that, despite their invariable protestations to the contrary, civil servants regularly do exercise such power, usually to advance an unstated middle-of-the-road, consensual point of view. This may be true to some extent — as Sir Anthony Part (ex-Permanent Secretary DTI) once said, 'the Civil Service always hopes that it is influencing Ministers towards the Common Ground'. Civil servants may also have strong personal views on some issues which will occasionally affect their conduct and flavour their advice. They are also likely to be more interventionist and decisive in areas where ministers have no interest, are weak or vacillating. Finally, they will be likely to fight hard to defend their own 'empires' — their ministries — and to control promotions and movement of staff within them.

All this suggests a substantial role, certainly, but hardly a dominant one. The fact is that senior civil servants are deeply influenced by their own professional ethos. They are moulded by a deeply conforming experience which enthrones the virtues of anonymity, caution, loyalty, discretion and (despite their cynical humour) respect for the democratic process. Politicians are weaned on an altogether stronger brew of assertion, self-promotion and power. A strong and able Minister usually has no difficulty in commanding the enthusiastic compliance of the civil servants. Indeed, Mrs Thatcher was in power for so long that her political credo became sufficiently

**Ponting's view
of the Civil
Service**

Clive Ponting resigned from the civil service after rising to the rank of
Assistant Secretary in the Ministry of Defence. His book *Whitehall:
Tragedy and Farce* (1985) contained some scathing criticisms.

'Amateurism'

The word that has caused the greatest offence to the top Civil Service
was the basis of the Fulton critique — 'amateur'. The senior ranks of the
Civil Service believe strongly that they are professionals — professionals
in the art of government. But this means knowledge of how Ministers
really operate; and this as we have already seen is a seedy and cynical
world. The mandarins can only justify themselves on the basis that there
is a separate function of operating the Whitehall machine in which
knowledge detracts from so-called professional objectivity and is
therefore positively harmful.

This is a bogus claim invented and sustained with great determination
to provide a justification for the administrative class. It is encapsulated in
the views of Sir Warren Fisher, Head of the Civil Service, to the Royal
Commission on the Civil Service in 1930:

> Let us guard ourselves against the idea that the Permanent Head
> of a department should be an expert: he should not be anything of
> the kind. Instead he should be a man of such breadth of
> experience that he will soon find himself picking out the essential
> points; and remember, there is a great deal to be said for a fresh
> eye.

In other words the mandarins can be left to get on with oiling the wheels
of government, confident in their arrogance that they can master any
problem, however complex or specialized, and come to sound
judgements, perhaps with help of other 'good chaps' they happen to
know.

This 'amateurism' has left an appalling catalogue of failure in
Whitehall.

Life in the Civil Service

Much of the life of the Civil Service is physically squalid. The staff are
poorly accommodated in badly decorated buildings, with inadequate
typing and photocopying facilitites, and surrounded by petty regulations.
In the Ministry of Defence until the early 1970s the 'modern' invention of
the roller towel was unknown and an old lady with a trolley used to
come round once a week distributing new towels and pieces of cheap
gritty soap. The canteens are all too often depressing places tucked
away in the basement, generally justifying their nickname of the 'Greasy
Spoon'.

But much of the work even at the top of the Civil Service is equally
depressing. The amount of personal responsibility is very limited. An
individual rarely takes a decision on his own partly because as the work
gets divided up into smaller and smaller units the degree of overlap
increases. The job of a senior civil servant is not to take decisions but to
consult others, to coordinate views, to produce pieces of paper which
are agreed by everybody. The invention of the photocopying machine
has reinforced this tendency with a vengeance. Now everybody who has
even the slightest interest in any aspect of a subject will receive a copy
of a paper and will in turn send copies of his comments, often only of
marginal interest, to everybody else. So the mountain of paper
accumulates.

The work of the top Civil Service is always conducted in unfailingly
polite terms. No instructions are ever issued, instead they are couched
in terms like 'I should be grateful if . . .' The idea that Whitehall is just

> one big game is reflected in the language used. Civil Service prose is scattered with cricketing terms such as 'straight bat', 'googly', and comments on a draft are normally required by 'close of play'. One Deputy Secretary sitting in a departmental promotion board once described a young administrator as 'not Test standard; but a good county player'. He was promoted.

well known for it to inform and direct the behaviour of civil servants almost automatically. Some students of *Yes, Prime Minister* (successor to *Yes Minister*) even noticed a subtle change in recent years. The plots were updated to take account of the Thatcher effect: Sir Humphrey did not always get his own way and he was often bested by an arguably more assertive Jim Hacker. Whether the script will have to be rewritten for a Major effect remains to be seen.

The two most distinctive features which emerge from this examination of central administration are first, the intrinsically political character of the administrative process and secondly, the variety of structures and processes by which it is carried out. This variety is both a reflection of the nature of the tasks of government and the result of centuries of *ad hoc* development. There are signs that the programmes and changes run on apace without any systematic thinking about the deeper implications for our system of government. Good government requires effective administration.

References and Further Reading

Bagehot, W., *The English Constitution* (1867; Fontana, 1963).
Birch, A.H., *Representative and Responsible Government* (Allen & Unwin, 1964).
Cmnd 3638, *The Civil Service* (The Fulton Committee Report) (HMSO, 1968).
Cmnd 8616, *Efficiency and Effectiveness in the Civil Service* (HMSO, 1982).
Cmnd 9058, *Financial Management in Government Departments* (HMSO, 1983).
Cmnd 9841, *Civil Servants and Ministers: The Government's Response* (HMSO, 1986).
Departments of Environment and Transport, Internal Training Calendar (1988/9).
Drewry, C. and Butcher, T., *The Civil Service Today* (Blackwell, 1988).
Efficiency Unit, *Improving Management in Central Government: the Next Steps* (HMSO, 1988).
Gray, A.G., 'A framework for the study of public administration', *Public Administration Bulletin*, No. 19 (1975).
Gray, A.G., 'The individual accountability of ministers', Chapter 3 of W.D.A. Jones (ed.), *Political Issues in Britain Today*, 3rd edn (Manchester University Press, 1989).
HC 92i, Treasury and Civil Service Committee, *Civil Servants and Ministers: Duties and Responsibilities* (HMSO, 1985–6).
Hennessy, P., *The Cabinet* (Blackwell, 1986).
Hennessy, P., *Contemporary Record* (Winter 1988).
Hennessy, P., *Whitehall* (Secker & Warburg, 1989).
Lynn, J. and Jay, A., *Yes Minister, Vol I* (BBC, 1981).
Lynn, J. and Jay, A., *Yes Minister, Vol II* (BBC, 1982).
Lynn, J. and Jay, A., *Yes Minister, Vol III* (BBC, 1983).
Ponting, C., *Whitehall: Tragedy and Farce* (Hamish Hamilton, 1985).

21 Administering Local Government

Andrew Gray and Bill Jenkins

This chapter examines the historical development of local government, its internal operation and the complex and continuing debate over finance. The recent tensions between central and local government are also explored and the chapter concludes with some thoughts on local government's possible future.

In 1988 Nicholas Ridley, then Secretary of State for the Environment, sketched out his vision of local government in the 1990s. For Mr Ridley, whose Department is responsible for financing and overseeing local government, the future role of local authorities should be a minimalist one. The 'enabling council' would have as its major function not the traditional one of providing services such as education and housing at the local level but that of specifying a range and level of services and then monitoring, and to a lesser extent regulating, other institutions that would provide these (Ridley, 1988).

Mr Ridley's ideas are certainly in tune with New Right thinking, in particular with those who see a strong state as necessary to free individual initiative and entrepreneurial activity. For others, however, Mr Ridley's remarks are a further challenge to local government which has been under continued attack for over a decade. The elements that make up this attack include increasing central control over the finance of local government, an erosion of its functions and an attempt to constrain those who take part in it. For the champions of local democracy the last decade has been one of general gloom and despondency. They see recent developments as continued evidence of an increasing state of centralization coupled with the erosion of the political pluralism that local government represents.

So is local government needed? For example, few people appear to know the identity of their councillor or bother to vote in local elections. Further, local authorities have been accused of behaving irresponsibly in their management of spending. On these and other grounds it is possible to make a case for curbing the powers of local government or, in the extreme, for replacing it with some form of local administration.

Many would challenge such a case as it represents a model of a centralizing state that is undemocratic and inefficient. As long ago as the middle of the last century J.S. Mill (1861) argued that local government was necessary as a buffer against the state, as a provider of local services and as a source of political education. These thoughts find modern echoes in the report of the Widdicombe Inquiry (Cmnd 9797, 1986) which was established to examine the conduct of local authority business.

Widdicombe saw the value of local government in its ***pluralism*** (the dispersal of state power), ***participation*** (its contribution to local democracy) and ***responsiveness*** (its ability to provide for local needs through the delivery of local services).

Local government is a form of decentralization. The case for its existence can be made in terms of democratic theory and the efficient delivery of a range of services. However, crucial to this argument is the idea of ***localism***, i.e. that there exist areas that have specific local needs best dealt with by a local political system. This should be close to individuals, responsive to their local demands and, therefore, democratic and accountable.

Britain has unitary, not federal, government. Federalism (for example in the USA) often gives a good deal of autonomy to decentralized units and enshrines this in a written constitution. Consequently, decentralized units have specific rights and defined areas of autonomy. In a unitary system this is not formally the case. The autonomy of local government in Britain is constrained by Parliament and subject to its ultimate authority. In legal terms local government can only do what Parliament permits.

Now this formal position may not represent the true reality. In particular the pattern of central–local relations may change. Nevertheless, how far any system of local government could or should be autonomous is a matter of continued debate. Yet if there *is* a case for local government how should it be structured and organized: on ***efficiency grounds*** (the most efficient way to deliver local services), in terms of a ***natural locality*** or in ***political terms*** (where the votes are and even where the money is)? Such questions are crucial to understanding the evolution of the local government system in the UK, not least since, as the following sections indicate, they have shaped in different ways the historical development of local government from its formalization in the late nineteenth century to the current controversies of today.

The Structure of Local Government

Early attempts at reform

Local government in Britain is as old as the parish church and the parish pump. A fear of unchecked local power has been tempered with a suspicion of the state and a championing of the village Hampden immortalized in Gray's Elegy. Consequently, over the years a vast maze of structures presided over by a variety of administrative and political authorities developed. However, with the coming of the industrial revolution this situation became unsatisfactory and unacceptable. By the mid-nineteenth century local government in Britain was seen as 'a chaos of areas, authorities and rates' (Byrne, 1983, p.28). This led to the emergence of a movement to reform its structure. The search for this structure was (and is) a search for an agreed set of ***territorial and functional jurisdictions***. How functions should be organized is of crucial importance. As the state has grown during the twentieth century the question of what tasks local government should be responsible for has changed with changing circumstances (see Table 21.1).

Driven by dissatisfactions with this chaos, a political 'reform' movement developed which through the Municipal Corporations Acts (1833, 1882), the Local Government

Table 21.1   *Current local government tasks*

Task	County council	Non-metropolitan district
Arts	x	
Consumer protection	x	
Education	x	
Environmental health		x
Fire Service	x	
Highway maintenance	x	
Housing		x
Leisure, recreation and museums	x	
Planning (structure)	x	
Planning (local)		x
Police	x	
Rate collection		x
Refuse collection		x
Refuse disposal	x	
Social Services	x	

Note: This is a selective list of tasks; for a more complete list see Byrne (1983), Appendix 2. Prior to 1987 there were also differences between the functions of metropolitan counties and districts and between the Greater London Council and the London Boroughs. After the abolition of the GLC and the metropolitan counties most functions were allocated to the district level

Acts (1888, 1894) and London Government Act (1889) dragged local government from '*ad hoc*ism' to an integrated and structured system. What emerged (see Table 21.2) was a mixed system involving a three-tier structure comprising counties, districts and non-county boroughs, and parishes and a separate system of county boroughs based mostly on large towns. In the three-tier structure the counties were responsible for functions such as planning, education and police, the lower units for housing, public health, amenities, etc. The county boroughs were to all intents and purposes semi-autonomous carrying out most functions themselves.

This structure, together with regular local elections, gave Britain an organized and coherent system of local government. However, within thirty years the system was under strain from demographic, economic and political pressures. In particular *suburbanization* (the flight from the cities) eroded the financial base of many of the county boroughs and caused problems for the efficient delivery of services. Elsewhere other demographic changes called into question the viability of smaller units which appeared to be neither organizationally nor financially capable of carrying out their functions.

Although these developments were not simultaneous, together they led to political differences over territory, tax and status (Alexander, 1982). They also coincided with a loss of autonomy as local government became financially more dependent on central government. For these reasons it became increasingly difficult to relate the demands of delivering services efficiently to concepts of localism. Such matters set the scene for the post-Second World War debate on local government reform.

Table 21.2 *The structure of local government in England and Wales before 1974*

Tier	County boroughs	County government			London government
First	CBs (83)	Administrative County (58)			London County Council
Second	—	Non-county borough (260)	Urban district (522)	Rural district (469)	Metro boroughs and City of London
Third	-—	—	—	Parishes (11,000 +)	—

Notes: Examples and populations:
Counties: 30,000 to 2.4 million, e.g. Devonshire
County boroughs: 33,000 to 1.1 million, e.g. Exeter
Non-county boroughs: 2,000 to 100,000, e.g. Newark non-county Borough
Urban districts: 2,000 to 123,000, e.g. Brentwood Urban District
Rural districts: 1,000 to 86,000, e.g. Crediton Rural District
Before 1965 reorganization of London

Source: adapted from Gray, 1979

Reform efforts after the Second World War

Between 1940 and 1970 several important criticisms were made of the local government system:

1. There were too many small authorities.
2. There existed a great disparity of size even amongst authorities of the same type.
3. The division of functions among authorities was often fragmented and illogical.

Yet from the viewpoint of local and central government there appeared to be little political capital to be gained from any change, especially since there was no agreed criterion on which any reform could be based. Should reform maximize efficiency (of service delivery), democracy/localism, simplicity or some mixture of the three? For some time these questions were avoided by successive governments. However, in the early 1960s an examination of Greater London proved that change was possible after all.

The government of London has long been a problem, not least in terms of organizing the relationships between the metropolitan centre, the outskirts and the neighbouring counties. The task of solving this was given to the Royal Commission on Greater London (known as the Herbert Commission) which produced a scathing attack on the established order (Cmnd 1164, 1960). Herbert recommended that the old world be replaced by a system based on a concentration of units and functions. For once the government acted and in the London Government Act of 1963 the boundaries were almost totally redrawn giving a system that was to last until the mid-1980s. Among Herbert's creations was the Greater London Council (GLC); among its casualties the county of Middlesex.

Herbert's structural solution demonstrated that reform was possible and implementable. Perhaps encouraged by this, the Labour government set up a Royal Commission on Local Government in England (1966) and separate enquiries to examine local government in Scotland and Wales. The analyses and conclusions of these reports have certain similarities but also particular differences. The principal issues were raised by the Maud Royal Commission on which this account now concentrates.

The Royal Commission conducted substantial research. Its report (Cmnd 4040, 1969) accepted the case for the existence of local government in the UK and argued that ideally this should perform efficiently; attract and hold public interest; deal with other parts of national government and adapt to social and economic changes (Byrne 1983, p.49). The Commission believed the system failed to achieve these: there were too many small units, fragmented politics and inefficiencies of service delivery. Given this analysis the Commission outlined criteria that any new structure should seek to achieve. These included the maximization of efficiency and democracy and a fit with current demographic patterns. Unfortunately many of these ideas were not necessarily compatible.

In its final report the Commission offered two solutions, neither of which was eventually implemented. The majority recommended a unitary solution. Aside from the metropolitan areas that were to have a two-tier system (like London) England was to be divided into fifty-eight unitary areas, in each of which a single authority would carry out all functions. This solution was criticized strongly in a minority report which argued for a two-tier structure based on city regions. In all events neither alternative materialized, since although the majority report was accepted by the Wilson government, this lost office in 1970.

The new Conservative government set out its own reforms in a White Paper (1971) that was the basis of the Local Government Act (1972). The resulting structure taking

Table 21.3   *The structure of local government in England and Wales after 1974*

Tier	Shire county government	Metropolitan county government	London government
First	Shire county (47)	Metropolitan county (6)	Greater London county (1)
	County district (333)	Metropolitan district (36)	London borough and City (32 + 1)
Second	(Parishes)	(Parishes)	—

Notes: Examples and populations:
Shire county: 109,000 to 1.4 million, e.g. Derbyshire
County district: 25,000 to 425,000, e.g. Canterbury
Metropolitan county: 1.2 million to 2.8 million, e.g. Greater Manchester
Metropolitan district: 174,000 to 1.1 million, e.g. Stockport
In 1987 the Greater London Council and the metropolitan counties were abolished and their functions transferred to districts or joint boards of districts

Source: adapted from Gray 1979

effect in 1974 was a two-tier solution that treated the metropolitan conurbations separately from the counties. Thirty-six metropolitan districts were created within six metropolitan counties. Elsewhere the two-tier system was based to a large extent on the majority of existing counties. The main victims were the old county boroughs who lost status, functions and financial independence in the new system. They were not the only casualties. The counties were slimmed from fifty-eight to forty-seven (England and Wales) and the districts from 1,249 to 333 (see Figures 21.1, 21.2).

Local government structure in the 1980s

In 1986 Mrs Thatcher's Conservative government abolished the Greater London Council and the Metropolitan Counties established under Herbert and the Peter Walker reforms of 1972–4. It argued that these bodies were wasteful, performed few useful functions, were distant from their electors and would not be missed. Following their removal their functions were passed on to the lower-tier authorities (e.g. the London boroughs) and to systems of joint boards.

Metropolitan Districts
A Wigan
B Bolton
C Bury
D Rochdale
E Salford
F Manchester
G Oldham
H Trafford
I Tameside
J Stockport

(Note: the names on the map represent the pre-1974 councils,
     with county boroughs shown in bold type)

The new metropolitan districts are listed (A–J).
The names on the map represent the pre-1974 districts and county boroughs (C.B.) Note
how the reorganization has reduced the number of authorities sharply

Figure 21.1 *Map of the Metropolitan county of Greater Manchester after 1974 (Source: Redcliffe Maud and Wood, 1974)*

(Note: the names on the map represent the pre-1974 councils, with the county boroughs shown in bold type)

The new districts are listed on map (A–H). The names on the map represent the old districts and the county boroughs (C.B.). Again, note how the reorganization sharply reduces the number of districts

Figure 21.2 *Map of the county of Cheshire after 1974 (Source: Redcliffe Maud and Wood, 1974)*

The debate over the development and fate of these authorities was embedded in the politics of the 1980s, not least the increasing tensions in central–local relations (see below). However, part of the problem also goes back to the reorganization of UK local government in the 1960s and 1970s. In particular, it can be argued that the logic of the Walker reforms had more to do with politics than with the functional delivery of services, clearly demonstrating the problem of separating questions of geography and efficiency from those of political advantage. The new system also placed severe management demands on elected members and officers. Whether they were capable of coping with this is an issue to which we now turn.

Internal structures and processes of local authorities

Councillors and officers

Local government can be viewed as comprising a representative system of elected members and an administrative system staffed at the most senior level by professional officers. This system delivers a variety of services to its local environment (e.g. education, housing, libraries, etc.) and depends on people in such an environment for political and financial support. Such a system is ***complex*** and ***inter-dependent***. In particular each element needs the other to operate successfully; e.g. members need officers to develop and implement policy while officers need members to give political legitimacy to their activity. In theory at least both need the public whom they are supposed to serve.

Given certain residential qualifications any adult over the age of twenty-one can stand in the regular elections to the councils. Such an achievement may be difficult without the help of (i.e. adoption by) a political party. But who are the councillors? A stereotyped view of them is that they are middle-class, middle-aged and male — a picture that recent surveys have shown to be near the truth. Thus, an official investigation in 1977 revealed that 50 per cent of councillors were over the age of 54, 83 per cent were male, 76 per cent were owner-occupiers and less that 25 per cent had a background in manual work (Robinson Committee, 1977). As the Widdicombe researchers demonstrated ten years later, this situation was little changed although, as Stoker (1988, p.35) notes, the new statistics conceal a more diverse situation. In particular, the Widdicombe research indicated that in urban areas councillors were more likely to be younger and that this was more probable for the Labour and Liberal parties than the Conservatives (Cmnd 9799, 1986). The Widdicombe research also indicated strong links between party and such factors as employment and economic status. Not surprisingly perhaps, Labour councillors are more likely to have a background in manual occupations and to have lower incomes. However, even in the Labour party, male domination persists and no major party registered more than 20 per cent of councillors as women.

In recent years there has been much talk of the politicization of local government and, in particular, the role of political parties. However, for many if not most aspiring councillors, the political party is ***the way*** on to the council and the party group that shapes policy and makes major decisions. In Town Hall, as in Westminister (and increasingly so since 1974), parties are the major force in local politics (Cmnd 9797, 1986). Following election the major party takes control, elects its leaders and chairs the powerful committees.

So what power does an individual councillor have? As executive authority is exercisable only by the council operating as a corporate body, the legal answer is very little. Further, councillors are normally part-time, unpaid (aside from attendance allowances and expenses) and untrained. Even if the situation is changing, many still see this as a cause for concern.

The permanent officials of local authorities constitute a career service rooted in the traditional local government professions (highway engineering, education, law). Consequently, prior to the 1980s it would have been rare to find departmental heads in local authorities who did not have a professional qualification and an extensive background in their particular field. Local government thus differs from the civil service in being more specialist, with greater mobility between authorities, all of whom are employers in their own right.

The service is further differentiated between senior officers, middle management and what might be termed field operatives (e.g. teachers, social workers and office staff). As with senior civil servants, the formal role of the senior local government officer is policy advice, implementation and the management of services. Also like civil servants, they are formally politically neutral. So, given the difficulties faced by the members (see above), is there a danger of the dominance of the elected member by the unelected and professional official? Perhaps, but such a view would be too simple, neglecting as it does the interdependence of councillor and officer, a factor that emerges if one examines the internal structures and processes of any local authority.

Councils and committees

The structure of a typical local authority is deceptively simple (see Figure 21.3) but like most formal organizational structures hides a more complex reality. The council itself is the supreme decision making body acting as a corporate entity arriving at its decisions through a series of regular meetings held throughout the year. However, since it would be impossible to conduct all business in full council, much is delegated to committees (usually service based) whose operations are then keyed in to the cycle of full council meetings. There are some powers that cannot be delegated (i.e. setting the community charge) but there is much that can be, with the result that fully delegated issues may be only reported back to full council and never debated.

Committees consist of elected members served by officers. The major council committees are functionally based (housing, social services, education, etc.) with others devoted to areas such as personnel and finance. Traditionally local government operations have been dominated by the service–committee relationship: councils relate to matters of detail through their committees and the committees relate directly to the departments. The relationship between the council and its activities is, therefore, filtered through committees. This has many advantages but it also has a number

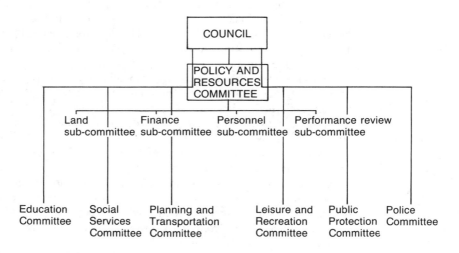

Note: actual structures may vary

Figure 21.3 *Local authority committee structure (shire county)*

of serious weaknesses, not least in the strategic coordination and management of council business.

Attempts at internal reform

The above and related issues were the focus of a number of attempts to introduce internal reform to local authorities in the late 1960s and early 1970s and ran parallel to the restructuring of the local government system as a whole. The most influential of these were the Maud Report (1967) and the Bains Report (1972).

Maud focused on the councillors and the committee system. He advocated a greater involvement on the part of councillors backed up by better training, a simpler structure and more emphasis on management. These ideas fell on stony ground; however, their thrust and analysis were echoed in the Bains Report (1972). The message of Bains (together with the Patterson Committee in Scotland) was *corporate management*: the power of functional departments should be weakened and the minds of officers and members focused on the corporate good. A reorganized committee structure included a central management committee (known as the Policy and Resources Committee) would coordinate the policies and priorities of the council; a chief executive would head a chief officers' management team. In this way individual departmental and committee interests were to be set aside for the greater good of the council as a whole (see Figure 21.4).

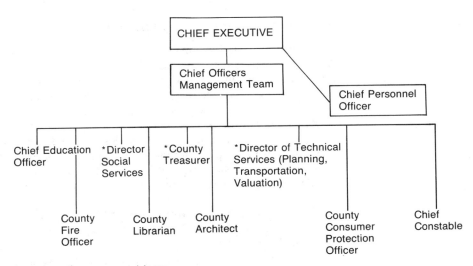

*member of management team

Notes: 1. Actual structures may vary
2. Chief Constable is not an officer of the County but an Officer of the Crown. However, police work has claims on the total resources of the council through the police committee

Figure 21.4 *Local authority departments and chief officers (shire county)*

By 1975 the majority of new authorities had appointed chief executives, formed policy and resources committees and talked of corporate strategies. Whether these affected councillor and officer behaviour was another matter for, by the late 1970s, the Bains reforms in most councils were more shadow than substance. As Stoker (1988, Chapter 4) observes, there were many reasons for this, not least that the reforms were inappropriate in a changing organizational and political environment that put traditional local government under new sets of pressures. Many forces were at work here, but of particular importance was an intensification of party politics following the reorganization of 1974.

Local Government and Local Politics

Many people believe that the politicization of local government is a recent phenomenon linked to the rise of left-wing councils and that, as a consequence, party politics have little place in local government. The first of these assumptions is a myth and the second can be strongly challenged. Historical and political analysis shows that politics are inherent in local government while the development of its parties was identifiable even before the beginning of the twentieth century, especially in the big cities. However, as Young (1986) notes, as each of the mass parties developed nationally the nature of local politics changed. By the early post-war period, the political nature of much of local government was firmly established.

Local politics after reorganization

The presence and activity of national parties in local government developed steadily if somewhat unevenly. By the 1960s it could be found at its strongest in the cities (Labour) and shire counties (Conservative) and at its weakest in smaller units such as districts. However, in the wake of reorganization in 1974 the nature of local politics in certain areas began to change. In particular, party pressure on members and officers *intensified* and *polarized*, especially as the difference between competing parties became wider and often more acrimonious. These forces could be seen in the increasing influence of party groups controlled by leaders and subjected to whipping procedures, a greater involvement by councillors in the detail of council matters and (here and there) increasingly strained relationships between councillors and officers.

Were such developments directly attributable to the 1974 reorganization and the creation of large authorities? This is part of the explanation, but taken alone it is far too simple, neglecting broader changes in British politics and the need for local government to respond to pressures in a changing world. There is considerable evidence, too, of a breakdown of consensus between and within parties in the 1970s. On the right the eclipse of Heath saw the embryonic beginnings and then development of the Tory party under Thatcher. On the left the world of traditional socialism was disturbed by the emergence of a radical left, the splitting of the party via the Social Democrats (SDP) and a call for a return of power to the grass roots of the movement.

Turnout in UK local elections has usually been low (*c.* 40–50 per cent compared with 75 per cent in general elections) and, as the Widdicombe Committee observed, many people also view local party politics as an 'alien presence'. However, Widdicombe also argued that party politics were inevitable and desirable in shaping local accountability. The new political movements were therefore driven by a rationale of creating a new politics and gathering new converts. Often this crusade was directed at a local level, not least by the former Liberal Party with its idea of community politics. Apathy came to be seen less as an inevitable human trait than as a product of a particular type of political system and some saw a local base as necessary to fashioning political commitment. This trend was followed in a different way by Labour. The idea of *local socialism* gained ground, especially in the cities (Gyford, 1985). Here the old Labour political organizations, seen as corrupt, inefficient and little interested in electors, were challenged, broken up and replaced by the radical left. But the Tory party was also changing its face in the counties and even in the cities (Wandsworth) traditional loyalists were replaced by a new breed of accountants and businessmen who talked of 'managing' local government and reducing its overloaded functions.

Those developments led to increasing friction, both inside and outside local government. Inside, the appearance of highly committed councillors influenced and strained internal relationships; outside, particularly in the case of Labour-held urban authorities (e.g. the GLC, Liverpool, etc.), there were hostile clashes with central government and even with the Labour party itself. Local politics have, therefore, changed in shape and nature influencing both the conduct of local government and the character of central–local relations. Yet this politicization is less the result of 'loony leftism' (or even 'loony rightism') than an outcome of wider changes in British political life, a fact pointed out by the Widdicombe Committee in 1986.

The Widdicombe Report

The Widdicombe Report (Cmnd 9797, 1986) offers a comprehensive investigation into aspects of British local government. Established by the Conservative Government, a Committee under the chairmanship of David Widdicombe QC was instructed to enquire into the conduct of local authority business. Its terms of reference included a brief to examine the rights and responsibilities of elected members and the roles of officers. It was also asked to suggest ways to strengthen 'the democratic process'. Finance and structure were excluded from the scope of its inquiry. The Committee's report contained eighty-eight recommendations, backed up by four substantial research volumes.

Widdicombe's analysis and recommendations were essentially modest. It argued that local government was characterized by diversity and citadels of the left and right were the exceptions rather than the rule. Undoubtedly, in some councils tensions had increased, and at its worst local politics had become a malign influence. However, Widdicome stated that political organization in local government was inevitable for the foreseeable future and directed its recommendations at accommodating this.

The report came out strongly for elected local people making decisions, for consolidating the role of councillors and for councils operating in a political framework (Jones, 1986). It acknowledged the role and importance of central government in setting the framework for local politics but it also argued that if local government was really *government* then political tensions with the centre may be inevitable and if really *local* other demands and problems may arise. These arguments were not what the government wanted to hear. A committee established to reveal the excesses of local government had, in many respects, produced an informed defence of the system. The government's official response took some time to appear and was confined to issues that fitted with its own wider vision of the future role of local authorities: limiting the political activities of council employees, promoting accountability and strengthening the financial regime (Cm 433, 1988). The White Paper proposed barring a large proportion of senior council officers from holding political office or taking an active part in political activity, banning the employment of party political advisors, setting tough rules for the composition of council committees and, in broader terms, limiting local government's discretionary spending powers which it claimed had been misused to finance anti-government political propaganda. The bulk of these proposals were incorporated into the Local Government Bill of 1989.

Local Government Finance and Central–local Relations

Financial questions have dominated the recent debate on local government: is local spending too high, does the centre need to control local government finance so closely, is a community charge an improvement over the rates? Such questions, however, are neither new nor simply financial but reflect inherent tensions not least between the role of central government as paymaster and policy maker and 'autonomous' local government.

The local financial system

To understand local finance it is necessary to understand how local government spends and raises its money. This may seem merely technical. In fact, the structural nature of the financial system together with the way it has developed has resulted in a number of fundamental political problems.

At its simplest, local authority expenditure is divided between revenue and capital: *revenue* refers to matters of a short-lived nature (salaries, office supplies, etc.) while *capital* relates to longer-term projects such as school building. Revenue is paid for out of current income, capital from borrowing, including from the money markets or the issuing of bonds. Such borrowing has implications for economic policy; thus governments have kept a careful eye on it, restricting its size and bringing it into line with macro-economic objectives. This has resulted in a range of controls that have, in turn, strained relations.

To fund current expenditure local government traditionally relied on three main sources of income: *charges, central government grants* and *rates*. Charges were paid directly by clients for services (e.g. rents), grants came as a subsidy from the central government and rates were a locally determined tax on the beneficial occupiers of domestic or business property. In 1990 the rates were replaced by a different tax known as the community charge (see below). The tri-partite system had existed

Gross Income
and
Expenditure
for an English
County
Council

% of Gross Expenditure	Service	Gross Expenditure £m	Income £m	Net Expenditure £m	Cost Per Week to the Average Domestic Ratepayer £
52.4	EDUCATION	399.0	53.7	345.3	3.07
12.7	HIGHWAYS	96.3	43.5	52.8	0.47
10.7	POLICE	81.0	7.6	73.4	0.65
10.3	SOCIAL SERVICES	78.2	15.7	62.5	0.55
2.8	FIRE	21.3	1.4	19.9	0.18
1.4	LIBRARIES	10.8	0.7	10.1	0.09
4.7	OTHER SERVICES	35.9	12.1	23.8	0.21
5.0	CONTINGENCY	37.9	–	37.9	0.34
100.0	Total	760.4	134.7	625.7	5.56

SUMMARY OF THE REVENUE BUDGET 1987 / 88

Gross expenditure on "Other Services" includes

Waste Disposal £5.8m
Probation £5.3m
Magistrates' Courts £5.2m
Land Drainage £4.8m
Planning £1.8m
Trading Standards £1.8m

The "Contingency" consists of two separate elements. The first is a sum set aside to provide for increases in pay and prices. This year we have allowed 4% for prices and 5% for pay. The second element is a special sum set aside to provide for unexpected costs falling upon the County Council during the year (for example as a result of exceptional weather conditions). There will be no change in the County Council's working cash balance of £18.7m.

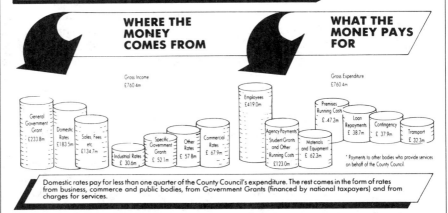

WHERE THE MONEY COMES FROM

WHAT THE MONEY PAYS FOR

Domestic rates pay for less than one quarter of the County Council's expenditure. The rest comes in the form of rates from business, commerce and public bodies, from Government Grants (financed by national taxpayers) and from charges for services.

The above figure is reproduced from an information leaflet sent to ratepayers in the county of Kent in 1987. It indicates where Kent County Council (KCC) obtains its money (gross income) and what this is spent on (gross expenditure). The table illustrates main items of expenditure in revenue terms for the county. Note that in this instance the bulk of the revenue expenditure is taken up by education, highways, the police and social services.

Source: Kent County Council, 1987–8.

since the late nineteenth century. After 1945, however, grants increased so that by the mid-1970s they contributed over 60 per cent of total income, implying an increasing financial dependence of local authorities on the centre. In such a world if grants were cut back (as they were) and if charges failed to rise (as they did), then the choice for local government was either to raise rates or to cut services.

Originally, grants tended to be specific (i.e. awarded for the financing of specific services). More recently, however, and especially since 1945, many of these were replaced by a ***block grant*** (for many years known as the Rate Support Grant (RSG)), the use of which was not specified by central government but left to the local authority to spend according to its needs.

After 1965, the RSG was made up of three main elements: needs, resources and domestic. The first two of these elements were designed to allow an authority to provide a given standard of service and to compensate for differences in revenue-raising capacity. Yet how were factors such as 'need' to be calculated? The answer lay in central government computers and mathematical and statistical formulae. The results were intensely debated not least because the mathematics appeared weighted by the political preferences of the government. Unsuccessful attempts to refine these methods meant that by the mid-1970s the credibility of the grant system was severely undermined (Travers, 1986).

The third part of the RSG, the domestic element, was a device to support domestic ratepayers. This highlights another controversial issue in local government finance, i.e. the rates. Rates were a property tax of ancient origin. They were also the one independent source of revenue available to local authorities. The rating system allowed local authorities to raise taxes on domestic and commercial properties subject to certain exemptions. This was done by giving each property a rateable value to reflect the rent it would raise on a commercial basis. The intention was to update these values frequently but for administrative and political reasons revaluations were often postponed or cancelled. As a consequence, even by the mid-1970s, the traditional rating system was in serious difficulties.

As a tax, rates had a number of strengths: they were simple to administer, difficult to evade and cheap to collect. They were also local in nature supplying a reliable source of income on a regular basis. However, they were also unfair and regressive, taking little or no account of an individual's ability to pay. For domestic ratepayers this effect was cushioned in the 1960s and 1970s by measures such as rebates for lower income groups and by the domestic element in the RSG. However, this meant that more of the rates bill was forced onto increasingly complaining industrial and commercial ratepayers. Rates should not, however, be seen in isolation. They were part of a system of local government finance which by the mid-1970s was displaying structural weaknesses. In particular, high grant levels led to a situation where small fluctuations in grant and price inflation could result in wild and large surges in rate demands. In 1974 a series of such rate rises led to what the government described as a 'crisis' in local government finance. To examine this it set up a committee of enquiry, the Layfield Committee.

The Layfield Committee: analysis and recommendations

The Layfield Committee sat for two years and reported in 1976 (Cmnd 6453). It argued that local government finance was characterized by confusion. It considered that the system confused responsibilities, weakened local accountability and led to an increasing degree of centralization. This was not in itself wrong but it meant that neither the government nor the local authorities were willing to accept responsibility for spending levels (Jones, 1978). For Layfield the way out of this muddle was to increase either central control or local accountability. The majority of the committee favoured local solutions, including a greater range of income-raising sources for local authorities. These included a local income tax together with a simplification and reduction of the grant system.

Layfield's proposals met with a chilly response from the Labour government who advocated instead the retention (with some minor changes) of the status quo (Cmnd 6813, 1977). However, the tone of the Green Paper signalled other changes that

The Rates

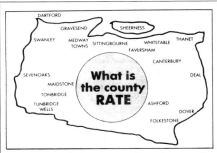

The County Council exists to provide a wide range of personal and other services for everyone in Kent.

In order to pay for these services the County Council needs to levy rates.

IN 1987/88 THE COUNTY RATE WILL BE 170.60p, AN INCREASE OF 4.7% OVER 1986/87

THIS IS THE LOWEST COUNTY RATE INCREASE FOR 19 YEARS

The level of this rate is calculated in the following way:-

- The Council estimates how much money it needs to provide your services during the year

- It subtracts from this the amount expected from Government Grants and Direct Income.

- The remainder (£339.8m this year) must come from rates

- The £339.8m is divided by the Penny Rate Product of £1,991,847 to calculate the required rate in the pound

WHY HAS THE RATE INCREASED?

	p in the £	£ million
In 1986/87 the County Rate was	162.97	317.4
Inflation will cost ratepayers	10.89	21.7
Of this, 5.8p (£11.5m) relates to the estimated cost of the proposed restructuring of teachers pay.		
Net additions to budget to improve services	3.96	7.9
	177.82	347.0
Increased Government grant will save ratepayers	−3.61	−7.2
Increased rateable value will reduce the required rate by	−3.61	
So in 1987/88 the rate will be	170.60	339.8

IMPROVED SERVICES

The 1987/88 budget provides for improvements to many of your services. These include:
- More social workers and resources to help prevent family breakdown, child abuse etc.
- Better staffing for old peoples homes and more community support to maintain elderly people in their own homes.
- Additional resources for mental health services and community support for the mentally handicapped.
- Improved pupil/teacher ratios in secondary schools.
- Developments in vocational training in colleges.
- More money for structural maintenance of pavements, roads and streetlighting.
- 31 additional firemen.
- 36 extra policemen for the County's ports, patrolling the M25 and combatting drugs related crime.

HOW MUCH WILL I PAY . . .

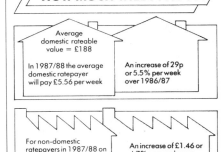

The percentage increase for domestic ratepayers is a little higher than that for non-domestic ratepayers because domestic rate relief remains unchanged at 18.5p in the pound.

HOW THE RATE IS COLLECTED

Your District Council adds the County Rate to its own rate and then reduces the total by 18.5p for Domestic Rate Relief. This sum is then multiplied by the Rateable Value of your property to give the total amount of rates due. This is collected by your District Council who pass over the amount due to the County Council.

Enquiries concerning methods of paying your rates or claiming rate rebate should be made to your District Council.

This figure is reproduced from an information leaflet issued by Kent County Council in 1987. It explains how the County calculates the rate it has to raise. it also indicates why, in the County's view, the rate has had to increase and what this will mean for the average ratepayer.

Source: Kent County Council, 1987–8.

were soon to gather pace, namely, 'that, whatever happened, the Government wanted greater central control over local government spending' (Travers, 1986, p.77).

In 1975 Tony Crossland, then Secretary of State at the Department of the Environment (DOE), told a local government conference that the spending party was over. From that date central efforts to squeeze local government quickened. These efforts were only partially effective; as the centre restricted the totals the local authorities cut back sharply on capital projects but much less rapidly on revenue expenditure (jobs and services). This did not please the Treasury and the arrival of Mrs Thatcher's first Administration in 1979 coincided with the Treasury's determination to introduce further controls.

The search for control in the 1980s

The Local Government Planning and Land Bill (1979) was a massive piece of legislation covering a wide range of issues from new systems of capital controls and allocations to ways of compelling local authorities to publish more information about their activities. The Bill sought to reorganize the grant system and link it with specific controls to enable high spenders to be identified and financially penalized. The RSG was replaced by a new block grant based on a system of need assessment known as Grant Related Expenditures (GREs).

The government's stated objectives were, first, to offer a fairer and more comprehensible allocation system to enhance local authority accountability and, secondly, to discourage high spenders. This was done by comparing local authorities' projected expenditure with what the centre calculated it should spend (its grant related expenditure (GRE)). The more the former exceeded the latter the more grant would be lost (a device known as the 'taper').

Details of the technical operation of these arrangements can be found elsewhere (Travers, 1986). Here it is sufficient to note that the new system differed from earlier regimes in its detailed central government intervention. Previously the centre influenced authorities by altering the *totals* of the RSG. Under the new arrangements the theory was that controls would be exerted *selectively* on *classes of local authorities*. If grant was cut back these authorities would either have to reduce spending or raise money via the rates. This would force over-spenders to subject themselves to greater local accountability.

This complex system was reinforced (in January 1981) by a further system of 'targets' and 'penalties'. These arose from a belief in Whitehall that even GREs would not get local government spending under control rapidly. 'Targets' and 'penalties' were much cruder affairs. In the first round all local authorities were told to cut expenditure back by 5.6 per cent on what they had spent in 1979 or they would suffer penalties, i.e. if an authority spent above its target its Block Grant was cut. This initiative caused serious problems as authorities now had two (often incompatible) systems to contend with. In the short term chaos reigned and the pressure on current spending remained upwards.

Following the local elections of May 1981, many of the new Labour urban authorities (for example, the GLC under Ken Livingstone) began to implement their commitments to extend local services and subsidize local transport. Pressures on spending intensified and some authorities attempted to meet financial shortfalls through raising a supplementary rate. This was forbidden by the government in 1982. From then until the general election of 1983 relationships between centre and local government continued to deteriorate. The problems of dealing with the over-spenders, coupled with Treasury paranoia over a loss of control of public expenditure, shaped the Conservatives' 1983 election manifesto. In this two major strategies to deal with local government were offered: the abolition of the GLC and the Metropolitan Counties, and the capping of the rates. The manifesto contained no overall commitment to examine and reform local government finance (*The Economist*, 1985).

New proposals to 'rate-cap' authorities were announced in the White Paper *Rates* (Cmnd 9008, 1983). The subsequent legislation allowed the Secretary of State at the Department of the Environment to 'designate' local authorities whose spending was considered 'excessive'. Once designated the local authority could appeal to have its limit increased but if this appeal was turned down the Secretary of State's mandate was absolute. This set the scene for further confrontations between government and local authorities.

The operations of the local government financial system have become steadily more complex and obscure. The nature of central intervention intensified from a hands-off policy of controlling totals to a much more detailed involvement, where many of the decisions about a local authority's spending might be taken not in the town hall but within the Department of the Environment. If the latter is exceptional and the overriding objectives have been the management of the economy and the protection of the ratepayers from unaccountable local authorities, it nevertheless goes against the arguments of Layfield, who wished to separate **central control** from **local accountability**.

The Audit Commission, finance and creative accounting

One of the creations of the early reforms of the 1980s was the Audit Commission, an independent body established under the Local Government Finance Act (1982) to control local authority audit and to conduct and promote studies to improve the economy, efficiency and effectiveness of local government.

The Commision took its brief seriously, examining not only activities such as refuse collection, further education and arrears on housing rents but also some of the financial systems that linked local authorities to the centre. One of these studies was on the Block Grant System (Audit Commission, 1984). In this the Commission argued that the system had too many incompatible objectives including the control of aggregate expenditure, the distribution of grant to reflect the differences in need and resources and the limiting of rate increases. The Commission considered this to be a strange mixture of political and financial tasks asking more than the system was capable of. However, as the financial screws on local government tightened, authorities (particularly urban, Labour-controlled councils) began to fight back by designing dubious but legal financial schemes to balance their books, maintain their budgets and deliver services. These strategies, known as 'creative accounting', brought such authorities into direct confrontation with the Audit Commission over their accountability for the management of public funds.

In its simplest form creative accounting involved the adoption of various financial strategies whereby an authority gained breathing space for itself. Examples of these included 'debt rescheduling' (where interest payments were deferred until a future date), 'capitalization' (where items such as housing repairs were transferred to the capital account thus avoiding grant penalties) and 'leaseback' (where the authority raised loans on its own possessions and properties sometimes from finance organizations it owned itself) (Stoker, 1988, Chapter 7).

The Audit Commission looked on this behaviour with some horror, especially since the implications of these strategies were that twenty years hence local taxpayers (or central government) might be footing large bills left by long-departed councillors. The Commission therefore sought to tighten audit, limit creativity and increase individual and collective accountability. The Government's attitude was more forceful. As each set of strategies appeared it sought to strengthen the financial regime to prevent them. This was to lead to the abolition of the rates and a further tightening of the controls on capital expenditure.

Paying for local government: the community charge debate

The question of reforming local government finance in any total sense was never discussed in the 1980s outside the demands for Treasury control over local spending. Within this framework, however, continual lip service was paid to rating reform and in 1981 a Green Paper *Alternatives to Domestic Rates* posed a number of alternatives without coming to any firm conclusion. According to the Green Paper any new system had to produce the following:

1. Increase local accountability.
2. Keep the costs of administration and collection within acceptable limits.
3. Assist proper financial control.
4. Be suitable for all tiers of local government.
5. Be integratable with the existing tax system.

Against this background the rates and major alternatives, such as a sales tax, a local income tax and a poll tax, were discussed.

In Scotland in 1985 the threat of the political repercussions from a rate revaluation sent shudders through the Conservative party. The commitment to 'do something about the rates' was finally seized in another Green Paper *Paying for Local Government* (Cmnd 9714, 1986). This argued that existing arrangements for local finance had long-standing flaws, not least the limited connection between *voting* and *paying* for local services and the operational complexity of the grant system. It argued that the government had a duty (linked to its goals of macro-economic management) to control the totals of local authority spending. Given this mandate it wished to replace the old arrangements with a simpler, more efficient and more accountable system. In particular it recommended the following:

1. The abolition of domestic rates and their replacement with a per capita *community charge* (the so-called *poll tax*, as it is essentially a tax on each of an authority's electors).
2. Non-domestic (business rates) to be taken away from local authority control and to be set, collected and distributed by central government.
3. A simplification of the grant system with part to be allocated on a per capita basis and part allocated according to need.

There followed intense debate over these proposals, particularly the community charge. Ministers claimed that its introduction would increase accountability and raise interest in local politics. It would also be easy to understand and was fair when linked to systems of rebates and to general levels of taxation. The issue of accountability was of great importance. In the government's view, low interest in local politics and the ability of many authorities to generate high levels of expenditure without electoral penalty arose from the fact that many electors either did not pay or escaped from rates. Such a system was also cushioned by the system of business rates which again could be increased without electoral consequences. The community charge, coupled with the removal of business rates from local authority control, was intended to counter this. By making nearly all adults liable for the charge it was argued that authorities would be forced to account for their spending and that excesses would be immediately visible and felt by electors. The community charge was therefore advocated as introducing a much needed strengthening of local accountability.

There was, however, considerable criticism of the community charge; it was unfair, would involve substantial administrative costs, would threaten individual freedom and liberties and was based on a spurious idea of accountability. The argument of unfairness centered on the charge bearing no relation to ability to pay or to the type of property occupied. Questions concerning collection and individual liberties relate to systems needed to establish and administer the charge. Many more individuals would be involved than with the rates and their location and registration would involve a great deal of detective work on the part of the local authorities. Further, in terms of accountability, the government's logic was questioned: critics argued that local spending would still be subject to stringent central controls that would inevitably influence community charge levels. 'Local accountability' was therefore a highly limited concept since local discretion over activities and finance would be even more tightly controlled than before.

A commitment to abolish the rates was included in the Conservative election manifesto in 1987 and, in December of that year, the Local Government Finance Bill sought to implement the proposals of the Green Paper with minimal change. The passage of the Bill was hotly debated with criticisms coming from Labour and Tory MP's alike. The local government community was also strongly opposed to the legislation, although the only concession to their concerns was the decision to make the transition from rates to community charge a once and for all affair rather than a phased change over a number of years.

In the House of Commons a major concern, especially of Tory back-benchers was the perceived unfairness of the charge. It was therefore proposed that a banded charge be introduced linked to income level and tax status. This amendment was only just fought off by the government. Elsewhere critics argued that any claim for increased accountability was illusory since government would not only continue to play a major role in funding local authorities via grants but also that this role would intensify with the centralization of business rates. This suspicion was confirmed by the government's moves to replace rate capping by poll tax capping. If there was a true link between community charge and local accountability such a system would be superfluous. In terms of a centralized system of control, however, such restrictions were clearly required.

The implementation of the community charge

Scotland was the laboratory for the community charge. In 1989 Scottish local electors received their first bills while in England and Wales local authorities began to compile community charge registers. In Scotland these changes were met with a good deal of spirited protest as, spearheaded by the Scottish National Party, the public was urged to join an active campaign of opposition under the slogan of 'can't pay, won't pay'. The Labour party was less absolute in its stance, caught between on the one hand its opposition to the charge and on the other its reluctance to urge electors to break the law. In the meantime the Government dismissed these difficulties as teething problems.

The implementation of the charge in England and Wales in 1989–90 was also far from smooth. In November 1989, Chris Patten, then Secretary of State for the Environment, introduced to the House of Commons the basis of what he called 'a simpler and more understandable' method of finance. His statement included details of standard spending assessments (SSAs) on which the new grants to local authorities were to be based. It also set out the details of transitional arrangements from the old system and calculated the average community charge as £276.

Few MPs, either Conservative or Labour, totally understood what Mr Patten had to say. Even Mr Speaker remarked that the Minister had made 'a very complicated statement' while one Conservative back-bencher described it as 'mystery wrapped up in enigma'. However, what did become clear was that the Department of Environment's formula for SSAs would penalise rural and county authorities and that the projected poll tax figure seemed to have been seriously underestimated. It was also thought that the new uniform business rate (UBR) was likely to have serious political consequences.

The concern over the business rate was well founded. Details announced in January 1990 brought relief in northern cities but huge increases in the south of England. Over 60 per cent of businesses nationwide faced increases and bodies such as the Confederation of British Industry (CBI) were not persuaded by Government arguments that regional inequalities were being reduced.

In the Commons' vote on local government spending in January 1990 the Government majority was cut to 36 by a back-bench revolt and as the new local government financial year approached it became clear that the average poll tax bills for Conservative authorities would be over 30 per cent above the Government estimate and 36 per cent higher in others. Exceptions to this included the London boroughs of Wandsworth (£148) and Westminster (£188). Some Conservative councillors resigned in protest at the reforms but the Government blamed excessive spending by Labour authorities and threatened to use poll tax capping powers. Local authority associations, however, blamed the rises on serious underfunding compounded by errors in the calculation of SSAs, inflation, and the high costs of collecting the charge. The public, or at least active sections of it, also made its opposition felt in some of the most intense protests (including rioting) ever seen against Government policy.

In an effort to regain control and the initiative Chris Patten moved to use his charge capping powers. However, he had some trouble in finding a formula that did not penalise Conservative as well as Labour local authorities. Eventually twenty authorities, all Labour controlled, were charge capped. Yet, when Brent (expenditure up 1.4%) was capped and Berkshire (expenditure up 20.6%) was not, it was argued that not only was the system in a state of chaos but that Mr Patten was behaving in a biased and partisan fashion. The chosen authorities decided to test the Secretary of State's powers in the courts and the case eventually reached the House of Lords. The courts supported the Secretary of State's claim that under the legislation, he was the sole arbiter of 'fairness'. However, in other cases, on lesser issues, some judgements were in favour of the local authorities.

By mid-1990 it was clear that the implementation of the community charge had run into serious difficulties, not least in terms of convincing the majority of the population it was either legitimate or fair. In the face of such opposition a Cabinet committee was established to look into the issue and Chris Patten gained £3 million from the Treasury to cushion the effects of future charge levels. Meanwhile even *The Times* had suggested a return to the rates (an idea close to the Labour Party's policy response), while Michael Heseltine had proposed the abolition of county councils, the introduction of directly elected mayors and poll tax charges banded according to income levels.

In the run up to the local government elections of May 1990 it had been suggested that the community charge was an electoral albatross dragging down the Conservative party. It was also whispered by some in the party that only a change of leadership would allow them to escape from this and that Heseltine was one of the few politicians who could rescue the party. In the event, while the Conservatives did badly in the May elections (loosing over 200 seats), they did not do as badly as some had feared. Hence the Party Chairman Kenneth Baker was able to announce that the holding of the two 'flagship' London boroughs of Westminster and Wandsworth, against the general trend, vindicated the effectiveness of the poll tax as an instrument of electoral accountability. This interpretation of events was strongly challenged. However, after this, talk of a leadership challenge faded from the scene, at least for six months.

The future of local government finance

It is doubtful if the issue of the community charge can be said to have been the direct cause of the downfall of Mrs Thatcher (described in Chapter 29). Nevertheless, once Geoffrey Howe had made his fateful speech in the House of Commons in early November 1990 and Michael Heseltine had entered the leadership lists, the issue of the poll tax had a direct influence on the leadership campaign. Of direct relevance was the policy's unpopularity and the electorate's perception of charge levels as the Government's responsibility. This view had filtered through to a number of Conservative MPs in marginal constituencies who saw the tax as an electoral disaster. Sensing this, Michael Heseltine made poll tax reform a plank of his leadership challenge. Mrs Thatcher's supporters sought to belittle these proposals but, within a week, the Prime Minister had resigned and all three candidates for the leadership, Heseltine, Hurd and Major were talking of the need to reform the poll tax system. Meanwhile, former ministers were having a crisis of conscience. Some talked of having being bounced into the original decision to introduce the poll tax while, most significantly, Nigel Lawson, former Chancellor of the Exchequer, argued that the Treasury had always opposed its introduction, had believed the new system unworkable and had fought to modernize and retain the rates.

In November 1990 John Major became Prime Minister. He appointed Michael Heseltine as Secretary of State in the Department of the Environment and gave him the brief to undertake the far reaching review of the poll tax that Heseltine had promised in his leadership campaign. To assist Heseltine Sir George Young, another opponent of the tax, was also given a ministerial post at Environment. The press welcomed these appointments with remarks that Heseltine had been given 'a poison chalice' and that his campaign had only led him to the job he had held eleven years previously. There can be, therefore, no doubt that Mr Heseltine's task was far from easy. The result, the Council Tax, will be introduced in 1993. It confirms what we have already seen, that the reform of the local government financial system has bedevilled governments for years, partially at least since any investigation of local government finance has too often been separated from that of structure. Mr Heseltine's arguments before and after he reassumed his mantle of Secretary of State at Environment demonstrated that he was aware of this issue. Yet, how far such a realisation will shape future proposals of the 1990s remains uncertain. What might be more probable is that this show is destined to run and run.

Local Government in the 1980s: A Shrinking World?

For the advocates of local government the 1980s were not a happy decade. It is argued that during this period central–local relations became more antagonistic, financial discretion was minimized and now, through further policies, local government is becoming increasingly marginalized as functions are removed from it (e.g. education, housing) or it is bypassed in favour of private sector bodies (e.g. in inner city development).

This view may neglect that historically there have always been tensions between central and local government and that the erosion of local powers has been a feature of developments dating back at least to the end of the Second World War (Alexander, 1989). However, what may be different about the latest onslaught is that for pragmatic, political and ideological reasons a number of successive, if often separately inspired, policies have eroded many of the traditional functions of local government and possibly redefined its role. These include the policies for local government finance discussed in detail above, efforts to liberalize or privatize local government activities and, finally, more specifically designed initiatives to expose particular services (e.g. education and housing) to market forces and consumer choice.

Privatization

Privatization came to local authorities in the early 1980s with the selling off of council houses to their tenants. This initiative of the Conservative government, known as 'right to buy', proved immensely popular with voters. The reactions of local authorities to it were mixed. Some Tory authorities (e.g. Wandsworth) pursued it vigorously. Labour authorities resisted both for ideological reasons and on the grounds that the dilution of housing stock via sales would damage local housing policy.

The 'right to buy' initiative constitutes one strand of privatization in local government. As Stoker (1988, Chapter 8) observes, others involve the deregulation of council services (e.g. transport), the instruction to contract out local government activities (e.g. direct labour organizations, sports centre management) and the bypassing of local government in the implementation of major policy initiatives (e.g. inner cities).

The government's case for deregulation and contracting out is that many local government services are cosy monopolies protected from market forces and the harsh winds of competition. This leads to inefficient operations, poor management, unnecessary subsidization and powerful and recalcitrant unions. In terms of deregulation, local authorities involved in public transport were therefore forced to reorganize their operations into businesses, seek value for money and expose themselves to competition. For city-dwellers the most visible effect of this was the appearance of fleets of mini-buses (which often failed to run on Sundays and holidays). For the rural dweller it often resulted in fewer or no buses at all.

Contracting out was a strategy first used in the National Health Service (NHS). The argument here is that in-house services should be put out to tender and awarded to the lowest bidder. Unlike the NHS, contracting out was not initially forced on local authorities although some Tory councils moved in this direction with enthusiasm, especially in the areas of refuse collection and office cleaning. However, under the Local Government Act (1989) authorities were forced to put a range of services out to tender. The specified services included cleaning, catering, refuse collection and sports centre management. Reactions to this initiative were mixed; however, some authorities welcomed these moves not least since the threat of 'be efficient or else' might have a galvanizing effect on outdated work practices and industrial relations.

Competitive tendering might also have the effect of drawing public and private sectors closer together in the provision of public services. This theme featured in different ways in various other policy initiatives (e.g. housing, care for the elderly and urban development). Indeed in urban renewal the tendency has often been to bypass local authorities who, in the government's eyes, have often stifled opportunities through over-zealous application of planning regulations and a failure to take a businesslike approach to economic matters. Hence, in some instances development responsibilities were given to Urban Development Corporations such as in London Docklands and Liverpool.

Housing and education

One of the major justifications for local government is that it provides the abilities to plan, coordinate and deliver local services in response to local needs. The government took the view that this was not being achieved. Instead there existed local state monopolies insensitive to consumer demands and resistant to central policy. This contributed to falling education standards, deteriorating public housing and dissatisfied customers and clients who had little control or say over the services they received.

In the case of housing these issues came to a head in the late 1980s when the government decided on a shift of policy. Rather than continue investment in the current public housing system, it proposed to launch policies to revitalize the privately rented sector. This was to be done by the creation of an internal market that would give council tenants freedom to choose from a variety of landlords. The right to buy legislation was also to be extended. These proposals were set out in a White Paper (Cm. 214, 1987) and were the basis of the Housing Act (1988). Here the government stated that its aim was to create a more 'businesslike' framework for the management of council housing in which local authorities were to cease to be major providers of housing and instead adopt a 'strategic role' in housing provision. These aims were incorporated into the Housing Act which proposed the following:

1. To open up the private rented sector by amending the 1977 Rent Act to remove restrictions from private landlords.
2. To allow council tenants to 'choose' a landlord, in particular by allowing them to transfer to a housing association, trust or private landlord.
3. To create bodies called Housing Action Trusts (HATs) that would take over some of the worst council estates, renovate them and sell them off.

This legislation had a bumpy passage through Parliament, especially in terms of what voting mechanism would be used to allow tenants to make choices about their landlord. Tenants also appeared wary of their new potential freedoms, stating (in surveys) that they preferred the council to the private sector as landlord and, in the case of estates named as potential HATs, often demonstrating forcefully that this was an honour they could do without. For local authorities, however, the housing legislation and tough new regulations on housing finance appeared to make a redefinition of their future role inevitable (Gray and Jenkins, 1988).

The late 1980s also saw major changes in education policy, again posing serious questions for local government. Of particular importance here were the proposals on schools 'opting out' of local authority control and of delegated financial management to the schools themselves. These initiatives were core parts of the Education Act (1989). In the case of opting out it was argued that it was important to create an internal market that would be parent (consumer) driven, offer greater choice and raise standards. It would therefore be possible for schools to 'opt out' of local authority control if the Secretary of State for Education agreed. Against this, however, it was argued that such moves might fragment the strategic management of education and weaken those who were left behind.

In the case of delegated financial management to schools, further changes in local authority responsibility must inevitably follow. It is planned that by 1993 the responsibility for a school's financial management will lie with the school itself (i.e. its governors and headmaster). Schools will therefore have a delegated budget (worked out by formula) and must manage their affairs within this. Whether individual schools are, or will be, ready for this change is a matter for debate. However, question marks clearly exist over the future role of Local Education Authorities (LEAs). The government's stated intention is that LEAs will retain responsibilities for strategic planning, setting budgets, monitoring performance and, if necessary, regulating the new fragmented world of education. How far such hopes are likely to be mirrored in reality remains to be seen.

In 1988 the Audit Commission published a paper entitled *The Competitive Council*.

Unashamedly managerialist in tone, it advocated 'well managed' authorities that were responsive, understood their customers, had clear and achievable objectives and monitored progress. But a different and even more radical vision of local government's future can be found in publications from the right-wing think-tank, the Adam Smith Institute (1989), which put forward proposals for local authorities to become private limited companies known as 'community companies'. Such an arrangement, it was claimed, could be compatible with the principles of local democracy. Other suggestions in this paper included a cabinet-style government for authorities, increasing adoption of private providers to deliver services and further use of contracting out and charging.

Whatever the feasibility of either of the above perspectives, it is clear that local government has come a long way from the Maud Report and the 1974 reorganization. In particular many of the assumptions concerning the value and role of local government are now being questioned. In the last decade a series of policies have not only constrained local government in financial terms but have also slimmed and redefined its role as a prime service deliverer for the welfare state. This raises questions of what local government should be and what it should do in the next decade. Should it accept that its future is to play an 'enabling' role of the form suggested by Mr Ridley (1988) or has it a more directive part to play?

Looking back over recent history even local government's friends would not argue that it has always performed effectively (and even efficiently) either in terms of facilitating local democracy or in the management and delivery of services. There have therefore been many calls for local government to give greater emphasis to its electors as clients and consumers and to adopt mechanisms that might allow a greater degree of participation in local affairs. Moves by some authorities to decentralize services to smaller and more approachable units that are 'closer to the customer' and the demand for 'a new management of local government' together with a public service orientation that values service *for* the public rather than *to* the public reflects this new mood (Stewart and Clarke 1987). This, of course, is in part a call for a return to *localism*. But such an idea of localism linked to the idea of a *community* differs sharply from that of right-wing thinkers. For many of the latter, the world is made up of individuals whose basic rights need to be protected by a strong state. Yet such a system may be inherently inefficient relying as it does on markets or quasi-markets to achieve a strategic purpose.

At the start of this chapter we noted the values of local government as recorded by the Widdicombe Committee, namely *pluralism, participation* and *responsiveness*. To these we would add *strategic direction*. The task of local government in the 1990s may be to seek structures and processes that combine and coordinate these. This will not be easy since, as has been demonstrated, simultaneous maximization of these values may not be possible. However, the danger of not moving along this path may be the erosion of the checks and balances provided by local government together with the growth of an increasingly centralized and authoritarian state.

References and Further Reading

Adam Smith Institute, *Wiser Counsels* (Adam Smith Institute, 1989).
Alexander, A., *The Politics of Local Government in the United Kingdom* (Longman, 1982).

Alexander, A., 'The decline of local government', *Contemporary Record*, **2**(6), 2–5 (1989).

Audit Commission, *The Impact on Local Authorities' Economy, Efficiency and Effectiveness of the Block Grant Distribution System* (HMSO, 1984).

Audit Commission, *The Competitive Council*, Management Paper Number One (Audit Commission, 1988).

Byrne, T., *Local Government in Britain*, 2nd edn (Penguin, 1983).

Cm 214, *Housing: The Government's proposals* (HMSO, 1987).

Cm 433, *The Government Response to the Widdicombe Committee of Inquiry* (HMSO, 1988).

Cmnd 1164, *Royal Commission on Local Government in Greater London 1957–60* (The Herbert Commission) (HMSO, 1960).

Cmnd 4040, *Report of the Royal Commission on Local Government in England* (The Redcliffe Maud Report) (HMSO, 1969).

Cmnd 4584, *Local Government in England* (HMSO, 1969).

Cmnd 6453, *Report of the Committee on Local Government Finance* (The Layfield Committee) (HMSO, 1976).

Cmnd 6813, *Local Government Finance* (HMSO, 1977).

Cmnd 8449, *Alternatives to Domestic Rates* (HMSO, 1981).

Cmnd 9008, *Rates* (HMSO, 1983).

Cmnd 9714, *Paying for Local Government* (HMSO, 1986).

Cmnd 9797, *The Conduct of Local Authority Business* (The Widdicombe Report) (HMSO, 1986).

Cmnd 9799, *The Conduct of Local Authority Business*, Research Volume II: The Local Government Councillor (HMSO, 1986).

The Economist, 'How the Tories muffed reform', 16 March 1985, 38–40.

Gray, A.G., 'Local government in England and Wales', in B. Jones and D. Kavanagh (eds), *British Politics Today* (Manchester University Press, 1979).

Gray, A.G. and Jenkins, W.I., 'Public administration and government in 1987', *Parliamentary Affairs*, **41**(3), 321–39 (1988).

Gyford, J., *The Politics of Local Socialism* (Allen & Unwin, 1985).

Jones, G.W., 'Central–local government relations', in D. Butler and A.H. Halsey (eds), *Policy and Politics* (Macmillan, 1978).

Jones, G.W., 'Introduction to special feature on the Widdicombe Report', *Local Government Studies*, **12**(6), 20–6 (1986).

Mill, J.S., *Representative Government* (1861, reprinted in Dent's Everyman Library with *Utilitarianism and Liberty*, 1910).

Redcliffe Maud, Lord and Wood, B., *English Local Government Reformed* (Oxford University Press, 1974).

Report of the Committee on the Management of Local Government (The Maud Report), (HMSO, 1977).

Ridley, N., *The Local Right: Enabling not Providing* (Centre for Policy Studies, 1988).

Stewart, J. and Clarke, M., 'The public service orientation: issues and dilemmas', *Public Administration*, **65**(2), 161–77 (1987).

Stoker, G., *The Politics of Local Government* (Macmillan, 1988).

The New Local Authorities: Management and Structure (The Bains Report) (HMSO, 1972).

The Remuneration of Councillors, Vol. 2 (The Robinson Committee) (HMSO, 1977).

Travers, T., *The Politics of Local Government Finance* (Allen & Unwin, 1986).

Young, K, 'Party politics in local government: a historical perspective', in Cmnd. 9801, *The Conduct of Local Authority Business*, Research Volume IV (1986).

Mrs Thatcher's Impact upon Whitehall

Peter Hennessy

The place is St George's House in the shadow of Windsor Castle; the occasion, an Anglo−American seminar on bureaucracy; the time, the spring of 1984, well into Mrs Thatcher's second term; the speaker is a neat, precise, bespectacled Englishman in his forties, sporting a watch and chain.

'The British civil service', he declares, 'is a great rock on the tideline. The political wave, Labour or Conservative, rolls in, washes over it and ebbs. The rock is exposed again to the air virtually unchanged.' He pauses, 'But Mrs Thatcher has been applying sticks of dynamite to that rock.'

The speaker was Clive Priestley, a former Whitehall Under-Secretary held in high esteem by the former Prime Minister for the work he had done as chief of staff to Lord Rayner of Marks and Spencer, her efficiency adviser. Mr Priestley's remarks were addressed to Mrs Thatcher as dynamiter of bureauratic waste, a subject to which I shall return. But there are observers in Parliament, the Press and Whitehall itself who believe that more than one stick of dynamite was applied by the demolition expert in Number 10, with damaging results to the constitutional masonry.

Alleged Attacks on the Civil Service Since 1979

A hostile expert in blast effects might draw up the following assessment:

1. Politicization of the senior ranks of the civil service by the application of informal 'Is he one of us?' tests to top appointments.
2. Deliberate bypassing of traditional, neutral Whitehall advice as evidenced by the abolition of the Central Policy Review Staff in 1983, the subsequent build-up of her own Downing Street Policy Unit and the discouragement of plain speaking or the parading of inconvenient facts at meetings with officials.
3. A conscious attempt to reduce civil service morale by parsimonious pay deals, hostility towards Whitehall unions, the deunionization of the Government Communications Headquarters (GCHQ), plus cuts in staff and promotion prospects.
4. The vigorous pursuit of leakers, trivial as well as serious, through the Courts if necessary and the refusal to draft a code of ethics to protect the conscience-stricken official.

There is *prima facie* evidence to support each indictment on the charge sheet. If the case *were* proven, the years between 1979 and 1990 would indeed have witnessed a truly over-mighty premiership upsetting, it not overturning, important constitutional conventions.

Politicization of upper ranks

In constitutional terms, the most serious charge is politicization of the upper ranks. The opportunity was there, the gift of prime ministerial longevity. Between 1979 and 1985, forty-three Permanent Secretaries and 138 Deputy Secretaries departed the scene through retirement, which is virtually a complete turnover in the top two grades in which Prime Ministers traditionally take an interest.

Mrs Thatcher undoubtedly took a closer interest than any PM in recent memory. This had its own effect. The half-dozen top officials who comprised the Senior Appointments Selection Committee (which submits a short-list of candidates to No. 10) certainly watched how she reacted at meetings to individuals in the promotion frame. This, they reckoned, had much more to do with personal chemistry than anything ideological. Mrs Thatcher had an unconcealed preference for the can-do official rather than the snag-obsessed bureaucrat.

There was, however, sufficient concern in high Whitehall places for Sir Douglas Wass (a former Permanent Secretary to the Treasury) to call for a Royal Commission, shortly after his retirement in 1983, to investigate this and other aspects of the civil service. Mrs Thatcher was not an admirer of the Royal Commission as a means of investigation and so the highly respected Royal Institute of Public Administration (RIPA) conducted an independent inquiry instead. In the process of clearing Mrs Thatcher, the RIPA's report captured the personality factors which had caused the issue to arise in the first place:

> To some extent [the report stated] the appointment process has become more personalized in the sense that at the top level 'catching the eye' of the Prime Minister (in a favourable or unfavourable manner) may now be more important than in the past . . . However, we do not believe that these appointments and promotions are based on the candidate's support for or commitment to particular political ideologies or objectives.

Despite Mrs Thatcher's acquittal, two genuine problems remained. One was given voice by Lord Bancroft, the former Head of the Home Civil Service who had gone into early retirement after the disbandment of the Civil Service Department in 1981. Bancroft, in a television interview in 1986, said the idea that his old service had been politicized was 'wholly misplaced' but there were dangers of a more insidious kind. 'The dangers', he explained,

> are of the younger people, seeing that advice which ministers want to hear falls with a joyous note on their ears, and advice which they need to hear falls on their ears with a rather dismal note, will tend to make officials trim, make their advice what ministers want to hear rather than what they need to know.

There is a second, related danger. The *impression* of politicization, however unjustified, is abroad. It could be cited as a precedent by a future Labour government wishing to apply its own 'one of us' test. Neil Kinnock has set his face against such a notion. But if it ever happened it would undo the Northcote−Trevelyan principle of a career, politically neutral civil service capable of serving any democratic government. The constitution would have changed and the origins of the process, rightly or wrongly, would be traced back to the Thatcher years.

Bypassing of neutral civil service advice

There is much more substance to the view that Mrs Thatcher had little use for the traditional, on-the-one-hand/on-the-other-hand style of civil service advice. She made no secret of her preference for ministers and civil servants who came to her with solutions rather than problems. And she would listen to unpalatable advice if she admired the track record and warmed to the personality of its giver. There were a number of instances, however, where top flight officials who could have expected to reach Permanent Secretary rank under another PM, Labour or Conservative, had a metaphorical black mark against their names after clashing with 'she who must be obeyed', as some in the Cabinet Office came to call Mrs Thatcher.

Reduction of civil service morale

In terms of pay, pensions and conditions, Mrs Thatcher did believe the civil service was privileged when she took office. On pensions she failed to secure the deindexing she was after. Far from recommending abolition, the Scott inquiry urged in 1981 that the principle of inflation-proofing be extended, though with the reduction of inflation the steam went out of the issue.

On pay, the government unilaterally abandoned the system whereby Whitehall remuneration was determined by fair comparison with comparable outside bodies on the grounds that it was flawed and inflationary. The twenty-two week civil service strike of 1981 was the result. Defeat and victory are crude words with which to judge outcomes but, however the dispute is viewed, the unions did not win. Since the subsequent Megaw inquiry into civil service pay, some progress has been made towards a more flexible system of bargaining which reflects particular skills and needs, though, as yet, the abandonment of national pay bargaining in favour of a regional pattern has still be to achieved.

Pay is probably the greatest single sapper of morale. According to the unions, since 1979 civil service pay awards have fallen by about 30 per cent behind the national average. Pay is closely followed by the truncation of promotion prospects — the inevitable consequence of the Government's success in reducing the size of the civil service from the 732,000 it inherited to 600,000 by the end of the second term. Morale may be unmeasurable but the lack of it was acknowledged by Sir Robert Armstrong as Head of the Home Civil Service when appearing before a Commons select committee and he raised it as a priority for his successor, Sir Robin Butler.

Morale has also been affected by factors other than pay or promotion. The feeling that many current ministers share the anti-civil service prejudice of the public at large has depressed the 3,000 or so policymakers who work closely with them. The deunionization of GCHQ in 1984, despite the offer of a no-strike agreement by the unions, created an unfavourable reaction from top to bottom of the civil service. In general terms, for the gifted and ambitious, Whitehall was no longer *the* place to be. An outward flow of marketable talent was sufficiently marked by 1986 for it to be the subject of an inquiry by the Prime Minister's Efficiency Unit.

Hounding of leakers

Another contributory factor was the manner in which leakers, great and small, were pursued. Few in Whitehall would have quarrelled with the dismissal of Sarah Tisdall (the Foreign Office clerk who disclosed details of cruise missile siting to a newspaper) or Clive Ponting, but their charging under Section 2 of the Official Secrets Act was another matter, while similar treatment afforded to Robin Gordon-Walker for leaving documents on a train was thought wildly overdone. The disquiet was compounded by the government's unwillingness to adopt a code of practice on civil service ethics as suggested by the top officials' union, the First Division Association. That such disquiet should have rumbled for so long at so high a level in the service was evidence of the degree to which relationships had decayed between some ministers and some senior civil servants.

Impact of Rayner

A canter through the critics' charge sheet, however, is a seriously incomplete way of examining Mrs Thatcher's stewardship of the civil service. Her premierships will be remembered for much more. For example, when the Thatcher archive is broken open at the Public Record Office in the twenty-first century, historians would do well to concentrate on a Cabinet Paper dated April 1980 with the title *The Conventions of Government*. In effect, it was Lord Rayner's charter for the better management of the state. Its cumulative impact was considerable and, in so far as these things are knowable, permanent.

In an interview in 1986, Lord Rayner described the actions proposed in the document:

> There were three: a short-term getting rid of paperwork; a medium-term getting down to individual activities or discrete parts of government and improving the way they perform; and thirdly, lasting reforms, bringing about the changes and the education and the experience during the career of a civil servant which would [enable] him to manage the substantial amounts of work that would unquestionably come his way.

For all three, Rayner received crucial and consistent backing from the Prime Minister who insisted his authority was on a par with that of the Head of the Home Civil Service and the Permanent Secretary to the Treasury.

Taking the proposals in the order he prescribed, Rayner concentrated his early fire on the raw materials of bureaucracy — paper and rules. There was a blitz against a profusion of administrative forms, thirty-six in a year for every man, woman and child in the United Kingdom. Five years after war was declared on 'bumf' 27,000 forms had been scrapped, 41,000 redesigned and £14m saved as a result.

Whitehall procedures were subjected to the Marks and Spencer treatment. The huge rulebooks of the tax and benefits system were simplified. Rayner found one defunct tax form which absorbed the time of 400 officials. In his investigation of government research and development establishments he found Ministry of Agriculture vets breeding their own rats for experimental purposes at a cost of £30.00 per rodent when the little beasts could be bought for £2.00 commercially. Turning his penchant for the revealing statistic to the civil service as a whole, Rayner calculated that it cost every man, woman and child £3.00 a week just to keep it in being before it did anything. His reward was to be called 'a remarkable and wonderful person' in the House of Commons by the Prime Minister.

As for those 'discrete parts' of government activity mentioned by Lord Rayner, a rolling 'scrutiny programme' was launched using bright, brave officials with full Downing Street backing to investigate chunks of work — payment of benefits, supply of food to the Armed Forces, the provision of Government statistics and the maintenance of departmental property. As a result, by the end of Mrs Thatcher's second term more than £1 billion had been saved, a tidy sum when you consider what it buys — the M25 motorway, twenty-two hospitals or the Chevaline missile improvement to the Polaris force. The problem with the scrutiny approach is that it proved exceedingly hard to extend it from the £13 billion administrative costs of government to the £100 billion (at 1987 prices) devoted to the huge spending programmes where the big economy and value-for-money prizes lie.

The other area of resistance to Raynerism was to what his Cabinet paper called 'lasting reforms' — i.e. those intended to change civil service culture to something more akin to the private sector. It was not so much a matter of civil servants showing reluctance to absorb new concepts of efficiency and effectiveness and the courses provided to teach them at the Civil Service College. It was more a matter of finding effective procedures which would act as a genuine surrogate for private sector profit-and-loss disciplines in the big businesses — tax collection, benefit payment, weapons procurement — which Whitehall was obliged to run and from which it could not withdraw if the going got tough or unremunerative.

Rayner's 1982 financial management initiative (known universally as the FMI) went some way towards devolving discretion to line managers and imbuing both ministers and officials generally with a sense of cost and the efficient use of resources. But by the late 1980s it seemed to many, both inside Whitehall and without, to have consumed its initial momentum while falling short of a permanent, self-sustaining revolution in the central management of the state, its servants and its budgets.

Ibbs and *The Next Steps*

This certainly seems to have been the view of Sir Robin Ibbs of ICI, who succeeded Rayner as the PM's Efficiency Adviser in 1983. Before the 1987 election he prepared, in considerable secrecy, a report for Mrs Thatcher entitled *The Next Steps*. A genuine transformation of Whitehall management, he argued, would require: first, a division of the civil service into its small, 20,000-strong, policy making core, with the remaining 580,000 engaged in delivering goods and services; secondly, that the delivery side be seen for what it was, a series of businesses, and split up accordingly into freestanding agencies within the pubic service or limited (if regulated) companies outside it. It was the most dramatic reform proposal since Northcote—Trevelyan 130 years earlier and, if adopted in full, would have ended the tight central control over every pound spent and official employed which has been the basis of Treasury power since the end of the First World War.

By the end of 1989, the pace with which *The Next Steps* programme had developed surprised most 'Whitehall watchers', accustomed as they were to see the more ambitious civil service reforms gradually subside into the quicksands of inertia. Ten executive agencies were up and running with a further ten expected within a year. By the end of the century, it was predicted, three-quarters of the civil service would be working in one or other version of these new managerial hybrids. What is more, some of the first ten, Her Majesty's Stationery Office in particular, had achieved a degree of freedom from Treasury control over pay and recruitment which few observers had expected.

Peter Kemp, the Cabinet Office civil servant charged with implementing *The Next Steps* programme as its project manager, saw it as special kind of enterprise, a way 'of getting the best of both worlds, filling a gap in the management armoury of this country . . . it's a public sector owner and broad public sector rules with a private sector approach to running businesses because that's what many Civil Service activities are.'

The project, however, still faced its greatest test when Mr Kemp spoke those words — the restructuring of the really vast Whitehall 'businesses' on an agency basis, the Employment Service and the Social Security network in particular. In their way they are to *The Next Steps* what British Telecom was to the privatization programme — if they fail to match expectations, the enterprise could falter; if they surpass hopes, the pace will quicken still further.

Whatever the ultimate fate of *The Next Steps*, Mrs Thatcher has already had more impact on the management of the civil service than *any* previous prime minister. Gladstone's was a revolution in recruitment; Lloyd George's in the machinery of government; Mrs Thatcher's managerial revolution along Rayner lines appeared to be largely, if not wholly, irreversible.

In the course of achieving it did she — by her close involvement in top appointments, her determination to strip it of privileges and to tighten internal discipline — reduce the civil service to the condition of her personal poodle? I think not.

The civil service is a fixed, national asset as permanent (we hope) as parliamentary democracy in Britain. In that sense it is leased by successive governments to whom its loyalty should be instantly on tap. But it is not a Prime Minister's or even a Cabinet's individual possession; it has not been for over a century and there is no real sign of it becoming so now. (The moment it does, the internal balance of the Whitehall—Westminster part of the constitution really will have changed.) Contrary to some appearances, Mrs Thatcher did nothing to alter that position or the understandings upon which it was based. These, along with extensions of the franchise, are the greatest political gifts from the nineteenth to the twentieth century.

Further Reading

Hennessy, P., *Whitehall* (Secker & Warburg, 1989; Fontana, 1990).

This Concluding Comment is an adaptation of Hennessy, P., 'Mrs Thatcher's Poodle?' *Contemporary Record*, **2**, No. 2, 2–4 (1988).

PART VII The Judicial Process

The judicial function of government is often glossed over superficially in politics courses and textbooks. This is partly because it is held to be politically neutral, outside or above politics and hence of scant interest. A number of recent developments and critiques, however, have questioned whether the judiciary is as neutral as its senior practitioners would have us believe. Politics, as we learnt in the introduction, is:

> essentially a process which seeks to manage or resolve conflicts of interest between people, usually in a peaceful fashion.

The law is clearly a key instrument in this process as it establishes a commonly accepted set of rules according to which citizens can live their lives, both in relation to each other and to the institutions of government.

These rules or laws are formulated in the legislature and implemented by the executive, but enforcement and interpretation of the law is the business of the courts assisted by the police. The alternative is an anarchy where intimidation and violence will surely prevail: the rule of law is the foundation of civilized society and fundamental to the working of the political system. To be generally accepted and effective the law must fulfil certain basic requirements:

1. Exact and detailed information about it must be freely available.
2. There must be certainty that the law will act in cases of violation.
3. Everyone should be treated equally before the law.
4. Judges should be honest, impartial and independent of any interest.

To satisfy conditions 3 and 4 the law must clearly be politically neutral. But is this possible? It all depends upon what is meant by political. Defenders of the system would claim that the law is above politics and that judges, whatever their own views might be, interpret and apply it with commendable impartiality irrespective of political creed, race, class or gender. Critics, however, claim that the law itself defends the interests of the wealthy and influential groups in society; that by being part of this group themselves judges cannot but be biased towards defence of its interests and reinforcement of the dominant values which underpin them.

Chapter 22:   **The Judiciary**
Philip Norton
Concluding Comment: Law and Order Moves up the Political Agenda

22 The Judiciary

Philip Norton

Britain does not have a system like the USA where the Supreme Court acts as the ultimate interpreter of the constitution and pronounces upon the constitutionality of Congressional and state laws together with the actions of public officials. Britain's judiciary has to bend its knee to the sovereignty of Parliament: it cannot make rulings on the constitutionality of Acts of Parliament. This chapter analyses the interface between politics and the law covering the judicial relationship to the legislature, the courts, judges, 'judicial activism' and the impact of membership of the European Community.

The literature on the judicial process in Britain is extensive. Significantly, virtually all of it is written by legal scholars; few works on the courts or judges come from the pens of political scientists. To those concerned with the study of British politics, and in particular the process of policy making, the judicial process is deemed to be of peripheral interest.

That this perception should exist is not surprising. It derives from two features that are considered to be essential characteristics of the judiciary in Britain. First, in the trinity of the executive, legislature and judiciary, it is a subordinate institution. Public policy is made and ratified elsewhere. The courts exist to interpret (within defined limits) and apply that policy once enacted by the legislature; they have no power to strike it down. Secondly, it is autonomous. The independence of the judiciary is a much-vaunted and essential feature of the rule of law, described by the great nineteenth century constitutional lawyer A.V. Dicey as one of the twin pillars of the British Constitution. The other pillar — parliamentary sovereignty — accounts for the first characteristic, the subordination of the judiciary to Parliament. Allied with autonomy has been the notion of political neutrality. Judges seek to interpret the law according to judicial norms that operate independently of partisan or personal preferences.

Given these characteristics — politically neutral courts separate from, and subordinate to, the central agency of law-enactment — a clear demarcation has arisen in recent decades, the study of the policy making process being the preserve of political scientists, that of the judiciary the preserve of legal scholars. There has been little overlap between the two. Consequently, few texts on British politics draw out and emphasize the role of the judiciary. Yet in practice the judiciary in Britain has not been as subordinate or as autonomous as the prevailing wisdom assumes. The dividing line between politics and the law is blurred rather than rigid.

A subordinate branch?

The judiciary is subordinate to Parliament (in legal terms, the Queen-in-Parliament) in that it lacks the power to strike down any Act of Parliament as being contrary to the provisions of the constitution or to any other superior body of law. It was not always thus. Prior to the Glorious Revolution of 1688, the supremacy of statute law was not established. In *Dr Bonham's Case* in 1610, Chief Justice Coke asserted that 'when an Act of Parliament is against common right and reason, or repugnant, or impossible to be performed, the common law will control it, and adjudge such act to be void'. A few years later, Chief Justice Hobart declared that an Act 'made against natural equity, as to make a man judge in his own case' would be void (*Day* v. *Savadge*, 1615). Statute law had to compete not only with the common law — law based on custom and precedent — but also with the prerogative powers of the Crown. The courts variously upheld the power of the king to dispense with statutes and to impose taxes, without the consent of Parliament, when necessity demanded.

The Glorious Revolution put an end to this state of affairs. Thereafter, the supremacy of statute law, under the doctrine of parliamentary sovereignty, was established. The doctrine is a judicially self-imposed one. The common lawyers allied themselves with Parliament in order to remove the prerogative powers of the king and the prerogative courts through which he sometimes exercised them. The supremacy of Parliament was asserted by statute in the Bill of Rights of 1689. 'For the common lawyers, there was a price to pay, and that was the abandonment of the claim that they had sometimes advanced, that Parliament could not legislate in derogation of the principles of the common law' (Munro, 1987, p.81). Parliamentary sovereignty — a purely legal doctrine asserting the supremacy of statute law — became the central tenet of the constitution. However, the subordination of common law to statute law did not — and does not — entail the subordination of the judiciary to the executive. Courts retain the power of interpreting the precise meaning of statute law once passed and reviewing the actions of ministers and other public agents to determine whether they are *ultra vires*, that is, beyond the powers granted by statute. Government decisions — or those of any other public body — which are not taken within powers granted by statute enjoy no legal force. The courts cannot strike down Acts of Parliament; but they can quash the actions of ministers which are not sanctioned by such Acts.

A government thwarted in its policy goals by having a particular action struck down as *ultra vires* may, of course, seek parliamentary approval for a Bill which gives statutory force to the action taken; in other words, to give legal force to that which the courts have declared as having — on the basis of existing statute — no such force. But seeking passage of a Bill is not only time-consuming, it may also prove politically contentious and publicly damaging, conveying the impression that the government, having lost a case, is trying to change the rules of the game. Though, as we shall see, it is a path governments have variously taken, it is one they would prefer to — and often do — avoid.

The power of judicial review thus provides the judiciary with a potentially significant role in the policy cycle. It is a potential which for much of the past century has not been realized. However, recent years have witnessed an upsurge in *judicial activism*, judges being far more willing both to review and to quash ministerial actions. It is an activism which coincides with another development that has enlarged the scope for such activism: British membership of the European Communities. Membership of the Communities has added a new judicial dimension to the British Constitution. The courts, whether they wanted to or not, have found themselves playing a more central role in the determination of public policy.

An autonomous branch?

The judiciary is deemed to be autonomous of the other two branches of government. Its independence 'is secured by law, by professional and public opinion' (Wade and Phillips, 1977, p.50). Since the Act of Settlement, senior judges have held office 'during good behaviour' and can be removed only by the Queen following an address from both Houses of Parliament. (Only one judge has been removed by such a process: Jonah Barrington, an Irish judge, was removed in 1830 after it was found he had misappropriated litigants' money and had ceased to perform his judicial duties.) Judges of inferior courts enjoy a lesser degree of statutory protection. (In 1977 a Scottish judge — Sheriff Peter Thomson — was removed by Order in Council after campaigning for a Scottish Plebiscite, continuing to do so after being warned about his activities. He had been found guilty of misbehaviour on two occasions by a judges' enquiry and declared unfit for office.) Judges' salaries are a charge upon the Consolidated Fund: that means that they do not have to be voted each year by Parliament. By its own resolution, the House of Commons generally bars any reference by Members to matters awaiting or under adjudication in criminal and most civil courts. By convention, a similar prohibition is observed by ministers and civil servants. MPs also generally recognize the convention that judges should not be criticized.

For their part, judges by convention refrain from politically partisan activity. Indeed, they have generally refrained from commenting upon matters of public policy, doing so not only of their own volition but also for many years by the direction of the Lord Chancellor. The Kilmuir Guidelines issued in 1955 enjoined judges to silence since 'every utterance which he (a judge) makes in public, except in the course of the actual performance of his judicial duties, must necessarily bring him within the focus of criticism'. These guidelines were relaxed in the late 1970s but effectively reimposed by Lord Hailsham in 1980. For judges to interfere in a contentious issue of public policy, one that is not under adjudication, would undermine public confidence in the impartiality of the judiciary. Similarly, for politicians to interfere in a matter before the courts would be seen to challenge the rule of law. Hence, the perceived self-interest of both in confining themselves to their own spheres of expertise.

However, the dividing line between judges and politicians — and, to a lesser extent, between judicial and political decision making — is not quite as sharp as these various features would suggest. In terms of personnel, memberships of the executive, legislature and judiciary are not mutually exclusive. There is, particularly in the higher reaches, some overlap. The most obvious and outstanding example is to be found in the person of the Lord Chancellor. He is the head of the judiciary and exercises major judicial functions; most judges are either appointed by him or on his advice. He is also the presiding officer of the House of Lords (albeit a position entailing no significant powers) and a member of the Cabinet. A number of Lords Chancellor have been prominent party politicians, most recently and most notably Lord Hailsham, Lord Chancellor for eleven years (1970−4 and 1979−87), a former contender for the leadership of the Conservative party. Other members of the government with judicial appointments are the Law Officers: the Attorney General, the Solicitor General, the Lord Advocate for Scotland and the Solicitor General for Scotland. The Attorney-General and Solicitor-General lead for the Crown in major cases as well as serving as legal advisers to government. In Scotland, the Lord Advocate and Solicitor-General for Scotland perform somewhat broader functions, including the control of public prosecutions.

The highest court of appeal within the United Kingdom is the House of Lords. For judicial purposes, the Lords constitutes a judicial committee of the House, though all of the members of the committee are members of the Upper Chamber. Some Members of Parliament serve as or have served as Recorders (part-time but salaried judges in the Crown Court) and many sit as local magistrates. Judges in the High Court, Court of Appeal and Court of Session are barred by statute from membership of the Commons and any MP appointed to a judgeship becomes ineligible to remain in the House. No such prohibition exists in the case of the House of Lords. The overlap in judicial and political powers is not quite so great as the overlap in personnel would suggest. By convention, peers holding judicial office refrain from partisan comment in the House of Lords, confining any contributions to debates on legal matters. The Law Officers are deemed — and expected — to act independently of the government in exercising their judicial and advice-giving functions; their legal opinions given to ministers are customarily treated as confidential. There is thus some attempt to generate a 'Chinese wall' between judicial and political activity.

The separation of judicial and political, however, is not complete. Judges do not operate in a judicial vacuum. A number of judicial decisions result each year in public controversy. Sentences in rape cases regarded by MPs and members of the public as unduly lenient, for example, may provoke the Lord Chancellor to request transcripts of the proceedings. In extreme cases he may take the step of issuing a reprimand, an action likely to influence not only the offending judge but also other members of the judiciary in future behaviour. In November 1988, a judge — Sir Harold Cassel — gave a light sentence to a man convicted of indecent assault on his twelve-year-old stepdaughter. In his judgement, Sir Harold asserted that the man's actions were the likely consequence of his wife's pregnancy, his wife not being able to fulfil his sexual needs. The case attracted immediate media and parliamentary attention. The Lord Chancellor, Lord Mackay, called in the papers of the case and subsequently issued a reprimand. It was then announced that the judge was to retire on health grounds. (It was announced by the Lord Chancellor's Department that the judge had actually written his resignation the day before he made his comments in court.)

The Lord Chancellor may, then, intervene in particular cases. So too may the Home Secretary, who has the power to refer cases back for consideration to the Court of Appeal if new evidence comes to light. Recent years have witnessed particular pressure on the Home Secretary to refer back a number of cases, which he did for example in the case of the 'Guildford Four', resulting in the convictions being quashed. Nor are the Lord Chancellor and Home Secretary alone in having

Lord Hailsham of St Marylebone

Quintin Hogg, Lord Hailsham of St Marylebone, has the distinction of having been Lord Chancellor for a total of twelve years. He also has the distinction, with Lord Home, of having served *twice* in *both* Houses of Parliament.

Quintin Hogg was born in 1907 and — like his father — had an active career as a lawyer and politician. He was called to the Bar in 1932 and became a Queen's Counsel (QC) in 1953. He was Conservative MP for Oxford from 1938 (when he won a famous by-election) to 1950, when he succeeded his father as Viscount Hailsham. He served as a government Minister from 1956 to 1964. In 1963, he took the first opportunity possible to renounce his peerage. (He had announced his intention to do so in order to seek the premiership in succession to Harold Macmillan — instead, the leadership went to another peer, Lord Home, who also then renounced his title.) From 1963 to 1970, Hogg was Conservative MP for St Marylebone. In 1970, upon the return of a Conservative government, he was given a life peerage and appointed Lord Chancellor. He held the position throughout the period of the Heath government and, with the return of the Conservative party to office in 1979, was again returned to the Woolsack by Margaret Thatcher. He served until 1987.

As Lord Chancellor, Hailsham proved willing to use his prerogative to sit as a judge. His period as head of the judiciary witnessed a number of innovations, though he opposed radical reform of the legal system itself. Following his retirement, he was a vocal opponent of the Government's 1989 proposals for a restructuring of the legal profession.

Throughout his period of public office, Hailsham proved willing to give his opinion on a wide range of issues and had a reputation for intellectual arrogance. His opinions encompassed religious, political and judicial issues.

power to intervene in the judicial process. Certain powers also reside with the Attorney General and his Scottish equivalent. In particular, the Attorney General may intervene to prevent prosecutions being proceeded with if he considers such action to be in the public interest. He also has responsibility in certain cases for initiating prosecutions, for example under the Official Secrets Act, and — though he takes decisions in such matters independently of his government colleagues — he remains answerable to Parliament for his decisions.

Judges themselves do not completely stand apart from public controversy. The past decade has witnessed a tendency on the part of several judges to justify their actions publicly and in 1988 the new Lord Chancellor, Lord Mackay, allowed some relaxation of the Kilmuir rules in order that judges may give interviews. One judge in particular — Judge Pickles — made use of the opportunity to appear frequently on television. Thus, though the two generalizations that the judiciary constitutes a subordinate and autonomous branch of government — subordinate to the outputs of Parliament (Acts of Parliament) but autonomous in deciding cases — remain broadly correct, both are in need of some qualification. The courts are not as powerless nor as totally independent as the assertion would imply.

For the student of politics, the judiciary is therefore an appropriate subject for study. What, then, is the structure of the judicial system in Britain? Who are the people who occupy it? To what extent has the judiciary become more active in recent years in reviewing the actions of government? And what has been the effect of membership of the European Communities?

The Courts

Apart from a number of specialized courts and tribunals, the basic organizational division of courts is that between criminal and civil. The basic structure of the court system in England and Wales is shown in Figure 22.1. (Scotland and Northern Ireland have different systems.) Minor criminal cases are tried in magistrates' courts, minor civil cases in county courts. Figure 22.1 also shows the higher courts which try serious cases and the routes through which appeals may be heard. The higher courts — the High Court, the Crown Court and the Court of Appeal — are known collectively as the Supreme Court. At the head of the system stands the House of Lords.

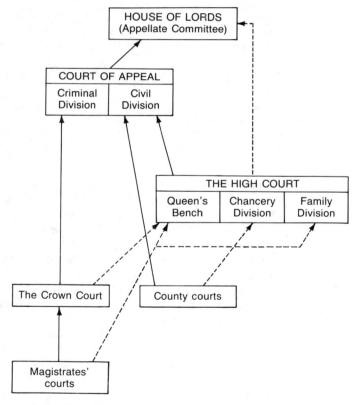

Appeals possible to higher courts as shown by arrows, usually through the immediate superior court or, in certain cases (indicated by dotted lines), through another route

Figure 22.1   *The court system in England and Wales*

Criminal cases

More than nine out of every ten criminal cases in England and Wales are tried in magistrates' courts. This constitutes each year approximately 2 million cases. (In excess of 2 million before 1987, slightly less than 2 million in 1987 as a result of the introduction of fixed penalty fines for summary motoring offences.) The courts have power to levy fines, the amount depending upon the offence and to impose prison sentences, though in no case exceeding six months. The largest single number of cases tried by magistrates' courts are motoring offences (see Figure 22.2). Other offences tried by magistrates range from allowing animals to stray on a highway and tattooing a minor to burglary, assault, causing cruelty to children and wounding. It takes on average between 100 and 130 days from the offence taking place for it to be tried. Once before a court, the majority of minor offences are each disposed of in a matter of minutes; in some cases, in which the defendant has pleaded guilty, in a matter of seconds. The courts also have a limited civil jurisdiction, primarily in matrimonial proceedings, and have a number of administrative functions in the licensing of public houses, betting shops and clubs.

Magistrates themselves are of two types: stipendiary or lay. Stipendiary magistrates are legally qualified and serve on a full-time basis. They sit alone when hearing cases. Lay magistrates are part-time and, as the name implies, are not legally qualified, though they do now receive some training in their spare time. They are drawn from the ranks of the public, typically those with the time to devote to such public duty (for example, housewives, local professional and retired people), and they sit on a bench of between two and seven in order to hear cases, advised by a legally qualified clerk. London and some of the larger cities have stipendiary magistrates. The rest of England and Wales relies on lay magistrates.

Until 1986, the decision whether to prosecute — and the prosecution itself — was undertaken by the police. Since October 1986, the Crown Prosecution Service (CPS), headed by the Director of Public Prosecutions, has been responsible for the independent review and prosecution of all criminal cases instituted by police forces in England and Wales, with certain specified exceptions. In 1987–8, the CPS dealt with some 1.5 million defendants in magistrates' courts. In Scotland, responsibility for prosecution rests with the Crown Office and Procurator Fiscal Service. Members of this service — like the CPS in England and Wales — are lawyers.

Appeals from decisions of magistrates' courts may be taken to the Crown Court or, in matrimonial cases, to the Family Division of the High Court or, on points of law, to the Queen's Bench Division of the High Court. In practice, appeals are rare: less than 1 per cent of those convicted appeal against conviction or sentence. The cost of pursuing an appeal would, in the overwhelming majority of cases, far exceed the fine involved. The time of the Crown Court is taken up instead with hearing the serious cases — known as indictable offences — which are subject to a jury trial and to penalties beyond those which a magistrates' court may impose. In 1987–8, the CPS proceeded against some 135,000 defendants in the Crown Court.

The Court itself is divided up into six court circuits and a total of nearly one hundred courts. The most serious cases will be presided over by a High Court judge, the most senior position within the court; other cases will be heard by a Circuit judge or a Recorder. High Court and Circuit judges are full-time, salaried judges; Recorders

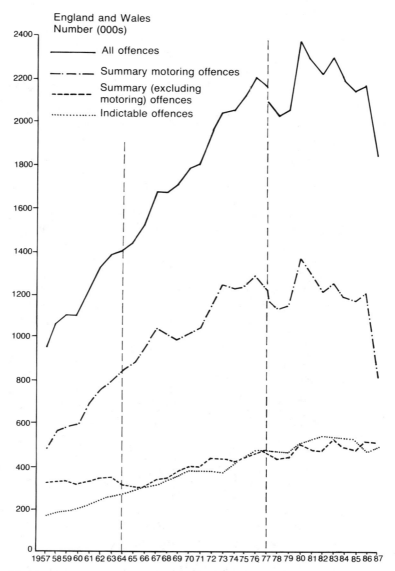

Figure 22.2 *Defendants proceeded against at Magistrates' Courts by type of offence (Source: Home Office, 1988)*

are legally qualified but part-time, pursuing their normal legal duties when not engaged on court duties.

Appeals from conviction in a Crown Court may be taken on a point of law to the Queen's Bench Division of the High Court but usually are taken to the Criminal Division of the Court of Appeal. Appeals against conviction are possible on a point of law and on a point of fact, the former as a matter of right and the latter with the leave of the trial judge or the Court of Appeal. Of 93,000 defendants sentenced by the Crown Court in 1987, 6 per cent (5,400) appealed. The Appeal Court may quash a conviction, uphold it or vary the sentence imposed by the lower courts. (Appeals against sentence — as opposed to the conviction itself — are also possible with the leave of the Appeal Court.) Since 1 February, 1989, the Attorney-General has had the power to refer to the Court sentences which appear to the prosecuting authorities to be unduly lenient. In such cases, the Court is vested with the power to increase the length of sentence imposed by the lower court.

The Court of Appeal comprises judges known as Lords Justices of Appeal and five judges who are members ex officio (the Lord Chancellor, the Lord Chief Justice, the Master of the Rolls, the President of the Family Division of the High Court and the Vice-Chancellor of the Chancery Division), though the composition varies from the criminal to the civil division. Appeals in criminal cases are usually heard by three judges. Though presided over by the Lord Chief Justice or a Lord Justice, judges of the Queen's Bench may sit on the court.

From the Court of Appeal, a further appeal is possible to the House of Lords if the court certifies that a point of law of general public importance is involved and it appears to the court — or to the Lords — that the point ought to be considered by the highest domestic court of appeal. For the purposes of such an appeal, the House of Lords does not comprise all its members; instead, the case is heard by an Appellate Committee. The work of the committee is undertaken by the Lord Chancellor, Law Lords known as Lords of Appeal in Ordinary (appointed to the Lords in order to carry out this judicial function) and those members of the Lords who have held high judicial office. Between five and ten will sit to hear a case, the hearing taking place in a committee room of the House of Lords but with the judgement being delivered in the chamber. Before 1966 the House considered itself to be bound by precedent (that is, by its own previous decisions); in 1966, the Law Lords announced that they would no longer consider themselves bound by their previous decisions, being prepared to depart from them when it seemed right to do so.

Civil cases

In civil proceedings, some minor cases (for example, involving the summary recovery of some debts) are dealt with in magistrates' courts. Most cases involving small sums of money, however, are heard by County Courts; more important cases are heard in the High Court. County courts are presided over by Circuit judges. The High Court is divided into three divisions: the Queen's Bench Division, which deals principally with matters of common law; the Chancery Division which deals with equity cases; and the Family Division, dealing with domestic cases (most of its time is taken up with divorce cases). The High Court comprises the Lord Chief Justice, who presides over the Queen's Bench Division; the Lord Chancellor, who is nominally President of the Chancery Division (but never sits, the presiding officer in practice being the Vice-Chancellor of the Division); the President of the Family Division; and up to a total of seventy-five judges known as puisne (pronounced *puny*) judges. In most cases judges sit alone, though a Divisional Court of two or more may be formed, especially in the Queen's Bench Division, to hear applications for writs of habeas corpus and writs requiring a public body to fulfil a particular duty (mandamus), to desist from carrying out an action for which it has no legal authority (prohibition) and to quash a decision already taken (*certiorari*). Jury trials are possible in certain cases tried in the Queen's Bench Division (for example, involving malicious prosecution or defamation of character) but are now rare.

Appeals from magistrates' courts and from County Courts are heard by Divisional Courts of the High Court: appeals from magistrates' courts on points of law go to a Divisional Court of the Queen's Bench Division, in matrimonial proceedings to a Divisional Court of the Family Division. Appeals from County Courts in bankruptcy cases go to a Divisional Court of the Chancery Division. From the High Court — and certain cases in County Courts — appeals are taken to the Civil Division of the Court of Appeal. In the Appeal Court cases are normally heard by the Master of the Rolls sitting with two Lords Justice of Appeal.

From the Court of Appeal, an appeal may be taken — with the leave of the Court or the House — to the House of Lords. In rare cases, on a point of law of exceptional difficulty calling for a reconsideration of a binding precedent, an appeal may go directly, with the leave of the House, from the High Court to the House of Lords.

Cases brought against Ministers or other public bodies for taking actions which are *ultra vires* will normally be heard in the Queen's Bench Division of the High Court before being taken — in the event of an appeal — to the Court of Appeal and the House of Lords.

Tribunals

Many if not most citizens are probably affected by decisions taken by public bodies, for example those determining eligibility for particular benefits (such as social security) or compensation for compulsory purchase, and post-war years have witnessed the growth of administrative law, providing the legal framework within which such decisions are taken and the procedure by which disputes may be resolved.

To avoid disputes over particular administrative decisions being taken to the existing, highly formalized civil courts — overburdening the courts and creating significant financial burdens for those involved — the law provides for a large number of tribunals to resolve such disputes. There are now tribunals covering a wide range of issues, including unfair dismissal, rents, social security benefits, immigration, mental health and compensation for compulsory purchase. Those appearing before tribunals will often have the opportunity to present their own case and to call witnesses and cross-examine the other side. The tribunal itself, as the name indicates, will normally comprise three members, though the composition varies from tribunal to tribunal: some have lay members, others have legally (or otherwise professionally) qualified members; some have part-time members, others have full-time members. Industrial tribunals, for example, each comprise an independent chairman and two representatives drawn from either side of industry (an employer and trade unionist); more specialized tribunals, such as Land Tribunals (for cases involving land valuation), have professionally qualified members.

Tribunals offer the twin advantages of speed and cheapness. As far as possible the formalities of normal courts are avoided. Costs tend to be significant only in the event of an appeal. Appeal procedures vary widely, depending upon the provisions of the relevant Act. The Employment Appeal Tribunal — to hear appeals from industrial tribunals — is headed by a High Court Judge. An appeal from this Tribunal is possible to the Court of Appeal. The Immigration Appeals Tribunal — to hear appeals from decisions of Immigration Adjudicators — consists of a President, two Vice-Presidents, two part-time legally qualified Chairmen and a number of non-legal members. No avenue of appeal against decisions of the Tribunal is prescribed by statute. In 1987 the Employment Appeal Tribunal received 721 appeals and the Immigration Appeal Tribunal received 1,256.

The Judges

At the apex of the judicial system stands the Lord Chancellor and the Law Officers. As we have seen, these are political appointments and the holders are members of the government. Below them are the professional judges. The most senior are the Law Lords, the Lords of Appeal in Ordinary, limited in number to a maximum of eleven. They are appointed by the Crown on the advice of the Prime Minister and they must have held high judicial office for at least two years. By virtue of their position they are members of the House of Lords and remain members even after ceasing to hold their judicial position. Indeed, they constitute the earliest form of life peers, the first Lord of Appeal in Ordinary being created under the Appellate Jurisdiction Act of 1876.

The other most senior judicial appointments — Lord Chief Justice, Master of the Rolls, President of the Family Division and the Lords Justices of Appeal — are also appointed by the Crown on the advice of the Prime Minister. The Lords Justices are drawn either from High Court judges or barristers of at least fifteen years' standing. Other judges — High Court judges, Circuit judges and Recorders — are appointed by the Crown on the advice of the Lord Chancellor. They are usually drawn from barristers with at least ten years' standing, though a solicitor of ten years' standing is eligible for consideration for appointment as a Recorder and a Recorder of five years' standing may be appointed a Circuit judge. Magistrates are appointed by the Lord Chancellor.

The attraction in becoming a judge lies only partially in the salary (see Table 22.1) — the top earners among barristers can achieve incomes in excess of £100,000; more especially it lies in the status that attaches to holding a position at the top of one's profession. For many barristers, the ultimate goal is to become Lord Chief Justice, Master of the Rolls or a Law Lord.

Judges, by the nature of their calling, are expected to be somewhat divorced from the rest of society. However, critics — such as J.A.G. Griffith in *The Politics of*

Table 22.1 *Judicial salaries, 1 January 1991*

Position	Annual salary £
Lord Chief Justice	95,750
Lord of Appeal in Ordinary and master of the Rolls	88,500
Lord Justice of Appeal	85,000
High Court judge	77,000

**Lord
Donaldson of
Lymington**

Lord Donaldson — then Sir John Donaldson — was appointed Master
of the Rolls in 1982, in succession to Lord Denning. Whereas Lord
Denning aroused political controversy because of some of his judicial
decisions, his successor aroused political controversy because of a
previous position he had held.

   John Donaldson was born in 1920 and educated at Cambridge.
After war service he was called to the Bar in 1946 and became a
Queen's Counsel (QC) in 1961. From 1966 to 1979, he was a Judge of
the High Court, Queen's Bench Division. During this period he also
served as President of the short-lived National Industrial Relations
Court, created by the 1971 Industrial Relations Act. The court was
viewed as an anti-union body by trade union leaders and Labour
politicians. In 1979, Donaldson was appointed a Lord Justice of
Appeal. Three years later, his appointment as Master of the Rolls
generated adverse comment from several union leaders and Labour
politicians, suspicious of his activities on the NIRC. In 1988, Donaldson
was created a life peer. Like his predecessor and all other judges in
the Upper House, he sits on the cross-benches.

the Judiciary (1977) — contend that this professional distance is exacerbated by social
exclusivity, judges being predominantly elderly upper-class males. Though statutory
retirement ages have been introduced, they are generous in relation to the normal
retirement age: High Court judges retire at seventy-five, Circuit judges at seventy-
two. In 1988, more than one-third of judges were aged over sixty-five. All judges
bar one are white and almost exclusively male; only 4 per cent of judges are female,
the proportion declining markedly in the upper echelons. All Law Lords are male
as are all but one of the twenty-seven Lords Justice of Appeal. (The exception is
Dame Ann Butler-Sloss.) At the beginning of 1988, there were two women among
the seventy-nine High Court judges; by the end of the year the number was reduced
to one with the retirement of Dame Rose Heilbron; both served in the Family
Division. There were no women judges in either the Queen's Bench or Chancery
Divisions. Of 401 Circuit judges, seventeen were women. The one non-white judge
sits at Southwark Crown Court.

   In their educational background judges are also remarkably similar. The majority
went to public school (among Law Lords and Lords Justice, the proportion exceeds
80 per cent) and the vast majority graduated from Oxford or Cambridge Universities;
more than 80 per cent of Circuit judges did so and the proportion increases the further
one goes up the judicial hierarchy. Judgeships are also almost exclusively the preserve
of barristers. It is possible — just — for solicitors to become judges. A solicitor
of at least ten years' standing is, as we have seen, eligible for appointment as a
Recorder and a Recorder of five years' standing may be considered for appointment
as a Circuit judge. Few, however, have taken this route: less than 3 per cent of
Circuit court judges have been drawn from the ranks of solicitors.

   Judges thus form a socially and professionally exclusive or near-exclusive body.
This exclusivity has been attacked for having unfortunate consequences. One is that
judges are out of touch socially, not being able to understand contemporary everyday
life, reflecting instead the social mores of thirty or forty years ago. (One judge —
now the Master of the Rolls — once interrupted a murder trial to enquire: 'What

Barristers and solicitors

> Barristers — of whom there are about 4,000 — constitute the specialists in the legal profession, offering advice in their particular area of expertise and enjoying an exclusive right to plead cases in superior courts. They deal with clients only through solicitors. Solicitors constitute the general practitioners of the profession, dealing with the day to day legal problems of citizens. They deal directly with members of the public — there are firms of solicitors in virtually every town — and since 1984 have been able to advertise their services.
>
> Barristers are trained in one of the four Inns of Court and are gathered together in their professional organization known as the Bar. Solicitors become such having taken a Common Professional Examination and having taken Articles (an apprenticeship) with an existing firm of solicitors. Their professional organization is the Law Society.
>
> At the beginning of 1989, the Lord Chancellor's Department published three Green Papers proposing major changes in the organization of the legal profession. Foremost among the proposals were that barristers should lose their monopoly on the right to plead cases before superior courts, with such a right being enjoyed by any lawyer who had attained a certain level in terms of education and training; that judgeships be open to any lawyer with a certain minimum experience; and that both barristers and solicitors should be permitted to form multi-disciplinary practices.

is snogging?') The male-orientated nature of the judiciary has led to claims that judges are insufficiently sensitive in rape cases. The background of most judges has also led to allegations of inbuilt bias — towards government and towards the Conservative party. These have been put most forcefully by J.A.G. Griffith. Senior judges, he contends, by their education and training have 'acquired a strikingly homogeneous collection of attitudes, beliefs and principles, which to them represent the public interest' (Griffith, 1977, p.193), a public interest that is construed to favour law and order and the interests of the state — at times of threat — over those of the individual; and their perception involves usually 'the promotion of certain political views normally associated with the Conservative Party' (Griffith, 1977, p.195). Occasions when the courts have found against government are, he argues, the exceptions to the rule.

The criticisms levelled by Griffith have not been taken up by many writers. Griffith himself was writing at a time when government increasingly wished that cases of the courts finding against it were as rare as he implied. However, the claims that judges are on occasion out of touch with prevailing wisdom and, not unrelated, drawn from a too-narrow professional background have been variously taken up by the media and, to some extent, accepted by government. The reprimand of Judge Cassel in 1988 was an illustration of official concern at a decision that offended public propriety.

Of longer-term significance, various attempts have been made to reduce the professional exclusivity of the bench by opening it up more to solicitors. A pilot scheme to recruit more judges from the ranks of solicitors was established in December 1988.

The impartiality of judges

Judges are appointed by the Lord Chancellor — always the politically appointed government senior law officer — usually from the ranks of the country's 4,000 barristers. In January 1987 the journal *Labour Research* examined the backgrounds of 465 judges.

Education
Of the ten Law Lords (including the Lord Chancellor) nine had been to public school and eight to Oxbridge. Of the twenty-three judges in the Court of Appeal 80 per cent went to public school (three to Eton, three to Westminster, two to Charterhouse) while 86 per cent had been to Oxbridge.

Age
Seven of the ten Law Lords and 42 per cent of the Court of Appeal Judges were over sixty-five.

Race
Only one judge was black.

Gender
Only seventeen were women.

Politics
Drewry has commented that

> Up to the 1920s it was accepted practice for Lord Chancellors to use judicial patronage to reward the party faithful. Harold Laski showed that of 139 appointments to the higher judiciary between 1832 and 1906 80 judges had been MPs at the time of their appointment and 63 of those had been appointed when their own party was in power ... It would nowadays be almost unthinkable for party political considerations to have any influence on judicial appointments.
>
> *Social Studies Review*, January 1986

Some dispute this last point but in any case it does not acquit judges from the accusation that they may be politically biased. *Labour Research* reinforces the well-known criticisms of Griffith by pointing out that a sizeable minority of the judges they studied has been active in politics: the biggest proportion on the right. Appeal Judge Lawton had even been founder of the Cambridge Union of Fascists and a Fascist candidate. Drewry also quotes a revealing admission by Lord Justice Scrutton from 1923 which sums up much of what the judiciary's critics are saying:

> The habits you are trained in, the people with whom you mix, lead to your having a certain class of ideas of such a nature that, when you have to deal with other ideas, you do not give as sound and accurate judgements as you would wish. This is one of the great difficulties at present with Labour. Labour says: 'Where are your impartial judges? They all move in the same circle as the employers, and they are all educated and nursed in the same ideas as the employers. How can a labour man or a trade unionist get impartial justice?' It is very difficult sometimes to be sure that you have put yourself into a thoroughly impartial position between two disputants, one of your own class and one not of your class.

Griffith argues that the conception of the 'public interest' shared by judges tends to favour the protection of property and 'the promotion of certain political views normally associated with the Conservative Party'. In his view judges tend to reflect a consistent bias against trade unionists and those subscribing to minority views or participating in picketing or demonstrations.

Dearlove and Saunders agree and urge that judges be made more accountable.

> Should we continue to trust the judges as defenders of our rights and give them carte blanche to behave as they will, or should we devise some democratic mechanisms to render them accountable and restrain their independence and power?
>
> Dearlove and Saunders, 1984, p.137.

Judicial Activism

The common law power available to judges to strike down executive actions as being *ultra vires* or contrary to natural justice was not much in evidence in the years prior to the 1960s. Courts were generally deferential in their stance towards government. This was to change in the period from the mid-1960s onwards. Though the composition of the higher judiciary changed little — comprising the same elderly, Oxbridge-educated males as before — the attitude of senior judges changed notably. Worried apparently by the perceived encroachment of government on individual liberties, they proved increasingly willing to use their powers of judicial review.

In four cases in the 1960s, the courts adopted an activist line in reviewing the exercise of powers by administrative bodies and, in two instances, of Ministers. In *Conway* v. *Rimmer* (1968) the House of Lords ruled against a claim of the Home Secretary that the production of certain documents would be contrary to the public interest; previously such a claim would have been treated by the courts as conclusive. In *Padfield* v. *Minister of Agriculture, Fisheries and Food* (1968), the Lords held that a Minister could not employ discretionary powers if their exercise thwarted the object of the Act conferring those powers, a case that involved considering why, and not just how, a decision was made (Norton, 1982, pp.137−8). It was a demonstration, noted Lord Scarman, that judges were 'ready to take an activist line' (Scarman, 1974, p.49). This activist line was maintained in the 1970s during the period of Labour government from 1974 to 1979, and in the 1980s during the Conservative Government of Margaret Thatcher. There were four cases in the latter half of the 1970s that proved especially controversial, the courts in each case finding against a Minister. In *Congreve* v. *Home Office* (1975), the Court of Appeal struck down the Home Secretary's decision to revoke the television licences of those who had bought new licences before the introduction of new licence fees; the Home Secretary responded by obtaining statutory power to raise licence fees without giving advance notice. In the *Tameside* case in 1976, the Court of Appeal — upheld by the House of Lords — struck down a direction by Education Secretary Shirley Williams to Tameside Council to implement a scheme to convert five grammar schools to comprehensive schools and sixth-form colleges. The Council, the Court of Appeal held, had not acted 'unreasonably', the only basis on which the minister was empowered to issue her direction.

In the following year, in *Laker Airways* v. *Department of Trade*, the Court of Appeal struck down as *ultra vires* 'guidance' given by the Secretary of State for Trade to the Civil Aviation Authority, holding that it conflicted with the provisions of the 1971 Civil Aviation Act. (Under the guidance, the Authority would have denied a licence to Laker Airways to operate its Skytrain service to the USA.) In an equally controversial case, *Gouriet* v. *Union of Post Office Workers*, the Court of Appeal reviewed the decision of the Attorney General to refuse his consent to a relator action brought by a private citizen against the Union of Post Office Workers. The Court decided that the citizen, John Gouriet, had standing to pursue such an action. However, the House of Lords reversed the Court's decision, holding that a refusal by the Attorney General to give his consent to a relator action was not reviewable by the courts.

Various Conservative Ministers in the 1980s also fell foul of the courts, though judicial activism was not confined to the actions of Ministers. In 1981 the High Court decided that Environment Secretary Michael Heseltine had not validly exercised his statutory powers when he refused to listen to representations made late to him by various London boroughs concerning his decision to reduce the rate support grant to them. The same year, the Greater London Council fell foul of the Court of Appeal, which upheld an appeal of Bromley Borough Council against the GLC's decision to introduce a supplementary rate precept to finance its policy of reduced fares on the underground. The Court — upheld by the House of Lords — held that the GLC had abused its powers and its action was *ultra vires*.

In 1984, the House of Lords upheld the government's right to ban, on grounds of national security, membership of trade unions at the Government's Communication Headquarters in Cheltenham, but in so doing criticized the government for acting 'unfairly' in failing to consult trade unions about the decision. The following year, the High Court quashed a decision by Transport Secretary Nicholas Ridley to require the GLC to pay £50 million to support the London Transport Authority set up in 1984. The decision was reversed by legislation. Also in 1985, the Court of Appeal held that the Secretary of State for the Environment had exceeded his powers, though not acting unreasonably, in issuing guidance to local authorities on expenditure limits that discriminated between high-spending and low-spending authorities. The House of Lords reversed the decision, finding that the Minister had not exceeded his power and, furthermore, that the Minister's action, having been approved by the House of Commons, was not reviewable by the courts. Lack of adequate consultation was also the issue in a case brought by the Association of Metropolitan Authorities against the Social Services Secretary when he sought comments on regulations made under the provision of the Social Security and Housing Benefits Act of 1982. The High Court declared that he had failed to comply with the duty imposed by the 1982 Act.

The government had more success in various subsequent cases involving judicial review. In September 1986, the High Court turned down an application by a leading member of the Campaign for Nuclear Disarmament for a declaration that the Home Secretary had exceeded his powers in issuing a warrant for the interception of his telephone calls. In 1987 the Court of Appeal turned down an appeal by the Northumbria Police Authority against a decision of the High Court that the Home

Secretary had power to supply equipment to police forces without the consent of the police authority. Later that year the High Court upheld an application from an inmate of Wandsworth Prison, transferred from a Spanish prison where he was serving a term of imprisonment, that the Home Secretary had misdirected himself

Lord Denning

A judge for almost forty years, Lord Denning established a reputation as one of Britain's most prominent — and controversial — jurists. For twenty years he served as Master of the Rolls, until his retirement in 1982 at the age of eighty-three.

Born in Hampshire in 1899, Alfred Denning was educated at Oxford and was called to the Bar in 1923. He was Recorder of Plymouth in 1944, a Justice of the High Court from 1944 to 1948, a Lord Justice of Appeal from 1948 to 1957 and a Lord of Appeal in Ordinary from 1957 until his appointment as Master of the Rolls in 1962. He was knighted in 1944, became a Privy Counsellor in 1948 and was created a life peer in 1957. Among various tasks for which he achieved public prominence was his Inquiry into the Profumo Affair in 1963.

As Master of the Rolls, he was known for his controversial decisions. He was particularly concerned to ensure that judges, and in particular the House of Lords, were not too rigidly bound by precedent. In clashes between a 'be consistent' and 'be fair' stance, he increasingly favoured the latter. In an interview with Alan Paterson (1982, p.137), he declared:

> I take firmly the view that judges oughtn't just to be saying 'I am only going to apply the law'. I think that the law ought to be developed, the judge ought to do justice in the particular case, not leave it to Parliament years afterwards, who don't do anything about justice in a particular case. It means that the poor individual has got to go away without justice.

His desire to 'do justice' in particular cases produced controversial, highly publicized reasonings and not infrequent overruling by the House of Lords.

in deciding he had no power to reduce the term of the sentence to one he would have served had he been convicted of the offence in an English court. The court allowed an appeal direct to the House of Lords, which overturned the decision of the High Court.

In February 1990 the High Court overruled government guidelines on the administration of the Social Fund introduced in 1988. This measure had replaced an open-ended commitment by the government to provide financial assistance to people needing basic household equipment with a finite sum of £200 million per year. From this pool, each local social security office was given an allocation which, according to government guidelines, could not be exceeded. This arrangement was challenged by the Child Poverty Action Group, supported by the Sheffield Law Centre. They maintained that local officers were being bound by a government ruling rather than 'guidance'. The eventual judgement from the High Court declared that while local officers should take budget allocations into account, they should not be bound by them. Government guidance was held to be 'unlawful insofar as it puports to indicate that there is no power to make payments excluding the local office allocation'. The government decided not to appeal against the ruling. The Labour party was quick to exploit the situation, claiming that the judgement left the government's social security policy 'in tatters'.

From these cases, it is clear that there is no consistent pattern of the courts finding against government. Nor is there any consistent pattern of the government seeking to reverse judicial adjudications by the introduction of retrospective legislation. What is apparent is an increase in the number of cases of judicial review. (See Figure 22.3.) The courts are willing to cast a critical eye over decisions of ministers in order to ensure that they comply with the powers granted by statute and are not contrary to natural justice. *The Economist* (18 November 1989) comments, 'Judicial review of central-government decisions has become so common that all civil servants are now briefed on the dangers of falling foul of the "judge on your shoulder" as one internal Whitehall document puts it.'

Judges also enjoy a certain leeway in the interpretation of legislation. As Drewry (1986) points out:

> Although judges must strictly apply Acts of Parliament, the latter are not always models of clarity and consistency. Politicians themselves often 'fudge' the wording of a statute in the pursuit of compromise. This leaves the judges with considerable scope for the exercise of their creative skills in interpreting what an Act really means. Some judges, of which Lord Denning was a particularly notable example, have been active and ingenious in inserting their own policy judgments into the loopholes left in legislation.

This willingness to interpret legislation and review ministerial actions and the response of government to a number of cases in which the courts have found against it have fuelled the debate on whether or not a Bill of Rights should be introduced in Britain, putting certain fundamental rights beyond the reach of government. Supporters of such a measure contend that it would strengthen the position of the courts, the principal defendants of individual liberty. This greater activism has also coincided with a development that has added a new judicial dimension to the British constitution: membership of the European Communities.

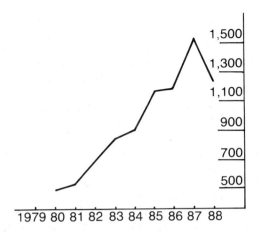

Figure 22.3 *Applications for judicial review (Source:* The Economist, *18 November 1989)*

The European Communities and the Courts

The European Economic Community was established by the Treaty of Rome of 1957. Britain acceded to the treaty in 1972. The European Communities Act of the same year gave effect to the legal nuts and bolts necessary for membership. Britain became a member on 1 January 1973.

The 1972 Act gave legal force not only to existing EC law but also to future law. When law has been promulgated by the Commission and Council of Ministers, it takes effect within the United Kingdom. Parliamentary assent is not required. Furthermore, under the provisions of the Act, questions of EC law are to be decided by the European Court of Justice, or in accordance with the decisions of that Court, and all courts in the United Kingdom are required to take judicial notice of decisions made by the European Court. Cases in the UK which reach the House of Lords must be referred to the European Court for a definitive ruling and requests may be made by lower courts to the Court for a ruling on the meaning and interpretation of the Treaties. In the event of conflict between the provisions of EC law and those of an Act of Parliament, the former are to prevail.

The question that has most exercised writers on constitutional law since Britain's accession to the EC has been what British courts should do in the event of the passage of an Act of Parliament that explicitly overrides EC law. The question remains a hypothetical one. Though some doubt exists — Lord Denning when Master of the Rolls appeared to imply on occasion that the courts must apply EC law, Acts of Parliament notwithstanding — the generally accepted view among jurists is that the courts, by virtue of the doctrine of parliamentary sovereignty, must apply the provisions of the Act of Parliament (see Bradley, 1985, pp.32–40).

Given the absence of an explicit overruling of EC law by statute, the most important question to which the courts have had to address themselves has been how to resolve apparent inconsistencies between EC and domestic law. During debate on the European Communities Bill in 1972, Ministers made clear that the Bill essentially provided a rule of construction; that is, the courts were to construe the provisions of an Act of Parliament, in so far as it was possible to do so, in such a way as to render it consistent with EC law. This has been the position that the courts have adopted. However, what if it is not possible to construe an Act of Parliament in such a way? In such a situation, is it possible for an Act of Parliament or parts of an Act to be suspended by the courts? The presumption until 1990 was that it was not. The constitutional waters, however, became muddied in that year. When Spanish fishermen challenged the provisions of the 1988 Merchant Shipping Act as being contrary to EC law, the High Court granted interim relief, suspending the relevant parts of the Act. This was then overturned by House of Lords, which ruled that the courts had no such power to suspend the application of an Act of Parliament. The European Court of Justice, to which the question was then referred, ruled in June 1990 that an Act could be suspended, though also providing the courts with the powers of injunction — suspending the application of legislation until the case was decided. The following month, the House of Lords granted orders to the Spanish fishermen preventing the Transport Secretary from withholding or withdrawing their names from the register of British fishing vessels, the orders to remain in place until the European Court had decided the case. The provisions of an Act of Parliament were thus in effect being put in cold storage until it could be determined whether they fell foul of EC law. English courts acquired a new power.

The courts have thus assumed a new role in the interpretation of EC law and the court system itself has acquired a supranational dimension. The European Court serves not only to hear cases that emanate from British courts but also to consider cases brought directly by or against the EC Commission and the governments of member states. At any one time it will be considering judgements on a number of cases to which the UK government is a party. Thus, for example, in the first six months of 1988, the Court was considering its judgement, or delivered its judgement, in twenty-two cases that were referred from UK courts, in nine cases brought by the UK government against the EC Commission, and in seven cases brought by the Commission against the UK government. The UK government also intervened or submitted comments in almost forty cases in which it was not a plaintiff or defendant.

Of cases referred from UK courts, one was brought by a student against the Secretary of State for Scotland. The student, Steven Malcolm Brown, challenged restrictions placed by the UK government on the eligibility of students and migrant workers from other member states of the EC for admission to higher education and grants for maintenance. In its judgement, the Court rejected Brown's claim that students from another member state had an unconditional right to whatever maintenance allowances that the UK made to its own students. However, it did uphold Brown's challenge to the UK requirement that a migrant worker had to be employed in the UK for nine months before being entitled to a maintenance grant (*Case 197/86: Steven Malcolm Brown* v. *Secretary of State for Scotland*).

Among cases brought by the UK Government against the Commission was one in which it challenged a Directive concerning minimum standards for the production of laying hens kept in battery cages (*Case 131/86: UK* v. *EC Commission*). The basis of the government's challenge was that the text of the Directive differed from that considered by the Council of Ministers. The Court upheld the government's challenge. The Directive was subsequently reintroduced after the correct procedures had been followed.

Of cases brought against the government by the Commission, one concerned the definition of 'medical services'. When the government exempted medical goods such as spectacles from Value Added Tax under the terms of the 1983 Value Added Tax Act the EC Commission claimed that the exemption was in breach of an EC Directive which allowed only for exemption for medical services. The government claimed that the supply of goods such as spectacles was an integral part of medical treatment. The Commission thus sought a declaration from the Court that the government had failed to fulfil its obligations under EC Council Directive 77/388. After hearing submissions, the Court found in favour of the Commission and issued the declaration that it sought (*Case 353/85: EC Commission* v. *UK*) in February 1988. There is thus a significant judicial dimension to British membership of the European Communities, involving adjudication by a supranational court, and the greater the integration of member states of the EC — especially with the completion of an internal market — the greater the significance of the courts in applying EC law. Integration involves harmonization and harmonization requires EC Directives in order to achieve it. Though cases heard by the European Court may not individually appear of major importance, collectively they produce a significant body of case law that constitutes an important constraint upon the actions of the UK Government. Each year that body of case law grows larger.

Figure 22.4 shows how judgements of the European Court of Justice affecting the UK have grown since 1979. The figure also reveals another interesting aspect of the European dimension. In 1949 Britain was a co-founder with nineteen other nations of the Council of Europe, an institution separate from the EC, dedicated

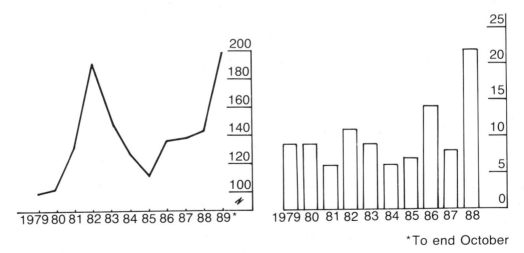

*To end October

Figure 22.4(a) *Number of registered applications to the European Commission of Human Rights concerning the UK*
(b) *Judgements of the European Court of Justice affecting the UK*
(Source: The Economist, 11 November 1989)

to the defence of parliamentary democracy. In the same year Britain also signed the European Convention on Human Rights which is administered by the European Commission of Human Rights at Strasbourg under the aegis of the Council of Europe. Britain, of course, has no Bill of Rights setting out citizen rights which cannot be overruled by legislation but increasingly British cases involving alleged violations of human rights are being referred to Strasbourg: the chart reveals a doubling of such applications during the 1980s from one to two hundred.

Though not at the heart of the policy making process in Britain, the courts nonetheless constitute actors in the political system. The doctrine of parliamentary sovereignty denies them the political role played by courts, such as those in the USA, which have the power to strike down legislation and executive actions as being contrary to the provisions of the Constitution. However, their task of interpreting the law passed by Parliament and the power to determine whether ministerial actions are within the powers granted by that law ensure that they are able to have an impact in the domain of politics. A combination of judicial concern about the growing powers of government — exemplified by Lord Hailsham's 1976 Dimbleby Lecture and tract, *Elective Dictatorship* — and Britain's membership of the European Community has produced an activism on the part of the judiciary in Britain and imparted to the British Constitution a new judicial dimension. The greater willingness and the new opportunities of judges to inject themselves more into the determination of political issues has generated concern among some politicians — fearful of the role that the courts may play as challengers to the power of government via Parliament — while at the same time alerting many jurists to the more central role that the courts may play as defenders of the individual against what they see as an increasingly powerful state. To judges, a more active and powerful judiciary constitutes the means to limit an over-powerful government. To politicians keen to defend the prerogatives of Parliament, it constitutes a 'non-elective dictatorship', denying the opportunity for political issues to be resolved by political means.

References and Further Reading

Bradley, A.W., 'The sovereignty of Parliament — in perpetuity?' in J. Jowell and D. Oliver (eds), *The Changing Constitution* (Oxford University Press, 1985).

Dearlove, J. and Saunders, P., *Introduction to British Politics* (Polity Press, 1984).

Drewry, G., 'Judges and politics in Britain', *Social Studies Review* (January 1986).

Griffith, J.A.G., *The Politics of the Judiciary* (Fontana, 1977, 2nd edn 1981).

Hailsham, Lord, *Elective Dictatorship* (BBC Publications, 1976).

Munro, C.R., *Studies in Constitutional Law* (Butterworths, 1987).

Norton, P., *The Constitution in Flux* (Basil Blackwell, 1982).

Paterson, A., *The Law Lords* (Macmillan, 1982).

Scarman, Lord L., *English Law — The New Dimension* (Stevens, 1974).

Wade, E.C.S. and Phillips, G.G., ed. A.W. Bradley, *Constitutional and Administrative law*, 9th edn (Longman, 1977).

Law and Order Moves up the Political Agenda

During the 1980s law and order moved dramatically up the political agenda investing the police, sentencing and penal institutions with increasing political importance. The chief reason is that — as we saw in Chapter 22 — indictable crimes since 1979 have increased by 50 per cent with an even more alarming increase in violent crime. Half of all such crime is committed by youngsters (predominantly males) under 21. Criminals have been reassured by the declining ability of the police to bring them before the courts while the public have become highly alarmed. Everyone now lives with the fear of crime: many have suffered as victims or as friends and relations of victims, others regularly view television programmes like *Crimewatch* while many more read alarming stories in the national press or in the local press which invariably feature tales of nearby wrong-doings.

Alexis de Tocqueville, when he visited the USA in the nineteenth century, examined jails first on the premise that the penal system offers the best barometer of the moral health of the country. On this criterion Britain is in a sickly state. In 1979 the Conservatives, correctly judging the public mood, came out strongly as the party of law and order. Their view is that criminals are responsible for their own actions: they weigh up the odds and make clear moral and rational decisions before breaking the law. If crime is on the increase it follows that penalties need to be toughened and the number of police increased. The 1987 manifesto stressed this view of crime as a breakdown in moral values: 'The origins of crime lie deep in society: in families where parents do not support or control their children; in schools where discipline is poor; and in the wider world where violence is glamorised and traditional values under attack'. Labour has responded with an alternative analysis which lays the stress on economic and social factors as the causes of crime and on Mrs Thatcher's role in exacerbating them.

> The callous individualism, poverty and frustration it causes, the dereliction of the urban environment and the continuous cuts in public services which have marked the Thatcher decade are responsible for much of this increase [in crime]. We attack the source of crime when we invest in improving the conditions of our cities and rural areas.
>
> *Meet the Challenge, Make the Change*, 1989, p.60

The Conservative problem is that their policies do not seem to be working. Since 1979 spending on law and order has increased by over 50 per cent to £5 billion per year in 1989; more offenders (49,000 in 1989) are being imprisoned for an average of 20 per cent longer; sentencing is anomalous with the imprisonment of offenders being ten times as likely in Dorset as in Bedford; police numbers have increased by 13 per cent and spending by 55 per cent; police pay has increased to the point where a London constable earns almost as much as a university professor. And yet crime figures continue to explode and public confidence in the police has slumped in the face of revelations of corruption, fabrications of evidence and beatings up. In 1959 a Royal Commission revealed that 83 per cent of polled respondents had a 'great deal of respect' for the police, 16 per cent had 'mixed feelings' and no one had 'little respect'. In 1989 a Mori poll returned figures of 43, 41 and 14 per cent, respectively, for the same questions.

Writing in the *Sunday Times* (11 February 1989) Simon Jenkins, a rightward-leaning journalist, declared 'No area of public policy is in such dire need of reform as crime . . . Crime is the Passchendale of Whitehall. The more money wasted on fighting it the more is demanded by the generals for 'just one push'.

The Economist (10 February 1990) quotes a disillusioned Westminster Tory: 'In my opinion the police need a jolly good kick up the backside. They get bloody well paid and they're not much good at catching criminals.' In February 1990 the Home Secretary David Waddington's right-wing credentials helped him with support for an initiative which would reduce prison numbers by introducing more non-custodial sentences for non-violent offenders. Reformers within the Conservative party would probably like to carry this policy further, shake up the administration, management and training of the police and rein in their constantly increasing pay. But this is unlikely. To quote *The Economist*'s jaundiced Conservative again, 'We can't actually kick their [the police's] bottoms because our own supporters wouldn't stand for it.' And here is the nub of the Conservative dilemna.

Every Home Office Minister discovers quickly that there are no easy answers to law and order problems yet Conservative voters thirst for them unrelentingly in the form of tougher sentences and more police. It is the party conference which annually provides the knee jerk stimulus to any Home Office Minister threatening to go 'soft' on crime. As a result judges, police and the prison service can ask for what they want and stand a good chance of getting it: in the words of Simon Jenkins they operate 'a union stranglehold on ministers more intense and more costly than anything the TUC attempted in the Wilson/Callaghan years'.

Will voters eventually turn to the Labour analysis that the roots of crime lie in society and that the police are merely struggling to control the consequences of Conservative social and economic policies? This also seems unlikely in that the authoritarian response to crime seems to permeate society irrespective of party. Conservative policies may indeed be to blame but as law and order deteriorates ironically it may be the Conservatives — as the 'tough' party on this issue — who reap the political dividend.

References and Further Reading

Benyon, J. and Bourn, C. (eds), *The Police: Powers, Procedures and Properties* (Pergamon Press, 1986).

Downes, D., *Law and Order: Theft of an Issue* (Fabian Society, 1983).

Jones, B., 'Crime and punishment', in B. Jones (ed.) *Political Issues in Britain Today* (Manchester University Press, 1989).

Labour Party, *Meet the Challenge, Make the Change* (1989).

Lea, J., and Young, J., *What is to be done about Law and Order? Crisis in the Eighties* (Penguin, 1984).

Northam, G., *Shooting in the Dark: Riot Police in Britain* (Faber and Faber, 1986).

Reiner, R., *The Politics of the Police* (Harvester Wheatsheaf, 1985).

PART VIII Policy Making and Policy Areas

Since the introductory chapter this book has divided up the main features of British politics and examined each one individually. This approach is inevitable and necessary for study purposes but it can contribute towards a fragmented impression of the system and disguise the fact that it is still indivisible, all of a piece: like a car engine all of its parts work most or all of the time to achieve motion. This final section aims to correct that tendency by concentrating upon key policy areas — economic, welfare, foreign, Northern Ireland and Europe.

23 The Policy Making Process

Bill Jones

This chapter provides a general view of how policy is made in British government. It begins with an overview of the system and then, drawing together some of the threads dealt with in foregoing chapters, moves on to study the policy making process itself. It concludes with a short case study of the privatization of British Telecom.

Two Overviews of the British Political System

The functions of government

It is helpful to contrast the British political system with that of the USA. It is well known that the eighteenth-century framers of the constitution wrote into their 1787 document a strict separation of powers. The legislature (Congress) and the executive (the Presidency) were to be separately elected for terms of differing length with the judiciary (the Supreme Court) appointed by the President for life. In diagrammatic form the functions can be represented by three separate and independent circles (see Figure 23.1).

The purpose of this arrangement was to disperse power to institutions which would check each other and ensure that no branch of government became overmighty. In

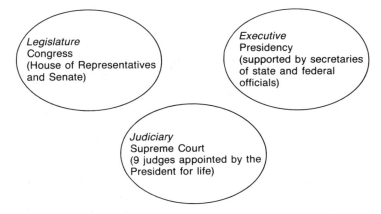

Figure 23.1 *Functions of government: USA*

Britain, however, there never was such a separation. The three functions overlap significantly. There is only one election to the legislative chamber, the House of Commons, and the majority party in that chamber, of course, invariably forms the executive. The crucial overlap between the legislative and executive spheres therefore comprise Prime Minister, Cabinet and the other seventy or so junior ministers. The judiciary is similarly appointed by the executive; not by the Prime Minister, but by the Lord Chancellor, the government's chief law officer, who sits in the Cabinet and presides over the House of Lords. It is he who sits at the centre of the three-circled web, together with the monarch — who once dominated all three spheres but now merely decorates them (see Figure 23.2).

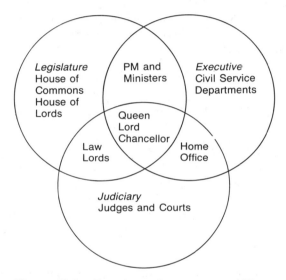

Figure 23.2 *Functions of government: UK*

The US constitution ensures that the President cannot be overthrown by Congress — except through impeachment — but looser party discipline means the President cannot regularly command Congressional support for his policies; indeed, like President Bush his party may be in the minority in Congress. The British Prime Minister in contrast has relatively more power: provided the support of the majority party is sustained he or she leads both the executive and legislative arms of government. However, loss of party support can bring down the British Prime Minister as it did Chamberlain in May 1940. This possibility clearly acts as a constraint upon potential prime ministerial action but the fact is that parties in government very rarely even threaten to unseat their leaders through fear of the electoral consequences. (Hence the extraordinary nature of Thatcher's downfall in 1990.)

The executive's power is further reinforced by: the doctrine of parliamentary sovereignty which enables it to overrule any law — constitutional or otherwise — with a simple majority vote; and considerable residual powers of the monarch via the Royal Prerogative. The House of Lords' power of legislative delay only and local government's essentially subservient relationship to Westminster complete the picture of an unusually powerful executive arm of government for a representative democracy.

Representative and responsible government

Represented in a different way the British political system can be seen as a circuit of *representation and responsibility*. Parliament *represents* the electorate but is also *responsible* to it via elections. In their turn ministers *represent* majority opinion in the legislature (though they are appointed by the prime minister, not elected) and are responsible to it for their actions in leading the executive. Civil servants are not representatives but as part of the executive are controlled by ministers and are responsible to them. Figure 23.3 illustrates the relationship.

This of course is a very simplistic view but it does express the underlying theory of how British government should work. The reality of how the system operates is infinitely more complex, as Figure 23.4 — itself highly simplified — seeks to illustrate. Earlier chapters have explained how the different elements of British government operate in practice.

Political parties dominate the system, organizing the electorate, taking over parliament and providing the Ministers who run the civil service.

The Prime Minister as leader of the majority party can exercise considerable personal power and in recent years has become more akin to a presidential figure.

The judiciary performs the important task of interpreting legislation and calling Ministers and officials to account if they act without statutory authority.

Civil servants serve Ministers but their permanence and their professionalism, their vested interests in searching for consensus and defending departmental interests raise suspicions that they occasionally or even regularly outflank their ministers.

Pressure groups infiltrate the whole gamut of government institutions, the most powerful by-passing Parliament and choosing to deal direct with Ministers and civil servants.

The media has increasingly usurped the role of Parliament in informing the public and providing a forum for public debate. Television is a potent new influence the impact of which is still to be fully felt.

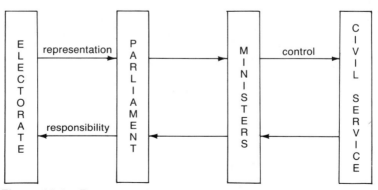

Figure 23.3 *Representative and responsible government*

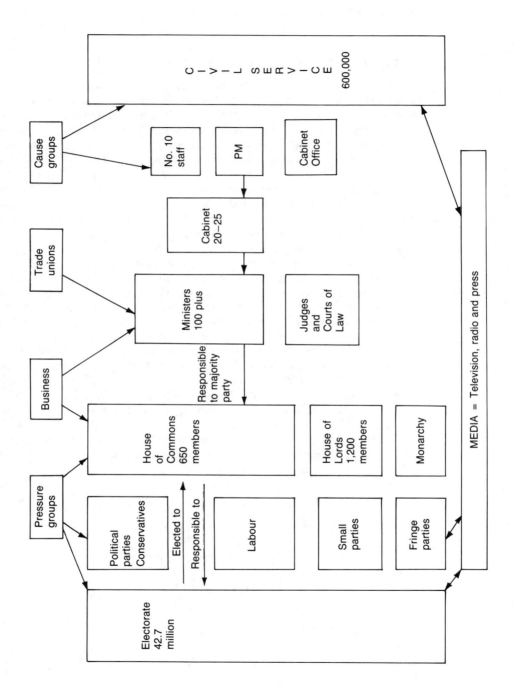

Figure 23.4 *Elements of UK central government*

Does the reality invalidate the theory? It all depends upon how drastically one believes Figure 23.4 distorts Figure 23.3. Indeed, Marxists would declare both to be irrelevant in that business pressure groups call the shots that matter, operating behind the scenes and within the supportive context of a system in which all the major actors subscribe to their values. Tony Benn would argue that the executive has become so dominant at the expense of the legislature that the PM's power can be compared with that of a medieval monarch. As we have seen, Britain's constitutional arrangements have always allowed great potential power — potential which strong prime ministers like Mrs Thatcher have been keen and able to realize when given the time. But I would maintain, and cite in support, the analyses offered by the authors of this book, that the essential features of the democratic system portrayed in Figure 23.3 just about survive in that: party dominated governments are removable, Parliament still applies watchdog controls (and just occasionally reminds the executive by biting), the electorate has a choice between parties, civil servants *will* obey their political masters and pressure groups *influence* but do not dictate.

How then is policy made in this system designed in the nineteenth century but stretched to meet the demands of the late twentieth century? This is the topic addressed by the rest of this chapter.

How Policy is Made

Policy can be defined as a set of ideas and proposals for action culminating in a government decision. To study policy, therefore, is to study how decisions are made. Government decisions can take many forms: Burch (1978) distinguishes between two broad kinds, as follows:

1. Rules, regulations and public pronouncements (e.g. Acts of Parliament, Orders in Council, White Papers, Ministerial and departmental circulars).
2. Public expenditure and its distribution. The government spends over £200 billion per annum mostly on public goods and services (e.g. education, hospitals) and transfer payments (e.g. social security payments and unemployment benefit).

Figure 23.5 portrays the government as a system which has as its *input* political demands together with resources available and its *output* as the different kinds of government decisions. The latter impact upon society and influence future inputs. So the process is circular and constant.

Students of the policy process disagree as to how policy inputs are fed into government and, once 'inside', how they are processed. Both Burch and Wood (1983) and Jordan and Richardson (1987) review these different analyses as models. Eight of them are summarized below.

1. *The conventional model.* This is the 'official' explanation of policy making found in Central Office of Information publications and the utterances of civil servants in public (though seldom in private). This maintains that Parliament

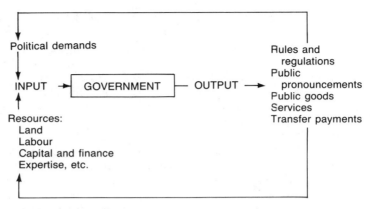

Figure 23.5 *The policy process (Source: Burch, 1978)*

represents and interprets the public will through its representatives, who formulate executive policies which are faithfully implemented by civil servants.

2. *The ruling class model*. This is effectively the Marxist interpretation, that those empowered with taking key decisions in the state — civil servants and politicians — subscribe consciously or unconsciously to the values of the dominant economic class. According to this view most policy outputs will have the effect of protecting dominant group interests.

Institutional theories

These attribute decisive importance to differing elements within the political system.

1. *The pluralist model*, often associated with the US political scientist Robert Dahl, assumes that power is dispersed within society to the various interest groups which comprise it — business, labour, agriculture and so forth — and that they can 'make themselves heard effectively at some crucial stage in the process of decision' (Jordan and Richardson, 1987, p.16). According to this view interest groups interact and negotiate policy with each other in a kind of free market, with government acting as a more or less neutral referee.
2. *Corporatism* is associated with the work of Philippe Schmitter and is offered as an alternative to pluralism. This model perceives an alliance between Ministers, civil servants and the leaders of pressure groups in which the latter are given a central role in the policy making process in exchange for exerting pressure upon their members to conform with government decisions. In this view therefore interest groups become an extension — or even a quasi form — of government. Corporatism has also been used pejoratively by British politicians of the left (Benn), right (Thatcher) and centre (Owen) to describe the decision making style of the discredited 1975–9 Labour government.
3. *The party government model*. The stress here is on political parties and the assertion that they provide the major channel for policy formulation.
4. *The Whitehall model* contends that civil servants either originate major policy

or so alter it as it passes through their hands as to make it substantially theirs — thus making them the key influence on policy.

Nature of decision making

These theories concentrate upon the way in which decision makers set about their tasks.

1. *Rational decision making*. This approach assumes that decision makers ought to behave in a logical, sequential fashion. Accordingly they will identify their objectives, formulate possible strategies, think through their implications and finally choose the course of action which on balance best achieves their objectives.
2. *Incrementalism*. This approach, associated with the work of Charles Lindblom, denies that policy makers are so rational and argues that in practice they usually try to cope or 'muddle through'. They tend to start with the status quo and make what adjustments they can to manage or at least accommodate new situations. In other words policy makers do not solve problems but merely adjust to them.

It is clear that some of these models are basically descriptive while others, like the rational choice or conventional models are also prescriptive — they offer an ideal approach as to how policies should be made. It is also obvious that echoing somewhere within each approach is the ring of truth. It would not be too difficult to find examples in support of any of the above models. The truth is that policy making is such a protean, dense area of activity that it is extremely difficult to generalize. Nevertheless, the search for valid statements is worthwhile, otherwise our political system will remain incomprehensible. We will therefore look at the process in greater detail in a search for some generally true propositions about it.

The policy cycle

If they agree on nothing else policy study scholars seem to agree that policy making can best be understood as a cycle. Analyses of the cycle can be quite sophisticated. Hogwood and Gunn (1984) discern a number of stages: deciding to decide (issue search and agenda setting); deciding how to decide; issue definition, forecasting; setting objectives and priorities; options analysis; policy implementation, monitoring and control; evaluation and review; and policy maintenance succession or termination. For our purposes, however, the three familiar stages will suffice: initiation, formulation and implementation.

Policy initiation

Each government decision has a long and complex provenance but all must start somewhere. It is tempting to think they originate in the minds of single individuals but they are more often the product of debate or a general climate of opinion involving many minds. Policy initiatives, moreover, can originate in all parts of the political system. Figure 23.6 depicts six groups of policy initiators starting from the periphery and moving in towards the nerve centre of government in No. 10.

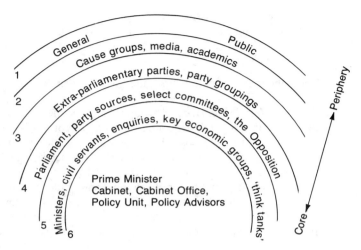

Figure 23.6   *Policy initiatives*

1. General public

The public's role in policy making is limited to (the not unimportant function of) voting for a particular policy package at general elections. They do have other occasional opportunities, however, for example the referendums on the EEC and Scottish and Welsh devolution in the 1970s and pressures which can be built up through lobbying MPs, as when Sir Keith Joseph was forced to withdraw his proposals to charge parents for a proportion of their children's university tuition fees.

2. Cause groups, media and academic experts

Cause groups. Many cause groups operate in the wilderness and many also stay there but some do influence public opinion and decision makers and achieve action on issues like abortion, capital punishment and the environment. Others achieve success on specific issues like Des Wilson's campaign to reduce lead in petrol. Certain policy 'environments' will include a bewildering array of pressure groups, all of whom seek to lean on the policy making tiller. Local government associations are particularly important in areas like education, housing and social services.

The media. Media coverage heavily affects the climate in which policy is discussed and important policy proposals occasionally emerge from television programmes, newspaper editorials, articles in journals and so forth. One editorial on its own would have little effect but a near consensus in the press might well stimulate action. Occasionally ideas are picked up from individual journalists — *Observer* columnist Alan Watkin's proposal that Labour concentrate on the theme of the Conservatives' 'Squalid Society' was discussed in Shadow Cabinet for example — though in the event Neil Kinnock turned it down. Other media figures who used to be consulted regularly on policy matters by Mrs Thatcher included such people as Rupert Murdoch, the press magnate, and journalists Brian Walden and Woodrow Wyatt.

All these agencies in the outer rim interact to provide that intangible climate of discussion which encourages the emergence of certain proposals and inhibits others. Each policy environment has its own climate created by its specialist press, pressure groups, academics, practitioners and the like who frequently meet in conferences and on advisory committees. An interesting feature of these bodies, however, is that from time to time they are blessed with favour, their arguments listened to, their proposals adopted, their leaders embraced by government and given advisory or even executive status.

Academics. Part III explained how policy emerged out of an ideological framework and pointed out how academics and philosphers and other thinkers had contributed towards these frameworks. The most obvious influences on the left would include Karl Marx, R.H. Tawney, Harold Laski, William Beveridge and incomparably in the economic sphere J.M. Keynes. Right-wing writers would include figures like David Hume and Michael Oakeshott and (on economics) two overseas academics Friedrich Hayek and Milton Friedman. Academics specializing in specific policy areas like transport, housing, criminology and so forth also regularly come up with proposals, some of which are taken up or drawn upon. Economists in particular plied Mrs Thatcher with advice. Most of this she rejected with some scorn except for the selected few with whom she agreed, like Patrick Minford and Sir Alan Walters who (until his resignation in October 1989) had been plucked from the outer rims of influence to sit in the inner sanctum as No. 10's economic adviser. On other occasions academics can be suddenly welcomed in by Departments, as when the Foreign Office began to use them extensively when the fall of the Shah of Iran revealed that they had been reading events in that country more accurately than the diplomats. In July 1990 much publicity was given to a seminar of six academics convened at Chequers to discuss the implications of German reunification. Colin Brown (*The Independent*, 17 July 1990) revealed that such seminars were regular features of Mrs Thatcher's policy making style. They were kept confidential and involved 'sympathetic' academics.

3. Extra-parliamentary parties

Both the Labour and Conservative extra-parliamentary parties are more influential in opposition than in government. As Chapter 14 discussed, Labour's system of internal democracy gave a substantial policy making role to the trade unions, the National Executive Committee and the party conference during the 1930s and 1950s. The Conservative party is far less democratic but Conference can set the mood for policy formulation, the Research Department can initiate important proposals and the Advisory Committee on Policy did much to reformulate the main outlines of Conservative policy in the late 1970s.

Party groupings — many of which have contacts with Parliament — can also exert influence. The Fabian Society has long acted as a kind of left-wing think tank (see below) and in recent years the left-wing Labour Coordinating Committee was influential in advising Neil Kinnock as he shifted Labour's policies towards the centre.

4. Parliament

The role of Parliament in initiating policy can be considered under two headings.

1. ***Party sources. In government*** parliamentary parties have to work through their back-bench committees though individual MPs seek to use their easy access to ministers to exert influence and press their own solutions. One Conservative MP, David Evans, pulled off the remarkable coup of convincing the Prime Minister that the identity card system introduced by Luton Town Football Club should be compulsorily introduced nationwide. His success was shortlived: the scheme was dropped in January 1990.

   The ***opposition*** is concerned to prepare its policies for when and if it takes over the reins of government. As we saw in Chapter 14 Kinnock wrested future policy making out of the party's NEC with his Policy Review exercise 1987—9, involving leading members of his front-bench team in the process. The opposition, however, also has to make policy 'on the hoof' in reaction to political events. It is their function and in their interests to oppose, to offer alternatives to government — but this is not easy. Opposition spokesmen lack the detailed information and support enjoyed by government; they need to react to events in a way which is consistent with their other policy positions; they need to provide enough detail to offer a credible alternative yet they must avoid closing options should they come to power. All these difficulties were apparent in Labour's tortuous reactions to the government's repatriation of Vietnamese Boat People from Hong Kong in 1989—90.

   Party groups like the Bow Group, Monday Club, Tribune and Campaign Group can all have peripheral — but rarely direct — influence on policy making.

2. ***Non-party sources.*** The fourteen select committees regularly make reports and recommendations, some of which are adopted. Most of these represent cross-party consensus on specific issues like the successful Home Affairs Committee recommendation that the laws allowing arrest on suspicion (the 'sus' laws) be abolished, but others like the Social Services Committee, chaired by Frank Field, have offered a wide-ranging and coherent alternative to government social policy. Individual MPs probably have a better chance of influencing specific, usually very specific, policy areas through the opportunities available to move Private Member's Bills (see Chapter 17).

5. Ministers, Departments, official enquiries and 'think tanks'

Strong-minded ***ministers*** will always develop policy ideas of their own either as a reflection of their own convictions or to get noticed and further their ambitions. Michael Heseltine, in the wake of the Toxteth troubles, probably shared both motivations when he submitted a paper to the cabinet called 'It Took a Riot' proposing a new and un-Thatcherite approach to inner city regeneration: the policy was partially implemented in Merseyside but not elsewhere. Such major initiatives are not the province of ***civil servants*** but through their day to day involvement in running the country they are constantly proposing detailed improvements and adjustments to existing arrangements. Such initiatives are not necessarily the preserve of senior officials: even junior officers can propose changes which can be taken up and implemented.

A Royal Commission used to be the precursor to major policy changes (for example, the Redcliffe Maud Royal Commission on Local Government 1966–9), but Mrs Thatcher was not well disposed towards such time-consuming essentially disinterested procedures and during the 1980s none were set up. Departments, however, regularly establish their own *enquiries*, often employing outside experts, which make important policy recommendations.

Right-wing 'think tanks' were especially favoured by Mrs Thatcher. *The Economist* (6 May 1989) notes how she spurned Oxbridge dons — the traditional source of advice for No. 10 — and suggests that 'the civil service is constitutionally incapable of generating the policy innovation which the prime minister craves'. Instead, as a reforming premier she instinctively listened to the advice of 'people who have been uncorrupted by the old establishment'. Think tank advice was often channelled to Mrs Thatcher via the No. 10 Policy Unit. Their radical suggestions acted as a sounding board when published and helped push the climate of debate further to the right. If new ideas are received in a hostile fashion ministers can easily disavow them — on 8 February 1990 a think tank suggested that Child Benefit be abolished: Mrs Thatcher told the Commons that her government had no 'immediate' plans to do this. The 'privatization' of government advice in the form of think tanks has been a striking feature of Mrs Thatcher's impact upon policy making. John Major is rumoured to be less receptive to such influences.

6. Prime Minister and Cabinet

This is the nerve centre of government, supported by the high-powered network of Cabinet committees, the Cabinet Office, the No. 10 Policy Unit and policy advisors. After a period of ten years in office it is likely any prime minister will dominate policy making. Chapter 8 made clear that while many sought to whisper policy suggestions in her ear Mrs Thatcher's radical beliefs provided her with an apparently full agenda of her own. The evidence of her personal impact on major policy areas is plain to see: privatization, trade union legislation, the environment, the exchange rate, sanctions against South Africa, the poll tax and Europe — the list could go on and on. She was also unusual, however, in taking a personal interest in less weighty matters like her (somewhat ill-starred) attempt to clean up litter from Britain's streets following a visit to litter-free Israel.

Harold Wilson saw himself as a 'deep lying half-back feeding the ball forward to the chaps who score the goals'. Mrs Thatcher was not content with this role: she wanted to score the goals as well. Wilson also said a Prime Minister governs by 'interest and curiosity': Mrs Thatcher had insatiable appetites in both respects and an energy which enabled her to feed them to a remarkable degree. Under her, assisted by a constitution which delivers so much power to the executive, the office of Prime Minister took on a policy initiating role comparable to that of the US President.

From this brief and admittedly selective description it is clear that:

1. Policy can be initiated both at the micro- and macro-levels from within any part of the political system but the frequency and importance of initiatives grows as one moves from the periphery towards the centre.
2. Even peripheral influences can be swiftly drawn into the centre should the centre wish it.

Think Tanks

The Institute of Economic Affairs is the grand-daddy of the think tanks. Founded in 1957 by Arthur Seldon and Ralph (now Lord) Harris, financed by Mr Anthony Fisher, owner of Buxted Chickens, and inspired by Mr Friedrich Hayek, it kept free-market economics alive when academic opinion had pronounced it brain-dead. Few listened to it until Sir Keith (now Lord) Joseph turned to it in 1974. Gradually its members were transformed into guardians of Thatcherite orthodoxy. It now has a new director: Mr Graham Mather, a lawyer and former policy setter at the Institute of Directors. The IEA has spawned some smaller semi-autonomous units: the IEA **Health Unit** (soon to become the Health and Welfare Unit), founded in October 1986 and directed by Mr David Green; and the **Centre for Research into Communist Economies.**

The Centre for Policy Studies was founded by Sir Keith Joseph in 1974, with Mrs Thatcher as vice-chairman. Originally designed as a quasi-academic body, it rapidly expanded its brief, becoming a hard-headed rival to the soft-hearted Conservative research department. Under its current director of studies, Mr David Willetts, it has become the most influential of the think tanks. People in Whitehall and Fleet Street feel that it 'knows in its bones what Thatcherism is about'.

The Adam Smith Institute. Founded in 1977 by two graduates of St Andrew's University, Mr Madsen Pirie and Mr Eamonn Butler, the Institute has acted as a cheer leader for radical Thatcherism. Whatever its merits, the Institute is not as important as it sometimes pretends: if it were, Mrs Thatcher would be little more than a footnote in its glorious history.

The Social Affairs Unit was founded in 1980 under the directorship of Mr Digby Anderson. The most fogeyish of the tanks (Mr Anderson regularly writes for the *Spectator* and the *Sunday Telegraph*), it is concerned less with advocating free-market economics than with promoting social morality and preserving the social fabric.

The left is belatedly getting into the think-tank business. Last year several left-wing grandees, notably Baroness Blackstone (once in the original government Think Tank), launched the **Institute of Policy Research**. Formally independent from the Labour party, it raised one-third of its money from trade unions, the rest from private donors. Its director, Mr James Cornford, adopts a discreet profile. And, earlier this year the Social Democratic party inaugurated **The Social Market Foundation**, which has so far produced a cracking pamphlet on social markets by Mr Robert Skidelsky of Warwick University.

Source: *The Economist*, 6 May 1989

3. Each policy environment is to some extent a world unto itself with its own distinctive characteristics. Higher education policy making, for example, will include, just to begin with: the Prime Minister, Cabinet, No. 10 Policy Unit, right-wing think tanks, numerous parliamentary and party committees, the Departments of Education and Employment, the Treasury, the funding councils for the universities and polytechnics, the Committee of Vice Chancellors and Principals, the Association of University Teachers and other unions, *The Times*

Higher Education Supplement, together with a galaxy of academic experts on any and every aspect of the subject.

Policy formulation

Once a policy idea has received political endorsement it is fed into the system for detailed elaboration. This process involves certain key players from the initiation process, principally civil servants, possibly key pressure group leaders and outside experts (who may also be political sympathizers) and, usually at a later stage, Ministers. In the case of a major measure there is often a learning phase in which civil servants and Ministers acquaint themselves with the detail of the measure: this may require close consultation with experts and practitioners in the relevant policy environment. The measure, if it requires legislation, then has to chart a course first through the bureaucracy and then the legislature.

The bureaucratic process

This will entail numerous information-gathering and advisory committee meetings and a sequence of coordinating meetings with other ministries, especially the Treasury if finance is involved. Some of these meetings might be coordinated by the Cabinet Office and when Ministers become involved the measures will be progressed in Cabinet committees and ultimately full Cabinet before being passed on to Parliamentary Counsel, the expert drafters of parliamentary bills.

The legislative process

As Chapter 17 explained this process involves several readings and debates in both chambers. Studies show that most legislation passes through unscathed, but controversial measures will face a number of hazards which may influence their eventual shape. Opposition MPs and Lords may seek to delay and move hostile amendments but more important are rebellions within the government party: for example the legislation required to install the Community Charge, or Poll Tax, in 1988–9 was amended several times in the face of threatened and actual revolts by Conservative MPs. The task of piloting measures through the legislature falls to Ministers closely advised by senior officials and this is often when junior Ministers can show their mettle.

From this brief description it is clear that three sets of actors dominate the policy formulation process: Ministers, civil servants and pressure group leaders and experts. Some scholars calculate that the key personnel involved in policy formulation might number no more than 3,500 but, as in policy initiation, Mrs Thatcher also played an unusually interventionist role in this process. Reportedly she regularly called Ministers and civil servants into No. 10 to speed things up, shift developments onto the desired track or discourage those with which she disagreed.

The implementation process

It is easy to assume that once the government has acted on something or legislated on an issue it is more or less closed. Certainly the record of government action reveals any number of measures which have fulfilled their objectives: for example, the Attlee government wished to establish a National Health Service and did so, the Thatcher government wished to sell off council houses to tenants and did so. But there are always problems which impede or sometimes frustrate implementation or which produce unsought-for side effects. Between legislation and implementation many factors intervene. Jordan and Richardson (1982, pp.234–5) quote the conditions which Hood suggests need to be fulfilled to achieve perfect implementation:

1. A unitary administrative system rather like a huge army with a single line of authority. Conflict of authority could weaken control, and all information should be centralized in order to avoid compartmentalism.
2. The norms and rules enforced by the system have to be uniform. Similarly, objectives must be kept uniform if the unitary administrative system is to be really effective.
3. There must be perfect obedience or perfect control.
4. There must be perfect information and perfect communication — as well as perfect coordination.
5. There must be sufficient time for administrative resources to be mobilized.

To fulfil wholly any, let alone all, of these conditions would be rare indeed, so some degree of failure is inevitable with any government programme. Examples are easy to find.

Education

The 1944 Education Act intended that the new grammar, technical and secondary modern schools were to be different but share a 'parity of esteem'. In practice this did not happen: grammar schools became easily the most prestigious and recruited disproportionately from the middle classes. The government could not control parental choice. To remedy this comprehensive schools were set up in the 1950s and 1960s but it was the middle-class children who still performed best in examinations. Reformers also neglected one crucial and in retrospect blindingly obvious factor: comprehensives recruit from their own hinterlands so inner city schools are predominantly working class with lower standards while suburban schools are more middle class with higher standards. The government made policy on the basis of inadequate information.

The economy

Burch and Wood (1983, pp.167–8) record how recent governments have consistently planned on the basis of public expenditure plans which in the event were exceeded: an estimated increase of 12 per cent in 1971 for the year 1975 proved to be 28.6 per cent in practice. The government lacked control over its own spending departments. Following the stock market crash of 1987 Chancellor Nigel Lawson lowered interest rates to 9.5 per cent to avoid the danger of a recession. This measure, however, led to an explosion of credit fuelling an inflationary spending boom which required high interest rates to bring it under control. High interest rates in their turn went on to produce economic recession in 1990. The government chose to ignore relevant information offered by advisers in 1988.

Social security payments

Many claimants report that a necessary service to which they have entitlement has been transformed by state employees and the restrictions they have been told to enforce into a humiliating time consuming obstacle course.

Inner city policy

In the wake of her 1987 victory Mrs Thatcher resolved to attack the problems of the inner cities. In March 1988 the Action for Cities initiative was launched with considerable fanfare. In January 1990 the National Audit Office reported that it had achieved only 'piecemeal success' (*The Guardian*, 25 January 1990); departments had 'made no overall assessment of inner cities "special requirements" ' and there was 'insufficient information to assess the strategic impact of the various programmes and initiatives involved'. Programme failure often results from the operation of constraints which constantly bear upon policy makers.

Constraints upon policy makers

Financial resources

Policy makers have to operate within available financial resources which are a function of the nation's economic health at any particular time, and the willingness of key decision makers, especially in the Treasury, to make appropriate provision from funds available to government.

Political support

This is initially necessary to gain endorsement for a policy idea but support is also necessary throughout the often extended and tortuous policy making process. Support at the political level is also crucial but it is highly desirable within the bureaucracy and elsewhere in the policy environment. Resistance to policies can kill them off en route and anticipated resistance is also important; as Jordan and Richardson (1982, p.238) hypothesize, 'There are probably more policies which are never introduced because of the *anticipation* of resistance, than policies which have failed *because* of resistance'.

Competence of key personnel

An able, energetic Minister is likely to push policy measures through: a weak Minister is not. Civil servants need to be up to the task of rapidly mastering the detail of new measures: their failure will impede the progress of a measure and limit its efficacy.

Time

New legislative initiatives need to carve space out of a timetable so overcrowded that winners of Private Members' ballots are lobbied by Departments themselves to adopt bills awaiting parliamentary consideration. The whole system is, moreover, arguably over centralized and, some would say, chronically overloaded.

Timing

Measures can fail if timing is not propitious. Just after a general election, for example, is a good time to introduce controversial measures. Mrs Thatcher, it will be recalled, was unable to secure the sale of British Leyland to an American company in the spring of 1986 because she had lost so much support over the Westland episode.

Coordination

Whitehall departments divide up the work of government in a particular way: proposals which fall between ministries are often at a disadvantage and the job of coordinating diverse Departments is not, in the view of critics, managed with particular efficiency. Burch, p.110 also notes that

> Too often policy making becomes a conflict between departments for a share of the limited resources available. This is ... especially true of expenditure politics when departments fight for their own corner at the cost of broader policy objectives.

Personality factors

Key decision makers are not as rational as perhaps they ought to be. They might have personal objectives — ambition, desire for image and status and rivalries — which lead them to oppose rather than support certain policy objectives.

Geographical factors

A bias in favour of the south east is often detectable in government policies — for example, in the granting of defence contracts — partly because decision makers in our centralized system live in the home counties, partly because the south east has a buoyant economy and partly for political factors: this after all is the Conservative heartland. (For a subtle and controversial analysis of territorial politics in the UK see Jim Bullpitt (1983).)

International events

The increasing interdependence of the large economies have made events like the quadrupling of oil prices in the early 1970s major constraints upon policy making. In some cases these constraints are formal as when the International Monetary Fund attached strict public expenditure conditions to its 1976 loan to Callaghan's Labour government. Political events like the Falklands can clearly have an enormous impact upon major policy areas while the 1989 revolutions in the communist countries changed the whole context within which foreign policy is formulated.

The influence of Europe

Treaty obligations and the growing power of Community institutions have imposed increasingly powerful constraints upon the freedom of action which British policy makers have enjoyed.

Constraints upon policy makers

1. Financial resources
2. Political support
3. Competence of key personnel
4. Time
5. Timing
6. Coordination
7. Personality factors
8. Geographical factors
9. International events
10. The influence of Europe

Policy Formulation and Implementation: The Case of the Privatization of British Telecom

This chapter concludes with an examination of policy formulation and implementation in the case of the privatization of British Telecom (BT) in 1984.

While Conservative ideology had long argued for minimal state interference official policy on privatization was very cautious as late as 1978. 'Denationalization' reported a Conservative policy study group in that year 'must be pursued cautiously and flexibly, recognizing that major changes may well be out of the question in some industries' (Lee, 1989, p.139). The 1979 manifesto had spoken only of selling just under a half share in selected industries. On 21 November 1980 a bill was presented separating the postal from the telephone side of the General Post Office. On 27 July 1981 British Telecom came into being. Shortly afterwards Sir Geoffrey Howe inaugurated the age of privatization with the announcement that several industries were being considered for this treatment: the biggest was British Telecom.

Figure 23.7 characterizes in a very simplified form the policy process which any measure has to negotiate.

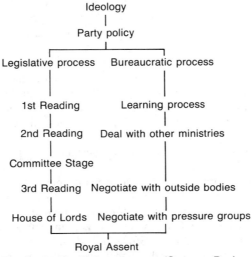

Figure 23.7 *Policy process (Source: B. Jones,* Is Democracy Working?, *Tyne Tees Television, 1986)*

Legislative process

When the Bill to privatize BT was introduced it faced great opposition. The Post Office Engineering Union (POEU) had three sponsored MPs in the Commons, led by John Golding who went on to become its General Secretary (under its changed name, the National Communications Union). Golding spoke for eleven hours in the Committee stage but it was the general election which caused it to lapse in May 1983. Mrs Thatcher was quick to reintroduce an amended form of the Bill after the election and, after a speedy progress helped by the guillotine, it became an act on 12 April 1984.

By common consent the second Bill was a much more workable piece of legislation. In a Tyne Tees TV programme in August 1986, John Golding claimed some of the credit. Having realized that the large Conservative majority would ensure the Bill's eventual success, he decided to cut his losses by pressing for the best possible terms for his members. Most of the important work took place in the corridors and at the Committee Stage rather than on the Floor of the House which was thinly populated during the debate stages. Golding claims his own advice and expertise was often sought by ministers and civil servants alike as the Bill was discussed and amendments moved.

Bureaucratic process

The bureaucratic process in this case to some extent preceded and to some extent continued in parallel with the legislative process. It began with a *learning process* when civil servants had to negotiate with BT officials and experts. Jason Crisp of the *Financial Times*, who followed these discussions closely, testified that talks were 'frequent, frantic, often very bad tempered'. Then negotiations with other *ministries* ensued, especially with the Treasury which was primarily interested in the huge increases in revenue privatization would produce. Inevitably, the Department of Trade and Industry was more concerned with achieving a particular kind of settlement, and one which worked, and negotiations with the Treasury were consequently not always smooth.

Next came consultations with the City where most of the finance was expected to originate. The DTI and the Treasury were clearly determined not to overprice BT's shares. The 1983 election manifesto had listed British Gas, Rolls Royce, British Steel and others as future candidates for privatization: they could not afford the failure of such a major test case as BT. The City financiers, like all potential buyers, had an interest in talking the price down and this they assiduously did.

Finally, negotiations with outside pressure groups took place. In 1980 the British Telecom Union Campaign was formed with the POEU to the fore. With the help of a public relations company and an advertising agency it orchestrated a campaign to frustrate the Bill and when that failed, to soften its impact upon trade union members. The POEU, in its booklet, *The Battle for British Telecom*, tells the story of how it put pressure on 800 key opinion makers in industry and in the programme already referred to (Tyne Tees, 1986) John Golding told how the relevant pressure groups were mobilized over rural services, especially the provision of kiosks. The response from the likes of the NFU, the local authority associations and the Womens'

Institutes was so overwhelming that civil servants 'begged' him

> to call off the campaign because the Department was absolutely inundated by resolutions and letters that came from all those traditionally Conservative supporting bodies. But of course we kept the campaign on and . . . The ministers caved in and made certain that they protected the rural services as far as it was possible.

A number of points can be made about the way in which this decision was made which also serve as a conclusion to this Chapter.

1. **Result differed from intention**. According to party ideology the main thrust of privatization is to reintroduce competition and to spread public ownership of shares. At the end of the three-year process, competition seemed to have taken a back seat. (Though Mercury Communications was licensed to compete with BT and in 1990 this duopoly ended and other enterprises were considered as licensed competitors.) And while nearly two million people helped produce the £4 billion flotation (within two years BT doubled in price to about £8 billion) the numbers had decreased to under 1.6 million owning only 12.6 per cent of the BT stock. The result of all the pressures bearing upon the process therefore produced an outcome substantially different from the original intention.

2. **Complexity**. Given the dense complexity of the process, it is small wonder that the public loses touch with all the various twists and turns through Parliament and the corridors of Whitehall. Nor is it surprising that many governments shrink from major initiatives when such mountains of vested interests have to be moved. Mrs Thatcher's governments were indeed unusual in taking so many major initiatives — trade union reform, abolishing the Metropolitan counties, privatization — and succeeding in pushing so many through.

3. **The limits of majority rule.** The case of BT illustrates that a large majority is no substitute for workable legislation. On occasions even opposition MPs have to be called upon to provide the necessary expertise.

4. **The opportunities for influence and consultation are considerable.** Throughout the legislative and bureaucratic processes the opportunities for individuals and pressure groups to intervene and make their point are considerable.

5. **The professionalism of civil servants.** Civil servants are often accused of being generalists — experts on nothing — but in the case of BT they mastered an immensely technical field with remarkable speed. There is no evidence either that they dragged their heels over the privatization of BT or did anything other than loyally carry out the bidding of their political masters. The irony, however, is that the team which privatized BT dispersed soon afterwards, lured by private sector employers impressed with the know-how the privatization process had bestowed upon them.

References and Further Reading

Bullpitt, J., *Territory and Power in the United Kingdom* (Manchester University Press, 1983).
Burch, M., 'Policy making in central government', in B. Jones and D. Kavanagh, *British Politics Today* (Manchester University Press, 1978).
Burch, M. and Wood, B., *Public policy in Britain* (Martin Robertson, 1983).

Haclo, H. and Wilkavsky, A., *The Private Government of Public Money* (Macmillan, 1981).

Hogwood, B. and Gunn, L.A., *Policy Analysis for the Real World* (Oxford University Press, 1984).

Hood, C.C., *The Limits of Administration* (Wiley, 1976).

Hood, C.C. and Wright, M. (eds) *Big Government in Hard Times* (Martin Robertson, 1981).

Jones, B., *Is Democracy Working* (Tyne Tees TV, 1986).

Jordan, A. and Richardson, J., *Governing Under Pressure* (Martin Robertson, 1987).

Jordan, G. and Richardson, J.J., 'The British policy style or the logic of negotiation', in J.J. Richardson (ed.), *Policy Styles in Western Europe* (Allen and Unwin, 1982).

Lee, G., 'Privatisation', in B. Jones, *Political Issues in Britain Today*, 3rd edn. (Manchester University Press, 1989).

Lindblom, C., *The Intelligence of Democracy* (The Free Press, 1965).

Lindblom, C., 'Still muddling, not yet through', *Public Administration Review*, **39**, 517–25 (1977).

Lindblom, C. (ed.), *The Policy Making Process* (Prentice Hall, 1980).

Mack, R., *Planning and Uncertainty* (Wiley Interscience, 1971).

Ponting, C., *Whitehall: Tragedy and Farce* (Hamish Hamilton, 1986).

Schmitter, P. and Lehmbruch, G. (eds), *Trends Towards Corporatist Intermediation* (Sage, 1979).

24 Economic Policy

Michael Moran and Bill Jones

This chapter begins by examining the nature and purposes of economic policy. It then looks at the machinery of policy — at the main institutions involved, and at their relationships with each other. The final section turns from machinery to substance — to some of the most important debates and issues raised by the politics of economic policy.

The Nature of Economic Policy

It may be thought a simple matter to identify 'economic policy': 'policy' consists in the choices made and rejected by government; 'economic' refers to that set of institutions and activities concerned with the production and distribution of goods and services; economic policy therefore consists in those choices made or rejected by government designed to affect the production of goods and services in the community.

This is, it will be plain, a very broad definition. Many activities of government not commonly thought of as 'economic' become so if we rigorously follow this guideline. Thus policy towards the arts — for instance, the provision of subsidized opera and theatre — is directed to influencing the price at which particular artistic services are provided to the community.

A broad definition of economic policy is highly revealing, for two reasons. First, it alerts us to the fact that the boundaries of 'economic policy' are moving all the time. For example, in recent years government has increasingly pictured education in economic terms. It conceives the primary purpose of schooling to be the production of one of the community's most valuable economic assets — a competent and educationally adaptable work force. Thus, to an increasing extent policy towards schools has been conceived as a facet of economic policy.

One of the primary features of economic policy is, therefore, that it has wide and constantly changing boundaries. This connects to a second factor making a 'broad' definition of policy appealing: there is constant struggle and argument over the making and control of policy. British government works in part by a series of conventions which allocate subjects to particular institutions. An issue defined as purely concerned with education, for instance, will be in the domain of the Department of Education and Science and the teaching profession. Until recently, for example, the content of the school curriculum was thought of as such a purely 'educational' matter. But the growing belief that the quality of education, by affecting the quality of the work-force, in turn shapes the fortunes of the economy, has introduced economic considerations into arguments about the curriculum — and has destroyed the idea that choices about what is to be taught in schools are to be made only by those concerned with education.

This example illustrates that in economic policy making arguments about what is, and what is not, relevant to the economy are of more than definitional significance. They are part of the process by which different groups in government try to gain control over particular areas of decision. If, for instance, the task of reviving the decaying parts of Britain's inner cities is pictured as one concerning the renovation of the physical environment, it will naturally be thought of as the responsibility at national level of the Department of the Environment. If, by contrast, it is pictured as a task of reviving a declining part of the industrial economy, it will more naturally be thought of as the proper responsibility of the Department of Trade and Industry. The 'boundaries' of economic policy are, therefore, uncertain and disputed. But if the boundaries are open to argument, there is nevertheless considerable agreement about where the heart of economic policy lies. The most important parts concern government's own 'housekeeping', and its wider responsibilities for economic management.

Government has to make choices concerning the raising and distribution of its own resources: it has, in other words, to make choices concerning its budget in the same way as a firm or a family makes choices. But the choices made by government about how much to spend, where to allocate the money and how to raise it, have a special significance. This significance is partly the result of scale: government is the biggest institution in the British economy and has a correspondingly great effect on the rest of society. Decisions by government about how much to spend and how much to tax crucially affect the prosperity or otherwise of the economy at large. But the significance of public spending and taxation choices also lie in their purpose, for they are important *instruments* which government can and does use to influence the course of the economy. This connects to a second 'core' aspect of economic policy.

Complementing its role as a major appropriator and distributor of resources in Britain, government has a second major economic policy responsibility — to 'steer the economy'. The implied comparison with steering a vessel or a vehicle, while not exact, is nevertheless helpful. Like the pilot of a vessel, government possesses *instruments* of control which can be manipulated to guide the economy in a desired direction; and like a pilot it has available a variety of *indicators* telling it how successfully these instruments are working. Among the most important instruments of control used by British government in recent decades are the budgetary instruments to which we have already referred. By varying the total volume of public spending, or the level of taxation, government is able to increase or depress the total amount of activity in the economy. By targeting its spending on particular areas — like education, or the inner cities, or as subsidies to particular industries — government can also try to influence particular economic groups in the economy.

The image of 'steering the economy' was particularly important in the twenty-five years after the end of the Second World War (Brittan, 1971). Mrs Thatcher's administrations, as we have seen in earlier chapters, denied that government could control the economy in the way that was attempted in the past. During the 1980s 'Thatcherites' asserted that government could only hope to create the right conditions for a freely functioning market economy; competitive forces, for better or worse, would do the rest. Yet the government still does try to 'steer the economy'. It has objectives — like the control of inflation — which it seeks to achieve, and instruments of control which it uses to that end. After the 1970s, therefore, the direction of economic steering and the instruments of control changed; but all governments in post-war Britain have been engaged in steering the economy.

The Machinery of Economic Policy

When we refer to the 'machinery' of something we are usually speaking of more than the mechanical parts of which it is composed; we also mean the process by which those parts combine in movement. So it is with the machinery of economic policy making: we mean not just the institutions, but the process by which they interact to produce choices.

If we look at a formal organization chart of British government we will see that it is hierarchical in nature with elected politicians — Ministers — at the top. It would be natural to assume, therefore, that the machinery of economic policy making worked by reserving the power to make policy to a few people at the top of government and reserving the task of carrying out policy to those lower down the hierarchy. But perhaps the single most important feature of policy making is that there is no simple distinction to be made between a few at the top who 'make' policy and a larger number lower down in government who 'implement' or 'execute' policy. More perhaps than in any other area of public affairs, *economic policy making* and *policy implementation* are inseparable. Those at the top of government certainly have the potential to make broad decisions about the direction of policy. But the substance of economic policy is determined not only by broad strategic judgements; it is also shaped by the way large numbers of organizations in *both the public and private sectors* translate those into practical reality. The best way of picturing the machinery of economic policy making, therefore, is not as a hierarchy in which a few take decisions which are then executed by those further down the hierarchy, but rather as a set of institutions in the centre of the machine which negotiate and argue over policy with a wide range of surrounding bodies in both the public and private sectors.

The centre of the machine

At the centre of the machinery of economic policy making is *the Treasury*. At first glance the Treasury looks an insignificant institution. It is tiny by the standards of most central departments. What is more it plays little part in the execution of economic policy. Vital tasks like administering schemes for financial support of industry and regulating the activities of particular sectors and occupations are carried out elsewhere, notably by the giant Department of Trade and Industry. The Treasury's importance essentially lies in three features. First, it is universally recognized as a vital source of policy advice about economic management, not only to its political head, the Chancellor of the Exchequer, but also to other senior Ministers, notably the Prime Minister. Secondly it is, as its title implies, in effect the keeper of the public purse: it is the key institution in decisions about revenue-raising (taxation) and about the volume of public spending. The latter process is organized around a virtually continuous cycle of bargaining between the Treasury and the 'spending departments' to fix both the level of spending commitments and the proportionate allocation of resources between competing claimants (Heclo and Wildavsky, 1975).

Thirdly, the Treasury shares with the Bank of England a large measure of control over policy towards financial markets. These matters include the terms on which the government borrows money, intervention to affect the level of interest rates throughout the economy and the 'management of Sterling' — in other words intervention in foreign exchange markets to influence the rate at which the pound is exchanged for other foreign currencies. Although in most of these activities the Bank of England acts as the agent of government, it only does this in close, virtually continuous, consultation with the Treasury. These responsibilities are especially important because the management of financial markets has since the mid-1970s become a key task of economic policy. Consequently the **Bank of England** should now be placed alongside the Treasury at the core of the machinery of economic policy, despite the fact that it is not a government department, nor even located in the area around Westminster where most of the major departments have their headquarters.

The Bank of England is the nation's 'central bank'. This means that it is a publicly owned institution (though it only became so in 1946) with responsibility for managing the national currency. It also has a legal responsibility to oversee and safeguard the stability of the country's banking system and a more general responsibility to oversee the stability of financial markets. It is, as we have already seen, also the Treasury's agent in managing public debt and in interventions to influence levels of interest rates in the economy. The Bank's headquarters are located in the City of London and this symbolizes its distinctive character. Although a public body and part of the core of the machinery of policy making, it retains a tradition of independence. Its Governor, while nominated by the Prime Minister, is usually a considerable and independent figure, in both the City of London and in international gatherings of other 'central bankers'. Likewise employees of the Bank are recruited separately from, and paid more than, civil servants (Moran, 1986).

The Bank's importance in the machinery of economic decision making rests on two factors. First, it plays a major part in the execution of decisions increasingly considered to be the heart of economic policy — those concerning the management of conditions in financial markets. Secondly, as a result of its continuous and deep involvement with the markets it has an established position as a source of advice about the policy options best suited to the successful management of these markets.

Describing the Treasury and the Bank of England as the centre of the machinery of economic policy does not amount to the same thing as saying that these two institutions dominate policy. As we will see in a later section there is considerable room for argument about the extent of Treasury and Bank of England power. However, it is undoubtedly the case that the two have a continuous role in the discussions about the strategic purposes and daily tactics of economic policy which occupy so much of modern government. No other *institution* in government specializes in this activity at such a high level.

The Treasury's and the Bank's position at the centre of the machine is nevertheless shared with others. All governments in modern times have viewed economic policy as a primary responsibility and as a major influence on their chances of re-election.

This means that economic management is never far from the minds of senior ministers. Two departmental members of the Cabinet usually occupy Treasury posts: the Chancellor of the Exchequer; and the Chief Secretary to the Treasury, whose main responsibility is managing at the highest level the negotiations over expenditure plans between the Treasury and the 'spending' Departments. Given the importance of economic policy, Prime Ministerial participation in consideration of strategy and tactics is now customary.

'Prime Ministerial' here partly means the individual who happens to be the occupant of that position at any particular moment. The Prime Minister is both figuratively and physically close to the machinery of economic policy making: his/her residence and that of the Chancellor adjoin, while the Treasury itself is barely a footstep away from No. 10 Downing Street. However, 'Prime Ministerial' involvement in economic policy denotes more than the involvement of a particular personality. It happened to be the case in the 1980s that Britain had in Mrs Thatcher an unusually commanding Prime Minister with a particular interest in, and firm grasp of, the mechanics of economic policy (Riddell, 1983). Consequently, she was a central figure in the machinery. Any modern Prime Minister is, however, likely to be an important part of the machine. The precise position will depend on changing factors: the abilities and interests of a particular individual; the personal relations between the Prime Minister and the Chancellor; and the wider popularity and authority which the Prime Minister can command. Prime Ministerial involvement need not consist only of personal intervention. It can also take the form of participation by the staff of the Prime Minister's own office and from institutions closely connected to the Prime Minister, notably the Cabinet Office. Prime ministerial economic advisors can also exert considerable influence: in 1989 the Chancellor Nigel Lawson actually resigned over the role performed by Mrs Thatcher's adviser Sir Alan Walters.

Prime Ministerial participation in the machinery of economic policy making may now be described as 'institutionalized' — which means that it is part of the established procedures, irrespective of the capacities and outlook of the individual who at any particular moment happens to occupy No. 10 Downing Street. It is less certain that the same can be said of the Cabinet, a body which once was indeed indisputably a dominant participant. It is true that the Cabinet retains a role irrespective of particular circumstances, such as the style of an individual Prime Minister. Thus the weekly meetings of Cabinet will always contain agenda items which bear on central parts of economic strategy. More important still, the network of Cabinet Committees which now do much business in place of full Cabinet are important forums for consideration of strategy and tactics. The Cabinet system retains a particular important role in deciding public spending. Although the process is dominated by direct bargaining between the Treasury and the individual departments, it is still accepted that it is at Cabinet committee level that irreconcilable differences between a Department and the Treasury are effectively resolved.

Nevertheless, the extent of collective Cabinet involvement in economic policy making has since the end of the 1970s been uncertain. The importance of individuals remains: after all, three Cabinet Members — the Prime Minister, the Chancellor and the Chief Secretary to the Treasury — are all indisputably part of the core machinery while others, like the Secretary of State for Trade and Industry, have an obvious concern with key matters of economic policy. But what may have declined is the collective consideration of strategy and tactics by Cabinet institutions — either in full Cabinet or in committee. Whether this is due to the style of leadership practised by Mrs Thatcher, who dominated her Cabinets in the 1980s, or whether it is due to longer-term changes in the significance of the Cabinet, is at present uncertain; but if it is due to long-term changes it is plainly important; and if due to Mrs Thatcher's leadership style it is also revealing, since its shows that the Cabinet's place in the machinery is dependent on the style of the particular Prime Minister who happens to be in office.

The observation that the Cabinet's role in the machinery is uncertain should not be taken to mean that Cabinet Ministers and their Departments are unimportant. Indeed, since we saw earlier that no simple division can be made between the 'making' of policy and its 'implementation' it follows that Departments, in the act of executing policy, in effect also 'make' it by shaping what comes out of the government machine. This is manifestly the case with, for instance, the Department of Trade and Industry which, in its multitude of dealings with individual firms, industries and sectors plays a large part in deciding what is, in practice, to be the goverment's policy towards a wide range of industries.

The machinery of economic policy stretches not only beyond the central institutions like the Treasury to other central Departments; it also encompasses what is sometimes called 'quasi-government' and even institutions which are in the private sector. It is to these matters that we now turn.

Quasi-government

One of the striking features of British government is the small proportion of the 'public sector' which is actually accounted for by what we conventionally think of as the characteristic public institution — the central department headed by a Cabinet Minister located in central London. Most people who work in the public sector are not 'civil servants', and most of the work of the public sector is done by institutions which do not have the status of civil service departments. This is an especially noticeable feature of the machinery of economic policy. It has become conventional to speak of this range of institutions as 'quasi-government' organizations. By this is meant that they have many of the marks of public bodies: they are usually entrusted with the task of carrying out duties prescribed in law; they often draw all, or a proportion of, their funds from the public purse; and the appointment of their leading officers is usually controlled by a Minister and his Department (Barker, 1982). Yet in their daily operations they normally work with some degree of independence of Ministers and are usually less subject than are civil service departments to parliamentary scrutiny. In economic policy it is helpful to distinguish between two categories of quasi-government institution: ***nationalized corporations*** and a more diverse category best labelled ***independent specialized agencies***.

Nationalized corporations are a comparatively standard organizational type. They normally work under a charter prescribing such matters as the constitution and powers of their governing board. The corporation form has been used for activities as different as delivering broadcasting services (the BBC) and mining coal (British Coal). They have responsibility for providing particular kinds of goods and services (although the boundaries of their appropriate activities are often unclear). Most nationalized corporations provide goods or services through the market, deriving the bulk of their revenue from sales. But they are also linked to central government. It is common for a corporation to have a 'sponsoring Department' in Whitehall. The 'sponsor' will be expected to 'speak for' its corporation inside central government, but it is also an instrument for exercising control over the corporation.

The exact powers of central departments over nationalized corporations have long been a source of dispute and disagreement, but it is undoubtedly the case that central government can appoint chairmen of the industries, can influence the prices they charge customers, can determine the terms on which they can borrow, or attract subsidies, and can influence the kinds of investment they make.

From 1945 to the end of the 1970s the nationalized corporation was a major instrument of government policy — and was itself in turn a major influence over the shape of economic policy. In the 1980s 'privatization' reduced the size and significance of the nationalized corporation in the machinery of economic policy; yet it remains a significant presence. Free standing, specialized agencies have, if anything, become more important in recent years. They cover a wide range of areas, and take a variety of organized forms. They have become one of the most important means by which economic policy is 'delivered' — and, in being delivered, shaped. Two examples will illustrate their range and importance. Since the end of the 1970s the Manpower Services Commission (latterly renamed the Training Commission) emerged as the major organization delivering government policy on manpower training and retraining — a key part of government economic policy since it is directed to the single greatest problem facing modern economic policy, unemployment. A second major example is provided by the attempts to solve yet another major problem, the declining economy of Britain's inner cities. Here, one of the chief instruments of policy has been Urban Development Corporations, given the specialized task of reviving the economies of particular areas. It is worth stressing that such bodies do not just carry out policy decisions made elsewhere; they shape policy by their control over the details of its execution and their role in policy advice.

There are many reasons why 'quasi-government' is important in the machinery of economic policy, but two are particularly significant. The first is that central government departments simply do not have the resources and knowledge to carry out the full tasks of the public sector; the system would become impossibly overloaded if the effort were made to control everything through a handful of government departments in London. The second reason is that the 'quasi-government' system offers some protection against control by politicians, especially Members of Parliament. It is much harder for a Member of Parliament to scrutinize and call to account an agency or a nationalized corporation than to do the same thing with a civil service department headed by a Minister.

The machinery of economic policy stretches into 'quasi-government'; but it also, we shall now see, reaches into the private sector.

The private sector

It may seem odd to include privately owned institutions like business firms in the machinery of policy. But it will become obvious when we realize two things: that economic policy is made in the process of execution, not just by a few people at

Central
economic
decision
makers

Prime Minister
Chancellor
Chief Secretary to the Treasury
Governor of the Bank of England
Senior Treasury Officials
Economic Advisers
Cabinet Office
Key Cabinet Committees
Secretary of State Department of Trade and Industry
Cabinet
Quasi-Government
Nationalized corporations
Independent specialized agencies
Private Sector
Business Firms
Banks

the top handing down decisions to be routinely carried out elsewhere; and in executing policy government relies widely on private bodies.

One of the most striking examples of this is provided by the banking system in Britain. Almost all British banks are privately owned; yet without the services provided by the banks any government's economic policies would come to nothing. For instance, the whole payments system, on which the economy depends, is administered by the banks. This includes, for example, the circulation of notes and coins throughout the population and the processing of cheques and other forms of payment. In some of the most technologically advanced sectors of the economy, like the nuclear power industry, firms in private ownership work in close partnership with government to implement jointly agreed policies (Ward, 1983).

We have now examined the nature of economic policy and the means by which it is formed and put into effect. But economic policy is more than definitions and machinery; it is the single most important source of debate about, and arguments in, British politics. Those debates are our next concern.

Themes and Issues in Economic Policy

Economic policy has been the single most important, and the single most contentious, area of British politics in modern times. Arguments about who runs the economy, about the causes of Britain's economic failures and about the proper way to remedy those failures have been at the heart of political divisions in the country. Understanding economic policy and understanding the political system with which it is so clearly bound up necessarily involves understanding the nature of these debates and issues. In this section, therefore, we look at key areas of debate — who controls policy, and why has it been so ineffective in reversing decline; how far the government can perform its own 'housekeeping', in the shape of controlling public spending; and the impact of 'Thatcherism', the most important ideology in modern politics, on the conduct of economic policy.

Who controls economic policy?

The arguments about who, if anyone, has the decisive influence over the shape of economic policy, is an argument about the location of power — a classically political question. It has prompted a variety of answers — many of them in effect critical of the way the economy has been governed. Formally, of course, the answer to the question is plain: Britain is a constitutional democracy and ultimate control of policy is in the hands of the people's elected representatives. More critical accounts have looked elsewhere — either to parts of the civil service or to powerful organized groups in the wider economy. We examine each of these in turn.

A Treasury elite view

The view that economic policy in Britain is controlled by a Treasury elite does not assert that all important decisions are taken by senior Treasury officials — but it does argue that the shape of economic policy and of arguments about policy are moulded by thinking closely in line with the Treasury's view of the world (Pollard, 1982). Three grounds can be produced for this argument. The first we have already encountered in our previous section. Inside the machinery of policy making itself the Treasury is uniquely placed to influence the content of decisions: it has formal powers, for instance over spending decisions; is always led in Cabinet by a major political figure, the Chancellor of the Exchequer; has traditionally attracted the most able civil servants of each generation, many of whom subsequently carry Treasury views elsewhere when they become heads of lesser departments; and has historically enjoyed a supreme position inside government as the authoritative source of information and advice about economic policy choices. Secondly, it can be argued that in the decisive crises of recent economic history it is the Treasury's concerns which have been dominant. Thirdly, it has been argued that the Treasury itself is part of a wider alliance of financial interests located in the City of London who have shaped economic policy with an eye on international rather than on home interests. In particular, the links between the Bank of England and the Treasury are often seen as ensuring that financial interests control policy (Blank, 1979).

Against this view three points can be made. First, although the Treasury is undoubtedly powerful and prestigious, as a small Department dealing mostly in policy advice, rather than in the actual carrying out of decisions, it is often at a considerable disadvantage. Secondly, while the Treasury has undoubtedly been decisive in many critical events, its record of lost battles is also a long one. For example, during most of the period since the Second World War public spending has been higher than the Treasury would have wished. Finally, it is not obvious that there is a single 'Treasury' view of the world, as distinct from positions on particular problems; it is indeed a Department where sharp argument about policy choice is encouraged.

Opponents and supporters of the 'Treasury domination' view tend to argue on the assumption that the critical influences on economic policy lie somewhere inside the machinery of government. By contrast, a 'veto group' account suggests that the shape of economic policy is moulded by forces in the wider economy — usually at the point where it is being put into effect.

The 'veto group' argument

We emphasized at the start of this chapter the extent to which the 'making' and 'implementation' of economic policy were intertwined. The 'veto group' argument stresses the significance of this point. It also points to a feature emphasized in our chapters on the social and economic context: that because Britain is a market economy, no policy can operate effectively without the cooperation of the institutions which keep a market economy functioning. Different views exist, however, as to which groups in the market place have so much power that they can place a veto over the policies of government.

Some observers stress the power of business as a veto group (Coates, 1984). They argue that the rules of a market economy give to business firms crucial capacities to facilitate or obstruct economic policy. The characteristic long term economic aims of all governments — the creation of jobs, industrial investment, expansion of production — all depend, in a market economy, on decisions taken largely by private enterprises. They will only take these decisions if induced to do so by the hope of profits. All economic policy, so the argument runs, is ultimately at the mercy of business which, if not convinced of the rightness of a policy, can exercise a 'veto' by declining to put resources behind that policy. Because the controllers of capital possess this veto they are, even in conditions where they do not use the veto, the decisive influence over the content of policy.

The private ownership of capital is undoubedly a key to understanding the conduct of economic policy in Britain. But alongside capital as a resource must be set *labour*. It has commonly been argued that labour, especially when organized into trade unions, is actually a more significant veto group than is capital. The most important version of this argument asserts that workers, when organized into unions, are in a position where they can prevent the introduction of a policy, or destroy it in the process of implementation. This is possible because life in a community like Britain is tolerable only if groups of workers voluntarily supply their labour (Finer, 1973; Brittan, 1975). Through the organized strike weapon, or even its threatened use, teachers, power workers, nurses or any of a host of other groups can veto policy quite as effectively as can a powerful business corporation.

The argument that unions are a powerful veto group was especially popular in the 1970s, when the country's economic crisis was widely associated with industrial disputes which did, indeed, disrupt everyday life. In other words, there exists a connection between arguments about who controls economic policy and arguments about the nature of Britain's economic problems. We now examine, as our second major theme, the debate about the causes of the country's economic decline.

The causes of Britain's economic decline

The long-term purpose of economic policy is to create the conditions for continuing and growing prosperity. Measured by that standard, British economic policy has been a great success. The nation as a whole, and almost every social group within it, is now much richer than was the case a generation ago. But another aim of economic policy has been not only to make the country prosperous, but to maintain Britain's place as a leading world economic nation. Nobody disputes that in this respect policy has failed — though as we shall see in the next section some argue that 'Thatcherite' solutions in the 1980s reversed this history of failure. Here we look at three of the most important sets of explanations offered for the inability of policy to stem decline.

A historically inevitable decline

It is appropriate to begin with a view which challenges the notion that economic policy can indeed be described as a failure. The United Kingdom is a small island state which for a brief moment in the nineteenth century led the world economically — just as she led it politically. It is unrealistic, such an argument runs, to expect such domination to endure. For many years after the end of the Second World War the more rapid economic growth rates of other nations were thus viewed as a process of 'catching up' on the lead originally opened by Britain in the nineteenth century. By the early 1960s this was a doubtful argument; by the 1980s it was more doubtful still. Other economies had not only closed Britain's lead; they had accelerated past her. The strikingly greater economic success of states of a similar size to Britain — like Germany and Japan — suggested that there was nothing natural about Britain's condition. Furthermore, while the country continued to grow more prosperous it was plain as long as two decades ago that many of the industries on which this prosperity had been founded were in decay, and were not being replaced by comparably successful new ones. If Britain's economic decline is inevitable, this inevitability must lie in some British characteristics which obstructed the development of appropriate remedial policies. 'Cultural' explanations of failure address this problem.

Cultural explanations of economic policy failure

A 'cultural' explanation traces failure to the attitudes and assumptions of powerful groups in British society (Barnett, 1972; Wiener, 1981). According to this view a successful economy demands that the ruling groups in a nation promote economic change, technical research and economic and administrative efficiency. These traits have been held to be conspicuously absent among the rulers of Britain. Economic policies have been made in an amateurish and ill-informed manner because competence and efficiency were less highly valued than social connections and the possession of a 'gentlemanly' style. Even more damaging, economic policy has been guided by a set of attitudes unsympathetic to manufacturing industry — the very bedrock of the country's historical economic power. This distaste for the 'ungentlemanly' nature of manufacturing industry spread even to the leaders of business itself, leading to a decay of enterprise as the heirs to industrial fortunes turned to gentlemanly ways of life, instead of pursuing business success.

One of the obvious difficulties with this argument can be expressed as follows. Even if it is indeed the case that crucial interests in the British economy have been unsympathetic to industry and to innovation, why has it proved so hard to dislodge them — as they have indeed been dislodged in other, more successful, economies? One explanation for this may lie in the idea that Britain is an example of a 'weak' state.

A 'weak state' and policy failure

The 'weakness' of a state is quite distinct from its size. Britain has long had a large state sector. 'Weakness' refers rather to the style of policy making — in other words, to the way in which public policy makers wield the state power vested in them (Dyson and Wilks, 1983). Two features have marked the British policy style, especially in the area of economics: it has been 'consensual'; and central government has played a relatively small part in the actual carrying out of policy. By 'consensual' is meant a preference for bargaining and compromise, as an alternative to the imposition by government of its will. This has been connected to the second feature, for it has been usual to rely on a wide range of institutions — local government, nationalized corporations, privately organized pressure groups, corporate bodies like universities and professional associations — to assist in the implementation of policy. This reliance on the cooperation of a wide range of institutions and groups forced a consensual style of policy making because, obviously, cooperation would not happen if policies were imposed in an atmosphere of hostility. But the price of this arrangement, so the argument runs, has been a weak state: in other words, a policy style which has been forced to accommodate interests in the community, when the creation of an efficient and internationally competitive economy often demanded that these interests be confronted.

The objections to the view that economic policy making has been of poor quality because of the policy style imposed by a 'weak state' arrangement are twofold. First, it is not at all clear that a consensual and cooperative policy making approach are indeed irreconcilable with successful policies: many of Britain's more successful competitors, like Germany and Japan, also have 'consensual' policy making characteristics. Secondly, the 'weak state' view neglects the variety found even within the field of economic policy making (Wright, 1988). Until recently, for instance, the framing of budgets in Britain was done without any serious consultation between the Treasury and outside interests — indeed, the whole affair was conducted in great secrecy only to be revealed on Budget day itself.

This brings us directly to the issue of the control of public expenditure.

Public expenditure policy

Economic policy comprises a number of very important areas like: dealings with foreign economies and international agencies, management of the economy and the raising of revenue. The control and allocation of public expenditure, however, is of particular interest as it affects all of us as consumers of government services. As Burch and Wood (1983) explain, the process involves no more than 200 people 'and is somewhat obscure and more or less closed to public scrutiny' (p.138). Since the early 1960s this policy area has been the responsibility of the Public Expenditure Survey Committee (PESC) comprising the chief departmental finance officers plus senior Treasury officials. The Treasury has a fifty-strong section specializing in expenditure matters and they assist in liaising and coordinating with internal departments. PESC operates according to an annual cycle with an expenditure White Paper appearing early in the year and with bids submitted in mid-year becoming the subject of extended and tough negotiations with Treasury officials before next year's figures are gathered together some time in December. Public expenditure is planned currently according to a three-year cycle, so each year's White Paper updates a forward-rolling programme.

The lead Cabinet minister on this is the Chief Secretary to the Treasury. It is his job to keep departmental bids under control; the measure of his success is how often the Star Chamber — an informal court of appeal for department ministers chaired by a senior Cabinet member — is obliged to meet (during 1988 it did not meet at all when John Major held this office). The Chancellor also has a big say and inevitably so does the Prime Minister. Other Cabinet and junior Ministers are drawn in as necessary, often to advise the Cabinet Committee on future economic strategy which regularly addresses the overall shape of public expenditure plans. Consideration by the full Cabinet is intermittent: some discussion of broad strategy in the summer and a more detailed discussion towards the end of the annual cycle in December. By that time most of the major decisions will have been taken and Cabinet has often little more to do than endorse what has been agreed elsewhere. The whole process is highly centralized, therefore, and secretive in that recipients of government funding — local government, nationalized industries — are consulted beforehand but are informed of the outcome usually without any explanation of how and why decisions are made.

How successful has this policy making process been? Keeping government expenditure under control has been a constant problem for all recent administrations. Labour came unstuck through regularly overestimating economic growth but Denis Healey reined in public expenditure in the late 1970s from 48 per cent of GDP in 1975−6 to 42 per cent in 1977−8, partly through the use of finite cash limits upon

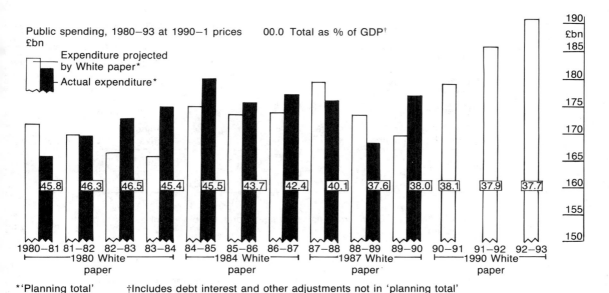

Figure 24.1 *Public spending 1980−93 (Source:* The Economist, *3 February 1990)*

Pence in every pound

Receipts			Expenditure
Income tax	24	10	Defence
		2	Foreign and Commonwealth Office
		1	Agriculture, Fisheries and Food
Corporation tax	12	1	Trade and Industry
		2	Employment
Capital gains tax	1	3	Transport
Inheritance tax	1	1	Environment — housing
Value added tax	15	2	Environment — other environmental services
		4	Home Office and legal departments
Local authority rates and community charge	11	10	Education and Science
Duties on petrol, alcoholic drinks and tobacco	10	12	Health
Petroleum revenue tax and oil royalties	1	26	Social Security
National Insurance and other contributions	17	5	Scotland
		2	Wales
Interest and dividends	4	3	Northern Ireland
Gross trading surpluses and rent	2	2	Chancellor's departments
		1	Other departments
Other duties, taxes, levies and royalties	5	2	Reserve
Other receipts	3	9	Gross debt interest
General government borrowing requirement	−6	3	Adjustments (net of privatisation proceeds)
Total	100	100	Total

Cash totals £194,300 million

Note: Differences between totals and the sum of their component parts are due to rounding.

Figure 24.2 *Planned receipts and expenditure of general government 1988—9 (Source:* Britain 1990: An Official Handbook*)*

spending in specific areas: Departments had no option but to cut their coat according to the cloth available. Mrs Thatcher's Chancellors have been keen to retain such devices and, assisted by economic growth, have been able to reduce expenditure from 46 per cent in 1980 to 38 per cent of GDP in 1989 (see Figure 24.1). But they have not been able to reduce absolute levels of spending.

The first Thatcher government planned for a 3 per cent cut over the four-year period 1980—4 and Ministers were encouraged to find prime ministerial favour through making cuts rather than courting departmental popularity with proposed increases. Unfortunately, as Figure 24.1 shows, this did not happen: expenditure increased by 6 per cent. The two subsequent White Papers in 1984—7 and 1987—90 also planned reductions but registered increases. The 1990—3 White Paper abandoned such ambitions and anticipated an 8 per cent increase. Figure 24.2 shows how spending was allocated in 1989 while Figure 24.3 reveals how certain major services have fared over recent years together with their projected allocations into the early 1990s.

Certain observations can be made on the basis of these figures:

1. **Continuity** is the most obvious feature: change where it is registered is mostly gradual and over time. Much of this continuity is accounted for by spending which has been committed over a period of years.

2. **Changing emphases** between programmes can be attributed to policy decisions deriving from party ideology. Thus spending on law and order increased by 53 per cent 1980—9 while trade and industry spending fell because the £3 billion being paid to nationalized industries in 1980 had been reduced to £300 million

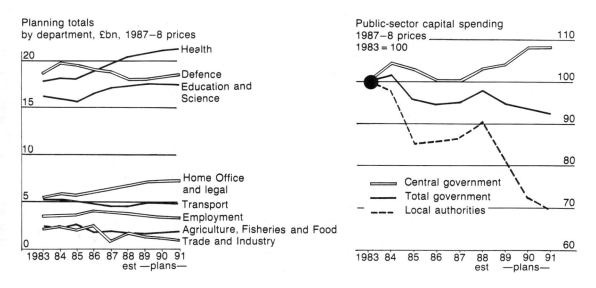

Figure 24.3 *The trend of spending (Source:* The Economist, *2 March 1990)*

by 1987 — in 1988 they actually made an overall profit. In one sense, though, Conservative ideology back-fired in expenditure terms. In 1980 Mrs Thatcher aimed to cut growth in social security payments to under the rate of inflation within two years; in the event they increased by 30 per cent as a result of unemployment caused by recession and a high interest rate policy.

3. *Factors beyond government control.* The major element in the social security bill is determined by demographic factors, especially the increasing proportion of the population who are elderly. The same goes for health spending but increased allocations in this sector still have to be approved and are not automatic as in social security.

4. *Peripheral functions suffer first.* Central decision makers have tried to protect their own areas by cutting peripheral functions like local government. Thus housing, a local government function, has been heavily cut by 67 per cent between 1979 and 1989. Figure 24.3 shows how local government capital spending as a whole has been badly hit.

5. *Electoral considerations always apply. The Economist* noted on 4 February 1989 that 'After four years in which the real level of public spending has been flat, it will rise by 7.6 per cent between 1989—90 and 1991—2, the year in which the next general election will probably be held'.

The debate about Thatcherite economic policy

'Thatcherism', a short-hand to describe the economic policies pursued throughout the 1980s by Margaret Thatcher's Conservative governments, is now so familiar to political argument that it is necessary to recall that it has quite recent origins. Those origins lie in the policy failures preceding Mrs Thatcher's election to office in 1979, and the debate prompted by those failures — debates sketched earlier in this chapter. Thatcherism had two elements: it was an attempt to introduce historically different policies; and an attempt to replace the 'consensual and cooperative' policy style of British government with a more centralized and directed way of doing things (Gamble, 1988).

The most consistent features of the substance of Thatcherism as economic policy are threefold. The first involves an attempt to radically change the structure of ownership in the community: in the 1980s the government 'privatized' nearly half of what had been publicly owned in 1979. Secondly, Thatcherism attempted to change the structure of rewards: it cut the tax bills of the very rich, while also reducing the real value of many welfare benefits, especially those to the unemployed. The expectation behind this change was that increasing the rewards of success would stimulate enterprise beneficial to all. Making unemployment more unattractive economically would encourage the unemployed to take jobs at lower wage rates, thus reducing both unemployment and the overall pressure of wage demands. Finally, Thatcherism withdrew or reduced subsidies to many industries, compelling the closure of many concerns and the more efficient operation of the rest in the face of international competition.

These changes in substance were accompanied by a change in the style of economic policy making. Precisely because Thatcherism involved an attempt to radically alter the substance of policy, it was compelled to break with the consensual and cooperative approach. Many reforms, such as those bearing on trade unions, were imposed upon groups whose cooperation was usually sought in the past. Many policies — such as obliging inefficient manufacturing to reorganize or to close — were pursued in spite of protests from representatives of manufacturing industry.

This break with consensus and cooperation helps explain why, despite its domination of economic policy making in the 1980s, judgements about the Thatcherite solution remain deeply divided. The case for Thatcherism can be summarized under three headings. The first is that, however painful the experience of closing down large parts of manufacturing industry may have been, it was only the recognition of the inevitable, in conditions where British industries simply were not efficient enough to find markets for goods. Secondly, a change to a more centralized and directive style of policy making was necessary because the traditional cooperative approach was responsible, at least in part, for the failed policies of the past. Finally, comparison of Britain with other economies shows that Thatcherism is not unique. Across the world governments are, almost regardless of party, introducing economic reforms resembling the Thatcherite programme. This suggests that Thatcherism in Britain was a necessary adjustment to changing patterns in the world economy, without which Britain would lose even its present modest place in the international economic hierarchy.

The alternative, critical judgement of Thatcherite economics can be summarized under two headings. First, the most distinctive consequence of Thatcherite economic policies has been to eliminate important parts of manufacturing industry, in a world where the manufacture and sale of finished goods is still the characteristic sign of an advanced industrial economy. In other words Thatcherism has only hastened what is sometimes called 'deindustrialization'. Secondly, the shift away from a consensual policy style, combined with a deliberate strategy of increasing the rewards to the rich and enterprising, carries great dangers for social peace and harmony.

The fall of Mrs Thatcher, her replacement by John Major, and the Conservatives' subsequent victory in the 1992 General Election have given the debate about Thatcherite economic policy a new aspect. Mr Major's personal style is very different from that of his predecessor. He is gentler in his language, and less obviously demanding in his advocacy of radical change. One of the major issues in economic policy in the coming years will be the extent to which the Major style also marks a break with the substance of Thatcherism. Early experience suggests that neither in the substance of policy, nor in the emphasis on pushing ahead at the expense of affected interests, has there been any great break. The poll tax excepted, none of the important domestic Thatcherite reforms have been reversed; and important further advances — such as the partial privatisation of British Rail — are intended.

References and Further Reading

Barker, A., *Quangos in Britain* (Macmillan, 1982).

Barnett, C., *The Collapse of British Power* (Eyre Methuen, 1972).

Blank, S., 'Britain: The politics of foreign economic policy. The domestic economy and the problems of pluralistic stagnation', in P. Katzenstein (ed.), *Between Power and Plenty* (Wisconsin University Press, 1979).

Brittan, S., *Steering the Economy* (Penguin, 1971).

Brittan, S., 'The economic contradictions of democracy', *British Journal of Political Science* 129−59 (1975).

Burch, M. and Wood, B., *Public Policy in Britain* (Martin Robertson, 1983).

Coates, D., *The Context of British Politics* (Hutchinson, 1984).

Dyson, K. and Wilks, S. (eds), *Industrial Crisis* (Martin Robertson, 1983).

Finer, S., 'The political power of organised labour', *Government and Opposition*, 391−406 (1973).

Gamble, A., *The Free Economy and the Strong State: The Politics of Thatcherism* (Macmillan, 1988).

Heclo, H. and Wildavsky, A., *The Private Government of Public Money* (Macmillan, 1975).

Moran, M., *The Politics of Banking*, 2nd edn. (Macmillan, 1986).

Pollard, S., *The Wasting of the British Economy* (Croom Helm, 1982).

Riddell, P., *The Thatcher Government* (Martin Robertson, 1983).

Ward, H., 'The anti-nuclear lobby: An unequal struggle?' in D. Marsh (ed.), *Pressure Politics* (Junction Books, 1983).

Wiener, M., *English Culture and the Decline of the Industrial Spirit — 1850−1980* (Cambridge University Press, 1981).

Wright, M., 'Policy community, policy network and comparative industrial policy', *Political Studies*, 593−612 (1988).

25 Welfare Policy

Dennis Kavanagh

Social policy — covering such public financial services as health, education and social services — has been a contentious area since Mrs Thatcher ended the post-war consensus. This is related to different visions about public spending. Labour claims that the government should support the needy through the redistribution of resources gathered through taxation and spent on public services; Conservatives question the amount of such spending: it may be beyond our means and contribute towards a 'dependency' culture. Opinion polls show the public largely supports Labour on this issue. This chapter takes a closer look at social policy, focusing on the four major areas of social security, health, housing and education.

In the course of the twentieth century the role of central and local government in providing welfare for citizens has expanded greatly. Before 1914 the state had started to provide pensions for a limited number of old people, and insurance against ill-health and unemployment. But today the state is the major provider of education, health and social security and plays a considerable role in providing housing. Some 30 per cent of Britain's GDP goes in spending on these services. In 1988−9 the total bill for social security amounted to £48.5 billion, or 32 per cent of public spending, with half of this going on state pensions. Richard Rose (1985, p.369) calculated that nearly 90 per cent of all families receive a state welfare benefit and more than 30 per cent of families rely on public transport, receive a pension, medical treatment or state education: 'Through public employment, pensions, unemployment benefits, and other social security payments, the British Treasury provides incomes for about one third of the population' (1985, p.370).

The traditional 'classic' role of the state in providing defence and maintaining law and order has been gradually overtaken by its role in providing welfare. It has become, according to some, a 'nanny state'. The change in role is reflected in the pattern of state expenditure and public employment. The National Health Service alone has over a million employees, making it the largest employer in Western Europe. Various reasons have prompted this expansion of the welfare role of government.

1. In part it has been a consequence of the country's *economic growth*. Generally, more affluent states spend a great proportion of their national income on welfare.
2. In part it has been stimulated by the growth of *collectivist ideas* and a concern for equality. It is interesting that in the USA, where state provision in health, education and housing is more modest, collectivist ideas are less developed. There

is more private spending on education and insurance welfare for needs in the United States.

3. In part there has been ***demographic pressure***, as numbers of claimants have increased. For example, the number of old age pensioners has more than doubled in the post-war period and today exceeds 10 million. They are heavy users of the hospital system, as well as being recipients of pension payments. There has also been an increase in the numbers unemployed in the past decade: the figure exceeded 3 million in 1982, though reduced to under 2 million by 1990.

4. Salaries and wages for employees in the welfare services account for a large part of the expenditure.

For much of the post-war period there was something of a consensus between the parties on the role of the welfare state. There was also much popular support for it although the Labour and Conservative parties disagreed about details, notably about how to pay for services. On the whole the Conservatives favoured more selectivity in the provision of services, while Labour was insistent that there should be universal provision. The Labour party reacted against the negative memories of means-tested benefits which were common in the inter-war years, but in practice there was little difference when the parties were in government from 1945 until the mid-1970s. Ironically the major criticisms during this period came from supporters of the welfare state — people like Professor Titmuss and Peter Townsend — who argued that provision was inadequate and should be increased.

Richard Titmuss believed the development of the welfare state was 'connected with the demand for one society; for non-discriminatory services for all without distinction and class, income or race; for services and relations which would deepen and enlarge self respect; for services which would manifestly encourage social integration.' Paul Wilding adds that the idea was that 'the rich man and poor man would collect the same pension from the same post office counter and sit next to each other in the same doctor's waiting room' (Wilding, 1990).

When the consensus broke it did so for a number of reasons:

1. The forced reining back of public spending in the wake of the 1976 IMF loan.
2. The erosion of faith in a number of welfare professions and in the idea that government action could ultimately resolve social problems.
3. High levels of inflation in the 1970s and the general decline in the authority of Keynesian economics.
4. The growth of a coherent and well articulated critique from the ***new right*** founded upon, as Wilding observes,

> one vital belief — *private provision is always better:*
> (a) *economically* because it is not damaging to the economy and because it will be more efficient;
> (b) *politically* because it does not make government the creature of particular interests; and
> (c) *socially* because it does not make people dependent and because it offers choice and makes providers accountable to consumers.
>
> Wilding, 1989, p.188

Social Security

The starting point for the modern social security system is contained in the document *Social Insurance and Allied Services* (1942), by William Beveridge. Beveridge wanted to construct a system which would protect people against what he termed 'Want, Disease, Ignorance, Squalor and Idleness'. His report recommended that existing *ad hoc* and means-tested schemes for pensions, unemployment and sickness benefits be consolidated into a universal national insurance scheme. Flat rate benefits would be paid as of right in return for flat rate contributions. In addition, there would be a 'safety net' of means-tested national assistance benefits for those not covered by social insurance. Beveridge also wanted room to be left for personal initiative, to prevent undue reliance on the state.

The main planks of the social security system were contained in a number of legislative acts by the 1945 Labour government. The Family Allowances Act (1945) granted a non-contributory allowance, to be paid to the mother, for each child after the first. In 1946 the National Insurance Act introduced a new scheme of insurance for loss of income arising from unemployment, sickness, retirement and widowhood. In 1948 the National Assistance Act provided supplementary benefit for the groups who were not covered under previous legislation. The same year saw the introduction of the National Health Service; this provided free medical treatment to patients.

In the post-war period spending on social security has doubled as a share of government expenditure: it constitutes the biggest single item of government spending, £50 billion in 1990. This spending covers many services: pensions, family allowances, unemployment and industrial injury benefits, rent rebates and housing benefits and supplementary benefits. There has been a particular increase in the numbers relying on supplementary benefit. In 1986 the numbers reached 5 million, covering large numbers of the unemployed, old age pensioners and single parents. What was originally a 'safety net' for small numbers was now a major source for millions. This had never been envisaged by Beveridge.

Criticisms

Among a number of criticisms of the social security system the following have been frequently voiced:

1. The rising cost which the country arguably can ill afford. Welfare spending is also difficult to control as it is based on entitlement. Between 1990–3 spending will increase by 12.5 per cent, nearly half the increases going to old age pensioners (see Figure 25.1).
2. Many benefits are not concentrated on those in need. This is in part a criticism of the universal nature of many of the benefits. For example, the millionaire receives the same basic state pension as a retired coal miner. In addition there is a poor take-up by many who are entitled to supplementary benefit.
3. Economists of the new right argue that because some benefits are granted too 'easily', they weaken the work ethic and an individual's sense of self reliance.

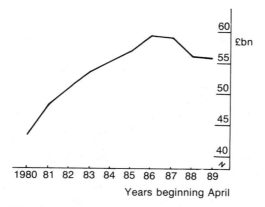

Figure 25.1 *Social security: government expenditure (Source:* The Economist, *4 February 1990)*

Some argue that by making it more difficult to obtain unemployment benefit people would have more incentive to seek and find employment. Ministers sometimes speak of their battle against the culture of 'dependency', i.e. people relying on state handouts rather than their own efforts.

4. The creation of the so-called poverty trap, under which people who increase their earnings may lose various benefits and actually end up poorer.

5. Paradoxically, it is the middle class who benefit proportionately more from some welfare services than the lower paid.

> Professionals, managers and employers receive about 40 per cent more NHS expenditure per ill person than semi and unskilled manual workers . . . In education the top fifth of households in terms of income receive about three times as much public expenditure on education per household as the poorest fifth. They receive five times as much university expenditure.
>
> Wilding, 1990

Since 1979 the Conservatives have taken a number of steps to reduce the burden of welfare expenditure. They have regularly revised downwards the numbers entitled to unemployment benefits, encouraged the private provision of pensions, lengthened the period of disqualification from getting unemployment benefit, refused to uprate some benefits in line with inflation and trimmed back the State Earnings Related Pensions Plan (SERPS). But the government has failed to slow the rise in state spending: the rise in unemployment has been a drain on the public purse and fear of electoral unpopularity has stopped the government from taking radical measures.

The National Health Service

The establishment of the NHS by the 1945 Labour government was one of that government's proudest achievements. Virtually all general medical and dental care was to be provided free from general expenditure. At one time, strange to say, it was anticipated that demand would actually decline as illnesses were cured. In fact demand for the NHS has soared. Among the pressures which make for greater spending on health are the following:

1. The growth in the number of aged people and increase in the life-span of people.
2. Developments in new technology (e.g. heart surgery) and drugs which mean that more illnesses are able to be tackled.
3. The pressures for pay of employees, which account for more than half of spending on the NHS.
4. Some argue that because the service is 'free' — in the sense that there is no relation between the services received and payments made — then there is no restraint on demand.

Much had been written and spoken by the Conservatives when in opposition in the late 1970s about introducing market forces into the NHS. However, once in office the (Labour initiated) Royal Commission on the NHS reported, endorsing a state funded service and roundly rejecting any shift towards increased charges or private insurance. It insisted that by comparison with other health services the NHS was unusually cheap. Opinion polls revealed that the public agreed. The NHS — the jewel in the crown of Attlee's post-war achievements — has clearly won a special place in the hearts of British people.

The Conservatives have boasted about the real increases in pay in health spending which have been achieved since 1979. During the 1980s spending rose by 30 per cent; 23 per cent more in-patients were treated and 16 per cent more than a decade before. A 9 per cent increase has been designated for the period 1990−3 (see Figure 25.2).

Yet much publicity is given to alleged neglect and underfunding: long waiting lists, shortages of staff and beds and dissatisfaction of staff and patients. If one takes account of the growth of the elderly (who are heavy users of the NHS) and new and more expensive technology the NHS requires real increases of at least 1 per cent per annum simply to 'stand still'. The opposition parties argue that even greater

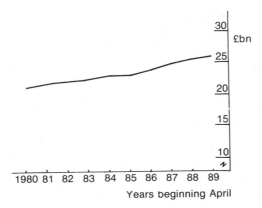

Figure 25.2 *Health: government spending (Source:* The Economist, *3 February 1990)*

levels of spending are required. The Conservatives have tried to encourage more private health care which at present only covers 7 per cent of the population. They argue that 'going private' is a way of relieving pressure on the NHS and increases total national spending on health.

The Labour party objects to private health care on the grounds that something as important as health should not be subject to the demands of the economic market, i.e. ability to pay. It also claims that private provision, like a private education service, leads to unequal treatment: it regards health as a natural right of democratic citizenship whereby everyone should be treated equally, through taxation, to the NHS and, moreover, in a free society people should be able to spend their money as they choose.

'The National Health Service is safe in our hands', said Mrs Thatcher during the 1983 election campaign, suggesting that it would not be the object of radical change. After yet another swingeing election victory, however, in 1987 the NHS moved up Mrs Thatcher's agenda. She had perhaps presaged her intentions during the 1987 election campaign when at a press conference she had defended her personal use of private health facilities because 'I want (to enter hospital) at a time I want and with a doctor I want . . . I exercise my right as a free citizen to spend my own money in my own way'. In January 1988 Mrs Thatcher suddenly announced a 'Prime Ministerial Review' of the NHS which she personally chaired comprising Kenneth Clarke and David Mellor from Health, John Major from the Treasury and Malcolm Rifkind and Peter Walker from the Welsh and Scottish Offices, respectively. The review took far less time than the previous Royal Commission — a form of enquiry which the Prime Minister disliked — and in the following year the White Paper *Working for Patients* was published. The main recommendations were that: hospitals and GPs be given finite budgets out of which patient care could be funded; NHS Hospital Trusts be set up to run larger hospitals independent of the health service administration (the so-called 'opting out' idea); an internal market to be developed whereby services could be bought by one NHS institution from another; the exclusion of local authority representatives from NHS management; and the break-up of the Department of Health into a Policy Board and a Management Executive concerned with day to day running. The Expenditure White Paper of January 1990 envisaged that the reforms would have no discernible effect upon total spending plans apart from £300 million allocated for implementation.

Supporters of the NHS were relieved that the radical ideas of some of the right-wing think tanks — notably the extension of private health insurance — had been turned down but great concern was voiced at the enthronement of management principles; the emergent outlines of privatization of NHS institutions; and the possible enlargement of the two-tier system whereby the rich receive the best treatment while the poor and the old are forced to accept an increasingly impoverished and inefficient service. Labour, under Robin Cook, has pursued an alternative theme of democracy in health care proposing the abolition of regional health authorities, parliamentary sanctioning of appointments to governing health bodies and the fusion of family practitioners' authorities with district health authorities. In addition Labour proposes that pay be linked to the quality of service given and that funding be increased to the point where an adequate service can again be given to the public.

Housing

In the aftermath of the devastation caused by the Second World War, the main housing problem facing the country was slum clearance and simply building more houses. The Labour government began a crash programme and relied heavily on the local authorities. In 1979 the total number of houses built by private enterprise and local authorities has ranged between some 250,000 and 370,000 annually. Since 1979 the figure has fallen as spending on housing has been slashed by more than 50 per cent.

But there has been a difference of emphasis between the parties. For much of the post-war period the Conservatives have been more supportive of building houses for private purchase, while Labour has encouraged public housing, i.e. houses built by local authorities and then rented to tenants. Private home ownership is very much a part of the Conservative ideology. In its 1987 manifesto the party said 'Buying their own home is the first step most people take towards building up capital to hand down to their children and grandchildren. It gives people a stake in society — something to conserve. It is the foundation stone of a capital-owning democracy.' Labour, on the other hand, is more inclined to see housing as a public service.

Britain has one of the highest proportions of houses which are privately owned. In 1951 29 per cent of homes were owner-occupied (compared to 18 per cent owned by local authorities, and 45 per cent rented from a private landlord). By 1987 the respective figures were 64, 26 and 10 per cent. In recent years the housing agenda has moved on a number of fronts.

1. The *extension of the right to buy for council tenants*. Under the Housing Act (1980) the Conservative government gave tenants in England and Wales of local authorities and new towns and non-charitable housing associations the right to buy their houses and flats, at generous discounts. The policy was extended under the Housing and Building Act (1984). At first the Labour party and a number of Labour-controlled authorities resisted this policy and the party was associated with lack of freedom of choice and forms of petty control over tenants. Since the 1983 election Labour has accepted the sales policy and one can now talk of a consensus on it. Since 1979 over a million council tenants have bought their own homes and flats under this legislation and sales are expected to average 120,000 a year until 1992.

2. Both parties, but particularly the Conservatives, are aiming at *a revival of the rented sector*. By the 1960s rented accommodation was in steep decline and in 1987 represented only 8 per cent of all dwellings. Because of the subsidies in mortgage tax relief and for council houses there is less economic incentive to rent. Moreover, rent controls in recent years have made landlords reluctant to rent houses.

3. There is also a growing debate between the parties over housing *subsidies*. Local housing subsidies have been cut by the Conservatives since 1979, while tax relief on mortgage interest payments has remained untouched. Labour and the Alliance parties would reduce such tax relief to the standard rate. At present people with large mortgages can claim tax relief at their top rate (40 per cent).

Why owning your own home could be bad for you and for Britain

Writing in the *Sunday Times* (29 January 1990) columnist Robert Harris summarized some of the arguments against Britain's obsession with owner-occupation: 57 per cent of the population in 1979, 68 per cent in 1990 and an anticipated 75 per cent by the year 2000.

1. ***Employment mobility***. People in rented accommodation are readier to move to fill vital skill shortages in other regions than those with their own homes; people living in the north are virtually excluded by the cost of housing from moving into the south east. The Centre for Economic Policy Research calculates that this 'mobility trap' has pushed up British wage levels by 4 per cent in recent years. US manual workers are eighteen times more likely to move to another region than their British equivalents.
2. Most of ***Britain's advanced competitors*** have a lower percentage of home-owners: 40 per cent in West Germany, 52 per cent in France, 59 per cent in Italy.
3. ***Britain's housing wealth*** represents a colossal £1,000 billion. Investment which could be fed into the economy is being assiduously ploughed by Britons into their own homes.
4. The ***inflationary credit boom in 1988–9*** was caused by low interest rates which in turn encouraged many home owners to borrow against the soaring values of their houses. 'Millions were in the happy position of knowing that their homes were earning more each week than they were. Small wonder that the nation went on an eighteen month spending spree.' Entry into the European Monetary System will cause problems for the housing market because of the fear that the reductions in interest rates which this is likely to entail would almost certainly fuel another spending boom. To make matters worse the Treasury actually encourages all this by annually giving a subsidy to owner occupiers of £7 billion in the form of mortgage tax relief.

Harris concluded: 'In the name of having the "freedom" to buy a home many do not feel "free" at all but, rather, compelled to take out a mortgage beyond their real means. We would probably all be happier — and certainly as a nation wealthier — if we would shed this obsession with owning our own homes.'

4. As part of their policy of by-passing or weakening local authorities over housing, the Conservatives legislated in 1988 to allow tenants to opt out of local authority control and form their own tenant cooperatives.

Patterns of housing tenure seem to have political consequences. Working-class council tenants divide more than 2 to 1 for Labour, whereas working-class home-owners divide 2 to 1 to the Conservative party. With some two-thirds of the electorate now either owning or purchasing their own homes, this is in theory an advantage for the Conservative party.

Education

For the first twenty years or so after 1945 there was a broad agreement between the parties about education. The framework was laid down by the Butler Education

Act of 1944. This established a tripartite system of secondary education, in which pupils at the age of eleven went to grammar or secondary modern or technical schools. Control of the running of schools was left to local authorities and the churches.

However, from the 1960s the agreement collapsed as Labour advocated comprehensive secondary education. The arguments against academic selection for entry to grammar schools were, first, that it was unfair to select at the age of eleven and too many people were wrongly allocated anyway; secondly, because the division into grammar and secondary modern schools often correlated with social class (i.e. children from middle-class homes went to the former, those from working-class homes to the latter) it was thought to be unequal. In 1965 the Labour government asked local authorities to submit schemes to end selection and introduce comprehensive education. When the Conservatives came to office in 1970 they rescinded that instruction. Labour reintroduced it in 1974 and the Conservatives rescinded it again in 1979. Under the 1976 Education Act Labour required local education authorities to submit comprehensive proposals (seven had refused). Secondary education is a classic case of adversary politics in action. Central government policies have varied, with changes in party control in Westminster. In fact, comprehensives have almost become the norm and over 90 per cent of secondary schoolchildren are educated in them.

As with other areas of the welfare service some of the divisions between parties are to do with the debate over resources. For example, although the level of real expenditure in education has not altered dramatically since 1979 (see Figure 25.3), Conservatives can boast of a sharp improvement in pupil—teacher ratios and an increase in spending per child over this period. In fact, both figures are largely a consequence of the reduction (17 per cent) in children of school age. There were similar improvements under the 1974–9 Labour government.

Under the Conservative government there has been a sustained attack on the role of local authorities in education. Consider the following:

1. The abolition of the Burnham pay bargaining machinery, on which representatives of the local authorities sat.

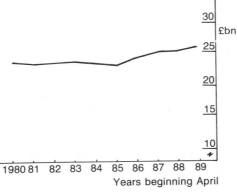

Figure 25.3 *Education and science: government expenditure (Source: The Economist, 4 February 1990)*

2. The ending of local authority control of polytechnics and the creation of a new Polytechnics and Colleges Funding Council.
3. The expansion of the assisted-places scheme (for pupils to attend independent schools) from 25,000 to 35,000. In addition, a scheme of City Technology Colleges has been set up in inner cities. Both schemes are designed to draw off talented children from state schools and operate outside the local authorities.
4. In the Education Act (1988) parents and governors of state schools may, in a ballot, opt for independent status and be freed from local authority control.
5. The government also plans to introduce a national core curriculum, to be followed by all state schools, with national tests for children starting at age seven.
6. There has been a major expansion of training programmes in further education, under the control of the Training Commission (later renamed the Training Agency).

The above steps amount to a major reform of the education system. The role of the local authorities has been greatly reduced. At all levels education is encouraged to be more vocational and job-related. In the past Conservatives have complained of schools being used for 'social engineering': particularly of the 'anti-racism', 'anti-sexism' and 'peace' courses being promoted by left-wing authorities. Tory radicals would like to go much further and virtually dismantle state education. They would like parents to be given education vouchers which they can redeem at the school of their choice.

Labour's view

Labour still adheres to comprehensive education, a battle that has been largely won. By 1987 there were barely a hundred local authority grammar schools still in existence. In office the party is pledged to end some of the Tory party's initiatives; it will end the charitable status of fee-paying private schools and end the Assisted Places Scheme. But it does not reject the idea of a core curriculum and testing. Interestingly, the Labour Prime Minister James Callaghan floated some of these ideas in his 1976 speech at Ruskin College which was supposed to launch a debate on education. In the following decade it is clear that the Conservatives managed to make most of the running on the issues of standards and parental choice.

Changes in the 1980s, however, have not produced an educational system which meets with the approval of Mr Eric Bolton, the HMI senior chief inspector of schools at the DES. In February 1990 he produced a widely publicized report. While 70 per cent of state schools were deemed to offer a reasonable service or better, 30 per cent were judged not to meet basic requirements: hundreds of thousands of pupils were said to be 'getting a raw deal'. The report concluded that 'The overarching picture must not hide the fact that there are serious problems of underachievement; of poor teaching and inadequate provision'. Serious weaknesses were identified in the teaching of English, mathematics, science, modern languages and technology. At Question Time on 6 February 1990, Mrs Thatcher described it as 'a good report which highlighted things which need to be done . . . the educational service is in far better shape than it has been before'. This view did not meet with approval even from some of her own supporters: The *Sunday Times* on 11 February 1990 described the government's record in education as a 'disgrace'.

Welfare is likely to be a major issue in British politics in the next few years. The combination of rising costs of welfare services and a Conservative government determined to restrain the growth of public spending is one pressure. Another is the determination of some influential forces in the Conservative party to reduce the role of the state as provider of such services.

More privatization of pensions, private health insurance, greater use of charges for services, and of vouchers, e.g. in education, are likely to be encouraged. Many such Conservatives believe that the present arrangements are a drain on the 'productive' economy; a burden on the taxpayer and are therefore a disincentive to effort; a limit on personal choice; if people kept more of their money, rather than pay it in taxes, they could finance their pensions, health care and their children's education.

But criticisms do not come only from the right. Many on the left claim that some services (e.g. higher education and commuter services) and subsidies (e.g. tax relief on private pensions and mortgage interest) help the better-off. Others, like Wilding, are insistent that the achievements of the welfare state should not be overlooked.

References and Further Reading

Friedman, M. and Friedman, R., *Free to Choose* (Penguin, 1980).

George, V. and Wilding, P., *Ideology and Social Welfare* (Routledge & Kegan Paul, 1987).

Hadley, R. and Hatch, S., *Social Welfare and the Failure of the State* (Allen & Unwin, 1981).

Johnson, N. *Reconstructing the Welfare State: A Decade of Change, 1980–1990* (Harvester Wheatsheaf, 1990).

Lee, G., 'The politics of housing', in B. Jones, *Political Issues in Britain Today* (Manchester University Press, 1989).

Loney, M., *The Politics of Greed* (Pluto, 1986).

Mishra, R., *The Welfare State in Crisis* (Harvester Wheatsheaf, 1984).

Moon, G. and Kendal, I., 'The NHS review', *Talking Politics*, (Winter 1989–90).

Robins, L., 'Issues and developments in education', in B. Jones, *Political Issues in Britain Today* (Manchester University Press, 1989).

Rose, R., *Politics in England* (Faber and Faber, 1985).

Seldon, A., *Whither the Welfare State* (Institute of Economic Affairs, 1981).

Wilding, P. (ed.), *In Defence of the Welfare State* (Manchester University Press, 1987).

Wilding, P., 'The Debate about the welfare state', in B. Jones, *Political Issues in Britain Today* (Manchester University Press, 1989).

Wilding, P., 'Equality', *Talking Politics* (Winter 1989–90).

26 Northern Ireland

Anthony Seldon

This chapter looks at the political conflict in Northern Ireland, focusing first on a chronological analysis of the origins and development of the conflict, and then turning to possible solutions.

The Conflict

Origins

The origins of the Northern Ireland conflict lie deep in the long history of conflict between Britain and Ireland since the late middle ages (for chronology see box at the end of this chapter). From the twelfth until the early twentieth century Ireland was an element within the British state. Its constitutional position developed from that of a colony to full theoretical equality with the other components of the United Kingdom, secured by the Act of Union in 1800. But Irish participation in the British state was at best reluctant and in 1919—21 the larger part of Ireland, the south and west, won effective independence by force. Northern Ireland was a product of Irish independence. A substantial fraction of the population in Ulster, the north eastern province of the island, struggled to preserve the Union with Britain and in 1920 secured partition: six of Ireland's thirty-two counties were detached from the rest, remaining within the United Kingdom to form the new political unit of Northern Ireland (see Figure 26.1). Its population was largely Protestant, though with a substantial Catholic minority — around one-third.

The nature of the Anglo—Irish conflict developed considerably in the course of eight centuries. It began as a conflict between a colony and its imperial masters. During the sixteenth and seventeenth centuries religious differences came to overlay the earlier but persistent colonial struggle and the Reformation brought about the creation of a British Protestant state, while the bulk of the Irish population remained Catholic. Religion became the basis of political allegiance and within Ireland Britain established the ascendancy of a small Protestant minority, holding a monopoly of land and political power, with the Catholic population dispossessed of both. Finally, in the late eighteenth and nineteenth centuries the rise of European nationalisms superimposed a third layer of conflict, or refashioned the other two: a largely Catholic Irish nationalism developed, aiming at the creation of an independent Irish state, or at the very least, a greater measure of autonomy for Ireland within the United Kingdom. The Protestant Irish were largely alienated from the nationalist movement and became strong defenders of the Union; their continued dominance in Ireland depended on maintaining the link with Britain.

Scale:
0 20 40 60 80 Kilometres
0 10 20 30 40 50 Miles

COLERAINE
Londonderry
ULSTER
DERRY
ANTRIM
DONEGAL
Strabane
TYRONE
Lough Neagh
Belfast
Omagh
Lisburn
DONEGAL BAY
FERMANAGH
MONAGHAN
ARMAGH
DOWN
Armagh
Crossmaglen
SLIGO
LEITRIM
CAVAN
LOUTH
MAYO
ROSCOMMON
LONGFORD
IRISH SEA
CONNAUGHT
MEATH
WESTMEATH
GALWAY
OFFALY
Dublin
DUBLIN
KILDARE
Galway
LAOIS
WICKLOW
GALWAY BAY
CLARE
LEINSTER
CARLOW
KILKENNY
TIPPERARY
WEXFORD
LIMERICK
MUNSTER
WATERFORD
KERRY
CORK
Cork

Legend:
▦ Northern Ireland
•••••••••• Province borders
–·–·–·– Border between Northern Ireland and the Republic of Ireland
———— County boundaries
■ Largest cities

Figure 26.1 *The four ancient provinces and the thirty-two counties of Ireland; the nine counties of Ulster and the six counties of Northern Ireland (Source: McCullagh and O'Dowd, 1986)*

Ulster was the area of greatest Protestant strength in Ireland from the late seventeenth century, when the British had fostered Protestant emigration from the mainland, particularly from Scotland. The north east thereby acquired, and has retained, a religious and political identity quite distinct from that of the rest of Ireland. Opposition to the twin phenomena of Catholicism and Irish nationalism was strongest and most militant there and Ulster Protestants were prepared to defend the Union by force. The background to partition in 1920 was the formation of a powerful Protestant political and military movement demanding separation of Ulster from the rest of Ireland, which for many Nationalists helped to legitimize the use of force against the British in the south and west.

Views on partition

The historical argument as to how and why partition took place in 1920 is crucial to understanding the present-day conflict in Northern Ireland. There have been two principal schools of thought. The first, defended mainly by hardline Nationalists in Ulster itself, argues that partition was something artificial, imposed and sustained in Ireland by the British with the use of force. Through partition, in this view, Britain sought to retain a foothold on Irish soil after losing the war of independence 1919—21; its motives were basically imperial, viewing Ireland as of potential military significance. According to hardline Nationalists, Protestant—Catholic divisions in Ireland as a whole were not the reason for partition, but merely an excuse for it; similarly, the religious differences within Northern Ireland itself are held to have been fostered and manipulated by Britain to justify its continued presence.

Most British commentators and moderate Nationalists in both parts of Ireland have come to hold a very different view of the reasons for partition. A new nationalism has emerged in the Republic over the last twenty years, repudiating the hardline old nationalism. This body of opinion argues that partition was the product of deep divisions between the Catholic and Protestant communities in Ireland, rather than the outcome of outside British intervention deliberately fostering Irish quarrels; most British and Irish commentators would now say that the Irish partitioned Ireland, not the British. This view challenges whether Britain had any strategic or other reasons to want a foothold in Ireland or the means to bring about and to sustain partition in the absence of real divisions within Ireland. Ultimately the reasons for partition and for the continued violence in Northern Ireland are held to lie in the failure of the Catholic and Protestant communities to appreciate and to respect each other's political feelings and traditions. It is consistent with this viewpoint to see British policy as having contributed significantly to the problem; similarly, the policies of the Republic and of Nationalist politicians may be open to censure. But the essence of the problem is held to be one of internal conflict.

These differing views as to the origins of partition lie at the root of hardline Nationalist and British/moderate Nationalist disagreements as to the reasons for the present-day troubles in Northern Ireland, as well as shaping profoundly the debate about solutions (or their absence). As often with deeply entrenched and opposed interpretations of events, the dispute is rooted in values rather than evidence and is not easily resolved by argument.

Stormont rule 1920−72

Strangely, perhaps, one of the few areas where one can find some common ground between the two schools is in discussion of the period of Unionist government in Ulster, 1920−72: the record of that government is almost universally condemned. When partition took place in 1920 Britain devolved power for local Ulster government from Westminster to a regional Parliament at Stormont in Belfast. The Stormont administration was dominated throughout its fifty-year existence by the Unionist party representing the Protestant population, Catholics being wholly excluded from power. In lower tiers of government Catholic influence was minimized by gerrymandering and narrow franchises; official discrimination against Catholics was widely practised.

Westminster took little interest in the condition of Northern Ireland until the 1960s when a civil rights movement developed among Ulster Catholics. Stormont then found itself under pressure internally and from London to liberalize and began to do so, slowly. This resulted in much friction within the Unionist party. Almost all subsequent

Note: The figures show the percentage of the population in each district which is Catholic. The areas shaded are those districts in which Catholics represent over half the population

Figure 26.2 *Roman Catholics as a percentage of the population in the Republic of Ireland (Source: McCullagh and O'Dowd, 1986)*

commentators have agreed that the pace was too slow and that Stormont had become too discredited in Catholic eyes to reform itself effectively in any case.

Alongside the emphasis on the depth of Catholic grievances there is some recognition in the literature that the Protestant community felt itself threatened by the large Catholic minority within Ulster, much of it openly hostile to the Northern Irish state, and in many ways Protestant politics reflected not simply their position as an insecure majority in the north but also their minority status in the island as a whole (Figure 26.2). But whatever the reasons for the discriminatory character of the Stormont regime, its ultimate impact was to create a situation in Ulster that greatly increased Unionist fears and insecurities.

Governmental Response to the conflict since 1969

The single greatest consequence of the outbreak of the troubles has been the ending of Northern Ireland's political isolation and the enforced involvement of London in governing the province. In many ways London's involvement has been reluctant. Westminster devolved power to Northern Ireland in 1920 largely because Irish politics were messy and unpleasant in the eyes of many British politicians; little has changed. More than that, the policy of successive British governments since the 1970s has been that only internal solutions have any chance of achieving long-term peace and stability in Northern Ireland: London has officially seen its role as one of creating the conditions in which local Ulster politicians can resume a large measure of self-government. There has been a fear that long-term government from London may undermine the capacity or the willingness of local politicians to play a constructive part, leaving the initiative to the paramilitaries. Many commentators have perceived just such a trend as the conflict has run on.

At Westminster itself the major parties have usually pursued agreed 'bipartisan' policies towards Northern Ireland, despite tension between them at particular points, notably 1970–2. The Northern Ireland issue does not fit straightforwardly into the ordinary categories of British party politics. None of the British parties from the mainland contest seats in the province and thus they have no local Ulster electorate to worry about. Nor is the British public on the mainland deeply moved by the Ulster question; aside from moments of crisis, events in Northern Ireland have little political impact on the mainland and few votes are to be won or lost on Ulster policy. Ministerial posts in Ulster carry little weight or prestige within government, one Secretary of State for Northern Ireland referring to his own department as 'the dustbin of British politics'.

Yet despite the absence of division on party lines, there have been disagreements among British policy makers concerned with Northern Ireland, less on questions of principle than on how best to manage and contain the crisis. There have been *activists* and *passivists* in London: the activists have sought by direct initiative to bring the two communities together in Northern Ireland and to strengthen British relations with the Republic; the passivists have seen direct initiatives as frequently counterproductive and destabilizing, seeking quieter ways of encouraging constitutional politics while minimizing the level of violence. The passivists perhaps have tended to be the more pessimistic, perceiving little prospect of an internal settlement or much value in the closer involvement of Dublin. But one should not over-emphasize the distinction: in practice neither school of thought has hoped to do more than check the deterioration in the province and containment has been the deepest aim of British policy.

In a wider context British governments have made extensive diplomatic responses to the troubles and in particular since the early 1970s the improvement of relations with the Irish Republic has been a major goal of policy, successfully pursued, despite periodic crises and setbacks. The root of this rapprochement lies in changed attitudes within the Republic — the virtual eclipse in mainstream politics of the old nationalism, with its emphasis on unification as the principal and immediate aim of the Republic's diplomacy with Britain. Both major parties in the south of Ireland have come to align themselves with the new nationalism, perceiving that unification without the consent of the Ulster Protestants would be a physical and political disaster for the Republic and that the immediate requirement is an internal settlement in Ulster. In practice, like Britain, the Republic has come to see its role in the short-term as one of containment; unification has become a policy for the long-term only. From this perception a fertile Anglo—Irish diplomacy has developed. In turn closer relations with Dublin have greatly helped Britain in selling its Ulster policy on the international scene, particularly in the USA.

1969—72

The beginnings of London's forced intervention in Northern Ireland politics came in the summer of 1969. In the face of serious rioting in both Belfast and Londonderry the Stormont government requested military help to maintain public order. The army came under the control of London and a cabinet decision was required before its deployment could take place. The Labour government of the day agreed the request, but with foreboding. It seems that British withdrawal was discussed among ministers closely involved in the crisis, though the option was quickly dismissed.

At the same time as sending in the troops, London reaffirmed Britain's long-standing 'constitutional guarantee' to Northern Ireland: that there would be no change in the constitutional status of the province unless the majority of the population wished it. The guarantee remains in place to the present day.

From summer 1969 until March 1972 London worked with the Stormont administration to stabilize the situation. Stormont came under significant pressure to reform in order to meet Catholic grievances and significant changes were made. London's influence in Belfast was strong: the Northern Ireland government was dependent on military aid and received a considerable subsidy from the British Exchequer; behind these levers of influence the British government also had the power (through Parliament) to suspend Stormont altogether and take direct control of the province. But for as long as possible London sought to keep at arms' length, trying to sustain the existing devolved regime and to reform it from within, despite its unacceptability to the Catholic population and increasing ineffectiveness in security policy. Stormont was responsible for the police in Northern Ireland and there was consequently an unhelpful division of responsibility for security between London and Belfast.

During 1970—1 these factors contributed to a significant rise in the level of political violence. It seems to have been at this stage that extreme Republican politics became militarized and the IRA revived as a terrorist force. Protestant paramilitary organizations emerged in response. Stormont persuaded London to introduce internment without trial in August 1971 in a desperate atttempt to contain the violence, but the measure was dramatically counterproductive: over the following eighteen months the disturbances massively increased. The level of casualties (military and civilian) rose from twenty-five in 1970 to 174 in 1971, and then climbed to 467 in 1972 — the single worst year of the troubles to date. London reacted by abandoning the attempt to sustain Stormont, which was suspended in March 1972. Involvement could no longer be kept at arms' length.

Direct rule after 1972

Stormont was replaced by 'direct rule' from London. A Secretary of State for Northern Ireland was appointed in the British Cabinet, heading a newly created Northern Ireland Office with branches in London and Belfast. The new Department took over not only the functions of Stormont but much of the political role of local government at lower levels.

Direct rule was intended to be a temporary expedient. Ministers announced that they intended to devolve power back to Northern Ireland as soon as practicable and over the course of 1972−3 a political and diplomatic strategy was framed to achieve this by the first Northern Ireland Secretary, William Whitelaw. The new devolved government would be on *power sharing* lines, involving representatives of both communities in the formation of a joint executive, both Unionist and Nationalist, responsible to an assembly elected by proportional representation — effectively a permanent and enforced coalition between the two communities. At the same time there would be recognition of an 'Irish dimension' of the problem by the creation of a new 'Council of Ireland', made up of delegates from both north and south, through which the Belfast and Dublin governments might consult on matters of common interest.

In June 1973 the new assembly was elected. Over the summer and autumn negotiations went ahead to form an executive and to finalize political arrangements with the Republic, which culminated in the Sunningdale Agreement of December 1973. The power-sharing executive took office under a Unionist Prime Minister and with a Nationalist Deputy in January 1974. This was the high point and greatest achievement of British activism in Ulster, but it proved a crushing disappointment. From the first the new executive's Unionist members found themselves under political threat within their own community; the course of the troubles since 1969, and the destruction of Stormont particularly, had traumatized and radicalized Unionist politics to such a degree that sharing power even with moderate and constitutional Nationalist politicians was difficult. But the creation of the Council of Ireland, proposed under Sunningdale, though not implemented immediately, proved a disastrous additional burden to the Unionist leaders. The 'Irish dimension' was the price of Catholic participation in the new government — the Nationalists would not have agreed to take office without it — but it helped to destroy the new government. Unionist supporters of power sharing were all but eliminated at the British General Election of February 1974 and were eventually forced into resignation in May 1974 by a general strike organized by anti-power sharing Unionists among whom paramilitaries were prominent. The executive collapsed.

Passivists in the ascendancy after 1984

The destruction of power sharing produced little visible change in British policy. Devolution on power-sharing lines still remained the goal. But the disappointments of 1974 helped to push the passivists into ascendancy in the making of British policy in Northern Ireland and high level interest in London shifted away from Ulster. Expectations were low. Though attempts were made to keep the politicians talking, through a Constitutional Convention in 1975−6 and a devolution plan in 1977, little political progress was made and direct rule began to assume a permanent look. Political violence began to fall in 1977 and it became possible to reduce the army presence and to restore the strengthened and reformed police force to primacy in maintaining order. Internment was phased out. New and tougher anti-terrorist powers were introduced by the Prevention of Terrorism Act 1974, and in the later 1970s there were clear signs that the IRA was on the defensive. Critics of government policy were claiming at this stage that security was the government's only real concern and that political initiatives were merely cosmetic; it seems that there was some hope among Ministers and their military advisers that the IRA was losing the capacity to sustain its terror campaign.

If such hopes were entertained, they proved illusory. In 1981 hunger strikes in Belfast's Maze prison by Nationalist prisoners, mainly IRA, produced an increase in violence and significant political gains for the IRA's political wing, Sinn Fein. Ten hunger strikers died, one of whom, Bobby Sands, had been elected to Westminster at a by-election. It became plain that the IRA was far from beaten and that it was capable of gaining new ground within the Catholic community, as well as winning sympathy, to a lesser extent, in the Republic.

The hunger strikes of 1981 produced a renewed phase of activism in British policy and a revival of interest by London in Ulster policy. A local initiative in 1982 ('rolling devolution') was boycotted by the major Unionist and Nationalist parties, but London's priority lay with a revival of the 'Irish dimension' rather than the long-standing commitment to power sharing. Circumstances in the Republic made a diplomatic initiative hopeful at this point, while an internal settlement was plainly out of reach: both major parties in the south were anxious to head off the rise of Sinn Fein and to do what they could to prop up the moderate Nationalist party in the north, the Social Democratic and Labour Party (SDLP).

Hillsborough Agreement, November 1985

The outcome, after lengthy negotiations, was the Hillsborough Agreement of November 1985. The Agreement took the form of an international treaty between Britain and Ireland, giving the Republic a consultative role in the running of Northern Ireland and reaffirming that the province would remain a part of the UK as long as the majority of its population wished it. The British commitment to power sharing was also reaffirmed. The Republic made clear that it intended to use the new machinery to pressure Britain on a whole range of issues affecting the minority in the north.

The apparent impact of the Agreement since 1985 has been to diminish further the chances of an internal settlement. Although the political rise of Sinn Fein was checked and the SDLP strengthened by the involvement of the Republic, the Protestant reaction to the Agreement has been bitter and wholly negative. It is true that neither Protestant policians nor paramilitaries have been able to dislodge the Agreement, as they were able to overturn the power-sharing executive in 1974, but recognition of their impotence has not brought Unionist leaders to the conference table. Nor has the Agreement achieved any visible improvement in the level of violence. Finally, Anglo—Irish diplomacy since 1985 has been marked by considerable conflict, with continuing arguments about the impartiality of the administration of justice in Northern Ireland, extradition of terrorist suspects from the Republic and incidents arising from the operation of the security forces. Critics of British policy since 1985 repeat the charges made in the late 1970s: that London has returned to a passive stance. Direct rule is likely to continue for the indefinite future.

McCullagh and O'Dowd provide, in Table 26.1, a useful distinction between 'negotiable' issues on which the major players in the conflict are prepared to talk and those 'non-negotiable', on which there is a complete stalemate.

Possible Solutions

Many suggestions have been made over the years as to how to 'solve' the Ulster problem (see Figure 26.3). Solutions take their shape, first of all, from the proposer's perception of the problem to be solved. But solutions depend also upon the proposer's perception of a satisfactory outcome: for some the Ulster problem would be solved if the violence stopped, but for others far more would be required.

Unification

The old nationalism, favoured still by hardliners in the north but out of favour among politicians in the south, has the simplest and most confident answer: it claims that immediate unification and British withdrawal are the solution to the Northern Ireland problem. Partition was unnatural, the product of a lingering British colonialism towards Ireland; continuing divisions between Catholic and Protestant in the north are merely the **result** of partition — a deliberate creation of British policy in fact — and would disappear if the British presence were to be removed.

But unification faces the counter-argument that Protestant opposition to the ending of partition is profound and not likely to be ended by British withdrawal. Many in Britain and in the Republic argue that a civil war would result from an attempt to unify Ireland against the will of the Ulster Protestants, with the Protestants likely to seek independence for Ulster — reducing the size of the territory, perhaps, and seeking somehow to purge it of at least a part of its Catholic population. The Republic would not be able to prevent a terrible escalation of violence from present levels. Ulster would be destabilized, and perhaps also the Republic.

The new nationalism now dominant in the Republic has created considerable

Table 26.1 *Positions of the major political forces in Northern Ireland*

Non-negotiable issues

Constitutional Unionists*	British Government	Constitutional Nationalists†	Republicans‡
1. British sovereignty	1. British sovereignty	1. Recognition of Irish dimension in Northern Ireland	1. Irish sovereignty: a unitary Irish State
2. No institutionalized political or administrative links with the Republic of Ireland	2. Self-determination for the NI majority	2. Need for institutionalized links between NI and the Republic of Ireland	2. British withdrawal from NI
3. Protestant self-determination	3. Suppression of the IRA	3. Need for partnership/power-sharing in NI	
4. Suppression of Sinn Fein and the IRA			
5. No power-sharing as of right in NI			

Negotiable issues

Constitutional Unionists*	British Government	Constitutional Nationalists†	Republicans‡
1. Cooperation with the Republic on matters of mutual interest	1. Institutionalized links and cooperation with the Republic	1. Unionist position within a united Ireland	1. Position of Unionists within a united Ireland
2. Expanded consultative role for Constitutional Nationalists within a devolved government in NI	2. The forms of devolution in NI	2. Reforms of security	2. Timing of British withdrawal
3. Greater recognition of Nationalists' cultural identity within NI		3. The forms of partnership administration for NI	

Notes: *Represented by the main Unionist parties; the Protestant paramilitaries share the general position of Constitutional Unionism, although the Ulster Defence Association (UDA) has mooted the possibility of an independent Northern Ireland.
†The Irish Government and the Social Democratic and Labour Party (SDLP).
‡Sinn Fein and the IRA.

Source: McCulloch and O'Dowd, 1986

'Stormont' Parliament*		Direct Rule from Westminster					
Unionist rule	Some reforms	Sunningdale	Convention	Anglo–Irish dialogue	Rolling devolution	New Ireland forum	Anglo–Irish treaty
1922–68	*1968–72*	*1973–4*	*1975*	*1980*	*1982*	*1984*	*1985*
Majority rule	Majority rule	Power-sharing executive	Elected consultative Assembly	Inter-governmental discussions aimed at by-passing the deadlock	Elected Assembly	Constitutional Nationalist Assembly including SDLP and political parties in the Republic of Ireland	Established a consultative inter-governmental Conference with Secretariat in Belfast to deal on a regular basis with: — political, legal and security matters — promotion of cross-border cooperation
One-party government	One-party government	Council of Ireland	Convention Report favoured majority rule with committee role for Constitutional Nationalists	Review of the totality of relations within these islands	Power to be gradually devolved in proportion to degree of cross-party cooperation	Report favoured Unitary State Option	Joint declaration by both governments that any change in NI status will require majority consent
	Administrative reforms Local government reforms Replacement of 'B' Specials by the Ulster Defence Regiment	Initiative defeated by Loyalist General Strike, May 1974	Report shelved by British government	Joint studies on possible new institutional structures, citizenship rights, security matters, economic cooperation and measures to encourage mutual understanding	Nationalist and Republican boycott	Outlined Federal State and Joint Authority Options	
						All options rejected by British government	Boycotted by Unionists and rejected by Sinn Fein
1921–68	1968–72	1973–4	1975	1980	1982	1984	1985

*The 'Stormont' Parliament was suspended on 24 March 1972, and the Westminster government assumed direct responsibility for Northern Ireland

Figure 26.3   *Some of the attempts to solve the Northern Ireland problem (Source: McCullagh and O'Dowd, 1986)*

common ground between London and Dublin as to Ulster's immediate needs: both sides perceive an internal settlement between the two communities as essential to progress and argue that consent is the only means of arriving at such a settlement; force will achieve nothing. Yet unification remains the genuine long-term goal of most of the new nationalists, north and south; part of the aim of the new nationalism is to engineer Protestant consent to Irish unity by demonstrating that the Nationalist is not insensitive to the Protestant Unionist viewpoint. Here there is a real contrast with British policy makers, whose goal in promoting an internal settlement has been to engineer Catholic consent to the status quo, with a view to ending the violence — an altogether less ambitious 'solution'. (One must note, however, that the British Labour Party is at present committed to the idea of unification by consent and proposes, if returned to office, to seek ways of persuading Protestant opinion to accept an end to partition.)

Power sharing

Power sharing remains the favoured model for an internal settlement in both London and Dublin, and also among moderate Nationalists in Ulster itself. It has no significant Protestant support; Unionist politicians have not forgotten the events of 1974.

Unionist solutions

Among Unionists a different range of solutions is canvassed. On the extreme fringes, some favour outright independence for Ulster, believing the British to be over-anxious to appease Dublin and the Catholic minority, possibly as a prelude to enforced unification. But a revolt from Britain has few friends in Unionist Ulster: the violence involved and the effects upon the economy of severing the British link would probably be devastating. Most Protestants in any case genuinely wish to remain British though independence may well be their second preference in the event of British withdrawal.

Many Unionists favour a return to a Stormont-type devolved government, without power sharing, often claiming also that a tougher security policy could end the violence. Such an approach has been rejected repeatedly by successive British governments through their adherence to power sharing, on the grounds that the Catholic community must be involved in the process of governing Ulster if peace is to be achieved. On the security issue, Britain has stated openly that no level of military effort can defeat the IRA: there is no 'military solution' available.

Finally, some Unionists urge full integration of Ulster within the United Kingdom — the elimination of a regional administration in Northern Ireland and of the separation between party politics in Ulster and the mainland. But again successive British governments have rejected the proposal, explicitly recognizing that Ulster differs from the rest of the United Kingdom in the existence of the 'Irish dimension'. Much Unionist opposition to the Hillsborough Agreement derives precisely from a denial of this idea of Ulster's distinctiveness, fearing that it represents the first step towards its expulsion from the Union.

Ireland: A
Chronology of
Key Events

Origins of the conflict

1170 Henry II of England begins conquest of Ireland

1542 Henry VIII proclaimed King of Ireland. Ulster remains Gaelic

1603 Ulster now comes under firm English governmental control. Gaelic order vanquished and settlement of Ulster by 175,000 mostly Scots Presbyterians begins

1641 Catholic revolt involving massacre of Ulster Protestants (Portadown). Cromwellian suppression follows (1649–50)

1688 James II deposed by William and Mary ('Glorious Revolution'), but James still recognized as King by Catholic Ireland

1689 *Seige of Londonderry* Protestants by forces of James II

1690 *James defeated at the Battle of the Boyne:* Protestant ascendancy now assured

1782 Irish Parliament set up in Dublin under Henry Gratton, inspired by American Revolution

1790s *Birth of Irish republicanism — Wolfe Tone*, inspired by French Revolution — attempt at French revolutionary intervention

1798 Insurrection of Tone's 'United Irishmen' suppressed

1801 *Act of Union:* Dublin Parliament disappears and Ireland becomes an integral part of the UK

1820s *Daniel O'Connell's* Catholic Association succeeds in achieving Catholic emanicipation in 1829 but fails in the 1830s and 1840s to force *Repeal* of the Act of Union. O'Connell father of Constitutional–Nationalism

1845–8 Famine, and Young Ireland Movement: violent rising in 1848 suppressed

1860s *Fenian movement* (Irish Republican Brotherhood) gathers momentum and develops a strategy of separatism, republicanism and violence. 1867 insurrection fails

1870s Irish party in Westminster captured and transformed by *Charles Stewart Parnell* into an organized, disciplined and popularly based political party

1886 Gladstone converted to Parnell's policy of Home Rule for Ireland within the Empire and subject to the Westminster Parliament introduces *First Home Rule Bill*. Defeated in the House of Commons following Liberal defections led by Joseph Chamberlain.

1893 *Second Home Rule Bill* passes House of Commons but defeated in the Lords. Gladstone concludes Home Rule is not possible while the House of Lords' powers remain unaltered

1905 *Sinn Fein party* founded by Arthur Griffiths and rapidly captured by the IRB (Fenians)

1910 Constitutional crisis following the House of Lords rejection of Lloyd George's 'People's Budget' leads to the return of a Liberal government *dependent* for its Parliamentary majority on Irish Nationalists

1911 *Parliament Act:* House of Lords veto replaced by delaying powers

1912 *Liberals introduce Third Home Rule Bill*, which provokes militant reaction by Ulster and Irish Unionists: *'Home Rule is Rome Rule'; 'Ulster Will Fight'*

1912–14 Ireland dividing into armed militias for and against Home Rule

1914 War with Germany. *Home Rule Bill* placed on The Statute Book but not to be implemented until the conclusion of war and then not without further debate

1916 *Dublin Easter Rising.* Fifteen leaders executed. Sinn Fein now overtakes the Nationalist party as the voice of 'Catholic' Ireland

1918 *Sinn Fein wins* a majority of seats at The General Election and in 1919 sets up the First Dáil as an alternative Parliament. IRA formed in

1919 from IRB

1919–21 *Anglo–Irish War* between IRA and 'Black and Tans' — military auxiliaries

1920 *Government of Ireland Act partitions Ireland*

1921 *Anglo–Irish Treaty* — confirms Partition and establishes Irish Free State

Ulster: emergence of a 'mini-state'

1920–21 *The Government of Ireland Act 1920 and Anglo–Irish Treaty 1921* establish the boundaries of the partitioned island. The Ulster 'State' consists of six of the nine historic counties which make up the Province of Ulster. Its Parliament — Stormont — meets for the first time on 5 June 1921

1922–72 *The Unionist Party dominates* the politics of Northern Ireland. The Roman Catholic minority is represented by the residual elements of the old Nationalist party but a portion looks to the remnants of Sinn Fein and the IRA who have not accepted the 1920–1 Anglo–Irish arrangements.

The 'Troubles'

1968 *The Civil Rights Movement* emerges with new demands related to jobs, housing and discrimination which starts the process of destroying the Stormont Parliament and the monolithic Unionist Party. The IRA re-emerges and the British government reluctantly gets sucked into the Ulster Crisis

1969–72 British troops deployed in Belfast and Londonderry as peacekeepers, ostensibly to protect Catholics from Protestant forces of 'law and order'. The position quickly changes and British troops find themselves confronting IRA as well

1972 *Stormont Parliament prorogued* and Ulster now directly ruled from Westminster via a Northern Ireland Secretary of State and Northern Ireland Office in Belfast

1973 *Sunningdale Conference; New Assembly elections*

1974 *Power-sharing Executive established* to deal with all internal Northern Ireland affairs. Representatives of the Official Unionist, Social Democratic and Labour and Alliance parties participate in Executive. Opposed by Ian Paisley's DUP and Ulster Loyalist Workers' Council whose strike brought it down in May 1974

1980 *Anglo–Irish Council established* to break the deadlock by reviewing the 'totality of relations within these islands'.

1982 *Northern Ireland Assembly reconvened.* Unionist parties oppose revival of power-sharing and Nationalist and Republican parties, i.e. SDLP and Sinn Fein, boycott the body. *Hunger strikes* — ten republicans die, including Bobby Sands

1985 *Anglo–Irish Agreement.* Both governments accept that the present constitutional status of Northern Ireland can only change with the consent of the majority. Establishes regular ministerial meetings via a consultative inter-governmental conference. A permanent secretariat of civil servants from both Britain and Ireland is located in Belfast to deal with political, security and legal questions, and to promote cross-border cooperation. Vigorously opposed by Unionists and rejected by Sinn Fein as irrelevant

1990 Prime Minister Haughey supports initiative by Secretary of State for Northern Ireland, Peter Brooke, to open up all-party talks between Nationalists and Unionists

Source: John McHugh, Manchester Polytechnic

Repartition

Among less commonly urged solutions is repartition: a redrawing of the border between Northern Ireland and the Republic to remove from the province those border areas wholly Catholic and Nationalist in composition, notably South Armagh. Repartition could not solve the problem in the sense of removing the Nationalist community from the north, leaving a purely Protestant and Unionist Northern Ireland: the two populations are geographically intermingled. Most judge that repartition would bring at best marginal benefits, and that it would have few supporters within Northern Ireland: Unionists would see it as a step towards unification, and Nationalists as an attempt to entrench partition. To attempt repartition would probably, therefore, damage the prospects for an internal settlement.

Direct rule

For some people direct rule is itself a solution (a solution in the sense of preventing a potentially greater problem from coming into existence — an Irish Lebanon) securing a basic stability that no other option could guarantee. Few can admit to seeing direct rule in this way; certainly not the British government, with its rooted faith in devolution and power sharing. Yet direct rule has many supporters, if only as second best. For almost everyone in Northern Ireland there are worse things imaginable, even if there are also better.

References and Further Reading

Arthur, P., *The Government and Politics in Northern Ireland*, 2nd edn. (Longman, 1984).

Arthur, P. and Jeffrey, K., *Northern Ireland Since 1968* (Blackwell, 1988).

Birrel, D., 'Northern Ireland: The obstacles to power sharing', *Political Quarterly* (1981).

Boye, K. and Hadden, T., *Ireland: A Positive Proposal* (Penguin Special, 1985).

Byrd, P., 'Northern Ireland', in B. Jones, *Political Issues in Britain Today* (Manchester University Press, 1989).

Clancy, P., Drudy, S., Lynch, K. and O'Dowd, L. (eds), *Ireland: A Sociological Profile* (Dublin Institute of Public Adminstration, 1985).

Connolly, M., *Politics and Policy Making in Northern Ireland* (Philip Allen, 1990).

Farrell, M., *Northern Ireland: The Orange State* (Pluto Press, 1980).

McCullagh, M. and O'Dowd, L., *Social Studies Review*, (March 1986).

Rose, R., *Northern Ireland: A Time of Choice* (Macmillan, 1976).

27 Britain and the European Community*

Michael Moran

This chapter is concerned with the role of the European Community (EC). We start by looking at the events which gave the Community a central place in the politics of the United Kingdom; we then look at the most important institutions of the European Community; and finally we sketch the debate about the relationship between Britain and Europe which has been central to British politics for over three decades.

The political system of the United Kingdom is shaped by a wide range of influences. Some of the most obvious are internal to the country — the class structure, our legal system, the formal organization of the institutions of government. But Britain, like other states, exists in a wider international political and economic system. The nature of British politics cannot be grasped without some understanding of these influences from abroad. Historically, world events were central to the development of British politics. In the second half of the nineteenth century, for instance, one of the most important influences on internal British politics arose from the fact that Britain, by virtue of her empire and her pioneering role in the industrial revolution, was the leading state in the world political system.

International influences and connections have therefore long been important. But in the last two decades they have acquired a particularly vital role in the shaping of British politics. The most significant reason for this is the United Kingdom's membership of the European Community (the EC). Strictly speaking there exist three 'communities': the European Economic Community; the European Coal and Steel Community; and the European Atomic Energy Community. Britain joined the second and third of these on her accession to the EC in 1973. Since 1967 the institutions of the three communities have been merged (Gregory, 1983, p.11).

In the past, the influence of institutions beyond the borders of Britain, though often very great, could nevertheless still be pictured as something external to the political life of the country — as an aspect of foreign policy. The EC is different. Much that concerns the workings of Community institutions is part of the fabric of the domestic political system in Britain; and British policies on the Community, we will see, are shaped by influences very like those that shape other areas of policy at home. In

* I am grateful to my colleague Simon Bulmer for his comments on an earlier version of this chapter.

other words, the institutions of the EC have some claim to be considered an integral part of the British politics, rather than belonging to the world of foreign affairs.

The central role of EC institutions in British political life is, moreover, growing, and will continue to grow as a result of the preparation for a 'Single European Market' by 1992, when frontiers will come down and the movement of people, goods and services will become unrestricted. Europe, moreover is increasingly important to the British economy both from the point of view of trade (see Table 27.1) and aid: for example Britain will receive one billion pounds in regional aid from the EC during the period 1990–3.

Historical Development

The European Economic Community dates its existence from the Treaty of Rome, which was signed in 1957 and which came into effect at the start of the following year. The original treaty had six national signatories: Belgium, France, the Federal Republic of Germany, Italy, Luxembourg and the Netherlands. Of these by far the most important were France and Germany. The aim of the treaty was the progressive establishment of a 'common market' between the member states. This involved a commitment to the lowering, and eventual abolition, of barriers to trade between the members of the EEC, the creation of a common external barrier against outsiders, the elimination of practices which would hinder competition within the common market and the elimination of national barriers to the movement of goods, services and capital (Nugent, 1989, pp.39–40).

Although the EEC did not come into existence until the late 1950s its origins lie much earlier. After the end of the Second World War in 1945, the states of the Western European continent were suffering varying degrees of economic and political devastation. They faced two great problems. The first was posed by the challenge from the Soviet Union, which after the war had emerged as a 'superpower' controlling a wide range of nominally independent countries in Eastern Europe. The second was how to rebuild their shattered economies without resurrecting the disastrous

Table 27.1   *Britain's foreign trade; geographical distribution of UK imports and exports, percentage share*

	1970 Exports	Imports	1975 Exports	Imports	1987 Exports	Imports
EEC*	30.2	27.3	32.6	36.9	49.4	52.7
Rest of Western Europe	16.0	14.2	15.3	14.2	9.5	13.7
USA	11.6	12.9	9.2	9.8	13.8	9.7
Canada, Australia, New Zealand	9.4	12.6	7.3	6.1	4.4	2.9
Oil exporting countries	5.9	9.1	11.7	13.6	6.5	1.8
Japan	1.8	1.5	1.5	2.8	1.9	5.8

*France, Belgium, Luxemburg, Holland, West Germany, Italy, Irish Republic, Denmark and Greece are included throughout; Spain and Portugal in 1987

Source: Lindskaer-Nielsen *et al.*, p.166

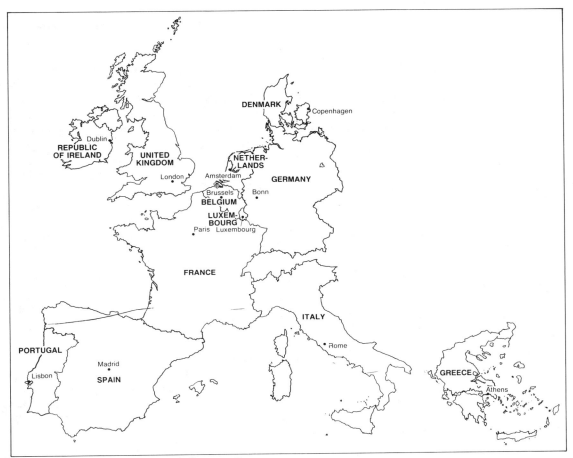

Figure 27.1 *Map of European Community*

nationalist competition that had culminated in the catastrophe of all-out war after 1939. Many of the most important political leaders in post-war Europe, especially in France and West Germany, believed that integration between national economies was the only way to reconstruct Europe and to eliminate the possibility of future military conflict. The setting up of the European Economic Community was therefore part of a long-term process of negotiation and institution-building designed to create a more unified European economic and political system. The most important predecessor of the EEC was the European Coal and Steel Community (ECSC), established in 1952 following the Treaty of Paris in 1951. The ECSC had the same signatories as had the Treaty of Rome six years later. Coal and steel were part of the foundation of the aggressive German wartime machine; the foundation of the ECSC thus marked an important symbolic break with the nationalist past.

The movement to integrate the economies of Western Europe aroused little initial enthusiasm in Britain. Successive British governments stood aside from the European Coal and Steel Community and from the EEC. Their indifference was due to the country's domestic mood after the war and to the legacy of past international commitments. The sense of crisis and the desire for renewal which lay behind much of the pressure for European integration was absent in Britain. The country had come out of the Second World War in a spirit of confidence: it had successfully resisted invasion and conquest; it was an important member of the alliance which had conquered Germany in 1945; its political institutions were believed to have worked well in organizing the war effort: and, by contrast with the ruined economies of other parts of Western Europe, much of its production remained functioning and able to take advantage of demand in world markets.

Britain's connections with the non-European world were also uniquely strong. There existed a close political relationship with the USA; we retained important trading links with some members of the 'old' Commonwealth, like New Zealand; and much of the Empire was intact. These reasons — the lack of any sense of identification with the post-war crisis of European institutions, and the country's strong non-European links — explain why the United Kingdom was so unenthusiastic about the early efforts to create economic integration in Europe.

In the late 1950s and the early 1960s, however, the most important sections of the country's leadership — the top of the ruling Conservative party, the leaders of the business community, the higher echelons of the civil service — all became convinced that Britain should apply for membership of the European Economic Community (Camps, 1964, pp. 274−366). The reasons for this shift in outlook were twofold.

1. The country's non-European connections weakened: the Empire was largely dissolved in favour of a much looser grouping of Commonwealth nations; a disastrous attempt at military intervention over the Suez Canal in 1956 showed that the country was no longer a major world military power; and the pattern of economic trade altered, with European markets growing in importance at the expense of some of Britain's old partners.
2. The confidence in British institutions that had kept the country aloof from the European integration movement disappeared. From the later 1950s the United Kingdom's economy showed signs of serious difficulties, with lower growth and higher inflation than most of her chief competitors. By contrast, the economies of the member states of the EEC were vigorously successful. It seemed that the process of integration was itself a source of economic dynamism.

This reasoning lay behind two British applications for membership in the 1960s (1961 and 1967). Both of these were vetoed by the French President, Charles de Gaulle, who did not believe that Britain's non-European links, especially her connections with the USA, would allow her to be a full-hearted member of the Community. But President de Gaulle was replaced in 1969 by a more accommodating French leader, President Pompidou. At the beginning of June 1970 the EC invited the United Kingdom to apply to start membership negotiations. In the second half of the same month the Conservatives, led by Mr Edward Heath, displaced Labour as the governing party in a General Election. The accession of Mr Heath to the premiership considerably increased British pressure for entry. Mr Heath had managed the first unsuccessful entry negotiations, and more than any other British political leader had tied his career to accomplishing Britain's integration into Europe. At the start of 1972 a Treaty of Accession was signed. In October of the same year the European Communities Act became law. Britain finally became a member of the EC in January 1973.

From six to twelve

The EC that Britain joined in 1973 was different from the Community created fifteen years before, and different also from that now existing in the 1990s. Britain's own entry was part of a continuing change in the Community's membership. With her in 1973 entered two other states — the Republic of Ireland and Denmark — whose trading relations bound them particularly closely to the British economy. These countries were followed into membership by Greece (1981) and by Spain and Portugal in 1986. Thus what was originally a close-knit group of six states created out of a long period of institution-building has been transformed into a politically and economically diverse collection of twelve nations.

The Community has not only grown in size; it has also in recent years made important changes in its institutions and in the substance of the treaty that binds its members. The European Parliament, which at first was composed of representatives nominated from the separate national parliaments, has been a directly elected body since 1979 (Lodge, 1983).

Single European Act

The most widely discussed change in the terms of Community membership is the Single European Act, which was passed in the United Kingdom Parliament in 1986 and which came into force Community-wide in 1987. This commits members to the creation of a single European market by the end of 1992 — a commitment involving the adaptation of many previously distinct national regulations, with the object of creating common competitive conditions throughout the EC. The Act also explicitly introduces the principle of majority voting in the Community's main decision making institution, the Council of Ministers, on a range of issues concerned with the creation of the single market (Lodge, 1989).

In short, the EC that Britain joined in 1973 was far more than an economic club. It was a varied and constantly changing system of political and economic institutions. We should now look briefly at the most important of these institutions.

The Institutions of the European Community

Four institutions of the European Community are especially important for the workings of British politics: the *European Commission*, the *Council of Ministers*, the *European Court* and the *European Parliament*.

The Commission

There are seventeen European Commissioners working out of Commission headquarters in Brussels. The Commissioners are in practice the nominees of the governments of the member states, with larger members (like the United Kingdom and the Federal Republic of Germany) entitled to two, while smaller states like the Republic of Ireland have one. Commissioners are nominated for four-year periods. But while they are the nominees of individual governments, they are far from being the servants of their home states or of the governing party in those home states. Most British commissioners are active and experienced politicians with established reputations at home. They expect to make an independent impact in Brussels and, where they are young enough to have continuing political ambitions, to enhance their domestic reputations. The Commission is therefore a decidedly political institution, with Commissioners allocated responsibilities for distinct policy areas. Commissioners sit at the top of a bureaucracy — in other words at the head of an organization which performs many classic 'civil service' functions. It prepares legislative initiatives to be considered by the Council of Ministers. It is responsible for monitoring the implementation of regulations in member states and, where regulations are not properly carried out, for bringing cases for enforcement to the European Court. This activity demands a considerable staff: of the 20,000 or so employed by the European Community around 11,000 alone work in the Commission (Nugent, 1989, p.59). One Commissioner serves as President of the Commission.

The Council of Ministers

Although the Commission is the institution most commonly associated with the EC, it is in key respects subordinate to the Council of Ministers. The Council formally consists of the ministerial representatives of the member states or their nominees. In practice it is less a single forum than a network of institutions. The so-called 'General Council', the most wide-ranging, is composed of the Foreign Ministers of the national governments. The 'Technical Councils' are not, as the name implies, concerned only with technicalities. They are the forums where the Ministers from member states with standard departmental portfolios, like Finance or Agriculture, meet. Partly 'shadowing' these General and Technical Councils are two 'Committees of Permanent Representatives' (COREPER), drawn from the staffs of the permanent representatives maintained by all the member states in Brussels. The importance of the Council of Ministers can be succinctly stated: whatever the Commission proposes, it is in the meetings of the Council that the Community directives and regulations binding on members are agreed. The workings of the Council are therefore central to the argument about how far membership of the European Community has resulted in a transfer of legal sovereignty from Westminster to Brussels (see below). For most of the Community's history Council decisions depended on unanimity, allowing any national government to veto a proposal to which it had a particularly marked objection. The single European Act, however, 'entrenches majority voting in the Council of Ministers on matters relating to the SEM's (Single European Market's) attainment' (Lodge, 1989, p.36). In other words, it is now possible for the British Government to be overruled in the Council.

The Council of Ministers should be distinguished from the European Council. The latter is a gathering of the heads of member governments, normally accompanied by their Foreign Ministers, plus two Commissioners, meeting at least twice-yearly. The European Council is, by virtue of its membership, therefore a forum in which some of the most important issues affecting the whole Community can be discussed at the highest level. In practice its meetings are extensively publicized diplomatic occasions when major world issues affecting the Community, or the most important issues dividing member governments, are discussed, and occasionally even settled.

The European Court

The European Community is the product of treaties between states. This fact conveys one of its most important but neglected characteristics: it is a legal creation, and the way the law of the Community is interpreted and applied is a major determinant of how the EC functions. This is why the ***European Court of Justice*** is a Community institution of the first rank. The Court, based in Luxembourg, consists of thirteen judges, twelve of whom are in effect nominated by the separate member states. The Court's importance for the workings of British politics lies in its power to interpret, and to order the enforcement of, the legal obligations created by EC treaty. Its acts of interpretation and enforcement under treaty mean that its decisions can override both domestic courts and Parliament in Britain. In Nugent's words: 'The Court of Justice has played an extremely important part in establishing the Community's legal order. Whether it is acting as an international court, a court of review, a court of appeal, or a court of referral (roles which, in practice, greatly overlap), it is frequently as much a maker as an interpreter of law' (Nugent, 1989, p.154).

The European Parliament

The European Parliament is not, as its name might suggest, the legislature for the European Community. As we have already seen, the preparation of legislation is largely controlled by the Commission, while the formal and the actual power to change proposals into policy lies in the Council of Ministers. The Parliament's major formal powers — to dismiss the Commission and to reject the budget for the Community institutions proposed by the Commission — can be exercised only with a two-thirds majority. The budgetary powers of the Parliament are nevertheless of some significance: the Parliament rejected the EC budget for five individual years in the 1980s. But the power to dismiss the Commission, while theoretically awesome, is in practice insignificant. A more realistic source of parliamentary influence with the Commission lies in the so called 'cooperation procedure' introduced under the Single European Act. The procedure allows Parliament to offer amendments to drafts of legislation coming from the Commission. According to Lodge, in the first year of the cooperation procedure the Commission accepted 70 per cent of Parliamentary amendments; of these, 30 per cent were accepted in turn by the Council of Ministers (Lodge, 1989, p.36).

As far as British politics are concerned, however, the European Parliament remains the most marginal of the main Community institutions. Members of the Parliament are not — a few Northern Ireland politicians apart — significant figures in domestic politics. The Parliament remains essentially a supplementary arena for continuing some of the domestic partisan battle. More significantly perhaps, it is also a supplementary arena for attempting to secure the redress of grievances. For instance, in the campaign to secure redress for the 'Birmingham Six' (allegedly wrongly convicted and imprisoned for pub bombings in 1974) the Parliament was used to

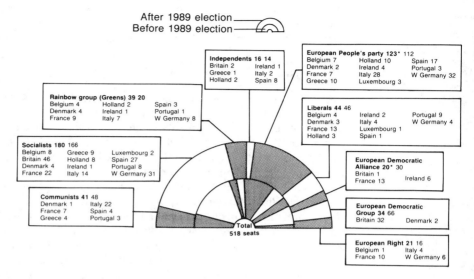

After 1989 election
Before 1989 election

Independents 16 14
Britain 2   Ireland 1
Greece 1   Italy 2
Holland 2   Spain 8

European People's party 123ʹ 112
Belgium 7   Holland 10   Spain 17
Denmark 2   Ireland 4   Portugal 3
France 7   Italy 28   W Germany 32
Greece 10   Luxembourg 3

Rainbow group (Greens) 39 20
Belgium 4   Holland 2   Spain 3
Denmark 4   Ireland 1   Portugal 1
France 9   Italy 7   W Germany 8

Liberals 44 46
Belgium 4   Ireland 2   Portugal 9
Denmark 3   Italy 4   W Germany 4
France 13   Luxembourg 1
Holland 3   Spain 1

Socialists 180 166
Belgium 8   Greece 9   Luxembourg 2
Britain 46   Holland 8   Spain 27
Denmark 4   Ireland 1   Portugal 8
France 22   Italy 14   W Germany 31

**European Democratic
Alliance 20ʹ** 30
Britain 1   Ireland 6
France 13

Communists 41 48
Denmark 1   Italy 22
France 7   Spain 4
Greece 4   Portugal 3

**European Democratic
Group 34** 66
Britain 32   Denmark 2

Total
518 seats

European Right 21 16
Belgium 1   Italy 4
France 10   W Germany 6

Figure 27.2   *Seats in the European Parliament after 1989 election*

publicize Europe-wide calls for a further judicial review of their case. Figure 27.2 shows the strengths of different political groups in the European Parliament. There are 518 MEPs of which the United Kingdom has allocated eighty-one seats.

The European Debate

The debate about the relationship between the United Kingdom and the EC has provided one of the great controversies in British politics — comparable in importance to the divisions over the Corn Laws in the nineteenth century or the arguments about tariffs and free trade in the early decades of the twentieth century. Like those earlier debates the 'European Debate' is about both external and internal matters — about the United Kingdom's place in the international system and about what interests and forces should predominate in British politics. In the European debate three broad positions can be distinguished: the separatist, the federal and the confederal.

Separatists oppose British membership of the European Economic Community. As we saw earlier, until the close of the 1950s most of the country's political and economic leadership belonged to this camp. After the changed climate of opinion that led to the first application for entry in 1961, the debate between opponents and advocates of membership created an important line of political division in Britain. In part this line corresponded to existing class divisions, and thus to the established lines of battle between the main political parties and their allies. On one hand the Conservative party and its supporters in the business community supported entry, in the belief that gaining freer access to the rich markets of Europe was one of the main ways of halting Britain's economic decline. On the other hand, a sizeable section of the Labour party and an even larger group in the trade union movement opposed membership, fearful that competition in a larger market would damage the domestic economy and would make planning by a British government more difficult, or even impossible (Moon, 1985, pp.161—89). But although the parties initially divided in this way, the European debate also split them internally. The Conservative party had been a proud supporter of Empire, and contained many who valued the traditional connections stemming from Empire more highly than the new connections with Europe. There were also many in the party who were strong supporters of British nationalism and the sovereignty of Parliament, in opposition to the perceived threat of integration in a wider European organization. In the Labour movement, by contrast, a large section of the leadership, especially in the Parliamentary Labour Party, advocated British membership of the EEC as a remedy against economic decline.

These arguments came to a head and were largely settled in the period between June 1970 (when the negotiations for Britain's eventually successful application began) and June 1975, when a national referendum endorsed the country's continuing membership of the Community. In the parliamentary votes on the terms which had been negotiated for entry (October 1971) and on the principles of the European Communities Bill empowering Britain's entry (February 1972), voting was largely along party lines, with Labour opposing and the governing Conservatives supporting. There was nevertheless a large minority of Labour members who declined to vote with their party, and a smaller minority of Conservative members who voted with the Labour opponents of entry. In the February 1974 General Election Mr Enoch Powell, the best known of the Conservative critics of entry, advised voters to support the rival Labour party in order to reject what he called a 'new European superstate' (Butler and Kavanagh, 1974, pp.103—5).

This intervention suggested for a moment that 'Europe' might create a reformation of the party system, on pro- and anti-European lines. But the Labour government that was returned after the General Election of February 1974 announced that it would 'renegotiate' the terms of British membership. The terms of this renegotiation were put to the electorate in the referendum of June 1975, with members of the Government campaigning on different sides, but with its leading figures recommending that Britain remain within the Community. To the question 'Do you think Britain should stay in the European Community?' 64.5 per cent of those voting answered 'yes'. Since that vote 'separatism' has ceased to be a significant force in British politics. Although the Labour party — reflecting the dominance of the left in the early 1980s — as late as the 1983 General Election retained the theoretical option of withdrawal in its manifesto, the debate in British politics has shifted to that between advocates of a 'federal' and a 'confederal' Europe.

While the arguments between the separatists and the advocates of entry were often elaborate they turned on a relatively clear choice: should the United Kingdom sign a treaty of membership with the Community? The divisions between the *federalists* and the *confederalists* are considerably more complex. The arguments cannot be reduced to a debate between defenders and critics of British sovereignty. According to Hinsley, sovereignty is 'the idea that there is a final and absolute political authority in the political community . . . and no final and absolute authority exists elsewhere' (Hinsley, 1966, p.26). As we have already seen, British membership involved surrender of that final authority — in some jurisdictions to the European Court, and in some to the Council of Ministers, where the Single European Act allows the Council to proceed by majority vote. Federalists argue that this process is an inevitable and necessary accompaniment of the creation of a single market. In a much discussed speech in 1988 the French President of the European Commission, Jacques Delors, envisaged that within a decade 80 per cent of economic legislation would originate in the Community.

The Delors Plan envisaged three stages: first, the further development of the European Monetary System whereby the exchange rates of member states are sustained in a stable relationship; secondly the establishment of new EC institutions; and thirdly the creation of a central bank and a European currency: complete monetary union. In an equally widely discussed intervention Mrs Thatcher responded in a speech in Bruges defending a confederal vision of 'cooperation between independent sovereign states'.

But if the broad terms of a debate between federal and confederal Europe are clear, the identity of those who consistently advocated one or the other vision were less so. Mrs Thatcher's own position was ambiguous, for while she used the language of a confederal Europe, it was her own administration which ensured the passage of the Single European Act through the British Parliament. The ambiguities were partly the product of the particular costs and benefits of Community measures for different interests within Britain. She was enthusiastic about the idea of a single market — a very Thatcherite idea. However the notion of a 'social Europe', in which British employment and welfare legislation is raised to the level existing in member states like the Federal Republic of Germany, is attractive to the Labour party and its trade union allies. By contrast, it is intensely unattractive to many in the Conservative party and the business community. It threatens to eliminate the competitive advantage conferred on British business under the more freely regulated labour markets created by the Thatcher government's economic and industrial relations policies of the 1980s.

Mrs Thatcher also resisted cooperation with the first stage of the Delors Plan. Her opposition to UK membership of the ERM, backed by her economic adviser Sir Alan Walters, was the issue which led her Chancellor Nigel Lawson to resign in 1989. (Lawson was in favour of joining 'sooner rather than later' but was 'opposed to European monetary union because I don't want to see political union', *The Times*, 13 February 1990.) This raised fears among some — Sir Geoffrey Howe and Michael Heseltine included — that a two-tier Europe would emerge in which Britain would be left behind. Others applauded her opposition: on 16 May 1989 151 Tory MPs signed an Early Day Motion declaring that the aims of the Delors Report were 'completely unacceptable'. Labour, once in favour of withdrawal from the Community, were able to discover a new enthusiasm for the EC which they used to exploit Conservative differences and positive popular attitudes towards the EC during the June 1989 elections to the European Parliament: they ended up winning handsomely by forty-two seats to the Conservatives' thirty-two.

In October 1990 Britain joined the ERM; allegedly Mrs Thatcher had finally backed down before a united front of her Chancellor, John Major and her Foreign Secretary, Douglas Hurd. Her rumoured reluctance, however, was given expression in November by some noisy anti-European rhetoric at the Despatch Box. For her Deputy Prime Minister this was the last straw. Sir Geoffrey Howe added his name to those of Heseltine, Brittan, Lawson and Ridley as a Cabinet minister resigning over the issue of Europe. Sir Geoffrey's subsequent scathingly critical resignation speech opened the door for Michael Heseltine to challenge Mrs Thatcher in the annual leadership elections. Her own resignation, therefore, on 22 November, 1990 was importantly connected with Europe, an issue on which wide divisions still exist within the Conservative Party.

'Federal' and 'confederal' positions are therefore in part the product of the impact of Community measures on domestic interests in Britain. To that degree the debate about the future shape of Europe resembles that elsewhere in the Community. But in Britain there exists a particular feature. The United Kingdom is the least European-minded of all the large members of the EC. Her political leaders came late to the idea of European membership, and only after the apparent failure of alternatives — a striking contrast with, for example, the Federal Republic of Germany, where European integration 'was adopted as one of the foundations of the West German state' (Bulmer and Paterson, 1987, p.5). Surveys of public attitudes to the benefits and costs of community membership have found over a long period that the British have been among the least enthusiastic in Europe about the EC, a suggestion strengthened by the evidence of low turnout in the three direct elections to the European Parliament. What Bulmer and Paterson suggest about the German case is perhaps even more true of Britain: 'European policy is conditioned by much the same set of factors which shape domestic policy.' (1987, p.3). The continuing debate between confederalism and federalism, and the outcomes in policy terms of that debate, will be heavily influenced by the way European policy affects the different economic and political interests within Britain and by the way popular attitudes to Europe evolve at home.

The early years of John Major's premiership suggest that this argument will be decisively settled against those, like Mrs Thatcher, suspicious of moves to greater integration. The signing of the Maastricht Treaty, and its ratification by Parliament in 1992, marked a significant increase in the significance of Community institutions. More important still, perhaps, it marked the eclipse within the Conservative Party of the anti-federalist wing.

References and Further Reading

Bulmer, S. and Paterson, W., *The Federal Republic of Germany and the European Community* (Allen & Unwin, 1987).

Butler, D. and Kavanagh, D., *The British General Election of February 1974* (Macmillan, 1974).

Camps, M., *Britain and the European Community 1955–1963* (Oxford University Press, 1964).

Gregory, F., *Dilemmas of Government: Britain and the European Community* (Martin Robertson, 1983).

Hinsley, F., *Sovereignty* (Watts, 1966).

Lindskaer-Nielsen, J. et al., *Contemporary British Society* (Akademisk Forlag, 1989).

Lodge, J., 'The European Parliament', in J. Lodge, (ed.), *Institutions and Policies of the European Community* (Pinter, 1983).

Lodge, J., 'The political implications of 1992', *Politics,* **9**(2), 34–40 (1989).

Moon, J., *European Integration in Britain Politics 1950–1963: A Study of Issue Change* (Gower, 1985).

Nicoll, W. and Salmon, T.C., *Understanding the European Communities* (Philip Allan, 1990).

Nugent, N., *The Government and Politics of the European Community* (Macmillan, 1989).

28 Foreign Policy

Anthony Seldon

Chapter 2 addressed the subject of Britain's post-war role in relation to the rest of the world. This chapter takes up the story of foreign and defence policy during the 1980s.

Prime Ministers and Foreign Policy

Prime Ministers habitually like to dominate foreign policy, and hence their Foreign Secretaries. This tendency was in evidence when Britain was still a great power, as when Chamberlain (1937–40) and Churchill (1940–5, 1951–5) were PMs, and it still held true when Britain had declined to second power status. Thus both Mr Heath (1970–4) and Mrs Thatcher (1979–90) devoted considerable time and energy to Britain's overseas affairs.

With Mrs Thatcher, the tendency increased with the passing years. She was, of course, totally dominant in the Falklands War of 1982, but in those early years her attention was far more absorbed by domestic affairs. In addition, in Lord Carrington (1979–82) she possessed a strong Foreign Secretary who did not welcome too many interventions from 10 Downing Street. Mrs Thatcher never trusted Carrington's successor, Francis Pym (1982–3), and after the 1983 General Election victory lost no time in replacing him with a man she valued much more highly, Geoffrey Howe (1983–9).

Yet over the years she increasingly came to dislike his favoured policies, especially on Europe, and felt that he was becoming far too closely identified with her least favourite of any Whitehall department, the Foreign and Commonwealth Office. Tensions rose throughout 1987 and 1988 and culminated in Mrs Thatcher, in effect, sacking Howe as Foreign Secretary in July 1989, replacing him by the relatively young and inexperienced John Major, who many thought at the time would become little more than a mouthpiece for Mrs Thatcher's wishes. Mr Major did not last long enough in that office for anyone to draw any conclusions because after three months he was smartly translated into the Treasury to take the place of Nigel Lawson, who had resigned over disputes with Alan Walters, a PM adviser, over British commitment to Europe. Douglas Hurd, his successor as Foreign Secretary, was an ex-diplomat possessed of considerable independence and self assurance but his freedom for manoeuvre was restricted by the machinery which the Prime Minister had established. The key Overseas and Defence Cabinet committee was chaired by Mrs Thatcher and she received independent advice upon foreign policy from special advisers (Sir Anthony Parsons held this post for a while after 1982) and above all her personal

The three Foreign Secretaries of 1989: Geoffrey Howe, John Major and Douglas Hurd. John Major was to become Chancellor of the Exchequer in October 1989 and Prime Minister in November 1990.

secretary, Charles Powell, also an ex-foreign office man who was widely regarded as an *eminence grise* at the Thatcher court.

As we saw in Chapter 2, in the early post-war years, Britain liked to see herself as enjoying a special position in international affairs, being uniquely at the centre of three 'overlapping circles' of the Commonwealth, Europe and the Atlantic relationship. Being the only 'member' to belong to each of those three, Britain harboured the essentially romantic view that she had a vantage point giving her weight and authority in world affairs. The reality, however, is that power in international relations is critically dependent upon economic might, and as Chapter 2 explained, as Britain's economy declined post-war so too did her ability to remain a major actor on the international stage.

Paradoxically, while Mrs Thatcher succeeded in establishing a reputation as a forceful and influential stateswoman, the changes she helped bring about in the international system pushed Britain further toward the position of a 'middle power', strong enough to carry weight as a key member of the North Atlantic Treaty Organization and the European Economic Community and the leader of the Commonwealth but weak enough to be eclipsed by the USA/USSR in discussions of a military nature, such as the reduction of nuclear weapons, and a political nature, such as regional security in Central America and Central Asia. After years of resisting the drift into a role as one of a number of European powers, the Thatcher government had to reconcile itself to that position.

The 'special relationship' with the USA

Thatcher, like previous Conservative Prime Ministers such as Churchill and Macmillan (1957–63), put great value upon the 'Atlantic Alliance' with the USA. Like them, she saw the alliance as a vehicle to maintain Britain's status as one of the world's 'great powers'. Britain, lacking the necessary financial, industrial and military resources does not do this through independent assertion of her power, as she could do before 1945; rather, she serves as a bridge between the USA and Western Europe and, even more significantly, between the USA and the USSR.

The 'special relationship' with the USA was reinforced by Thatcher's admiration for the policies of US President Ronald Reagan (1981–9). Reagan's economic programme of monetarism, coupled with tax cuts and emphasis on the private sector of production, paralleled the domestic thrust of 'Thatcherism'. In foreign policy, Reagan's anti-Soviet rhetoric in the early 1980s was eagerly backed by the Thatcher government. When Carter (1977–81) was still President Britain had been the most prominent European supporter of the December 1979 decision by NATO to deploy US Cruise and Pershing II missiles in Western Europe. Despite vocal demonstrations by the Campaign for Nuclear Disarmament (CND) and other anti-nuclear groups against the deployment, the Government held its ground. When the USA entered negotiations in November 1981 with the USSR on the reduction of strategic nuclear weapons, Thatcher again gave unwavering support to the position of the Reagan administration, despite complaints by the opposition Labour party that the USA was trying to impose unreasonable terms upon the USSR.

With Reagan in the White House, Anglo–American relations became arguably closer than at any point since the war. It was a remarkable example of the ability of individual leaders to affect the direction of a nation's foreign policy. After George Bush became President in January 1989 (who as a Republican shared many of Reagan's policy views, and who had indeed been Reagan's Vice-President) relations remained initially close. It became obvious very early on, however, that whereas President Bush valued a close relationship with Mrs Thatcher and Britain, he wanted to take US foreign policy in his own direction. West Germany quickly reasserted itself, for example, as the more important ally to the USA. The 'special relationship' was strengthened, however, by Thatcher's firm support for Bush over the Gulf crisis after Iraq invaded Kuwait in August 1990.

Relations with the USSR

When Mrs Thatcher came to power in 1979 the USSR was still ruled by the iron hand of Brezhnev, and she had little opportunity and no desire to change the hardline policy Britain had followed ever since the start of the Cold War. Brezhnev's death, followed by the deaths in quick succession of Andropov and Chernenko, changed all that. A new climate was soon felt and Mrs Thatcher, to her credit, was quick to realize the new opportunities.

In 1985 the Thatcher government attempted to become a full-fledged actor in the arms controls discussion between the USA and the USSR. The Prime Minister met the new Soviet leader, Mikhail Gorbachev, in London and announced that 'he was a man we could do business with'. While Britain continued to back the US bargaining position, Thatcher had declared her wish to serve as a go-between to speed up the negotiations. After the Reykjavik summit between Reagan and Gorbachev in Autumn 1986 ended in apparent failure over arms control, Thatcher again presented herself as a helpful mediator, culminating the effort with a high-profile visit to Moscow in March 1987. The Prime Minister could then claim some credit for subsequent progress in American–Soviet negotiations, whose fruits included the December 1987 agreement on reductions in intermediate-range nuclear weapons.

Mikhail Gorbachev's election as General Secretary of the Communist Party of the USSR in March 1985 led to improved relations between Britain and the USSR and an extensive programme of reforms in the USSR itself.

Britain and Europe

Meanwhile, the Thatcher government tried to establish a role in Europe and the Commonwealth which would not only confirm the prominence of British influence in those groupings but also protect British economic and diplomatic interests. Immediately after her first victory as Prime Minister in May 1979, Thatcher served notice that the EEC would have to reduce the price of Britain's participation in the organization. She noted that while Britain financed 20 per cent of the EEC budget, it received less than 10 per cent of the receipts of the Community; Britain's net contribution (gross contribution minus receipts) to the EEC would be more than £1 billion in 1980. A particular target of the British was the Common Agricultural Policy (CAP), the subsidy of European farm products financed by two-thirds of the Community's budget. The Prime Minister contended that the CAP was financed by the money of British taxpayers but benefited continental farmers, notably those in France and West Germany.

After a heated clash with leaders of the other EEC countries at the Dublin summit in November 1979, Thatcher obtained a temporary settlement which provided more than £3 billion in budget 'rebates' to Britain between 1980 and 1984. The long-term problem of EEC receipts and the CAP was more difficult to solve. An interim agreement at Copenhagen in 1985 raised contributions by member countries from 1 per cent of value-added tax to 1.4 per cent and established the principle that Britain would get an annual rebate of two-thirds of its net contribution, but no deal was reached on the CAP. Relations with the EEC remained difficult, however. Deep divisions opened up within the Conservative party with Mrs Thatcher remaining lukewarm towards plans for further integration in the monetary sphere, and others in her party far less concerned by the apparent threats of an erosion of British sovereignty. John Major's accession to power in November 1990 marked a more favourable attitude towards closer cooperation with European partners. (See also chapter 27.)

The Commonwealth

The Thatcher government obtained a significant victory for British prestige with its negotiation of an agreement for legal independence of Southern Rhodesia, later renamed Zimbabwe, in 1980. The problem had persisted since the leadership of the white minority in Rhodesia declared independence in 1963 and Britain, under the Labour PM Harold Wilson, imposed economic sanctions against the country. After April 1979 elections indicated support for a government headed by the leader of the whites, Ian Smith, and a leader of one section of the blacks, Bishop Abel Muzorewa, many Conservative Members of Parliament wanted recognition of the new regime and the lifting of sanctions. Thatcher hinted that she would support such measures but the Foreign Secretary, Lord Carrington, persuaded her that no government could survive which did not include the rebel leaders Robert Mugabe and Joshua Nkomo. British diplomacy through the ensuing Lancaster House negotiations provided for representation of all groups in the new state, and British troops ensured that a cease-fire held before elections and the full independence of Zimbabwe in Spring 1980.

Commonwealth issues receded in importance until 1985—6 when the problem of South Africa and her policy of racial apartheid threatened to split the group. With tension and internal violence increasing, pressure grew upon the USA and Western European countries to impose economic sanctions against the white minority regime in Pretoria. After prolonged resistance to sanctions, the Reagan adminstration was pushed by the US Congress and public opinion to take limited measures; European countries like France did likewise, and the EC began to consider joint sanctions. Despite the demands of black African states and other Commonwealth members such as India and West Indian countries for action, the Thatcher government refused to impose any financial or trade restrictions upon South Africa. The imposition of a state of emergency by the South African government, followed by the detention of thousands of blacks and anti-apartheid activists, worsened the situation. Black African and West Indian nations, as well as India, boycotted the Commonwealth Games in Edinburgh, and a public row arose in Britain when it was reported that the Queen was concerned that Thatcher's intransigence on sanctions would wreck the Commonwealth. Although the immediate British domestic crisis passed and the South African issue had little or no bearing upon the May 1987 elections, reports of black African resentment against the Thatcher Government persisted. The dispute erupted at the Commonwealth conference of heads of government in October 1987 in Vancouver, Canada. Thatcher accused the banned anti-apartheid movement, the African National Congress, of being 'terrorists', while leaders such as Robert Mugabe of Zimbabwe and Kenneth Kaunda of Zambia accused the Prime Minister of sacrificing all moral interests for the sake of greed and British trade with South Africa. Even non-African leaders such as Brian Mulroney of Canada and Bob Hawke of Australia publicly joined in condemnation of British policy. Tensions reached new peaks when in the summer of 1989 British cricketers announced their intention to take part in a 'rebel' tour of South Africa. In the event, the tour was cancelled in February 1990 in the face of the demonstrations which preceded and accompanied the release from prison of the black African ANC leader, Nelson Mandela. Mrs Thatcher welcomed his release, but refused to support the maintenance of economic sanctions on the De Klerk regime. In the face of considerable opposition, especially from European partners, she used the release of Mr Mandela as a reason for relaxing certain economic and cultural sanctions Britain already had in place.

The Falklands war

The most significant crisis in foreign policy for the Thatcher Government, however, happened outside the 'three rings' of Atlantic alliance, Europe and Commonwealth. In April 1982 Argentina, frustrated by decades of inconclusive negotiations, invaded the Falkland Islands, a British territory (population 1,800) in the South Atlantic. The invasion caught the British by surprise and led to the resignation of the Foreign Secretary, Lord Carrington, and the near-resignation of the Defence Secretary, John Nott. Within weeks, however, the Thatcher government was able to turn the disaster into a diplomatic and military victory. Britain obtained United Nations condemnation of the invasion, and EC sanctions against Argentina. A British task force sailed 8,000 miles and, despite tenuous supply lines and numerical inferiority in manpower, inflicted an overwhelming naval, air and land defeat upon the Argentines. Argentina surrendered in early June and Britain reasserted its sovereignty over the Islands.

After the fall of the military government in Argentina and its replacement by an elected civilian regime many countries, notably the USA, urged Britain to negotiate a long-term settlement with Argentina over the islands. The Thatcher government, however, adamantly refused to discuss the issue, arguing that Argentina never ended the state of belligerency against Britain and that the sovereignty of the islands was beyond negotiation. Instead, Britain maintained a military garrison of 2 to 3,000 men and built up the infrastructure of the islands. In January 1987, a new airport with runways suitable for heavy civilian and military aircraft was opened, 30 miles from Port Stanley, the capital of the islands. By the end of the 1986–7 financial year, Britain had spent £2.6 billion, almost £1.5 million per resident, to defend and develop the territory.

Defence policy developments

The cornerstone of the defence strategy was the commitment to the Atlantic alliance and NATO. Besides supporting the deployment of Cruise and Pershing nuclear missiles in the early 1980s, the Thatcher government maintained its commitment to Britain's independent nuclear deterrent, notably the development of the Trident missile system to be operational in the mid-1990s. Opposition to Trident came not only from anti-nuclear protesters but also from those who were concerned at the escalating costs of the project and the possibility that Trident would be rendered obsolete, even before its deployment, by more advanced missile systems.

The sweeping Conservative victory over Labour which had favoured unilateral disarmament of Britain's nuclear deterrent, in June 1983, gave the Thatcher government a renewed mandate for its policy of nuclear defence, although opinion polls continued to show a majority of people against the development of Trident. The government pressed ahead, arguing there was no alternative to Trident, although estimates of the project's cost reached £9.9 billion in 1987. In January 1987, Minister of Defence George Younger reaffirmed that Trident was the only option for an independent deterrent.

Less publicized but just as significant in Britain's defence policy within NATO was a commitment, made in the late 1970s, to increase real spending on defence by 3 per cent per year through to 1985–6. As a result, British spending on defence increased 27 per cent in real terms between 1978–9 and 1985–6. Britain had sustained its commitment to keep 55,000 troops in West Germany. Planned reductions in naval forces, recommended by the 1981 defence review, were mitigated by Britain's involvement in the Falklands War.

This maintenance of Britain's defence capability was not unopposed within the government, however. The Treasury, determined to control public expenditure, argued for cutbacks in the defence programme; the conflict led to the move of Francis Pym from Defence Secretary to Leader of the House of Commons in 1981. With the expiration of NATO's commitment to 3 per cent real growth in defence budgets, the Treasury had gained the upper hand in the battle with the Ministry of Defence. Spending on defence was scheduled to decrease from £18.1 billion in 1986–7 to £17.1 billion in 1989–90 (1986–7 prices).

Table 28.1 Forces on active service in the mid-1980s

Country	Army	Navy	RAF	Royal Marines
Ascension		1 helicopter detachm't	Victor tankers Hercules transports 1 helicopter detachm't 4 Harriers ½ squadron RAF Regt (Rapier air defence missiles)	
Belize	1 armoured recce troop 1 field artillery battery 1 engineer squadron 1 infantry btn			
Berlin	1 infantry brigade			
Brunei	1 Gurkha infantry btn 1 flight helicopter			1 infantry company
Canada	1 army training unit			
Cyprus*	1 armoured recce squadron 1 engineer support squadron 1½ infantry btns 1 helicopter detachm't		1 helicopter detachm't 1 squadron RAF regt 1 armoured recce squadron	
Diego Garcia		Naval liaison party		
Falklands	1 infantry btn	3–5 frigates or destroyers 1–2 nuclear submarines	8–10 Phantoms 4–6 Harriers 1 helicopter detachm't 1 RAF Regt detachm't (Rapier air defence missiles)	
Gibraltar	1 infantry btn 1 artillery detachm't	1 frigate		
Hong Kong	1 infantry btn 4 Gurkha infantry btns 1 Gurkha engineer regt 1 squadron army helicopters	Patrol boat detachm't	1 squadron helicopter	
Indian Ocean		Periodic navy group deployments (aircraft carrier, frigate/destroyer, submarine)		
Lebanon				
N. Ireland	1 armoured recce unit 1 engineer squadron 8 infantry btns 1 marine commando 2 helicopter squadrons 11 btns Ulster Defence Regiment	Patrol boat detachm't	1 helicopter detachm't 1 squadron RAF Regt 1 engineer squadron	
Sinai	1 army detachm't in MFO			
W. Germany	1 corps HQ 3 armoured divs 1 artillery div.		1 Tactical Air Force	
W. Indies		1 frigate or destroyer		

*Britain also contributes ½ infantry battalion and 1 army helicopter detachment to the United Nations (UNFICYP contingent).
Source: adapted from *The Economist*, 17 December 1983.

The constraints on defence spending, combined with the increasing cost of an independent nuclear deterrent, force difficult choices for British policy makers. One option is to abandon commitments outside NATO, such as the maintenance of the Falklands garrison and the despatch of British frigates in summer 1987 to assist in protection of shipping in the Persian Gulf. Such a decision, however, would represent a retreat from Britain's attempts to maintain its status as an international power (Table 28.1). Another option is to reduce Britain's NATO commitments, but this risks alienation of the USA, which has called for a greater European contribution to the organization, and countries in Western Europe. The option of holding down the salaries of members of the armed forces would be a reversal of Thatcher's policy of keeping military wages competitive with those in the private sector and would yield only marginal savings.

Facing these decisions and the possible completion of arms control negotiations between the USA and the USSR, the Thatcher government began to consider the option of a European nuclear deterrent. Combined with the move by the EC to forge a single European market, the concept of a European defence system independent of NATO revives the possibility of a 'third force' in international politics, a vision dating to the Labour government of 1945.

References and Further Reading

Barber, J., *Who Makes British Foreign Policy?* (Open University Press, 1976).
Baylis, J., *British Defence Policy: Striking the Right Balance* (Macmillan, 1989).
Byrd, P. (ed.), *British Foreign Policy Under Thatcher* (Philip Allan, 1988).
Freedman, L., *Britain and the Falklands War* (Basil Blackwell, 1988).
Smith, M., Smith, S. and White, B. (eds), *British Foreign Policy: Tradition, Change and Transformation* (Unwin Hyman, 1988).

Britain and the World in the Wake of the 1989 Revolutions

The extraordinary events of 1989—90 in the communist world threw both British foreign and defence policy into confusion. When communism was born in 1917 the establishment of the Soviet Union had been hailed by liberals as the beginning of the end for right-wing tyrannies and by Marxists as the unravelling of an inevitable historical process. Capitalism was destined to collapse through its own internal contradictions and a classless communism would replace it. After 1945, backed by Soviet military power, such predictions had some credibility, especially when Eastern Europe, China and North Korea joined the communist camp.

At the height of the Cold War it had been thought by Western states that the line against communism had to be held by the West, otherwise regimes close to it would be subverted and would collapse like 'dominoes'. During 1989, however, a series of internal revolutions in Eastern Europe saw the communist regimes themselves collapse — perhaps more like a pack of cards than a row of dominoes. Subsequent events exposed these governments as inefficient, corrupt and as tyrannical, if not more so, than some of the right-wing regimes they had replaced after the Second World War. China brutally suppressed attempts at liberalization by the massacre of demonstrators in Peking but the Soviet Union, perhaps in order to control internal pressures for democracy, chose to embrace them.

When he came to power in 1985 Mikhail Gorbachev inherited a fossilized bureacratic, one-party state in which party members enjoyed unfair privileges; an economy so inefficient it could not provide adequate food and basic consumer goods; and simmering discontents amongst the scores of national groups which for seventy years had been suppressed by communist hegemony. His policies of openness (*glasnost*) and reconstruction (*perestroika*) had been designed to revolutionize this state of affairs but while those policies struggled to make an impact at home they provided the signal for the popular uprisings which swept through Eastern Europe. Having laid waste these regimes the movement rolled back into the USSR, sweeping out the old guard and ending the communist party's traditional monopoly of power. Having initiated the storm Gorbachev was forced to ride it out — at considerable risk to his own position.

The implications of these events for British foreign and defence policy are still unclear but the repercussions will be felt until the end of the century and beyond. Richard Perle, former adviser to Ronald Reagan and nicknamed the 'Prince of

Darkness' for his hawkish views was now in a strange position of discounting the credibility of a Soviet strike through Eastern Europe; Mr Bush announced a 2.6 per cent cut in defence spending in January 1990 and proposed that the US garrison in Europe be cut by a further 50,000 men. (At the same time, however, spending on nuclear weapons and 'Star Wars' was to be maintained if not increased.)

In Britain two main tendencies could be identified in the arguments circulating around foreign and defence policy. A somewhat crude but useful distinction can be drawn betwen *idealists* and *realists* in foreign policy. Idealists stress the power of ideas, the need for trust and the possibilities of international cooperation, especially in the field of disarmament. Realists, on the other hand, believe that security in an unsafe world can only be achieved by nations through their own military and economic power and those of their allies.

Idealists, found usually on the left of the political spectrum, welcome developments behind the Iron Curtain and claim some of the credit through the pressure they have exerted over the years for issues like disarmament and human rights. Tony Benn has claimed the events in the communist world vindicate those in CND who had long maintained the USSR did not want to attack the West. Now that Gorbachev had proposed huge defence cuts to help rebuild the Soviet economy so, it was claimed, Cold War thinking and levels of defence expenditure should be abandoned. Idealists pointed out that Britain's defence spending at 4.3 per cent of GNP was the highest of European NATO members. A reduced figure of 2 per cent — the classic peacetime British defence budget — would produce a 'peace dividend' of over £11 billion per annum.

It also follows, according to the idealist view, that Britain no longer needs to shadow so slavishly US foreign policy or to act as junior constable to that country's 'world policeman' role. The task now, say idealists, is to bury the Cold War, turn swords into ploughshares and help Gorbachev and Eastern Europe to develop genuine democracies and productive economies.

The *realist* position, espoused substantially by Mrs Thatcher, the Ministry of Defence and others including Michael Hesletine, is diametrically opposed. According to this view it has been the tough defence stance of the West which has preserved peace since the war and enabled the forces of freedom and democracy to develop within communist countries. It would be foolish, say realists, to slacken our guard when so many momentous and destabilizing changes are taking place. History shows that the death of tyrannies is often followed after short hopeful interregnums by the birth of new ones: thus the Tsar was replaced by Stalin, the Shah of Iran by the authoritarian ayatollahs. It follows that NATO should not be allowed to crumble and demobilize, nor should the nation drop its guard against other potential enemies: where would we have been in 1982, for example, without the means to defeat Galtieri and in 1991 to stand up to Saddam Hussein? Realists are also concerned about the growing power of Germany, especially as the freeing of East Germany from communism has led to a reunified Germany. They seek to locate this burgeoning power within a widened Europe — both east and west — which would at the same time head off the kind of federalism envisaged by the Delors Plan.

1989 will go down in history as a year of revolution to rank with 1789 and 1848. In 1990 much relief was being expressed at the abandonment of an experiment begun over seventy years ago which went badly wrong. There was hope also that a new era of peace, international cooperation and disarmament would ensue and pressure was put upon the government to break away from its Cold War mentality and hasten in this direction. But there are others who warn that as long as Soviet military power remains intact its very existence represents a threat and while Soviet intentions currently seem more benign than hitherto who can predict how they might change in the future? These voices also go on to point out that the power vacuum opened up in what used to be the Communist world has also ushered in an unpredictable and possibly even more dangerous phase in international affairs which can only be successfully negotiated through caution, traditional diplomacy and reliance upon sustained military strength.

Mrs Thatcher quite clearly inclined towards the latter view:

> Great plans for peace can precede great wars. Cool headedness, commonsense and vigilance are never more important than when Europe is convulsed by change.
>
> 11 February 1990

29 The 1992 General Election

Bill Jones

'We will win the election with a clear working majority.'

John Major, 13 March 1992

'The election was about hope and fear, and fear won. People hung onto the Tories even in this time of recession because of this problem of trust.'

Neil Kinnock, 2 July 1992

The result of the 1992 General Election was the biggest electoral upset in British politics since 1970, when the Conservatives similarly defied poll predictions of defeat and delivered a majority on the day. This chapter explains the background to the election, analyses the four weeks of the campaign, examines the results and finally looks briefly at why Labour lost.

Background

John Major takes over the reins

For someone as allegedly grey and boring as John Major, he has led an extraordinarily interesting life in recent years. Consider his progression. In July 1989, Geoffrey Howe was removed from the Foreign Office; the unassuming Mr Major took his place. Three months later he was drafted in to replace Nigel Lawson when the Chancellor resigned after a public row. And just over a year later, in November 1990, he replaced Margaret Thatcher as Conservative Party leader and Prime Minister. Those who quipped that he had risen without a trace had a point. Outside Westminster he was almost unknown; his low key, vocabulary-starved verbal style had disqualified him from most media platforms. Even within government circles he was an unknown quantity: certain Conservative MPs could be forgiven for fearing their party had blundered into selecting a second-rater for the highest office in the land.

Mr Major's performance in foreign affairs soon provided reassurance. His tough line over the Gulf War early in 1991 proved successful, as was his promotion in its aftermath of a 'safe haven' for Iraq's beleaguered Kurdish minority. In December 1991, his deft handling of the Maastricht negotiations over future European economic integration enabled him to satisfy Conservative pro-Europeans and Euro-sceptics alike — no mean feat. But on the home front life was much tougher. Whilst Major fastidiously eschewed triumphalism in the wake of the Gulf War, many believed Michael Heseltine as leader would have cashed in by calling a General Election and winning it handsomely. Rightly or wrongly, Mr Major acquired a reputation for dithering — of being a little *too* fair, *too* tolerant — too weak perhaps.

The state of the economy did not help. Chancellor Norman Lamont cut a sorry figure as his successive predictions that the 'green shoots of recovery' were evident were successively proved wrong. At the Despatch Box, Mr Major fared less well than his predecessor against an ebullient Neil Kinnock, buoyed up for much of 1991 by substantial opinion poll leads. A possible June election gave way to expectations of one in October, and, after that, November. When Major announced he would wait until the spring of 1992, there seemed substance to the Opposition jibe that he 'could run, but could not hide'. Commentators in the press began to detect 'the smell of death' about a party which had been in power for thirteen years.

The 'phoney' election campaign

From the spring of 1991, both parties engaged in an unofficial election campaign. Despite the repetitive wearisomeness of it, they had little choice. Mr Major was hoping the economy would improve so that he could call the election, but the catalogue of dire economic statistics — bankruptcies, repossessions, soaring unemployment, zero or minus economic growth — kept his party teetering nervously on the starting line. To offset the bad news, Mr Major did his best to expunge the memories of Mrs Thatcher's fearsome style by being relentlessly nice and of her animus against the public sector by handing it billions of pounds. Labour was caught in the same limbo. As each possible election date approached, the 1989 Policy Review, designed to eradicate Labour's early eighties extremism, was dusted down and reissued with minor alterations, a new title and much public fanfare. Neither party could afford to relax in case the other gained an unassailable lead. In January 1992, the Conservatives seized the initiative and a poll lead by attacking Labour's expenditure plans, which, they alleged, would lead to huge tax increases. By February Labour had made up the difference and again drawn narrowly ahead. This remained the situation until 11 March, when Mr Major finally announced an April election.

The Issues

Despite Mr Major's attempts to distance himself from his unpopular predecessor, the election campaign inevitably focused on the record of the Thatcher years. The Conservatives stoutly defended this record, whilst the opposition parties did their best to rubbish it.

Economic management

The Conservatives claimed the eighties had been 'a decade of remarkable achievement for the British economy': from being the sick man of Europe during the sixties and seventies, Britain's economy averaged 3 per cent growth per annum — more than that of any country except Spain. Business investment grew at a record 45 per cent between 1986 and 1989, whilst manufacturing productivity, at 4.5 per cent per annum throughout the decade, outstripped that of all our leading competitors, including Japan. All this had been achieved through a revival of the entrepreneurial spirit and supply-side reforms which had, for example, loosened the grip of trade unions and reduced the incidence of strikes to the lowest level for 100 years. On top of this, the Conservatives claimed 3.5 million jobs had been created between 1983 and 1991, and that the number of new businesses operating in 1990 was one-third higher than in 1979. At the same time, the National Debt had been reduced by £30 billion and in 1988/89 the proportion of public expenditure to Gross Domestic Product (GDP) had fallen to 39.5 per cent — the lowest level since the 1960s.

The Conservatives admitted that the recession which began in 1989 was, with the wisdom of hindsight, caused by 'unnecessary further stimulus', to the economy in the form of low interest rates during the previous two years. But they were quick to point out that: opposition parties had urged even lower interest rates; most economies experience a downswing after a period of rapid growth; and economic recession was an international phenomenon. Having said all this, the best Mr Major could say about future economic prospects was that 'all the ingredients are in place to come out of recession'.

Labour and the Liberal Democrats hotly disputed this record which they saw as one of incompetence and missed opportunities. The 'economical miracle' was dismissed by Labour as a 'mirage' produced by selective statistics: if the two recessions were included with the boom years, the annual growth rate worked out a mere 1.7 per cent. Labour charged that during their period of office the Conservatives had: destroyed one-fifth of our manufacturing base; allowed the industrial infrastructure to crumble; squandered £100 billion of oil revenues; given massive tax cuts to the already rich; and irresponsibly initiated a credit boom which could only be curbed by recession-causing high interest rates. In consequence Britain had sunk to the bottom of the international growth league, was suffering from record falls in manufacturing investment and faced all the hardship of rising unemployment and house repossessions. In their policy statements both Labour and the Liberal Democrats accepted a modified market economy, with Labour stressing co-operation between government and industry and the establishment of a National Investment Bank, and the Liberal Democrats stressing the need for more savings and closer financial integration into the European Community.

Taxation

The Conservatives claimed to have shifted the tax burden from direct income, e.g. income tax, to taxes upon spending, e.g. VAT. In this way, they argued, people had been given a greater incentive to work hard whilst at the same time gaining the power to choose how to spend their money. The standard rate of income tax, they pointed out, has been reduced from 33p to 25p in the pound and the higher rate from 83p to 40p. On 10 March, Norman Lamont's Budget introduced a new tax band of 20p in the pound for the first £2,000 of taxable income. The Conservatives accused Labour of expenditure plans which would cost £35 billion per year or the equivalent of 10p extra on income tax.

Labour dismissed these calculations as bogus, insisting that their pledged increases amounted to just over £3 billion; any further spending would be wholly dependent on 'the harvest of growth'. Labour counter-accused the Conservatives of being the party of highest taxation: in 1979 the proportion of national income taken by all forms of taxation had been 34.75 per cent; by 1991 it had increased to 37.75 per cent. Labour also insisted that VAT, standing at 17.5 per cent, would be pushed up even further if the Conservatives won the election. Labour's Shadow Budget promised to increase tax thresholds, taking three-quarters of a million people out of tax altogether. A new top rate of 50 per cent would be introduced for earnings over £40,000 and the immunity from National Insurance Contributions (NICs) would be ended for incomes over £20,000 per year. Labour claimed that eight out of ten people would benefit from their redistributive tax and spending proposals.

The Liberal Democrats pledged an increase of 1p on income tax, generating £2 billion to be spent on education. They proposed an overhaul of the taxation system involving three new tax bands, which would also incorporate NICs.

Privatization

The Conservatives saw privatization as one of their major success stories. After 1979 the state-owned sector was reduced by 60 per cent, with nearly fifty major businesses privatized. Nearly one million workers were returned to the public sector and from making huge tax-funded losses these concerns had been transformed into profit-making enterprises. Sales had generated over £30 billion for the nation and helped share-ownership increase from one in ten of the adult population in 1979 to one in four in 1990. The Conservatives promised to privatize coal and British Rail if they won the election. Labour promised that electricity and water would 'be restored to public control', but abandoned plans to do the same for British Telecom and Gas. There would be no privatization of British Rail.

The welfare state

Mrs Thatcher had attacked the welfare state for being enormously costly, inefficient and over protected. Better, she argued, to allow individuals and families to take more responsibility for their own welfare. She saw privately funded welfare services as a more efficient alternative. Mrs Thatcher did not allow, however, for the widespread public support for such institutions: she was forced to abandon more radical reforms in favour of the introduction of 'internal markets' in both health and education. Mr Major, whilst keen to see these reforms through to their conclusion, was much more supportive of welfare institutions. In the autumn of 1991 he fed in an extra £4 billion and his Citizens' Charter promised higher standards of public services, together with a battery of consumer rights and means of redress. The Conservatives vigorously denied that they had ever starved the welfare state of adequate funding. They claimed that, between 1979 and 1991, spending in real terms increased: 55 per cent on the NHS; 50 per cent on education and 41 per cent on social security.

In the housing field, moreover, they could boast that 1.2 million Council tenants had bought their own properties on advantageous terms under the right-to-buy policy.

Labour charged that, on the contrary, the welfare state had been allowed to atrophy, citing closed wards, crumbling NHS buildings and waiting lists approaching the million mark. The 'reforms' constituted a progressive 'privatization' of the Health Service, in which a two-tier system would dispense good treatment to the rich and inadequate care to the poor majority. Both Labour and the Liberal Democrats promised to increase a range of social security payments. In particular Labour promised to increase child benefit to £9.95 and pensions by £5 per week for single people and £8 for couples. Both parties promised to abolish the Social Fund and restore benefits for 16- and 17-year-olds.

Law and order

Labour and the Liberal Democrats made much of the huge increase in notifiable offences: 2.5 million in 1979 to over 5 million in 1992. Despite massive increases in police spending the 'clear up rate' (the percentage of crimes which the police were able to solve) fell from 41 per cent in 1979 to 34 per cent in 1990.

Both opposition parties argued that increased crime was the price society had to pay for a decade of Thatcherite policies, in which the rich had been favoured at the expense of the poor. The Conservatives rejected this attack upon their record and the link with social deprivation, pointing out that crime did not increase dramatically during the 1930s when unemployment was also high. Their explanation was that a deterioration in social values had occurred as a result of the 'progressive' thinking of the 60s, which tended to blame 'society' for criminal activity rather than the individual perpetrator.

Constitutional change

Whilst the Conservatives remained unimpressed by calls for constitutional change, Labour moved dramatically towards the Liberal Democrats' position. Both opposition parties called for: separate assemblies for Scotland and Wales, regional assemblies for England, single tier local authorities, a reformed House of Lords, a Freedom of Information Bill and a strengthening of Citizens' Rights. Whilst not endorsing electoral reform — the centre point of the Liberal Democrats' constitutional programme — Labour left the door ostentatiously ajar for post-election discussions.

An Historic Contest

As the parties squared up to each other, media comentators reflected on the significance of the contest. If successful, the Conservatives would enter unknown territory. No party since the dawn of parliamentary democracy in the early 19th century had ruled for longer than thirteen years. Psephologists also pointed out that no governing party entering the election behind in the polls had succeeded in winning. Despite their fractional lead, the hill facing Labour seemed easily as steep. A win for them would require a much greater electoral swing than any since 1945. The apparent level pegging of the two big parties also seemed to offer the first major role for a third party in peacetime for over sixty years: in a hung parliament the Liberal Democrats would occupy a pivotal role.

Everyone expected Labour to win seats, but how many? Remember, 'swing' is calculated by adding what one party has lost to what another has gained and then dividing by two: this figure reflects the average amount of movement of support from one party to another. In 1987 votes cast on the British mainland divided into 43 per cent for the Conservatives, 32 per cent to Labour and 23 per cent to the SDP/Liberal alliance. To deny the Conservatives an overall majority, Labour needed a swing of 4.5 per cent; to become the biggest party 6.2 per cent and to win an overall majority a massive 8.5 per cent. As always the marginals — those constituencies with thin majorities — would decide the contest. Labour needed to win a daunting 97 to put Mr Kinnock in Number 10.

The campaign

During the first few days the Conservatives lost the initiative in the election race which control of the starting pistol should have given them. The City had reacted coolly to Lamont's election Budget and opinion polls confirmed that the public felt the same. The Conservative campaign already looked threadbare: low on vision and high on negative themes. Their approach seemed to reflect American studies which reveal that attacking your opponent is a more cost-effective way of winning support than setting out your own policy stall. Douglas Hurd set the initial tone for the front bench politicians by describing the difference between Mr Kinnock and John Major as that 'between a pilot and a weather cock'. The predominantly pro-Tory tabloid press invariably struck a less cerebral note. 'Planning applications', *The Sun* informed the nation, 'including loft conversions, home extensions and garages — will have to be approved by gay and lesbian groups if Labour are elected'.

Labour strategists had decided that attacking the Conservative record was not enough. Striking new proposals would have to be offered as well. On 17 March the Party made its big play. In a brilliantly choreographed presentation outside the Treasury building John Smith revealed his dramatically redistributive Shadow Budget. However far to the centre Kinnock had moved the Labour Party, this was unmistakenly a socialist taxation programme. *The Economist* (20 March) judged it a 'big political gamble', allowing the Conservatives to claim that 'Labour plans the biggest tax rise ever in peacetime Britain and that many people who do not consider themselves rich — middle income managers, head teachers, policemen — will be hit.' *The Times* leader (17 March) weighed in with 'from now on this battle is not between Tweedledum and Tweedledee. It is about something real.' In *The Guardian* on the same day Hugo Young doubted the wisdom of Labour's strategy, but in a television debate on their respective budgets the calm Mr Smith easily bested the less-than-convincing Norman Lamont.

With all three manifestos out Peter Kellner in *The Independent* (19 March) spoke for most commentators in judging that Labour had won the first week. In *The Sunday Times* (22 March) Andrew Neil suggested that, had it not been for the widely

Some campaign quotes

'England does not love coalitions.'

Disraeli, 1852

'Modern elections are about prosperity.'

The Times leader, 14 March 1992

'The tragedy of the Labour Party is not that their aims aren't sincere, it's just that they have this absurd obsession that high earners are rich.'

Andrew Lloyd Webber, 21 March 1992

'He isn't a bad fellow.'

Neil Kinnock on John Major, 26 March 1992

'Every other party has had him, it's only fair the Conservatives should now.'

Paddy Ashdown on David Owen's endorsement of John Major, 5 April 1992

'If you vote for the Conservatives, you betray your country.'

Enoch Powell's advice to a Huntingdon voter, 6 April 1992

'Governing well is a dull business. Mr Major is good at it and getting better.'

Simon Jenkins, 7 April 1992

'If there is a lesson to learn from this election it is not to pay too much attention to opinion polls when placing bets.'

Graham Sharp, William Hill Bookmakers, 10 April 1992

'Whatever people say about us, we got the campaign right.'

David Cameron, member of the 'Bratpack', 10 April 1992

publicized separation of the Duke and Duchess of York, Labour would be more than three points ahead in the poll of polls: 'the Tory party had campaigned with all the energy of a sleepwalker.' The chief problem was diagnosed as Major's lack of campaigning talent. Kinnock, often verbose, tense and muddled on television, came alive at public meetings, rousing the faithful with genuine oratory and natural theatricality. TV coverage of his campaign fully conveyed the excitement and enthusiasm he was generating. By contrast Major could not invest his cleverly drafted set-piece speeches with any passion or sense of drama. The ploy of seating him on a stool in a room full of supporters produced pleasant conversation but poor television. The same was generally true of his face-to-face interviews with the likes of Brian Walden, the Dimblebys and others.

Towards the end of the second week the sorry state of the Conservative campaign itself became a news story with the youthful team in Central Office — labelled the 'Bratpack' — attracting hostile comment. The Conservatives reacted by encouraging Major to be more aggressive. Mrs Thatcher was drafted in to do some walkabout campaigning — a move which at least one poll suggested was counter-productive. She did succeed in making the headlines, however, when a woman in Marple Bridge, Cheshire, first offered her a bunch of daffodils and then beat her over the head with them.

At this stage of the campaign an extraordinary sequence of events came to the Conservatives' aid. On the evening of Tuesday 24 March a Labour Party election broadcast (PEB), featuring actors, told the story of two little girls each waiting for the same ear operation. One, with wealthy parents, had the operation done privately but the other had to suffer a long and painful wait. This slick piece of television, designed to highlight long hospital waiting lists, ignited a row of surreal proportions. Labour had claimed the film was based on a real-life case but held back the name of the family involved for fear of tabloid intrusions. On the following morning, however, the name of the girl, Jennifer Bennett, was revealed in the *Daily Express* and *The Independent*. It also transpired that, whilst her father had collaborated in the making of the film, her mother, daughter of a former Conservative mayor of Faversham, had opposed it and did not believe the film was a fair representation. Chris Patten, Chairman of the Conservative Party, launched a furious attack on Kinnock for this 'sleazy and contemptible film' whilst Health Secretary William Waldegrave likened it to Nazi propaganda. Labour counter-attacked by publicizing supporting documentary evidence and alleging Conservative collusion in leaking Jennifer's name to the press. At a press conference shortly afterwards William Waldegrave was forced to admit the Central Office had put the consultant at the centre of the case in touch with *The Daily Express*. The row continued for three days. As Nicholas Wapshott commented (*The Observer*, 29 March) 'the election slipped from their [political parties'] control and veered off in a direction of its own.' The row damaged both main parties but benefited the Liberal Democrats. The weekend commentators judged that Labour's campaign had narrowly avoided disaster, but the Conservatives came in for much harsher criticism. Andrew Neil in *The Sunday Times* described the campaign as 'a shambles'; Mrs Thatcher detected no 'oomph' or 'whizz' or many signs of life at all.

Monday 30 March was Mr Major's birthday. He had little to celebrate but remained calm and, in public at least, unswervingly confident. His new electioneering ploy was to stand on a box and address people through a megaphone — as he had done in the old days when campaigning to become a Lambeth councillor. Whilst this injected some life and bite into his campaign it also showed him in an undignified light. Polls showed the approval ratings gap between Major and Kinnock was rapidly narrowing. On Wednesday 1 April a number of polls showed Labour's lead extending to an average of four points — a margin which would have given them an overall majority. *The Times* poll recorded that, with John Smith as leader, Labour would be the beneficiary of a further 4.5 per cent swing. Some commentators dubbed this 'Red Wednesday'. Labour's stock had never been higher.

That evening Labour held a rally for ten thousand people in Sheffield. The Shadow Cabinet were introduced as the next government. Neil Kinnock descended from the heavens in a red helicopter and entered the hall to a pop star's reception. Famous names endorsed Labour's cause on a huge video screen. Labour's victory was assumed to be a foregone conclusion: it all seemed over bar the voting. The next day *The Independent* reported that 'it was corny, manipulative and totally successful'. But many who saw film clips of the rally on television news were repelled by what they felt was Labour's gloating triumphalism. Toes curled with embarrassment, moreover, when Neil Kinnock roared a Jerry-Lee-Lewis-like 'Well alright' not once but three times. A visitor from Czechoslovakia was horrified by a spectacle which she likened to the official adulation organized for former East European communist rulers.

During the last week of the campaign Labour moved the agenda away from economic and welfare issues towards constitutional change, especially voting reform. Labour strategists thought that a more accommodating position on these issues would encourage Liberal Democrat defections and pave the way for post-election negotiations in the event of a hung parliament. The newspapers were full of speculative articles on the role which the small parties might play in such negotiations. The Conservatives totally rejected constitutional change and plugged away ever more insistently at their twin themes of Kinnock's unsuitability and Labour's tax plans — which they claimed would put an average of £1,250 per year on individual tax bills. The negative campaign in the tabloid press reached a new pitch of intensity as successive opinion polls indicated a Conservative defeat. On Wednesday 8 April William Hill offered odds of 1:4 on Labour becoming the biggest party whilst *The Times* conceded that Kinnock looked 'electable'. In *The Independent* Alexander Chancellor wrote that 'the Tories appear to be resigned to a spell in opposition.' On election day itself the newspapers reported 'a late surge' to the Conservatives, but most experts still confidently expected a hung parliament.

The exit polls taken for the BBC and ITV suggested a similar outcome, but as the results filtered through a different story was revealed. When Basildon voters returned Conservative David Amess against most poll predictions it became clear that the pollsters had misread the public mind. After flirting with Labour and the Liberal Democrats it seemed as if a decisive number of votes had swung back to the Conservatives in the last days of the campaign. Against all the odds John Major's calm optimism had been justified. Neil Kinnock conceded defeat in the early hours of the Friday morning.

The results

By the time all the results had come in on 10 April John Major remained Prime Minister with a reduced but workable majority of twenty-one.

Instead of trailing Labour by 1 per cent as the polls had predicted, the Conservatives trounced them by a full seven points. The national swing to Labour was only 2 per cent but they managed 3.5 per cent in the marginals, suggesting that their targeted campaigning had been effective and that some tactical voting for Labour by Liberal Democrats may have taken place. Indeed, the story in the marginals was complex: some wafer thin Conservative majorities survived whilst healthier ones were overcome.

The Liberal Democrats, after such a spirited campaign, were disappointed with their smaller share of the vote but must have been relieved to lose only two seats and pleased that one of their gains was at the expense of Chris Patten, the much criticized but finally vindicated Party Chairman. No such luck for the two remaining SDP MPs, who both departed the political stage. The turnout at 78 per cent was surprisingly high, suggesting that talk of voter apathy had underestimated the election's importance to the nation. The Conservatives managed to garner more votes than any other party has ever polled. A record number of women were also returned to Westminster: 58 compared with 41 in 1987.

John Major

After his election as Conservative leader in November 1990, one wit commented, 'Two weeks ago Britain knew nothing about John Major; now the whole world knows nothing about John Major.' In reality, quite a bit is known of his unusual biography.

He was born in 1943, the son of a one-time music hall performer who became a successful businessman in the 1930s and then fell on hard times. Perhaps the only Prime Minister in history to have experienced downward social mobility, his family moved from a smart suburb to a flat in Brixton. John Major did not enjoy his time at Rutlish Grammar School, Wimbledon; he was described as 'cheeky' and admits he was something of a rebel. Leaving school at 16, Major worked at several jobs, including labouring, and spent a while in 1961 on the dole (£2.87 a week unemployment pay). At the age of 21, he joined the Standard Bank as a trainee and served some time abroad in Africa. Upon his return, his chance came when he was picked out to become personal assistant to Lord Barber, Edward Heath's former Chancellor.

Around this time, he became active in local politics, choosing the Conservatives as the party which offered choice and incentive to those with energy and ambition. He became a successful Chairman of Housing in Lambeth, winning the admiration of no less an opponent than Ken Livingstone. In 1979 he entered Parliament as MP for Huntingdon and climbed the ladder as whip and then junior minister in the DHSS. His ability was soon recognized and he was promoted to become Nigel Lawson's number two, as Chief Secretary to the Treasury.

In July 1989, Major was catapulted into the Foreign Office and, three months later, when Nigel Lawson resigned, the Treasury. When he put his name forward for the second round of the party leadership contest on 22 November 1990, he was seen as too inexperienced and lacking in personality. With the backing of Norman Tebbit and Margaret Thatcher, however, he emerged as the candidate of the right, with support in the centre and left, who had the best chance of uniting the party and winning a fourth election victory for the Conservatives. On 9 April 1992, he demonstrated that this trust had not been misplaced.

Table 29.1 *The 1992 election results*

| | Seats | | Votes | |
	1987	1992	1987	1992
Conservatives	376	336	42.2	42.5
Labour	229	271	30.8	35.2
Liberal Democrats	22	20	22.6	18.3
SNP	3	3	1.2	1.9
Plaid Cymru	3	4	0.5	0.5
Others	17	17	2.7	3.3
Conservative majority	102	21		

Why were the polls wrong?

Once, during a television programme on a by-election result, Peter Kellner of *The Independent* said he was prepared to 'put his house' on the exit poll being right about the winner. After the 1992 election, it is doubtful he would be so cavalier with his property. Most of the fifty or so polls during the campaign predicted a hung parliament, but instead of an average 1.3 per cent lead for Labour, the result was a 7.6 per cent lead for the Conservatives. The ITN exit poll got the percentage nearly right at 41–37 per cent, but still predicted a hung parliament in terms of seats. Pollsters are careful to remind us that polls are only a snapshot of the public's changing views and are accurate only within a plus or minus 3 per cent margin of error. In 1987, the polls' margin of error was 1.5 per cent, and in 1983, 1 per cent, but nothing had prepared them for the 1992 result. Why did this happen? The debate continues, but a number of explanations have been offered:

A late swing amongst undecided voters which the pollsters were unable to pick up. Usually 80 per cent of voters have made up their minds before the campaign; this time the figure was much lower at 63 per cent.

The don't knows, who, at 5 per cent, represented an unusually large percentage of respondents just before polling day, are thought to have voted disproportionately for the Conservatives.

Secret voters. ICM's re-interviewing of its eve-of-poll respondents indicated that a high percentage of people who had refused to divulge their voting intentions eventually voted Conservative, a view supported by MORI's inquest.

Respondents may have lied through a sense of guilt at voting for the low taxation, low spending Conservatives. As *The Times* suggested (13 July 1992), 'Promising a Tory vote was unfashionable.'

Protest votes. Some voters may have vented their anger against the Government to poll questioners, as in a by-election, but returned to the fold on election day.

Sampling error. Most respondents were interviewed on the street on the same day — a practice which some experts say favours Labour. Weekend polls by Harris tended to produce Conservative leads. Psephologist David Butler argues that telephone polls are cheaper and more reliable.

Differential turnout. MORI claims that Conservatives displayed a greater willingness to turn out and vote than Labour supporters.

Non-registration. A significant number of people polled, maybe 1 per cent, had not registered to vote in order to avoid poll tax payment. As such people were more than likely to be Labour voters, this could explain some of the distortion.

The conclusion of the Market Research Society's own in-house study was that, through methodological weaknesses, pollsters have consistently overstated Labour's strength and understated Conservative support by between 1.5 and 2 per cent since 1959. The polling organizations angrily rejected this. Another explanation which the polling organizations were unhappy to accept was that the result was itself a *consequence* of the polls. According to this view, favoured by the Labour Party, a significant number of voters perceived a Labour victory and a hung parliament as likely, realized they did not want this, and swung back into the Conservative camp.

The results in detail

The regions

London was the region most heavily studded with Labour target seats but despite some poll predictions of an 8 per cent swing it was only 4.6 per cent on election day, delivering the smaller-than-hoped-for harvest of twelve extra seats. The *South* witnessed a 4.5 per cent swing to Labour but this produced only five gains for Labour and four for the Liberal Democrats, drawn mostly from the South West. The *North* remained a Labour stronghold but the swing, at 2 per cent, was much less than predicted: in South Yorkshire and Tyne and Wear it was negligible. Of eighteen target seats in the North West Labour won only nine and picked up a bare two more in the rest of the region. The *Midlands* registered the biggest swing of 5.2 per cent (6.3 per cent in the East Midlands) but here again, at twelve gains, Labour's pickings were thin.

Scotland had been expected to be the graveyard for up to seven of the ten Scottish Conservative MPs, but on the day the pendulum swung sensationally the other way — by 3.5 per cent — and produced a net increase of one for the Government party. *Wales* was more complex: an overall swing of 3 per cent to Labour produced three Conservative gains, three Labour and one for Plaid Cymru in Cardigan and Pembroke.

Overall the 1992 election did not radically alter the electoral geography of Britain. The South remained predominantly Conservative and the North Labour, but the swing to the Tories in Scotland was a surprise.

Class

The surprising story told by Table 29.3 is how the Conservative vote held up in all social groups. Where Labour did gain substantially it was at the expense of the Liberal Democrats rather than the Conservatives. The C2s, which both parties

Table 29.2 *Voters and seats in the regions (excluding Northern Ireland)*

	Votes cast % of total*				Change since 1987, % points				Swing**	Seats won			
	Con.	Lab.	Lib. Dem.	Nat.	Con.	Lab.	Lib. Dem.	Nat.	Con.	Con.	Lab.	Lib. Dem.	Nat.
London	45.3	37.0	15.2	—	−1.2	5.6	−6.1	—	−4.6	48(−10)	35(+12)	1	—
South	52.3	20.3	25.9	—	−1.7	3.8	−3.1	—	−4.5	144(−7)	7(+5)	6(+4)	—
Midlands	46.6	36.3	15.9	—	−1.2	6.3	−5.8	—	−5.2	74(−12)	46(+12)	0	—
North	36.9	46.0	16.1	—	0.3	3.9	−5.0	—	−2.0	53(−10)	107(+11)	3(−1)	—
ENGLAND	45.5	33.9	19.2	—	0.8	4.4	−4.6	—	−3.8	319(−39)	195(+40)	10(+3)	—
SCOTLAND	25.7	39.0	13.1	21.5	1.6	−3.4	−6.1	7.4	3.5	11(+1)	49(−1)	9	3
WALES	28.6	49.5	12.4	8.8	−1.0	4.4	−5.5	1.6	−3.0	6(−2)	27(+3)	1(−2)	4(+1)
GREAT BRITAIN	42.5	35.2	18.3	2.4	−0.5	3.7	−4.8	0.7	−3.0	336(−40)	271(+42)	20(+1)	7(+1)

* Total votes cast: 32,834,263. Votes cast for 'others' are excluded.
** A plus sign indicates a swing to Conservative, a minus sign a swing to Labour.
Source: Adapted from *The Economist*, 18 April 1992

Table 29.3   *Class and voting*

% of 1992 voters	Social groups	1987			1992			
		Con.	Lab.	LD	Con.	Lab.	LD	% swing (− to Labour, + to Conservative)
19	AB professional	57	14	26	56	20	22	− 3.5
24	C1 white collar	51	21	26	52	25	19	− 1.5
27	C2 skilled	40	36	22	38	41	17	− 3.5
30	DE skilled	30	48	20	30	50	15	− 1.0
4	Unemployed men	21	56	20	24	52	17	+ 3.5
3	Unemployed women	23	54	19	26	51	16	+ 3.0

Source: MORI, *The Sunday Times*, 12 April 1992

Table 29.4   *Housing and voting*

% of 1992 voters	Social groups	1987			1992			
		Con.	Lab.	LD	Con.	Lab.	LD	% swing (− to Labour + to Conservative)
	HOMEOWNERS							
36	Middle-class	57	15	26	56	21	20	− 3.5
31	Working-class	43	32	23	41	39	17	− 5.5
67	Owner-occupier	50	23	25	49	30	19	− 4.0
7	Private tenant	39	37	21	33	40	21	− 4.5
	COUNCIL TENANTS							
2	Middle-class	28	41	24	34	40	18	+ 3.5
21	Working-class	21	58	18	22	58	15	+ 0.5

Source: MORI, *The Sunday Times*, 12 April 1992

targeted, registered a sharply increased Labour vote but nowhere near the hoped-for upper forties. The 1 per cent swing in the DE category — Labour's main constituency — gave little comfort to the Opposition, but they did better amongst the professionals. The swing to the Conservatives amongst the unemployed appears extraordinary at first sight but is explained by the fact that unemployment in 1992 was boosted by a recession which hit the Conservative-dominated South particularly hard.

Housing

Table 29.4 suggests that high interest rates and repossessions led to some disillusionment amongst working class owner-occupiers but council tenants — 23

Table 29.5 *Sex, age and voting*

% of 1992 voters	Social groups	1987			1992			% swing (– to Labour + to Conservative)
		Con.	Lab.	LD	Con.	Lab.	ID	
7	Men 18–24	42	37	19	39	35	18	– 0.5
7	Women 18–24	31	42	24	30	43	19	– 2.0
9	Men 25–34	41	33	24	40	37	17	– 2.5
10	Women 25–34	37	33	27	40	38	18	– 1.0
16	Men 35–54	42	32	24	40	37	19	– 3.5
17	Women 35–54	47	27	25	46	32	19	– 3.0
17	Men 55 +	45	31	23	43	38	17	– 4.5
17	Women 55 +	46	32	20	49	32	17	+ 1.5
9	Men 65 +	47	30	22	44	38	16	– 5.5
9	Women 65 +	46	33	20	51	31	17	+ 3.5
23	Pensioners	47	31	21	48	34	16	– 2.0
49	Men	43	32	23	41	37	18	– 3.5
51	Women	43	32	23	44	34	18	– 0.5
100	TOTAL	43	32	23	43	35	18	– 2.0

Source: MORI, *The Sunday Times*, 12 April 1992

per cent of the population — swung fractionally to the Conservatives (perhaps reflecting the popularity of the right-to-buy programme).

Sex and age

Table 29.5 reveals that, as in 1987, young men voted disproportionately Conservative and young women disproportionately Labour. Small swings to Labour were registered for both groups in 1992. Paradoxically, however, older men were more likely to change their vote to Labour whilst older women swung to the Conservatives. Labour must have been disappointed that their proposed pension increases did not make any substantial inroads into this latter group.

Trade unionists

Table 29.6 shows a slight shift overall to Labour, with much bigger swings amongst the over-55s and trade unionists living in the Midlands.

Taken overall, the election suggested that not a lot had changed since 1987. True, Labour came much closer to the Conservatives, who, had they lost an extra dozen MPs, would have lost their overall majority. But Labour managed to win only an extra sliver of the nation's sympathies and remained a party locked up in the north and in the lower income brackets. The Liberal Democrats saw their support fall all over the country and in every social group and must be wondering how they can mount a bridgehead out of the Celtic fringe.

Table 29.6   *Trade unionists and voting*

% of 1992 voters	Social groups	1987			1992			
		Con.	Lab.	LD	Con.	Lab.	LD	% swing (− to Labour + to Conservative)
23	Members	30	42	26	30	47	19	−2.5
15	Men	31	42	25	30	48	18	−3.5
8	Women	29	41	27	31	44	21	−0.5
3	18−24	29	46	23	30	42	20	+2.5
5	25−34	28	47	23	28	49	19	−0.5
10	35−54	29	40	29	31	45	20	−1.5
5	55+	36	37	24	33	49	16	−7.5
10	ABC1	37	30	30	36	36	24	−3.5
8	C2	28	47	24	27	52	17	−3.0
5	DE	22	56	19	24	59	13	−0.5
9	North	25	50	21	25	53	14	−1.5
6	Midlands	35	39	24	32	49	18	−6.5
8	South	33	34	32	35	38	26	−1.0

Note: Tables 29.3−6 were based upon MORI's aggregate analysis of over 22,000 voters in Great Britain during the election, statistically weighted to reflect the election results, *The Sunday Times*, 12 April 1992

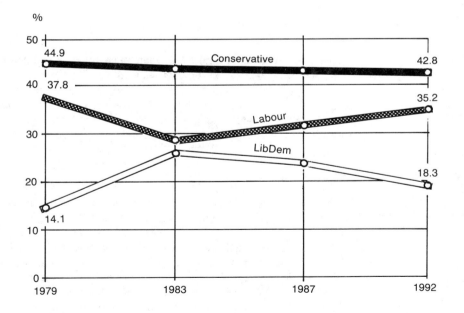

Figure 29.1   *Percentage of vote won by the major parties, 1979−92*

The panels of voters polled throughout the campaign by *The Sunday Times* and *The Independent on Sunday* revealed that some 11 million voters — 'churners' as the psephologists call them — changed allegiance during the four-week period. Beneath the apparently calm surface great waves of opinion were surging across the political spectrum. The Conservatives, however, emerged with more or less the same share of the vote as in 1979 (see Figure 29.1), suggesting that they have been able to keep the same coalition of voters together through the dog days of Thatcherism, the poll tax fiasco and the longest recession for sixty years. How did they do it? Why did Labour lose?

Labour's Defeat

Post mortems into Labour's shock defeat abounded in the summer of 1992, both outside and within the Party. Reasons adduced included the following.

A last-minute swing

Even allowing for poll distortions a major late shift of opinion must have taken place, as in the 1970 election. Labour's own enquiry suggested that 13 per cent of voters did not make up their minds until the last twenty-four hours. Why did so many voters flood into the Conservative camp at the last minute? Labour's Director of Communications, David Hill, believed it was Labour's apparent success, as reflected in the polls, which caused the reaction: 'the more people considered the prospect of Labour winning the more they were worried by it. . . . when people faced up to the prospect of a Labour victory [they] did not want it.'

Labour's image

Labour's post-election polling revealed a fundamental lack of trust. Some of it focused on Neil Kinnock and was partly explicable by the years of vilification he had suffered in the tabloid press. But the autopsy also detected a wider problem. The Party was associated in the public mind with negative images of trade union conflict, declining industries, minority interests and intra-Party strife. 'One major long term problem', according to Hill, 'appears to be that we carry too much baggage from the late 1970s and early 1980s to persuade people that they can fully trust us.' 'Changes in policy stance and style', offered the report, 'had not completely overcome public distrust . . . . Labour was perceived as a party of the past and one which holds back aspirations and tends to put the clock back.'

Labour's campaign

Nicholas O'Shaughnessy from Cambridge University believed Labour's American presidential-style campaign put Kinnock in a starring role which 'encouraged voter doubts about him to surface — about his competence, circumlocutory evasiveness — as well as irritation at his overblown bonhomie'. He also suggests that British political culture was resistant to transatlantic political marketing (*Independent on Sunday*, 12 April). John Curtice comments, 'Mr Kinnock was never an electoral asset for Labour during the campaign; in the final days he may have become a liability' (*The Guardian*, 13 April). Labour's own enquiry admitted errors. General Secretary Larry Whitty thought the row over Jennifer's ear had 'demeaned the campaign and blurred our high ground image'; it had been 'wrongly briefed and poorly researched' and led to a 'serious crisis in the campaign'. The triumphalism of Sheffield was also thought to be an error as was an ill-handled focus on electoral reform in the vital last week, which enabled the Conservatives to win support by arguing that votes for the Liberal Democrats would put Labour into power. By contrast the Tory campaign may have been lacklustre but, according to Whitty, 'it was crude and it worked.' O'Shaughnessy comments, 'it was crass and unsubtle but it may nevertheless have been effective in planting doubts about Labour from early on. Marketing need not be sophisticated to be effective.'

The tabloids

In the wake of their victory the former Conservative Party Treasurer Lord McAlpine congratulated the tabloid press for effectively winning the election. The *Sun* responded with the headline (12 April) 'It's the Sun wot won it.' Neil Kinnock agreed, citing the unremittingly negative attacks upon himself and his Party which, in the final weeks, alleged that a Labour victory would lead to greatly increased immigration. Labour's enquiry calculated that 400,000 votes were swung by the tabloids in the last week; MORI's research, based on over 22,000 voters, reinforced this claim and the proposition that the tabloids could have made the crucial difference.

Taxation and the economy

The pro-Tory tabloids also did more than their bit to convey negative messages, some of them distorted, about Labour's taxation plans. Taxation did not figure highly in voters' priorities as reported to pollsters but Major's belief that the issue was a 'sleeper' which would come through on polling day was apparently vindicated. An NOP poll on 2 April reported an 8 per cent lead for the Conservatives on taxation; on 9 April the lead had leapt to 21. Despite Labour's assertion that eight out of ten people would benefit from their spending proposals, voters were more moved by Conservative assertions that tax and interest rates would soar under Labour. Chris Patten's reiterated message that 'you can't trust Labour' struck home. Ironically, the recession possibly served in the end to help Major: the public were dissatisfied and disillusioned with the Conservatives for causing the recession but trusted them more than Labour to get the country out of it. Voters 'hung onto nurse for fear of worse'.

An indistinct message

Some commentators and not a few Labour politicians blamed Neil Kinnock's drive for the centre ground. Whilst this cleared out much that was both unpopular and obsolete, it did not offer any distinctive or exciting alternatives. Claims were made that Labour had abandoned socialism, virtually embraced capitalism, and tried to convince the country that it could run a free enterprise economy better than the Conservatives. Faced with this, perhaps voters proved the truth of Harry Truman's observation: 'When there is a choice between true conservatives and those in pragmatic approximation thereto, the voters will always opt for the real thing.'

Labour's election inquest identified five tasks for the future: reassure Labour's bedrock supporters of council tenants, the unemployed and pensioners; convince suburban dwellers that Labour will improve their standard of living; attract women aged over 35 repelled by the Party's 'macho' image; overhaul local Party organization; and persuade the Press Complaints Commission to enforce media recognition of the difference between political reporting and comment. Labour's performance in the May 1992 local elections revealed that the Conservative success was no fluke: the Conservatives polled 45 per cent of the vote to Labour's 30 per cent and the Liberal Democrats' 19 per cent — a 7.5 per cent swing to the Tories. If Labour could not win in the favourable circumstances of 9 April what chance have they of winning under their new leader John Smith? The Boundary Commission's redistribution of constituency boundaries will give the Conservatives at least an extra twenty safe seats in any election held after 1995. Some Labour politicians still argue that 'one more heave' will do it, but others argue for drastic remedial measures: a weakening or severance of the link with trade unions, beginning with the abolition of the block vote; the development of a new dynamic programme; and an overhaul of Party organization and structure. Others still argue that if the mould could not be broken in 1992 after thirteen years of Tory rule it will need a new understanding between Labour and the Liberal Democrats to prevent Tory hegemony extending into the twenty-first century.

References and Further Reading

Conservative Party, *The Conservative Manifesto 1992: The Best Future for Britain* (Conservative Party, 1992).

Conservative Research Department, *The Campaign Guide 1991* (Conservative and Unionist Central Office, 1991).

Cowling, D. (ed.), *The ITN Guide to the Election, 1992* (Boxtree, 1992).

Crewe, I., 'Voters made fools of pollsters and pundits' (*The Times*, 11 April 1992).

Curtice, J., 'Labour's slide to defeat' (*The Guardian*, 13 April 1992).

Fabian Review: Election Special, May 1992.

Green Party, *Manifesto for a Sustainable Society* (Green Party, 1991).

'How Labour lost' (*The Economist*, 18 April 1992).

Labour Party, *Meet the Challenge, Make the Change: The New Agenda for Britain* (Labour Party, 1989).

Labour Party, *Labour's Election Manifesto: It's Time to Get Britain Working Again* (Labour Party, 1992).

The Liberal Democrats, *The Liberal Democrat Manifesto 1992: Changing Britain for Good* (Liberal Democrats, 1992).

McKie, D., *The Election: A Voters' Guide* (Fourth Estate, 1992).

O'Shaughnessy, N., 'Why a "flawless" campaign flopped' (*The Independent on Sunday*, 12 April 1992).

Plaid Cymru, *Wales in Europe* (Plaid Cymru, 1992).

Rallings, C. and Thrasher, M., 'How and why the votes were cast' (*The Sunday Times*, 12 April 1992).

Smyth, G. (ed.), *Can the Tories Lose? The Battle for the Marginals* (Lawrence and Wishart, 1991).

Sparrow, N., 'Total recall on the forecasts' (*The Guardian*, 12 May 1992).

Waller, W., *The Almanac of British Politics*, 4th edn (Routledge, 1991).

Index